TODAY'S
HOTTEST COLLECTIBLES

From the publishers of *Warman's Today's Collector* & *Toy Shop*

© 1998 by
Krause Publications, Inc.

Published by

krause publications

700 E. State Street • Iola, WI 54990-0001

Please call or write for our free catalog.
Our toll-free number to place an order or obtain a free catalog is 800-258-0929
or please use our regular business telephone 715-445-2214
for editorial comment and further information.

Library of Congress Catalog Number: 98-84625

ISBN: 0-87341-372-5

Printed in the United States of America

TODAY'S HOTTEST COLLECTIBLES

Contributing Editors

Sharon Korbeck

Daisy Cain

Mike Jacquart

Guy-Michael Grande

Shawn Brecka

Beth Wheeler

Liz Isham Cory

Robert Ball

Joanne Ball

Cover Design/Photography

Ross Hubbard

Chris Pritchard

Page Design

Jackie Michalowski

The editors wish to thank the dozens of contributors/experts nationwide who provided information, pricing and photos for this project. They graciously gave of their talents and patiently waited for this book to be published. You'll find them listed at the end of their respective chapters.

CONTENTS

INTRODUCTION

What Are Your Collectibles Worth?

What's it worth?

That's the question people ask me most frequently since I work for a collectibles publishing company. And as editor of *Toy Shop* magazine, I am often able to offer estimates of values on toys.

But outside that arena, I'm just like all those people asking the questions — another rummage sale scavenger hoping to unearth a treasure among dusty books, dirty curtains, rusty bikes and broken toys.

I may find what I believe is a great item at a sale and be willing to pay the asking price. I know it's worth more than the quarter or dollar I may pay . . . but how much more?

You've all been in that situation. That's why we published this book — for all of you fans of garage sale bargains hoping to turn 50 cents into 50 dollars or more.

Beanies, Barbies and Baseball

Today's Hottest Collectibles offers collecting tips, trends and values for more than 90 of today's top collecting categories from action figures to world's fair memorabilia.

Don't know what that McCoy cookie jar you picked up is worth? You'll find more information about cookie jar collecting and pricing inside.

Think you might have found an original 1959 Barbie doll? We'll give you tips on how to tell and list prices on new and old Barbie dolls.

And even if you don't find your exact collectible listed, you'll get a better feel for what similar items are selling for on the active secondary market.

Don't find many "good" toys at rummage sales anymore? Ever notice how many thrift shops mark up older board games, fast food toys and dolls as collectibles? That's because toys are some of today's most actively-collected items. And while you'll find lots of information on toys in this book, you'll also find chapters on old standbys like salt and pepper shakers, Elvis, pottery, Disney and Western collectibles.

Collectible? *Those* Old Things?

You may also be surprised by some of the chapters we've included — chapters that might make you say, "Who would have thought anyone would collect those old things?" Often overlooked items like lunch boxes, insulators, puzzles and old kitchen ware have loyal followings and escalating prices. And don't forget Beanie Babies — they're one of the fastest-growing collectibles with values rising at insanely rapid rates.

Today's Hottest Collectibles will aid the garage sale fanatic or antique shop browser in their collecting strategies. And while the book hits on the highlights of more than 90 categories, it also offers a road map to follow for more detailed information. Lists of clubs and publications direct readers to collectors sharing their interests.

But the more than 10,000 prices listed in this volume are the real boon to collectors wanting to value their own possessions or just wanting to get a sense of the market.

We hope you'll learn more about collectibles in general through this book. But we've also hoped we've piqued your interest in other areas.

Lots of Experts Inside

Dozens of people — experts in their respective fields — contributed to this book. You'll find most of their addresses listed in the chapters to which they contributed. Editor's Note: Not all contributors provided the values for the chapters. In-house editors also worked to compile values from various sources, like prices realized at auctions or shows and dealer lists.

Abbreviations used in individual chapters are explained in those chapters. Two abbreviations common in collecting — MNP/MNB (Mint no Package/Mint in Box) may be used throughout the book. Those refer to items in Mint — like new — condition either in or out of original Mint condition packaging.

WHAT ARE REPRODUCTIONS?

When spending any money on antiques and collectibles, a collector wants to be sure he knows what he's getting. That's why it is especially important to be aware of reproductions that may be circulating as authentic antiques.

Here are some terms relating to reproductions that collectors may want to be aware of. Notice the subtle differences in each description.

- A **reproduction** is an exact copy of a period piece.

- A **copycat** is a stylistic reproduction, similar in shape, form and decoration to a period piece, but not an exact copy.

- A **fantasy piece** is a shape or form that did not exist during the initial period of manufacture or licensing.

- A **fake** is an object deliberately made to deceive, usually a one-of-a-kind item.

There are books and other publications designed to alert collectors and dealers to reproductions. One to consider is the *Antique & Collectors Reproduction News*, Box 71174, Des Moines, IA 50325.

ACTION FIGURES

The action figure hobby is one of the fastest growing areas of collecting. For proof, walk through the toy section of any store and look at the vast number of figures—Star Wars, Star Trek, Spawn and many others, as well as the numerous sizes, ranging from 3-3/4 inches to 12 inches. It's been speculated that action figures bring more collectors into toy collecting than G.I. Joe, Hot Wheels and model kits combined!

Even new figures originally priced at $5-$10 have jumped 50 percent or more in just a few years as buyers become more aware of the figures' future potential.

Action figures date back to the 1960s. Prior to that time, boys often played with toy soldiers made of iron, lead or plastic with no movable parts.

The 1960s saw American culture and technologies change in countless aspects of everyday life, including how toys would be made and sold. Mattel's Barbie doll, marketed on television commercials, was taking the toy world by storm. No one dreamed boys would play with dolls, but toy executives believed boys would play with dolls if they were called "action figures." Hasbro's 12-inch G.I. Joe action figure was unveiled at Toy Fair in 1964.

Mego joined Hasbro and Ideal as a major player in the action figure market when it released its first superhero series in 1972, eight-inch cloth and plastic figures called the Official World's Greatest Super Heroes. It later added figures based on TV characters from shows like *Planet of the Apes, Star Trek* and *The Dukes of Hazzard*.

Five years later, another action figure milestone unfolded when Kenner released the first toys based on the smash film *Star Wars*. As well as being the first to capitalize on the film's success, the company also introduced a new, smaller size for its figures. Unlike G.I. Joe (12 inches) and Mego figures (eight inches), Kenner's *Star Wars* figures stood only 3-3/4-inches tall, a smaller size that's remained another standard industry size today.

General Guidelines: Action figures in original packages (boxes or on blister cards) command the highest prices. Don't pass up unpackaged figures, though—look for ones in the best possible condition and those with a recognizable character. But be aware that action figures without boxes can be difficult to identify.

The fewer figures that were made, the more the figure will likely be worth. Fewer figures are usually made of females or those of minor characters like aliens (as opposed to major characters) so they're often harder to find and generally worth more to collectors.

Related accessories like vehicles, play sets and weapons can be worth just as much if not more than original boxes.

Clubs
•Captain Action Collectors Club
P.O.Box 2095, Halesite, NY 11743

•Action Figure Mania
515 Ashbury St.,San Francisco, CA 94114

•Classic Action Figure Collectors Club
P.O.Box 2095, Halesite, NY 11743

•National Big Jim Collectors Association
904 Woodland Dr., Wheeling, IL 60090

•Star Trek: The Official Fan Club
P.O. Box 111000, Aurora, CO 80011

HOT TIP!

Because fewer were made, female action figures tend to command higher prices than their male counterparts. Likewise, villain figures often command higher prices than the more common hero figures.

Honey West, karate outfit, 1965, Gilbert, $45 Excellent.

Princess Wildflower, Best of the West, 1974, Marx, $50 loose.

VALUE LINE

Prices listed are for figures Mint in Package.

Alien, Kenner, 1990s
Lasershot Predator $12
Swarm Alien $11
Queen Alien $25
Scorpion Alien $15
18-inch Alien $500

A-Team, Galoob, 1980s
Amy Allen $30
Hannibal $20
Murdock $25
Viper $15

Batman, The Animated Series, Kenner, 1990s
Killer Croc $30
Phantasm $25
Poison Ivy $30

Mr. Freeze $20
15-inch Batman $50
Bruce Wayne $10
Catwoman $25
Joker $20
Ninja Robin $15

Batman, Legends of, Kenner, 1990s
Catwoman $13
Joker $13

Batman Returns, Kenner, 1990s
Catwoman $12
Robin $12
Penguin $15
Penguin Commandos $40
Bruce Wayne $20
Any Batman $15

Fantastic Four, Toy Biz
Human Torch $6
Medusa $6
Mr. Fantastic $8
Silver Surfer $8
The Thing $7

Planet of the Apes, Mego, 1970s
Astronaut Burke $100
Astronaut Verdon $100
Cornelius $60
Dr. Zaius $90
Galen $100
Gen. Ursus $100
Zira $125

Spawn, McFarlane Toys, 1990s
Angela $20
Badrock $12
Overtkill, gold $16
Pilot Spawn, black $13
Malebolgia $50
Tremor $15
Troll $15
Twitch and Sam $13
Vampire $15
Vertebreaker $15
Violator $15
Werewolf, brown $19

Spider-Man, Toy Biz
Alien, Slasher $5
Carnage Unleashed $8
Peter Parker $8
Spider-Man Web Racer $5
The Lizard, red shirt $5

Starting Lineup, Kenner
Alonzo Mourning, 1996 .... $12
Brett Hull, 1994 .... $8
Cal Ripken $45
Deion Sanders, 1996 .... $12
Dennis Rodman, 1996, orange hair $20
Eric Lindros, 1996 .... $13
Eric Metcalf, 1996 .... $8
Grant Hill $35

Astronauts in Mattel's 1967-1970 Major Matt Mason series. From left to right are Major Matt Mason, $40 Mint no Package(MNP); Doug Davis, $50 MNP; Jeff Long, $75 MNP; and Sergeant Storm, $50 MNP.

Arturs Irbe, 1994 .... $30
Jim Carey, 1996 .... $16
Joe Montana $42
Joe Sakic, 1996 .... $13
Johnny Unitas, 1989 .... $20
Kevin Greene, 1996 .... $12
Mark Messier, 1996 .... $13
Marshall Faulk, 1995 .... $35
Nolan Ryan $60
Reggie Jackson $25
Ron Francis, 1996 .... $10
Steve Bono, 1996 .... $8
Willie Mays $20

Star Trek, Mego, 1970s
12-inch Mr. Spock $60
12-inch Kirk $50
8-inch Kirk $50
8-inch Mr. Spock $25
8-inch Zatanite $150
8-inch Klingon $150

Star Trek, Playmates, 1990s
Worf $20
Picard $20
Ferengi $25
Borg $20
Romulan $30
Data $12
Q $12
Wesley Crusher $12

Starsky and Hutch, Mego, 1976
Hutch $45
Starsky $45
Huggy Bear $50
Capt. Dobey $50

Star Wars, Kenner, 1970s
Original 12 (3-3/4-inch) figures
Luke $300
Leia $275

Stormtrooper $20
Tusken Raider $225
R2-D2 .... $125
Jawa, vinyl cape $1,400
Jawa, cloth cape $180
C-3P0 .... $125
Obi-Wan Kenobi $225
Han Solo $500
Chewbacca $180
Darth Vader $225
Death Squad Commander $100
12-inch Darth Vader $200
12-inch Luke $250
12-inch IG-88 .... $500
12-inch Boba Fett $350

Super Powers, Kenner, 1980s
Aquaman $35
Robin $50
Penguin $40
Mr. Miracle $200
Wonder Woman $20
Lex Luthor $15
Flash $20
Darkseid $15
Batman $55

Toy Story, Thinkway, 1990s
Talking Woody $40
Talking Buzz $40
5-inch Kicking Woody $8
5-inch Hamm $8
5-inch Flying Buzz $8
5-inch Crawling Baby Face $10

World's Greatest Super Heroes, Mego, 1970s
Aquaman $150
Batman $150
Batgirl $300
Captain America $200
Clark Kent $500
Joker $150
Robin $150
Supergirl $450
Isis $250
Incredible Hulk $100
Falcon $200
Mr. Mxyzpltk $100
Tarzan $100
Wonder Woman $250

ADVERTISING COLLECTIBLES

You've come a long way, baby! That's what advertising has done since it first appeared as the symbols and pictures that hung over the entrance way to shops and stores way back when. It wasn't until the invention of printing in Germany in the mid-1400s that advertising really got going. Newspapers followed in the 1600s, and modern advertising began in earnest in the 1800s and especially in the early part of the 20th century. Magazines, tins, paper items, bottles and ceramic objects all carried advertising, often in highly colorful and beautiful artwork. The nostalgia bug is probably mostly responsible for the popularity of advertising items.

The field of collectible advertising is broad. It might be one of the most popular collecting categories of all (along with toys, glass and pottery). The better and brighter the artwork on a particular piece of advertising memorabilia, the more valuable it usually is.

Condition, of course, is a major factor, along with the company that produced the item. When considering condition, keep in mind that items that are 50 or 100 years old aren't normally found in Mint, pristine condition.

Collectors tend to collect by item (beer, coffee, tobacco), company (Coca-Cola, John Deere, Hershey's) or type of material (tins, bottles, signs). One of the reasons advertising pieces can get so pricey is there are so many different collecting groups after them. For example, a DeLaval match holder in the shape of a cream separator is collected by people looking for DeLaval items, match holders and farm-related collectibles.

Collectors should be aware of reproductions and fantasy items. Many are obvious reproductions as they are marked as such, but other items are not marked and can often fool the uninitiated.

Don't overlook current advertising items offered as premiums. For instance, Ragu recently offered a disposable 35mm camera with Ragu advertising on it just for buying a few bottles of spaghetti sauce. There probably weren't many of these items produced, and few people probably had enough interest to send for one. Add to this equation that of the people who ordered them, many likely used the camera, leaving those still Mint in Package even harder to come by. This nice-looking advertising piece will probably be somewhat desirable to those who collect disposable cameras with advertising.

Don't overlook current store displays. The large standees are interesting items, as are some of the smaller cardboard signs. Store managers often toss these items, so you might be able to get them free for the asking. Especially look for advertising with celebrities such as Michael Jordan.

Neat Stuff to Look For

Tobacco: Do you have Prince Albert in a can? Many people do. The first tobacco advertisement supposedly appeared around 1790. Since then, there have been innumerable advertising items created for cigarettes, cigars and pipes. Collectors can look for tins, cigar boxes, tobacco tags, signs, postcards, ashtrays and lighters, along with flat paper items of all kinds. Most collectors focus on one area of items or a particular brand of tobacco. Collecting everything isn't realistic because these items can be extremely pricey. Many reproductions exist in this area.

Kitchen: The kitchen is a good place to begin collecting advertising items. There are innumerable coffee, spice, peanut butter, tea, candy and oyster tins available. As is the rule in collecting anything, focus in on one area. Oyster and peanut butter tins have increased greatly in value over the past five years. Small spice tins, even recent ones from the 1960s and 1970s, are usually marked at a minimum of $3- $5.

Other tins: Typewriter and phonograph needle tins are very neat and becoming very expensive. Fuse box tins is another up-and-coming area.

Toiletries: People are collecting all the "unmentionable" tins and bottles that spent their lives in bathrooms such as tins and bottles. Cough syrup, cough drop, deodorant, salve and hair tonic containers of all sorts are now highly collectible. Most are also reasonably priced, from $10-$35. Talcum powder tins, along with prophylactic tins, are likely the two hottest powder room items going today. Talcum powder tins depicting babies are extremely popular. Many collectors treasure these items for their nostalgia and, often, their humorous claims and/or phrases.

Toys: You simply can't beat the combination toys and advertising. Dolls and banks are two of the more common types of advertising toys. Some of the more popular advertising characters that have had toys made in their likenesses are found on cereal boxes (Quisp and Cap'n Crunch are two good examples). Many companies today still offer toy premiums.

Signs: Perhaps the most desirable form of advertising is signs, especially the metal signs with enamel. Because of their purpose (to be hung on the wall), they look great on collectors' walls. Signs can run from $50 into the thousands. Any original sign, no matter what the subject, is worth buying; however, be aware of the many reproductions on the market. Reproductions sell for $10 and up.

Sign, Buster Brown Health Shoes, 9-1/2" x 9-3/4", reverse on glass, Buster and Tige, framed.

Clubs

•Advertising Association of America
 P.O. Box 1121, Morton Grove, IL 60053

•Advertising Cup & Mug Collectors of America
 P.O. Box 680, Solon, IA 52333

•Campbell's Soup Collector Club
 414 Country Lane Court, Wauconda, IL 60084

•Cigarette Pack Collectors Association
 61 Searle St., Georgetown, MA 01833

•Dr. Pepper Collectors Club
 P.O. Box 153221, Irving, TX 75015

•National Pop Can Collectors
 P.O. Box 7862, Rockford, IL 61126

•Painted Soda Bottle Collectors Association
 9418 Hilmer Dr., La Mesa, CA 91942

•Pepsi-Cola Collectors Club
 P.O. Box 1275, Covina, CA 91722

•Porcelain Advertising Collectors Club
 P.O. Box 381, Marshfield Hills, MA 02051

•Tin Container Collectors Association
 P.O. Box 440101, Aurora, CO 80044

VALUE LINE

Bottles

Anasarcin Diurectic Elixir, label, cork, NM $35
Ballard's Horehound Syrup, 4 oz., cork, label, with box,
  directions, EX $20
Cuticura Resolvent for Affections of the Skin, two labels,
  embossed, NM $38
DeWitt's D&C Expectorant, label, screw cap, with box,
  NM $25
Dr. Drakes Glessco Children's Coughs, label, with box,
  NM $25
Dr. Guns Cough Remedy, embossed/labeled bottle, with box,
  EX $18
Dr. Koenig's Hamberg Drops, clear labeled bottle, EX $25
Dr. Pierce's Golden Medical Discovery, full, with box $20
Dr. W.H. Bull's Chill Syrup Cure, cork, label, with box,
  instructions, EX $145
E. Merck & Co., Apiol Fluid Green, 1 oz., cork. Label, paper
  cap, NM $35
Eucaline Malaria Chill Tonic, label, screw cap, sealed,
  NM $45
Gardner-Barada Urinary Urisepetin, label, wrapped,
  NM $48

Golden State Liniment, B.F. Hewlett, clear, 5", EX $15
Grandma's Absorbo, label, full jar, with box and directions,
  NM $30
Hobson's Sarsaparilla, Pfeiffer, cork, label, with box, EX $40
Humphrey's Homeopathic No. 12 Lencorrhea, EX $18
Karl's Clover Root, for constipation, full, with box, EX ... $65
Kings Discovery, label, screw cap, with box, EX $23
McLean's Tar and Wine Compound, screw cap, label,
  instructions, EX $8
Mrs. Winslow's Syrup, screw-top bottle, EX $18
Parke Davis Orange Extract for Soda Fountain, label, EX $40
Powers & Weightman Benzoali Ammonium, label, foil cap,
  EX $40
St. Joseph's Lax-Ana Tonic, label, cork, NM $25
Swanson's 5 Drops, label, cork, with box, NM $30
Triena Laxative for Infants, with box, EX $8
W.S. Merrell Genitone, two labels, amber, NM $65

Phonograph Needle Tins

Edison Bell, Chromic Needles, England $350
Embassy Radiogram, England $28
Golden Pyramid, Medium, England $175
Golden Pyramid, Radiogram, England $155
Marschall, five-pack of needle tins, Germany $125
Marshal, Germany $28
Natural Voice $28
Songster Needles, five-pack of needle tins $125
Taj Mahal, Extra Loud Tone $28
Verona Needles, five-pack of needle tins $125
Verona Needles, unopened $28

Signs

Bartle's, button sign $250
Blackhawk Beer, sign $375
Dorne's Carnation Chewing Gum sign $800
Francisco Auto Heater, tin sign $1,850
Grecian Cream, sign $5,500
Orange Crush, button sign $425

Tins

Adams Gum $450
Addressograph, typewriter ribbon tin $65
Amolin Deodorant, 2-1/2" h, NM $25
Amolin Deodorant Powder Tin, with box, 3-1/2" h, MT .. $30
Anusol Hemorrhoidal Suppositories, 1-1/4" x 1-1/2", MT $25
Babs Tablets for Diseased Throats, NM $25
Battle Creek Lacto Dextrin, 9-1/4" x 5" x 5" $48
Bee Brand Cloves, EX $15
Ben-Hur Spice, EX $16
Bon Ami, VG $17
Bonnie Day Talcum, 6", EX $15
Breethem Sweet as Babys, NM $45
Caandettes Antibiotic, 1-3/4" x 4", EX $10
Campbell's Tomato Soup tin pail, J. Chein, 5-3/4" h $48
Cascaret (for constipation), 1-1/2" x 2-1/2",EX $12
Caswell's Coffee $275
Chase & Sanborn Seal Brand Coffee, 5" h, 4-1/4" d $10
Chase & Sanborn Tea, 4-3/4" x 3-3/4" x 3-3/4" $15
Climax Peanut Butter, 160 oz., 1923, EX $125
Comfort Foot Cooler Talc, EX $30

Sign, Campbell's Soup Campbell Kid character, metal, 23-1/4" x 14-1/2".

Core-Ga Dental Powder, sample, 2-1/4" h, VG $20
Cosmo Shear Pins $15
Credo Peanut Butter, VG $80
Dixie Peanut Butter, EX $100
Doan's Ointment, 1 oz., blue and white with graphics, EX
    .... $65
Don't Fear Smoke and Fume Respirator, rare, NM $195
Dream Girl Talc, NM $50
Dr. Hobb's Kidney Pills, 1-1/2" x 2 1/2", EX $40
Dr. Scholl's Foot Powder, full, 1930s, NM $38
Dr. Whetzel's Quick Relief Asthma, EX $45
Dr. Wood's Cold Remedy, 2" round, EX $25
Dupont Superfine FF Gunpowder, 6-1/4" x 4", oval $85
Dutch Boy Liquid Drier, 5" x 2-1/2", NM $30
Feen-a-Mint, die-cut display with 24 unopened, wrapped
    boxes, NM $225
Fixaco (medical tin), 1-1/4" x 2", NM $30
Freeman's Face Powder, NM $35
Gold Bond Toilet Powder, EX $35
Golden Sun Spice, NM $20
Great Seal Talc Toilet and Baby Powder, EX $65
Happy Home Peanut Butter $450
Helps Cool and Soothe Throat, EX $10
Hills Cascara Cold Tablets, EX $8
Hollister's Golden Nugget Tablets, NM $65
Jergens Miss Dainty Talcum $75
Kerite Tape, 4-1/2" x 4-1/2" x 2" $6
Killark Auto Fuses $17
Kingsman Asthmatic Powder, Capitol Drug, NM $65
LaJean Scalp Pressing, black advertising, NM $25
Liggett's Candy Sticks, 1 lb., EX $145
Lucky Brown Hair Dressing, black advertising, NM $35
Mackintosh's Toffee de Luxe, 3-1/4" x 4-1/2", oval, worn $18
Man-Tan Rectal, sample tin, EX $10
Maryland Beauty Brand Oyster, one gallon $270
May Breath Mouth Deodorant, VG $12
Merrit's Guest Size Hair Promade, sample, NM $25
Mexene Chile Powder Seasoning, round, 3-1/2", EX $30
Miller Line, typewriter ribbon $35
Nyals Huskeys Throat Lozenges, EX $30
Old Dutch Cleanser can, 5" h, EX $15
Oysters Huitres, EX $15

Parke Davis, raw drug tin, Life Root Herb, NM $145
Paul Hanna Compound for Coloring Gray Hair, litho tin,
    unopened, NM $70
Porter's Laxative, 2" x 1-1/2", EX $20
Queen Hair Dressing, sample, 1-1/2", NM $20
Rawleigh's Cold Tabs small yellow, EX $8
Rawleigh's Talcum and Baby Powder, baby graphics,
    EX $165
Red & White Spice, chili, EX $15
Remington, typewriter ribbon $45
Remrandco, typewriter ribbon $45
Rose Marie Tea, 5" x 3-1/2" x 3-1/2" $22
Royal Scarlet Spice, EX $20
Royal Shield Spice, EX $20
Rupert Talc, 4" x 4-3/4", NM $65
Sanette Adhesive Tape, 1-1/4" h, EX $15
Singleton Oysters, 9 oz., EX $20
Stop Cough, Tom Hoges & Sons, VG $65
Sweet Georgia Brown, sample, NM $18
Sylvan Carnation Talc, 4-1/2", VG $65
UCA Salve, NM $9
Van Dyk Coffee, screw top, VG $45
Vicks, test sample, NM $30
Wellman Cayenne Spice, EX $30
White Rose Tea Balls, 10" h, EX $45
White Witch Talc, NM $95
Williams Talcum, EX $35
Wickham's Peanut Butter, G $55
WonderBrand, typewriter ribbon $40
Wu Lung Tea, VG $30
Zefinges Black Currant Pastilles, EX $15

Toys

A&W, plush Root Bear hand puppet $5
Big Boy, doll, vinyl figural, 9-1/4", 1973 .... $35
C&H Sugar, doll, "Hawaiian Huggables" Hula Girl, 14" . $28
California Raisins, plastic wind-up toy, Nasta, 1987,
    MOC $24
Commercial Travelers, 6" ceramic bank, man with coin head
    and money body $125
Crest, Toothpaste Man Telephone, 11-3/4" $70
Domino's Pizza Noid stuffed doll, 20" l, 1988, Acme, EX $45
Eskimo Pie Ice Cream, doll, print on cotton, 14" $35
Esso, playing cards, complete, 1950s $30
Folger's Coffee, puzzle in a can, EX $15
Franklin Life Insurance, doll, print on cotton, 12" $35
Hershey's Reese's Plush Bear, 1989, Hershey's, 16" h, EX
    .... $18
Kellogg's, paper doll, Dandy the Duck, 13" x 17", 1935,
    uncut, Mint $75
Kellogg's, paper doll, Dinky the Dog, 13" x 17", 1935,
    uncut, Mint $75
KFC, bank, Colonel Sanders, 10" tall, EX $50
McDonald's, Ronald inflatable punch bag, 13" h, 1980s,
    EX $10
McDonald's, 1984 Olympics, clear glass mug $5
Pepsodent, puzzle, radio premium, Molly Goldberg and
    Family, 8" x 10", 1932 .... $35

Poppin' Fresh, vinyl figure, 7-1/4" h, 1971 .... $30
Poppie Pillsbury, vinyl figure, 6" h, 1971 .... $30
Pops Rite Popcorn, doll, "Puffy," print on cotton, 11" $35
Toys R Us, doll, Geoffrey Giraffe, bendable sponge body,
   "I'm a Toys R Us Kid," 12" $35

Trays

American Line, tip tray $245
Bartel's, serving tray $995
Fredericksburg Beer, tip tray $275
Leisy Brewing Company, tip tray $475
Loux Ice Cream, tray, 1913 .... $950
Mity-Nice Bread, tip tray $145
Moxie, tip tray $650
Ohio Art, tip tray, tin litho, "Home of the World Famous
   Etch A Sketch-Ohio Art is the World of Toys" $28
Old Reliable Coffee, tip tray $300
Weld's Ice Cream, serving tray $195
Yuengling Prize, beer tray $240
Yuenglings, tip tray $275

Miscellaneous

Allied Radio, catalog, 1938, 160 pp., pictures dozens of
   radios $25
Alpine Air Coolers, paper fan, wood handle, G $4
Beechnut Gum, display, 1916 .... $3,000
Borden's Baby Brand Condensed Milk, jar in original box
   5" h x 3" d $32
Budweiser, salt and pepper, Bud Man, 1990s, Ceramarte,
   Mint $38
Budweiser, telephone, beer can shape $60
Burger Chef, Triple Play Funmeal Box, 1977, first kid's
   meal promotion $50
Burger King, Toy Story floor display, 1995 .... $315
Carter's Ink, print, framed, "Carter's Kittens," 13" x 12",
   EX $125
Dairy Queen, salt and pepper, girls, 4" h, 1960s $195
DeLaval Cream Separator, brochure, 24 pp., 1928, EX ... $18
Heinz Ketchup, salt and pepper, bottles, plastic, 4" $24
Hotpoint, refrigerator bottle, Hall China, blue,NM $75
International House of Pancakes ceramic chicken,
   toothpick or mint dish, 1960s, minor chip $24
John Deere, pencil, celluloid, EX $18
Kellogg's, salt and pepper, Snap and Pop,2-1/2" h $60
KFC, salt and pepper, plastic, Colonel and Mrs. Sanders,
   4" tall, Margarot Corp., 1972, EX $195
M&Ms Candy, cookie jar, Mars, 1982, Mint $375
McDonald's, Happy Meal box, 1980s, Mint $15
McDonald's, Speedee paper hats, 1950s-60s, Mint $35
Michelin Man, air compressor, 1930s $550
Necco Wafer, display, 1940s $525
Nichol Kola, metal sign, 33" h x 57" w, EX $225
Pepsi, Bathing Girls Decals, 1940s $2,400
Pillsbury, napkin holder, Pillsbury Doughboy, ceramic, 5"
   square, marked "1988 The Pillsbury Company" $24
Pillsbury, spoon rest, Pillsbury Doughboy, ceramic, 8",
   marked "1988 The Pillsbury Company" $24
Planter's Peanuts, cookie jar, Mr. Peanut, Benjamin &
   Medwin $85
Planter's Peanuts, salt and pepper, Mr. Peanut, 5",
   Benjamin & Medwin $35

Quaker Oats plastic mug, F&F Mold and Die Works,
   Dayton, Ohio, 3-1/2" h $14
Ralston Purina, dog bowl ashtray, ceramic, 5-7/8"d $35
RCA Victor, record catalog, 550 pp., 11-1/4" x 8-1/2",
   Nipper on cover, 1948, EX $30
Reddy Kilowatt, holiday cookbook, 24 pp., 1950s $17
Reddy Kilowatt, tea apron, plastic, "Reddy Kilowatt —
   Your Electric Servant," 1950s, Mint $35
Sambo's coaster, "10 cents;" red, white and blue coffee
   cup, 3" d, 1970s, Mint $10
Sharples Cream Separator, match safe $350
Shawmut Rubbers, Tacoma Wash., pocket mirror, Zodiac $55
Smokey Bear, cardboard poster, full color, 16-3/4" x 14",
   1956 .... $60
Smokey Bear, novelty mug, embossed Smokey, "Prevent
   Forest Fires," 1950s $55
Smokey Bear, salt and pepper, full figure, 4", 1950s $85
Spitz's Bread, original advertising art, 32-1/2" w x 12" h,
   G $125
Stag Beer, metal advertising sign, 18" w x 13-1/2" h;
   1954, EX $125
Star-Kist, telephone, Charlie the Tuna, 10", 1987, Mint ... $80

Box, Waltke's Baby Doll Soap, Proctor & Gamble, 2-1/2" x 4" x 1-1/2".

StayPuft Pencil Sharpener, 1987 Columbia Pictures, China, 3" h, EX $20
St. Charles Evaporated Cream, cow clock $1,250
Tappan, chalkware chefs, 9-1/2" h, flat backs, 1940s, for pair $95
Texaco, metal key chain charm, EX $15
Tyson, egg timer, 3-3/4" h $38
War Poster, Government Bonds $350
Woolsey's Paint, pocket mirror $350
Wrigley's Gum display, tin $850

Tobacco Items

Bloodhound 10 Cent Cuts, cardboard box, NM $95
Brown's Mule, diecut display, cardboard box w/15 plugs, NM $135
Camel, ad, "Read the truth: when they learn to smoke, they flock to Camel," 1928, NM $43
Camel, Chesterfield, Luckies, Old Gold, framed pin-up poster, woman in shorts, EX $28
Cannon Ball Chewing Tobacco, memo booklet giveaway .. $8
Chesterfield, magazine ad, 1938, NM $4
Chesterfield Plant, postcard, 1950s, EX $5

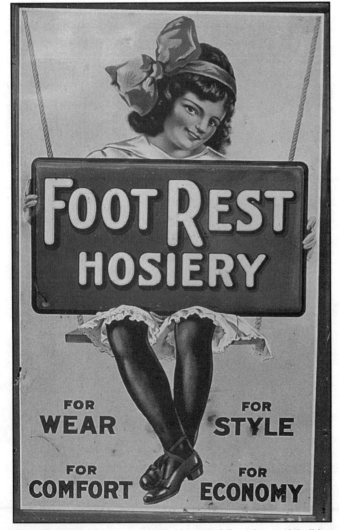

Sign, Foot Rest Hosiery, 11-3/16" x 17-1/4", embossed tin litho on cardboard, yellow ground behind letters.

Day's Work, diecut display cardboard box w/12 plugs, EX $75
Egyptienne Luxury, cardboard cigarette box, 1909, NM ... $25
Friends, die-cut display cardboard box w/12 unopened pouches, EX $135
George Washington, cardboard pouch, unbroken seal, NM $55
Hillbilly, cloth pouch, unbroken seal, 1910, NM $35
Hit Parade, magazine ad, 1957, NM $3
J.K. McKee & Co. Confectionery and Cigars letterhead, EX $12
L&M, magazine ad with James Arness, 1959, NM $4
L&M, postcard, EX $5
London Life, cardboard cigarette box, 1910, NM $20
M. Melachrino and Co., cigarette cardboard box, NM $28
Model Tobacco Co. Plant, postcard, 1957, EX $5
Model, cardboard tobacco pouch, unopened, seal intact, Series 113, EX $30
Old English Curve Cut, cardboard box, 4-3/4" x 3-3/4", EX $25
Our Advertiser, 2-1/4 oz. cloth pouch, unopened, EX $25
Our Advertiser, 7 oz. cloth pouch, unopened, NM $65
Prince Albert, magazine ad, NM $3
Red Fox Chewing Tobacco, memo booklet giveaway $8
RJR, postcard, Winston cigarette plant, 1940s, NM $6
RJR, stock certificate, 1948, EX $25

Tobacco Signs

Camel Cigarettes and Prince Albert, cardboard sign w/Santa, 1941, EX $195
Camel Cigarettes, Christmas cardboard sign w/Santa Claus, 1936 .... $365
Camel Cigarettes, "So Mild So Good, Sold Here," tin sign, series #973, 24" x 8", NM $175
Granger Rough Cut, heavy cardboard sign, man and woman, 1930s, EX $45
L&M, round diecut tin sign, EX $85
Prince Albert, tin sign, The National Joy Smoke Sold Here," EX $125
RJR, cash value tin sign, NM $115
Verada Cigarette, ashtray, porcelain, NM $105

Tobacco Tags

American Navy, NM $10
B.F. Hanes, Our Senator, EX $20
Bird in Hand, NM $18
D.H. Spencer & Son, Calhoun, NM $18
F.G. Flynt, Pride of Winston, EX $18
Harvey's National Leaf, NM $7
Irwin & Poston, Sweet Mash, NM $25
J.G. Flynt, Pride of Winston, NM $20
Lash's Select, EX $7
P.H. Hanes, Early Bird, EX $10
P.H. Hanes, Just Out, NM $12
Piedmont #11, EX $12
R&W, Ogburn and Hill, EX $7
RJR, Home Dew, embossed, NM $10
RJR, Mickey, NM $8
RJR Strawberry, EX $9
Spargar Bros., Cream of NC, NM $55
Stater Bros., Days Work, NM $8

Sun Cured, Ram's Horn, NM $7
Taylor Bros., Cannon Ball, NM........................... $12
Taylor Bros., Ram's Horn, NM $10

Tobacco Tins

Allen & Ginter Dixie Chop Cut Plug, barrel tin, 4-1/2" x 3",
EX $250
Arcadia Tobacco, horizontal box, 4" x 2-1/2" x 1", VG.... $10
Auto Tobacco, horizontal flat box tin, 1/2" x 3-3/4" x 2",
VG $15
Bagdad Tobacco, pocket tin, 1-1/4" x 3-3/4" x 2-1/2", EX $60
Belfast Cigars, vertical box tin, 7" x 6" x 3", NM $28
Benton Tobacco, vertical box tin, 2-1/4" x 4-1/2" x 3-1/4",
VG $20
Black and White Tweenies, small flat cigar tin, 1/2" x 3-1/4"
x 3", EX $75
Blue Boar, cylindrical tobacco tin, 5", NM $15
Bond Street Tobacco, pocket tin, 1" x 4-1/2" x 3" EX $18
Briggs Tobacco, pocket tin, 1" x 4-1/2" x 3", EX $15
Bridley's Mixture, cylindrical tobacco tin, 3-3/4" x 5-1/2",
NM $8
Bugler, cylindrical tobacco tin, 5" x 4-1/4", NM $15
Camel, horizontal flat cigarette tin, 3/4" x 5-1/2" x 4-1/4",
EX $25
Cameron's, horizontal box tobacco tin, 1-1/4" x 3-1/4" x
4-1/2", EX $40
Carolina Gem Long Cut, square corners, EX $125
Chesterfield Cigarette, small round tin, 3-1/4" x 2-1/2",
EX $15
Chesterfield Cigarette, flat horizontal tin, 3/4" x 5-3/4" x
4-1/2", EX $12
Christan Peper, vertical box tobacco tin, 6-1/4" x 4-3/4" x
3-3/4", NM $12
Cinco, horizontal box cigar tin, 1" x 8" x 5", EX $10
Columbia, horizontal box tobacco tin, 2" x 4" x 2-12",
VG $30
Dill's Best, cylindrical tobacco tin, 2-3/4" x 5", NM $25
Dixie Queen, lunch pail tobacco tin, 4" x 7" x 5", NM ... $85
Dutch Masters, horizontal box cigar tin, 4" x 3" x 1", VG $12
Dutch Masters, cylindrical cigar tin, 5-1/4" x 5-1/2", NM $25
Edgeworth, horizontal box tobacco tin, 3/4" x 3" x 2",
NM $10
Edgeworth, sample tobacco tin, 3/4" x 2" x 3", VG $20
Eight Brothers, cylindrical tobacco tin, 6" x 5", EX $10
Eight Brothers, cylindrical tobacco tin, 5" x 5", NM $13
Eight Brothers, cylindrical pail tobacco tin, 6-1/4" x 4-3/4",
EX $85
F.F. Adams & Co. Peerless, cylindrical pail tobacco tin,
6-1/4" x 4-3/4", NM $85
Friends, cylindrical tobacco tin, 5" x 5", NM $25
Gail & Ax, Navy lunch pail tobacco tin, 6" x 5" x 4", GD . $20
George Washington, key top canister, EX $30
George Washington, slip top canister, 1926 stamp, EX ... $65
Half and Half Tobacco, pocket tin, 1" x 4-1/2" x 3", NM $20
Half and Half Tobacco, collapsible pocket tin, 1" x 4-1/2"
x 3", EX $17
Half and Half Tobacco, pocket tin, 5" x 4-1/4", NM $20
Half and Half, cylindrical tobacco tin, 8", NM $10
Handsome Dan, horizontal box tobacco tin, 4" x 3" x 1",
VG-EX $50
Hiawatha, horizontal box tobacco tin, 2" x 5" x 3", EX ... $60

Just Suits, horizontal box tobacco tin, 3" x 4" x 6", EX .. $25
Kentucky Club, vertical box tobacco tin, 4" x 4-1/4" x 6",
MT $20
Kentucky Club, pocket tobacco tin, 1" x 4-1/2" x 3", NM . $20
La Pallina, horizontal box cigar tin, 1-1/2" x 5" x 3-1/2",
EX $10
Lady Churchill, horizontal box cigar tin, 1-1/2" x 5" x
3-1/2", EX $20
Lucky Strike, horizontal box tobacco tin, 2" x 4-1/2" x 3",
EX $15
Lucky Strike, pocket sample tobacco tin, 3/4" x 3-1/4" x
2-1/2", EX $45
Lucky Strike, horizontal box flat cigarette tin, 1/4" x
6" x 4", EX $15
Manola, vertical box cigar tin, 5-1/4" x 3-1/2" x 3-1/2",
EX $40
Maryland Club, horizontal box tobacco tin, 2" x 4-1/4" x
2-1/4", EX $12
Mayo's, lunch box tobacco tin, 5" x 7-3/4" x 3-1/2", EX $75
Melachrino, horizontal box, assortment, Egyptian cigarette
tin, 2-3/4" x 9-3/4" x 1-1/4", EX $10
My Pal, horizontal box tobacco tin, 3" x 4-3/4" x 3-1/2",
EX $20
Ogden's, cylindrical tobacco tin, 4" x 4-1/4", NM $15
Old Chum, vertical box tobacco tin, 6" x 3-1/2" x 4-1/2",
EX $30
Old English flat square tobacco tin, 1/2" x 3-1/4" x 3-1/2",
VG $10
Old English, horizontal box tobacco tin, 2-1/4" x 3-1/2" x
3-1/4", EX $15

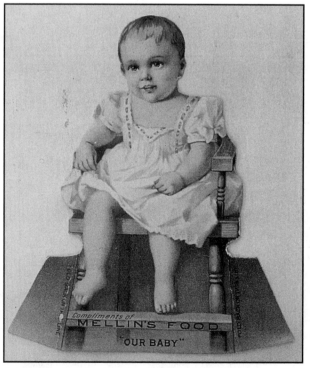

A baby food trade card illustrated by Maud Humphrey
Bogart, $17.

Old English, horizontal box tobacco tin, 2-3/4" x 4-3/4" x 3-1/2", NM $25

Old English, horizontal box tobacco tin, 2-3/4" x 4-1/2" x 3-1/2", EX $25

Old Virginia, cylindrical box tobacco tin, 4" x 4-1/2", EX$10

Omar Cigarettes, horizontal box tobacco tin, 1-1/4" x 8-1/2" x 5-3/4", EX $15

Orcico, vertical box cigar store tin, 5-1/2" x 6" x 4", EX . $275

Patterson's Seal, lunch pail tobacco tin, 5" x 6-1/2" x 4-1/2", EX $65

Pearson's Red Top Snuff, tin, paper label, EX $25

Penn's, square box tobacco tin, 6-1/2" x 6-1/2" x 1-3/4", EX $20

Piper Heidsieck Chewing, square flat tobacco tin, 1/2" x 3" x 3", VG $10

Player's Cigarette, horizontal box tin, 1-1/2" x 4-3/4" x 3-1/4", Mint $15

Player's Cigarette, horizontal flat box tin, 5" x 7-3/4" x 3-1/2", NM $20

Prince Albert, key top, 1926, unopened, Mint $85

Prince Albert, pocket tobacco tin, 1" x 4-1/2" x 3", NM . $20

Prince Albert, round canister top, EX $30

Red Jay, square box tobacco tin, 4-1/2" x 6-1/2" x 6-1/2", EX $60

Repeater, horizontal box tobacco tin, 1-1/4" x 3-1/2" x 2-3/4", VG $45

Revelation, pocket tobacco tin, 1" x 4" x 3-1/2", EX $15

Revelation, pocket tobacco tin, 1" x 3" x 3-1/2", EX $15

Revelation, sample pocket tobacco tin, 1" x 3" x 3-1/2", EX $50

Sail, cylindrical tobacco tin, 5-1/4" x 4-1/2", EX $15

Senator, vertical box tobacco tin, 4-1/2" x 3-3/4" x 2-1/2", EX $50

Sir Walter Raleigh, pocket tobacco tin, 1" x 4-1/2" x 3", EX $20

Stag, pocket tobacco tin, 1" x 3-1/2" x 2-3/4", VG-EX .. $50

Summer-Time, cylindrical tobacco tin, 5-1/2" x 4", NM $10

Surbrug's Golden Sceptre, tobacco tin, 3-1/2" x 2-1/2" x 1-1/2", EX $35

Sweet Burley Light, round tobacco tin, 2" x 8", EX $45

Sweet Caporal, horizontal box tobacco tin, 3/4" x 5-3/4" x 4-1/2", NM $15

Sweet Caporal, horizontal flat cigarette tin, 3/4" x 5-3/4" x 4-1/2", EX $15

Sweet Cuba, lunch pail tobacco tin, 4-1/2" x 7-1/2" x 4-3/4", G $25

Target, cylindrical tobacco tin, 5" x 4-1/4", VG $10

Three States, horizontal box tobacco tin, 1" x 4-1/2" x 3-1/4", G $9

Three States, horizontal box tobacco tin, 2-1/4" x 4-1/2" x 3-1/4", EX $45

Tiger, horizontal box tobacco tin, 2-1/4" x 3-1/4" x 6", EX $40

Tops Snuff, paper label, unopened, EX $18

Tuxedo, cylindrical tobacco tin, 4" x 4-1/4" x 3-1/2", VG $15

Tuxedo, pocket tobacco tin, 1" x 4-1/2" x 3", EX $20

Twin Oaks, pocket tobacco tin, 1" x 4" x 3-1/4", VG $60

Union Leader, pocket tobacco tin, 1" x 4-1/2" x 3", EX .. $10

Union Leader, pocket tobacco tin, 1" x 4-1/2" x 3", NM. $15

Union Leader, lunch pail tobacco tin, 5" x 7-1/4" x 5", VG $15

Union Leader, horizontal box tobacco tin, 3" x 6" x 3-3/4", EX $25

Velvet, pocket tobacco tin, 1" x 4-1/2" x 3", EX $35

Velvet, cylindrical tobacco tin, 6" x 5", EX $10

Webster, horizontal box tobacco tin, 1-1/2" x 3-1/2" x 5-1/4", EX $20

World's Navy, square box tobacco tin, 2-1/2" x 7-1/4" x 6-1/2", EX $30

Yale, horizontal box tobacco tin, 1-1/4" x 4" x 2-1/2", EX $13

Tin, Shamokin Packing Co., Pure Lard 2 lb. pail, wire handle, Indian motif, blue ground top, 4-3/4" diameter, 4" bottom, 4-3/4" high, $25.

Advertising pinback button, tin, $8-$15.

ANIMATION ART

One of the big pushes in collecting and investing in the 1980s and 1990s is animation art. Galleries feature animation art nationwide, and major auction houses sell it for thousands of dollars. Why has this historically-discarded art become such a major collectible?

1. **Limited availability.** Through the years, studios destroyed a majority of their animation cels, making those that survived even more valuable.
2. **Beauty.** Animation art pieces are great display items and conversation pieces.
3. **Nostalgia.** Just like Barbie dolls and Hot Wheels cars, people remember fondly the cartoons of their past. What better way to bring back those warm feelings of youth than to have an original piece of animation art from those cartoons?

Combine these three elements and you have the makings for an explosive marketplace. And that's just what has happened. Witness the five-figure prices paid for some of the most popular animation art — *Lady and the Tramp* cel, $57,500; Peter Pan and Tinkerbell cel, $21,850; *Snow White and the Seven Dwarfs* cel, $85,000.

Animation art is not cheap, but there are many items that retail in the hundreds and low thousands.

History: Winsor McCay's 1909 *Gertie the Dinosaur* is frequently referred to as the first animated cartoon. But the celluloid process — an animation drawing on celluloid — is attributed to Earl Hurd. These early pioneers paved the way for the giant in animation, Walt Disney. To this day, Disney Studios remains the leader in animation. Disney animation cels are truly expensive. At a recent auction, an original production cel of Mickey Mouse garnered a bid of more than $400,000.

Contemporary cels from such films as *Beauty and the Beast*, *Pocahontas*, *The Lion King* and *Hercules* are made through computerization, so limited-edition animation art has been produced for the collector market. They are hand-painted reproductions of famous scenes and even newly created scenes not in the movie. These limited-edition items are made in editions of 250 to 2,500. Values can be in the thousands of dollars.

Serigraphs, or sericels, are silk-screened cels that look similar to limited-edition cels, but no work is done by hand. They are often produced in editions of 5,000. Sericels are the most affordable items of animation art, usually selling for less than $300.

Warner Brothers characters are second only to Disney characters in collectibility. Bugs Bunny is king of the Warner line, with the Road Runner, Wile E. Coyote, Daffy Duck, Taz and Marvin the Martian not far behind.

With a successful movie and television show, cels featuring MTV's Beavis and Butthead are hot sellers today.

Foreign animation art from countries such as Japan is currently underappreciated and undervalued. Termed "Japanimation," this art is some of the more affordable on the marketplace, with some original productions cels in the $100 to $200 range.

Definitions

12-Field: 10" x 12" cel or drawing.

16-Field: 12" x 16" cel or drawing.

Animation Cel: Sheet of clear acetate or nitrate hand-painted and placed over a background and photographed. These are photographed in sequence; the sequence, when projected, creates the illusion of motion.

Animation drawing: Original production drawings created by an animator from which the cels are later created.

Courvoisier: A cel set-up created and sold by the Courvoisier Galleries in the late 1930s to early 1940s. Characters were often trimmed to image, glued to the background and covered with a protective top cel. Backgrounds used include wood veneer, polka dots, stars and hand-painted watercolor backgrounds. The original set-ups were framed in an off-white mat, included penciled name of the character and a "Walt Disney Productions" stamp, with labels attached to the back.

Disneyland Art Corner: Cels sold at Disneyland from the mid 1950s to the early 1970s. Cels are trimmed, set against a litho background and have a gold seal attached to the back of the mat.

Disney Seal: Sold in the 1970s, these are full cels that are laminated and embossed with "Original hand-painted movie film cel." These seals are larger than those used today.

Pan (Cinemascope): Cel or drawing up to 12" x 30".

Production: Any cel or drawing created for the production of an animated film, but doesn't mean the piece appears in the film.

Publicity or Promotional: A non-production cel created for promotional purposes.

Sericel from 1937 film *Snow White and the Seven Dwarfs*, $250.

Reproduction or Limited Edition: A non-production hand-painted cel created specifically for collectors. Produced in limited quantities, usually 250 to 2,500. They were not used in a film and were created to resemble original production art, either reproducing a scene or creating new scenes. Mostly made in the last 20 years.

Serigraph cel (Sericel): Non-production silk-screened cel similar to a limited edition, but no work is done by hand. Often produced in editions of 5,000. These are not animation cels.

Publications
Animation Film Art, P.O. Box 25547, Los Angeles, CA 90025.

Animation Magazine, 4676 Admiralty Way, Ste. 210, Marina, Del Ray, CA 90292.

In Toon!, P.O. Box 217, Gracie Station, New York, NY, 10028.

Storyboard/The Art of Laughter, 80 Main St., Nashua, NH   03060.

Clubs
•Greater Washington Animation Collectors Club
  12423 Hedges Run Dr. #184, Lake Ridge, VA 22192

DID YOU KNOW?

•One second of film requires more than 20 animation cels.

VALUE LINE

Disney
Aladdin, Aladdin plucks a tasty treat for Princess Jasmine, limited edition, framed size 16" x 34" $2,500

Aladdin, Aladdin and lamp, sericel, framed size 19" x 22" $275

Alice in Wonderland, Down the Rabbit Hole, limited edition, framed size 18" x 38" $2,000

Bambi, Bambi and Faline, sericel, framed size 18" x 21" $275

Bambi, Bambi and Thumper, limited edition, framed size 18" x 21" $2,250

Beauty and the Beast, Belle and the Beast, limited edition, framed size 20" x 24-1/2" $2,500

Beauty and the Beast, Belle and the Beast by the fire, Sericel, framed size 19" x 22" $275

Cinderella, Bruno, color model animation cel, 3" x 5" ... $800

Cinderella, Lady Tremaine, original animation production drawing, signed by Frank Thomas, 7-1/2" x 4" $500

Cinderella, limited edition, hand-inked and hand-painted, framed size 18" x 21" $2,850

Cinderella, panoramic-size sericel of entire cast, framed size 17" x 38" $650

Cinderella, perfect fit, sericel, framed size 18" x 21" $275

Donald Duck, Alpine Climbers, Donald fighting with eagle and getting slapped by eagle, original animation production drawings, price for pair $1,200

Donald Duck, Lonesome Ghosts, Donald emerging from box, original animation production drawing, 4" x 4" . $450

Donald Duck, Mickey's Circus, Donald with fish in bill, original animation production drawing, 4" x 4" $495

Donald Duck, from 1938 short *Donald's Better Self*, original animation production cel, 5-1/2" x 9" $1,800

Donald Duck, from 1961 short *Mathmagic Land*, original animation production cel, 5" x 4" $650

Donald Duck, 1950s/1960s original animation production cel, Disneyland set-up with gold seal, 6" x 8" $600

Donald Duck, 1985 television commercial, original animation production cel, 9-1/2" x 5-1/2" $450

Dumbo, Dumbo and his mother inside the circus tent, limited edition, framed size 18" x 21" $1,850

Dumbo, Dumbo and Baby Mickey, original production cel, framed size 16" x 18" $700

Dumbo, original animation art story drawing of Dumbo, matted and framed, 8" x 11" $1,900

Goofy, Batter Up, sericel, framed size 16" x 26" $375

Goofy, Goofy Golf, sericel, framed size 34" x 20" $450

Goofy, 1985 television commercial, original animation production cel, 10" x 6" $350

Fantasia, centaur, original animation art production cel, 8" x 6" $3,900

The Jungle Book, Mowgli, Baloo and Bagheera, limited edition, framed size 18" x 21" $1,850

The Jungle Book, Mowgli and Bagheera, sericel, framed size 19" x 22" $275

Lady and the Tramp, Lady and Tramp over a color laser background, original animation production cel, framed, 7" x 4-3/4" $4,900

The Lion King, pan-sized sericel, framed size 17" x 38" $650

The Lion King, Rafiki teaches Simba, sericel, framed size 17" x 20" $275

The Lion King, Simba introduces Pumbaa and Timon to Nala, limited edition, framed size 20" x 25" $2,650

Mickey, Camping Out, Mickey and Minnie, original animation art production drawing, 3" x 4" $450

Mickey, Canine Caddy, Mickey swinging golf club, original animation art production drawing, matted and framed, 6" x 7-1/2" $950

Mickey, Mickey's Elephant, Mickey holding a saw, original animation art production drawing, 4" x 2-1/2" $525

Mickey, Puppy Love, Mickey holding flowers and candy, original animation art production drawing, matted and framed, 3-1/2" x 3-1/2" $850

Mickey, Society Dog Show, Mickey dragging Pluto, original animation art production drawing, 5-1/4" x 6" $575

Mickey, Steamboat Willie, original animation art production drawing, 3-1/2" x 6-1/2" $2,400

101 Dalmatians, Cruella, limited edition, framed size 18" x 21" $2,000

101 Dalmatians, Double Wedding (Perdita and Pongo, Anita and Roger), limited edition, framed size 18" x 32" $2,000

101 Dalmatians, Pongo with puppy on his head, original animation art production cel, Disneyland mat and gold seal $3,800

101 Dalmatians, Puppy Disguise, sericel, framed size 19" x 22" $275

Peter Pan, Hook, original animation production drawing, 10" x 4-1/2" $975

Peter Pan, John readying for battle, original animation production drawing, 16-field paper, 6-1/2" x 6-1/4" . $375

Peter Pan, Lost Boys, original animation production drawing, 5-1/2" x 6-1/2" $600

Peter Pan, Michael yanked up pirate sail, original animation production drawing, 3" x 10-1/2" $425

Peter Pan, one of the Lost Boys and Indians, original animation art production cel, 12-1/2" x 9" $950

Peter Pan, Peter Pan in headdress, original animation production drawing, 5-1/4" x 5-1/2" $595

Peter Pan, Peter Pan, original animation production drawing, 6-1/2" x 4-3/4" $750

Peter Pan, Peter Pan, original animation production drawing, 7" x 3-1/2" $850

Pinocchio, Coachman, original animation production drawing, green highlights, 5" x 8-1/2" $850

Pinocchio, Jiminy and Gideon, original animation art production cel, 9-1/2" x 8-1/2" $4,500

Pinocchio, Pinocchio, Figaro and Cleo, original animation art production cel, original paint, Courvoisier set-up with original label $13,500

Pinocchio, Pinocchio and Jiminy, original animation art production cel, Courvoisier set-up $11,000

Pinocchio, Stromboli, original animation production drawing, red accents in ax, 7-1/2" x 7-1/2" $700

Pluto, *Donald's Garden*, Pluto fighting with gopher for bone, 2-3/4" x 10" $475

Pluto, *Just Dogs*, original animation art production model drawing of Pluto and different poses of the same dog, framed $950

Pluto, *Mickey's Elephant*, Pluto as devil $350

Pluto, *Society Dog Show*, Pluto and judge, 6-3/4" x 8-1/4" $400

Robin Hood, Robin and Little John, framed, 6-1/2" x 11" $900

Sleeping Beauty, Briar Rose, original animation art production cel over a color laser background, 4-1/2" x 3-1/4" $1,950

Sleeping Beauty, Briar Rose and forest animals, original animation art production cel over a color laser background, matted and framed, 7" x 9" $2,900

Sleeping Beauty, Briar Rose close-up of face with cape, original animation art production drawing, 7-1/2" x 4-1/2" $450

Hand-painted cel from Disney's *The Lion King*.

Sleeping Beauty, Briar Rose full-figure pose, original animation art production drawing, 5-1/2" x 2-1/2" ... $495

Sleeping Beauty, Briar Rose full-figure pose, original animation art production drawing, 6-1/2" x 2-1/2" ... $495

Sleeping Beauty, Briar Rose with berry basket, original animation art production drawing, 9-1/2" x 5" $395

Sleeping Beauty, goon, original animation art production drawing, 4-1/2" x 3" $250

Sleeping Beauty, Maleficent and Diablo, original animation art production cel over a color laser background, 7-1/2" x 6" $4,900

Snow White, Bashful, original animation art production drawing, key drawing, red highlights, 4-1/2" x 3-1/2" $850

Snow White, blue bird on Snow White's fingers, original animation art production cel, Courvoisier set-up with labels $14,500

Snow White, raccoon and his reflection, original animation art production cel, Courvoisier set-up with labels, original Courvoisier framing, 3-1/2" x 2-1/2" $950

Sword in the Stone, Wart as squirrel and lady squirrel, 5" x 10" $550

Winnie the Pooh, Pooh, Eeyore, and Piglet, 1980s, sericel with Disney seal $195

Winnie the Pooh, Pooh and Piglet with matching production background from an educational 1980s, original animation art production cel $950

Winnie the Pooh, Tigger Bouncing, 1980s, original animation art production cel $195

Winnie the Pooh, Tigger, 1980s, original animation production drawing $125

Winnie the Pooh, New Adventures of Winnie the Pooh, Rabbit, 1970s, original animation production drawing, 4-1/2" x 2-3/4" $125

Other Characters

Beavis and Butthead, original production cel $500

Bugs Bunny, Bugs and Daffy Duck, *Hunting Season*, limited edition, signed by Chuck Jones, framed size 18" x 21" $850

Bugs Bunny, Bugs, Daffy and Elmer, limited edition cel, signed by Chuck Jones, framed size 18" x 21" $950

Bugs Bunny, *A Hare Grows in Manhattan*, limited edition, framed size 16" x 34", signed by Virgil Ross $845

Bugs Bunny, *Little Red Riding Rabbit*, limited edition, framed size 18" x 21", signed by Virgil Ross $795

Bugs Bunny, Show Biz Bugs, 4-panel scene, limited edition, framed size 18" x 39", signed by Virgil Ross $995

Bugs Bunny, *A Wild Hare*, Bugs and Elmer Fudd, limited edition, framed size 16" x 18", signed by Virgil Ross $650

Daffy Duck, *Daffy Duck's Fantastic Island*, 1981, original animation art production cel of Daffy in grumpy mood, signed by Friz Freleng, Warner Bros. Seal, matted and framed, 4-3/4" x 2-3/4" $850

Daffy Duck, 1960s, original animation production drawing, matted and framed $500

Elmer Fudd and Daffy Duck, *Duck Hunting*, limited edition cel, framed size 18" x 21", signed by Friz Freleng $950

Fat Albert and the Cosby Kids, Filmation Studios, 1970s, tempera background sheet, framed $900

Felix the Cat, *Biker Felix*, limited edition, signed by Don Oriolo, framed size 18" x 21" $600

Felix the Cat, Felix and his magic bag, limited edition, signed by Don Oriolo, framed size 18" x 21" $600

Felix the Cat, Felix time line, limited edition, signed by Don Oriolo, framed size 18" x 36" $700

Felix the Cat, Felix Dentist, limited edition, signed by Don Oriolo, framed size 16" x 18" $400

Foghorn Leghorn, 1960s, original animation art production $325

Garfield, original production cel, Garfield and Grandma from Garfield's Christmas, signed by Jim Davis, framed size 16" x 18" $400

Garfield, original production cel, Garfield and Odie, signed by Jim Davis, framed size 16" x 18" $500

Garfield, original production cel, Garfield, Odie and Jon, signed by Jim Davis, framed size 16" x 18" $600

Garfield, original production cel, Garfield dancing, signed by Jim Davis, framed size 16" x 18" $400

Garfield, original production cel, Garfield wondering where Odie is with the remote control, signed by Jim Davis, framed size 16" x 18" $300

Garfield, original production cel, No applause, just throw lasagna!, signed by Jim Davis, framed size 16" x 18" $400

Garfield, original production cel, Odie, signed by Jim Davis, framed size 16" x 18" $300

Japanimation, original production cel, Akira $175

Japanimation, original production cel, Dragon Ball $175

Japanimation, original production cel, Gall Force $175

Japanimation, original production cel, Genocyber $150

Japanimation, original production cel, Robot Carnival .. $150

Marvin the Martian, limited edition, signed by Chuck Jones, framed size 16" x 18" $675

Marvin the Martian, Marvin and Hugo, 1980s $1,400

Pink Panther, Anteater, original production cel, 4-1/2" x 4" $125

Pink Panther, Inspector, early cel in grease pencil $150

Popeye, limited edition cel, edition size of 250 .... $450

Ren & Stimpy, original production cel $500

Road Runner, 1980s, original animation art production $350

Road Runner and Wile E. Coyote, Acme Bird Seed, limited edition, signed by Chuck Jones, framed size 16" x 29" $1,325

Road Runner and Wile E. Coyote, chase scene, limited edition, signed by Chuck Jones, framed size 16" x 18" $1,195

Sylvester, original production cel, gouache on full celluloid, accompanied by original layout drawing, 1960, mounted, framed, glazed, 17" x 32" $400

Tasmanian Devil, Taz in Dallas Cowboys uniform, from 1980s/1990s television commercial $550

Tasmanian Devil and Sam, in front of Cactus Saloon, limited edition cel, framed size 16" x 18", signed by Friz Freleng $950

Tom and Jerry, Tom, Jerry and Tuffy, 1940s/1950s, 4" x 5" $450

Tom and Jerry, Jerry, 1940s/1950s, model drawing, 3-1/2" x 5" $450

Tom and Jerry, Jerry and lady Cat from *Love Me, Love My Mouse*, cel, 5-1/4" x 2-1/2" $300

Tom and Jerry, *Tom and Jerry The Movie*, original production multi-cel setup, reproduction background, gouache on full celluloid, unframed, signed by Bill Hanna and Joe Barbera, 11" x 14" $250

Tweety and Sylvester playing tennis, sericel, signed, framed size 16" x 18" $700

Wile E. Coyote, 1980s, original animation production drawing $300

Yellow Submarine, John Lennon and Ringo Starr, Heinz Edelman, King Features, 1968, 7-1/2" x 9" gouache on celluloid $2,500

Warner Brothers, limited edition cel featuring eight Looney Tunes characters, 30" x 20", signed by Friz Freleng $1,775

Warner Brothers, limited edition cel featuring 18 Looney Tunes characters, 40" x 34", signed by Virgil Ross $1,895

ART DECO

Although the style Art Deco dates between 1920-1940, the term itself was not coined until the Art Deco revival of the 1960s. At the time, the sleek, clean style known as Art Deco was referred to as modernism, although some purists will claim clear differentiation between the two. Whatever one chooses to call it, the style was a clear departure from the swirling excesses of Art Nouveau. Most art historians agree true Art Deco began slowly in the early 1900s and attained the height of its glory in the Exposition Internationale des Arts Decoratifs et Industriels Modernes, held in Paris in 1925.

After the abundantly embellished motifs of Art Nouveau, the clean geometric lines and form-that-follows-function philosophy of Art Deco was a welcome breath of fresh air.

Although the lines are strong and simple, Art Deco is actually very sumptuous and luxurious. The use of exotic woods, precious metals, exquisite fabrics, ivory, mother-of-pearl, snakeskin and animal hides implies understated refinement. The devotion of Art Deco designers to fine craftsmanship, the clean geometric lines and avoidance of prettiness in embellishment is a fine combination.

As with any design style, some Art Deco pieces were designed and produced with the elite in mind, while others were produced for the average consumer. For the most part, those differences are reflected, now and in the 1920s, in price differences. In a few instances, simple functional pieces made of modest materials are disproportionately expensive, due to the name of the designer.

Clarice Cliff pottery is a perfect example. Cliff, a self-taught decorative British painter, worked her way up to designer, from line painter, in a famous pottery factory. Her challenge was to decorate styles of blank pottery whose sales had slumped in recent years and generate enough interest to sell off the remaining stock of blanks. The success of her designs is the stuff of which legends are made and today, a teapot featuring one of her signature designs can sell for thousands.

Art Deco examples can be found in paintings, furniture, pottern, fashion and almost any other works.

Bareaux set, mirror, brush, powder box; unmonogrammed, black and chrome.

Clubs:
- National Coalition of Art Deco Societies
  One Murdock Terrace, Brighton, MA 02135-2817
  Newsletter: NCADS Bulletin

- Art Deco Society of California
  Suite 511, 100 Bush St., San Francisco, CA 94104

- Art Deco Society of Chicago
  5801 N. Lincoln, Chicago, IL 60659

- Art Deco Society of Cleveland
  3439 West Brainard Rd. #260, Woodmere, OH 44122

- Art Deco Society of Detroit Area
  PO Box 1393, Royal Oak, MI 48068-1893

- Art Deco Society of Los Angeles
  PO Box 972, Hollywood, CA 90078

- Art Deco Society of Louisiana
  PO Box 1326, Baton Rouge, LA

- Art Deco Society of New York
  385 Fifth Ave., Suite 501, New York, NY 10016
  Newsletter: Modernist

- Art Deco Society of Northern Ohio
  3439 West Brainard Rd. #260, Woodmere, OH 44122

- Art Deco Society of the Palm Beaches
  820 Lavers Circle #G203, Del Ray Beach, FL 33444

- Sacramento Art Deco Society
  PO Box 162836, Sacramento, CA 95816-2836

- Art Deco Society of San Diego
  PO Box 33762, San Diego, CA 92163

- Art Deco Society of South Carolina
  856-A Liriope Lane, Mount Pleasant, SC 29464

Publications
Collector's Guide To Art Deco by Mary Frank Gaston (Collector Books, 1994)

The Echoes Report
Deco Echoes Publications
PO Box 2321, Mashpee, MA 02649
508-428-2324

4-1/2" ash tray and cigarette box, pottery.

1936 McClelland Barclay plaque, 8-7/8".

Museums

•Walter Gropius House
  68 Baker Bridge Rd., Lincoln, MA 01733
  617-259-8843

•The Newark Museum
  49 Washington St., Newark, NJ 07101-0540
  201-596-6550

•Virginia Museum of Fine Arts
  2800 Grove Ave., Richmond, VA 23221-2477
  804-367-0888

VALUE LINE

Magazines and ephemera

Theatre June, 1927 (cover only)	$30
Judge May, 1924	$20
Spur (large format magazine from 1938 and 1939)	$10
Modern Priscilla June 1923 (cover only)	$10
Needlecraft Magazine July, 1928	$16
Child Life July, 1938	$10
Picture Play April, 1922	$23
Colliers (1922)	$28
American Home (1930s)	$10
Western Business October, 1931 (cover only)	$15
Valentines, Easter, anniversary cards (1920s-1930s)	$5 ea

Glass

Four etched deep leaf cordials	$35
Pair clear candleholders	$27

Amethyst art glass vase in brass stand	$595
Piano candy dish	$125
Six-sided water pitcher with two etched panels of female figure	$500
Blue glass vase w/etching (signed)	$275
Pair marigold cornucopia vases (Jeanette Glass Co.)	$35
Black glass box w/ pewter lid	$75

Decorative Pottery

Dish w/ painted floral design (Japan)	$25
Pink vase in shape of hands (Nelson McCoy)	$48

Fiestaware

Small green tray	$35
Small plate	$7-$12
Cobalt pitcher w/ chip	$35
Lamp of nude female figure	$400
Pair green cornucopia wall vases (Hall)	$55

Kitchen Items

Chrome electric teapot w/cord	$38
5-pc stove-top set (s&p, sugar, flour)	$75
4-pc chrome coffee set	$110
Chrome 2-slice toaster	$75
Chrome toaster	$50
Chrome 2-slice toaster (Sunbeam)	$80
Covered refrigerator containers (Hall China Co.) blue	$30
yellow	$32
orange	$35
Yellow pitcher (Hall China Co.)	$40
Yellow tea pot (Bauer)	$125
Ceramic salt & pepper shakers	$45

Light blue tinted glass picture frame, tin-plated corner mounts, 4" x 5", Ginger Rogers picture.

Jewelry

Elaborate rhinestone bracelet $45
Simple rhinestone bracelet $35
Clip w/rhinestones and red stone $30
Pair rhinestone shoe slips $30
Mesh bag w/rhinestone clasp $95
Small silver mesh bag $37
Large black mesh bag $53
Tiny silver mesh bag $53
Rhinestone necklace w/matching earrings $95
Pair 10K gold cufflinks w/diamonds $250
Onyx and sterling earrings w/rhinestones $75
Bakelite bracelet $28
Blue enamel belt buckle (2 pc) $69
Rhinestone dress clip $75

Desk Items

Cast-iron letter stand $75
Electric clock w/round face and blue glass
   (in working order) $55
Wooden clock with female figure (small) $175
Celluloid desk set $150
Dog bookends c1937 (Rockwood) $475
Iron foyer lamp $125
Brass Scottie bookends $250
Hollow metal Scottie bookends $45

Perfume Bottles

Danse Galante eau toilette $35
Nuit de Gala (Francois Gerard) $45
Tiny Shalimar w/blue top $20
Chypre Moiret Paris $55
Pink glass w/glass stopper $42
California Perfume Co. $75
Black-glass perfume atomizer $50

Compacts

Illinois Case Co. (square w/watch, powder, and rouge) $95
All-in-one (Richard Hudnut) $75
Coty "envelope" $50
14K gold (no mark) $625
Pentagon-shaped compact w/lipstick $150

Garments

Beaded white silk dress (early 1930s) $150

Bar Ware

Glass cocktail shaker w/"Sweet Ad-aline" and two
   drunks $32
Glass cocktail shaker w/bellhop $35
Chrome seltzer dispenser $45
Glass seltzer dispenser w/etched words $30
Glass ice bucket w/chrome handle $35

Smoking Accessories

Chrome cigarette case w/attached lighter $25
Marble ashtray w/figurine $140
Sterling silver cigarette lighter $55
Cigarette case w/lighter (Ronson) $49
Chrome ashtray (floor model) $150
Glass cigarette box (Heisey) $160

Furniture

Small mahogany chifferobe (minimal embellishment) ... $350

Bronze wash Spalter, celluloid faces, marble base, 5" high, 5" base.

ART POTTERY

In the early 1870s, the art of ceramic and china painting caught the attention of the public as a form of self-expression and potential field of employment, mainly for women. By 1879, ceramic mania had swept the country and potteries were springing up from sea to shining sea.

Pockets of successful potteries were centered in areas known for their indigenous clay. (One such well-known pocket was centered around Zanesville, Ohio.) In these pockets, the business of pottery-making flourished, with each company working feverishly to develop new paste recipes, shapes, glazes and painting techniques; guard their precious trade secrets; and market lines of decorative ware to an adoring public.

The popularity and demand for decorative ware peaked and then dimmed with the economic crisis of the late 1920s and '30s. By the late 1940s, many once-prolific potteries had closed their doors forever.

Because these potteries are no longer producing their wares, collectors find the American art pottery pieces produced between 1880 and 1950 particularly desirable. A beginning collector would profit from reading a few library books and attending a museum exhibition or two before jumping into this highly competitive market.

Although the demand for well-known collectibles is keen, pieces by lesser-known potteries are still available at very reasonable prices, making this a good collecting category for beginners.

General Guidelines: An undamaged piece commands a higher price than one with even minor blemishes: no chips, cracks, flakes, crazing, or hairlines. With a few exceptions, a well-known pattern, preferably one advertised in a catalog, is more desirable than an unknown pattern. A marked piece is more desirable than an unmarked piece. The marked piece of a well-known design, or a rare-but-known design, in pristine condition, signed by the artist, commands the highest price of all.

Why do two similar pieces by the same manufacturer vary so much in price? Regional differences can account for some fluctuation. Demand by competing collectors in a specific area can cause artificially high prices.

Collecting Terms

Au Gratin. Small covered casserole dish.

Baker. An open dish for baking pies, vegetables, etc.

Earthenware. Pottery made of clay fired at temperatures lower than porcelain. It is considered good for everyday use because it is cheaper to produce than porcelain.

Flint enamel glaze. A finish usually applied to yellow ware consisting of powdered metallic glazes sprinkled on a coat of wet, clear glaze. When fired, the melting metal produced streaks of brilliant blue, green, white, and orange.

Gadroon. Dinnerware with molded-rope decoration.

Lug. Small tab handles on a bowl or jardiniere.

Paste. A mixture of clay and chemicals from which pottery pieces are made.

Roseville vase, 9-3/4" high, Rozanne Woodland, beige ground, brown tiger lily, tan stem, leaves. E.E. on base.

Red ware. Represents the widest category of American pottery, due to the availability of the raw material-red clay. The pieces are relatively fragile.

Rockingham. Clay glazed with dark brown, sometimes mottled glaze.

Scroddled or agate ware. Ceramic pieces made of mottled or swirled colors created by incompletely mixing several different clays. When fired, they would create a variegated effect. This is felt to be the least-known American ceramic product.

Toby jug. A mug or pitcher with the face or entire figure of a person.

Vitreous or vitrified. Non-porous pottery which resists stains.

Yellow ware. Common, inexpensive American pottery, which takes its name from the color of the clay. Often associated with pie plates and mixing bowls, plain or decorated with a simple colored band or sponged glaze.

Popular Manufacturers

A.E. Hull Pottery Company. Founded in 1905 by Addis Emmet Hull, William Watts, and J.D. Young in Crooksville, Ohio. Ceased production in 1986. Popular designs include Blossom Flite (mid 1950s), Bow Knot (late 1940s), Butterfly (mid 1950s), Calla Lily/Jack In The Pulpit (late 1930s), Capri (early 1960s), Crab Apple (mid 1930s), Dogwood/Wild Rose (mid 1940s), Ebb Tide (mid 1950s), Iris/Narcissus (mid 1940s), Magnolia (matte finish-mid 1940s; gloss finish-mid 1950s), Morning Glory.

General Guidelines: Distinctive markings on the bottom of Hull vases help with identification. Early stoneware pottery has an "H." The famous matte pieces, a favorite of most collectors, contain pattern numbers. For example, Camellia pieces are marked with numbers in the 100s, Iris pieces have 400 numbers and Wildflower pieces have a "W" preceding the number. Most of Hull's vases re also marked with their height in inches, making it easy to determine their value. Items made after 1950 are usually glossy and are marked "hull" or "Hull" in large script letters. Hull collectors are beginning to seriously collect the glossy ware and kitchen items.

McCoy Pottery.
Founded in 1848 by W. Nelson McCoy and W.F. McCoy near what is now Zanesville, Ohio. It was passed down through four generations of McCoys, and was sold to De-signer Accents in 1985; ceased production around 1990. Popular lines include: Hobnail, Lily Bud, Stretch Animals, Butterfly, Blossomtime, Wild Rose, Cascade, Brocade, Rustic, Harmony, Floraline, Antique, Starburst, and Golden Brocade.

General Guidelines: Several marks were used by the McCoy Pottery Co. Take the time to learn the marks nad the variations. Pieces can often be dated based upon the mark. Most pottery marked "McCoy" was made by the Nelson McCoy Co.

Red Wing Potteries Inc.
Founded in Red Wing, Minne-sota in the early 1900s; discontinued production in 1967. The Red Wing Stoneware Company (established 1878) and the Minnesota Stoneware Company (1883) merged in the early 1900s to form the Red Wing Union Stoneware Company. The well-known art ware was develop in the early 1930s and the name officially changed to Red Wing Potteries Inc. in 1936. The lines included vases, flower arrangers, figurines, etc.

General Guidelines: Red Wing Pottery can be found with various marks and paper labels. Some of the marks include a stamped red wing, a raised "Red Wing U.S.A. #_____," or an im-pressed "Red Wing U.S.A. #___." Paper labels were used as early as 1930. Some pieces were identified only by a paper label that was easily lost. Many manufacturers used the same mold patterns. Study the references to become familiar with the Red Wing forms.

Rookwood Pottery.
Founded in 1880 by Maria Longworth Nichols (in an old schoolhouse purchased by her father at a Sheriff's auction) in Cincinnati, Ohio; ceased production in 1967. Items include lamps, tea pots, chocolate pots, sugar bowls, cream-ers, vases, jardinieres, mugs, steins, candlesticks and ginger jars — initially these were purchased blanks and Rookwood empha-sized surface decoration. Later, the company was known for its complex clay blanks (erroneously call earthenware, but more closely resembling a semi-porcelain). Rookwood had more than 500 glazes, but eight glaze lines comprised the company's iden-tity: Cameo, Dull Finish, Standard, Aerial Blue, Sea Green, Iris, Mat and Vellum.

General Guidelines: With very few exceptions, all pieces of Rookwood Pottery were marked and dated. The vast majority of pieces — all but the very earliest — will display the famous "R" and "P" with the "R" reversed and the letters conjoined, surrounded by flames. In the very early years, counting the flames would de-termine the year of issue. By 1901 the date was indicted with a Roman numeral.

Production pieces (cast, undecorated) of Rookwood Pottery are usually available for about $40 and up. Most in demand, how-ever, are the artist-signed pieces. Expect to pay at least $300 and often more depending on quality, scarcity and condition of the piece. Very high quality pieces can bring thousands.

Roseville Pottery Company.
The facilities of J.B. Owens Pottery in Roseville, Ohio was sold in 1890. The company was incorporated in 1892 with Charles S. Allison as the first president and George F. Young as general manager. Young eventually be-came principal stockholder, and four generations of his descen-dants subsequently managed the firm. In 1900, Young hired Ross Purdy to develop Rozane, Roseville's first art line. The original Rozane line was renamed Rozane Royal in 1904. Roseville made more than 150 different lines or patterns.

General Guidelines: The prices for Roseville's later com-mercial ware are stable and unlikely to rise rapidly becaus it is readily avialable. The prices are strong for the popular middle-period patterns, which were made during the Depression and pro-duced in limited numbers. Among the most popular patterns from this middle period are Blackberry, Cherry Blossom, Falline, Ferella, Jonquil, Morning Glory, Sunflower and Windsor. Desirable Roseville shapes include baskets, bookends, cookie jars, ewers, tea sets and wall pockets. Most pieces are marked, however dur-ing the middle period paper stickers were used. These often were removed, leaving the piece unmarked.

Shawnee Pottery Company.
The Shawnee Pottery Co. was incorporated in the state of Delaware in 1936, and operated out of a complex of buildings in Zanesville, Ohio. Shawnee pot-tery was an inexpensive, mass-produced pottery that was sold by large retailers. Shawnee began production in 1937 in the midst of the Great Depression and continued into the new decade of the 1940s. It survived during the World War II years with a greatly curtailed, though highly profitable, operation. The late 1940s and early 1950s were the booming years for Shawnee; this was when it produced most of the figural lines and corn dinnerware that is so highly collected today. Production during the late 1950s and into the 1960s consisted mainly of corn dinnerware, ashtrays, kitchenware and non-figural floral items such as planters and vases.

General Guidelines: Shawnee pottery was made with a va-riety of marks, each indicative of a certain time period of produc-tion. Wares produced pre-WWII and into the early 1940s were generally marked with an incised U.S.A. on the glazed bottom. Later, the U.S.A. mark was combined with a three or four digit number. Post-war items often had the embossed word Shawnee on the bottom, along with U.S.A. and a number. In 1953, Shawnee began producing lines under the name Kenwood, and this name appears on many of those pieces along with U.S.A. and a number.

Prices have increased dramatically during the 1990s, dictated in large part by supply and demand. Figural items such as cookie jars, pitchers and creamers have always been preferred to non-figural items such as planters and vases. Miniatures are some of the least-expensive yet most highly sought-after Shawnee items. These miniatures are mostly non-figural pre-WWII items averag-ing three inches high and made as small vases, baskets, etc. in solid colors. Finding what is considered a "mint" condition piece is difficult, and any defects decrease the value considerably.

One of Shawnee's policies was to sell all of its "seconds" to outside decorators, who would then add gold trim, decals or handpainted features such as hair, bugs, patches, etc., to cover flaws on the pottery and sell these decorated items to higher-priced gift shops and stores. Items that have been decorated in this way are highly sought and often command from 50 to 100 percent more than the same item decorated plain.

Weller Pottery. Founded by Samuel A. Weller in 1872 near Zanesville, Ohio. The first pieces were sold door-to-door until the business grew large enough to open a factory in 1882, in Zanesville. Eventually, the business became one of the largest potteries in America, at one point owning three plants. It ceased production in 1948. There are well over 100 Weller patterns.

General Guidelines: Because pieces of Weller's commercial ware are readily available, prices are stable and unlikely to rise rapidly. Forest, Glendale and Woodcraft are the popular patterns in the middle price range. The Novelty Line is most popular among the lower-priced items.

Contributor to this chapter: Shawnee Pottery, Pamela D. Curran, 904-760-6600.

REPRODUCTION ALERT!

Unfortunately, Nelson McCoy never registered his McCoy trademark, a fact discovered by Roger Jensen of Tennessee. As a result, Jensen began using the McCoy mark on a series of ceramic reproductions made in the early 1990s. While the marks on these recently made pieces copy the original, Jensen made objects which were never produced by the Nelson McCoy Co. The best known example is the Red Riding Hood cookie jar, which was originally designed by Hull and also made by Regal China.

A mark alone is not proof that a piece is period or old! Knowing the proper marks and what was and was not made in respect to forms, shapes and decorative motifs is critical in authenticating a pattern.

Commemorative Shawnee cookie jars were produced from 1992-95 by Mark Supnick, and these are well-marked and dated as new. Several other companies, however, are reproducing cookie jars, corn ware and banks that may mislead the new collector. A company in Tennessee is making new Smiley Pig and Puss 'n Boots cookie jars, and some jars are marked with the word McCoy. Any known Shawnee design found with the word McCoy on the bottom should be considered to be a new piece.

An Ohio company that is reproducing Shawnee is calling itself The Shawnee Pottery Co. of Zanesville, Ohio, and has been marking its items with the name Shawnee, just as the original company marked its wares. To date the company is making Farmer Pig and his wife cookie jars, Smiley and Winnie bank cookie jars, and a set of six banks in the likeness of original Shawnee figurines. Don't be misled into thinking the original Shawnee Pottery Co. is back in business; it is not.

Clubs/Associations

•American Art Pottery Association
  PO Box 525, Cedar Hill, MO 63016

•Collectors of Illinois Pottery & Stoneware
  1527 East Converse St., Springfield, IL 62702

•Dedham Pottery Collector's Society
  248 Highland St., Dedham, MA 02026-5833

•North Dakota Pottery Collectors Society
  PO Box 14, Beach, ND 58621-0014

•Pottery Lovers Reunion
  4969 Hudson Dr., Stow, OH 44224

•Red Wing Collectors Society Inc.
  PO Box 184, Galesburg, IL 61402-0184

•Rosevilles of the Past Pottery Club
  PO Box 656, Clarcona, FL 32710-0656

•Shawnee Pottery Collectors Club
  PO Box 713, New Smyrna Beach, FL 32170-0713

Publications

American Pottery and Porcelain Identification and Price Guide by William C. Ketchum, Jr. (Avon Books)

Art Pottery of America by Lucile Henzke (Schiffer Publishing)

Art Pottery of the United States by Paul Evans (Scribner)

Roseville Pottery For Love or Money by Virginia Hillway Buxton (Tymbre Hill, 1977)

Shawnee Pottery, The Full Encyclopedia by Pamela Duvall Curran, P.O. Box 713, New Smyrna Beach, FL, 32170

VALUE LINE

Hull

Pre-1950 Patterns

Bow knot, B 3, 6" vase	$200
Bow knot, B 7, 8-1/2" vase	$275
Bow knot, B 13, double cornucopia	$295
Bow knot, B 28, 10" d, plate	$1,200
Dogwood (Wildflower), 504, 8-1/2" vase	$150
Dogwood (Wildflower), 507, 5-1/2" teapot	$350
Dogwood (Wildflower), 514, 4" jardiniere	$110
Iris, 405, 4-3/4" vase	$80
Iris, 406, 7" vase	$125
Iris, 412, 7" hanging planter	$175

Jack-in-the-Pulpit/Calla Lily, 500/32, 10" bowl $185
Jack-in-the-Pulpit/Calla Lily, 505, 6" vase $125
Jack-in-the-Pulpit/Calla Lily, 550, 7" vase $140
Magnolia, 4, 6-1/4" vase $55
Magnolia, 8, 10-1/2" vase $150
Magnolia, 14, 4-3/4" pitcher $55
Magnolia, 22, 12-1/2" vase $250
Magnolia (Pink Gloss), H 5, 6-1/2" vase $30
Magnolia (Pink Gloss), H 17, 12-1/2" vase $200
Open Rose (Camelia), 105, 7" pitcher $225
Open Rose (Camelia), 114, 8-1/2" jardiniere $375
Open Rose (Camelia), 120, 6-1/2" vase $110
Open Rose (Camelia), 140, 10-1/2" basket $1,300
Orchid, 301, 10" vase $325
Orchid, 306, 6-3/4" bud vase $145
Orchid, 311, 13" pitcher $650
Pinecone, 55, 6" vase $150
Poppy, 606, 6-1/2" vase $200
Poppy, 607, 8-1/2" vase $250
Poppy, 609, 9" wall planter $450
Rosella, R 1, 5" vase $35
Rosella, R 8, 6-1/2" vase $75
Rosella, R 15, 8-1/2" vase $85
Stoneware, 26 H, vase $80
Stoneware, 536 H, 9" jardiniere $110
Thistle, #53, 6" $150
Tulip, 101-33, 9" vase $245
Tulip, 109-33, 8" pitcher $235
Tulip, 110-33, 6" vase $150
Waterlily, L-8, 8-1/4" vase $145
Waterlily, L-18, 6" teapot $225
Waterlily, L-19, 5" creamer $75
Waterlily, L-20, 5" sugar $75
Wildflower, 54, 6-1/2" vase $145
Wildflower, 66, 10-1/2" basket $2,000
Wildflower, 76, 8-1/2" vase $325
Wildflower, W-3, 5-1/2" vase $55
Wildflower, W-8, 7-1/2" vase $85
Wildflower, W-18, 12-1/2" vase $250
Woodland (matte), W1, 5-1/2" vase $95
Woodland (matte), W10, 11" cornucopia $195
Woodland (matte), W25, 12-1/2" vase $395

Post-1950 Patterns (Glossy)
Blossom Flite, T8, basket $125
Blossom Flite, T10, 16-1/2" console bowl $125
Blossom Flite, T11, candleholders, price for pr $75
Butterfly, B4, 6" bonbon dish $45
Butterfly, B13, 8" basket $150
Butterfly, B15, 13-1/2" pitcher $185
Ebbtide, E3, 7-1/2" mermaid cornucopia $195
Ebbtide, E7, 11" fish vase $167
Figural planters, 27, Madonna, standing $30
Figural planters, 82, clown $50
Figural planters, 95, twin geese $50
Parchment & Pine, S-5, 10-1/2" scroll planter $85
Parchment & Pine, S-15, 8" coffeepot $125
Serenade (Birds), S7, 8-1/2" vase $55
Serenade (Birds), S15, 11-1/2" ftd fruit bowl $110

Red Wing vase, 8-1/8", light blue glaze, impressed mark and "1151."

Sunglow, 51, 7-1/2" cov casserole $50
Sunglow, 80, cup and saucer wall pocket $65
Sunglow, 95, 8-1/4" vase $45
Tokay (Grapes), 4, 8-1/4" vase $95
Tokay (Grapes), 12, 12" vase $125
Tokay (Grapes), 19, large leaf dish $95
Tropicana, T53, 8-1/2" vase $500
Woodland, W-6, 6-1/2" pitcher $65
Woodland, W-9, 8-3/4" basket $110
Woodland, W-13, 7-1/2" shell wall pocket $75

McCoy
Ashtray, Seagram's VO, Imported Canadian Whiskey,
    black, gold letters $15
Baker, oval, Brown Drip, 9-1/4" l $12
Bank, sailor, large duffel bag over shoulder $20
Basket, black and white, emb weave ext, double handle . $25
Bean pot, brown, #2 .... $35
Bean pot, brown, #22 .... $60
Birdbath $28
Bowl, 8-1/2" x 3", green $50
Casserole, open, Brown Drip $4
Center bowl, 5-1/2" h, Classic Line, pedestal, turquoise,
    brushed gold $35
Chuck Wagon, El Rancho $150
Coffee Server, El Rancho $125
Cookie jar, cov, Coffee Grinder $50
Cookie jar, cov, Colonial Fireplace $150

McCoy flower pot with attached saucer, green.

Cookie jar, cov, Cookstove, black $35
Cookie jar, cov, Cookstove, white $35
Cookie jar, cov, Covered Wagon $155
Cookie jar, cov, Jug, red label with Coca-Cola logo $80
Cookie jar, cov, Kookie Kettle, black $55
Cookie jar, cov, Mr. and Mrs. Owl $155
Cookie jar, cov, Oaken Bucket $40
Cookie jar, cov, Pontiac Indian $400
Cookie jar, cov, Potbelly stove, black $50
Cookie jar, cov, Puppy, with sign $135
Cookie jar, cov, Sad Clown $125
Cookie jar, cov, Schoolhouse $225
Cookie jar, cov, Strawberry, white $35
Cookie jar, cov, Tea Kettle, black $40
Cookie jar, cov, Tourist Car $150
Cookie jar, cov, Train, black $150
Cookie jar, cov, W.C. Fields $400
Cookie jar, cov, Woodsey Owl $345
Creamer, brown drip, 3-1/2" h $6
Creamer, Elsie the Cow $20
Custard Cup, vertical ridges, green $5
Decanter, Apollo Mission $30
Dog food dish, emb Scottie $15
Flower arranger, black $15
Flower bowl, Grecian, 12"d, 3"h, 24k gold marbling $24
Hanging basket, stoneware, mkd "Nelson McCoy," 1926 $20
Jardiniere, 6" d, glossy black, mkd "McCoy 6" $65
Jardiniere, 6" d, yellow, 1940s $60
Jardiniere, 7" d, Spring Woodline, c1960 .... $45
Jardiniere, 7" d, Swirl, black matte $38
Mug, Surburbia, yellow $10
Mug, Willow Ware, brown, c1926 .... $15

Pitcher, brown, Drip, 5" h, 16 oz $9
Pitcher, elephant, figural, tan glaze, c1940 .... $32
Pitcher, water lily, c1935 .... $20
Planter, Arcature, green and yellow $30
Planter, Wishing Well $18
Reamer, green glaze, 8" d, 1948 .... $12
Salt and pepper shakers, pr, figural, cucumber and mango,
    1954 .... $20
Spoon rest, Butterfly, dark green, 1953 .... $15
Spoon rest, Penguin, black, white and red, 1953 .... $20
Sugar, cov, emb face and scrolls, red glazed cover $10
Teapot, Brown Drip, short spout $20
Teapot, Grecian, 1958 .... $30
Teapot, Sunburst Gold, 1957 .... $25
Vase, Blossomtime $40
Vase, Bud, green $18
Vase, Double Handles, green, 8" h, 1948 .... $50
Vase, Maroon Gloss, 6" h, 1940s $35
Vase, Swan, pink $25
Vase, Triple Lily, 8-1/2" h, 1950 .... $90
Vase, Wheat, 8" h, 5" d, yellow, brown tint $45

Red Wing

Ashtray, horse's head, black or ochre $75
Basket, white, semi-gloss $32
Bean pot, cov, Tampico $35
Beverage Server, cov, Tampico $125
Bookends, pr, fan and scroll, green $20
Bowl, Cloverleaf, glossy, gray int, yellow ext. $32
Bowl, Spatterware, #4 .... $85
Butter dish, rect, Bob White $45
Candleholders, pr, Medieval $50
Candy dish, 3 part, hexagon, gray, semi-gloss $15
Casserole, cov, Tampico $25
Celery tray, Random Harvest $12
Cereal bowl, Damask $7.50
Cereal bowl, Pompeii $9
Chop plate, 12" d, Capistrano $20
Compote, blue and brown $60
Compote, blue fleck $45
Compote, orchid cherub $60
Console set, bowl and matching candlesticks,
    Renaissance Deer $120
Cookie jar, Katrina, beige $125
Cookie jar, King of Tarts, blue speckled $1,200
Creamer and sugar, Smart Set $85
Crock, two gal., birch-leaf dec $50
Cruet, Town and Country, chartreuse $25
Cup and saucer, Bob White $18
Cup and saucer, Capistrano $15
Cup and saucer, Magnolia $7.50
Cup and saucer, Tampico $10
Custard Cup, Fondos, green and pink $18
Flower block, Dolphin $35
Fruit bowl, Lute Song $9
Gravy boat, Driftwood, blue $19
Leaf dish, 11" x 11", green $60
Nappy, Lotus $8.50
Pitcher, Bob White $35

Pitcher, Brushed Ware, 8-1/4" h $225
Planter, Birch $25
Planter, Loop shape, green and silver $50
Plate, 6-1/2" d, bread and butter, Bob White $7.50
Plate, 6-1/2" d, bread and butter, Pepe $4
Plate, 6-1/2" d, bread and butter, Pompeii $5
Plate, 6-1/2" d, bread and butter, Random Harvest $6
Plate, 10" d, dinner, Bob White $10
Plate, 10" d, dinner, Lotus $8.50
Plate, 10" d, dinner, Town and Country, blue $9.25
Platter, Town and Country, chartreuse $18
Relish, Town and Country, blue, 7" x 5" $12
Salad bowl, Pheasant, blue and green $45
Salt and pepper shakers, Bob White, pair $30
Salt and pepper shakers, Brittany, Provincial $15
Shell, ftd, 11" x 9" $80
Teapot, yellow rooster, gold trim $75
Trivet, Minnesota Centennial $75
Vase, calla, blue and yellow $80
Vase, classic shape, 9" h, swan handles, cream, high glaze,
    mkd "Rumrill" $75
Vase, fan shape, 7-1/2" h, #892, blue, pink int $48
Vegetable bowl, Lute Song, divided $24
Vegetable bowl, Town and Country, chartreuse $15
Wall pocket, Gardenia, matte ivory $35
Warmer, 2 step $35

Rookwood
Ashtray, fox, beige high glaze, 6-3/4" d $325
Ashtray, harp, light green high glaze, 5-1/2" d $210
Ashtray, rook, butterscotch high glaze, 6-1/2" wide $250
Ashtray, rook, green mat glaze, 6-1/2" wide $270
Ashtray, rook, white mat glaze, 6-1/2" wide $250
Bowl, flower, wax primrose glaze, 12-1/2" d $625
Bowl, squat with banded dentil work, brown mat glaze,
    6" d $200
Compote, three elephants, burnt orange mat glaze, 5-3/4"
    high, 11" d $450
Jar, lidded, art deco, pink mat glaze, 6" $250
Jar, lidded, beige high glaze, 6-1/2" $349
Jiggered plate with knotted edges, 7" d $175
Urn, two-handled, white mat glaze, 12-1/2" high,
    10-1/2" d $525
Vase, art deco, pink mat glaze, 8-1/2" $350
Vase, beet red high glaze, 5" $245
Vase, blue high glaze with dark accents, 7" $275
Vase, butterfly design, yellow-green high glaze,
    4-1/2" high $140
Vase, charcoal with turquoise high glaze, 7" $350
Vase, cobalt blue high glaze, 10-1/2" high $400
Vase, crab apple motif, green glaze, 4-1/4" $175
Vase, deco motif, green mat glaze, 5-1/2" $175
Vase, deco motif, pink mat glaze, 5-1/2" high $300
Vase, diamond pattern, turquoise mat glaze, 5" high $300
Vase, flared lip, turquoise and gray high glaze, 7" high . $410
Vase, floral motif, brown high glaze, 6" high $175
Vase, fluted, two-handeled, cream high glaze, 8" $200
Vase, footed, blue highlights on maroon porcelain glaze,
    4-1/2" $275

Vase, incised decoration around base, light blue mat
    glaze, 5-1/2" $150
Vase, incised leaf design, mat green glaze, 5" high $175
Vase, leaf motif, light brown high glaze, 5" $150
Vase, lidded with decorative border, rose mat glaze,
    5-1/2" $210
Vase, Mexican motif, yellow-green high glaze, 5-1/2" .. $175
Vase, narrow neck, dark blue mat glaze, 7" $150
Vase, pink mat glaze, 5-1/2" $170
Vase, raised pattern, light blue mat glaze, 7" $350
Vase, tall with incised diamond pattern, pink and green
    mat glaze, 11-1/4" high $425
Vase, tulip, pink and green mat glaze, 5" $130
Vase, two-handeled with deco design, green mat glaze,
    6-1/2" high $110
Vase, waterlily design, turquoise high glaze, 6" $215

Roseville
Ashtray, Silhouette, brown $35
Basket, 10" d, clematis, brown $65
Basket, 10" d, Magnolia, green, mkd "385-10" $95
Basket, 10" d, Peony, yellow flowers $95
Basket, 10" d, Pine Cone, mkd "308-10" $215
Basket, 10" d, Rozana, ivory, mkd "1-66-2-2" $95
Bookends, pair, Foxglove, blue $125
Bookends, pair, Snowberry, pink $135
Bookends, pair, Zephyr, brown $115
Bowl, Apple Blossom, 8" d, green $45
Bowl, Carnelian II, blue and purple $95
Bowl, Corinthian, 6-1/2" d $55
Bowl, Magnolia, 10" d, blue $65
Bowl, Monticello, blue $85
Bowl, Panel, 5" d, brown $45
owl, Wisteria, blue, 2 handles, 2-1/2" x 6-1/2" $325
Candlesticks, pair, Baneda, pink, 4-1/2" h $575
Candlesticks, pair, Bleeding Heart, blue $95
Candlesticks, pair, Clematis, blue, mkd "1158-2" $85
Console bowl, Luffa, green, 13" d $265
Console bowl, Ming Tree, mkd "528-10" $75
Console bowl, Pine Cone $80
Cornucopia, Bittersweet $50
Cornucopia, Ivory II, 8", Art Deco $65
Cornucopia, Water Lily, brown $55
Creamer and sugar, Seascape, brown dec $140
Ewer, Bushberry, 6" h, blue $75
Ewer, Columbine, 7" h, blue $70
Ewer, Freesia, 6" h, green $65
Ewer, Gardenia, 6" h, brown $50
Ewer, Silhouette, 10" h $65
Ewer, Snowberry, 10" h, blue $95
Floor vase, Velmoss, green, 14" h $375
Flower frog, Fuchsia, green $195
Hanging basket, Mock Orange $265
Jardiniere, Florentine, 8' d, brown $95
Jardiniere, Imperial I, 9" x 9", small burst bubble $175
Jug, Cherry Blossom, brown, 4" h $265
Mug, Pine Cone, 4" h, brown $125
Planter, Artwood, yellow, 1056-10" $125
Planter, Earlam, green, 89-8 .... $200

Soap dish, Donatello $175
Sugar, cov, Snowberry, pink $125
Urn, Freesia, 8" h, green $95
Vase, Apple Blossom, pink, 7" h, #382 .... $125
Vase, Apple Blossom, pink, 8" h, #385 .... $165
Vase, Apple Blossom, pink, 10" h, #388 .... $250
Vase, Carnelian II, blue, 8" $185
Vase, Clematis, dark green, 6" h, #103 .... $90
Vase, Ferrella, 8" h, orange, mkd "506-8" $225
Vase, Foxglove, 6" h, blue, double open handles, mkd
    "44-6" $95
Vase, Freesia, brown $95
Vase, Futura, 6" h $195
Vase, Imperial II, 468-5" $165
Vase, Rosecraft, 5" d, black, mkd "158-5" $95
Vase, Thorn Apple, blue $85
Vase, Tuscany, gray, 9" $185
Vase, Wisteria, brown, 630-6 .... $375
Wall pocket, Corinthian, 12" l $225
Wall pocket, Donatello, 11-1/2" l $175
Wall pocket, Florane, handle $125
Wall pocket, Florentine, 9-1/2" l, brown $135
Wall pocket, Imperial II, #1264, orange and green $450
Wall pocket, Mostique, 9-1/2" l $195
Wall pocket, Tuscany, pink $125
Wall pocket, Wincraft, 5-1/2" l $175
Window box, Ming Tree, 11-1/2" l, blue $125

Shawnee

Prices listed here are for those Shawnee items in very good condition with no hairlines, crazing, chips, stains, discoloration or damage of any kind.

Ashtray, arrowhead 4-1/2" w $150
Ashtray, flair #408 .... $12
Ashtray, flying geese #403 .... $25
Aster vase, 5" h $8
Auto #506 .... $15
Bank, tumbling bear $175
Birds on driftwood #502 .... $45
Blackie the cat #642 .... $15
Bookends, setter (dog) heads, pair $45
Boy at gate 4" h $10
Boy and wheelbarrow #750 .... $22
Calla lily planter #181 .... $14
Canopy bed #734 .... $100
Chihuahua and dog house #738 .... $25
Chinese girl with book #574 .... $12
Clock, trellis $50
Cookie jar, Smiley Pig, 11-1/4" h, handpainted
    shamrocks $250
Cookie jar, Smiley Pig, 11-1/4" h, yellow neckerchief,
    gold, decals $350
Cookie jar, Winnie Pig, 11-1/4" h, blue collar $300
Cookie jar, Winnie Pig, 12' h, Clover Blossom $375
Cookie jar, Smiley Pig, 10-1/2" h, bank head, chocolate
    pants $400
Cookie jar, Winnie Pig, 10-1/2" h, bank head,
    butterscotch coat $425
Cookie jar, Puss 'n Boots, short tail, 10-1/4" h $175

Cookie jar, Puss 'n Boots, 10-1/4" h, gold & decals $425
Cookie jar, Muggsy dog, 11-1/4" h, blue bow $450
Cookie jar, Lucky elephant, 11-3/4" h, cold paint deco ... $90
Cookie jar, Sailor boy, 11-1/4" h, cold paint deco $100
Cookie jar, Sailor boy, 11-l/2" h, gold and decals $600
Cookie jar, Dutch boy, 11-1/4" h, cold paint deco $85
Cookie jar, Dutch girl, 11-1/2" h, handpainted tulip on
    skirt $175
Cookie jar, Drum major, 10" h, plain $400
Cookie jar, Jo Jo Clown and seal, 9" h, plain $350
Cookie jar, Winking Owl, 11-1/2" h, plain $125
Cookie jar, Little Chef, 8-1/2" h, yellow, green,
    or caramel, ea $100
Cookie jar, Pensylvania Dutch jug, 8-1/4" h, marked
    U.S.A. 75 .... $175
Cookie jar, Fern ware, 8-3/4" h, octagonal shape, marked
    U.S.A $80
Cookie jar, Basketweave canister, 7-3/4" h, yellow, green,
    or blue $75
Cookie jar, Corn King, #66 .... $250
Corn King range salt and peppers, 5-1/4" h, #77 .... $35
Corn King table salt and peppers, 3-1/4" h, #76 .... $25
Corn King sugar bowl w/ lid, #78 .... $35
Corn King creamer, #70 .... $30
Corn King casserole, large, #74 .... $70
Corn Queen mixing bowl, #5 .... $35
Corn Queen mug, #69 .... $50
Corn Queen teapot 30-oz, #75 .... $95
Corn Queen covered butter dish, #72 .... $45
Creamer, elephant, plain $30
Creamer, elephant, gold & decals $200
Creamer, Puss 'n Boots, yellow/green #85 .... $40
Creamer, Puss 'n Boots, white, gold/decals $200
Creamer, Smiley Pig, peach flower $70
Creamer, Smiley Pig, clover blossom $95
Donkey and basket #671 .... $22
Duckling and egg #753 .... $15
Dutch windmill #715 .... $25
Elephant #759 .... $15
Fawn and log #766 .... $30
Figurine, Mumpy Kitty 5" h $35
Figurine, crane 5-1/4" h $12
Figurine, dolphin 1-3/4" h $15
Figurine, flying bird 2-1/2" w $15
Figurine, Sealyham w/toothache 5" h $35
Figurine, spaniel 3-1/2" h $15
Figurine, standing lamb 2-1/4" h $15
Figurine, stippled bird $12
Figurine, terrier 6" h $22
Figurine, turtle 3-1/2" l $15
Floral planters and vases, 1950s, each $15
Flying mallard #707 .... $20
Frog on lily pad #726 .... $35
Giraffe and baby vase #841 .... $50
Globe #635 .... $25
Gondola 11-3/4" l $15
Kentucky colt 6-1/2" h $18
Lamb, black w/gold trim #724 .... $25

Leaf, red, planter #440 .... $14
Lobster covered sugar bowl #907 .... $30
Lobster creamer #909 .... $50
Lobster mug, 8-oz $100
Lobster french casserole, 10-oz $15
Miniature, Grecian pitcher 3" $12
Miniature, poinsettia jug 3" $12
Miniature, star pitcher 3" $12
Panda and Cradle #2031 .... $35
Piano #528 .... $25
Pie bird 5" h $40
Pitcher, chanticleer rooster $95
Pitcher, Little Bo Peep, gold and decals $250
Pitcher, Little Boy Blue #46 .... $135
Pitcher, Smiley Pig, flowers on chest $175
Rabbit and stump 3" h $12
Rooster #503 .... $25
Salt and pepper, Dutch Boy & Girl 5" h $35
Salt and pepper, lobster claw $50
Salt and pepper, milk cans 3-1/4" h $20
Salt and pepper, Muggsy 5" h $125
Salt and pepper, Puss 'n Boots, 3-1/4" h $35
Salt and pepper, Smiley Pig, peach, 5" h $110
Salt and pepper, Winnie and Smiley Pig, 5" h $125
Southern girl 7-1/4" h $20
Teapot, embossed rose $30
Teapot, Granny Ann, peach apron $125
Teapot, Granny Ann, lavender, gold/decals $225
Teapot, rosette flower $20
Teapot, Tom The Piper's Son, white deco $110
Teapot, Tom The Piper's Son, gold trim $225
Toby mug, 5-1/5" h $25
Valencia 10" dinner plate $18
Valencia teacup and saucer $30
Valencia salt and pepper shakers $20
Valencia 9" bowl $40
Valencia ball jug pitcher, 64-oz $45
Wall pocket, bird on cornucopia $18
Wall pocket, girl w/ rag doll #810 .... $30
Wall pocket, scottie dog $55
Wheat bowl, oval, marked U.S.A. $18

Weller

Ashtray, Coppertone, frog seated at end $100
Ashtray, Roma, 2-1/2" d $35
Ashtray, Woodcraft, 3" d $75
Basket, Melrose, 10" $145
Basket, Sabrinian $165
Basket, Silvertone, 8" $350
Bowl, 5-1/2" tall Ivory ware $80
Bowl, 4-1/2" tall Ivory ware $55
Bowl, 4" tall Ivory ware w/leaves $55
Compote, Bonito, 4" $75
Flower frog, figural, Muskota $125
Flower frog, figural, Silvertone, 1928 .... $100
Flower frog, figural, Woodcraft, figural lobster, c1917 .. $120
Jardiniere, Claywood, 8", cherries and trees $95
Jardiniere, Ivory, 5" $45
Jardiniere, Marvo, rust, 7-1/2" $85

McCoy french casserole, pink, $8.

Planter, blue drapery $60
Planter, Klyro, small $45
Planter, Sabrinian, 5" x 5" $170
Planter, Woodrose, 9"h $60
Vase, Art Nouveau, 9-3/4"h $225
Vase, Bonito, blue flowers, two small handles, 5"h $70
Vase, Burntwood, pin-oak dec, 11"h $150
Vase, Claremont, 5"h, two handles $60
Vase, Coppertone, 8-1/2"h $265
Vase, fan, 7"h, small flake $60
Vase, floretta, 7-1/2"h, grapes decoration, high-gloss
    glaze $175
Vase, forest, 6"h $165
Vase, Glendale Thrush $250
Vase, Hudson, floral dec., 7" high, signed "D England" $200
Vase, Hudson, floral dec., 7" high, signed "Timberlake" $375
Vase, Knifewood, 5-1/2"h, canaries, high glaze, nick on
    inside rim $125
Vase, Louwelsa, 10"h $210
Vase, marbleized, 6" $80
Vase, Muskota, boy fishing, c1915, 7-1/2"h $200
Vase, oak leaf, 7"h, double bud type, green and brown
    accents, blue ground $85
Vase, paragon, gold, base chip, 6-3/4" $145
Vase, Roma, grape dec., 6"h, scenic $65
Vase, Suevo, 7"h $115
Vase, Tutone, 4"h, three-legged ball shape $75
Vase, Woodcraft, 1917, smooth tree-trunk shape, molded
    leafy branch around rim, purple plums, 12"h $195
Wall pocket, Roma $195
Wall pocket, Sabrinian $475
Wall pocket, Suevo $195
Wall pocket, Sydonia, blue $225
Wall pocket, Woodcraft, 9"h, tree-trunk shape, molded
    leaves, purple plus $400
Wall pocket, Woodcraft, 10"h, conical, molded owl's
    head in trunk opening $300
Wall pocket, Woodrose, lilac $85

AUTOGRAPHS

Autograph collecting is the hobby of queens and presidents. It's true! Queen Victoria (in her childhood years), Franklin D. Roosevelt and John F. Kennedy all collected autographs. Ironically, collectors now avidly seek the autographs of these famous autograph collectors.

The past two decades have seen a tremendous growth in the popularity of autograph collecting. As an interest of some five million people in the United States, autograph collecting has joined the likes of trading cards and dolls as one of the most favored U.S. pastimes.

The cost for collecting can be minimal. Often, the price of a celebrity address book, a few stamps and a photo can net you a prized signature. On the other hand, the cost of collecting can be astronomical. Signatures of historically important figures will cost a pretty penny. Prices for some signatures have eclipsed the five-figure mark. Even some modern-day scrawls of living celebrities can run $100 or more.

Besides sports personalities, the most popular area of collecting may be the U.S. presidents. Other extremely hot areas are the signatures of the signers of the Declaration of Independence, U.S. Supreme Court Justices, vice presidents, first ladies, key individuals of the Civil War and other war heroes, royalty, entertainers and even criminals and other infamous personalities.

Obtaining Signatures

Getting autographs can be done through a reputable dealer, in person or through the mail. Items such as historical documents and manuscripts should be purchased from a dealer with a solid reputation and a return policy. A reputable dealer can evaluate the authenticity, condition, quality of the signature and the content of the document.

Signatures could be authentic (the actual person's autograph), secretarial (or ghost-signed), pre-printed, autopen, rubber stamp or a forgery.

A secretarial signature is the signature of the celebrity signed by a secretary or other such assistant. Walt Disney authorized his artists to sign his name. Experts can determine that a particular signature was written by an artist and determine which artist it was.

A pre-printed signature has been printed directly onto the document or photo or the negative. To tell if the signature is pre-printed on a glossy photo, hold the photo at an angle, up to a light. If the gloss is over the signature, you've probably got a pre-printed signature.

The autopen is a device that traces the signature onto the document. To find out if an autopen was used is a bit more difficult, as the autopen has become increasingly advanced. Autopen signatures have even ink-flow throughout, including the beginning and end of the signature. Another telltale sign of an autopen in use is that the signatures on several documents will match exactly. Autopens are used most often by high-demand celebrities, such as popular movie stars, athletes and government officials.

A rubber stamp may be used to place the signature on the item. These signatures may appear to be uneven in ink dispersion and/or smeared.

A forgery is an unauthorized copy of a signature. A reputable dealer can authenticate signatures.

If you get the autograph in person, you know it's authentic. If you get it by other means and have access to other authentic signatures from the celebrity, compare the signatures to determine authenticity. Signatures shouldn't appear identical; if they do, you may be looking at an autopen autograph.

This Babe Ruth autographed baseball sold for at auction for $3,066.

PRESERVING AUTOGRAPHS

Autographs on paper can deteriorate if not cared for properly. Most paper is highly acidic and will deteriorate over time. To prevent this, store the paper in acid-free protectors. Older papers, made before the late 19th century, should be kept separate from newer papers, since older paper isn't as acidic.

To avoid damage from moisture and light, keep autographs in a low-humidity, dark environment. If autographs are framed, they should be framed using special materials that shield the paper from ultraviolet light. The combination of acid-free protectors, darkness and low humidity will ensure proper protection of autographs for years to come.

Trends: The signatures of Civil War principles are very hot; even lesser-known Civil War participants are seeing the values of their signatures increase.

Also, vice presidents' and first ladies' signatures are getting more attention. This is due in part to the fact that presidential signatures have gotten so expensive.

Autographs of living celebrities are in demand, but not only those of current stars. Actors from 1960s and 1970s TV series and films can be found signing at autograph or movie memorabilia shows across the country. Sci-fi and horror stars are most in demand.

Finally, on a slightly morbid note, death is still one of the best things to happen to a signature. When a celebrity dies, that's the end of the signatures. If there's sufficient demand or the celebrity died at a young age and hadn't signed too much material, values can rise.

Clubs

•United Autograph Collectors Club
P.O. Box 6181, Washington, DC 20044-6168;

•Universal Autograph Collectors Club
P.O. Box 5262, Clinton, NJ 08809;

•The Manuscript Society
350 N. Niagara St., Burbank, CA 91505-3648;

Publications

Autograph Times, 1125 W. Baseline Rd #2-153-Q, Mesa, AR 85210

Autograph Collector, 510-A S Corona Mall, Corona, CA 91719-1720

The Autograph Review, Jeffrey W. Morey, 305 Carlton Rd., Syracuse, NY 13207

Space Autograph News, Mike Johnson, 862 Thomas Ave., San Diego, CA 92109-3940

Autograph Research, Mike Johnson, 862 Thomas Ave., San Diego, CA 92109-3940

TERMS AND ABBREVIATIONS

To understand autograph collecting, it is necessary to become familiar with some collecting terms. Listed below are some commonly-used terms.

4to: approximately 8" x 10"
8vo: approximately 6" x 8"
12mo: smaller than 6" x 8"
ADS (Autograph Document Signed): official document with the body of the document written in the hand of the signer.
ALS (Autograph Letter Signed): letter written completely in the hand of the person described and signed by the same person.

AMQS (Autograph Musical Quotation Signed): handwritten musical notes or a bar of music, signed.
ANS (Autograph Note Signed): commonly confused with an ALS, an ANS usually has no salutation or ending.
AQS (Autograph Quotation Signed): quotation (of the signer or another person) that is signed and written in the hand of the person described.
Autograph hand-written: autograph can appear as a signature by itself or it could be anything written in a person's own handwriting.
B/W: black and white photograph.
C: color photograph.
Circa, Ca. or C: term meaning "approximately," especially used with dates, when a specific date cannot be determined.
CS (Card Signed): signature on a card, usually a 3" x 5" or 4" x 6" index card.
DS (Document Signed): official document with the body of the document written or typed by another person or printed and signed by the person described.
Engraving: print made from a wood or metal surface that has had an image cut directly into it. After the image is cut into the plate, ink is forced into the lines that make up the image. The original surface of the plate is wiped clean, leaving ink only in the recessed image areas. A print is obtained by placing paper over the plate and running both the plate and paper through a printing press.
FDC (First Day Cover): envelopes printed especially for a new stamp, which are then canceled with a "First Day of Issue" designation.
FF (Free Frank): envelope mailed free of charge by a government official, member of royalty or other notable person who had the privilege of mailing correspondence at government expense. The signature is placed instead of postage and is often accompanied by the word "free."
Folio: approximately 12" by 18".
Foxing: yellow-brownish stain in paper that is caused by the oxidation of iron salts and minerals inherent in old paper.
Hand-coloring: applying watercolor by hand to a black-and-white printed image.
I (Inscribed): personalized.
IP (In Person): signature received in person.
ISP (Inscribed Signed Photo): personalized signed photo.
LS (Letter Signed): body of the letter is written by someone other than the person described as the signer.
Nd: no date
Ny: no year
Offsetting: very light impression of ink transferred to paper when a map or print has been folded and stored.
Paraph: an addition to a signature; a flourish or swirl, below or behind the signature proper.
Plate-mark: embossed line around the border of a map or print caused by the pressure of the printing press on the edge of the printing plate.
QS (Quotation Signed): quotation (of the signer or another person) that is signed. The quotation may be typed, printed or written in another hand.
Sig (Signature): signature of the person described, often found on a small card or as a "clipped signature" that was cut from a document or letter.

SP (Signed Photograph): photograph signed by the person/persons pictured.

TCS (Trading Card Signed): a signature on a trading card (sports or non-sports).

TLS (Typed Letter Signed): a typed letter that was signed.

Vellum: fine-grained lambskin or calfskin prepared especially for writing or binding books.

Watermark: marking in paper resulting from a design in the paper-mold, which is visible when the paper is held to the light.

Contributor to this section: Jerry Docteur, Pages of History, P.O. Box 2840, Binghamton, NY 13902.

TIPS FOR REQUESTING AUTOGRAPHS THROUGH THE MAIL

1. Always include an SASE (self-addressed stamped envelope) with sufficient return postage.
2. Be polite and courteous in your letter to the celebrity. Make the letter sincere. Mention that you enjoyed one of the celebrity's movies or were thrilled by his or her performance at a game.
3. Make the letter as brief as possible, one page or less.
4. You may either type or hand-write the letter. But always sign it by hand.
5. Be patient. Celebrities are busy. Many get hundreds and even thousands of requests per week.
6. Include an item you wish signed (an index card, a photograph etc.), but don't send a piece of memorabilia you don't want to lose.
7. Keep track of requests sent and received.

VALUE LINE

Presidents

George Washington, Signature	$5,500
John Adams, DS	$1,750
Thomas Jefferson, DS	$4,500
Andrew Jackson, ADS	$2,250
Martin Van Buren, ALS	$1,250
U. S. Grant, LS	$2,650
Benjamin Harrison, LS	$575
William McKinley, DS	$475
Theodore Roosevelt, TLS	$575
William H. Taft, ALS	$650
Woodrow Wilson, SP	$575
Calvin Coolidge, ALS	$550
Franklin D. Roosevelt, TLS	$725
Dwight D. Eisenhower, TLS	$325
John Kennedy, SP	$2150
Ronald Reagan, TLS	$225

Signers of the Declaration of Independence

John Hancock, Signature	$1,650
Josiah Bartlett, Signature	$210
Thomas McKean, DS	$360
Samuel Huntington, DS	$2,300
Roger Sherman, DS	$625

Civil War

Jefferson Davis, ALS	$1,550
William T. Sherman, ALS	$1,050
Philip H. Sheridan, ALS	$535
George B. McClellan, ALS	$440
Marcus Reno, Signature	$425
John C. Fremont, ALS	$530
Joshua Chamberlain, ALS	$1,800
Robert E. Lee, SP	$5,000
James Longstreet, SP	$1,800
Albert Sidney Johnston, ALS	$3,000

Supreme Court

Felix Frankfurter, SP	$550
John McLean, ALS	$525
Hugo Black, Signature	$40
Harold H. Burton, TLS	$100
Salmon P. Chase, ALS	$350
Oliver Ellsworth, DS	$175
Charles E. Hughes, Signature	$50
Potter Stewart, TLS	$75
Sandra Day O'Connor, TLS	$65
R. B. Taney, LS	$250
Earl Warren, TLS	$95
Fred M. Vinson, Postal Cover	$75

Sports

Hank Aaron, SP	$30
Muhammad Ali, SP	$50
Johnny Bench, SP	$30
Jim Bottomley, SP	$150
James J. Braddock, Signature	$110
Lou Brock, SP	$40
Frank Chance, SP	$1,250
Roberto Clemente, Signed Baseball Card	$200
Dizzy Dean, Signature	$50
Joe DiMaggio, SP	$125
Don Drysdale, SP	$50
Wayne Gretsky, SP	$60
Mickey Mantle, SP	$85
Babe Ruth, Signature	$600
Sam Snead, SP	$40

Entertainment

Lucille Ball, SP	$85
Jack Benny, SP	$60
The Beatles, Four Signatures	$1,400
Irving Berlin, Signature	$75
George Burns, SP	$45
Charlie Chaplin, SP	$750
Bette Davis, SP	$75
Walt Disney, Signature	$900
Billy Joel, SP	$40
Laurel & Hardy, SP	$800
Janet Leigh, SP	$25
Roy Orbison, SP	$100
Elvis Presley, Signature	$500
Christopher Reeve, SP	$50
Roy Rogers, SP	$40
Bruce Springsteen, SP	$75
Patrick Swayze, SP	$40
John Travolta, SP	$40
Ed Wynn, SP	$95

AUTOMOBILIA

Karl Benz and Gottlieb Daimler introduced the first successful gasoline-powered motor vehicles in 1886. Experimental horseless carriages existed earlier, and some motorized road-travel machines were built before 1800.

The American automobile industry began in 1896 when the Duryea Motor Wagon Co. mass-produced 13 cars of standard design. From that point, the auto industry introduced countless new developments and it didn't take long for the first cars to become outmoded and historically interesting.

By the mid 1920s, automotive trade magazines were publishing silver jubilee editions that celebrated the 25th anniversary of the industry. This focused attention on the history of the automobile and soon led to the formation of the first antique car clubs in the early 1930s.

In addition to vehicles, hobbyists collect automotive memorabilia, better known as automobilia. In the early days of the hobby, two types of collectibles — clothing and literature — got the automobilia ball rolling.

Clothing

When the hobby first began, most of the cars collected were built before 1916. These cars were from an era when motorists, driving in open-bodied cars, wore special clothing — such as dusters, cloth helmets, goggles and fur coats — to protect against the elements. Naturally old-car collectors want to look the part when driving their cars, and dressing up in vintage motoring garb has become part of the hobby.

When cars of the classic era (1920s-1940s) became popular, Gatsby-style clothing was the rage among car collectors. In the 1950s, the Model A Ford became a hot collectible and it was barbershop quartet-style duds that antique-auto lovers sought in thrift shops. Today, the rock-and-roll style clothing of the 1950s — like poodle skirts and saddle shoes — is popular with postwar car fanciers. Don't look now, but bell bottoms and double-knit leisure suits should be coming on strong as interest in 1970s cars develops.

General Guidelines: To be collectible, clothing must be in good or better condition. Items with the look of a specific era are especially desirable, as are articles of clothing made of fur or leather, like hats or jackets.

Literature

Old automotive literature has always been sought by antique-auto restorers. There has been a lot of material published about cars, from service manuals to magazines to travel guides.

Various companies published guides to help motorists buy the best cars at the right price. Other firms printed books that estimated values for second-hand cars. As early as 1902, Studebaker produced a press kit with photos to help publicize its electric cars. Hobbyists also go head-over-heels for sales brochures that illustrate their favorite car and all its features.

1915 Hood ornament, Louis Varonson, arms rotate.

The first car magazine was published around 1900 and thousands of other titles have launched and folded since, with hundreds still in circulation. All of these are collectible, as are books written about the romance or the history of the automobile. Books of this nature began appearing in good numbers after World War II.

Other collectible automotive literature includes old advertisements, posters, corporate reports, stock certificates, technical literature, publicity photos, promotional giveaways and showroom decorations.

General Guidelines: Collectors often seek automobile literature more for the subject than the condition of the book or manual, so items in lesser condition are collectible. However, paper items free of rips and stains are most desirable.

Badges, Mascots, Parts

In the early days of the hobby, there was a tremendous fascination with the many brands of automobiles that had been produced. In America alone, over 5,500 companies had built cars. Each of these marques had its own nameplate, badge or logo, distinctive radiator shape and hood or radiator mascot.

The nameplate was usually a brass name or initials affixed to the front of the radiator. The badge or logo decorated the top face of the radiator and sometimes the hubcaps. Radiator shapes ranged from barrel-like, as on the Franklin, to coffin-like, as on the Stanley Steamer. Mascots or ornaments sat atop the radiator caps of early cars. Later, when the radiator was moved under the hood, they decorated hoods. Mascot designs ranged from birds to elephants, naked ladies to Indian heads. Some were made by famous artists and sculptors.

Hubcaps, steering wheels, headlights, taillights and anything else that can be removed from an automobile also became common collectibles.

General Guidelines: Collecting badges and mascots is not as common as it was years ago, when such items could be found in salvage yards. Most newer collector cars don't have hood ornaments, and even the use of badges has slowed down in recent years. Complete collections put together years ago often find their way to high-end collectors. Muscle cars of the 1960s and 1970s usually have trim badges to set them apart from look-alike family cars and some of these decorative items are very rare and extremely valuable. Parts are more valuable as usable parts than they are as collectibles.

Dealer and Corporate Memorabilia

Car makers turned out all kinds of items bearing the name or logo of their product. Matchbooks used as sales premiums carried the same name and logo as the giant neon sign hanging outside the dealership. Today both the matchbook and the dealer sign have collector appeal, along with anything else the dealer owned, stocked or gave away.

Collectors have also been known to buy items such as factory security badges, corporate employment anniversary pins, sales contest prizes and myriad other items related to their favorite brand of car.

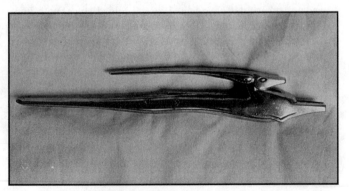

12" chrome antelope hood ornament.

General Guidelines: Corporate and dealer memorabilia is a very hot field. Old-car fans tend to be loyalists and will go to great (financial) extremes to get factory merchandise missing from their collection. Rarity is everything to serious buffs, and there are many rare trinkets. Promotional items with limited, or regional, distribution are most valuable.

License Plates

In the early days of the automobile, motorists made their own license plates, sometimes by decorating leather tags with house numbers. Porcelain plates were also used for a time. However, the metal plates used today have a long history.

States and territories use distinctive colors and designs on their plates. Special plates are made for trucks, taxis, official vehicles and school buses. In addition, unique designs have been created for presidential inaugurations, Vietnam veterans and United Nations ambassadors. The designs have changed many times over the years, as have the colors, though less frequently.

All of these factors make license plates attractive and appealing to collectors. The plates or "tags" are miniature artworks — produced in a more or less standard format — that reflect both history and creativity.

In addition to license plates, auto enthusiasts also collect old vehicle titles and registrations, tag toppers (small advertisements bolted onto the plates) and special license plate frames, such as those sold in Florida with palm trees in the frame design.

General Guidelines: License plates are often collected in series, such as collecting all the years and variations of plates issued by one state. Others collect specialty issues. Antique auto hobbyists collect plates from the year their favorite car was built. Plates should be in the best condition possible; however, most plates can be restored with minimal time, effort and cost. Therefore a rare plate in poor shape can still be worth more than a near-perfect common plate, as long as it can be restored.

Traffic Devices

After the invention of the automobile, it didn't take long for two horseless carriages to collide. After the first crash, it became obvious that traffic controls were essential. This led to stationary traffic signs which evolved into semaphore-style signals. These evolved into the common red/yellow/green traffic lights.

Early examples of stop lights, with only green and red lights, were perched atop ornate fluted cast-iron poles. Later, yellow caution lights were added.

Parking meters and reproductions of traffic signs are other popular collectibles.

General Guidelines: Stop lights are bulky and heavy and not usually available for sale, so they bring relatively high prices. Lights that function are most desirable.

Motorsports Memorabilia

Stock car racing has become *the* recent hot spectator sport. Most of the hot collectibles now have links to the National Association of Stock Car Auto Racing (NASCAR). Die-cast toy vehicles and apparel are especially collectible. Among the most popular items to collect are those associated with drivers Dale Jarrett, Dale Earnhardt, Kyle Petty, Rusty Wallace and Jeff Gordon.

General Guidelines: Historic memorabilia from the glory years of racing is becoming quite valuable. For newer racing collectibles, buy as much of the cheap stuff — lemonade boxes and coffee cans — as you can, since anything that depicts the driver can send its value skyrocketing. On the other hand, save some of your money to invest in high-end, limited-edition merchandise. This can be pricey, but worth it in the long run.

Clubs

•Automobile License Plate Collectors Association, Inc.
Gary Brent Kincade
P.O. Box 77, Horner, WV 26372
304-842-3773 / 304-269-7623

•Automobile Objects D'Art Club
David K. Bausch
252 N. 7th St., Allentown, PA 18102-4024
610-820-3001 / 610-432-3355

•Spark Plug Collectors of America
Jeff Bartheld
14018 NE 85th St., Elk River, MN 55330-6818
612-441-7059

•Hubcap Collector's Club
Dennis Kuhn
P.O. Box 54, Buckley, MI 49620
616-269-3555

•Antiques Motorcycle Club
P.O. Box 333, Sweetser, IN 46987

VALUE LINE

Autograph, Mario Andretti, photo	$20
Bottle, Fan Fuelers sports drink, 32 oz., Kyle Petty	$6
Bumper Sticker, Thunderbird, NASCAR Birds of Prey	$5
Clipboard, black plastic, Chevy Racing, red bow tie	$10
Decal, STP, checkered flag, Novi Indy race car, 1950s	$25
Hat pin, Jimmy Bryan, 200, 1986	$10
Helmet, brown leather, some aging	$75
Key Fob, Indianapolis car, brass, 1950s	$35
Mug, Indianapolis 500, frosted glass, Roger Ward, metal race car replica on handle, 1950s	$35
Order Form, flyer, Daytona 500 tickets, 1965	$5
Patch, jacket, Demolition Derby	$2
Plate, ceramic, Dale Earnhardt, 23k gold border, 6-1/2"	$30
Newspaper, National Dragster, 1964 issue	$2

Program, Late Model Championship Stock Car Race, 1958	$20
Rule Book, American Hot Rod Association, 1970	$15
Ashtray, metal, Snap-On Tools, 5" x 7"	$10
Catalog, JC Whitney, 1959	$20
Drive-In Speakers, good condition with wiring	$30
First-Aid Kit, Johnson & Johnson, tin, orig. contents, 5" x 7" box	$25
Flag Holder, gold colored, red and blue enamel, 1927	$75
Fuzzy Dice, 4" w, white with black dots	$5
Gasoline Gauge, Atwater Kent, 1909	$30
Gearshift Knob, simulated onyx, brass Saint Christopher medal center	$25
Gloves, pr., long gauntlet-style, black leather	$35
Hood Ornament, Liberty Bell, 1926	$16
Hood Ornament, Moon, crescent-shape, 1912-'28	$65
Hubcaps, set of four, Flipper, chrome	$90
Hubcaps, set of four, Pasco, screw-on, nickel-plated brass	$50
License Plate, Pennsylvania, school bus, 1969	$10
License Plate Tag Topper, State Farm Insurance	$13
Mirror, Argus, rearview	$45
Mirror, Vanity visor, bakelite frame, birds and flowers	$20
Owner's Manual, Buick Electra, Le Sabre and Wildcat, 1972	$7
Owner's Manual, Ford Thunderbird, 1961	$15
Owner's Manual, Plymouth, 1931	$15
Radiator Ornament, Ford, 1936, greyhound	$200
Reflector, red plastic, litho tin, 1950s	$15
Spark Plug, Blue-topped porcelain	$15
Spark Plug, Motormaster Blue Crown	$5
Steering Wheel Knob, ivory colored glass, blue and yellow swirls, "Rotary International" center	$45
Sunshade, cobalt blue, 1930s, heavy	$50
Tissue Dispenser, swing-out model, Hollywood brand	$50
Tray, carhop, 1950s	$25

Sales and Promotional Items

Ashtray, Chrysler Corporation, copper, 1933 World's Fair	$40
Badge, AAA Membership, white porcelain	$30
Badge, Humble Oil, plastic, red and silver	$15

Pennsylvania license plate, 1935.

Bell, Pontiac, hand held $30
Bird, Ford Falcon, plastic, 1960 .... $75
Blotters, Dodge/Plymouth, 1947 .... $10
Blotters, Firestone Tires, 1920s roadster, unused $8
Blotters, GMC Heavy Duty Trucks, 1951, unused $5
Calendar, Pennsylvania Ford, pocket, 1939 .... $10
Candy Container, 1930s sedan-shape, glass $15
Coin, commemorative, 1954 Corvette, gold colored $15
Cookie Cutter, metal, Chevrolet bow tie trademark $5
Fan, Ford, cardboard with wooden handle $10
Flashlight, Mopar Parts, red plastic, pocket size $10
Fork, Cadillac crest, silver-plated $35
Ice Scraper, Pontiac, red plastic $5
Magazine, Buick, May 1951 .... $5
Magnet, Mustang horse, vinyl $5
Matchbook, Plymouth, 1956 .... $4
Medallion, Chrysler, brass, 1939 .... $20
Pot Holder, Dodge, apple-shaped $10
Ruler, Pontiac, wood, 1938 .... $30
Service Mats, Chevrolet, paper, 1964 .... $10
Screwdriver, Chevrolet, metal handle, bow tie logo $25
Sign, Chrysler Motors/Mopar Parts, metal, flange $185
Sign, ESSO/Put A Tiger In Your Tank $110

Sign, Good Year Tires, emb. painted metal $55
Sunglasses, Chevrolet, 1962 .... $10
Thimble, Indiana Chevrolet, plastic, 1960s $5
Visor, Chevrolet, blue and white $5
Windshield Scraper, Pontiac, 1957 .... $5

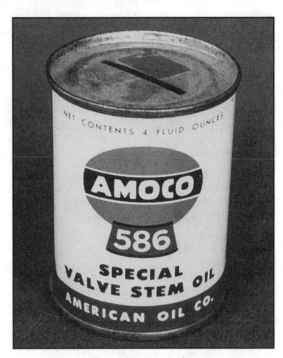

Tin oil can bank, $5.

Pontiac owner's manual 1950, 64 pages Pontiac owner's manual, 1950, 64 pages.

Elgin watch, $120.

BADGES

Everyone identifies the lawman by this symbol of his office, the badge. It is the single most recognizable part of his uniform and authority. It conveys the officer's oath of office and bestows his authority of law. This symbol of office can be found in the following categories: local, county, state and federal.

History: Badges have been a major instrument of identification since the mid-19th century. Metal insignia date back to the era of knights and before; under the rule of the Ming Dynasty in China, metal insignia was used to differentiate rulers' armies.

In the United States, the badge has been widely used since the Civil War era. The United States Marshal Service used them in the taming of the western frontier. Since the 1840s the United States Customs Service and established cities such as Boston, Baltimore, New York and Los Angeles have used the badge. As government bodies grew, different agencies were created to handle additional needs of the citizenry. As these agencies evolved new laws were created, thus creating an enforcement body. Hence the evolution of the instrument of office, the badge.

The heraldry of many local municipal, county and state governments can be found on badges. The United States government has adopted and uses only the eagle and federal shield as its design.

General Guidelines: Condition of the badge is a major factor in determining value. Most serious collectors want department-issued badges that exhibit some wear. Non-department issued badges are not as desirable. Beware of reproductions.

Badges come in a variety of metals and shapes. Most are manufactured by the use of a base metal and then plated in either brass, bronze, copper, silver or gold. They can be shaped like a shield, oval, circle or a star. Badges in their original state of issue are most desirable.

Badges are designed to be affixed by the use of a pin, lugs, screw post, belt or wallet clip. Missing fasteners will decrease value. Most badges issued after the 1950s have a maker's hallmark.

CAUTIONARY NOTE:

Collectors should consult state and local statutory laws concerning the purchase, trading or obtaining of law enforcement memorabilia. Some states have outlawed the possession of badges, patches and buttons by those other than law enforcement personnel.

Trends: Most badges are worth less than $300. Pricing depends on availability or rarity, metal, condition, and whether or not the badge is department-issued. Special presentation badges made of precious metals (sterling silver and/or gold, 10k, 14k, 18k) are eagerly sought by advanced collectors and can command a premium. Badges that were given or used by famous people or lawmen also command premium prices. For instance the D.E.A. badge given to Elvis Presley was auctioned for almost $10,000. A bid of $60,000 was made for the 14-karat gold U.S. Marshal badge given to General James Longstreet.

Publications

Federal Law Enforcement Badges by Kenneth W. Lucas Sr.

Badges of Law and Order by George E. Virgines

Badges of the United States Marshals by Raymond Sherrard/George Stumpf

The State Police & State Highway Patrol Badge Guide by William Mauldin

PCNEWS (Police Collectors News) RR 1 Box 14, Baldwin, WI 54002

Contributor to this section: Kenneth W. Lucas, 3052 Bel Pre Rd. #101, Silver Spring, MD 20906, 301-871-0877.

VALUE LINE

New York City, 1st Issue, 1845-1850s, Star .. $2,000-$5,000
New York City, 2nd Issue, 1857-1870 .... $1,000-$2000
New York City, 3rd Issue, 1870-1872, Acorn . $1,000-$2,000
New York City, 4th Issue, 1872-1889 .... $600-$1,200
New York City, 5th Issue, 1889-1898, Potsy . $1,200-$2,000
New York City, 6th Issue, 1892-1902 .... $600-$1,200

First issue, Boston Police, 1845-1850s.

New York City, 7th Issue, 1902-Present .... $400-$600
Boston, 1st Issue, 1845-1850s, Star .... $2,500-$4,500
Boston, 2nd Issue, 1854-1856 .... $1,500-$2,600
Boston, 3rd Issue, 1856-1868 .... $1,000-$2,600
Boston, 5th Issue, 1870-1879, Round .... $700-$1,500
Boston, 6th Issue, 1879-1922, Radiator .... $300-$600
Boston, 7th Issue, 1922-1959 .... $100-$200
Boston, 8th Issue, 1959-present .... $80-$150
Baltimore, 1st Issue, 1850-1860, Star .... $2,500-$4,500
Baltimore, 2nd Issue, 1860-1862, Faces .... $2,000-$3,000
Baltimore, 3rd Issue, 1862-1890, Star .... $300-$500
Baltimore, 4th Issue, 1890-1976 .... $45-$125
Baltimore, 5th Issue, 1976-present .... $300-$500
Philadelphia, 1st Issue, 1840-1850s, Oval .... $2,500-$4,000
Philadelphia, 2nd Issue, 1850-1861, Star .... $2,000-$3,500
Philadelphia, 3rd Issue, 1861-1890 .... $800-$1,600
Philadelphia, 4th Issue, 1890-1904 .... $400-$600
Philadelphia, 5th Issue, 1904-1930s .... $275-$450
Philadelphia, 6th Issue, 1930-present .... $50-$150
Pittsburgh, 1st Issue .... $1,000-$2,000
Pittsburgh, 2nd Issue, Current .... $50-$200
Toledo, 1st Issue, 1868-1870s .... $600-$1,000
Toledo, 2nd Issue, 1870-1880s .... $600-$1,000
Toledo, 3rd Issue, 1890-1900s, Wings .... $500-$1,000
Toledo, 4th Issue, 1920-1959 .... $150-$300
Toledo, 5th Issue, 1938-present .... $75-$150
Chicago, 1st Issue, 1870-1880s, Star .... $500-$1,200
Chicago, 2nd Issue, 1880-1890, Shield .... $700-$1,200
Chicago, 3rd Issue, 1890-1900, Star .... $175-$400
Chicago, 4th Issue, 1890-1955, Star .... $100-$300
Chicago, 5th Issue, 1955-present .... $300-$700
Kansas City, MO, 1st Issue, 1874-1910, Star .... $300-$600
Kansas City, MO, 2nd Issue, 1910-1925, Star .... $200-$500
Kansas City, MO, 3rd Issue, 1925-1932, Shield .... $200-$350
Kansas City, MO, 4th Issue, 1932-1939, Shield .... $150-$225
Kansas City, MO, 5th Issue, 1939-1980, Shield .... $100-$225
Kansas City, MO, 6th Issue, 1980-present .... $100-$225
New Orleans, 1st Issue, 1880-1911, Shield .... $400-$800
New Orleans, 2nd Issue, 1911-present .... $100-$250
Cincinnati, 1st Issue, 1860-1904, Shield .... $400-$800
Cincinnati, 2nd Issue, 1904-present .... $100-$200
Cincinnati, Sterling Silver Lt., Current .... $600-$800
Lexington, KY, 1st Issue, Star .... $750-$1,200
Lexington, KY, 2nd Issue, Shield .... $125-$175
Dallas, 1st Issue, 1880-1914, Shield .... $500-$1,200
Dallas, 2nd Issue, 1914-1945, Star .... $250-$600
Dallas, 3rd Issue, 1945-present .... $100-$250
San Francisco, 1st Issue, 1860-1920, Star .... $750-$2,500
San Francisco, 2nd Issue, 1920-present .... $400-$600
Los Angeles, 1st Issue, 1850-1869, Star .... $2,500-$10,000
Los Angeles, 2nd Issue, 1869-1909, Star .... $1,000-$3,000
Los Angeles, 3rd Issue, 1909-1913, Shield .... $300-$1,200
Los Angeles, 4th Issue, 1913-1923, Shield .... $300-$600
Los Angeles, 5th Issue, 1923-1940, Shield .... $250-$600
Los Angeles, 6th Issue, 1940-present .... $750-$1,500

State police/highway patrol
Alabama Highway Patrol, Current .... $90-$150
Alaska State Troopers, Current .... $700-$1,200

Cincinnati, Sterling Silver Lt., current.

Arizona Highway Patrol, Current .... $300-$450
Arkansas State Police, Current .... $75-$125
California Highway Patrol, current .... $500-$600
California State Police (Defunct) Last .... $350-$450
Colorado State Patrol, Current .... $400-$650
Connecticut State Police, Current .... $300-$400
Delaware State Police, Current .... $75-$125
Florida Highway Patrol, Current .... $75-$150
Georgia State Patrol, Current .... $200-$300
Hawaii, State of, Sheriff, Current .... $150-$200
Idaho State Police, Current .... $125-$200
Illinois State Police, Current .... $200-$275
Indiana State Police, Current .... $175-$275
Iowa State Patrol, Current .... $350-$450
Kansas Highway Patrol, Current .... $250-$375
Kentucky State Police, Current .... $300-$450
Louisiana State Police, Current .... $75-$175
Maine State Police, Current .... $100-$175
Maryland State Police, Current .... $1,000-$1,600
Massachusetts State Police, Current .... $200-$350
Michigan State Police, Current .... $350-$450
Minnesota State Patrol, Current .... $100-$175
Mississippi Highway Patrol, Current .... $250-$400
Missouri State Highway Patrol, Current .... $250-$300
Montana Highway Patrol, Current .... $400-$600
Nebraska State Patrol, Current .... $175-$250
Nevada Highway Patrol, Current .... $500-$700
New Hampshire State Police, Current .... $350-$550
New Jersey State Police, Current .... $750-$1,200
New Mexico State Police, Current .... $200-$450
New York State Police, Current .... $750-$1,200

North Carolina State Highway Patrol, Current .... $175-$250
North Dakota Highway Patrol, Current .... $375-$500
Ohio Highway Patrol, Current .... $500-$750
Oklahoma Highway Patrol, Current .... $150-$275
Oregon State Police, Current .... $300-$500
Pennsylvania State Police, Current .... $200-$275
Rhode Island State Police, Current .... $200-$300
South Carolina Highway Patrol, Current .... $150-$250
South Dakota Highway Patrol, Current .... $100-$250
Tennessee Highway Patrol, Current .... $175-$250
Texas Dept. of Public Safety, Current .... $100-$225
Utah Highway Patrol, Current .... $150-$250
Vermont. State Police, Current .... $150-$250
Virginia State Police, Current .... $750-$1,300
Washington State Patrol, Current .... $175-$350
West Virginia State Police, Current .... $125-$175
Wisconsin State Police, Current .... $125-$200
Wyoming Highway Patrol, Current .... $200-$400

Federal Law Enforcement

US Dept. of Agriculture
    Law Enforcement .... $125-$300
    Special Agent .... $250-$600
US Dept. of Commerce, Special Agent .... $300-$600
US Dept. of Defense
    Special Agent-DCIS .... $400-$750
    Special Agent-DIS .... $400-$750
    Naval Intell., Special Agent .... $250-$600
    WWII War Dept., Special Agent .... $750-$1,500
    WWI War Dept., Military Intelligence .... $1,500-$2,500
    Air Force, Security Police .... $45-$175
US Dept. of Energy
    USTVA-PSS .... $125-$175
Federal Officer $100-$175
US Dept. of Health & Human Service
    FDA-Agent .... $300-$600
    FDA-BDAC Agent .... $300-$600
US Dept. of Interior
    US Park Police .... $400-$600
    National Park Ranger .... $75-$300
    Fish & Wildlife .... $175-$300
    Bureau of Indian Affairs Law Enforcement....... $125-$350
US Dept. of Justice, Immigration Agent .... $175-$350
    Border Patrol .... $225-$300
    Drug Enforcement Adm. .... $300-$2,500
    Prohibition Service .... $600-$3,000
    F.B.I. $5,000
    US Marshal Service .... $300-$1,500
    US Marshal BiCent. .... $100-$300
US Dept. of Labor, Investigator .... $250-$500
    Special Agent .... $200-$350
    Employee Service .... $75-$125
US Dept. of State, Special Agent .... $600-$1,500
US Dept. of Transportation .... $175-$600
    F.A.A. .... $200-$600
    Railroad Police .... $750-$1,500
    Coast Guard Police .... $100-$250
    Coast Guard Intell. .... $400-$750
    Coast Guard Sp. Ag. .... $400-$600

US Dept. of Treasury, A.T.F. Agent .... $300-$750
    Special Ag. .... $600-$750
    Prohibition Service .... $750-$3,000
    Customs Agent .... $200-$450
    I.R.S. Agent .... $200-$300
    I.R.S. Special Ag. .... $200-$750
White House Police, 1st Issue, 1922-40 Unique
    1st Issue, Restrike .... $75-$125
    2nd Issue, 1940-51 .... $200-$400
    3rd Issue, 1951-63 .... $200-$350
    4th Issue, 1963-68 .... $300-$500
    5th Issue, 1968-69 .... $300-$500
    6th Issue, 1969-70 .... $300-$500
    Executive Prot.Sv., 7th Issue, 1970-78 .... $175-$300
Secret Service UD., 8 Issue, 1978-present $1,500
Secret Service, 1976 Bicentennial .... $300-$350
Secret Service, Special Agent Star, 1891-71 .... $2,500
Secret Service, Security Office .... $250-$600
Secret Service, Special Officer .... $250-$600
Bureau of Engraving & Printing Police .... $250-$600
US Capitol Police
    2nd Issue, 1890-20 .... $1,000-$1,500
    3rd Issue, 1920-35 .... $175-$250
    4th Issue, 1935-49 .... $175-$250
    5th Issue, 1950-69 .... $225-$350
    6th Issue, 1969-90 .... $225-$350
    7th Issue, 1990-present .... $300-$500
    1976 Bicentennial .... $250-$350
Washington, D.C.
    1st Issue, 1845-90 .... $750-$2,000
    2nd Issue, 1890-18 .... $300-$500
    3rd Issue, 1918-present .... $225-$350
    1976 Bicentennial .... $250-$350
    Police Academy Inst $250-400
    Chief of Police .... $400-$500
    Traditional Badges .... $100-$1,500

Lt. Gen. James Longstreet's U.S. Marshal badge,
14K, 1881-1882.

BANKS

Banks have been around as long as there have been coins to put in them. Made of cast iron, die-cast metal, plastic and other materials, they take all shapes and sizes, from cartoon characters like Popeye to historical figures like Uncle Sam and monuments like the Statue of Liberty. Often depicting scenes and situations both whimsical and well-known, some banks serve a dual purpose — holding change and advertising products.

Cast-iron banks include mechanical and still banks. Mechanical banks, which date back as far as 1869, perform some action when a coin is deposited. The complexity of a bank's design and mechanism is a key element in determining its value, along with its rarity and subject matter. Still banks feature no action when a coin is deposited.

Advertising banks are of interest to bank collectors and advertising collectors. Die-cast banks have been manufactured in the form of vehicles since 1981, when Ertl introduced its 1913 Model T Parcel Post Mail Service. Producing limited-edition runs that usually advertise prominent companies (ranging from Amoco to Winchester), die-cast bank manufacturers include First Gear, Racing Champions, Scale Models and Spec-Cast. These banks are of interest to bank collectors, die-cast collectors and brand-specific collectors.

General Guidelines: Banks in operational condition with much original paint are the most valuable. Popular themes, like Black Americana, can also make a bank more desirable.
Prominent cast-iron bank manufacturers include Arcade, Ives, Kenton and Stevens.

Building-shaped banks are regarded the single largest type of still banks, followed by animals, busts, people, clocks, globes, mail boxes and safes. Featuring monuments such as the Eiffel Tower, commemorative banks are particularly popular among collectors. Early cast-iron examples can be expensive. Due to rising values, many cast-iron mechanical banks have escalated into a price range reasonable only to the wealthiest and most major collectors. While still banks mirror this trend somewhat, their values are generally a fraction of mechanicals. Closer to the range of casual collectors, still banks have become attractive investment vehicles for those with modest means. Die-cast and plastic banks are the latest examples both available and affordable to average and beginning bank enthusiasts.

Trends: While cast-iron still and mechanical banks remain the most desirable collectible banks, die-cast examples continue to hold their popularity and are often more affordable.

The importance of condition on a bank's value can't be underestimated. Cast-iron banks in Near Mint condition, featuring all original parts and little paint wear, are rarely found. Such examples might likely bring two to five times as much as one in Average or Very Good original condition with no repairs or restoration. The use of replacement parts and dreaded refinishing or overpainting significantly depreciate a bank's worth.

Clubs

•Mechanical Bank Collectors Club of America
P.O. Box 128, Allegan, MI 49010
616-673-4509

•Still Bank Collectors Club of America
1456 Carson Ct., Homewood, IL 60430
708-799-1732

Trick Dog, Hubley, 1920s.

VALUE LINE

Advertising Banks

Alka-Seltzer, Speedy Figure, 1960s, vinyl	$250
Ballard Biscuits	$20
Big Boy, 1970s, vinyl	$35
Bosco, 1960s	$40
Bubble Yum	$20
Buddy L, Easy Saver, 1970s	$35
Buster Brown, 1980s	$45

Cap'n Crunch, 1975, molded vinyl $25
Chrysler Mr. Fleet figure, 1973 .... $350
Chuck E. Cheese, vinyl $25
Coca-Cola, 1950s $65
Coca-Cola, Linemar $450
Cocoa Puffs $30
Curad Taped Crusader figure, 1975, vinyl $35
Esso Oil, 1992, plastic $60
Esso Oil Tiger, vinyl $35
Eveready Batteries, 1981, vinyl $15
Farmer Jack Supermarkets, 1986, vinyl $30
Greyhound Bus, Jimson, 1960s, plastic $40
Howard Johnson's, 1950s, plastic $45
Husky Dog Food $5
Icee Bear, 1974, plastic $25
Ivory Soap $30
Keebler Ernie the Elf, ceramic $45
Kentucky Fried Chicken, 1970, plastic $25
Kentucky Fried Chicken, 1965, plastic $35
Kraft Cheeseasaurus Rex, 1992 .... $20
Magic Chef, 1960s, vinyl $20
Marky Maypo, 1960s, vinyl $45
Nestle Quik, 1980s $10
Oscar Mayer Wienermobile $20
Pepto Bismol, soft plastic $75
Pillsbury, tin $25
Planters Mr. Peanut, 1950s, molded plastic $15
Royal Gelatin King Royal, 1970s, vinyl $250
Spam $10

Ertl Die-Cast Banks

Values are for banks in Mint in Box condition.

4-H Clubs of America, 1913 Model T $35
4-H Clubs of America, 1917 Model T $30
4-H Clubs of America, 1905 Ford Delivery $35
AJ Seibert Co, 1913 Model T $125
AC Rochester #1 UAW, 1950 Chevy Panel $110
ACE Hardware, 1918 Runabout $75
Agway #1, 1913 Model T $300
Agway #2, 1918 Runabout $40
Alka-Seltzer #1, 1918 Runabout $140
Allied Van Lines #1, 1913 Model T $80
American Red Cross #1, 1913 Model T $75
Amoco, 1913 Model T $155
Anheuser-Busch #2, 1926 Mack $60
Arm & Hammer, 1913 Model T $105
Atlas Van Lines #1, 1926 Mack Truck $100
Barq's Root Beer #1, 1913 Model T $60
Bell Telephone #1, 1950 Chevy Panel $60
Breyer's Ice Cream, 1905 Ford Delivery $75
Canada Dry Ginger Ale, 1918 Barrel Runabout $40
Comet Cleanser, 1905 Ford Delivery $30
Dairy Queen, 1913 Model T $125
Dolly Madison, Step Van $65
Frito-Lay, 1950 Chevy Panel $40
Hamm's Beer, 1926 Mack Truck $70
Heineken Beer #1, 1918 Barrel Runabout $175
Henny Penny, 1932 Ford Panel $40
Hershey's Chocolate Milk, 1926 Mack Tanker $45

Professor Pug Frogs Great Bicycle Feat, J&E Stevens Co., designed by Charles A. Bailey, c. 1886.

Hershey's Kisses, 1950 Chevy Panel $135
NASA, Step Van $40
Pepsi-Cola, 1917 Model T $125
Stroh's Beer, 1918 Ford Runabout $55
Titleist Golf Balls, 1913 Model T $65
Wonder Bread #1, 1913 Model T $75
York Peppermint Patties #1, 1932 Ford Panel $105

Mechanical Banks

Values are for cast-iron banks in Excellent, operational condition.

Acrobat, J&E Stevens, 1883 .... $9,500
Artillery Bank, Shepard Hardware, 1892 .... $1,200
Bad Accident Mule, J&E Stevens, 1890s $3,800
Bill E. Grin, Judd, 1887 .... $2,200
Bird on Roof, J&E Stevens, 1878 .... $2,000
Boy and Bulldog, Judd, 1870s $1,850
Bulldog Savings Bank, Ives, 1878 .... $3,000
Butting Ram, Ole Storle, 1895 .... $12,000
Calamity, J&E Stevens, 1905 .... $35,000
Chief Big Moon, J&E Stevens, 1899 .... $5,000
Crowing Rooster, Keim & Co., 1937 .... $1,200
Dapper Dan, Marx, 1910 .... $900
Dinah, J. Harper & Co., 1911 .... $1,450
Eagle and Eaglets, J&E Stevens, 1883 .... $1,650
Feed The Goose, Banker's Thrift, 1927 .... $600
Fortune Teller, Nickel, Baumgarter & Co., 1901 .... $1,400
Girl Skipping Rope, J&E Stevens, 1890 .... $45,000
Haley's Elephant $650
Harlequin, J&E Stevens, 1907 .... $22,000
Horse Race, J&E Stevens, 1870 .... $8,000
Humpty Dumpty, Shepard Hardware, 1882 .... $4,000
Indian Shooting Bear, J&E Stevens, 1883 .... $4,500
Joe Socko, Straits Mfg., 1930s $650
Jonah and The Whale, Shepard Hardware, 1890s $4,500
Kiltie, J. Harper & Co., 1931 .... $3,000
Lighthouse, 1891 .... $3,000

Bismark Bank, J&E Stevens Co., designed by Charles A. Bailey, c. 1883.

Lion Hunter, J&E Stevens, 1911 .... $10,000
Little Jocko, Ferdinand Strauss, 1912 .... $2,200
Magician, J&E Stevens, 1901 .... $6,500
Mammy and Child, Kyser & Rex, 1884 .... $6,500
Merry-Go-Round, Kyser & Rex, 1888 .... $15,000
Milking Cow, J&E Stevens, 1885 .... $7,000
Minstrel, Saalheimer & Strauss, 1928 .... $900
Mosque, Judd, 1880s $2,000
Organ Grinder and Dancing Bear, J&E Stevens,
    1890s $7,500
Paddy and the Pig, J&E Stevens, 1882 .... $4,000
Punch and Judy, Banks & Sons, 1929 .... $7,000
Red Riding Hood, W.S. Reed, 1880s $18,000
Rooster, Kyser & Rex, 1900s $1,500
Safety Locomotive, Edward J. Colby, 1887 .... $2,200
Santa at the Chimney, Shepard Hardware, 1889 .... $4,000
Scotchman, Saalheimer & Strauss, 1930s $700
Starkie's Aeroplane, Starkie, 1919 .... $3,500
Sweet Thrift, Beverly Novelty, 1928 .... $450
Trick Pony, Shepard Hardware, 1885 .... $3,500
Turtle, Kilgore, 1920s $20,000
Uncle Sam with Carpet Bag, Shepard Hardware,
    1886 .... $8,000
Watch Dog Safe, J&E Stevens, 1890s $1,250
World's Fair, J&E Stevens, 1893 .... $1,850
Zoo, Kyser & Rex, 1890s $2,250

Still Banks

Values listed are for cast-iron banks in Excellent condition.
Air Mail on base, Dent, 1920 .... $1,000
Alamo, Alamo Iron Works, 1930s $450
Amish Boy, John Wright, 1970 .... $65
Amish Girl, John Wright, 1970 .... $65
Andy Gump, Arcade, 1928 .... $950

Arabian Safe, Kyser & Rex, 1882 .... $300
Aunt Jemima, AC Williams, 1900s $325
Barrel, Judd, 1873 .... $225
Baseball Player, AC Williams, 1909 .... $325
Battleship Maine, Grey Iron Casting, 1800s $3,000
Beehive, Kyser & Rex, 1882 .... $500
Billiken, AC Williams, 1909 .... $125
Billy Possum, JM Harper, 1909 .... $4,500
Boss Tweed, 1870s $3,500
Buster Brown & Tiger, AC Williams, 1900s $275
Campbell Kids, AC Williams, 1900s $350
Captain Kidd, 1900s $450
Cat on Tub, AC Williams, 1920s $200
Circus Elephant, Hubley, 1930s $350
City Bank with Teller, HL Judd $700
Covered Wagon, Wilton Products $25
Daisy, Shimer Toy, 1899 .... $175
Dog Smoking Cigar, Hubley $850
Doughboy, Grey Iron Casting, 1919 .... $850
Dutch Boy, Grey Iron Casting $850
Dutch Girl, Grey Iron Casting $850
Egyptian Tomb, Kyser & Rex, 1882 .... $750
Electric Railroad, Shimer & Toy, 1893 .... $6,000
Fido, Hubley, 1914 .... $145
GE Refrigerator, Hubley, 1930s $225
Gunboat, Kenton $1,800
Holstein Cow, Arcade, 1910 .... $350
Humpty Dumpty, 1930s $850
Ice Box, Arcade $650
Laughing Pig, Hubley $275
Lighthouse, Lane Art, 1950s $250
Limousine, Arcade, 1921 .... $2800
Lion on Wheels, AC Williams, 1920s $225
Little Red Riding Hood, JM Harper, 1907 .... $4,000
Main Street Trolley, AC Williams, 1920s $400
Mammy with Hands on Hips, Hubley, 1900s $400
Mermaid Boat, Grey Iron Casting, 1900s $850
Mulligan Policeman, AC Williams, 1900s $400
Nest Egg, Smith & Egge, 1873 .... $850
Newfoundland Dog, Arcade, 1930s $225
Organ Grinder, Hubley $350
Palace, Ives, 1885 .... $3,000
Pavillion, Kyser & Rex, 1880 .... $500
Pay Phone, J&E Stevens, 1926 .... $1,800
Puppo on Pillow, Hubley, 1920s $275
Rooster, Arcade, 1910 .... $350
Sailor, Hubley, 1910 .... $475
Santa Claus, Hubley, 1900s $950
Seal on Rock, Arcade, 1900s $500
Skyscraper, AC Williams, 1900s $150
Statue of Liberty, Kenton, 1900s $175
Thoroughbred, Hubley, 1946 .... $150
Three Wise Monkeys, AC Williams, 1900s $550
US Navy Akron Zeppelin, AC Williams, 1930 .... $500
Villa, Kyser & Rex, 1894 .... $850
Yellow Cab, Arcade, 1921 .... $2,400

BARBIE DOLLS

Everyone's favorite doll, Barbie, was first issued in 1959 by Mattel Toys and has consistently led the pack in sales and in collectors' value. While collecting Barbie and her friends has always been popular, special editions and reissues have fueled the dolls' popularity.

General Guidelines: Condition is everything when collecting Barbies because of the large number of dolls issued from the 1960s to present. Because the dolls were favorite playthings for baby boomers, finding examples in Near Mint condition (or still in the box) is difficult. But finding that box can add 50 percent or more to the value.

While some 1960s Barbies have sold for thousands of dollars, those in poorer condition or without boxes are worth much less.

Collector's Alert: Without the box, it may be virtually impossible to identify the name or date of a doll. The date found on a doll's buttocks is a patent date and often is not the same as the actual year of issue; many later Barbies bear 1960s trademark dates. Also, clothes may make the doll, but don't try to date a Barbie doll by her clothing. Fashions are often switched from doll to doll. Bringing the most value today are 1959 and 1960s dolls and fashions — all still in original packages. Holiday Barbies, porcelains and collector editions are gaining popularity among newer collectors. Ken, Midge, Skipper and other Barbie friends are collectible, but Barbie herself remains the most popular with collectors. Because so many were made, most regular issue, or "play," dolls from the 1970s to the present sell for $5-$25.

Don't overlook accessories. Barbie houses, vehicles, cases and other toys bearing the Barbie logo are also collectible. Vehicles still in the box remain the most valuable accessories.

Clubs
•Barbie Collectors Club International
P.O. Box 586
North White Plains, NY 10603

Publications
The Ultimate Barbie Doll Book by Marcie Melillo (Krause Publications).

VALUE LINE

All Barbie dolls/fashions are manufactured by Mattel. Prices listed are for dolls in Mint condition **without the box.** *Add 50 percent or more for Mint dolls in Mint original boxes.*

Dolls

Most regular issue Barbies, 1970s-present	$5-$25
American Girl Barbie, side part, 1965	$2,230
Bob Mackie Designer Barbies, 1990s	$150-$300
Francie, 1966	
Straight leg	$125
Bendable leg	$100
1967 bendable leg, African-American	$500
Great Eras Barbies, 1993-'94	$20-$30
Happy Holidays Barbie, red gown, 1988	$200
Happy Holidays Barbie, 1992-1995	$35-$100
Hawaiian Fun Barbie and Friends, 1991	$3

LOOKING OUT FOR #1

The first Ponytail Barbies all look somewhat similar to the non-collector, but there are subtle differences. The first Barbie, Ponytail Barbie #1 (No. #850, 1959), featured:

• holes in the bottom of the feet with copper tubes

• zebra-stripe swimsuit

• blonde or brunette hair w/soft curly bangs

• red fingernails, toenails, and lips

• gold hoop earrings

• white irises, severely pointed black eyebrows

• heavy, black facial paint

• pale, almost white, ivory skin tone

Ponytail Barbie #3, blonde, 1960, $450 MNB.
(Photo courtesy of McMasters Doll Auctions)

International Barbie Series, 1980-present .... $10-$65
Some of the most valuable include:
International Barbie Eskimo, 1982 .... $50
International Barbie Italian, 1980 .... $65
International Barbie Oriental, 1981 .... $55
International Barbie Royal, 1980 .... $65
Ken, original flocked hair, 1961 .... $60
Ken, painted hair, 1962 .... $40
Ken, bendable legs, 1965 .... $125
Malibu Barbie, 1970s $10
My First Barbie, 1980s, many variations .... $3-$10
Ponytail Barbie #1, 1959
Blonde $2,500
Brunette $3,500
Ponytail Barbie #3, 1960
Blonde $450
Brunette $525
Porcelain Barbies, 1989-present .... $100-$400
Rocker Series Barbie and Friends, 1985-86 .... $7
Skipper
Straight leg, 1964 .... $45
Bendable leg, 1965 .... $100
Statue of Liberty, 1996 .... $40
Teen Talk Barbie, 1992 .... $15
w/phrase "Math is Tough" $350
Toys R Us Exclusives, 1990-1994 .... $6-$25
Tropical Barbie or Ken, 1985 .... $3-$5
UNICEF Barbie, 1989 .... $7

Barbie Accessories
Double Barbie Case $25
Single Barbie Case $20
Fashion Queen Case $150
Skipper Case $25
Ken Case $25
Barbie Goes Travelin' Case $175
Barbie's Austin Healy Convertible $175
Ken's Hot Rod $200
Barbie Little Theatre $300
Barbie's Dream House, 1962 .... $65
Malibu Barbie Colorforms Set $15

Barbie Vintage Fashions, 1959-1966
*Prices listed are for fashions in Mint condition **without** original box.*
Barbie Skin Diver, #1608 .... $40
Beautiful Bride, #1698 .... $650
Candy Striper Volunteer, #0889 .... $125
Easter Parade, #971 .... $1,500
Fashion Editor, #1635 .... $350
Fraternity Dance, #1638 .... $195
Little Red Riding Hood/Wolf, #0880 .... $220
Nightly Negligee, #965 .... $55
Pajama Party, #1601 .... $20
Pan American Stewardess, #1678 .... $1,000
Roman Holiday, #968 .... $1,500
Skater's Waltz, #1629 .... $140
Solo in the Spotlight, #982 .... $125
Wedding Day Set, #972 .... $140

Bob Mackie Queen of Hearts Barbie, 1994, $125 MNB.

Tips of the Trade

Blondes may have more fun, but because fewer were usually made, corresponding brunettes are worth more. The same often holds true for African-American and other ethnic versions.

Don't forget the fashions! Barbie's attire throughout the years has changed with the times. Some of her fashions alone have sold for $2,000 still in the original package.

BASEBALL MEMORABILIA

It's no secret that many old baseball cards, and even some newer ones, are valuable. But perhaps even more valuable than those stacks of 1950s trading cards in the attic are other types of baseball memorabilia, including autographs, uniforms, equipment, statues, yearbooks, media guides, programs and ticket stubs — all of which have emerged as popular collectibles within the past few years.

Autographs

The most common autographed items are baseballs, 8-by-10 photos, and trading cards, but also popular among collectors are autographed programs, books, index cards, personal letters and documents (checks, contracts, etc.), and various types of equipment (shoes, bats, hats, jerseys, etc.).

General Guidelines: Several terms are helpful in determining the value of an autograph or when talking with autograph specialists and dealers. A "cut signature" is just a simple signature on a piece of paper. It is the least desirable type of autograph and generally the least valuable.

A "single-signed" baseball is an official league baseball signed by one player only. This is probably the most desirable type of autograph for serious collectors of baseball memorabilia. A single-signed baseball is generally worth more than an autographed photo, baseball card, or cut signature of the same player.

Values of autographs can vary from around $5 for a common player of marginal ability to thousands of dollars for a deceased Hall of Fame player like Babe Ruth or Lou Gehrig. The most important factor in determining the value of an autograph is, of course, the player involved. Autographs of Hall of Famers and future Hall of Famers are most in demand.

The significance of an autographed item can also greatly affect its value. For instance, Cal Ripken's signature on a baseball that was used in the game when he set the record for playing in the most consecutive games would be worth many times more than an "ordinary" Ripken autograph. Likewise, Paul Molitor's signature on a ticket stub or program from the game in which he got his 3,000th hit would be worth more than Molitor's signature on some other ticket stub or program.

A player's signing habits also affect value. Some players, like Hall of Fame pitcher Bob Feller and home run king Hank Aaron, are very cordial signers and have appeared at numerous shows to sign autographs. Other stars, like Mike Schmidt, have developed the reputation of being a tougher autograph, making their signatures more valuable. Age is also a factor. Obviously, fewer autographs exist for Cap Anson or Tris Speaker than for Duke Snider or Harmon Killebrew.

How do you know if the signature on your ball is real or fake? Examine the signature's style, the type of ball and the writing instrument. For instance, be suspicious of a ballpoint pen mark on an early 20th century autograph. Ballpoint pens didn't become common until the 1940s. Felt tips took over in the 1960s.

Forgeries can also be detected by uncommon breaks, peculiarities in pressure and movement in strokes and changes in thickness in the letters. Facsimile signatures also exist. These are exact reproductions of the player's signature, which are printed or stamped on the item. Some players have also used used ghost signers or "auto pens" to sign autograph requests. These, of course, are not considered authentic signatures and have little value, but often it takes an autograph expert to identify them.

In addition to single-signature baseballs, team-signed balls can also be especially valuable. These are balls signed by all members of a specific team, like the 1958 New York Yankees, for example. They should include the signatures of all key players — both starters and reserves — and the manager. The manager's signature can often be found on the ball's "sweet spot," the space between the two seams. The more complete the ball, the more valuable it is. Team balls of World Series champions, All-Star teams, etc. will also bring higher prices.

Even balls from recent teams like the 1981 San Francisco Giants and the 1989 Minnesota Twins can run $50 to $100. Naturally, the older the ball, the harder it will be to find. A team ball from the 1920 Detroit Tigers (including Ty Cobb's signature) is worth $1,700 to $2,500, and a ball signed by the 1929 New York Yankees (including Ruth and Gehrig) can fetch $4,000 or more! (Additional signatures on a ball — like those from umpires or broadcasters —can actually detract from a ball's value.)

Ty Cobb, tobacco insert card.

Bats

Like uniforms, authentic game-used bats are very collectible, and many can bring high prices, depending on the player involved. Again, don't confuse Major League game-used bats with models you can buy at the neighborhood sporting goods store. Authentic game-used bats must actually have been used by a player in a Major League game.

While bats used by Hall of Famers and popular superstars will be expensive, other games-used bats can be surprisingly cheap. For example, prices can range from as little as $15 for a Louisville Slugger used by Jerry Hairston in the late 1980s to $85 for a Louisville Slugger used by Tim Wallach in 1992.

Hartland Statues/Figurines

From 1960-1963, the Hartland Plastics Company in Wisconsin offered a line of 8-inch molded plastic statues featuring 18 star baseball players.

The statues sold well at baseball stadium concession stands and retail stores. They originally cost between $2 and $4 each. Up to 150,000 of some players (Babe Ruth, Willie Mays, Mickey Mantle, Yogi Berra, Hank Aaron, Ted Williams and Eddie Mathews) were sold, while there were only about 5,000 statues made of Dick Groat and about 10,000 depicting Rocky Colavito. Because of their scarcity, Groat and Colavito are now the two most valuable figures in the set, each worth more than $1,000 in top condition.

Others in the line included Warren Spahn, Duke Snider, Don Drysdale, Roger Maris, Harmon Killebrew, Luis Aparicio, Nellie Fox, Ernie Banks, and Stan Musial. Most players were shown in hitting poses, but others were shown pitching or fielding.

Note: In 1988, a Texas company bought the rights to the Hartland name, retooled the original molds and produced a 25th commemorative edition of each of the 18 original players, plus Roberto Clemente, Nolan Ryan, Honus Wagner and Cy Young. The 25th anniversary edition Hartlands are identified as such and should not be confused with the originals.

In addition to overall condition, prices for original Hartland statues are based on the degree of whiteness the statue has maintained. In other words, has it remained white, or has it faded to a cream or yellow color? Off-white statues are generally worth about half the value of a figure that has not faded.

Media Guides

Media guides, presented to the radio, television and newspaper reporters who cover major league teams throughout the season, came into general use during the 1940s and '50s. They are designed to provide the reporters with almost every imaginable kind of biographical and statistical tidbits to liven up a broadcast or story, from who's on first to the player's favorite hobbies. Minor league teams are also covered and, coupled with chronologies of team histories, have contributed to the guides' increases in page size from the 1950s to the 1990s. In recent years, some teams have begun offering their media guides to the general public, making them much more plentiful.

Periodicals

Periodicals like *The Sporting News, Sports Illustrated* and *Sport* are collected by many sports enthusisasts. Generally, only complete magazines in Good condition are considered collectible. For the most part, values depend on age and the cover subject. Issues with popular players on the cover (Mickey Mantle, Ted Williams, Joe DiMaggio, etc.) are most in demand and usually bring the highest prices. Pete Rose, Steve Carlton, Reggie Jackson and Carl Yastrzemski are among players from the 1960s and '70s who have appeared on the most covers. Rose, Yastrzemski, Willie Mays, Hank Aaron and Roberto Clemente remain among the most popular players from that era. Many collectors have covers autographed and framed.

General Guidelines: Common issues of *The Sporting News* from the 1910s in Very Good condition sell for about $50 each. Issues from the 1920s-1960s are generally valued at $10-$30 each. Issues from the 1970s-1990s tend to bring $15 or less. Issues of *The Sporting News* published during the regular season (April-October), especially Opening Day, All-Star and World Series issues, generally carry higher prices than those published during the baseball off season (November-March).

Among the more valuable issues of *The Sporting News*:
• Issue from the 1930s picturing Babe Ruth on the cover can be worth $300 to $500 each.
• Issues picturing Joe DiMaggio on the cover, dating from the 1930s and '40s, are generally worth around $100 each.
• Issues from the 1940s and early '50s picturing Jackie Robinson generally sell in the $75-$100 range.
• Issues from the 1950s and early '60s picturing Mickey Mantle are typically worth around $100.
• Issues with Hank Aaron on the cover, dating from the 1950s through the early '70s, usually sell in the $25-$60 range.

Most issues of *Sports Illustrated* are valued at $5-$30 each. Exceptions include the first cover of *Sports Illustrated* with Milwaukee Braves great Eddie Mathews ($250) and the April 11, 1955 issue with San Francisco Giant greats Willie Mays and Leo Durocher on the cover ($100).

Most issues of *Sport* magazine are also priced in the $5-$20 range. Exceptions include the September 1946 issue with Joe DiMaggio on the cover ($400-$450), the September 1948 issue with Joe DiMaggio and Ted Williams on the cover ($95) and the October 1956 issue with Mickey Mantle on the cover ($30-$60).

Programs

Many fans who have attended a Major League game have purchased a souvenir program to keep score in. Others have purchased them as reading or historical material or perhaps to have it autographed by a player. This will increase its value.

General Guidelines: Condition is critical. Although unmarked programs are preferred by most collectors, programs someone kept score in also have intrinsic value because they give a history of what happened in the particular game.

Program design and attractiveness also add to a program's value, especially the cover design or subject. Values given are for programs in Excellent condition which show little wear and tear. Age will also affect value.

Ticket Stubs, Schedules

Ticket stubs do not command high prices unless they are from a World Series, All-Star or playoff games, or from a game in which a significant achievement or record occurred.

Complete, unused tickets are worth more than ticket stubs and are generally from playoff or World Series games that were never played (a seven-game series completed in six games, for instance) or one in which a baseball milestone occurred.

Shortly after Nolan Ryan won his 300th game in 1990, unused tickets (purchased by speculators solely for resale to the collectibles market) were being offered for $60. Other examples of tickets or stubs tickets that command high prices include the sixth game of the 1977 World Series (when Reggie Jackson hit three home runs) and the 1956 World Series contest when the New York Yankees' Don Larsen pitched a perfect game. A ticket stub from that game sold for $532 in a 1992 auction. It was autographed, framed, and included a photo of the final pitch and a copy of the box score.

Other complete, unused tickets from memorable contests can bring prices in the hundreds, but in general, ticket stubs are rarely worth over $25.

Baseball schedules, or "skeds" for short, are also popular with many sports memorabilia collectors. Although the most common form is a pocket schedule, skeds come in all shapes and sizes. Pocket schedules are commonly provided by major league teams' ticket offices. Other schedules are printed on matchbook covers, cups, brochures, decals, magnets, rulers, napkins, place mats, stickers, key chains and plastic coin purses.

To be collectible, schedules should be in good shape, with no tears, creases, writing, etc. Schedules for defunct teams are often worth more, as are hard-to-find schedules and those featuring team or player photos.

Uniforms

Authentic uniforms — the actual game-used pants and jerseys worn by the players themselves — are among the most valuable of all sports collectibles. But don't confuse them with the replica jerseys commonly seen in department stores and ballpark souvenir stands. Those replica jerseys are great for showing off your favorite team colors, but they have almost no value as a collectible.

When it comes to actual game-worn uniforms, the old flannel styles are the most valuable. They often contain other materials such as wool, cotton or a blend of various fibers. Flannels were used in Major League Baseball until 1973, when doubleknits, made primarily of polyester-based fabrics, were introduced.

Since then, mesh jerseys, not unlike those used by many teams in the other major sports, have also been worn, primarily as pregame jerseys for batting practice or spring training contests. Pregame jerseys, although collectible, are not as desirable as game-used jerseys.

Until the early 1980s, the idea of making uniforms available to typical fans was considered off base. Some jerseys were sold through charity auctions, while a few lucky fans were fortunate enough to obtain one from a team or a player. But those sales or giveaways were rare.

Changes began to occur in 1978 when the Philadelphia Phillies sold an entire lot of 1977 game-used jerseys to a New Jersey dealer, who then advertised them in hobby papers. This practice of bulk sales to dealers has been continued by many teams in various sports, thus allowing more and more authentic jerseys to enter the collectibles market.

A game-used uniform must have been worn by the player. It shouldn't be falling apart, but it should show some evidence of laundering. A jersey used for an entire season should show some visible wear. The collar and armpits should indicate sweat or laundering out perspiration. Letters and numbers should feature an even degree of wear.

For authentification purposes, game-worn jerseys must exhibit the proper tags, generally identifying the player's name and the year the uniform was issued. Various types of tags exist, and their locations on the uniform vary (usually found on the collar or the shirt tail). Uniform experts should be consulted to verify the authenticity of a jersey.

A typical knit game-worn uniform may sell for $100 to $200, but prices can escalate, depending on the player, the team, and the significance of the uniform. Jerseys worn during record-breaking games, All-Star Games, World Series games, etc. are more valuable. Some uniforms can bring hundreds or even thousands of dollars. Prices for newer uniforms, not just older ones, can bring high prices. For instance, a Baltimore Orioles uniform with an All-Star patch worn by Cal Ripken Jr. in 1993 can bring nearly as much money ($2,295) as a uniform worn by Pee Wee Reese for the 1956 Brooklyn Dodgers ($2,800).

World Series Programs

Programs from early All-Star games and World Series games are worth more than programs from regular-season games. For instance, a program from the first All-Star game held in Chicago in 1933 is worth around $2,000 in Excellent condition. Even an All-Star Game program from as recent as 1975 can bring $35-$60.

World Series programs generally command the highest prices. They've been published every year since 1903, except for 1904. A different program, each full of statistics, pictures, biographies and special covers was offered for both teams in the series until 1974. Since that time, the programs have been a joint effort of the teams and have been distributed by Major League Promotion Corp.

The price range for original World Series programs in Excellent condition is from $5-$10 for recent examples to $25,000-$35,000 for a 1903 program. Programs for the teams which win the series generally are more valuable than those for the losers.

Yearbooks

It wasn't until the 1940s and '50s that yearbooks were produced by teams on a regular basis. During the 1950s, the Jay Publishing Company of New York printed a series of *Big League Books* which served as the official yearbooks for major league teams. Jay Publishing stopped issuing them in 1965.

Most yearbooks from the 1960s are not extremely valuable. Prices generally run in the $10-$100 range. Rare yearbooks from the 1950s can bring more money, and autographed editions are even more valuable.

Yearbooks from a team's first year of existence are generally more valuable than succeeding years.

VALUE LINE

Autographs

The values below are for autographed 8-by-10 photos. Values for autographed baseballs will be higher — perhaps twice as high for current and recent players, and many times higher for older players. Values for "cut signatures" will be less than the value shown. The list includes current players, popular retired players and Hall of Famers.

Hank Aaron	$30
Grover Cleveland Alexander	$700
Roberto Alomar	$20
Brady Anderson	$17
Cap Anson	$3,500
Luis Aparicio	$15
Richie Ashburn	$18
Jeff Bagwell	$24
Ernie Banks	$20
Cool Papa Bell	$50
Albert Belle	$30
Johnny Bench	$30
Yogi Berra	$20
Dante Bichette	$15
Vida Blue	$14
Wade Boggs	$24
Barry Bonds	$35
Bobby Bonds	$12
Lou Boudreau	$12
George Brett	$35
Lou Brock	$20
Ken Boyer	$70
Ellis Burks	$12
Roy Campanella	$500
Jose Canseco	$17
Rod Carew	$25
Steve Carlton	$25
Gary Carter	$20
Joe Carter	$15
Alexander Cartwright	$3,000
Orlando Cepeda	$15
Frank Chance	$2,000
Roberto Clemente	$600
Will Clark	$20
Roger Clemens	$30
Ty Cobb	$1,200
Rocky Colavito	$20
Eddie Collins	$400
Eric Davis	$15
Dizzy Dean	$350
Bill Dickey	$50
Joe DiMaggio	$150
Larry Doby	$20
Don Drysdale	$45
Shawon Dunston	$10
Leo Durocher	$65
Dennis Eckersley	$18
Bob Feller	$15

Alex Fernandez	$12
Cecil Fielder	$17
Rollie Fingers	$15
Carlton Fisk	$20
White Ford	$20
Nellie Fox	$250
Jimmie Foxx	$950
Julio Franco	$14
Frankie Frisch	$195
Joe Garagiola	$18
Steve Garvey	$15
Lou Gehrig	$4,000
Bob Gibson	$25
Josh Gibson	$1,700
Tom Glavine	$20
Lefty Gomez	$50
Mark Grace	$15
Hank Greenberg	$150
Ken Griffey	$12
Ken Griffey Jr.	$35
Lefty Grove	$200
Ozzie Guillen	$12
Tony Gwynn	$25
Rickey Henderson	$22
Gil Hodges	$300
Rogers Hornsby	$700
Elston Howard	$150
Catfish Hunter	$15
Monte Irvin	$12
Reggie Jackson	$40
Fergie Jenkins	$15
Hugh Jennings	$1,500
Jackie Jensen	$150
Derek Jeter	$35
Walter Johnson	$1,300
Andruw Jones	$25
Chipper Jones	$20
Jim Kaat	$15
Al Kaline	$20
Wee Willie Keeler	$3,250
George Kell	$12
Mike Kelly	$5,000
Harvey Kuenn	$75
Harmon Killebrew	$15
Ralph Kiner	$15
Ryan Klesko	$18
Ted Kluszewski	$75
Chuck Knoblauch	$20
Sandy Koufax	$50
Harvey Kuenn	$75
Nap Lajoie	$1,000
Barry Larkin	$23
Don Larsen	$12
Tony Lazzeri	$500
Buck Leonard	$15
Kenny Lofton	$20
Fred Lynn	$15
Connie Mack	$400

Greg Maddux	$25
Mickey Mantle	$150
Juan Marichal	$15
Roger Maris	$250
Billy Martin	$75
Tino Martinez	$18
Don Mattingly	$25
Bill Mazeroski	$15
Fred McGriff	$15
Mark McGwire	$25
Paul Molitor	$25
Thurman Munson	$325
Dale Murphy	$16
Eddie Murray	$35
Phil Niekro	$15
Hideo Nomo	$28
Mike Piazza	$25
Cal Ripken Jr.	$45
Phil Rizzuto	$15
Robin Roberts	$12
Brooks Robsinson	$15
Frank Robinson	$20
Jackie Robinson	$600
Alex Rodriguez	$35
Babe Ruth	$2,500
Ryne Sandberg	$30
Mike Schmidt	$40
Red Schoendienst	$15
Tom Seaver	$30
Gary Sheffield	$20
Enos Slaughter	$12
Ozzie Smith	$22
Duke Snider	$19
Warren Spahn	$15
Tris Speaker	$700
Willie Stargell	$13
Casey Stengel	$130
Don Sutton	$15
Frank Thomas	$40
Joe Tinker	$900
Alan Trammel	$17
Pie Traynor	$300
Bob Uecker	$20
Robin Ventura	$18
Honus Wagner	$725
Larry Walker	$15
Lloyd Waner	$155
Paul Waner	$320
Earl Weaver	$15
Hoyt Wilhelm	$14
Bernie Williams	$25
Billy Williams	$15
Matt Williams	$17
Ted Williams	$90
Maury Wills	$20
Hack Wilson	$675
Dave Winfield	$30
Early Wynn	$20

Carl Yastrzemski	$30
Cy Young	$850
Eric Young	$12
Robin Yount	$25

Bats

Prices listed are for game-used bats. Hand-signed bats always command higher prices.

Hank Aaron, Hillerich & Bradsby, 1964	$2,850
Sandy Alomar, Adirondack, 1970s	$95
Dusty Baker, Adirondack, 1970s	$150
Chris Bando, Louisville Slugger, 1986-1989	$20
Don Baylor, Adirondack, 1968-1971	$110
Yogi Berra, Hillerich & Bradsby, 1950s, signed	$2,500
Wade Boggs, Louisville Slugger, 1993	$495
Glenn Braggs, Adirondack, 1989	$30
George Brett, Louisville Slugger, 1977-1979 signed	$1,850
George Brett, Louisville Slugger, early 1980s	$1,150
Lou Brock, Hillerich & Bradsby, 1965-1972	$625
Brett Butler, Louisville Slugger, 1980s	$150
Gary Carter, Louisville Slugger, mid-1980s	$275
Joe Carter, Louisville Slugger, 1986-1989	$195
Rick Cerone, Louisville Slugger, 1986-1989	$45
Cecil Cooper, Hillerich & Bradsby, 1977-1979	$50
Andre Dawson, Louisville Slugger, 1980-1983, signed	$395
Bucky Dent, Adirondack, 1980	$95
Joe DiMaggio, Hillerich & Bradsby, 1949-1960	$1,695
Dwight Evans, Hillerich & Bradsby, 1977-1979	$295
Carlton Fisk, Adirondack, 1971-1979, signed	$995
Gary Gaetti, Louisville Slugger, 1986-1989	$50
Ken Griffey Jr., Louisville Slugger, 1992	$795
Toby Harrah, Hillerich & Bradsby, 1984, signed	$40
Kent Hrbeck, Louisville Slugger, 1980-1983	$75
Reggie Jackson, Adirondack, 1971-1979	$695
Reggie Jackson, Adirondack, 1971-1979	$995
Mickey Mantle, Hillerich & Bradsby, 1964	$9,995
Mickey Mantle, Adirondack, handle crack 1961-1967	$8,500
Don Mattingly, Louisville Slugger, 1984	$795
Paul Molitor, Hillerich & Bradsby, 1977-1979	$695
Stan Musial, Hillerich & Bradsby, cracked 1950s, signed,	$5,500
Tony Pena, Louisville Slugger, 1986-1989	$50
Kirby Puckett, Louisville Slugger, 1986-1989	$395
Cal Ripken Jr., Louisville Slugger, 1990	$725
Pete Rose, Hillerich & Bradsby, 1972-1975 signed	$1,595
Ryne Sandberg, Adirondack, 1992	$625
Ryne Sandberg, Louisville Slugger, 1980-1983, signed	$1,295
Kevin Seitzer, Louisville Slugger, 1986-1989	$60
Frank Thomas, Worth, two-toned, 1993	$425
Lou Whitaker, Hillerich & Bradsby, 1977-1979	$495
Dave Winfield, Adirondack, cracked, 1993	$425
Carl Yastrzemski, Hillerich & Bradsby, 1977-1979 signed,	$795
Robin Yount, Louisville Slugger, 1984-1985, signed	$595

Hartland Statues/Figurines

Here are some prices for Hartland statues in Excellent to Near Mint condition.

Hank Aaron	$275-$350
Luis Aparicio	$250-$400
Ernie Banks	$275-$400
Yogi Berra	$250-$350
Rocky Colavito	$1,000-$1,300
Don Drysdale	$350-$525
Nellie Fox	$250-$350
Dick Groat	$1,800-$2,000
Harmon Killebrew	$500-$650
Mickey Mantle	$300-$400
Roger Maris	$450-$600
Willie Mays	$300-$400
Eddie Mathews	$175-$250
Stan Musial	$250-$350
Babe Ruth	$200-$300
Duke Snider	$450-$650
Warren Spahn	$150-$225
Ted Williams	$250-$350

Uniforms

Prices listed are for game-used uniforms. Home refers to the player's home uniform, and road refers to a uniform worn by a player in an away contest.

Johnny Bench, 1971 Cincinnati Reds, road	$7,500
Rod Carew, California Angels old-timers	$1,600
Steve Carlton, 1977 Philadelphia Phillies, home	$2,800
Roberto Clemente, 1957 Pittsburgh Pirates, road, restored	$15,000
Bob Gibson, 1968 St. Louis Cardinals, road, restored, signed	$7,500
Kirk Gibson, 1989 Los Angeles Dodgers, home, signed	$350
Moose Haas, 1978 Milwaukee Brewers, home	$185
Catfish Hunter, 1971 Oakland A's, road	$2,800
Bo Jackson, 1989 Kansas City Royals, home	$1,495
Harmon Killebrew, 1969 Minnesota Twins, home flannel	$6,995
Willie McGee, 1984 St. Louis Cardinals, knit	$400
Paul Molitor, 1988 Milwaukee Brewers, road	$975
Jack Morris, 1983 Detroit Tigers, road	$850
Nolan Ryan, 1984 Houston Astros, road	$3,495
Mike Schmidt, 1989 Philadelphia Phillies, road	$1,750
Ozzie Smith, 1982 St. Louis Cardinals, World Series home	$1,895
Carl Yastrzemski, 1969 Boston Red Sox, home, signed	$5,000
Robin Yount, 1992 Milwaukee Brewers, warm up	$1,295

Yearbooks

Los Angeles Angels, 1962	$85-$100
California Angels, 1983	$7-$12
California Angels, 1992	$12
Houston Astros, 1962	$175-$200
Houston Astros, 1966	$45
Houston Astros, 1992	$12
Philadelphia Athletics, 1949	$135-$200
Kansas City Athletics, 1955	$160-$200
Kansas City Athletics, 1960	$60-$80
Oakland Athletics, 1968	$100-$125
Oakland Athletics, 1974	$23-$30
Oakland Athletics, 1983	$10
Toronto Blue Jays, 1977	$35-$45
Toronto Blue Jays, 1992	$5-$6
Boston Braves, 1946	$350
Boston Braves, 1950	$150
Milwaukee Braves, 1953	$150-$175
Milwaukee Braves, 1957	$85-$100
Atlanta Braves, 1966	$60-$100
Atlanta Braves, 1973	$18-$25
Atlanta Braves, 1992	$10
Seattle Pilots, 1969	$175-$200
Milwaukee Brewers, 1970	$50-$75
Milwaukee Brewers, 1983	$12
St. Louis Cardinals, 1951	$200
St. Louis Cardinals, 1960	$40-$50
St. Louis Cardinals, 1967	$50-$75
St. Louis Cardinals, 1977	$12-$15
St. Louis Cardinals, 1991	$5-$6
Chicago Cubs, 1934	$275-$350
Chicago Cubs, 1941	$175-$250
Chicago Cubs, 1950	$90-$100
Chicago Cubs, 1957	$65
Chicago Cubs, 1985	$8-$10
Brooklyn Dodgers, 1947	$275
Brooklyn Dodgers, 1952	$150-$185
Los Angeles Dodgers, 1958	$150
Los Angeles Dodgers, 1965	$50
Los Angeles Dodgers, 1976	$12-$18
Los Angeles Dodgers, 1989	$6-$7
Montreal Expos, 1969	$45-$100
Montreal Expos, 1972	$20-$50
Montreal Expos, 1985	$6-$10
New York Giants, 1947	$185-$200
New York Giants, 1951	$100-$150
San Francisco Giants, 1958	$250
San Francisco Giants, 1969	$25-$35
San Francisco Giants, 1980	$8-$10
Cleveland Indians, 1948	$100-$150
Cleveland Indians, 1954	$95-$110
Cleveland Indians, 1966	$40-$45
Cleveland Indians, 1984	$6-$10
Seattle Mariners, 1985	$10
New York Mets, 1962	$300-$400
New York Mets, 1963	$125-$150
New York Mets, 1969	$85-$100
New York Mets, 1986	$7-$12
St. Louis Browns, 1944	$335
St. Louis Browns, 1953	$150-$275
Baltimore Orioles, 1954	$200-$225
Baltimore Orioles, 1960	$70-$90
Baltimore Orioles, 1970	$25-$40
Baltimore Orioles, 1984	$7-$10
San Diego Padres, 1969	$75

San Diego Padres, 1985 .... $6-$9
Philadelphia Phillies, 1949 .... $175-$200
Philadelphia Phillies, 1951 .... $500-$600
Philadelphia Phillies, 1961 .... $75
Philadelphia Phillies, 1967 .... $35-$55
Philadelphia Phillies, 1977 .... $15-$18
Pittsburgh Pirates, 1951 .... $175-$225
Pittsburgh Pirates, 1954 .... $90-$100
Pittsburgh Pirates, 1963 .... $35-$50
Pittsburgh Pirates, 1974 .... $20-$25
Pittsburgh Pirates, 1991 .... $5-$6
Cincinnati Reds, 1948 .... $175-$200
Cincinnati Reds, 1953 .... $100
Cincinnati Reds, 1962 .... $45
Cincinnati Reds, 1975 .... $18-$20
Cincinnati Reds, 1989 .... $5-$7
Boston Red Sox, 1951 .... $175-$200
Boston Red Sox, 1959 .... $70-$100
Boston Red Sox, 1969 .... $25-$30
Boston Red Sox, 1982 .... $10-$12
Kansas City Royals, 1969 .... $50
Kansas City Royals, 1971 .... $25-$35
Kansas City Royals, 1983 .... $7-$10
Detroit Tigers, 1955 .... $250-$275
Detroit Tigers, 1960 .... $70-$100
Detroit Tigers, 1965 .... $40-$60
Detroit Tigers, 1976 .... $15
Minnesota Twins, 1961 .... $185-$200
Minnesota Twins, 1964 .... $40-$75
Minnesota Twins, 1973 .... $20-$25
Chicago White Sox, 1952 .... $90-$100
Chicago White Sox, 1956 .... $70-$75
Chicago White Sox, 1970 .... $18-$20
New York Yankees, 1950 .... $275-$325
New York Yankees, 1952 .... $200-$250
New York Yankees, 1961 .... $100-$125
New York Yankees, 1967 .... $40-$70
New York Yankees, 1977 .... $2

Media Guides

*Like yearbooks, prices for media guides from a team's first
year of existence or the first year a media guide was issued usually are worth more than others. Overall, media guides tend to
bring lower prices than yearbooks because there is less demand
for them.*
*Following are general price ranges for media guides in Good con-
dition.*

1930s and earlier .... $75-$150
1940s .... $50-$80
1950s .... $40-$65
1960s .... $20-$40
1970s .... $7-$20
1980s .... $4-$8

Programs

Pre-1900 programs (rare) .... $500-$750
1900-1910 .... $200-$250

1920s .... $35-$75
1930s .... $20-$35
1940s .... $15-$25
1950s .... $10-$25
1960s .... $5-$25
1970s .... $5-$7

World Series Programs

*Values listed are for World Series programs in Good
condition.*

1903-1910 .... $8,000-$30,000
1910-1920 .... $2,000-$10,000
1920s .... $1,500-$4,000
1930s .... $400-$1,000
1940s .... $100-$350
1950s .... $100-$225
1960s .... $50-$150
1970s .... $20-$75
1980s .... $10-$20

All-Star Game Programs

*Values listed are for All-Star Game programs in Good
conditon.*

1930s .... $800-$3,000
1940s .... $350-$900
1950s .... $100-$500
1960s .... $60-$200
1970s .... $30-$100
1980s .... $15-$30
1990s .... $10-$20

Schedules

1901-1909 .... $150
1910-1919 .... $100
1920s $75
1930s $35
1940s $30
1950s $25
1960s $15
1970s $10
1980s .... $1-$2

BATTERY-OPERATED TOYS

Battery-operated toys are still made today, but the charming tin character toys and robots of the 1940s-1960s are the most collected today.

The heyday of battery-operated toys began in the 1940s with Japanese companies leading the charge. Popular wind-up and friction toys, often of vehicles or human and animal characters, were soon replaced by longer-lasting battery-operated versions.

Thousands of designs were made with toys featuring a variety of creative characters — from bubble-blowing monkeys to robots to cigar-smoking clowns. Disney and other cartoon characters like Popeye were also popular. The ingenuity of the Japanese created some truly unique novelty toys, valued today for their animation, design and humorous appeal.

Toys were often complex and could replicate several motions, such as walking, lifting or drumming. The tin lithography was usually quite interesting and detailed.

It is often difficult to identify the manufacturer of a battery-operated toy. Many companies used only initials to mark toys; some didn't mark them at all.

Major manufacturers of battery-operated toys from the 1940s-1960s include Marx, Linemar (Marx's Japanese subsidiary), Alps, Marusan, Yonezawa, Bandai and Modern Toy (MT).

The manufacture of tin toys dropped off in the 1960s in favor of cheaper methods and materials.

General Guidelines: While American-made Marx toys were popular, those made by Linemar and other Far East firms, were common.

To command top value, battery-operated toys should be operational and free of rust. But it is difficult to find most battery-operated toys in Mint condition in original boxes since the toys are highly susceptible to rust, corrosion and yellowing of fabric/plush.

Toys with character ties generally command more money. Space-related battery-operated toys, especially robots, are also popular.

Having the original box greatly increases the toy's desirability. Instructions were often printed on the box, and the name of the toy on the box often didn't match the toy exactly.

The complexity of the toy also determines value. A toy with three or more actions will generally be worth more than a toy that performs only one action. Even though they may be nice display pieces, toys that don't work command much less.

COLLECTORS' ALERT!

Check battery compartment for leaking batteries or corrosion that can damage toys.

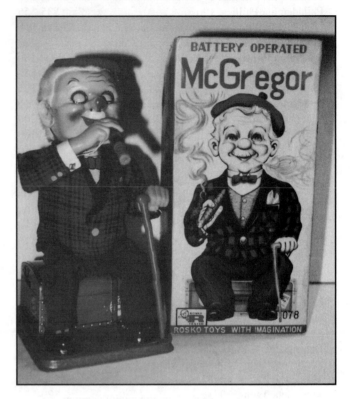

McGregor, 1960s, Rosko, $140 Excellent.

VALUE LINE

*Prices listed are for toys in Excellent to Near Mint condition **without original box**.*

Bartender, 1960s, TN	$45
Batmobile, 1972, ASC	$250
Big Loo, Marx, 1960s	$1,500
Bongo the Drumming Monkey, 1960s, Alps	$125
Bubble Blowing Bear, 1950s	$200
Bubble Blowing Popeye, 1950s	$1,200
Busy Secretary, 1950s	$200
Charlie Weaver, 1962	$65
Clown on Unicycle, 1960s, MT	$285
Cragstan Crapshooter, 1950s	$130
Cragstan Mother Goose, 1960s, Y	$125
Cragstan Roulette, Gambling Man, 1960s, Y	$220
Daisy the Jolly Drumming Duck, 1950s	$180
Dancing Sweethearts, 1950s, TN	$120
Disney Fire Engine, 1950s, Linemar	$660
Donald Duck, 1960s, Linemar	$275

Bubble Blowing Monkey, 1950s, Alps, $120 Excellent.

Drinking Captain, 1960s, S&E, $150 Excellent.

Doxie the Dog, 1950s, Linemar	$30
Drinking Captain, 1960s	$150
Drinking Dog, 1950s, Y	$115
Fairyland Loco, 1950s, Daiya	$90
Flintstone Yacht, 1961, Remco	$150
Godzilla, 1970s, Marusan	$105
Good Time Charlie, 1960s	$130
Great Garloo, 1960s, Marx	$450
Gypsy Fortune Teller, 1950s, Ichida	$600
Hootin' Hollow Haunted House, 1960s, Marx	$950
Indian Joe, 1960s	$90
Jolly Santa, 1950s	$200
Maxwell Coffee-Loving Bear, 1960s	$150
McGregor, 1960s	$140
Mickey the Magician, 1960s, Linemar	$1,200
Nutty Mad Indian, 1960s, Marx	$180
Picnic Bear, 1950s	$120
Pistol Pete, 1950s	$215
Popcorn Eating Bear, 1950s	$150
Rocking Chair Bear, 1950s	$140
Roller Skater, 1950s	$135
Sam the Shaving Man, 1960s	$180
Sammy Wong the Tea Totaler, 1950s	$200
Shoe Shine Monkey, 1950s	$195
Smoking Bunny, 1950s	$140
Smoking Elephant, 1950s, Marusan	$165
Smoking Popeye, 1950s, Linemar	$900
Smoky Bear, 1950s	$300
Sneezing Bear, 1950s	$270
Superman Tank, 1950s, Linemar	$925
Switchboard Operator, 1950s, Linemar	$400
Teddy the Boxing Bear, 1950s, Y	$175
Teddy the Rhythmical Drummer, 1960s, Alps	$120
Telephone Bear, 1950s	$280
Tom-Tom Indian, 1961, Y	$115
Topo Gigio Playing the Xylophone, 1960s	$440
Walking Bear w/Xylophone, 1950s, Linemar	$275
Walking Esso Tiger, 1950s	$300
Wash-O-Matic Washing Machine, 1940s, TN	$40
Western Locomotive, 1950s, MT	$60
Whistling Spooky Tree, 1950s, Marx	$750
Yo-Yo Clown, 1960s	$160
Yummy Yum Kitty, 1950s	$270
Zero Fighter Plane, 1950s	$230

BEANIE BABIES

Beanie Babies — those cuddly, understuffed beanbag animals — became all the rage in 1997, but were really introduced by Ty, Inc. in 1994. When the company began "retiring" (ceasing production of) specific animals, the collecting fever hit, with people scrambling to find scarce Beanie Babies and paying top dollar for them.

A secondary market quickly grew, and soon collectors were paying $50 or more for the tiny toys, which originally retailed for $5.

Over 100 Beanie Babies exist, from Twigs the giraffe and Tabasco the bull to Ziggy the Zebra and Hoppity the rabbit. A 1997 McDonald's promotion offered 10 Teenie Beanie Babies, smaller versions of the beanbags, which were offered with Happy Meals. A 1998 promotion offered 12 more.

General Guidelines: Retired Beanies and those with older hang tags sell for the highest prices. Variations in tags, colors and styles increase the collectibility of certain Beanies. Each of the newer Beanie Babies is labeled with its name, a poem and its birth date on a heart-shaped tag. Old tags are paper "To/From" style tags or a tag sewn into the animal.

Beanies with hang tags intact are more desirable than those without tags. Teenie Beanie Babies will have a higher value in original plastic bag packaging.

Regional variations (like the Canadian Maple bear) and special editions (like Princess, a Princess Diana commemorative bear) are highly desirable.

Snort the Bull (note the cream-colored feet) is still worth his issue price of $5. He is a variant of Tabasco (red feet), an earlier version that was retired in December 1996 and is worth about $100.

VALUE LINE

Ally the Alligator, retired, old tag	$25
Ally the Alligator, retired, new tag	$15
Baldy the Eagle, retired	$15
Bernie the St. Bernard	$12
Bessie the Cow, retired, old tag	$40
Bessie the Cow, retired, new tag	$20
Blackie the Bear, old tag	$30
Blackie the Bear, new tag	$5
Blizzard the Tiger, retired	$15
Bones the Dog, retired, new tag	$12
Bones the Dog, retired, old tag	$32
Bongo the Monkey, old tag, tail same color as body	$60
Bongo the Monkey, old tag, tail same color as face	$25
Bongo the Monkey, new tag, tail same color as body	$5
Bongo the Monkey, new tag, tail same color as face	$7
Bronty the Brontosaurus, retired	$400
Bubbles the Fish, new tag	$5
Bubbles the Fish, old tag	$40
Bucky the Beaver, new tag	$7
Bucky the Beaver, old tag	$28
Bumble the Bee, retired, old tag	$225
Bumble the Bee, retired, new tag	$200
Caw the Crow, retired	$195
Chilly the Polar Bear, retired	$700
Chocolate the Moose, new tag	$12
Chocolate the Moose, old tag	$35
Chops the Lamb, retired, old tag	$45
Chops the Lamb, retired, new tag	$65
Congo the Gorilla	$15
Coral the Fish, retired, old tag	$65
Coral the Fish, retired, new tag	$30
Crunch the Shark	$8
Cubbie the Bear, Chicago Cubs promo	$100
Cubbie the Bear, old tag	$35
Cubbie the Bear, new tag	$15
Curly the Bear	$40
Daisy the Cow, old tag	$30
Daisy the Cow, new tag	$10
Derby the Horse, old tag, fine yarn	$60
Derby the Horse, new tag, coarse yarn	$12
Derby the Horse, old tag, coarse yarn	$35
Digger the Crab, retired, new tag, red	$40
Digger the Crab, retired, old tag, red	$50
Digger the Crab, retired, old tag, orange	$295
Doby the Doberman	$15
Ears the Bunny, retired, old tag	$18
Ears the Bunny, retired, new tag	$12
Echo the Dolphin, retired	$12
Erin the Bear, green w/shamrock	$70
Flash the Dolphin, retired, old tag	$40
Flash the Dolphin, retired, new tag	$30

Fleece the Lamb $15
Flip the Cat, retired, new tag $25
Flip the Cat, retired, old tag $35
Floppity the Bunny $7
Flutter the Butterfly, retired $450
Freckles the Leopard $15
Garcia the Bear, retired, old tag $80
Garcia the Bear, retired, new tag $60
Glory the Bear $100
Goldie the Goldfish, old tag $30
Goldie the Goldfish, new tag $10
Gracie the Swan, retired $10
Grunt the Razorback, retired, new tag $85
Grunt the Razorback, retired, old tag $120
Happy the Hippo, retired, new tag, lavender $20
Happy the Hippo, retired, old tag, gray $325
Hippity the Bunny, retired $15
Hoot the Owl, retired, old tag $120
Hoot the Owl, retired, new tag $85
Hoppity the Bunny, retired $20
Humphrey the Camel, retired $625
Inch the Worm, retired, old tag, felt antennas $130
Inch the Worm, retired, new tag, yarn antennas $20
Inky the Octopus, retired, old tag, tan $200
Inky the Octopus, retired, old tag, pink $18
Inky the Octopus, retired, new tag, pink $12
Inky the Octopus, retired, old tag, gray $185
Jolly the Walrus, retired $15
Kiwi the Toucan, retired $75
Lefty the Donkey, retired $80
Legs the Frog, retired, new tag $20
Legs the Frog, retired, old tag $40
Libearty the Bear, retired, with flag $90
Libearty the Bear, retired, without flag $400
Lizzy the Lizard, old tag, tie-dye $300
Lucky the Ladybug, retired, old tag, spots glued on $100
Lucky the Ladybug, retired, new tag, spots on patterned
    fabric $12
Magic the Dragon, old tag, light pink stitching $40
Magic the Dragon, new tag, light pink stitching $20
Magic the Dragon, new tag, regular pink stitching $10
Manny the Manatee, retired, new tag $35
Manny the Manatee, retired, old tag $60
Maple the Bear Canadian exclusive $125
Mel the Koala $12
Mystic the Unicorn, old tag, fine yarn mane $50
Mystic the Unicorn, new tag, coarse mane $10
Mystic the Unicorn, old tag, coarse yarn mane $18
Nip the Cat, new tag, white paws $6
Nip the Cat, retired, old tag, white face/belly $175
Nip the Cat, old tag, white paws $35
Nip the Cat, retired, old tag, gold, no white $475
Nip the Cat, retired, old tag, gold, no white $475
Nuts the Squirrel $12
Patti the Platypus, retired, new tag, purple $20
Patti the Platypus, retired, old tag, purple $35
Patti the Platypus, retired, old tag, maroon $600

Peanut the Elephant, retired, old tag, light blue $20
Peanut the Elephant, retired, old tag, dark blue $1,500
Peanut the Elephant, retired, new tag, light blue $10
Peking the Panda, retired $1,000
Pinchers the Lobster, retired, new tag, red $15
Pinchers the Lobster, retired, old tag, red $25
Pinchers the Lobster, retired, old tag, orange $75
Pinky the Flamingo $10
Pouch the Kangaroo $12
Princess the Teddy Bear Princess Diana commemorative,
    purple bear w/rose $50
Pugsly the Dog $14
Quackers the Duck, retired, old tag, without wings $900
Quackers the Duck, retired, new tag, with wings $12
Quackers the Duck, retired, old tag, with wings $45
Radar the Bat, old tag $80
Radar the Bat, retired, new tag $60
Rex the Tyrannosaurus, retired $300
Righty the Elephant, retired, without flag $200
Righty the Elephant, retired, with flag $30
Ringo the Raccoon, new tag $15
Ringo the Raccoon, old tag $32
Roary the Lion $10
Rover the Dog, retired $12
Scoop the Pelican $12
Scottie the Terrier, retired $12
Seamore the Seal, retired, new tag $50
Seamore the Seal, retired, old tag $65
Seaweed the Otter, old tag $30
Seaweed the Otter, new tag $12
Slither the Snake, retired $500
Sly the Fox, old tag, brown belly $75
Sly the Fox, new tag, white belly $10
Sly the Fox, new tag, brown belly $40
Snip the Cat $10
Snort the Bull $12
Sparky the Dalmatian, retired $50
Speedy the Turtle, retired, old tag $35
Speedy the Turtle, retired, new tag $20
Spike the Rhinoceros $20
Splash the Whale, retired, old tag $50
Splash the Whale, retired, new tag $45
Spook the Ghost, old tag, not "Spooky" $75

Ally the Alligator.

Spooky the Ghost, old tag	$30
Spooky the Ghost, new tag	$25
Spot the Dog, retired, old tag, without spot	$1,150
Spot the Dog, retired, new tag, with spot	$20
Spot the Dog, old tag, with spot	$40
Squealer the Pig, retired	$12
Steg the Stegosaurus, retired	$300
Sting the Ray, retired	$55
Stinky the Skunk, old tag	$30
Stinky the Skunk, new tag	$12
Stripes the Tiger, retired, old tag	$60
Stripes the Tiger, retired, new tag	$12
Tabasco the Bull, retired	$150
Tank the Armadillo, retired, new tag, nine ridges	$65
Tank the Armadillo, old tag, seven ridges	$60
Teddy the Bear, retired, brown, new tag, new face	$15
Teddy the Bear, retired, brown, old tag, old face	$425
Teddy the Bear, retired, brown, old tag, new face	$80
Teddy the Cranberry Bear, retired, new face	$260
Teddy the Cranberry Bear, retired, old face	$400
Teddy the Jade Bear, retired, new face	$400
Teddy the Jade Bear, retired, old face	$300
Teddy the Magenta Bear, retired, new face	$325
Teddy the Magenta Bear, retired, old face	$400

Teddy the Teal Bear, retired, new face	$600
Teddy the Teal Bear, retired, old face	$375
Teddy the Violet Bear, retired, new face	$500
Teddy the Violet Bear, retired, old face	$400
Trap the Mouse, retired	$400
Tusk the Walrus, retired	$50
Twigs the Giraffe, retired, old tag	$35
Twigs the Giraffe, retired, new tag	$15
Valentino the Bear, new tag	$20
Valentino the Bear, old tag	$20
Velvet the Panther, retired, new tag	$20
Velvet the Panther, retired, old tag	$40
Waddle the Penguin, retired, new tag	$12
Waddle the Penguin, retired, old tag	$30
Waves the Whale, retired	$20
Web the Spider, retired	$415
Weenie the Dog, retired, old tag	$30
Weenie the Dog, retired, new tag	$15
Wrinkles the Dog	$12
Ziggy the Zebra, retired, old tag	$25
Ziggy the Zebra, retired, new tag	$10
Zip the Cat, retired, old tag, black, no white	$1,000
Zip the Cat, retired, old tag, white face/belly	$200
Zip the Cat, retired, old tag, white paws	$40
Zip the Cat, retired, new tag, white paws	$6

Baldy the Eagle.

Twigs the Giraffe, Pouch the Kangaroo and Blackie the Bear.

BEATLES & ELVIS COLLECTIBLES

Elvis Presley and The Beatles are undoubtedly the two most collected musical acts ever. Making their debuts about a decade apart, both inspired generations of young people to rock and roll. They also both put fear into the hearts of parents — Elvis with his gyrating pelvis and The Beatles with their radical long hair.

If either Elvis or The Beatles were newcomers today, their appearances wouldn't make a ripple. They would, however, still be relevant musically. The timelessness of their music and the popularity of Elvis and The Beatles in their primes has led to many collectibles that seem to rise in value every year.

Elvis Presley

Is Elvis alive and enjoying retirement on a secluded beach somewhere? If you've read the tabloids since the King's death in 1977, you might be convinced that he is. While that isn't likely, the tabloids do prove that Elvis is alive in people's hearts today. Witness his 29-cent U.S. stamp, which features a young Presley, that was tremendously successful several years ago.

Charting more than 30 "Top 40" hits (almost 20 #1 hits), Elvis has sold more than a billion records since cutting his first songs in the mid-1950s. He also starred in 31 feature films.

General Guidelines: Most Elvis collectibles date from 1956 to the present. The most valuable items are licensed items created during his lifetime; many are marked "Elvis Presley Enterprises." Items created after his death are considered fantasy items, designed purely as collector's items. These will not likely increase in value as investments.

There were several licensed items issued for Elvis. Among the licensed items are bookends, calendars, hair and body care products, wallets, belts, record players, handkerchiefs and buttons. (For more about Elvis records, see the "Records" chapter elsewhere in this book).

Licensed items can be worth several hundred dollars or more; however, even more expensive are one-of-a-kind Elvis items, such as items he wore while filming his many movies in the 1960s, his stage outfits and his autograph (which he signed generously during his career). Examples of forged Elvis autographs abound, however.

Elvis collectors who wish to expand their range of items can seek out items from the women in Elvis' life, like his wife Priscilla or daughter Lisa Marie, as well as items from Elvis' controversial manager, Colonel Tom Parker.

Clubs
•Elvis Forever TCB Fan Club
  P.O. Box 106, Pinellas Park, FL 34665

•Graceland News Fan Club
  P.O. Box 452, Rutherford, NJ 07070

•Graceland
  P.O. Box 16508, Memphis, TN 38186-0508
  800-238-2000

The Beatles

While Elvis was the king of rock 'n roll, The Beatles were the kings of rock 'n roll collectibles — there are many more Beatles items than Elvis items to collect.

These British imports — George Harrison, John Lennon, Paul McCartney and Ringo Starr — made their American debut on The Ed Sullivan Show. And what a debut it was. This television appearance propelled the Fab Four to the forefront of music in the 1960s and spawned Beatlemania. Not only did the band find tremendous popularity as a group, but each member met success on his own, with McCartney far outdistancing the other three on the solo front.

General Guidelines: Because of its mega-popularity, the group was featured on items ranging from dolls and bubble gum cards to lunch boxes and school bags. A majority of these collectibles date from 1964 to 1968. The Beatles' marketing efforts were definitely aimed at youth.

Collectibles based on the Beatles motion picture Yellow Submarine are some of the most popular today, probably due to the wild colors and graphics.

One-of-a-kind items, from autographs to drawings by John Lennon, are highly desirable and expensive.

Products officially authorized by the Beatles were marked either "NEMS" or "SELTAEB." "NEMS" was the acronym for Beatles manager Brian Epstein's company, North End Music Stores; while "SELTAEB," the group's American licensing company, was simply "Beatles" spelled backwards.

Paul McCartney Soaky, Colgate, 1965.

Clubs

•Beatles Connection
P.O. Box 1066, Pinellas Park, FL 34665

•Beatles Fan Club
397 Edgewood Ave., New Haven, CT   06511

•Beatles Fan Club of Great Britain
Superstore Publications
123 Marina, St. Leonards on Sea
East Sussex, England TN38 OBN

•Working Class Hero Beatles Club
3311 Niagara St., Pittsburgh, PA 15213

•Beatles PublicationsBeatlefan
P.O. Box 33515, Decatur, GA 30033

•Instant Karma
P.O. Box 256, Sault Ste. Marie, MI   49783

•Strawberry Fields Forever
P.O. Box 880981, San Diego, CA 92168

(See also Records chapter)

Authentic Beatle Wig, Lowell Toy Mfg. Corp.

VALUE LINE

Beatles

Alarm Clock, Yellow Submarine, 1968, Shefield
  Watch, MIB $4,000
Alarm Clock, Yellow Submarine, 1968, Shefield
  Watch, NM $2,000
Autographed photo, all four Beatles .... $2,500-$4,000
Bandage, from movie *Help!*, 3-1/2" long, unused,
  Curad bandage, sealed, 1965, rare, VG $50
Banks, Yellow Submarine, set of four bust figures of
  each Beatle, 7-1/2" h, plastic, 1968, VG $1,400
Box, ice cream bar, four-count, Hood Co., 1960s $400
Box, ice cream bar, four-count, Townhouse, 1960s $750
Box, licorice, held 24 pieces of Record Candy, 1960s ... $500
Bread, Ringo Roll (custom bag for loaf of bread), 1960s $600
Bubble gum cards, 165 cards w/original wrapper, 1964
  Topps $410
Bubble gum cards, *A Hard Day's Night*, unopened box
  of 24 packs, 1964 .... $400
Bubble gum cards, *A Hard Day's Night*, set of 55, 1964 $150
Bubble gum cards, *A Hard Day's Night,* unopened pack,
  1964 .... $60
Bubble gum, Chu-Bops packs, miniature records, 16
  different Beatles albums, 1986, each $2
Cake Decorating Figures, set of 4, plastic, EX $30
Candy, Beatle Bar wrapper, 1960s $50
Candy, Lollipop wrapper, 1960s $30
Candy, Ringo Candy Rolls, Argentina $50

Candy, Yeah Yeah Candy Sticks packs, World Candies,
  set of six $1,000
Candy, Yeah Yeah Candy Sticks box, held 25 two-stick
  boxes $750
Candy, Yellow Submarine Sweet Cigarettes box,
  Primrose Confectionery $250
Can, Nestle's Quik, Beatles doll offer, 1960s $1,000
Christmas Ornament, 1994, Hallmark, complete with
  box, stage and microphones, NM $125
Comic Book, *The Beatles Story*, Marvel, 1978 .... $15
Desk Set, Yellow Submarine, only one complete set
  known, includes pen holder, pencil holder cup,
  letter holder, desk pad, 1968, A&M Leatherline,
  for set .... $5,500 and up
Dolls, set of four Remco dolls, with instruments, no
  boxes, NM $400
Dolls, set of four Remco dolls, MIB $1,000
Drawing, Yellow Submarine, John Lennon, 8" x 5",
  original production drawing, matted and framed
  with a certificate of authenticity $400
Flasher Button, VariVue, George $20
Game, Flip Your Wig, Milton Bradley, 1964, EX $125
Guitar, Hong Kong, 4-7/8" Miniature, first names on
  guitar, rubber bands for strings, MIP $80
Guitar, Mastro, 21", Four Pops, red and pink plastic,
  four-string, Beatles faces and autographs on front,
  U.S., MIP $750
Guitar, Mastro, 5-1/2", Miniature pink plastic, Beatles
  faces on front, two rubber bands for strings, U.S.,
  MIP $125

Guitar, Mastro, 14-3/4", Junior pink and burgundy
plastic, four-string, Beatles on body and crown,
U.S., MIP $1,500
Guitar, Mastro, 21", Yeah Yeah, red and burgundy
plastic, six-string, Beatles faces and autographs on
body, U.S., MIP $2,500
Guitar, Mastro, 30", Beatle-ist, pink and burgundy
plastic, six-string, Beatles faces and autographs on
body, U.S., MIP $1,500
Guitar, Selcor, 21" Big Beat, red and orange plastic,
four-string, color photo sticker, autographs on
front, U.K., MIP $1,750
Guitar, Selcor, 32-1/2" Big Six, orange, red and
burgundy, 6-string plastic, issued in coffin-shaped
cardboard box, U.K., MIP $1,000
Guitar, Selcor, 14" Junior, orange body with color paper
photo, sealed with backing board, U.K., MIP $2,000
Guitar, Selcor, 32-1/2" New Beat, red and burgundy,
four-string, Beatles pictures and autographs on front,
U.K., MIP $750
Guitar, Selcor, 23" New Sound, red or orange and cream,
four-string, Beatles faces and autographs on front,
U.K., MIP $1,500
Guitar, Selcor, 31" Red Jet Electric, red and white, six-
string electric, Beatles sticker and autographs on
front, coffin-shaped cardboard box, U.K., MIP $1,200
Gumball charms, set of four, 3/4" diameter with loop,
reverse has song $30
Gumball rings, set of four with mini records attached $50
Gumball wallets, set of four, 1" wide, set $45
Hair Pomade, H.H. Cosmetic Labs, unused packet,
1964, 2-1/2" x 1", VG $100
Halloween Costume $95
Lunch Box, Yellow Submarine, steel, with Thermos
bottle, King Seeley, 1968, NM $500
Magazine, *Rolling Stone*, Jan. 22, 1981, John and
Yoko on cover, MT $20
Magazine, *Flip #1*, September 1994, Beatles on cover,
MT $23
Movie Poster, Concert for Bangladesh, 1971, one-sheet . $75
Movie Poster, *A Hard Day's Night*, 1964, one-sheet $300
Movie Poster, *A Hard Day's Night*, 1964, three-sheet ... $450
Movie Poster, *A Hard Day's Night*, 1964, six-sheet $550
Movie Poster, *A Hard Day's Night*, 1964,
24-sheet (billboard) $1,500
Movie Poster, *A Hard Day's Night/Help!*, combo, 1965,
one-sheet $650
Movie Poster, *A Hard Day's Night/Help!*, combo, 1965,
40" x 60" $750
Movie Poster, *Help!*, 1965, one-sheet $400
Movie Poster, *Help!*, 1965, three-sheet $650
Movie Poster, *Help!*, 1965, six-sheet $750
Movie Poster, *Help!*, 1965, 24-sheet (billboard) $1,500
Movie Poster, *How I Won The War*, 1967, one-sheet $400
Movie Poster, *Magical Mystery Tour*, 1967, one-sheet .. $350
Movie Poster, *Magical Mystery Tour*, 1967, three-sheet $600
Movie Poster, *Magical Mystery Tour,* 1967, six-sheet $70
Movie Poster, *Magic Christian* (Ringo, John Cleese and Peter
Sellers), 1969, one-sheet $50

George Harrison, John Lennon, Ringo Starr and Paul McCartney
dolls by Remco, 1964.

Movie Poster, *Yellow Submarine,* 1968, one-sheet $950
Movie Poster, *Yellow Submarine*, 1968, three-sheet $850
Movie Poster, *Yellow Submarine,* 1968, six-sheet $950
Movie Title Banner, *A Hard Day's Night*, 1964,
24" x 82" $500
Movie Title Banner, *Help!*, 1965, 24" x 82" $500
Movie Title Banner, *Let It Be*, 1967, 24" x 82" $500
Movie Title Banner, *Yellow Submarine*, 1968, 24" x 82" $600
Nodders, 1964, papier-mache, set of four $700
Notebook, three-ring binder, white with Beatles photo,
New York Looseleaf Corp., 1964, VG $175
Paperback, *The Beatles, Yesterday, Today and Tomorrow*,
1968 .... $14
Plate, bamboo, 12" diameter, Beatles photo in center,
colorful, 1966, NM $200
Poster, *A Hard Day's Night*, heavy paper stock, advertises
paperback book and movie 1964, 11" x 14" $400
Potato Chips, premium, Laura Scudder's Potato Chips
display card advertising Yellow Submarine stickers
included in each package, 1968 .... $500
Program, July 8, 1963, show at Winter Gardens in
Margate, U.K., VG $300
Promo Card, Let It Be, 1970, 5" x 5-1/4", black and
white, NM $25
Puzzle, Fan Club, black and white, marked "The Official
Beatles Fan Club," NM $45
Record Player, Beatles model #1000, VG $3,500
Souvenir Book, Hard Day's Night, Whitman, MT $20
Talcum Powder, Margo of Mayfair, U.K., NM $600
Thermos, blue, 1965, VG $175
Thermos, Yellow Submarine, 1968, NM $225
Tennis Shoes, high tops, Wing Dings, NM in original
box $900
Ticket, unused, pink and black print with photo,
Candlestick Park, last concert, Aug. 29, 1966, NM .. $450
Ticket, unused, white with black print, Suffolk Downs,
Mass., Aug. 18, 1966, VG $100
Ticket, unused, yellow with photo, Shea Stadium,
Aug. 23, 1966, NM $300

Tour Program, 1964, U.S., 12" x 12", VG $50
Water Color Set, Yellow Submarine, MIP $150
Wrapper, ice cream bar, Hood Co., 1960s $10
Wrapper, ice cream bar, foil, Townhouse, 1960s $100

Elvis Presley

The following are estimated values for some vintage Elvis collectibles. Most items shown are from the late 1950s, the period of greatest interest to serious collectors. Values shown are for items in Excellent or better condition. The "EPE" notation on many of the items indicates that it was licensed by "Elvis Presley Enterprises." Note that in some cases, prices are given for items still in their original packaging, a condition that increases the value substantially.

Anklets, 1956, EPE, two pairs attached to card $1,000
    Card only $300
Ashtray, 1956, EPE, facsimile autographed photo in
    glass $400
Elvis Presley autograph, "cut signature" on piece of
    paper .... $450-$600
    Autographed photo .... $500-$1,000
    Autographed picture sleeve or album cover ... $700-$1,200
    Autographed high school yearbook .... $4,000-$5,000
Autograph Book, 1956, EPE, line drawing of Elvis on
    front $450
Belt, 1956, EPE, leather $700
Belt, 1956, EPE, plastic $625
Belt Buckle, 1956, EPE, ... $250
Billfold, 1956, EPE $475
Binder, 1956, EPE, "Love Me Tender" zipper model . $1,000
Bolo Tie, 1956, EPE $200

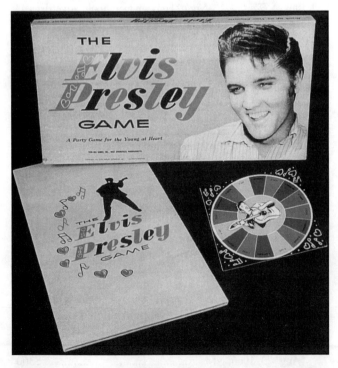

The Elvis Presley Game, 1957, Teen-Age Games, Inc., $800-$1,200.

Bookends, 1956, EPE, pair $600
Elvis books (dozens available), with dust cover .... $15-$50
    Without dust cover .... $10-$25
Bracelet, 1962, EPE, various styles .... $35-$65
Carrying Case, 1956, EPE, with insert $650
Ceramic Tile, 1956, EPE, "Best Wishes, Elvis Presley,"
    6-inch square $850
Charm Bracelet, 1956, EPE, with original card $150
    Bracelet only (no card) $100
Coaster, 1956, EPE, facsimile autographed photo in
    glass $150
Coin Purse, Key Chain, Elvis pictured in striped shirt ... $150
Cuff Links, 1958, EPE, in original box $400
    Cuff Links only, (no box) $250
Diary, 1956, EPE (with lock) $500
Dog Tag Bracelet, Key Chain, Anklet, 1958, EPE,
    (many styles) .... $20-$40
Dog Tag Necklace, 1958, EPE, on original card $85
    Necklace only (no card) $30
Dog Tag Sweater Holder, 1958, EPE, on original card .. $200
    Sweater Holder only (no card) $125
Doll, 1957, EPE, in original box with all clothing $2,000
    Doll, original clothing, no box $1,500
Earrings, 1956, EPE, picture of Elvis, on original card .. $250
    Earrings alone (no card) $150
Elvis Fan Club Membership Package, 1956,
    complete .... $300-$500
    Fan Club Membership Card $40
    "I Like Elvis and His RCA Records" Pin-On Button .. $75
    "Personal Note to You From Elvis" $100
Framed Portrait, 1956, EPE "Love Me Tender,
    Sincerely, Elvis Presley $500
The Elvis Presley Game, 1956, EPE, board game in
    box $1,000
Drinking Glass, 1956, EPE $200
Toy Guitar, 1956-57, EPE, Emenee, with carrying
    case .... $1,500-$2,000
    Guitar only (no case) $1,000
Song Book For Emenee Guitar Including Elvis Presley
    Song Hits $40
Handbag, 1956, EPE, clutch style $500
Handkerchief, 1956, EPE $300
Hats, EPE, Magnet, 1956, with mfg. tag $100
Hat, paper army to promote "G.I. Blues," 1960 .... $35
Hat, straw, "Elvis Summer Festival" $20
Hound Dog, 1956, EPE, 10-inch dog with "Hound Dog"
    hat $250
Hound Dog, 1972, 12-15 inches, "Elvis Summer
    Festival" $40
Jar, AML (112060), "Love Me Tender" $60
Jeans, 1956, EPE, Blue Ridge, with "Elvis Presley Jeans"
    tag $150
Keychain, EPE, Pictorial Products, 1956, flasher $20
Hawaiian Lei, promoting "Blue Hawaii" LP $100
Lipstick, EPE, Teen-Ager Lipstick Corp., 1956, on
    original card $1,000
    Lipstick only (no card) $275
Locket, 1957, EPE, heart shaped Elvis $40

Elvis magazines, 1956-1960 (hundreds exist) .... $25-$75

Elvis *TV Guides* (several different) .... $50-$200

Medallion, 1956, EPE, "I Want You, I Need You, I Love You;" "Don't Be Cruel;" "Hound Dog;" "Heartbreak Hotel" $150

Mittens, 1956, EPE, pair $350

Necklace, 1956, EPE, heart-shaped, engraving of Elvis, original card $225
    Necklace only (no card) $150

Opening Night Invitations, Las Vegas, Lake Tahoe, printed paper $15

Paint-by-Number set, 1956, EPE $500

Pajamas, EPE, pictures a singing Elvis, lists "Hound Dog," "Don't Be Cruel," others $400

Paperweight, "Sincerely Yours, Elvis $12

Patches, 1956, EPE, heart-shaped, "My Heart Belongs to Elvis Presley," "I Love Elvis Presley, and Elvis Presley is a Doll" on display card $100
    Single Patch (no card) $30

Tour Patches, ribbons (1970-77) $30

Pencils, 1956, EPE, Union Pencil Co., complete box, one dozen packs of Elvis Presley Pencils $2,000
    Single Pencil $15

Pencil Sharpener, 1956, EPE $125

Perfume, 1957, EPE, "Elvis Presley's Teddy Bear Eau de Parfum, 1957 picture of Elvis on label $275
    1965 version of above (1965 photo) $40

Phonograph, 1956, EPE, portable, facsimile autograph model $900

Printed Instructions, "How to Use and Enjoy Your RCA Victor Portable Phonograph" $75

Photo Album, 1956, EPE $350

Elvis Presley Photo Albums (souvenir and concert), 1956 "In Person Elvis Presley Country Music's Mr. Rhythm $400
    1956, "Elvis Presley Mr. Dynamite" $325
    1956, "Souvenir Photo Album Elvis Presley" $300
    1957, "Elvis Presley Photo Folio" $200
    1970-1977 Examples .... $25-$45

Pillow, 1956, EPE $500

Pin, 1956, EPE, framed picture of Elvis attached to a guitar, with original card $350
    Pin only (no card) $200

Pin, 1956, EPE Vari-Vue or Pictorial Productions, flasher $30

Pocket Watch, 1964, pictures Elvis wearing jacket and playing guitar, polished finish $200
    Above, but with knurled finish $35

Purse, 1956, EPE, clutch style, three pictures of Elvis, lists "Hound Dog," "Heartbreak Hotel," "I Want You I Need You I Love You" $350

Record Case, 1956, EPE $400

Ring, 1956, EPE, adjustable $100

Flasher Ring, 1957 .... $60

Scarves, 1956 EPE, three drawings of Elvis, lists "I Want You I Need You," "Love Me Tender," "Don't Be Cruel,"

"You're Nothing But A Hound Dog," reads "Best Wishes, Elvis Presley" $175

Scrap Book, 1956, EPE $300

Elvis Presley Sheet Music, (various picturing Elvis)
    1956-1959 .... $25-$50
    1960-1977 .... $15-$30

Shirt, 1956, EPE, Blue Ridge, gree-and-white striped ... $125

Shoes, 1956, EPE Faith Shoe Co., pumps, pair in box ... $500
    Pair of shoes without box $400

Skirt, 1956, EPE, Little Jeans Togs $650

Socks, 1956, EPE, Two pair of bobby socks on original card $200
    Card only $35

Statuette, 1956, EPE, 8-inch bronze figure $550

Teddy Bear, 1957 EPE, 24-inch with "Teddy Bear" and Elvis Presley" ribbons $275

International Hotel Bear, 1971, pink and white with pin on badge $40

Trading Cards, 1956, Topps, any one card .... $8-$12
    Complete set (66 cards) $600
    Unopened Pack of 1956 cards .... $50-$125
    Wrapper from 1956 set .... $35-$75

Trading Cards, 1978, Donruss, any one card .... 50-75 cents
    Complete Set .... $40-$50

Trading Cards, 1992-93, The River Group, One complete series $40

Wallet, 1956, EPE (several styles) $300

Barbie Loves Elvis gift set, 1990s, Mattel, $70.

BEER STEINS

Often called mugs, jugs or tankards, steins are drinking vessels with a handle and lid used for the consumption of beer. The word "stein" is derived from the German word "steinzeugkrug," which means stoneware jug or tankard. While beer steins date back to the 1500s, most of the steins of interest to collectors today were made in the last 100 years.

The bubonic plague in Europe ultimately led to laws in Germany requiring that drinking vessels be covered to keep flies out of the beer. The most common lids are made of pewter. From the late 1600s through the early 1800s, significant advances occurred in the production of beer steins. Better techniques were introduced for controlling the high temperatures needed to make stoneware, porcelain and glass. Decorating techniques using glazes, paints and enamel, as well as engraving, were refined to create beer steins with artistic merit.

Early Beer Steins

Faience steins: Porcelain steins made by dozens of small factories throughout Germany. They were usually decorated in blue, yellow, green, red and black.

Creussen steins: Made in Creussen, Bavaria in the late 1600s. They featured a hand-applied relief decoration, most commonly the Twelve Apostles. While some Creussen steins were left undecorated with only a dark brown glaze, the most desirable examples were decorated with white, yellow, blue and red. The productions of Creussen steins began once again around 1900. Thousands of copies were made using molds and glazes inferior to the originals.

Westerwald steins: Gray stoneware with a blue saltglazed decoration. First made in the 1600s, the most desirable examples were made in the 1700s. They are still made today.

Pewter steins: These steins from the 1600s and 1700s are very desirable when original pewtersmith's touch marks are present and an engraved design appears on the pewter. Pewter can very easily be copied, so reproductions do exist.

Glass steins: From the 1700s and early 1800s, clear glass was used. For added protection, a pewter rim was often applied to the base of the stein. Sometimes an engraver would enhance a glass stein with a family crest, a running stag, a building or some other design. Enameled decorations were relatively rare on early glass steins.

Other steins made before 1800 include porcelain (most notably from the Meissen factory), wood, silver and gold.

Early 1800s

Shortly after 1800, a change occurred in the type of steins that were made for the next 50 to 75 years. While glass, pewter and porcelain steins were still being made, other materials lost favor and were either discontinued or the volume of production was greatly reduced.

More colors of glass were introduced including blue, green, amber, red and yellow. Engraving, etching and cutting became common. Enameling gained popularity, and some very attractive tech-

German half liter stein, pewter top with ceramic center, marked "1635."

niques such as overlay (two layers of glass) were introduced. Pewter steins underwent few changes during this time, a few factories were beginning to produce porcelain steins.

Very simple relief stoneware steins were first made before 1850. They became the forerunner of what is know known as the pottery or stoneware relief stein.

The Golden Era

After 1850, an increasing interest in the decorative arts and their application to the manufacturing of beer steins in Germany led to the emergence of a large industry of beer stein manufacturers. The foremost of these was Villeroy & Boch, located in the town of Mettlach. Beer steins made by this company are called Mettlach steins.

Villeroy & Boch began to make stoneware steins in the late 1800s. The most notable steins produced by Villeroy & Boch were etched, but they also made other types of steins.

The production of Mettlach steins virtually stopped in about 1910. In 1976, Villeroy & Boch began to produce beer steins again, primarily limited editions.

Etched steins: Around 1900, many companies produced steins that looked similar to the Mettlach etched steins, but were usually of a lower quality. Some of the companies that produced these steins were Marzi & Remy, A.J. Thewalt, Simon Peter Gerz, Merkelbach & Wick, J.W Remy and Hauber & Reuther.

Relief steins: From the late 1800s until today, the most commonly-produced steins have been stoneware and pottery relief steins. Stoneware is gray, and pottery is tan or cream-colored. Stoneware steins are frequently colored with a blue salt glaze, and pottery steins can be decorated with various colored glazes. These steins were made by dozens of companies. Today, the relief stein industry thrives in Germany.

Glass steins: The emergence of highly-decorated porcelain and stoneware resulted in strong competition for glass stein manufacturers. Glass steins were produced in many different colors with enameled or transfer decorations. Pewter overlays were used to create designs over the glass, and engraved scenes became very popular.

Pewter steins: During the late 1800s, relief designs became popular on pewter steins. These designs were part of the mold and gave the manufacturers a competitive product at a reasonable cost. During the 1880s, a style was introduced that copied the form of earlier pewter steins but added a relief figure in a small window or niche in the front of the stein. These figures were of various workmen, such as a shoemaker or blacksmith, usually engraved with dates from the 1600s.

Character steins: Stoneware, porcelain, pottery and pewter were all used to make character steins shaped like people, animals, buildings and other objects. Two prominent manufacturers from the early 1900s were E. Bohne Sohne and Schierholz.

Porcelain steins: These steins feature many decorations including occupations, city scenes and floral patterns. They usually bear the name of the original owner, a mention of his occupation and a scene depicting his occupation.

Regimental steins: German soldiers in the Imperial Army frequently purchased a beer stein upon completing military service; these are called regimental steins. Most often made of porcelain, these steins depicted military life and carried the name of the owner and his service information, including the name of his unit and his service dates.

While some regimental steins can be found from earlier times, most are dated from 1890 to 1914. Many factors influence the desirability and therefore the collecting value. Size and overall attractiveness are very important, with later dated steins being taller and more elaborate. Scarce units such as aviation (Luftshiffer and Flieger) command premium prices.

Military & Third Reich steins: Many souvenir steins were made to commemorate the German war effort between 1914 and 1918. These are primarily half liter stoneware steins with transfer decorations. Military souvenir steins were also made during the Reichswehr period 1918-1934. The rise of the Third Reich in 1934 led to a resurgence in the volume of military stein production. Most Third Reich steins were produced between 1934 and 1939. Reichswehr and Third Reich steins were made of pottery, stoneware, porcelain, glass and pewter.

Brewery steins: Beginning in the late 1800s, German breweries distributed beer steins featuring their logos. The earliest were gray stoneware with an incised design colored with blue salt glaze. Around 1900, colorful transfer decorations replaced the incised designs. Both gray stoneware and tan pottery were used for these steins. Frequently, the pewter lid had a relief design with the brewery logo. Steins with matching logo lids are more desirable than those with plain lids.

Modern Steins

After World War II, it took a few years for the manufacturing of beer steins in Germany to revive. This occurred as a result of the demand from American tourists and servicemen for souvenirs. Until the early 1980s, most German stein production was devoted to relief pottery and stoneware steins.

In the 1980s, glass and porcelain became very popular. A strong demand by American collectors resulted in the creation of numerous limited-edition steins.

The largest producer of beer steins today is Ceramarte, a company in Brazil founded by German immigrants. Ceramarte started selling beer steins in the United States in the early 1970s. The company's earliest steins were actually unlidded mugs.

Mettlach stein, half liter, #2051, c. 1896, beige ground, green, browns, gilt trim, $700.

In the mid-1970s, Anheuser-Busch contracted with Ceramarte to make steins. Within a few years, the promotional efforts grew into a huge marketing effort that resulted in the production of more than 10 new Anheuser-Busch steins produced each year. Some of the earliest Anheuser-Busch steins have increased in value from around $10 to over $200.

General Guidelines: Steins over 200 years old are not likely to be in Mint condition, but condition is still important. Steins in perfect or near perfect condition command top prices. A small hairline crack will have only a minor effect on the value of a Faience or Creussen stein, but it will greatly reduce the value of a glass stein.

Contributor to this section: Gary Kirsner, Glentiques, Ltd., 1940 Augusta Terrace, P.O. Box 8807, Coral Springs, FL 33071.

COLLECTORS' ALERT!

Beware of reproductions. Many antique beer steins have been reproduced, and some of the reproductions are over 100 years old. Generally, they are easily distinguished from older steins because they were given contemporary factory marks.

Faience and Creussen reproductions are harder to detect. Faience reproductions are heavier and have poorly-painted decorations. Creussen reproductions are heavier, lack detail, and are frequently found to have been painted poorly with noticeable paint flaking. Both show signs of having been made in a mold rather than hand thrown.

Reproduction pewter steins use a lower quality pewter. Frequently, they have fictitious marks and poor workmanship. Reproductions of 18th century Westerwald steins are mold made and generally have current factory marks.

Glass steins require close examination to determine age. Reproductions are slightly heavier, very uniform and do not show any of the minute wear that old glass steins have due to normal handling. Most character steins that have been made recently have contemporary marks, but some do not. Usually a lower quality pewter indicates a reproduction.

Regimental steins have been reproduced since the early 1950s. While dozens of varieties exist, most can be detected by one of the following characteristics: the presence of a factory mark on the bottom of a porcelain stein (frequently a gold crown); a semi-nude scene in the porcelain lithophane; incorrect unit information on the stein or poorly-defined pewter parts.

Not all reproductions contain all off these signs, but most contain at least one. Third Reich steins are only 50 to 60 years old and therefore present a unique problem for collectors in that eproductions can easily be made using the same materials as the originals. Fortunately, most of the reproductions are easy to detect. The most common reproductions have a mark in gold on the base indicating a date, such as 1939. The lids are usually poorly defined — but accurate — copies of the original.

Half liter porcelain character stein by Ernst Bohne; imp. anchor mark.

VALUE LINE

Pre 1800s Steins

Prices listed are for original steins in Mint or Near Mint condition with original lids.

Faience stein, one liter, blue and white, Nurnberg factory, buildings .... $1,000-$2,000

Faience stein, one liter, blue and white, Nurnberg factory, religious figure .... $2,000-$4,000

Faience stein, one liter, Bayreuth factory, running horse .... $1,000-$1,500

Faience stein, one liter, Bayreuth factory, bird .... $500-$1,000

Faience stein, one liter, Berlin factory, buildings $800-$1,500

Faience stein, one liter, Crailsheim factory, St. George .... $5,000-$7,000

Faience steins, one liter, various scenes, ordinary quality .... $800-$1,200

Faience steins, one liter, various scenes, excellent quality $1,000- $2,000

Creussen stein half liter, Twelve Apostles, brown glaze .... $1,000-$2,000

Creussen stein half liter, Twelve Apostles, colored decoration .... $4,000-$6,000

Creussen stein one liter, Twelve Apostles, colored
   decoration .... $5,000-$10,000
Creussen stein one liter, Hunting scene, colored
   decoration .... $7,000-$12,000
Creussen stein one liter, Lunar scene, colored
   decoration .... $7,000-$12,000
Westerwald stoneware stein, half liter,
   18th century .... $400$1,000
Westerwald stoneware stein, one liter,
   18th century .... $500-$1,500
Pewter stein, half liter, 18th century, undecorated . $200-$400
Pewter stein, half liter, 18th century, decorated .. $400-$1,000
Pewter stein, one liter, 18th century, undecorated .. $300-$500
Pewter stein, one liter, 18th century, decorated ... $500-$1,500
Glass stein, half liter, 18th century, undecorated ... $300-$600
Glass stein, one liter, 18th century, undecorated .... $500-$800
Glass stein, half liter, 18th century, engraved
   decoration .... $600-$2,000
Glass stein, one liter, 18th century, engraved
   decoration .... $800-$2,500
Glass stein, half liter, 18th century, enameled
   decoration .... $1,000-$3,000
Glass stein, one liter, 18th century, enameled
   decoration .... $1,500-$4,000
Porcelain stein, one liter, Meissen, floral decoration,
   silver lid .... $3,000-$5,000

Early 1800s Steins

*Prices listed are for original steins in Mint condition with
original lids.*

Glass stein, half liter, c. 1840, engraved buildings or animals
   $400-$1,000
Glass stein, half liter, c. 1840, enameled, flowers .. $350-$600
Glass stein, one liter, c.1840, enameled, flowers ... $500-$900
Glass stein, half liter, c. 1860, overlay, blue and
   white .... $500-$1,000
Glass stein, one liter, c. 1860, blue, enameled
   flowers .... $400-$700
Glass stein, half liter, pressed glass, porcelain inlaid
   lid .... $50-$125
Pewter stein, one liter, early 19th century,
   undecorated .... $150-$300
Pewter stein, one liter, early 19th century,
   decorated .... $250-$500
Stoneware stein, half liter, relief, porcelain inlaid lid $75-$100
Stoneware stein, one liter, relief, porcelain inlaid lid $80-$120

The Golden Era

*Prices listed are for original steins in Mint condition with
original lids.*

Mettlach stein, half liter, 2090, etched $550
Mettlach stein, half liter, 2093, etched $700
Mettlach stein, half liter, 1675, etched $550
Mettlach stein, half liter, 2025, etched $425
Mettlach stein, half liter, 2778, etched $1,200
Mettlach stein, half liter, 2765, etched $2,400
Mettlach stein, half liter, 2030, etched $1,000
Mettlach stein, half liter, etched, various scenes . $400-$4,000
Mettlach stein, one liter, 2090, etched $700
Mettlach stein, one liter, 2500, etched $750

Mettlach stein, one liter, 2382, etched $1,000
Mettlach stein, one liter, 2580, etched $1,100
Mettlach stein, three liter, 1940, etched $1,200
Mettlach stein, three liter, 2428, etched $1,200
Mettlach stein, seven liter, 1161, etched $4,500
Mettlach stein, half liter, print-under-glaze, various
   scenes .... $150-$500
Mettlach stein, one liter, print-under-glaze, various
   scenes .... $150-$500
Mettlach stein, half liter, relief, various scenes ...... $150-$400
Mettlach stein, one liter, relief, various scenes ...... $200-$400
Mettlach stein, half liter, cameo, various scenes . $500-$1,000
Mettlach stein, half liter, Faience type, various
   scenes .... $400-$700
Mettlach stein, one liter, Faience type, various
   scenes .... $700-$2,000
Mettlach stein, half liter, Rookwood type, various
   scenes .... $350-$500
Etched steins, half liter, various scenes and
   manufacturers .... $100-$400
Etched steins, one liter, various scenes and
   manufacturers .... $150-$500
Character steins, half liter, stoneware, various
   figures .... $150-$600

1/2 liter regimental stein.

Character steins, half liter, pottery, various figures $150-$600
Character steins, half liter, porcelain, various figures .... $150-$3,000
Character stein, half liter, porcelain, Bismarck, by Schierholz $550
Character stein, half liter, porcelain, Singing Pig, by Schierholz $400
Character stein, half liter, porcelain, Uncle Sam, by Schierholz $1,600
Character stein, half liter, porcelain, Wrap Around Alligator, by E. Bohne Sohne $700
Character stein, half liter, porcelain, Devil, by E. Bohne Sohne $650
Regimental steins, half liter, porcelain, various common units .... $250-$600
Regimental steins, half liter, porcelain, various semi-common units .... $500-$900
Regimental steins, half liter, porcelain, various moderately rare units .... $600-$1,200
Regimental steins, half liter, porcelain, various rare units .... $800-$5,000
Military steins, half liter, WWI commemorative .... $100-$300
Third Reich steins, half liter, various scenes .... $200-$600
Pewter steins, half liter, various scenes .... $75-$200
Pewter steins, half liter, various niche scenes .... $300-$400
Pottery relief steins, half liter, various scenes .... $50-$200
Stoneware relief steins, half liter, various scenes ..... $40-$150
Porcelain steins, half liter, various floral scenes ...... $75-$125
Porcelain steins, half liter, various own scenes .... $75-$125
Porcelain steins, half liter, various occupational scenes .... $200-$500
Glass steins, half liter, enameled or transfer scenes $100-$300

Glass steins, half liter, engraved scenes .... $150-$500
Glass steins, half liter, pewter overlay .... $150-$400
Glass steins, one liter, pewter overlay .... $300-$500
Brewery steins, half liter, pottery or stoneware, various breweries .... $75-$400
Brewery steins, one liter, pottery or stoneware, various breweries .... $100-$500

Modern Steins

Prices listed are for original steins in Mint condition with original lids.

Villeroy and Boch, half liter, fairy tale scenes .... $100-$200
Villeroy and Boch, one liter, Four Seasons series .. $200-$250
Villeroy and Boch, half liter automobile scenes .... $100-$150
Character steins, half liter, porcelain, reproductions of Schierholz steins .... $250-$500
Character steins, half liter, porcelain, reproductions of E. Bohne Sohne steins .... $100-$150
Character steins, half liter, various pottery and stoneware steins .... $75-$200
Pottery steins, half liter, relief, various scenes (current retail) .... $50-$100
Pottery steins, one liter, relief, various scenes (current retail) .... $75-$150
Pottery steins, two liter, relief, various scenes (current retail) .... $100-$250
Limited-edition steins, various manufacturers .... $100-$300
Anheuser-Busch stein, half liter, The Bud Man (the first version) $300
Anheuser-Busch stein, one liter, 1976 U.S. Bicentennial $350
Anheuser-Busch stein, one liter, 1976 Centennial $350
Anheuser-Busch steins, half liter-one liter, various scenes .... $10-$500

Mettlach stein, #2092, signed "H. Schlitt", matte finish, $595.

Mettlach stein, #1132, $675.

BEVERAGE-RELATED COLLECTIBLES

America's love affair with soda is long-standing. But interest in collecting beverage-related advertising is also popular.

Nostalgia and colorful graphics attract collectors to beverage memorabilia. The artwork is eye appealing and collectors can identify with the realistic images portrayed in the advertising. Even the logos are presented in a bright and aesthetically-pleasing arrangement.

History: It could be said the soft drink industry started some 300 years ago with the introduction of carbonated water. Over the years, different flavors and extracts were added.

Toward the end of the 1800s, people wanted their favorite soda in portable containers. Soon the bottle was introduced, and early bottles were plugged with stoppers including simple glass marbles and rubber plugs with attached wires. These early bottle stoppers were not the best at maintaining freshness, however, so in 1903 Michael Owens introduced a bottle topping machine. Using a uniformly-sized bottle top, metal bottle caps called crowns became the accepted standard for proper soda bottling.

The economic and social consequences were phenomenal. Equipped with a cost-effective container, the soft drink industry exploded.

General Guidelines: Most collectors categorize soda collectibles into two distinct groups: pre- or post-1970. Pre-1970 items are desirable to collectors and can be further divided into vintage and collectible items. Vintage items are usually pre-1940, while collectible items fall into the 1940-1970 period. Post-1970 items are still too new to have any collector value. The majority of these items include licensed reproductions and limited-edition items.

Items in Excellent to Mint condition sell briskly even when their price is high. Rare items, such as vintage calendars and cardboard signs, may sell for premium prices even in lesser condition. Because paper and cardboard signs are easily torn or creased and are often found faded and trimmed down from their original size, examples in Mint condition command high prices.

The subject matter and visual appeal of the artwork plays a significant role in an item's collectibility. Pieces with women in bathing suits, movie stars and sports stars tend to be worth more.

Trends: The field has been and will always be dominated by Coca-Cola advertising (see **Coca-Cola** chapter for more information). Vintage Coca-Cola material is becoming hard to find and extremely expensive. Even collectible items from the 1940s and 1950s cost hundreds or thousands of dollars. In the last few years, collectors have been looking to other brands of beverage memorabilia to collect, including Pepsi Cola, Orange Crush, Hires Root Beer and Dr. Pepper.

1941 Pepsi cardboard bottle display, shows Pepsi and Pete, 14" x 14", with bottle, $600.

COLLECTORS' ALERT!

Because of the desirability of Coca-Cola collectibles, they have suffered from reproduction and fantasy items for many years. With the growing popularity of other soda pop brands, the rash of fakes has spread to include these brands.

It is important to differentiate between reproductions and fantasy pieces. A reproduction is a copy of an original piece. A fantasy item is a recent fabrication of a piece that was never manufactured.

In most cases, reproductions are produced with permission from the beverage company. Be aware, however, that some dealers may try to sell such items as originals.

Don't be tempted to try and restore damaged pieces made of tin or porcelain. Restoration may lessen an item's value. One-of-a-kind items, however, like vintage paper and cardboard signs, may be candidates for restoration due to their scarcity.

Don't place signs in direct sunlight. Even indirect sunlight will damage items over time. Advertising signs, especially paper and cardboard, should be displayed in areas without major temperature extremes or problems with humidity, mold or fungus. Old paper is brittle and can be easily damaged by improper handling. Storage in damp basements or hot attics should be avoided.

Clubs

•Pepsi Cola Collectors Club
P.O. Box 12 75, Covina, CA 91722

•Dr. Pepper 10-2-4 Collectors Club
3508 Mockingbird Lane, Dallas, TX 75205

•Root Beer Float
Dave & Kathy Nader
P.O. Box 571, Lake Geneva, WI 53147

•New England Moxie Progress
Judy Gross
445 Wyoming Ave., Milburn, NJ 07041

Contributors to this section: Craig and Donna Stifter, P.O. Box 6514, Naperville, IL 60540, 630-717-7949.

VALUE LINE

Prices listed are for pieces in Excellent condition. Ranges cover Good to Near Mint condition.

Cherry Smash

1912 calendar, all months listed in background, 7-1/2" x 15", girl on swing holding fan $575
1920s cardboard hanger sign, 6" x 11", cherries w/sundae $150
1920s cardboard hanger sign, 6" x 11", cherries w/fountain glass $150
1930s cardboard hanger sign, 5" x 11", "Please Everybody & Everywhere 5 cents" $125
1910s cardboard foldout window display, woman sitting with mansion in background $2,000

1930s Dr. Pepper aluminum hanging sign, 10" diameter, "Energy Up! At 10-2 and 4," $375.

1910s cardboard festoon, woman and man holding glasses on ends, mansion in middle $1,400
1930s cardboard bottle display topper, boy holding glass with cherries $35
1910s paper sign, 19" diameter, shows sundae $145
1910s paper sign, 14" x 32", colonial boy holding serving tray $375
1920s paper sign, 6" x 18", "Lunch With Us Today" above club sandwich, logo on right $150
1951 tin flange sign, 18" x 20", main part of sign is circular $250
1920s celluloid sign, 5" x 11", "Always Drink Our Nation's Beverage" $275
1920s syrup dispenser, ceramic potbelly, 14" x 9", "Always Drink" above cherry branch $1250
1930s syrup dispenser, glass and bakelite, w/paper labeled jug $275
1940s syrup dispenser, red glass and chrome, complete $425
1930s syrup jug, paper label, shows mansion scene $90
1912 celluloid watch fob $275

Coca-Cola (see Coca-Cola chapter)

Dr. Pepper

1937 calendar, complete pad $750
1944 calendar, complete pad $300
1948 calendar, complete pad $200
1954 calendar, complete pad $150
1964 calendar, complete pad $50
1968 calendar, complete pad $50
1930s clock, 15" diameter, composition material frame, glass front $225
1950s clock, 15" diameter, metal frame, glass front $200
1960s clock, 20" square, light up, metal and glass $200
1939 tin serving tray, girl holding two bottles, "Drink a Bite to Eat" $275
1910s flared drinking glass, name etched around flared top $1,200
1940s drinking glass, tapered with applied color label, "Dr. Pepper, Good for Life" $150
1940s cardboard six-pack bottle carrier $50
1930s tin six-pack bottle carrier $65
1940s mechanical pencil $40
1930s-1940s matchbooks .... $10-$15
1940s fan, shows bottle on front, "Drink a Bite to Eat at 10-2 and 4 o'clock" $100
1937 fan, shows girl holding bottle $275
1930s blotters .... $40-$60
1930s tin match holder $115
1940s cardboard signs, 15" x 25" .... $225-$375
1930s seltzer bottle $175
1930s cardboard cutout sign, 21" x 26", lady with bottle leaning on railing $675
1950s cardboard sign, 19" x 32", 2-sided, original wood frame $350
1930s aluminum hanging sign, 10" diameter, "Energy Up! At 10-2 and 4" $375
1930s porcelain sign, 9" x 21", "Drink Dr. Pepper, Good for Life" $200

1940s tin sign, 18" x 54", 10-2-4 clock above bottle and logo, yellow background $325

1960s tin sign, 14" x 48", shows bottle on white background $150

1960s tin sign, 11" x 28", "Drink Dr. Pepper" in red oval with silver background $65

1940s celluloid signs, 8.5"x11" .... $350-$600

1930s thermometer, 10-2-4 clock above bottle and logo $450

1940s thermometer, logo over bottle and 10-2-4 clock .. $225

1950s thermometer, bottle cap over "Frosty Cold" $175

1960s thermometer, plastic, bottle cap shaped $50

1940s tin menu board, 20" x 28", shows bottle with 10-2-4 clock and logo $225

1960s tin menu board, 20" x 28", "Drink Dr. Pepper" in oval logo $75

Hires

1890s embossed cardboard hanger sign, 7" x 11", shows extract package & centennial bottle $800

1907 "Pulveroid" hanging sign, 6" x 8", shows Hires kid, "Say! Drink Hires, 5 cents" $950

1890s paper sign, 17" x 19", image of trees spells out "H", display for extract $425

1900s tin sign, shows modified centennial bottle, black writing with yellow background $650

1950s cardboard sign, 8" x 24", shows Hires with food specials .... $35-$60

1940s cardboard sign, 20" x 36", with original frame ... $350

1910s cardboard sign, 15" x 21", art by Haskell Coffin . $875

1940s cardboard cutout, 18" x 32", shows bottle with menu $125

1930s cardboard cutout, 8" x 14", shows girl at refrigerator $275

1920s paper sign, 6" x 20-1/2", "Say! Drink Hires, 5 cents" $150

1940s heavy paper sign, 34" x 58", "So Good With Food" .... $250-$400

1940s canvas truck banner $325

1920s tin sign, 10" x 28", shows paper label bottle, "Hires in Bottles" $325

1940s tin sign, 18" x 60", shows bottle on slant $450

1940s tin sign, 13-1/2" x 42", "Hires to You!", shows bottle .... $125-$200

1950s tin sign, 10" x 28", shows bottle, "Drink Hires" . $100

1950s tin menu board, 15" x 28" $150

1918 celluloid sign, 7" x 10", Haskell Coffin art, shows two women $725

1920s celluloid sign, 8" x 11", "Enjoy Hires, Nature's Delicious Drink", shows woman $850

1950s celluloid, 9" diameter, "Drink Hires Root Beer" . $100

1910s oval tin cutout, 24" across, two women drinking from fountain glasses $1,800

1950s tin cutout in shape of bottle, 48" tall .... $275-$375

1900s reverse painted glass sign, shows Hires boy with mug $1,500

1950s thermometer, tin, bottle shaped, 18" tall ..... $125-$175

1960s thermometer, glass front, 15" diameter $65

1950s clock, glass and metal, 15" diameter $200

1960s clock, plastic, 15" square $50

1931 Pepsi tin sign, 13" x 39", shows "necked" waist bottle, "Here's Health," $1,200.

1907 Hires self-framed tin sign, shows Hires kid, $1,750.

1915 tin serving tray, 12" diameter, shows Josh Slinger $800
1900s tin serving tray, 12" diameter, shows Hires
  boy $1,200
1917 tin serving tray, 10-1/2" x 13-1/2", Haskell Coffin
  art $375
1900s syrup bottle, label in red on white under
  glass .... $250-$400
1890s centennial bottle, paper label .... $70-$125
1940 syrup jug with paper label $75
1900s checker board, shows Hires boy with extract
  box .... $250-$400
1904 celluloid pocket mirror, shows girl with roses in
  cheeks, without mug $425
1908 pocket knife, shows Hires boy pointing "To Your
  Health" $350
Metlach stoneware mug, shows Hires boy holding mug $300
Stoneware mug, straight-sided, shows Hires boy in suit $325

Moxie

1904 7" x 10-1/2" cardboard sign, lady leaning over
  chair $750
1950s 6" diameter cardboard cutout $45
1920s 8" x 11" cardboard cutout, lady holding sandwich
  and glass .... $275-$500
1950s 9" x 21" cardboard cutout, hand holding bottle $65
1940s 8" x 13" cardboard cutout, bust of boy baseball
  player, "He's Got Moxie 5 cents" $375

1930s 26" x 40" cardboard cutout, girl on swing,
  "The Swing is to Moxie" $575
1940s cardboard bottle display, girl with tennis racquet,
  "She's Got Moxie" $100
1940s cardboard bottle display, man holding up bottle,
  "You Need Moxie" $100
1930s 19" x 27" tin sign, horse on car speeding past
  billboard image .... $275-$500
1930s 19" x 54" tin sign, Moxie in hall of fame image . $350
1940s 7" x 10" tin sign, "Braces First — Chases
  Thirst" $125
1940s 12" x 18" tin flange sign, "Drink Moxie" $275
1950s 20" x 28" tin menu board, "It's Always a Pleasure
  to serve You" $75
1900s 5" x 7" reverse painted glass sign with chain for
  hanging $1,200
1920s tin thermometer, "Good at any
  Temperature" .... $300-$475
1950s tin thermometer, "Always a Pleasure to Serve
  You" $250
1970s tin thermometer, "Remember Those Days" $50
1912 8" diameter reverse glass tray with metal rim and
  handles, image of woman, "I Like It" $400
1915-1920 complete eight piece setting of Moxie Girl
  china $250
1915-1920 Moxie Girl china sugar bowl $100
1930s ceramic ashtray, image of pointing man $45
1940s glass dispenser with "Drink Moxie" label .. $175-$250
1930s bottle with paper label and embossing on neck $35
1940s embossed flared fountain glass $65
1910s etched straight-sided fountain glass $150
1940s milk glass mug, "Drink Moxie" label $100
1940s cardboard six-pack bottle carrier $10
1920s paper bottle bag, kid walking with dog on front
  and bottle on back $25
1920s paper bottle bag, image of two kids and baby in
  wood bottle box .... $30-$45
1920s slide bottle opener $30

Nehi

1935 calendar, complete pad, Rolf Armstrong art,
  girl in yellow gown w/white fur cape .... $150-$275
1936 calendar, complete pad $250
1938 calendar, complete pad, Rolf Armstrong art, sailor
  girl at helm, sailboats beyond $250
1930s cardboard sign, 12" x 18", lady reading
  newspaper, shows bottle $175
1950s cardboard sign, 11" x 28", table tennis scene $65
1930s tin sign, 20" x 28", "Curb Service Sold Here Ice
  Cold" $175
1940s tin sign, 42" x 15", "Drink Nehi" over bottle and
  "Ice Cold" $150
1950s tin sign, 15" x 42", "Drink Nehi Beverages,"
  shows slanted bottle $125
1940s tin sign, 17" x 45", "Drink Nehi Beverages" left
  of bottle on white oval $150
1940s tin flange sign, 13" x 18", "Drink Nehi Beverages,"
  shows bottle $225

1940s tin flange sign, 13" x 18", "Drink Nehi" above "Ice Cold," bottle on white at left $325

1940s tin menu board, 42" x 15", "Gas Today" around circular chalkboard area $500

1920s tin serving tray, shows bathing beauty caught up in ocean wave .... $100-$200

1940s fountain glass, applied color label, white band with Nehi logo $85

1940s cardboard six-pack bottle carrier $15

1950s cardboard four-pack bottle carrier, family package $10

1930s bottle opener $15

1940s matchbook .... $10-$15

1940s blotter, "Drink for Health and Happiness too Nehi" $10

1920s booklet, lists available premiums $5

Nesbitt's

1950s cardboard sign, 22" x 35", kid dressed as boxer .. $100

1950s cardboard sign, 20" x 36", clown with kids $325

1950s cardboard sign, 20" x 36", twins sitting at table .. $275

1953 calendar, complete pad $65

1950s picnic cooler $45

1950s tin menu board, 20" x 28" .... $50-$75

1950s push bar, tin plate on wire frame $80

1950s thermometer, 24" tall, name over thermometer and bottle $175

1950s thermometer, 18" tall, name over bottle and thermometer $175

1930s glass dispenser with original jug $225

1940s glass dispenser without jug .... $100-$175

1940s miniature bottle, decal label $10

1940s cardboard six-pack carrier $25

1940s porcelain door push bar, 32-1/2" long $165

1950s die-cut cardboard sign, 23" x 21", lady in hat & gloves with bottle $85

1940s tin sign, 49" x 16", "Drink & 5 cents" above image of bottle $275

Nu-Grape

1923 calendar, complete pad $425

1925 calendar, complete pad .... $250-$400

1939 calendar, complete pad $200

1941 calendar, complete pad $200

1949 calendar, complete pad $100

1951 calendar, complete pad $65

1956 calendar, complete pad $50

1930s cardboard sign, 12" x 36", shows girl holding up bottle $250

1949 cardboard sign, 18" x 32", "It's a Thriller" $75

1920s cardboard die-cut sign, 14" x 24", girl w/arm around large bottle .... $200-$350

1940s cardboard die-cut sign, 13" x 15", woman wearing beret $125

1940s cardboard die-cut sign, 14" x 16", woman with snowman $125

1920s tin sign, 10" x 24", "Drink Nu-Grape in Bottles and at Founts," bottle at left $325

1930s tin sign, 12" x 4-3/4", "Drink" at left of colorful bottle on yellow background $175

1930s tin sign, 36" x 14", "Drink A Flavor You Can't Forget" above hand holding bottle $275

1930s tin sign, 12" x 30", "A Favorite With Millions," bottle framed at left $175

1940s tin sign, 44" x 18", "You Need A" on ribbon banner around neck of bottle $225

1940s tin sign, 12" x 28", "You Need A Nu-Grape Soda," slanted bottle at right .... $75-$125

1940s clock, 15" diameter, light-up, face shows yellow logo over tilted bottle $250

1920s tin serving tray, hand holding bottle against bright light oval background $75

1940s cardboard six-pack carrier $20

1930s blotter $25

Orange Crush

1946 calendar, complete pad $275

1957 calendar, complete pad $50

1932 calendar, complete pad $575

1936 paper sign, 15" x 31", shows ballerina, Walt Otto art $425

1920s die-cut cardboard sign, shows "Served with red hots" $200

1920s Orange-Crush die-cut cardboard hanger sign, "Have a red hot with delicious Orange-Crush," $200.

1890s cardboard sign, $800.

1920s cardboard sign, 11" x 22", shows dispenser w/bottle and glass $325

1940s cardboard sign, 12" x 18", w/vanilla ice cream $50

1930s cardboard sign, 11" x 17", shows Crushy figure .... $75-$125

1920s die-cut cardboard sign, self standing, bathing beauty sitting on dock $650

1930s cardboard bottle display, wraps around bottle, shows glasses and oranges $500

1920s cardboard bottle display, baseball player boy wraps around bottle top $900

1930s fan pull in shape of oranges $50

1920s tin sign, 9" x 19-1/2", bottle on left side, orange background $475

1930s tin sign, 12" x 32", bottle on each end $350

1950s tin sign, in shape of bottle cap, 36" diameter .... $175-$275

1930s tin sign, 18" x 48", amber bottle & Crushy figure on left $325

1930s flange tin sign, 15" x 22", shows bottle in snow . $275

1960s tin sign, 12" x 28", "Enjoy a Fresh New Taste!" ... $85

1940s tin sign, 12" x 16", shows Crushy figure whistling $275

1930s tin door push, 3-1/2" x 10", "Come In! Drink Orange-Crush" $225

1950s flange tin sign, 14" x 18", "Enjoy" with bottle cap $175

1930s tin menu board, 18" x 24", shows Crushy figure w/bottle $200

1940s tin scoreboard, 23" x 36", chalkboard for baseball scoring $275

1950s celluloid sign, 9" diameter .... $75-$125

1940s celluloid sign, 9" diameter, shows whistling Crushy figure $200

1939 tin cutout sign in shape of bottle, 18" tall $300

1950s thermometer, tin, 16" tall, shows bottle $150

1950s thermometer, tin, bottle shaped, 30" tall $125

1940s thermometer, tin, 16" tall, shows bottle $175

1950s thermometer, glass front, 12" diameter .... $125-$175

1950s clock, glass & metal, 15" diameter, bottle cap on face $225

1930s tin serving tray, shows Crushy figure squeezing oranges $275

1950s tin serving tray, 12" diameter, shows bottle cap $65

1940s tin serving tray, 10" diameter, shows amber bottles $75

1930s dispenser with pump, "Wards Orange Crush", in shape of orange $1,250

1940s dispenser with pump, clear glass with metal base $350

1940s bottle, amber with applied color label $8

1920s bottle, embossed label $12

Pepsi

1909 calendar, complete pad, 10" x 18", woman holding glass next to table $3,250

1920 cardboard calendar, 5" x 7", Rolf Armstrong artwork, 12 months listed at bottom $3,800

1921 calendar, complete pad, 14" x 25", Rolf Armstrong artwork $2,300

1941 calendar, complete pad, 15" x 23", George Petty artwork $650

1941 calendar, support American Art series, 15" x 20" ... $65

1943 calendar, support American Art series, 15" x 20" ... $65

1944 calendar, support American Art series, 15" x 20" ... $65

1945 calendar, support American Art series, 15" x 20" ... $65

1946 calendar, support American Art series, 15" x 20" ... $65

1947 calendar, support American Art series, 15" x 20" ... $65

1948 calendar, support American Art series, 15" x 20" ... $65

1949 calendar, support American Art series, 15" x 20" .. $65

1950 calendar, six pages, 13" x 22" $375

1951 calendar, complete pad, 16" x 33", woman walking dog $650

1954 calendar, easel back $125

1919 cardboard sign in original wood frame, 23" x 28", Rolf Armstrong artwork $1800

1930s foil covered cardboard bottle display, 5" x 18" ... $385

1940 cardboard sign, easel back, gloss coated, Pepsi w/rum drinks, 6" x 12" $275-425

1941 cardboard cutout bottle display, Pepsi and Pete, 14" x 14" $525

1943 cardboard sign, 11" x 28", shows two kids, "Big Shot", Whitney Darrow, Jr. art $200

1945 cardboard sign in original wood frame, 11" x 28", "It's a Great American Custom" $325

1950 self-framed cardboard sign, 21" x 27", "Certified Quality" $275

1950 cardboard sign, 11" x 28", "More Bounce to the Ounce" $250

1951 cardboard sign, 11" x 28", Santa scene, "Your Good Old Friend" $285

1951 cardboard cutout sign, easel-back standup, woman holding glass, 20" x 48" $450

1951 cardboard cutout Santa sign, 20" tall .... $100-$185

1954 cardboard cutout, 16" x 20", "Have a Pepsi," woman holding coat over shoulder $185

1956 embossed plastic Santa sign, cardboard back, lights up, 26" tall $175

1960 cardboard sign, 37" x 25", "Be Sociable É Have a Pepsi" $150

1960 cardboard cutout sign, easel back, woman holding six-pack $125

1910 tin sign, 14" x 38", paper label bottle at left $2,100

1931 tin sign, 13" x 39", shows tapered waist bottle, "Here's Health" $1,800

1951 tin cutout in shape of bottle cap, 24" diameter $200

1960 mirror sign, 6" x 14", girl holding bottle $65

1960s tin door push bar with metal work, "Say 'Pepsi, Please!'" $85

1950s light up sign, plastic, 10" x 16", "Have a Pepsi" image of bottle cap $175

1950s tin thermometer, 27" tall, bottle cap and "More Bounce to the Ounce" $150

1940 tin thermometer, 16" tall. "Bigger Better," image of bottle $275

1956 tin thermometer, 27" tall, "Have a Pepsi" with bottle cap image $150

1951 clock, double glass front, 15" diameter, bottle caps used for numbers $750

1945 clock, 14" x 17", plastic and metal, bottle cap image in center of face $225

1961 clock, double glass, 15" diameter, "Think Young – Say 'Pepsi Please!'" $550

1964 transistor radio in shape of vending machine $145

Royal Crown Cola (RC)

1940 calendar, complete pad $200

1950 calendar, complete pad, Wanda Hendrix $100

1950 calendar, complete pad, Anne Blyth .... $100-$145

1952 calendar, complete pad, Loretta Young $175

1953 calendar, complete pad, Arlene Dahl $150

1956 calendar, complete pad $85

1959 calendar, complete pad $75

1963 calendar, complete pad .... $45-$65

1964 calendar, complete pad $65

1966 calendar, complete pad $65

1968 calendar, complete pad $65

1940s cardboard sign, 26" x 40", June Haver $185

1940s cardboard sign, 26" x 40", Veronica Lake $175

1940s cardboard sign, 26" x 40", Jeanette MacDonald . $175

1940s cardboard sign, 26" x 40", Mary Martin ..... $100-$150

1940s cardboard sign, 11" x 28", Claudette Colbert $75

1940s cardboard sign, 11" x 28", Mary Martin $75

1940s cardboard sign, 11" x 28", Barbara Stanwyck .... $50-$75

1940s cardboard sign, 11" x 28", Paulette Goddard $95

1940s cardboard sign, 11" x 28", Joan Caufield $95

1940s cardboard sign, 11" x 28", "My Mom Knows Best" $50

1940s cardboard sign, 11" x 28", "First choice, any time," in original frame $115

1950s cardboard cutout, 15" x 21", 3-D, "Enjoy today's modern RC" $225

1950s cardboard carton display cutout, little girl $100

1950s cardboard carton display cutout, little boy $100

Moxie enamel advertising sign, 18" x 9", yellow and red.

1940s tin sign, 12" x 29-1/2", bottle in white oval at right $175

1960s tin sign, 12" x 28", "Enjoy Royal Crown Cola" $75

1940s tin thermometer, RC on top with logo on bottom "Better Taste Calls for RC" $175

1940s tin thermometer, embossed RC logo on top and bottle at right $150

1950s tin thermometer, RC on top with logo on bottom "Best By Taste-Test" .... $100-$150

1940s clock, 15" diameter, glass and metal, logo in center of face $250

1950s clock, 16" square, glass and metal $100

1940s bottle, applied color label $7

1940s bottle, embossed $10

1940s cardboard 6 pack bottle carrier $25

1940s box of straws, box shows bottle, "RC makes you feel like new!" $200

1940s matchbook .... $5-$8

1940s fan, Joan Caulfield $45

1950s fan, all-American girl $30

1940s blotter .... $25-$35

7up

1950 calendar, complete pad, 9-1/2" x 20", woman holding bouquet of roses $375

1955 calendar, complete pad, 9-1/2" x 20" $300

1960 calendar, complete pad .... $15-$25

1930s cardboard easel-back sign, 4" x 6", advertise with liquor $35

1930s cardboard sign, 13" x 20", "Real 7up, sold here, fresh up" $40

1943 cardboard sign, 11" x 21" "Fresh Outlook" logo on top .... $150-$200

1949 cardboard sign, 11" x 21" "We're a 'Fresh Up' family!," family watching TV $45

1960s embossed foil covered cardboard sign, 12" x 16", shows bottles in bucket $85

1930s cardboard cutout bottle display, 7-1/2" x 12-1/4", shows peacock $75

1930s cardboard cutout, 8-1/2" x 10-1/2", "Morning noon and night 7up likes you" $50

1947 cardboard cutout hanging sign, 5" x 9-1/2", shows hand holding bottle $40

1950s cardboard bottle topper, Christmas theme $25

1940s 3-D cardboard bottle display, bottle sits in winter scene .... $75-$135

1947 tin sign, 19-1/2" x 27", hand holding bottle $275

1940s tin sign, 18" x 27", "You Like It...It Likes You" .. $200

1954 tin sign, 18-1/2" x 27", "Fresh Up," shows bottle top .... $75-$125

1955 tin cutout sign, school zone traffic guard, 23-1/2" x 59" $750

1930s tin string holder sign, 13" x 15-3/4" $450

1950s tin sign, 13" x 44", "Nothing does it like Seven-Up" $150

1930s tin flange sign, 14" x 18", circular in shape, "Real 7up Sold Here" $425

1940s tin flange sign, 14" x 18", circular in shape, "7up Sold Here" $350

1954 tin flange sign, 18" x 20", shows bottle .... $350-$475

1950s tin menu board, 18" x 28", "Nothing does it like Seven-Up" $50

1930s pair corner tin signs, 8" x 10-1/2", "Take Some Home" $165

1940s pair corner tin signs, 8" x 10-1/2", "Fresh Up! It Likes You" $145

1930s tin sign, 14" diameter, "Real 7up Sold Here" $100

1940s die-cut cardboard menu board, "Fresh Up with 7up... with lunch...it likes you" $150

1930s light-up sign, shield shape showing bottle attached to wood base $1,000

1950s plastic light-up sign, 11" square, "Fresh Up With 7up, Nothing does it like Seven-Up" $200

1940s tin embossed thermometer, bottle at right, "We Proudly Serve 7up" $250

1950s tin thermometer, bottle at right, "The all-family drink" .... $30-$50

1950s glass and metal thermometer, 10" diameter, "Fresh Clean Taste" $100

1960s glass and metal thermometer, 12" diameter, "7up The Uncola" $50

1940s clock, 15-1/2" square, wood frame, "We Proudly Serve 7up...It Likes You" $350

1950s clock, 14" diameter, glass and metal .... $175-$275

1960s clock, 15-3/4" square, "Get Real Action...7up Your Thirst Away!!" $150

1950s tin serving tray, 12-1/2" diameter, "Fresh Up with 7up Your Family Drink" $110

1950s Bakelite counter dispenser, three spigots, 7-1/2" x 11" $250

1960s plastic display bottle, 28" tall $65

1930s squat amber bottle, applied color label $95

1950s green glass syrup jug with paper label $20

1950s emerald green fountain glass, applied color label .. $20

1940s tin six-pack bottle carrier, "Fresh Up with 7up You Like It" .... $40-$60

1950s cardboard six-pack carrier, "Fresh Up 7up" $10

1960s box of straws, "Get Real Action...7up Your Thirst Away!" $145

1940s glass bottle display in shape of iceberg, shaped to hold bottle at slant $425

1950s tin Pepsi sign, $350.

BICYCLES

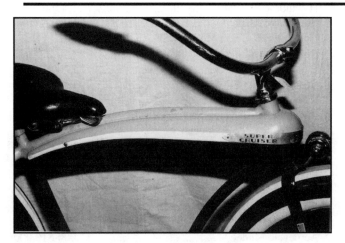

Detail of a 1939 Colson Firestone Bullnose boy's bike.

As far back as 1899, more than a million bicycles were produced in the United States. Over the next couple of decades, their numbers dropped steadily as bicycle styles waned and automobiles became more affordable. Bicycle manufacturing wouldn't benefit from a big upswing until 1933, when the Century of Progress Exposition featured Schwinn's revolutionary new balloon-tire model. Designed with the masses in mind, Schwinn's invention revived a flattened market and maintained its popularity for years to come.

Style wars followed between leading bicycle manufacturers soon thereafter until the realities of World War II resulted in frugally basic bikes. While post-war euphoria and prosperity flowed throughout the flashy new bicycle designs, these models were different in that they were aimed almost exclusively at the youth market; by this time, adults were far too busy driving their stylish new cars to bother with bikes. Reflecting the automobiles of the time, many examples of this new breed of bikes featured chrome fenders, wide whitewall tires, leather seats and plenty of accessories including automatic brake lights, hubcaps, baskets and even battery-operated radios. Today, all of these bicycles are in demand.

General Guidelines: Bicycles are perhaps the hottest vehicle collectible today. Featuring no complicated motors, requiring no special licenses to operate, and still readily available at many neighborhood garage sales, good, old-fashioned bicycles are bringing big bucks from collectors who are pedaling across the nation in search of the classic bicycles of their youth.

Unlike many other collectibles, bicycles usually don't suffer the unfortunate throwaway fate. When bikes were outgrown by their owners, most were saved for the family's next child. Because of this, many classic bicycles have survived. However, these two-wheeled wonders don't come cheap. Many are selling for as much as 10 times their original retail price.

Collectors' Alert: As bicycle collecting grows in popularity, more and more reproduction parts are becoming available. While purists want their bikes to be all original, some less serious collectors will often accept bikes with repro parts. Be sure you know what you're buying!

Trends: Classics manufactured during what are today considered the boom years of cycling — between 1933 and 1959 — are most in demand. More than 38 million bicycles were made during that time, along with some 17 million middleweights and banana-seat models, leaving the field wide open for discovery. Muscle bikes from the 1960s and 1970s are especially collectible. Unable to drive the souped-up hot rods of the day, kids settled for the next best thing — Schwinn Fastbacks and Raleigh Choppers, among others. These bikes featured slick, small tires, funky banana seats and high-rise handlebars.

Due to the fact that there are more men than women who collect bicycles — and also because boys are usually rougher on their bikes than girls are — boys' bikes are worth more than corresponding girls' models. Fewer boys' bikes manage to survive the rough treatment and make it to the collectible stage in good condition. Boys are also more likely than girls to customize their bikes by removing fenders, chain guards and the like resulting in models of depreciated value.

TIPS OF THE TRADE

- Design, popularity, scarcity and condition are four key factors in determining a bicycle's value.
- Go for quality over quantity. Investing in one or two really nice bicycles is better than gathering a dozen clunkers.
- Generally speaking, boys' bikes in nice condition are worth more than the corresponding girls' models.
- Deluxe versions of bikes — those with lights, speedometers, horns and other original accessories — are more popular with collectors than a stripped-down version of the same model.
- Novelty and character bikes are also popular. Some of the most popular specialty bikes include the Hopalong Cassidy model from Rollfast, the Donald Duck model made by Shelby, Monark's Gene Autry model and Huffy's Radiobike.
- While the really old "high-wheelers" from the 1800s can often sell for thousands — and most prewar bikes have more value than postwar models —bikes are not necessarily worth more because of age.
- Most collectors specialize, restricting their collections to one manufacturer, a certain era, or even a specific model.
- Once you have the bike in the condition you want, you can then concentrate on finding the corresponding memorabilia to go with it, including the original owner's manual, advertising and promotional literature.

Huffy Radiobike.

TWO-WHEELED WONDERS

The following are some of the leading manufacturers of bicycles collected today: Columbia, Elgin, J.C. Higgins, Monark, Murray, Rollfast, Schwinn, Shelby.

Clubs
•Classic Bicycle & Whizzer Club
35892 Parkdale
Livonia, MI 48150

VALUE LINE

Ranges listed are for bicycles in Excellent to Mint condition.

Columbia

Twinbar	$2,500-$4,000
3-Star	$300-$600
5-Star	$750-$2,000
Fire Arrow	$250-$450
Firebolt	$150-$400

Elgin

Bluebird	$5,000-$10,000
Blackhawk	$2,750-$4,000
Skylark	$1,500-$2,500
Robin	$3,000-$4,000
Twin 30	$650-$800
Twin 40	$1,750-$2,500
Twin 50	$4,000-$5,000
Twin 60	$6,000-$8,000

Miscellaneous

JC Higgins Color-Flow	$750-$2,000
JC Higgins Flightliner	$150-$400
Sears Spaceliner	$150-$350
Monark Silver King Hex Tube	$850-1,500
Monark Silver King Flo-Cycle	$2,750-$3,500
Monark Super DeLuxe	$750-$2,200
Monark Holiday	$650-$1,750
Shelby Airflow	$7,500-$10,000
Hawthorne Standard Duralium	$500-$700
Hawthorne Airflow	$2,750-$3,500
Huffman Champion Model 10SF	$750-$1,100
Rollfast Custom Built Model V-200	$2,500-$3,000
Evinrude Streamflow	$6,000-$8,000
Roadmaster Jet Pilot	$100-$300
Roadmaster Luxury Liner	$550-$800
Raleigh English Three-Speed	$100-$300

Novelty, Character & Specialty

Rollfast Hopalong Cassidy model	$2,000-$4,000
Monark Gene Autry model	$1,500-$2,750
Shelby Donald Duck model	$1,750-$3,500
Huffy Radiobike	$1,200-$2,500
Bowden 300 Spacelander	$6,500-$9,000

Schwinn Classics

Aerocycle Model 34	$7,000-$10,000
Model 35 DeLuxe	$3,500-$4,000
B-107 Autocycle	$1,200-$2,000
B-607 DeLuxe Autocycle	$1,200-$2,500
Phantom Model B-17	$1,000-$3,500
Panther Model D-27	$750-$2,200
Panther Girl's Model D-77	$700-$1,400
Starlet Model D-67	$350-$700
Mark II Jaguar	$500-$1,200
Corvette	$250-$450
Tiger	$150-$300
Flying Star	$150-$300
Wasp	$100-$300
Spitfire	$100-$300
Hornet	$200-$600
Traveler	$100-$300
Racer	$100-$300
Paramount	$500-$1,000

CYCLING SPOKE-N HERE

The Bicycle Museum of America may be the ultimate road trip for bike collectors. This Chicago-based nonprofit museum features a history of bicycles from the high-wheelers of the 1800s to today's modern bike models and tomorrow's futuristic designs. Featuring exhibits devoted to bicycle racing, advertising, art and the social history of cycling, the museum is aptly located just off the city's lakeshore bike path in Chicago's North Pier area. For more details, contact the Bicycle Museum, North Pier, 435 E. Illinois St., Chicago, IL 60611, 312-222-0500.

BLACK AMERICANA

Collecting Black Americana memorabilia has become a growing phenomenon. Over the past 10 years, prices of black memorabilia have doubled — even tripled — in some cases.

Black collectibles — often featuring now-derogatory phrases and stereotypical illustrations — were originally made to reinforce and maintain stereotypes, but they are now cherished by collectors worldwide.

Black memorabilia encompasses items that either depict African-Americans or can be directly attributed to a black artisan. Some of the important areas of Black Americana memorabilia include advertising, dolls, art, books and toys.

Unlike other collectibles, Black Americana offers education, emotional conflict, increasing value and a piece of history. There is some controversy as to the appropriateness of black collectibles. Some argue that they shed a negative light upon the race, while others see them as important historical artifacts that serve as a reminder of the past.

Early black collectibles may portray slaves, exaggerate peoples' features or depict blacks of great beauty. Pieces found that do not exaggerate the features are considered very rare. Pieces made prior to 1850 were probably handmade. After 1850, many were mass-produced and marked with the manufacturer's name. If the manufactured pieces are of great quality and rarity, they can fetch a price as high as the handmade pieces.

General Guidelines: Many early items made were paintings, toys and dolls; those in Good condition can be quite expensive. Throughout the first half of the 20th century, production of black memorabilia greatly increased. Rag dolls, cookie jars, decorative items and other household items were common. Also on the rise were the items created by black artists — mainly furniture and decorative items were produced, but they were often unsigned or unmarked.

Variety among black collectibles is abundant, from photography, pictorials and figures to novelties, dolls and toys. Additionally, there are famous characters, including Aunt Jemima and Amos n' Andy.

The largest area of black collectibles is postcards, photos and pictorials. The most common images are of black men and women. Children and babies are less common, and very rare are pictures of famous personalities and black military men. Postcards are the most common form of these pictorials. Most can be found for under $10. The most expensive rare pictorial images can cost more than $100.

Advertising Items

Advertising pieces and political memorabilia like trade cards, labels, fans, prints, posters, banks, signs and tobacco tins are the most common. These advertisements depict images such as children playing, servants or people engaged in stereotypical activites such as eating watermelon. These advertisements could be found for many items including tobacco, cleaning products, food and clothing. Political memorabilia, posters and buttons denounce racism and promote black rights. Posters range in value from $50 to $125, with the rarest fetching up to $500. Buttons can be found in the $15 to $50 range.

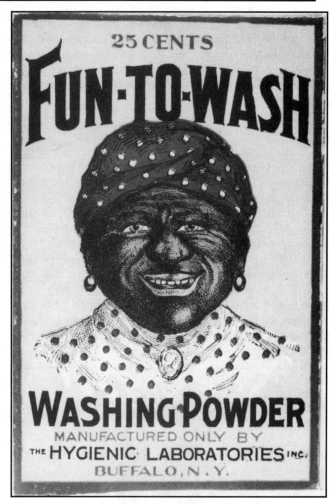

Advertising box, Fun-To-Wash, cardboard, Hygienic Laboratories Inc., Buffalo, N.Y., mammy, red turban, 7-1/4".

Paper Items

Books and magazines are another area of black collectibles. Items published by black authors are often rare, thus these will garner the highest prices. Black magazines, such as *Opportunity* and *Jet*, usually retail for $5 to $15. *Time* and *Life* magazines with blacks on the cover sell for $15 to $75. Books by authors such as Sojourner Truth, Booker T. Washington and W.E.B. DuBois can command top dollar.

Stamps/Currency

Blacks were pictured on coins, paper money and tokens. Booker T. Washington and George Washington Carver were on the silver half dollars. Confederate money may be found depicting blacks at work. Tokens known as slave tokens date back to the 18th and 19th centuries. The coins sell for $30 to $50; the paper money may bring $10 to $30, and tokens are so rare they are often only found in museums. Stamps that feature blacks are unusual, but can be found from most dealers for under $10, although some scarcer ones can go as high as $40.

Figures

Figurals and containers are another popular area of Black collectibles. These items are typically ceramic, but are also found made of wood or metal. The figurals are mostly of men, and the best examples date back to the late 1800s and early 1900s. The value of figurals is considerable, usually $100 and up, with the scarcest running into the thousands of dollars. Containers can hold many types of things, from cookies to tobacco to salt and pepper. These items can run into the hundreds of dollars. Beware of reproductions.

Toys

Toys and dolls are highly collectible, especially when found in Good or better condition. Since most toys were played with, finding ones without missing pieces, in working order and in good shape can be costly.

Top condition old toys are very expensive, due to their rarity. The range on the price of toys varies greatly, from as low as $40 on up to thousands of dollars.

Black dolls, especially golliwogs (with exaggerated, sterotyped features), are especially collectible. These dolls were made of cloth, wood, plastic, china, paper, vinyl and modern materials. Some of the more common dolls cost under $100; rarer dolls may sell for $400 or more. Also, look for rare blackface baseball and football bobbing head dolls that were made in the 1960s that can cost $400 to $1,200 each.

Tobacco humidor, chalkware, olive jacket, mustard hat, pants, 10-1/2".

VALUE LINE

Aunt Jemima

Oilcloth doll, 11" h, neatly stitched and stuffed, c1949, EX $95

Paper plate, Aunt Jemima's Restaurant, 1940s image of Aunt Jemima, red plaid bandanna, red lips and neckerchief, ivory ground, 9" d, MT $60

Placemat, Aunt Jemima at Disneyland, 13-3/4" x 9-3/4", color, *The Story of Aunt Jemima* in drawings based on N.C. Wyeth paintings, from first Aunt Jemima Restaurant at Frontierland in Disneyland, 1955, MT .. $35

Placemat, paper, 10-1/2" x 13-1/2", full color, "Story of Aunt Jemima" and her "Pancake Days," c1950s, MT . $35

Salt and pepper, Aunt Jemima and Uncle Mose, F&F Mold & Die Co., 5" h $65

Table card, Aunt Jemima Restaurant, 4-3/4" x 3", color, Aunt Jemima's face in die-cut relief, "Folks...It's a treat to eat out often...Bring the whole family...Time for Aunt Jemima Pancakes," 1953, MT $45

Golliwog Books by Enid Blyton

Amelia Jane Again, 1946, Dean & Son, 184 pp., b&w illustrations $70

Hurrah for Little Noddy, 1950, Saalfield, 48 pp., color illustrations, NM $85

Noddy Goes to School, no date, dust jacket, hardcover, 60 pp., color illustrations by Beek, MT $50

Noddy Goes To Toyland, no date, dust jacket, hardcover, 60 pp., color illustrations by Beek, MT $50

The Three Golliwogs, 1968, Dean & Son, 184 pp., b&w illustrations, EX $70

Where's Monkey, first story in 1930s *Collins Little Folks Annual*, England, 8" x 10", 96 pp., EX $90

Salt and Pepper Shakers

Black babies in basket, three-piece ceramic set, 1950s, Japan $125

Black clown minstrel, red clay, 2-1/2" h, 1950s, Japan,
EX $40

Black Jonah and the Whale, interlocking, brown-skinned
boy wears only red shorts, exaggerated ethnic features,
rides atop black whale, 1950s, with foil title label $95

Glamour girl native and alligator, ceramic, cute exaggerated
ethnic female caricature strikes a pose as a hungry
alligator looks on, girl is 4" h, vintage Japan $125

Liza and Rastus, die-cut, wooden, c1940s, 3" h, EX $30

Mammy and chef, ceramic, glazed light blue with cold
paint for the black and red, 4-3/4" h, EX $60

Mandy's Children, ceramic, brown-skinned boy holds a
basket of apples, girl holds bouquet of flowers, c
1980s $85

Naughty female nude, three-piece set, red clay, body forms
holder for two "large" shakers, 5" l x 2-1/4" h, Japan,
1940s $95

Sambo on alligator, ceramic, vintage Japan $125

Sambo on camel, ceramic, interlocking, 4-1/2" h x 4-1/2" w,
boy has brown skin tone, exaggerated ethnic features,
orange lips, bulging eyes and green shirt, EX $225

Trade Cards

Dixon's Stove Polish, mammy and cherub, pre-1900,
color litho, EX $27

Finnegan & Co., set of four, minstrels, pre-1900, color
litho, EX, for set $125

Domestic Sewing Machine Company, pre-1900, color
litho, EX $27

Edwin C. Burn Fine Shoes, color litho, EX $24

Jackson Wagon, pre-1900, color litho, EX $28

Miscellaneous

Advertising packing label for Small Black Brand, Delta
Packing Co., shows black baby $20

Alabama Coon Game, J.W. Spear & Son, Bavaria, c
1880s $245

Amos n' Andy Cloth Patch, "Check-Double Check,"c1930s,
fuzzy texture, embroidered features, 4-3/4" d, EX $60

Amos n' Andy Pepsodent radio premium, map and letter
in original mailing envelope, full-color, "Eagle's Eye
View of Weber City, Inc.," c1935, EX $95

Angel of Africa figure, ceramic, 1958, Artgift
Corporation $55

Barefoot Boys, cast-metal miniatures, 5" h, c1930s, EX $150

Birthday card, black girl with doll $15

Black Chef dinner bell, ceramic, c1930s, Japan, 3-1/2" h,
gold trim, side-glance eyes, blue trim on chef's hat .. $125

Bobbing head doll, Chicago White Sox, 1960s $400

Book, *All About Amos n' Andy and Their Creators*, hardcover, Correll & Gosden, 126 pp., 1929, EX $55

Book, children's, *Epaminondas and His Auntie*,
hardcover, by Sara Cone Bryant, illustrated in color by
Inez Hogan, 1938, 6-1/2" x 8", 16 pp., EX $125

Book, children's, *Little Brown Koko*, 8" x 11", hardcover,
dust jacket, first edition, 96 pp., illustrated, 1940,
EX $95

Book, *A Treasury of Stephen Foster*, hardcover, 9" x 12",
first edition, 1946, Random House, 224 pp.,
w/dust jacket, EX $75

Bowl, small white plastic bowl with picture of Weird Harold
at bottom, decal on side says "Come out of the ol' bowl
Weird Harold," from Fat Albert, 1976, General Foods $25

Cigarette paper, wrapper box titled "Blanco y Negro,"
Spain $25

Cookie jar, Someone's Kitchen, mammy, 1989,
Department 56, 11" h, MT $150

Condiment set, nude natives and straw hut, comical, Japan,
5" l x 3" h, EX $195

Covered sugar and creamer set, Someone's Kitchen,
Department 56, 1989, MT $125

Doll, plush Golliwog, 34", no tags $185

Doll, Shindana Baby Nancy, MIB, 12", vinyl, pink dress
trimmed with lace, spoon and baby bottle $50

Envelope cover, Deluth Imperial Flour, black chef with
bag of flour and loaf of bread, back has text and
picture of factory $50

Fairbanks Gold Dust Washing Powder, giant size, 1920s,
MIB, Gold Dust Twins busy at work, 9" h x 6" w x
2-7/8" d $75

Famous and Dandy, color plate, 1930s, inspired by
Amos n' Andy, MT $95

Mechanical wind-up toy, 6-1/4" base, 10-1/4" high, "Spic and
Span—The Ham's What I Am," Marx Toys, New York.

Aunt Jemima cookie jar, McCoy, 10-1/2" high, white dress, black face and hands, red bandanna, "Cookie" in red letters impressed script, $40.

Game, Smoky Holler, 1916, target, instructions and box cover are intact, color graphics, target is 10-3/4" l x 7" w, balls and box bottom are missing, EX $185

Glass, Jazz Band, Art Deco, c1930s, 4-3/4" h, stylized black musicians playing banjo, sax, tuba and drums, instruments are yellow, EX $42

Glasses, three shot glasses featuring comical scenes with black figures $60

Gone with the Wind, commemorative mammy teapot, fashioned after Hattie McDaniel's role, 1988 .... $125

Handbill, play, *Tourists in a Pullman Palace Car,* color, 3" x 5", features porters toting feather dusters, pre-1900, EX $38

Knox Gelatin, cookbook, *Dainty Desserts for Dainty People,* 4-1/2" x 6-3/4", 41 pp., c1924 .... $48

Lime Kiln Club, cigar box label, 7-1/2" x 6-1/4", color litho, busy scene depicting a multitude of ethnic stereotypes including an alligator hanging from the ceiling, c1883 .... $195

Little Black Sambo, print in original mailing envelope, c1940s, color, artist-signed, 11" x 9-1/2", EX $95

Mammy and Chef, spice shaker set of five, 3" h, fully embossed figures, c1930s $250

Mammy, folk art hand-painted egg, signed "Winona," 1984 .... $95

Merrythought, artist-signed ltd. ed. Golliwog, #118 of 500, tag is signed Oliver Holmes, with tags and labels, MT $125

Mini-bell, orange with picture of black man, paint loss on bell $30

Minstrel decanter, 8" h, hat is cork, outfit with red, yellow, white detailing, four shot glasses are suspended, late 1940s $95

Napkin doll, wooden, mammy, 6-1/4" h, skirt is slit to insert folded cocktail napkins as table centerpiece, facial features are hand-painted, blue skirt adorned with hand-painted flowers, jointed arms, EX $70

Noisemaker, tin with Caribbean figures, made in U.S. $12

Paper doll book, *Betty and Billy,* Whitman, 10" x 12", c1955, MT $125

Photo, framed b/w photo of black couple in Art Deco setting $20

Pin, Art Deco-style, decorative, black-skinned woman, goldtone metal with green stones which dangle from the back to form her eyes, turban has rhinestones, 2" . $70

Playing cards, double deck in box, Tamko Roof advertising, 1930s, EX $165

Pop-up book, *Little Black Sambo,* 1934, Blue Ribbon Press, 4" x 5", 60 pp., EX $125

Postcard, advertising, "Jocular Jinks of Kornelia Kinks," No. 5 Series "A," 1907 The H-O Company, EX $35

Postcard, embossed with silk insets, "Four of a Kind," caricatures of four young men wearing fancy silk enhanced clothing, "Germany" postmarked 1908 .... $40

Raphael Tuck Christmas greeting card, late 1800s, grotesque ethnic caricature in fine and colorful litho, 2-1/2" x 4", premium from "Pawtuxet Valley Auction and Bargain Rooms...Phenix, R.I." $40

Record, 78 RPM, *Tales of Uncle Remus For Children From Walt Disney's Song of the South,* 1947, Capitol Records, illustrated cover, three-record set, EX $90

Rollicking Rotary Minstrels Fund Raiser Show Program, 1918, brown-skinned minstrels with banjo, 8-1/2" x 11", EX $65

Sambo, musician ornament, vintage papier-mach and chenille, black skin tone, red lips, turban, yellow shoes, blue pants, paper horn, 2-1/2" $25

Sambo, hand-held dexterity puzzle, 25 cents price tag, figural hard plastic head in solid color, c1950s, MIB $38

Sheet music, *Dat's De Way To Spell Chicken,* 14" x 11", stereotype caricature of fellow at blackboard, "Tremendous Hit with Billy Clark of Hi Henry's Minstrels," c1903, EX $45

Smoking box, wood-hinged box with decal of black butler pointing to smoker sign, souvenir of Lake George, NY $95

Southern Biscuit Company, color tin, 10" d x 3-1/2" deep, ethnic servant serving biscuits to a Southern white family on plantation porch, embossed "FFV Richmond Virginia U.S.A.," 1926 .... $85

Spoon rest, pottery, mammy wall hanging, 8" x 6", dark brown pottery skin tone, bandanna features large embossed yellow polka dots, large rose lips and white teeth protrude, MT $165

Stereo view, "Dis am de pick of dat roost," Underwood & Underwood, c1901 .... $18

Stereo view, "Uncle Tom after Scraps," c1900 .... $18

Swizzle Sticks, glass, set of six, Black figures on top, for set $130

Tin, round, Licorice Mint Candies "Black Beau," shows black child on top of tin, VG $60

Toy, wooden, Black child playing xylophone while toy is pulled, Japan, paint loss, with box $90

BOARD GAMES

Once board games were thought of only as playthings, and were used, misplaced and casually discarded. Today, games of all kinds are being snatched by eager collectors for nostalgia and display purposes.

Board games came into their heyday in the mid-1800s, when boxes featured colorful and elegant lithography — the trademark of Victorian games made by companies like McLoughlin Bros., Bliss, J.H. Singer and Clark & Sowdon. In the late 1800s and early 1900s, Parker Brothers and Milton Bradley were the game giants and still are today. The now-defunct Transogram was also a major player in the 1950s-1960s.

General Guidelines: Game collectors seek everything from pre-World War II Victorian games to post-World War II games based on television shows. The three main collecting areas are Victorian games, sports games, and character-related (TV, Disney, comic, etc.) games.

Games most likely to increase in value are those featuring popular TV shows, science fiction characters (Godzilla, *Land of the Lost*, etc.), sports figures (Babe Ruth, Mickey Mantle, etc.) or early sports-themed games (particularly baseball) and Victorian games from the late 19th century.

All types of games — board, card, skill and bagatelle (handheld pinball) — are collectible, but the key is the condition of the box. Boxes with tears, fading colors or crushed edges are worth less than those in clean condition. To command top dollar, games should also be complete with all pieces, board and instruction sheet. Monopoly, Rook, Password, Trivial Pursuit, Scrabble, and other generic games which have been made for many decades have little collector value. Since so many were made for so many years, even the earliest editions see little appreciation.

Clubs
•American Game Collectors Association
P.O. Box 44, Dresher, PA 19025

Waterloo, 1895, Parker Brothers, $550 Excellent.

Game of Baseball, 1896, McLoughlin Brothers, $1,600 Excellent.

VALUE LINE

Prewar Games (1945 or earlier)
Prices listed are for games in Good condition.

Air Base Checkers, 1942, Einson-Freeman	$20
Alpha Football Game, 1940s, Replica	$70
Anagrams, 1885, Peter G. Thompson	$20
Astronomy, 1905, Cincinnati Game	$20
Babe Ruth's Baseball Game, 1926, Milton Bradley	$200
Bag of Fun, 1932, Rosebud Art	$15
Bally Hoo, 1931, Gabriel	$30
Barney Google and Spark Plug Game, 1923, Milton Bradley	$100
Bible Quotto, 1932, Goodenough and Woglom	$6
Black Sambo, Game of, 1939, Gabriel	$90
Buck Rogers in the 25th Century, 1936, All-Fair	$250
Checkered Game of Life, 1966, Milton Bradley	$240
Contack, 1939, Parker Brothers	$5
Dick Tracy Detective Game, 1937, Whitman	$40
Famous Authors, 1943, Parker Brothers	$10
Fire Alarm Game, 1899, Parker Brothers	$1,300
Fox and Hounds, 1900, Parker Brothers	$85
Great American Baseball Game, 1906, William Dapping	$145
Jack and the Bean Stalk, The Game of, 1898, McLoughlin Bros.	$550
Knute Rockne Football Game, Official, 1930, Radio Sports	$250
Little Colonel, 1936, Selchow & Righter	$75
London Bridge, 1899, Singer	$100
Lone Ranger Game, 1938, Parker Brothers	$40
Lotto, 1932, Milton Bradley	$6
Mickey Mouse Circus Game, 1930s, Marks Brothers	$180
Monopoly, 1935 ed. only, Parker Brothers	$20
Mother Goose, Game of, 1921, Stoll & Edwards	$30
Nellie Bly, 1898, Singer	$100
Object Lotto, 1940s, Gabriel	$15

The Six Million Dollar Man, 1975, Parker Brothers, $10 Excellent.

Ouija, 1920, William Fuld $20
Parcheesi, 1880s ed., Chaffee $90
Peg Baseball, 1924, Parker Brothers $105
Peter Coddle's Trip to New York, 1888, Parker Brothers .. $25
Red Riding Hood, Game of, 1898, Chaffee & Selchow . $200
Red Ryder Target Game, 1939, Whitman $75
Rival Policeman, 1896, McLoughlin Bros. $1,200
Rummy Football, 1944, Milton Bradley $35
Shopping, Game of, 1891, Bliss $900
Snow White and the Dwarfs, 1938, Parker Brothers $125
Teddy's Ride from Oyster Bay to Albany, 1899, Jesse
    Crandall $3,000
Three Little Kittens, 1910s, Milton Bradley $60
Treasure Hunt, 1940, All-Fair $20
Uncle Wiggily's New Airplane Game, 1920s, Milton
    Bradley $50
Walt Disney's Uncle Remus Game, 1930s, Parker
    Brothers $50
Wild West, Game of, 1889, Bliss $500
Winnie the Pooh Game, 1931, Kerk Guild $50
Wonderful Game of Oz, 1921, Parker Brothers $175
World's Fair Game, 1892, Parker Brothers $800
Yankee Doodle!, 1940, Cadaco-Ellis $30
Zippy Zepps, 1930s, All-Fair $350
Zoom, 1941, Whitman $35

Postwar Games (1946 to present)

Prices listed are for games in Excellent condition.

$25,000 Pyramid, 1980s, Cardinal $15
Abbott & Costello Who's On First?, 1978, Selchow &
    Righter $10
Addams Family, 1965, Ideal $100
Atom Ant Game, 1966, Transogram $70
Batman, 1978, Hasbro $30
Batman Batarang Toss, 1966, Pressman $250
Beatles Flip Your Wig Game, 1964, Milton Bradley $125
Beverly Hillbillies Game, 1963, Standard Toycraft $65
Bewitched Game, 1965, T. Cohn $80
Bionic Crisis, 1975, Parker Brothers $15
Boris Karloff's Monster Game, 1965, Gems $125
Bullwinkle Hide & Seek Game, 1961, Milton Bradley $40
Calling Superman, 1955, Transogram $85
Casper the Friendly Ghost Game, 1959, Milton Bradley .. $10
Charlie's Angels, 1977, Milton Bradley $10
Chutes & Ladders, 1956 ed., Milton Bradley $15
Cracker Jack Game, 1976, Milton Bradley $15
Davy Crockett Adventure Game, 1956, Gardner $75

Dr. Kildare's Perilous Night, 1962, Ideal $40
Dukes of Hazzard, 1981, Ideal $10
E.T. The Extra-Terrestrial, 1982, Parker Brothers $10
Elvis Presley Game, 1957, TeenAge Games $650
Family Affair, 1967, Whitman $40
Family Feud, 1977, Milton Bradley $15
Felix the Cat Game, 1968, Milton Bradley $25
Flintstones Game, 1980, Milton Bradley $10
Flying Nun Game, 1968, Milton Bradley $30
General Hospital, 1980s, Cardinal $20
Globetrotter Basketball, Official, 1950s, Meljak $100
Godzilla, 1960s, Ideal $250
Green Hornet Quick Switch Game, 1966, Milton
    Bradley $300
Happy Days, 1976, Parker Brothers $25
Hogan's Heroes Game, 1966, Transogram $85
Howdy Doody's Own Game, 1949, Parker Brothers $125
I Dream of Jeannie Game, 1965, Milton Bradley $75
James Bond Secret Agent 007 Game, 1964, Milton
    Bradley $35
KaBoom!, 1965, Ideal $15
King Kong Game, 1966, Ideal $15
Land of the Giants, 1968, Ideal $100
Land of the Lost, 1975, Milton Bradley $50
Life, The Game of, 1960, Milton Bradley $15
MAD Magazine Game, 1979, Parker Brothers $12
Magilla Gorilla Game, 1964, Ideal $65
Mickey Mantle's Big League Baseball, 1958, Gardner .. $250
Mystery Date, 1966 ed., Milton Bradley $60
Nancy Drew Mystery Game, 1957, Parker Brothers $65
O.J. Simpson See-Action Football, 1974, Kenner $150
Partridge Family Game, 1974, Milton Bradley $15
Password, 1963 ed. only, Milton Bradley $10
Pee Wee Reese Marble Game, 1956, Pee Wee
    Enterprises $295
Petticoat Junction, 1963, Standard Toycraft $55
Pink Panther Game, 1959, Remco $35
Popeye, Adventures of, 1957, Transogram $75
Ricochet Rabbit Game, 1965, Ideal $75
Risk, 1959 ed. only, Parker Brothers $50
Scooby Doo and Scrappy Doo, 1983, Milton Bradley $5
Scrabble, 1953 ed. only, Selchow & Righter $12
Simpsons Mystery of Life, 1990, Cardinal $7
Six Million Dollar Man, 1975, Parker Brothers $10
Star Trek: The Next Generation, 1993, Classic $25
Tarzan to the Rescue, 1976, Milton Bradley $15
Three Stooges Fun House Game, 1950s, Lowell $100
Trivial Pursuit, 1981, Selchow & Righter $10
Underdog Save Sweet Polly, 1972, Whitman $45
Untouchables, 1950s, Marx $160
Wacky Races Game, 1970s, Milton Bradley $40
Waltons Game, 1974, Milton Bradley $15
Wanted: Dead or Alive, 1959, Lowell $75
Weird-Ohs Game, 1964, Ideal $145
Welcome Back, Kotter, 1977, Ideal $15
Wizard of Oz Game, 1974, Cadaco $15
Wolfman Mystery Game, 1963, Hasbro $200
Yogi Bear Break a Plate Game, 1960s, Transogram $80
Zorro, Walt Disney's, 1966, Parker Brothers $75

BOTTLES

Many collectible bottles were made prior to the 20th century when glass was handblown. Hand blowing imparts a certain crudeness which is desirable, and it ensures no two bottles are exactly alike.

History: Glass making originated about 3,000 years ago in Syria or Egypt. Glass blowing began in ancient Phoenicia. The technique migrated to Europe where it was maintained in Venice and Germany.

Glass blowing was one of America's first industries. A glass house was established in Jamestown, Va., in 1608. American firms utilized European glassblowers until Americans learned the art. America led the way during the Industrial Revolution in the various techniques of making glass bottles.

Shortly after the turn of the 20th century, machines took over, and bottles became so uniform and common that most bottles from that time have little collectible interestwith few exceptions, notably milks, sodas, some fruit jars, perfumes and liquor decanters.

General Guidelines: Condition is of key importance. Cracks, chips, stains and mineral deposits greatly reduce value. Stains can be covered temporarily with oil, water or more permanently with epoxy.

Embossing on a bottle should be easily readable. Rare colors can appreciate an item's value; some items are rare in clear or aqua and some are rare only in more exotic colors. Be aware, however, that colors can be artificially changed or enhanced. The sun or mild ultraviolet light, for instance, can change some clear glass to light purple, which does not hurt its value.

Trends: Generally speaking, the older the category of bottle, the more stable the price. Rarity is a factor, but popularity of an item is more important.

Because of the abundance of bottles, even handblown examples, many collectors choose to specialize.
Flasks and bitters generally command high prices. Milk and painted label soda bottles are gaining popularity. Fruit jars are popular due to availability, but rare items can be pricey.

Medicine bottles are popular and relatively inexpensive. Labels, original boxes and contents enhance value.

One area of collecting that has been overlooked are household items such as stove and shoe polishes, bleaches, bluing, paste, insecticides and dyes. Such bottles are available for under $25 each.
Bottles from the Civil War era are especially collectible.

Determining Age

Machine-made bottles usually have a seam that runs up to and over the mouth of the bottle. Hand-blown bottles may have a seam which stops short of the mouth, or the lip will have been ground down.

Bottles made in the 1860s often have a pontil scar resembling a gray, black or red stain on the base. These scars were caused by the attachment to the base of a rod that held the blown bottle while the lip was applied. When the lip was finished, the rod was snapped off, leaving a pontil scar. Collectors find these pontil-scarred bottles especially desirable because of their age. New handmade bottles and glass items, if they are free blown, may also may

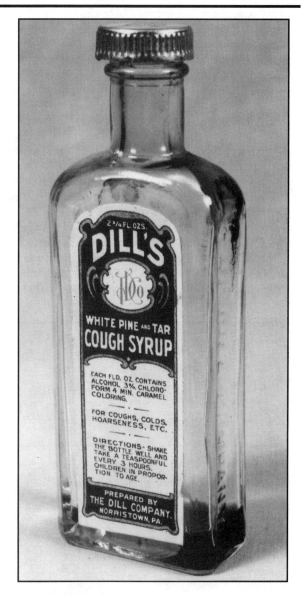

Medicine, Dill's Cough Syrup, paper label, embossed side and back, 5-7/8", clear.

have pontil scars.

Utilitarian bottles stopped having pontil scars when snap-case molds became popular after 1870. The lack of a seam can indicate free blowing without a mold or turning a bottle in a mold.

Clubs
•Federation of Historical Bottle Collectors (FOHBC)
P.O. Box 224, Dolton, IL 60419
708-841-4068

Perfume Bottles

Two types of fragrance bottles are collected — non-commercial and commercial. Non-commercial bottles are offered solely for the appeal of the container and not to house a specific scent, allowing the customer to use it as a receptacle for the scent of their choice. Commercial bottles are designed and produced to complement their contents; thus, the packaging of the product and the bottle design become important for attracting potential buyers.

The production of scent bottles involves glassmaking —including the complex skills of glass blowing and mold making — as well as bottle design, etching and engraving. Ohio's DeVilbiss company devised and supplied the classic bulb atomizer bottles prized by collectors today. Oriental and Middle Eastern influences were also prevalent in early bottle designs, a stylization that continued in popularity well into the 20th century.

Certain names and markings, like those of Lalique and Baccarat, command particular attention, as do specific types of glass. These include opaline, with unusual and colorful presentations dating to the era of Napoleon III, as well as the distinctive look of Venetian and millifiori glass (both of which were first produced as early as the 13th and 14th centuries). Specific compa-

nies, such as Meissen and Staffordshire, were also pioneers, creating scent bottles during the 17th and 18th centuries.

Many European glasshouses were, and still are, responsible for the manufacture and/or designing of bottles for fragrance companies throughout the world. These include French enterprises like Baccarat, Verreries Brosse (identified by a VB marking), Pochet et du Courval (identified by HP), Saint Gobain Desjonqueres and Lucien Gaillard. At the apex is Lalique, with the designs of both the commercial and non-commercial variety by founder Rene Lalique, and later his son Marc Lalique. The Lalique name can be found on bottles for specific scents by perfume icons like Coty, Worth, Roger et Gallet, Caron, Nina Ricci and numerous others.

General Guidelines: Collectors seek both commercial and non-commercial bottles. Some look for bottles by specific manufacturers, designers or fragrance companies. There are several collecting categories for commercial bottles both past and present: those of the regular, retail size; miniatures and purse-sized; and the large factice (display) bottles.

Many flacons have no identifying marks to indicate their manufacturing or designer origins; however, reference books often include this information.

Publications
Perfume and Scent Bottle Quarterly
International Perfume Bottle Association
P.O. Box 187, Galena, OH 43021

Mini-Scent Newsletter
c/o Arielle Hart
1123 N. Flores St. #21, West Hollywood, CA 90069

Contributors to this section: Bottles: Mike and Betty Jordan, 8411 Porter Ln. , Alexandria, VA, 22308; Perfume bottles: Joanne Ball

Czechoslovakian atomizer, clear blue glass stein, enameled floral top on gold ground.

VALUE LINE

Bitters
Embossed bottles are worth more than bottles with complete paper labels.

Atwoods Jaundice Bitters, Moses Atwood (aqua) $5
Big Bill Best Bitters (amber) $125
Brown Celebrated Indian Herb Bitters, Indian queen figural
    (amber) $350
California Wine Bitters, Los Angeles (green) $12,500
Doyles Hop Bitters, 1872, picture of hop leaves and berries
    (amber) .... $25-$50
Drake's Plantation Bitters Patented 1862, cabin figural
    (amber) .... $50-$100
Excelsior Aromatic Bitters (amber) $1,000
Ferro Quina Bisleri (amber) .... $10-$25
German Hop Bitters (amber) $50
Dr. J. Hostetters Stomach Bitters (amber) .... $25-$50
Iron Bitters, Brown Chemical Co. (amber) $35
Jacobs Cabin Tonic Bitters, Laboratory, Philadelphia
    (clear) $15,000

Kellys Old Cabin Bitters — Patented 1863 (green) $7,000
Lash's Bitters Co. New York-Chicago-San Francisco
    (amber)... $25
Mishlers Herb Bitters (amber) $75
National Bitters (amber) $300
Old Sachem Bitters and Wigwam Tonic (aqua)........... $4,500
Peruvian Bitters (amber) $200
Quinine Tonic Bitters (clear) $50
John Roots Bitters, 834, Buffalo, NY (blue green) $800
Sazuarac Aromatic Bitters (yellow olive) $600
Dr. Tompkins Vegetable Bitters (teal blue) ...... $1,500-$2,500
Utica Hop Bitters (aqua) $75
Vigo Bitters (amber) $50
Wahoo and Calisaya Bitters, Jacob Pinkerton (amber) .. $400
Yerba Buena Bitters (amber) $60
Zingari Bitters (amber) $175

Flasks

Prices listed are for pints unless stated otherwise.

Portrait Flasks

Columbia Bust/Eagle (aqua) $4,100
Lafayette/Liberty Cap (amber) $250
Taylor/Corn "Corn for the World" (aqua) $250
Washington/Eagle (aqua) $100
Washington/Jackson (aqua) $100
Washington/Taylor (sapphire blue)............................... $2,500

Picture Flasks

Anchor (amber)... $25
Baltimore Monument — A little more Grape Capt.
    Bragg/Grapes (Puce) $7,000
Eagle/Cornucopia (aqua) $150
Masonic/Eagle (Emerald green) $6,000
North Bend-Tippecanoe, cabin-shaped (emerald) $40,000
Sheaf of Wheat/Star (aqua) $50
Star (amber) $25
Success to the Railroad — locomotive both sides
    (aqua) $400

Fruit Jars

Prices are for quarts with complete original closures. Pints and half gallons are worth slightly more. Reproduction closures, clamps and other hardware are common and decrease value 10 to 25 percent.

Atlas EZ Seal (aqua) $5
Ball Perfect Mason (aqua) $1
The Canton Domestic Fruit Jar (cobalt blue) $5,000
Dexter (aqua) $30
Economy (clear or light purple) $5
Favorite (aqua) $1,500
Gem (aqua) $10
Hero (aqua) $25
Independent Jar (clear) $35
Jersey (aqua) $500
Kerr Economy Trademark (clear) $10
Louisville KY Glassworks (aqua) $500
Masons Patent Nov. 30th, 1858 (aqua) $5
National Super Mason (clear) $10
Ohio Quality Mason (clear) $10
The Queen (aqua) $20
The Reservoir (aqua) $400

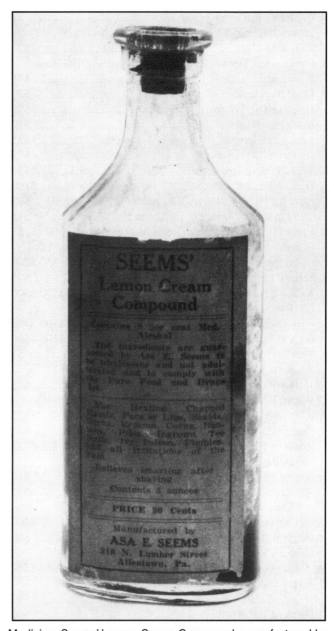

Medicine, Seems' Lemon Cream Compound, manufactured by Asa E. Seems, Allentown, Pa.; cork stopper, graduated markings on sides, 5-1/4" x 2".

Selco Surety Seal (aqua or clear) $10
Texas Mason (clear)... $25
Universal LF & C (aqua) $25
The Valve Jar Co., Philadelphia (aqua).......................... $250
Wan Eta Coco (amber or aqua) $15
Yeoman's Fruit Bottle (aqua).. $50

Medicines

Complete labels and contents greatly enhance value. Age is also important; look for pontil marks.

Ayers Hair Vigor (peacock blue) $45
Bromo Seltzer (cobalt blue)... $1
John Bull, Extract of Sarsaparilla, Louisville, KY
    (aqua) $150

California Fig Syrup (clear) $1

Dickey "Morter & Pestle" Pioneer 1850 chemist, SF
(cobalt blue) $75

Elepizone, A Certain Cure for Fits & Epilepsy, HG Root
(aqua) $75

Dr. D. Fahrnry & Son (amber) $50

Gargling Oil, Lockport, NY (green) $75

Halls Hair Renewer (teal blue) $50

Johnson & Johnson (bandage jar) (amber) $25

Kickapoo Oil (aqua) $75

Lyons Powder (red amber) $150

G. W. Merchant, Lockport, NY (aqua) $100

Newell's Pulmonary Syrup, Redington & Co. (aqua) $25

Owl Drug Co. "Picture of Owl," San Francisco (green) .. $75

Lydia Pinkham Vegetable Compound (aqua) $5

Rohrer's Wild Cherry Tonic Expectoral, Lancaster, PA
(amber) .... $50-$200

Schenk's Pulmonic Syrup (aqua) $75

Swaim's Panacea Philada (olive) .... $200-$300

Dr. Townsend's Sarsaparilla, Albany, NY
(amber) .... $100-$300

USA Hospital Dept (cobalt blue) .... $100-$300

Vaseline (Jar) (amber or clear) $1

Warner's Safe Kidney and Liver Cure, Rochester, NY
(amber) $25

Warner's Safe Kidney and Liver Remedy, Rochester, NY
(amber) $15

Yager's Sarsaparilla (amber) $35

Zoeller's Kidney Remedy (amber) .... $75-$125

Whiskey/Beer

Amber Beers (local breweries) .... $5-$10

Anheuser-Busch Brewing Co (any city) (amber) ...... $10-$25

A.M. Binninger & Co. 19 Broad St. NY, (Figural
Cannon) (amber) $500

Original Budweiser Conrad & Co. (aqua) $50

Casper's Whiskey Made by Honest North Carolina
People (cobalt blue) .... $350-$500

J. H. Cutter, Old Bourbon, A.P. Hotaling & Co. Sole
Agents (amber) $90

Denver Club Whiskey (aqua) $1,500

Golden Eagle Distilleries Co. (Eagle) San Francisco
(amber) $300

Forest Lawn - J.V.H. (Whiskey) (amber) .... $300-$500

Good Old Bourbon In A Hogs(Figural Pig) (amber) $250

Holmes & Spencer New Orleans (amber) $750

Jones & Banks Importers 58 Broad St. N.Y. (Whiskey)
(amber) $75

Kelloys Extra Bourbon Whiskey (amber) $75

London Jockey Club House Gin (green) $500

Millers Extra, E. Martin & Co. Old Bourbon (amber) ... $500

Nabob (Whiskey) (amber) $50

Old Jordan Whiskey (back bar bottle) (clear with gold
letters) $35

Pabst Brewing(amber) .... $5-$10

Phoenix Old Bourbon (amber) $250

Royal Imperial Gin, London (cobalt blue) $400

Schlitz Brewing Co. (amber) .... $5-$10

Star Whiskey, New York, W. Crowell Jr. (amber) $400

Louis Taussig & Co. SF (amber) $500

United We Stand Whiskey, Charles Kohn & Co.
(amber) $1,500

Van Duncks Genever, Ware & Schmitz (amber) $75

Wharton's Whiskey, 1850, Chestnut Grove (amber) $350

Yosemite Wine Co. Oakland CAL (clear) $50

Miscellanous Bottles

Cigar (amber), 1/2 pint $25

Coffin Shaped (amber) $15

Guaranteed Full Pint (any color) $5

Local company name and address in circle (any
color) .... $25-$50

Merry X-mas and Happy New Year (aqua), 1/2 pint $35

Pistol (amber) $25

Plain green or olive .... $15-$25

Union Made (any color) $5

Vertical ribs (amber), 1/2 pint $25

Avon Spring Water (green) $500

Bluing Bottles (aqua) $5

Bunker Hill Pickle (amber) $50

Carters Ink (clear) .... $5-$10

Coca-Cola (straight sided) (aqua or amber) .... $35-$50

Congress & Empire Spring, Saratoga N.Y. (green) . $50-$100

F. Dusch, This Bottle is Never Sold (blob-top soda)
(cobalt blue) $200

Empire Soda Works, San Francisco (blob-top soda)
(cobalt blue) $450

Franklin Spring Mineral Water Ballston Spa, Saratoga
Co. NY (green) $400

Frigid Fluid Co. (Embalming Fluid) (clear) $25

Glue or Paste (aqua or clear) .... $5-$10

Heinz Catsup (clear) $5

Insecticides (clear or aqua) .... $5-$10

Jamaica Ginger Beer (aqua) $600

Kinsella & Hennessy-Albany, NY (mineral water)
(green) $40

Lynch & Clarke-New York (mineral water) (green) $250

Milk, painted label (clear) .... $5-$25

Milk, round (amber) $35

Milk, square (amber) $10

Mouthwash (aqua or clear) $5

Mustard Barrels (aqua or clear) .... $10-$25

National Casket Co. Embalming Fluid (clear) $35

Oak Orchard Acid Springs Mineral Water $90

Pepper Sauce (fancy scrollwork design)(aqua) .... $50-$300

Pickles (cathedral type, fancy scrollwork design)
(aqua) .... $75-$300

Queen City Soda Works, Seattle (aqua) $250

John Ryan, Savannah, GA. (blob-top soda)
(cobalt blue) $125

Skull-Shaped Poison (cobalt blue) .... $1,000-$3,000

Sodas (blob-top, greens and blues) .... $50-$100

Snuff (square with short necks and dots on base) (amber) . $5

Tahoe Springs Natural Mineral Water (aqua) $300

Underwood Ink (cobalt) .... $75-$150

Vermont Spring, Saxe & Co. Sheldon, VT (amber) $300

J. Wise-Allentown, PA (blob-top soda, cobalt blue) $100

Ypsilanti Mineral Salts (aqua) $30

Perfume Bottles

19th century amethyst-colored flint glass cologne
bottle in loop design; 7" .... $500 and up

Mother-of-pearl coffret holding pair of decorative, blue
French opaline bottles; era of Napoleon III;
4-1/2" .... $500 and up

Napoleon III era French opaline bottle; green with
ormalu trim; stopper featuring Parisien architectural
drawing under glass; 2-1/2" .... $250-$350

Rare amberina cologne bottle; hexagonal design; 7-1/2";
nineteenth century .... $1,000-$1,500

Rare canary yellow cologne bottle by the New
England Glass Co.; hexagonal design; 6" .... $300-$500

Victorian cut glass "lay down;" heart-shaped; sterling
top; 5-1/4" $300

Engraved sterling purse bottle; 2-1/2" .... $125-$175

Gold Aurene atomizer; Steuben for DeVilbiss; circa
1927; 7" .... $400 up

Cameo glass atomizer; red/black designs; circa
1915 .... $200-$350

Lalique non-commercial bottle; marked R. Lalique;
elaborate etched and painted design, flat stopper;
4-1/2" .... $1,000 up

Pyramid-shaped porcelain bottle; hand-painted Oriental
designs in pink and grey; 5-3/4" .... $125-$175

Bohemian scent bottle; 19th century; citrine with
elaborate etchings; domed stopper; 7" .... $300-$500

Czechoslovakian flacon; mold-blown, frosted and
clear pink; etched designs, large stopper; 5" .... $250-$400

Glass flacon housed in jeweled brass filigree; large
openwork stopper, flared base; 1930s; 7" .... $200-$350

Commercial

Houbigant's Quelques Fleur; 7-3/4"; marked "Baccarat,
France;" gold stopper and French court scene
encircling base .... $250-$350

Caron's Fleurs De Rocaille with box; floral stopper; lacy
ruff .... $175-$250

Caron's Or et Noir; black velvet case; circa 1949 $250–$500

Elizabeth Arden's Cyclamen; Baccarat bottle; rare
boxed presentation .... $1,000 and up

Astris by L.T. Piver; Art Deco design in pink and
silvery gold; Baccarat; 4-1/2" .... $500-$1,000

Roger & Gallet Bouquet Largilliere; complete with
box and embossed seal; circa 1910 .... $500-$1,000

Corylopsis by Fantine; Victorian era; colorful
Oriental label; 5" .... $150-$250

Arly's Boheme; frosted insets on grey cut glass; 3"; circa
1915 .... $350

Diorissimo by Dior; mauve velour case with ribboned
top; urn-shaped bottle; 6"; circa 1956 .... $175-$250

Corday's L'Ardente Nuit; clear glass with frosted
stopper, footed design; circa 1930s .... $100-$150

Parfum Pour Brunes by Lionceau; boxed presentation
with pair of red Bakelite dice; 1930s $250

Shalimar by Guerlain; urn-shaped, 5-3/4" bottle, blue
"fan" top; mauve velour case .... $175-$275

Nikki by Orloff; double-eagle design with pleated "wings;"
brass top; circa 1939 .... $150

Jabot miniature by Lucien Lelong, with box; both
feature swirling "jabot" design .... $100 and up

Schiaparelli Succes Fou miniature with leaf design ..... $100+

Schiaparelli Shocking dressmaker-style miniature;
bulbous glass stopper and flowers .... $75-$100

Velour ball encasing three miniature Matchabelli
fragrances; 3-1/2" .... $125 and up

Boxed presentation of 10 miniatures of individual
Fragonard fragrances .... $125-$175

Factice

Guerlain's Mitsouko; triangular stopper; gold tassels;
Baccarat; 13-1/4" .... $900 and up

Nina Ricci's 12" L'Air du Temps; 13" frosted bird;
frosted, double–tiered stand .... $1,500 and up

Corday's Toujours Moi; 1925 design attributed to
Rene Lalique; gold trim; 8" .... $700 and up

Balmain's Jolie Madame; amber green bottle, flat
stopper; 12"; circa 1953 .... $200-$300

Oscar de la Renta's Ruffles; fan-shaped, Pochet
et du Couval bottle .... $275-$375

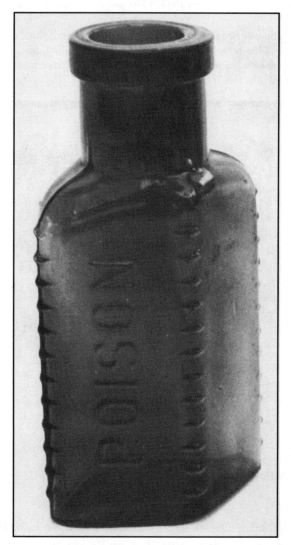

Embossed poison bottle, triangle front, curved back,
ribbed corners, blown, 3-9/16", amber.

BOY SCOUTING COLLECTIBLES

The Boy Scouts were founded in England by Robert S.S. Baden-Powell in 1907. The Boy Scouts of America was organized in 1910. Its success brought about copycat organizations, but — following the issuance of a federal charter in 1916 — the Boy Scouts of America emerged as the only scout group serving boys ages 12-18.

In 1930, the Cub Scout program was developed for younger boys. Bobcat, Wolf, Bear and Lion were the ranks for the three-year program. Lion was replaced in the mid 1960s with Webelos. The Sea Scout Program was organized in 1914 for boys interested in boating. A "Senior Scout" program, sometimes called Rovers, developed in the early 1930s and later changed into the Explorer Scout program. Air Scouts also flourished for a while in the WWII era.

Special gatherings called World Jamborees have been held every four years since 1920 (except during WWII). National Jamborees have been held in 1937, 1950, and every three to five years since.

The Boy Scout program has grown and changed with the century, but the three foundations — character building, leadership and fitness — continue to guide volunteer leaders throughout the country.

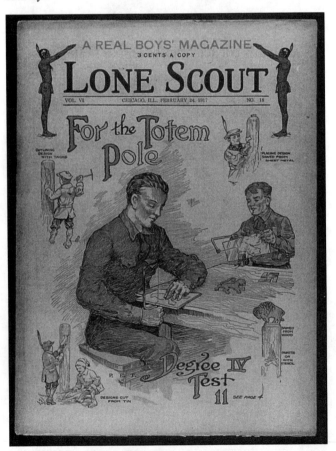

Lone Scout magazine, 1915-1925, kept boys in rural areas informed.

General Guidelines: Since many of today's collectors were Boy Scouts in the 1960s and 1970s, memorabilia from that time period is often available. Pre-World War II items, especially pre 1925, however, command the highest prices.

Officially sanctioned pocket knives, hand axes, flashlights, first aid kits, canteens and cook kits have all been available since the earliest days. A first aid kit with instruction booklet and contents from the 1930s could be worth three times as much as the empty container.

Uniforms

In the early days of the program, a military-style look was adopted, even to the point of using collar brass (copper) for unit identifications. Cloth patches for office, rank and skill were worn on the sleeves, and pins of rank and office were made for campaign hats. It was not until 1926 that a sash was developed to display merit badges.

In 1911, uniforms included a high collared shirt, over which was worn a large full square neckerchief rolled around the neck; laced knickers; long socks; spats and the campaign hat. Copper screw-back unit numbers were worn on one collar with a BSA monogram on the other.

After World War I, to eliminate the military look of the uniform, a spread-collared shirt replaced the high, straight-collared version. Troop numeral patches made of red felt with white embroidery were introduced.

Once the tan scout uniform was introduced in the mid 1920s, the other major changes have been the introduction of khaki, and with it standard long pants with fold-up button pockets. Early khaki shirts have pleated pockets while the later ones have plain pockets. The Cub uniform is blue, introduced first with knickers, then switching to long pants or summer shorts. The most recent uniform change came in 1983 with the introduction of the current design. All uniforms are marked with a label consisting of a tenderfoot seal and the wording "Boy Scouts of America." Prior to 1953 it also said "National Council — New York City;" after that just "National Council."

Neckerchiefs were originally a full square of 32 inches; later they were reduced to 28", and by the 1940s were usually cut to half of that on the diagonal. Commemorative neckerchiefs for World and National Jamborees, World's Fair Service Corps and Order of the Arrow Lodges are of interest to specialists. They were made in many ways. Some were printed, silk screened, embroidered or just had a patch affixed to them. Except for a very few cases, such as Order of the Arrow lodges and early Jamboree issues, lodge issues are of minimal interest.

Badges, Medallions, Medals and Awards

The earliest rank badges are embroidered on tan or wool cut square cloth. From 1916 to 1926 they also come in combination with troop offices and positions. There was a Tenderfoot, Tenderfoot Scribe and Tenderfoot Patrol Leader Scribe. These were available for Bugler, and for Second and First Class as well. A pocket patch for Eagle was introduced in 1924 to augment the medal.

In Paul Meyers' definitive study of the subject, he has provided these guidelines for dating rank patches. A collector needs to identify each distinguishing characteristic.

Cloth
1919-39/40-Coffee/Tan
1940/41-45-Sand-twill
1925-55 (Life and Eagle), 1925-1972 (Star)-Sea Scout blue & white cloth
1946-72-Khaki rough twill
1964/65-72-Khaki fine twill
1972-89-Colored Oval cloth backgrounds
1989-present-Tan cloth oval background, except Eagle

Borders
1913-61/62-Cut-edge cloth
1962-72-Embroidered cut edge
1972-present-Rolled edge border

Eagle details for Tenderfoot and First Class
1913-36-Squatty-crown
1936-37-Tall crown without center vertical line
1937-72-Tall crown with vertical line

Scroll details for Second Class
1913-36/37-High-smile scroll
1937-present-Low smile scroll

Exceptions: Life with embroidered cut edge introduced in 1955; Eagle with rolled edge border introduced in 1956.

Pins for the campaign hat were available for each rank. Many of these pins bear a "Pat.1911" date on the back, but were made that way well into the 1950s. The way to distinguish early pins from later styles is by the type and location of the pin; if it is a flat back, slightly indented behind the central shield, or totally embossed (a WWII variety to save metal). Two styles are currently available, with military clasp (wing) pins. Adults holding position of Scoutmaster and Assistant Scoutmaster and other troop positions wore First Class hat pins with enamel in the fleur-de-lis.

In the early years of scouting, some of the badges of office were combined with those of rank (see previous descriptions) or offered individually. In Mitch Reis' book on BSA Badges, Uniforms and Insignia, these major design types are noted for the Patrol Leader position: Two white bars 3/8" x 1-1/2" (1910-14); two felt bars on tan cloth (1914-33); embroidered green bars on tan cloth (1934-42); green bars on sand twill (1942-45); khaki cloth (1946-54); khaki cloth, coarse twill, cut edge (1955-64); khaki cloth, fine twill, cut edge (1965-71); 3" round, green background, Tenderfoot emblem and two bars (1972-89); 3" round, tan background, Fleur-de-lis and two bars (since 1989).

Patrols were identified by a four or five-inch long, single or bi-colored ribbons pinned to the sleeve at the shoulder. These were replaced in 1926 with a Patrol Medallion, a two inch square red felt with black border and animal or image silhouette. These were quickly replaced by a 2-inch round red felt patch. The third style is red felt with BSA below the animal design. In the 1950s the fourth style was introduced, black on red twill. This variety comes in gauze, cloth or plastic back types. Colored designs on colored cloths with colored borders began in 1972. In 1989, borders and backgrounds all became tan.

Merit badges have been around since 1910. They include square (1911-33); wide crimped (1934-35); tan rough twill narrow crimped (1936-42); tan fine twill narrow crimped (1942-46); khaki twill narrow crimped (1947-60); khaki twill rolled edge (1961-68); fully embroidered cloth back (1961-71); fully embroidered plastic back (1972-present); computer-stitched design (1993-present). The 1940s Air Scout program had four special fully embroidered blue background design merit badges.

With any stitching process and with multiple suppliers, variations abound. Even in recent times, the plastic on the badges had a blue tint to it, while the more recent employ a clear plastic. Finally, the required badges for Eagle all received a silver border (rather than standard green) in the early 1970s.

Medals
Widely collected are the Eagle Scout, Quartermaster, Ranger, Ace and Silver Award medals. There are numerous varieties of Eagle Scout medals, several Quartermasters (silver and non-silver) and two totally different designs for the Silver award. The Ranger (1944-51) and Ace (1942-48, two ribbon varieties) were earned in such limited quantities, they are rare. The presentation box, lapel pin, pocket card and wall certificate named to a recipient all enhance value.

Medals for lifesaving have been awarded since the earliest days. Until 1925 the design was a First Class emblem on a Maltese Cross suspended from a bar inscribed BE PREPARED. They were issued in gold, silver and bronze. Redesigned in 1926, the tricolored Honor Medal and Medals of Merit were introduced with a tenderfoot badge and palm branch within an enameled legend. All are uncommon, especially with the award certificate.

Contest medals are commonly encountered. They were issued with plain backs, thus some have been personally engraved. The first group issued by 1917 depicted specific events such as camping, cooking, hiking, knots, handicraft and swimming. Made in bronze, silver and gold colored metal on blue and red-white-blue ribbons, few survive in nice shape.

Patches
One of the most popular collecting area is that of Council Shoulder Patches (CSPs) and Order of the Arrow Lodge Pocket Flaps (OA Flaps). These are followed closely by official patches of the World Jamborees, National Scout Jamborees and national high adventure bases. Of local interest are camp patches and council or district event patches.

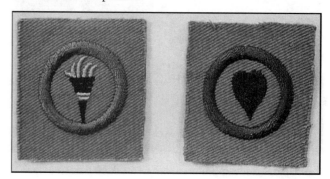

Boy Scout merit badges for Public Health and Personal Health.

World and National Jamborees

The World and National Jamborees, because of their uniqueness and rarity, have been a special niche in the collecting world. Jamboree pocket patches from 1935 and 1937 are the most valuable, bringing between $100 and $150, depending upon how well they were preserved and if they have moth holes. Beware of reproduction sets that appeared in the mid 1970s.

Jacket back patches are less common than pocket patches and staff patches are scarcer. Jamboree neckerchiefs from 1935 come in red or blue. Red is more common and worth between $90 to $125, while the blue is worth $125 to $150. Jamboree neckerchiefs produced since 1964 are worth $8 or less.

The highest lifesaving medal, honor medal for saving life with risk to one's own.

Clubs/Associations
- National Scouting Collectors Society
c/o Mrs. Billie Lee
806 E. Scott St., Tuscola, FL 61953

- American Scouting Traders Association
P.O. Box 210013, San Francisco, CA 94121-0013

- American Scouting Historical Society
Bill Topkis
11729 Henley Lane, Los Angeles, CA 90077

- The Scouter's Journal
P.O. Box 4100, Shawnee Mission, KS 66204-9874

- Scout Memorabilia
P.O. Box 1121, Manchester, NH 03105

Publications
Standard Price Guide to U.S. Scouting Collectibles by George Cuhaj (1998, Krause Publications)

Contributor to this section: George Cuhaj, 700 E. State St., Iola, WI 54990.

VALUE LINE

Boy Scout Handbooks

Original edition, scout standing with flag, 1910	$400-$600
1st and 2nd edition, scout holding hat up, 1911-1914	$75$125
3rd edition, scout signaling cover, 1914-1927	$40-$70
4th edition first cover, scout profile left, 1927-1940	$15-$30
4th edition second cover, Cub, Boy and Sea scouts, 1940-1946	$8-$15
5th edition first cover, patrol hiking, 1947-1949	$6-$10
5th edition second cover, Indian above three scouts by fire, 1950-58	$4-$8
6th edition, scout walking right, 1959-65	$3-$7
7th edition, three scouts and camp scene, 1965-71	$2-$6
8th edition first cover, plain green, scouts and telescope, 1972-77	$1-$3
8th edition second cover, group hiking, archer, back packer and others, 1975-77	$2-$4
9th edition, camp scene by lake, 1977-1989	$1-$2
10th edition, three photos of scout activities, 1990 and later	$1-$2

Rank Medals

Eagle, first type	$250
Eagle, full back with BSA, 1920s-1930s	$125
Eagle, flat back with BSA	$95
Eagle, full back with BSA	$75
Eagle, full back non-silver with pin back	$25
Sea Scout Quartermaster; silver	$125;
non-silver	$50

Explorer silver award type one (compass/anchor/wings design) $1,300;
    type two (eagle and compass design) $300
Explorer Ranger $850
Air Scout Ace Medal $1,500

Patrol Patches

Felt without BSA .... $10-$25
Felt with BSA .... $3-$15
Red twill, cloth back .... $1-$3

Community Stripes

Red on green .... $1-$4
White on red .... $.25-$1
Yellow on blue .... $.50-$3
Brown on dark green .... $1-$4
Blue on white or white on blue .... $2-$6
Full square neckerchiefs .... $2-$4
Kodak camera (folding) $225

Membership cards

Four-page corner Grommet, 1911-1917 .... $20-$30
Three-page fold, 1917-late 1930s .... $8-$15
Two-page fold, late 1930s-1940s .... $3-$5
One page, 1950s-1960s .... $.25-$1

National Jamboree Patches

1935, felt $125
1937 .... $80
1950 .... $15
1953 .... $10
1957 .... $8
1960 .... $8

Merit Badge Books

White cover, 1918-25 .... $10-$20
Brown cover, 1925-39 .... $3-$15
Standing scout, 1939-44 .... $4-$8
Red/white cover, 1944-52 .... $.50-$3
Red/photo cover, 1949-66 .... $.50-$3
Full photo, 1966-71 .... $.25-$1
Full photo green top,1971-79 .... $.25-$1
Full photo red stripe, 1980 and later .... $.25-$1
Air scout blue, 1940s .... $30-$50

The Lion Boy's Cub Book, 1930s.

The four highest awards for leadership from left to right: Eagle Scout for Boy Scouts; Quartermaster for Sea Scouts; Silver award for Explorers, late 1950s-64; and Ranger award for Explorers, late 1940s program.

BREWERIANA

Breweriana is the term used to describe items used by a brewery to market or advertise its products.

History: The rise of the brewing industry in the United States closely parallels the rise and success of our country as a whole. From the time Pilgrims were forced to land at Plymouth, Mass., beer has been an integral part of our culture.

William Penn, Samuel Adams and Thomas Jefferson all recognized the importance of beer and left their mark on the industry. Penn, who owned a small brewery as part of his Pennsbury Manor estate, sought to establish Philadelphia as a brewing center, which it became. Philadelphia beer was widely known in that era and recognized worldwide until national Prohibition intruded in 1919.

Brewing was primarily a very localized industry until after the Civil War. Most sizeable communities had a local brewer, and many households brewed their own beer. Two technological advances — efficient railroad transportation and mechanical refrigeration — changed the face of the industry. Once larger, more successful brewers were able to break out of localized markets, advertising became important.

From about 1870 until 1915 when prohibitionists began to hold sway, the brewing industry rode the crest of immigration, westward expansion and the industrial revolution. There were thousands of competing commercial breweries in the country and in those days — before television and radio — signs, trays, lithographed posters and giveaways were the most effective means of advertisement.

In 1919, Prohibition nearly wiped out an entire industry for 14 years. Upon repeal in 1933, 750 breweries reopened or began brewing again. Competition became intense as larger brewers poured millions of dollars into advertising. The industry slowly dwindled to less than 50 breweries by 1980, and partly because of the disappearance of most local and regional brands, interest in collecting breweriana grew.

Two of the oldest clubs for breweriana collectors were founded in 1970 — Eastern Coast Breweriana Assn. (ECBA) and Beer Can Collectors of America (BCCA). In 1983, a new brewing industry trend developed with the opening of the first two new breweries in many years. These tiny companies were the first of what has come to be called "micro" or "craft" brewers. By the end of 1996, there would be nearly 1,000 of these micro or pub breweries nationwide, reversing the trend of the past 60 years and creating a new supply of brewery collectibles.

General Guidelines: The effect of Prohibition on the American brewing industry has created a critical division of which collectors must be aware. Beer advertising items made or used before 1919 are called "pre-Prohibition" pieces. With the possible exception of embossed bottles, breweriana before 1870 should be considered extremely rare, from 1870 to 1890 very rare, and from 1890 to 1919 rare — with very few exceptions. All pre-Prohibition beer advertising is valuable and highly collectible.

Advertising items generally seen before 1919 include etched drinking glasses, cardboard coasters, lithographed metal signs and serving trays, lithographed posters and calendars, reverse painted glass signs, bottle labels, mugs and steins, pin-back buttons and cardboard, paper or metal signs. Workmanship and material was of high quality and highly detailed.

During Prohibition, many brewers attempted to stay in business through the manufacture of near-beer, malt syrup or soft drinks, so frequently the word "brewing" was dropped from the company name. Most brewery-related advertising from the Prohibition era (1919-1933) is considered rare and highly collectible.

Upon the repeal of Prohibition in 1933, brewing and beer advertising went wild in an apparent attempt to make up for lost time. Breweriana items introduced after 1933 include beer cans (first sold in January 1935), electric lights and signs, tap knobs for draft beer, statues and plastic signs and novelties.

Condition, age and rarity matter most, although an exception would be the market for new "collectible" beer steins. Often a false market is created by manufacturers and dealers selling limited-edition steins that number in the thousands. The values in this market have more to do with hype than age or rarity.

Materials are also important in some categories, with metal or glass signs commanding more interest than plastic or cardboard. Damaged or worn beer advertising items can still be quite valuable if rare or old.

Miniature beer bottle, Schlitz, brown glass, brown label, white/blue letters.

Types of Breweriana

Sports Collectibles. Sports figures have often served as beer spokesmen, and beer advertising and sporting events have been closely linked for nearly 100 years. Colonel Jacob Ruppert, the colorful owner of the New York Yankees during their heyday, made his fortune on the success of Ruppert Knickerbocker Beer.

Postcards and Ephemera. Perhaps more than any other industry, brewers used and issued scenic and advertising postcards to promote their products, breweries and even special events. Before Prohibition in 1919, many brewers owned parks and gardens which were frequently featured on postcards. Letterhead, trade cards, bottle labels and booklets are all items used by brewers which appeal to breweriana collectors as well as more general collectors of these items.

Glass and China. Even delicate and decorative household items have borne the mark of brewery advertising. At least one brewer, Horlacher (Allentown, Penn.), offered carnival glass dishes and other decorative plates and bowls as premiums. These turn-of-the-century giveaways all bear the brewery name on the back. Some larger breweries such as Pabst (Milwaukee) used brewery china bearing the company insignia in its brewery dining room or tap room.

Toys. Toy beer trucks and scale model railroad cars are currently popular collectibles. Some brewers issued toy trucks bearing their logo as early as the 1940s, long before toy collecting became a fad. Playing cards and games have been the target of brewery advertising.

Bottles. Early embossed beer bottles are important to breweriana collectors as often the sole link to early and short-lived breweries.

Cans. Beer in cans was first introduced in 1935 by the G. Krueger Brewing of Newark, N.J., but it did not catch on with the American public until after World War II. The first cans of Krueger beer or ale may bring $300 to $350 today.

Serious collectors seek pre-1960 "flat-top" or "spout-top" cans, with pre-World War II cans commanding top prices. Some 1964-1972 "pop-top" cans can be quite valuable with the rarest labels bringing as much as $500. Many 1970s and 1980s beer cans are readily available and not valuable today.

The statement "Internal Revenue Tax Paid" was required to appear on all packaged beer from mid 1935 until 1950. Only the earliest cans (rare and valuable) or those made after 1950 will not have these words somewhere on the label. The appearance of the "IRTP" statement makes a can more valuable.

Spout-top cans, also called cone-tops or crown-tops because they had a conical top which closed with a bottle cap, were made to be filled like a bottle. Nearly all spout-top cans are collectible; many are extremely rare. Prices range from $20-$25 for the most common to over $2,500 for the rarest brands. Spout-top cans were made from 1935 until the late 1950s.

Among the rarest and most desirable beer cans are those pre-WW II flat-top cans with opening instructions on the side of the label. Prewar flat-top cans range in price from $25 for a common brand like Pabst or Budweiser to over $2,500 for the rarest cans. Because of the numbers of cans produced and the amount saved by collectors, few cans made after 1975 are worth more than $5; most are worth much less. A can of 1970s Billy Beer is worth less than $1.

Beer tap knobs, from left to right: Fauerbach, Madison, Wis.; Koehler's, Erie, Pa.; Old Style, LaCrosse, Wis.; and Point, Stevens Point, Wis.

Misprinted cans are generally not worth more than perfect cans. Collectors prefer to display near perfect, bottom-opened examples whenever possible. Full cans are not more valuable than empty ones.

Trays. Often decorated with colorful scenes, trays were first used for beer advertising in the late 1880s. Pre-Prohibition trays are the most sought after and valuable. Early trays are normally characterized by low, flat rims and highly-detailed lithography. Themes include women, brewery or drinking scenes and detailed and ornate depictions of products or logos.

Trays produced after Prohibition are generally less detailed and often pictured only the brewery name or logo. Contemporary trays are cheaper, lighter, smaller and often less desirable.

The most valuable trays are those that depict women or factory scenes. Common trays start at around $5; rarer examples can command thousands.

Nearly all post-WWII trays sell for less than $50. Prewar trays, made of heavier gauge metal with higher-quality paint and design, range from $50 to $250. Pre-Prohibition trays start around $100 and can range upwards of $2,500 for Excellent rare examples.

Coasters. Meant to be used and discarded, coasters bear much more than a simple advertising message. Some include puzzles and poems, songs and slogans, ladies and limericks, facts and fantasies. The rarest coasters sell for $50 to $100, but most sell for less than $2. Ballantine Beer of Newark, N.J., was one of the most prolific coaster producers with nearly 300 to its credit.

Bottles. Beer bottles are less collectible than other breweriana. The most sought-after labels are those from the 1930s or earlier, especially unusual brands from small breweries.

Early embossed bottles are more collectible than the uniform brown bottles used after Prohibition. While the embossing makes each bottle unique, prices of early bottles do not approach the prices of other early breweriana. A typical 1880-1919 embossed beer bottle without a paper label will sell for $3-$15. The same bottle with a paper label in Good condition will sell for $15-$50.

Signs and Lights. Neon signs are the most popular, most fragile lighted signs. Collectors pay as little as $25 for some less popular brands, although the typical price for a recent vintage neon in working order is $75-$150. Older, rarer neons can range upwards to $500 or more.

Tin-on-cardboard signs consist of a piece of printed or painted metal folded over a heavy cardboard backing. What makes these signs collectible is their size (usually small), composition and variety. Those most in demand are 9-inch round "button" signs and those that are scenic or show the product.

These signs were first used before Prohibition, and any of that age are rare and in high demand. Pre-WWII signs range from $100 and up, while postwar signs generally start at about $25 and can go as high as $125. Production of these signs faded by the mid 1960s as cheaper materials replaced them.

Statues. Chalkware (plaster) statues feature a character or product. Although not always made of plaster, the statue is formed in a mold and painted to be colorful and eye-catching. Some rare or unusual examples have brought over $1,000.

Lithographs. Considered by those that collect or appreciate them to be the ultimate beer collectible, lithographed posters and calendars are the crowning achievement of the printer's art. Stone lithography as executed around the turn of the century captured ornate art and minute detail not possible in any other advertising medium.

Individually very rare by breweriana standards, lithographed posters from 1870 until 1919 are a solid investment. Low-end prices for a framed print which may be unique or one of a few known start at about $500. Beautifully-executed prints of women with subtle advertisement or ornately detailed factory scenes may bring $2,500.

Glasses and Mugs. One of the oldest forms of brewery advertising, a beer mug or a glass from an obscure local brewer is an antique treasure worthy of preserving. Many pre-Prohibition glasses and mugs bore painted or etched designs and were created as gifts, or simply as drinking vessels.

Beer can, Jones Brewing Co., Smithton, Pa., Stoney's Pilsener Beer.

Considering their age and rarity, pre-Prohibition glasses and mugs are frequently underpriced today. Many rare examples sell for less than $50. Post-Prohibition glasses, with painted or decal designs, were most frequently given to taverns to serve the customer. Prices range from $1 for common types and brands such as Budweiser up to $100 for an older glass from a small brewer. The craft brewery movement that has swept the country, beginning with the West Coast in 1983, has supplied collectors with a seemingly endless variety of new glasses. Many can be found for less than $5.

Can and Bottle Openers. The small, hand-held can or bottle opener was a necessary accessory to the invention of the bottle crown and the beer can. Breweries gave away millions of small metal openers bearing advertising of the brewery. Prices range from 25 cents to several dollars for most openers. Pre-Prohibition openers which frequently resemble a key (known as "church keys") may bring $10-$20. Prior to bottle openers, some brewers issued advertising corkscrews which are rare and highly valued.

Foam Scrapers. The uneducated browser at an antique market would be hard pressed to explain what looks like an oversized tongue-depressor with a beer name printed on both sides. This is a foam scraper used in the days before health departments to scrape the foam from the top of an overfilled glass. Foam scrapers fell out of favor by the 1950s and are highly collectible. Common brands such as Schaefer or Rheingold may bring only $5-$10, but rare or pre-Prohibition scrapers sell for $50-$100.

Tap Knobs. Tapper handles from the 1930s through the 1950s were small round knobs with a porcelain insert. All tap handles are collectible, but the primary interest is in these early ball knobs and other types of early draft beer dispensers. Modern plastic, wooden or composition tap handles bring $5 to $25. Designs from the 1960s are smaller and less showy and bring comparable prices. Tap knobs from the 1950s and earlier generally start at $25 and can reach several hundred dollars for rare or unusual brands.

Bottle Caps. A favorite collectible of children in a much simpler time, bottle caps have achieved recognition as a category of beer advertising memorabilia. Collecting beer caps (or crowns) offers the advantage of compact size and low cost. Many caps can be had for free or as little as five cents. Advanced collectors or specialists might pay as much as $5-$10 for a rare brand or pre-Prohibition crown.

FUTURE COLLECTIBLES?

Familiar with all the microbreweries that have been cropping up in the last 10 years? By the end of 1996, there were nearly 1,000 breweries in this country, a number which was last seen before Prohibition struck down the brewing industry in 1919. Many are microbreweries that sell their product either on premises or in a limited area.

Because of their small size and limited budget, most craft breweries do not produce many items of memorabilia. Items such as glasses and coasters from these microbreweries may prove to be wise investments.

Belmont Brewing Co. beer tray, Martin's Ferry, Ohio.

Clubs

•Eastern Coast Breweriana Association (ECBA)
P.O. Box 349, West Point, PA 19486
610-439-8245

•Beer Can Collectors of America (BCCA)
747 Merus Ct., Fenton, MO 63026-2092
314-343-6486

•National Association of Breweriana Advertising (NABA)
2343 Met-To-Wee Lane, Wauwatosa, WI 53226

•American Breweriana Association (ABA)
P.O. Box 11157, Pueblo, CO 81001-0157
719-544-9267

•The Microbes Micro Breweriana Collectors
P.O. Box 826, South Windsor, CT 06074

Contributor to this section: Lawrence Handy, 535 N. 8th St. Allentown, PA 18102.

VALUE LINE

Ashtray, O'Keefe's Old Vienna Beer, 6" d $5
Ashtray, Tuborg Beer, white milk glass $15
Backbar Bottle, James Garfield, b&w image of Garfield in
  front of red, white and blue shield, gold borders,
  1880 .... $2,860
Badge, American Brewers Association Convention, 1899,
  "ABA" inscription, enamel and brass plated $18
Beer Tray, Yosemite Lager $750
Bell, Sterling Beer, girl $73
Blotter, 3" x 7-1/2", Bergdoll Brewing Co., 60th
  Anniversary, black and yellow Louis Bergdoll portrait,
  Christmas holly design, 1909, unused $48
Bottle Opener, Fritz's Corner, Coeur D'Alene, Idaho $8
Bottle Opener, Miller Beer, 1955 .... $35

Calendar, 1907, Yuengling & Son Brewers & Bottlers,
  Pottsville, PA, four puppies at the bar, 34" x 26"
  frame $1,700
Clicker, Gunther's Beer, white litho tin, red letters, "The
  Beer That Clicks," Kirchof Co., 1930s $25
Clock, Busch, electrical, horse-and-rider scene, crossing
  valley near mountains of Busch $35
Clock, Lord Calvert, "Custom Distilled for Men of
  Distinction," black wood case, 11" x 12", 1940s $70
Clock, Piels Beer, 15" x 11" $85
Clock, Schlitz, lights, 1959 .... $60
Coasters, Acme Beer, Cereal & Fruit Ltd., Honolulu, red
  and black letters $7
Coasters, Brugh Brau Beer, McDermott, Chicago, black
  and gold letters $18
Coasters, Champagne Velvet Beer, Terre Haute Brewing,
  IN, man holding up glass of beer, red, blue and black $12
Coasters, Golden Age Beer, Fernwood Brewing, PA,
  center glass of beer, red, blue and yellow $50
Coasters, Gunther's Beer, Gunther Brewing, Baltimore,
  bear holding beer bottle, red, black and yellow $15
Cribbage Board, Drink Rhinelander Beer $25
Decanter, Old Crow $30
Display Bottle, Old Grand-Dad, 28" h, full $200
Doorstop, Hanley's Ale, cast iron, bulldog $565
Fishing Lure, Schlitz, bottle shape $8
Foam Scraper, celluloid, Goetz Brewery $18
Foam Scraper, Meister Brau $20
Glass, Philip Best, Milwaukee, etched $395
Glass, Colorado Three Star Beer, Trinidad, CO,
  enameled $310
Glass, Fox Head 400, Waukesha, WI, barrel shape $725

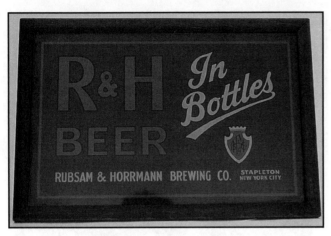

R&H Beer sign, New York City.

Glass, F.W. Cook Brewing Co., Evansville, IN, pre-Prohibition $185
Glass, Northwestern Beer, Superior, WI, enameled $270
Glass, Silver Bar Beer, Tampa, enameled $150
Ice Pick, Empire Lager, Black Horse Ale $30
Keychain Fob, Schlitz Beer, brass charm, beer-keg shape, Schlitz trademark script name, early 1900s $20
Lapel Stud, 3/4" x 7/8", Bert and Harry Fan Club, diecut brass, blue paint, cartoon figures, National Bohemian Brewery Co., Baltimore, c1950 .... $20
Map, Champagne Velvet, battle map of the Pacific $20
Medallion, bronze, Stroh's Run for Liberty $20
Memo Book, Pearl Beer, 1960-61 calendars $3
Menu, Old German Beer, Cafe Bischoff, York, PA, 1940 $10
Mugs, pre-Prohibition, Genesee Brewing Co., Rochester, NY $230
Mugs, pre-Prohibition, Hafemeister Brewing Co., Green Bay, WI $98
Mugs, pre-Prohibition, Schlitz, Milwaukee, salt glaze $45
Patch, Lucky Lager, 7-1/4" x 6-1/2", large red X, white ground, yellow and red letters $18
Peanut Dispenser, Miller Beer $15
Pinback button, American Beverage Co., "Hop Ale," red, white and blue $20
Pinback button, Bohemian Export, multicolored $2
Pinback button, Gluek's Beer, blue and white, 1911-20 .... $7
Pinback button, Budweiser Month, red letters, white ground, Anheuser-Busch logo, c1950 .... $25
Pinback button, Rupperts Beer/Ale, dark blue and yellow, c1930 .... $25
Radio, Bud Can, MIB $50
Shot glass, Henry Schnelten's Whiskeys, Quincy, IL, etched $20
Shot glass, Penn State, blue enamel logo $2
Shot glass, Peoria Co., Club Whiskey, Peoria, IL, etched $25
Shot glass, Shawhan Whiskey, Weston, MI, etched $25
Sign, Adam Scheidt, Norristown, PA, Valley Forge Special, diecut, woman holding bottle standing behind case of beer, cardboard, 11" x 20" $90

Sign, Ballantine, Newark, NJ, Ballantine Beer, diecut, 1960s pro-football schedule, cardboard, 12" x 20" $20
Sign, Falstaff Beer, Blacks in bar setting, lights, 11-1/2" x 18" $85
Sign, Old Dutch Bock Beer, Eagle, Catasaqua, PA, referee holds up hand of standing ram prize fighter, cardboard, 13" x 19" $85
Sign, Schlitz, lighted $85
Sign, Wunder Beer, Oakland, CA, cardboard, hanging type $65
Sign, Budweiser, 20" x 17", red and white $90
Sign, Coors, 22" x 23", red, white and gold $90
Sign, Old Topper Ale, 12" h, 12" w, glass, illuminated $44
Sign, Schlitz, 10-1/2" x 33-1/2", white $60
Statue, Ballantine, wood, white, red and gold $18
Statue, Budweiser, wood, black, white and red $20
Statue, Hamm's, ceramic, black, white and red $18
Statue, Pabst, ceramic, white, black, red $18
Statue, Piels, plastic, brown, gold, white and red $7
Tab, litho tin, Ballantine slogan, white litho, red letters, three-ring symbol, 1970s $10
Tap Handle, Schmidt City Club Beer, multicolored enamel design $85
Thermometer Tannhauser Beer, brass case, paper dial, eagle logo, 1896 .... $95
Tin, Chickencock Pure Rye, multicolored $225
Tip Tray, Ballantine & Sons, back hanger $25
Tip Tray, Octavio Bumadez, red border, blue center, liquor bottle image, 4-1/2" d $15
Tip Tray, Red Raven, 4" x 6", some damage from use .. $100
Token, Hamm's Beer $20
Tray, Ballantine's Ale, 12" d, 1940s $40
Tray, Bartels, 12" d, Bakelite $50
Tray, Berghoff Beer $70
Tray, Chester Pilsner, Ale and Porter, 12" d, blue and gold $75
Tray, Columbia, Preferred Beer, 12" d, red, white and gold $60
Tray, Eagle Brewery, Catasauqua Beer, 12" d, eagle illus $150
Tray, Falstaff, round, metal, maiden pouring beer $115
Tray, Genesee Cream Ale, 12" d, black, green and white .. $5
Tray, Hohenadel Beer-Ale, 13" d $45
Tray, Kaier's Beer, 12" d, green and white $20
Tray, Old Reading Beer, Reading, PA, 12" d $40
Tray, Muehlebach Beer $20
Tray, Neuweiler's Ale, Allentown, PA, 13" d, 1940s $35
Tray, Pabst Blue Ribbon, emb plastic, blue $8
Tray, Schaefer Beer $10
Tray, Silver Bar Ale, Tampa, round $70
Tray, Stegmaier's Beer, 13-1/4" d, red, black and gold $12
Tray, Tru-Blu Beer, Northampton Brewing Co., 12" d, horse and dog llus $50
T-Shirt, Bud Man, dated 1988, Jostens $10
Watch Fob, 1-1/2" d, diecut silvered brass, Anheuser-Busch, enameled red, white and blue trademark $60

CAMERAS

Photography and cameras have their beginnings in the early 1800s when Johann Zahn, a German monk, created the first fully portable wood box camera. It had a movable lens, an adjustable aperture and a mirror to project the image. In 1826 Joseph Nicephore Niepce discovered how to make the image "permanent" by projecting it onto a paper that was wet with a solution of silver chloride. The negative result could be made into a positive by putting it in contact with a sensitized metal plate, a process which was continued by Louise Jacques Mande Daguerre.

By the mid-1880s, nearly 500,000 daguerreotypes were sold, and the earliest all-wood cameras, with simple brass lenses and a small piece of metal which moved to expose the plate, were being produced.

Cameras with many refinements and adjustments developed rapidly. Some cameras were small, even concealable, while others were large and bulky. There were cameras in colors, cameras made of brass and other metals, and cameras made of Bakelite and plastics. For each period since the 1860s, the development of the camera has reflected the trends prevalent in the engineering and artistic communities.

General Guidelines: Common cameras — such as Polaroid, 8mm or newer black bellows cameras — are worth next to nothing. Cameras in poor condition are only valuable if they are quite rare or desirable, such as wooden exterior or rangefinder cameras. On the other hand, a special lens or accessory can double the value of some cameras. Only experience will allow a collector to ascertain the real value of many collectible cameras and related equipment, but here are some general guidelines:

- Wooden exterior cameras that held the wet-plates of the mid-1800s are valued in the thousands to tens of thousands of dollars when found in complete condition and with the appropriate accessories. They are extremely difficult to find.
- Turn-of-the-century and later bellows cameras are easy to find. Most black-bellows cameras made in this century are fairly common. Usually only those with interesting features, such as special shutters, features or colors, are of significant value. Colored cameras (those other than black) with colored bellows are popular; early folders with red bellows, especially those with elaborate brass shutters are also of interest.
- Disguised and hidden cameras have been made since the 1800s, and early examples of "detective" and satchel cameras are quite scarce and valuable. Well-made miniature cameras are of value, while cheaply-made tiny cameras from the mid-1930s to date are less prized.
- Quality rangefinder cameras, pioneered by Leitz, Nikon, Canon and several other European and Japanese manufacturers, are often of significant value. Cheap copies made by most makers in the United States are less valuable.
- Panorama, or wide-field cameras, are still being produced today but the older, well-made cameras — in Good condition — are of value.

- Stereoscopic cameras — made since the late 1800s — as well as the quality stereo cameras and accessories made in the 1950s, are popular and often valuable. As with many other groups of cameras, the more modern stereo cameras are bought and sold to be used as well as to be collected. This is often true with rangefinder and press cameras, as well as large plate cameras.
- Most 8mm and 16mm cameras and projectors, and most Polaroid cameras, are nearly worthless.

Clubs

- American Society of Camera Collectors
  4918 Alcove Ave. North, Hollywood, CA 91607
  818-769-6160

- National Stereoscopic Association
  P.O. Box 14801, Columbus, OH 43214

- Photographic Historical Society
  P.O. Box 39563, Rochester, NY 14604

- Camera and Memorabilia Enthusiasts Regional Association (C.A.M.E.R.A)
  William J. Tangredi
  Sec.15 Turner Ln., Loudonville, NY 12211

Contributor to this section: Harry Poster, P.O. Box 1883, South Hackensack, NJ, 07606.

VALUE LINE

Ansco Buster Brown Box, No. 2A, c1910-23, 2-1/2" x 4-1/4" on 116 rollfilm $12

Ansco Pioneer, c1947-53, plastic eye-level, 2-1/4" x 3-1/4" exposures on PB 20 film $5

Ansco Readyset Royal, No. 1, c1931-32, folding 120 roll film camera, textured leather covering resembling fur . $25

Agfa Paramat, c1963, 35mm half frame, Color-Apotar f2.8/30mm lens, automatic metering $30

Agfa Selecta, c1962-66, 35mm rangefinder camera, Color-Apotar f2.8/45mm lens, Prontor-Matic shutter .. $25

Argus Model M, c1939-40, small streamlined Bakelite camera, 828 film, Argus anastigmat 6.3 lens in collapsible mount $40

Argus V-100, c1958-59, 35mm rangefinder, made in Germany for Argus, Cintagon II f2/45mm lens $33

Autronic C3, c1960-62, heavy 35mm rangefinder camera, Cintar f3.5/50mm lens, metered automatic exposure ... $20

Ciro-Flex Model D, 1940s, common twin-lens reflex camera $30

Clarus Camera Mfg. Co., (Minneapolis), Model MS-35, 1946-52, 35mm rangefinder camera, interchangeable f2.8/50mm Wollensak Velostigmat lens $40

Retina Reflex III, 1961-64, German-made single-lens reflex camera, f2.8/50mm Retina-Xenar lens, Synchro Compur shutter, coupled exposure meter $90

Eiko Co., Ltd (Taiwan), Can Camera, c1977-83, plastic, shaped like beverage can, various product labels $30

Konishiro Kogaku (Japan), Pearlette, c1946, "Made in Occupied Japan," trellis-strut folding camera, 127 rollfilm, Rokuosha Optar f6.3/75mm lens, Echo shutter $35

Toakoki Seisakusho (Japan), Gelto D III, c1950, half-frame 127 film camera, postwar chrome body, f3.5/50mm Grimmel Anastigmat lens $90

1860s wooden "box-within-box" designed wet-plate camera .... $1,000-$10,000

1890s wooden or leather "detective" concealed camera .... $550-$2,250

Ordinary Kodak, 1890s all wooden early roll film camera .... $1,000-$2,000

Ihagee black bellows folder, complete with plate holders .... $35-$100

Kodak Brownie, folder or box style, 1915-1955 .... $5-$25

Black or black-and-chrome box camera, 1940s, various makers .... $5-$50

Graflex, 4" x 5" press camera, very clean .... $50-$250

Leitz Model IIIC Leica, rangefinder circa 1945 ..... $100-$200

Nikon S-series, chrome and black rangefinder with 50mm lens .... $200-$2,000

Burke and James, simple press cameras for glass plates .... $50-$100

Stereo camera, working, with case and slide viewer $75-$450

Rollicord (cheaper line of Rolleiflex) twin-lens camera .... $50-$150

Polaroid early rollfilm instant cameras .... $5-$15

8mm movie camera and projector, with reels .... $10-$25

Clarus USA-made, poorly crafted rangefinder........... $10-$25

Automatic Kodak Junior, No. 2C, 1916-27 .... $15

Boy Scout Camera, 127 roll film, green vest pocket, emb on bed, 1930-34 .... $40

Bullet, 127 roll film, c1935 .... $15

Instamatic, 314, lever wind, light meter, flash cubes, 1968-71 .... $12

Monitor Six-16, anastigmat special f4.5 lens, 2-1/2" x 4-1/4" exp, 616 roll film, c1939-46 .... $15

Pony, 135, Kodak Anaston f4.5 lens, 1950-54 .... $10

Weno Hawk-Eye Box, #7 .... $25

Advertising, Parliament $12

Ansco, Rediflex $10

Bell & Howell, Autoset Movie Camera, 8mm, interchangeable lenses, c1957 .... $15

Bell & Howell, Filmo Turret Movie Camera, 8mm, triple lens holder, variable speeds, c1938 .... $15

Character, Donald Duck, Herbert George Co. $50

Candid Camera Corp. of America, Perfex 44, 35mm, c1939-40 .... $80

Canon, Canonflex RP, fixed finder, canomatic lenses, 1960-62 .... $150

Ciro Cameras Inc., Delaware, OH, 35 rangefinder for 35mm film, 1949 .... $15

Nikon, Nikkorex Zoom-8, 8mm movie camera, f1.8 lens . $25

Revere, Ranger Model 81, 8mm movie camera, c1947 .... $10

Samei Sangyo, Japan, Samoca, 35mm, c1958 .... $35

Schneider Xenar, 70mm, f4.5 lens, c1934 .... $45

Scovill Mfg. Co., Klondike, c1898 .... $50

Spartus 35, 35mm, bakelite viewfinder, c1950 .... $10

Universal Camera Corp., Univex AF, compact, collapsing for Number 00 roll film, cast metal body $15

Vitar, 35mm, Flash Chronomatic shutter $15

Zeiss, Ikon, Tenax I, East Germany, 1948-53 .... $60

Eastman Kodak

Anniversary Box Camera, No. 2 Hawk-Eye Model C camera, tan with foil seal, given away on 50th anniversary of Eastman Kodak in 1930 .... $30

Bantam f8, 1938-42, Bakelite body, rectangular telescoping front instead of bellows $15

Cartridge Kodak, No. 4, 1897-1907, 4" x 5" exposure on 104 rollfilm, leather-covered wood body, polished wood int, red bellows $150

Medalist II, 1946-53, 2-1/4" x 3-1/4" frames on 620 rollfilm, Kodak Ektar f3.5/100mm lens, Flash Supermatic shutter $160

Camera-Related Items

Advertising Cooler, Kodak Disc Cameras and Film, vinyl, shoulder strap, 14" x 8" x 9" $8

Book, *Guide to Kodak Retina, Retina Reflex, Signet and Pony*, Kenneth S. Tydings, 1952 .... $9

Box, Eastman Kodak Developing Powders, "For Use in Brownie Tank Developer," c1900 .... $9

Catalog, Korona, 52 pgs, 1926 .... $25

Catalog, Kodak and Kodak Supplies, 1927, 64 pgs $18

Exposure Meter, Zeiss Ikon Ikophot, clear-plastic case, instruction booklet $18

Manual, Leica Reflex Housing, nine pgs, 1956 .... $5

Trade Card, T.P. Stiff, The Photographer, Brockton, MA, chlth, 3-1/3" x 4-1/4" $15

Sign, Kodak Film, 10" x 3-1/2" x 3-1/2", Kodak film box shape, lights up $40

Sign, Kodak Film, 18" x 14", two-sided, enamel on steel, nohanger $65

Box Cameras

AGFA-Ansco, various colors, sizes 2 and 2 .... $30

Kodak, Beau Brownie, Art Deco front, sizes 2 and 2A, pink $175

Kodak, Beau Brownie, Art Deco front, sizes 2 and 2A, other colors $75

Kodak, Brownie, various colors, sizes 2 and 2A $40

Kodak, Rainbow Hawkeye, various colors, sizes 2 and 2A $30

Kodak, Target Hawk-Eye, various models and colors $30

CANES

Canes have probably been around for as long as man. Imagine a caveman twisting his ankle while hunting or gathering berries. For his long walk back to the cave, he probably picked up a stick and used it for support. That's likely how the first cane was born.

Truly functional, canes eventually developed into status symbols and works of art, featuring fabulously carved and designed handles. Some canes even concealed guns, booze, dice and whips. For all these factors, there's little wonder as to why antique canes (or walking sticks) have become popular items to own. The number of serious cane collectors in the United States is relatively modest today — a few thousand or so. But that number is substantially higher than it was 10 or 15 years ago. It's likely there will be continued expansion in the cane market in the coming years (in the way of more collectors and steadily higher prices). But it's also likely that the universe of collectors is limited by the cost of canes. This isn't a hobby for the weak of wallet. A few antique canes can sell for $75 to $200, but many more run into the hundreds and even thousands of dollars.

Folk Art vs. Commercial

Collectors classify sticks into two categories — mass-produced (commercial canes) and individually-made (folk-art canes). Commercial canes were built by professional canemakers for the retail market (they were, however, far from the assembly-line variety).

Folk art canes were one-of-a-kind canes made by individual artists. Often, folk art canes were fashioned from one piece of wood and used by the maker. Folk art canes sometimes had carved handles and carved shafts. Of all antique canes, folk art varieties generally sell for the least, but that can still be pricey. For example, a mid-19th century folk art cane — likely American — that was incised with a horse race (in perfect and original condition) sold for $500 at a 1996 auction held by Malter Galleries. Others sold for $150 and up.

The attention paid to mass-produced canes, on the other hand, was on the handles. The handles could be of any type of material, including ivory, bone, tooth, tortoise shell, horn, gold and silver. Ivory was a favorite for cane handles in the 19th century, and it remains a favorite of collectors today. Ivory handles, depending on their quality and subject matter, can sell for several hundred to several thousand dollars. For instance, a 2-3/4-inch high ivory knob that contains all numbers on the skull pertaining to phrenology (with related explanation on the collar of the bust) was sold for $2,900 at a Malter Galleries sale.

Handles sported lions, boars, horses, dogs, cats, snakes, elephants, monkeys, birds, angels, flowers, hands, fingers, skulls, lady heads, lady legs, famous personalities and leaders, mythological characters and creatures, religious symbols and organizational symbols, to name a few. The most popular collectible canes were made in the United States, England, France, Japan and Germany.

Besides regular commercial canes, there are interesting examples known as system or gadget canes — canes that served more than one purpose. For example, some canes were used for exploding caps or as flashlights, while others held cigar cutters/match safes, alcohol, ladies' compacts, guns, pencils, swords, documents, golf clubs, cameras and stands, musical instruments, sundials, watches, microscopes, measuring devices, compasses and so on.

Would you pay $1,000 for a cane on which the ivory knob unscrews to reveal a whip with silver mounts? That's exactly what someone bid on a 19th century English masochist's cane at a Malter Galleries auction. Microscope canes are rare and valuable, often valued from $1,500 to $2,000 or more.

Strange as it might seem, there were even glass canes made, many in the latter part of the 19th century. These were often produced at the end of the day with leftover glass. The making of these fragile canes became a competition between individual glassmakers and factories as they tested their glass-making skills. Three glass canes sold from $125 to $200 at auction.

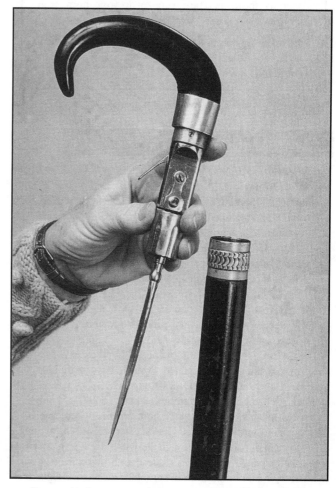

Gun and stiletto canes are very popular with collectors.

CANE TERMINOLOGY

Here are some terms used in collecting and identifying canes.

Crook: Handle shaped like a candy cane.

Knob: Round handle that fits into one's palm.

L-Shape: Handle shaped like an "L."

Opera: Handle precedes the shaft, with the shaft set about three-fourths of the way back on the handle.

Pistol Grip: Handle shaped like butt-end of a pistol.

T-Shape: Handle shaped like a "T."

Collar: A metal collar or band used to conceal the joining of the handle and shaft. Collar often made from bronze, silver or gilt.

Eyelet: Hole drilled through shaft toward the top of the cane, through which a cord was attached so that the owner could free his/her hands, but still hold on to the cane.

Ferrule: Located at the base of the shaft, the ferrule served to protect the end of the cane from wear and damage, such as splitting. They were made from horn, iron, bronze, brass, silver, metal, ivory and other elements.

Shaft: The long portion of the cane, most commonly made from various woods. Snakewood and rosewood are often found on antique canes.

VALUE LINE

Prices listed are auction results.

American Canes

American Occupation of Japan billiard-cue system stick, carved-and-painted design and map showing occupied islands of Japan on outer shaft, polychromed, mint, ca. 1945, 34-3/4" long $200

Decorative gold-filled presentation cane, 3-1/4" high, unusual long shape, mounted on snakewood shaft, horn ferrule, 19th century, 35" long $200

Decorative gold-presentation knob, 1-3/4" high, engraved "Father," mounted on snakewood shaft, horn ferrule, 19th century, 36" long $275

Decorative gold-presentation knob, 2" high, engraved monogram on top, mounted on snakewood shaft, horn ferrule, 19th century, 37-1/4" long $150

Flick stick, a.k.a. Canne Jet, turned horn knob, 1-1/4" high, real full-bark malacca shaft, horn ferrule, (when cane is swung, centrifugal force allows a steel blade, 6-3/4" long, to snap out and lock through the white metal trap door on the knob; by pressing a side steel band on the blade side, it is returned to chamber; blade etched and signed "WINCHESTER" with "USH" monogram), 19th century, 35-1/2" long $1,200

Folk Art, boxwood handle, 4.35" wide, carved with dog, hardwood shaft, chiseled bronze collar, iron ferrule, excellent patina, 19th century, 33-1/2" long $150

Folk Art, probably American, one piece of wood, incised all over with a horse race in various scenes, bronze ferrule, perfect and original condition, mid-19th century, 35-3/4" long $500

Glass, amber glass of square section with twisted base, slightly twisted handle, 1870, 36" $125

Glass, baton shape in pale green clear glass (made by competitive American glass companies to show off their skills) 1870, 35" long $200

Glass, clear glass around amber core, twisted base, slightly twisted handle, 1870, 40" long $175

Ivory handle, 4" wide, carved as eagle head with strong bill and glass eyes, fluted silver collar, mounted on a figged ebony shaft, horn ferrule, 19th century, 36-1/2" long $1,550

Marine cane, whale-tooth knob, 3-1/2" high, carved in shape of right fist holding a snake coiled about the wrist, snake in very high relief, shows long forked tongue, eyes inlayed with two colors of tortoise shell, finely scaled skin, hand with beautiful fingers and nails, buttoned cuff inlayed with Mother of Pearl, woven carved collar, thick and plain whale-bone shaft, silver collar, bronze ferrule, 19th century, 36-1/4" long ... $5,500

Masonic Folk Art, carved monkeys, birds, flowers, anchor, eagle, Masonic square and compass, carved in one piece of boxwood, brass ferrule, first half of 19th century, 33-3/4" long $650

1939 New York World's Fair, rare example with wooden shaft and handle, handle hand-carved into figure of egret, original World's Fair label, original finish, 39" $100

Repeater popper-system stick, 6-1/4" iron mechanism at lower end into which a roll of early exploding caps was placed, cane owner could tap the road repeatedly to celebrate Independence Day, etc., hardwood shaft, ball grip, 29-1/4" long $75

Sterling-silver opera handle, 4" wide, chiseled with flowers and hallmarked sterling on ebony shaft, horn ferrule, 19th century, 35" long $200

Walking stick, turned oak with curved grip, double-line design along shaft, silver ferrule, 33-1/2" long $40

Whale-bone cane, whale-tooth loop handle, 4-3/4" high, carved in shape of stylized snake with collar of baleen rings, mid-19th century, 33-1/2" long $400

Whale-bone cane, handle in shape of hammer, 3-1/2" wide, inlayed with four baleen rings, mid-19th century, 37-1/2" long $450

Continental Canes

Flashlight, crook handle, 6" high, lighting system on side (light activated when large metal band is turned), full function, 19th century, 36-3/4" long $275

Fruitwood handle, 3-1/4" high, carved in shape of shepherd's dog with opened mouth, mounted on rose wood shaft, horn ferrule, 19th century, 38-1/2" long $225

Mountain cane, large stag-horn handle, 5-1/4" high, detailed carving of wild boar hunt around handle, bear in horn's rose, oak shaft with bronze ferrule, 19th century, 38-1/2" long $350

Silver opera handle, 3-1/2" wide, chiseled with baroque decorations and flowers, mounted on snakewood shaft, horn ferrule, 19th century, 34-1/2" long $250

Silver-plated knob, 1-3/4" high, shape of long-haired dog, real full-bark malacca shaft, bronze ferrule, 19th century, 34-1/2" $225

Sword cane, elegant shape with plain stag-horn pistol-grip handle, 4-1/4" high, on its thin real full-bark malacca shaft, white metal ferrule, woven silver wire collar, elegant and faceted blade, 16-1/2" long, gilt decorations, ca. 1800, 33" long $500

Twisted grooved ivory knob, 1-3/4" high, original full-bark malacca shaft with ivory eyelets, gold string tassel, bronze ferrule, 18th century, 39-3/4" long $600

English Canes

15-kt knob, 1-1/2" high, hallmarked and signed "Swaine & Adeney London," mounted on snakewood shaft, horn ferrule, 19th century, 36-3/4" long $225

Gambler cane, large and plain turned-ivory knob, 2-1/2" high, glass top holding four dice that can be shaken for games on its red full-bark malacca, eyelets, long horn ferrule, mid-19th century, 33" long $650

Handle in shape of an ear of corn, 5-1/2" high, elegantly carved, Art Nouveau-style, mounted on snakewood shaft, horn ferrule, 19th century, 38-1/2" long $1,200

Ivory ball handle, 1-3/4" high, carved with a cat face on painted malacca shaft, bronze ferrule, Chester hall marked silver collar, 19th century, 34-1/2" long $650

Ivory handle, 4" wide, carved in shape of horse head with open mouth and glass eyes, on a half-bark malacca shaft, gilt collar, bronze ferrule, very rare, mid-19th century, 36" long $850

Ivory handle, 4-1/2" wide, carved in shape of crocodile head, moving long tongue and glass eyes, mounted on snakewood shaft, horn ferrule, metal collar, mid-19th century, 37" long $350

Ivory handle, 5-1/4", bust of Shakespeare, mounted on snakewood shaft, horn ferrule, mid-19th century, 38-1/4" long $1,500

Ivory knob, masochist's, 2" high, crest on real full-bark malacca shaft, unscrews to reveal thin long whip with silver mounts, inscribed "Lauric Oxford Street," 19th century, 35-3/4" long $1,000

Ivory knob, phrenology, large size, 2-3/4" high, mounted on ebony shaft, stag-horn ferrule, 19th century, 38-1/4" long $2,900

Ivory top, 3-1/2" high, carved in shape of feathered exotic animal head, eyes inlayed with ebony, thick full-bark malacca shaft, wide silver collar, bronze ferrule, 19th century, 37" long $500

Masonic ivory handle, 3" high, naturalistically well-carved in shape of skull on three whirls, good patina, mounted on coromandel shaft, horn ferrule, 19th century, 36-3/4" $1,700

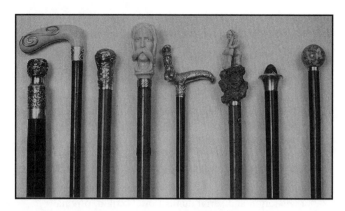

An assortment of handles, from the pistol grip to the knob.

Narwhal handle with consistent silver top, 2-1/4" high, fully hallmarked, dated 1889, mounted on rosewood shaft, stag-horn ferrule, 41-1/4" long $550

Narwhal with thick and attractive chiseled silver knob, 2-1/2" high, natural twisted and grooved Narwhal-tooth shaft, bronze ferrule, rare, 19th century, 33-1/2" long $1,600

Plain turned ivory knob, 2" high, inset rhino-horn horse head on top, mounted on snakewood shaft, horn ferrule, 19th century, 36-1/2" long $225

Smoker's system cane, L-shaped hammered-silver handle, 3-3/4" wide, (handle opens on two sides with a cigar cutter on the front and a match safe on the back), fully hallmarked London 1903 on stepped partridge shaft, bronze ferrule, turn of the century, 36-1/4" long $700

Toulouse Lautrec flask cane, silver knob, 2-1/2" high, full-bark real malacca shaft, bronze ferrule, Birmingham 1905 hallmarked silver knob unscrews to show concealed long flask with drinking glass (French artist Lautrec carried a similar cane), turn of the century, 35-3/4" long $375

Walking cane, all in leather, horn ferrule, decorated with woven cap and wide collar from same material, 19th century, 36-1/4" long $75

French Canes

Bulldog glove-holder cane, fruitwood handle, 2-3/4" high, natural oak shaft, horn ferrule, 19th century, 38-1/2" long $375

Ivory handle, 4" wide, in shape of dog head with long muzzle, open mouth, glass eyes, mounted on snakewood shaft, engraved silver collar, horn ferrule, 19th century, 37" long $450

Ivory handle, 4-3/4" wide, finely carved with foliage, mounted on snakewood shaft, ivory ferrule, 19th century, 34-1/2" long $275

Ivory handle, 5-1/2" high, carved with peacock facing snake on flowered tree branch on its pepper-bamboo shaft, bronze ferrule, 19th century, 36-3/4" long $850

Removable opera-glass handle, 3-1/2" wide, replaced ebony shaft, horn ferrule, turn of the century, 40" long $700

Silver-gilt engine-turned handle with Empire decorations, 6" high, mounted on snakewood shaft, horn ferrule, early-19th century, 35-3/4" $350

Stylized bone duck head as a handle, 3-1/4" high, original full-bark malacca shaft, replaced stag-horn ferrule, 19th century, 37-3/4" $500

Two-shot pistol cane, .22 caliber rim-fire cartridges with crook black-horn handle, 4-1/2" wide, patented in France in 1921 by C. Jorriot and bearing trademark registration and serial number on its collar, original but defective condition, 35" long $900

German Canes

Art Nouveau, silver handle, 5" wide, Eve's head and snake amid sinuously arranged flowers, mounted on snakewood shaft, horn ferrule, late-19th century, 34-3/4" long ... $650

Handle from Black Forest, 12-2/5" high, carved and color painted with two dwarfs in a tree, mounted on a rosewood shaft, horn ferrule, 19th century, 35-1/2" long $250

Ivory handle, 5-1/2" high, wild cock between a bird of prey and stag head with large horns, scene framed with oak leaves and acorns, real full-bark malacca shaft, bronze ferrule, early-19th century, 37-1/4" long $500

Large silver handle, 4-3/4" high, pointer head, mounted on deep-black ebony shaft, horn ferrule, turn of the century, 33-1/2" long $225

Silver crook handle, 4-1/2" wide, shape of reclining greyhound on ebony shaft, bronze ferrule, late-19th century, 37-1/2" long $700

Silver handle, 4-1/2" wide, in shape of lady dressed with a net, reclining on waves with malacca shaft, bronze ferrule, 19th century, 35-1/2" long $2,100

Japanese Canes

Ivory export handle, 4-1/4" high, carved in shape of monkey playing with dragonfly, mounted on a macassar ebony shaft, horn ferrule, 19th century, 39" long $250

Ivory handle, 3-3/4" wide, carved with stylized owl with inlayed eyes, mounted on rosewood shaft, horn ferrule, 19th century, 35-1/2" $275

Signed ivory handle, 7-3/4" high, carved with a dragon, mounted on a coromandel shaft, staghorn ferrule, plain silver collar, 19th century, 38-1/2" long $300

Signed ivory knob, 2-3/4" high, carved with fox, mounted on snakewood shaft, gilt collar, ivory ferrule, 19th century, 37-3/4" long $475

Signed ivory, 1,000 Faces, 1-1/2" high, carved with 20 different heads, mounted on a snakewood shaft, horn ferrule, 19th century, 36-1/4" long $600

Silver crook handle, 8-1/2" high, hallmarked, masterly chiseled with bamboo sprays, snakewood shaft, horn ferrule, 19th century, 36" $950

Staghorn handle, 5-1/2" high, carved with bird perched on flowers and leaves, mounted on snakewood shaft, gilt collar, horn ferrule, 19th century, 37" long $500

Other Canes

Austro-Hungarian, large ivory crook handle, 4-1/2" wide, bulldog at the end on real full-bark malacca shaft, replaced stag-horn ferrule, 19th century, 36" long . $1,000

Chinese ivory export handle, 4" wide, carved dragon, mounted on a macassar ebony shaft, horn ferrule, 19th century, 35" long $425

Russian enamel and hard-stone knob, 2-1/2" high, Empire decorations, style of Carl Faberge, fully hallmarked, perfect condition, mounted on ebony shaft, horn ferrule, late-19th century, 37-3/4" long $1,075

Swiss Alpine hiking stick, 6-1/4" wild-goat horn handle, wood collar, hardwood shaft, replacement brass ferrule, 32-1/4" long $75

Viennese, automated, 3-1/4" high, large fruitwood knob, monkey face on silver-ash shaft (when knob on back of the top is pushed, monkey rolls his eyes and pulls out long red tongue), plain gilt collar, bronze ferrule, 19th century, 37" long $1,500

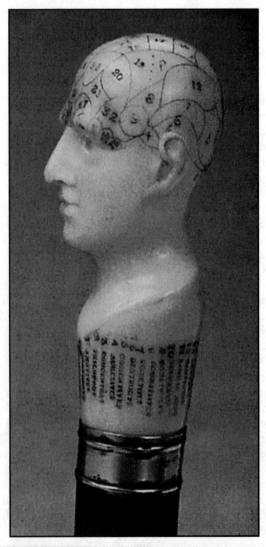

Rare and controversial phrenology cane, with areas of the skull marked and numbered.

CAROUSEL ART

The heyday of the American carousel was from 1880-1929, when nearly 4,000 carousels were carved. Few remain intact today. Many were destroyed by natural disasters; others withered away through neglect or destroyed as obsolete.

Collectors began paying attention to carousel animals as collectibles in the early 1970s.

Carousel animals — especially colorful, elaborate ones — by America's top carvers command top dollar at auction. One of the highest prices ever paid was $174,900 for a Philadelphia Toboggan Company St. Bernard.

General Guidelines: Animals by master carvers command top dollar. Names to look for include Gustave Dentzel, Allan Herschell, Daniel Muller and the Philadelphia Toboggan Company.

Horses from the outside row of a carousel, usually more elaborately detailed, are worth more than inside row horses. Menagerie animals typically sell for more than horses because far fewer were made.

Carousel art is equally valuable in restored or original condition. It is rare to find an animal with original paint.

Beware of reproductions. Original carousel horses are hollow, and virtually all have a "pole hole." Most antique carousel animals have glass eyes and are realistically carved, "horse-shaped" eyes.

CAROUSEL TRIVIA

- The word "carousel" comes from the 17th century Italian word "carosello," meaning "little war." It referred to a contest among horsemen who tried to catch clay balls filled with scented oil.

- Other names for a carousel are merry-go-round, jenny, flying Dutchmen, roundabout and carry-us-all.

- The Golden Age of the American carousel was 1880-1930, when 13 carousel builders produced 3,000-4,000 wooden carousels. Only about 160 of them survive today.

- American carousels always turn counterclockwise, so the carousel animals were more heavily decorated on the right side. English carousels, however, turn in a clockwise motion.

- Each carousel carried a single "lead horse," or "king horse," a figure more elaborate than the others.

- There are more than two dozen different types of animals, other than horses, found on American carousels. The rarest figures include kangaroos, buffalo, sea dragons and roosters. Also popular are lions, tigers, dogs, cats, rabbits, giraffes and donkeys.

Forty-two horse carousel circa 1910-1912 by Stein & Goldstein Co., Brooklyn, N.Y.

Values vary widely, depending on style, condition, row position, maker, decorations and size. The following are ranges for American carousel art. European carvings typically sell for less.

Aluminum kiddie carousel horses, carver Allan Herschell,
1950s .... $250-$500
Aluminum horses, Herschell and C.W. Parker,
1950s .... $500-$1,000
Transitional horses with aluminum heads and legs, carved
wooden bodies, Herschell .... $1,500-$2,000
Outside row horses, Herschell .... $2,500-$5,000
Second and third-row jumpers, Spillman Engineering and
Herschell Spillman .... $2,500-$5,000
Herschell frog .... $25,000-$35,000
Bear or cat, carver Gustave Dentzel .... $25,000-$35,000
Dentzel giraffe .... $20,000-$30,000
Herschell stork .... $20,000-$30,000
Herschell dog or chicken .... $5,000-$10,000
Dentzel rabbit .... $35,000-$50,000
Outside row jumper by a major carver .... $25,000-$35,000
Outside row standing horse by a major
carver .... $40,000-$55,000

Clubs
•The National Carousel Association
P.O. Box 4333
Evansville, IN 47724

•The American Carousel Society
3845 Telegraph Rd.
Elkton, MD 21921

Publications
The Carousel News & Trader, 87 Park Ave. West Suite 206
Mansfield, OH 44902, 419-529-4999

The Carousel Shopper, P.O. Box 47, Millwood, NY 10546

Outside row stargazing jumper by C.W. Parker circa 1918.

CAST IRON

Durable vintage cast-iron items — from banks and cookware to doorstops and toys — are popular collectibles today.

Early American settlers brought their knowledge of smelting iron from Europe. Small hand forges and foundries popped up in the New England colonies as early as 1642. With the advent of the Industrial Revolution in the mid-1850s came the development of a suitable high grade iron which could be cast inexpensively in quanitity. Smelting technology improved, and dozens of foundries followed.

Trends: The values of cast-iron collectibles have remained consistent. Several notable cast-iron banks have recently made headlines for garnering high auction prices. Griswold mania has swept through the cast-iron cookware field due to that manufacturer's prominence. Prices on doorstops have been relatively stable for several years. Most cast-iron collectibles haven't lost value or suffered as a result of the fluctuations in the antiques and collectibles market. As expected, rare examples in Excellent condition with original paint have commanded the highest prices and remain the most sought-after. Overall, prices are on the rise and cast-iron remains as solid a collectible interest as ever.

Banks

(See Banks chapter)

Cookware

Cast-iron cookware consists of an endless variety of functional kitchen utensils. Decorators use it to accent early American kitchens. Collectors appreciate both the artistic designs and high quality of workmanship.

Foremost and without peer for sheer quantity and quality in cast-iron cookware is the Griswold Manufacturing Company and its forebears — Erie, and Selden & Griswold. Two other cookware makers of significance are Wagner Manufacturing and Sidney Hollowware.

General Guidelines: Condition is everything to the serious collector. Avoid cracked, rusted, warped or badly-pitted cookware. Look carefully for hidden damage. A painted surface may conceal serious flaws. Ring a piece by tapping it lightly with a knife or small metal object. It should ring clear, like a bell; a hollow sound indicates damage.

Place a skillet or muffin pan on a flat surface and see whether it rocks or sits solidly. Avoid pieces that wobble; this indicates warping. Avoid pieces that have been sanded, sandblasted or subjected to a grinding wheel.

Many pieces of cast-iron cookware bear the markings of the manufacturer on the bottom, and some marks are rarer than others. Study a guide to the markings to learn which are the most common and most rare.

Doorstops

Cast-iron doorstops were first used by the British, and many were imported from England around the 1860s. Americans followed the British lead with figural doorstops and eventually created lighter examples. The most prolific production in America was from 1920 to the 1940s. Prominent companies that made doorstops include Hubley, Bradley and Hubbard, Littco and National Foundry.

Toys

Cast-iron toys came into play around the turn of the century and reigned until the 1940s, when the advent of other lightweight toys signalled their demise. Highly-detailed, most early cast-iron toys were modeled after airplanes, boats, wagons, cars and other vehicles of the time. Prominent makers of cast-iron toys include Arcade, Kenton, Dent, Hubley and Kilgore.

General Guidelines: As with cookware, condition is essential when determining the worth of cast-iron doorstops and toys. Original paint is of primary importance, as is the piece's overall condition. The best examples are undamaged and have bright, original paint, exhibiting no rust or chipping. Doorstops and toys with some chips, paint loss or a bit of rust are still worth something to avid collectors. However, an item's overall value is greatly reduced by missing paint or even worse, if it has been repainted.

Clubs

•The Griswold Cast-Iron Cookware Association (GACICA)
3007 Plum Street, Erie, PA 16508

•Cast Iron Cookware News
28 Angela Ave., San Anselmo, CA 94960

•Griswold Cast Iron Collectors' News & Marketplace
P.O. Box 521, North East, PA 16428

Cast-iron trivet.

Contributors to this section: Cookware: Joe Noto, 54 Macon Avenue, Asheville, NC 28801-1523. Doorstops: Craig Dinner, P.O. Box 251, Townshend, VT 05353-0251.

VALUE LINE

Cookware

Prices listed are for items in Good condition.

Ashtray, Griswold #00, common	$25
Cowboy Hat Ashtray, Griswold, rare	$1,000
Bolo Ovens, Griswold Kwik-Bake	$40
Broilers, Erie, Griswold & Wagner, w/out lid	$27
Coffee Grinders, Griswold, table or wall mounted	$500
Coffee Pots, various marks	$50
Coffee Roasters, three sizes	$1,200
Cuspidors, rare hourglass design	$1,500
Griddle display rack, chromed	$500
Metal skillet display rack, chromed	$250
Wooden skillet display rack	$500
Dutch oven display stand	$1,200
Waffle iron display stand	$1,200
Food chopper display stand, metal base	$800
Dutch oven, Griswold #13, rare	$1,000
Dutch oven, Griswold #6, #11, #12	$300
Chuck wagon dutch oven, Griswold, size #8 to #13.	$200
Barbecue dutch oven, Griswold	$300
Dutch oven, Wagner, size #6 to #11	$50
Food chopper, common	$15
Food chopper, rare #0	$50
Fruit & lard presses, various sizes	$125
Flop griddles, oval or rectangular	$150
Fluters	$150
Gas hot plates, one and two burners, common	$75
Gas hot plates, three or four burners	$300
Griddles, common	$25
Hammered Griswold, 1940s-50s	$100

Heat regulators, #300	$200
Kettles, uncommon	$200
Lemon squeezers, Griswold Classic	$125
Mailboxes, Selden & Griswold	$300
Mortar & Pestle, Griswold	$350
Muffin pan, Griswold #10 Popover, common	$25
Muffin pan, Griswold #13, #26, #2800, rare	$1,800
Oval roasters, Griswold	$350
Parlor stoves, Erie #40, #50, #60	$500
Parlor stoves, Erie gas heater #100, #150, #200	$200
Patty molds and bowls, common	$35
Patty bowl, The Junior #870	$200+
Pitchers, various logos	$100
Platters and servers, round or oval	$60
Pots and pans, various logos	$30
Sad irons	$75
Sad iron heaters, Erie Griswold domed #1314	$600
Skillets, slant Griswold Erie #1, very rare	$3,500
Skillets, Griswold #2, rare	$500
Skillets, Griswold #13, rare	$1,000
Skillets, Griswold wood handle, 1905-35	$3,000+
Skillets, Wapak Indian head #4, rare	$1,200
Skillet lids, Griswold, common	$40
Stove dampers, common	$10
Stove lid lifters, Erie or Griswold	$125
Tea kettles, Erie, Selden & Griswold, rare	$150
Tea kettle, Erie Spider, rare	$600
Tobacco cutters	$100
Trivets, 1950s	$30
Wafer iron, various designs	$300
Waffle irons, common	$60
Waffle iron, Selden & Griswold, rare	$500

Doorstops

Prices listed are for items in Good condition.

Boston Terrier	$35
German Shepherd	$75
Boxer, Hubley	$225
Cairn Terrier, B&H	$175
Pekingese, Hubley	$900
Sealyham, Hubley	$375
Setter, Hubley	$125
Fireside Cat, Hubley	$125
Poppies and Cornflowers, Hubley	$90
Marigolds, Hubley	$100
Delphinium, Hubley	$125
Jonquil, Hubley	$150
Tulip Vase, Hubley	$125
Nasturtiums, Hubley	$75

Pansy Bowl, Hubley $150
Poppies and Daisies, Hubley $100
Rose Vase, National Foundry $250
Cosmos, Hubley $400
Peacock $90
Rooster $225
Sleeping Cat, Hubley $250
Penguin, Taylor Cook $950
Elephant, B&H $175
Southern Belle, National Foundry $125
Colonial Woman, Littco Prod. $100
French Girl, Hubley $125
Small Mammy, Hubley $175
Medium Mammy, Hubley $275
Peter Rabbit, Hubley .... $175-$275
Li'l Red Riding Hood, Hubley $375
Drum Major $125
Cape Cod House, Eastern Specialty Mfg Co. $125
Highland Lighthouse $375
Windmill, National Foundry $75

Toys

Ranges listed are for toys in Good condition.

Air Force fighter plane, Arcade, 1941 .... $250
H-21 American Eagle, Hubley, 1960 .... $45
Lucky Boy glider, Dent, rare $500
Sea Gull flying boat, Kilgore $525
Battleship $50
Gunboat, Conestoga Mfg. $65
Circus Wagon, Arcade, 1920s $550
Ferris Wheel, Hubley $150
Buckeye ditch digger, Kenton,1930s $625
Huber steamroller $250
Jaeger cement mixer, Kenton, 1935 .... $425
Mack Ingersoll Rand air compressor truck, rare .... $2,500+
Panama steam shovel, Hubley $1,000
Ahrens-Fox fire engine, Hubley $350
Fire Chief car, Arcade, 1941 .... $250
Fire Patrol truck, Hubley, 1920s $600
Fire Pumper, Arcade, 1920s $450
Ladder truck, Hubley .... $100-$225
Dumping coal wagon, Ives $650
Hansom cab $250
Panama wagon, Wilkins .... $475-$625
Army tank, Arcade, 1937 .... $1,800
Bell Telephone truck, Hubley $225
Breyer's Ice Cream delivery van, Dent, 1932 .... $1,500
Checker Cab, Friedag, 1920s $2,500
Chrysler Airflow, Hubley $600
City Ambulance, Arcade, 1932 .... $650
Coach Bus, Dent, 1925 .... $950
Doctor's Coupe, Ford Model T $1,200
Double-Decker Bus, AC Williams .... $200-$350
Dump Truck, Hubley $1,000
Ford Coupe, AC Williams, 1936 .... $350
Futuristic Sedan, AC Williams $275
Greyhound Bus, Arcade $350
Harley-Davidson motorcycle, Hubley $1,200
Life Saver truck, Hubley, rare $425

Mack dump truck, Hubley $475
Motorcycle with sidecar, Kilgore $775
Police motorcycle, AC Williams $450
Pontiac Roadster, Kilgore $1,000
Pullman Railplane, Arcade $125
Racer, AC Williams $475
Reo Coupe with rumble seat, Arcade, 1931 .... $2,200
Roadster, Kilgore $225
Sedan, Hubley $275
Standard Oil semi-tanker, Kenton, 1933 .... $2,500
Taxi Cab, Arcade, 1923 .... $2,200
Texaco delivery truck, Hubley, c. 1935 .... $550
Water Tower truck, Kenton $650
World's Fair tour bus, Arcade $85
Wrecker, Arcade $125
Yellow Cab, Arcade $850

TIPS OF THE TRADE

• Baked-on food and carbon can be easily removed from cast-iron cookware with lye or oven cleaner.

CATALOGS

Vintage catalogs provide snapshots of life in different eras, and they truly are records of history. Today, catalogs are collected for their historical and nostalgic value as well as their colorful illustrations and useful and interesting information.

General Guidelines: Sears catalogs, in particular, command much collector attention. The first Sears "Big Book" appeared in 1896; today those issues may sell for $200 or more. Sears Christmas catalogs, first issued in 1933, can bring up to $300. Especially popular are catalogs that feature ads for the first Barbie dolls, G.I. Joe or other especially collectible toys.

The value of vintage catalogs depends on age, subject matter, rarity, demand and condition.

Christmas catalogs from J.C. Penney, Aldens and Spiegel are also in demand.

Specialized catalogs — for sporting goods, hunting supplies or toy manufacturers — have a following as well.

VALUE LINE

A.C. Gilbert Co., New Haven, CT, toys, 62 pgs. $17
Abercrombie & Fitch Co., New York, 1920, 166 pgs. $60
Allis-Chalmers Tractors, 1936, Milwaukee, 16 pgs. $30
American Brewers Supply, Pittsburgh, c1925, 138 pgs. ... $76
American Cabinet Co., Two Rivers, WI, 1905, 68 pgs. $63
American Rug & Carpet Co., New York, c1929, 24 pgs. .. $27
Atlas Shoe Co., Boston, 1912, 120 pgs. $24
Atwater Kent Mfg. Co., Philadelphia, 1929, radios,
    30 pgs. $48
Baldwin Locomotive Works, Philadelphia, 1907,
    32 pgs. $58
Bausch & Lomb Optical Co., Rochester, NY, 1919,
    microscopes and accessories, 112 pgs. $52
Bausch & Lomb Optical Co., Rochester, NY, 1921,
    12 pgs. $21
Bell & Howell Co., Chicago, c1929, Filmosound Projector,
    36 pgs. $16
Black & Decker Mfg. Co., Towson, MD, 1931, electric
    tools, 44 pgs. $18
Brown-Morse Co., Muskegon, MI, 1922, 32 pgs. $23
C.P. Barnes & Bros., Louisville, 1884, jewelry, 192 pgs. . $92
California Perfume Co., New York, c1929, 14 pgs. $14
Caterpillar Tractor Co., Peoria, IL, 1937, 8 pgs. $29
Chicago Mail Order Co., Chicago, 1927, 104 pgs. $9
Crown Hair Goods Co., New York, c1920, Beauty Hints
    for the Beauty Salon, 48 pgs. $82
Cundy-Bettoney Co., Inc., Boston, 1940, clarinets and
    flutes, 12 pgs. $43
Eimer & Amend, New York, 1903, chemical and physical
    apparatus, 418 pgs. $98
Encyclopedia Britannica, 1929, 30 pgs. $16
Enterprise Mfg. Co., Philadelphia, household goods,
    138 pgs. $72

Estate Stove Co., Hamilton, OH, c1910, 64 pgs. $28
Fiske & Co., Inc., Boston, 1911, brickwork, 40 pgs. $26
General Electric Co., Schenectady, NY, 1919, The
    Electric Ship, 39 pgs. $68
Groome & Co., Philadelphia, 1912, wine merchant's
    price list, 24 pgs. $34
International Harvester Co., Chicago, 1938, 32 pgs. $34
Iron City Sash & Door Co., Pittsburgh, 1939, 68 pgs. $32
J.C. Penney, Spiegel Christmas catalogs,
    1950s-1960s .... $75-$100
J.C. Penney, Spiegel Christmas catalogs,
    1970s-1980s .... $15-$40
J.L. Mott Iron Works, New York, 1895, 40 pgs. $46
J.R. Wood & Sons, Brooklyn, NY, 1922, jewelry,
    208 pgs. $110
John Deere, Moline, IL, 1956, Modern Farming with
    John Deere Quality Farm Equipment, 92 pgs. $32
Jordan Marsh & Co., Boston, 1885, spring and summer
    catalog, 120 pgs. $52
Kenneweg & Co., Cumberland, MD, 1891, wholesale
    groceries, 11 pgs. $14
Lake Submarine Co., Bridgeport, CT, 1906, 49 pgs. $92
Larkin Co., Buffalo, NY, 1914, 16 pgs. $25
Mahler Bros., New York, 1900, spring and summer
    clothing, 88 pgs. $46
Mead Cycle Co., Chicago, 1918, Ranger bicycles,
    64 pgs. $83
Morgan Sash & Door Co., Chicago, 1921, 96 pgs. $19
National Cloak Co., New York, 1902, 28 pgs. $34
National Trading Co., Chicago, 1924, Emma Post
    Barbour's New Bead Book, 28 pgs. $23
Ormond Manufacturing Co., Baltimore, 1878, sewing
    machines, 96 pgs. $73
Pabst Brewing Co., Milwaukee, c1896, 16 pgs. $110
Paige-Detroit Motor Car, Detroit, 16 pgs. $46
Parker Brothers, Inc., Salem, MA, 1929, games,
    12 pgs. $39
Patton Paint Co., Milwaukee, c1900, 14 pgs. $58
Philco Radio Corp., c1938, 12 pgs. $21
Piedmont Red Cedar Chest, Statesville, NC, 1912,
    56 pgs. $43
Proctor & Gamble Co., Cincinnati, 1918, Approved
    Methods for Home Laundering, 68 pgs. $32
Sears first Big Book 1896 .... $250
Sears, Wards catalogs 1900-1910 .... $150-$250
Sears, Wards catalogs 1911-1920 .... $100
Sears, Wards 1920s .... $70-$80
Sears, Wards 1930s .... $50-$60
Sears, Wards 1930s Christmas .... $100-$300
Sears, Wards 1940s $50
Sears, Wards 1940s Christmas $75
Sears, Wards 1950s $40
Sears, Wards 1950s Christmas $75
Sears, Wards 1960s $30

Ten decades of Sears catalogs, from 1896 (far left, top) to 1993 (bottom right).

Sears, Wards 1960s Christmas .... $75-$100
Sears, Wards 1970s $20
Sears, Wards 1970s Christmas $35
Sears, Wards 1980s $12
Sears, Wards 1980s Christmas $20
Sears final Big Book, 1993 .... $7
Spiegel, Chicago, Stern Co., 1936, 48 pgs. $19
Shear, Packard & Co., Albany, NY, 1867, Improved
    American Hot Air Gas Burning Cooking Stove,
    42 pgs. $63
Standard Mail Order Co., New York, c1924, men's and
    women's clothing, 64 pgs. $16

Star Motor Co., of NY, New York, c1915, The Star Car,
    built by W.C. Durant, 24 pgs. $63
Stetson Paint & Varnish, Chicago, 1934, 42 pgs. $68
Steuben Glass, New York, 1947, 24 pgs. $32
Studebaker Corp., of America, Detroit, 1914, 32 pgs. $93
Sutcliffe Co., Louisville, 1923, sports equipment,
    64 pgs. $48
U.S. Playing Card Co., Cincinnati, 1900, 138 pgs. $97
Westfield Mfg., Westfield, MA, 1922, Columbia
    bicycles, 16 pgs. $76
White Hall Pottery Works, Stone Hall, IL, c1930, 44 pgs. $26
Wilson Furniture Co., Louisville, 1912, 24 pgs. $30

CHILDREN'S BOOKS

There's nothing like going back to your childhood to collect items that made you happy. Big Little Books (BLB) and Little Golden Books (LGB) are two collectibles that do bring back very happy memories. There is hardly a person alive who doesn't remember reading (or having been read to) these classic children's books.

Today, BLBs and LGBs represent a growing collecting area. Besides the nostalgia aspect, these are hot collectibles because they are easy to obtain and often inexpensive. They are frequently found at rummage sales and flea markets for a fraction of their retail collectible price.

These books are colorful and can be displayed rather easily. They often feature characters from comics, television, radio and cartoons, making them especially collectible.

General Guidelines: Condition is essential. Near Mint and Mint examples of the BLBs and LGBs are uncommon. They are priced at a premium. Books with torn or missing pages, writing on the cover or inside pages and/or chewed-on covers are common; these are valued at 10 to 20 percent of an Excellent condition book. Occasionally, there are warehouse finds of LGBs printed in the 1960s (usually, one box of books is discovered); these books are worth about twice as much as a Near Mint book would be worth, simply because this condition is very difficult to acquire.

Big Little Books

Whitman first published BLBs in the early 1930s ("Big Little Book" was a Whitman trademark). These thick (several hundred pages), small-format, pulp paper books proved to be so popular that other publishers — Saalfield, Goldsmith, Van Wiseman, Lynn, Dell and World Syndicate — copied this concept. The books were illustrated with a full-page drawing on the right-hand page with the story on the left. The original cover price of BLBs was 10 cents, still affordable during the Great Depression.

The first BLB published was *The Adventures of Dick Tracy Detective*. This book can fetch anywhere from several hundred dollars to $1,000, depending on condition. Dick Tracy was featured on about 30 different BLBs. Showcasing popular characters proved successful for the titles. Don Winslow, Flash Gordon, Buck Rogers, The Lone Ranger, Charlie Chan and other popular personalities found their way onto the covers of these books. Disney characters were also well represented.

Collections often focus on characters. For example, some attempt to get a copy of each Dick Tracy book or Donald Duck book. Collecting by artist is also becoming popular, with the work of such famous artists as Al Capp and Alex Raymond being featured in BLBs.

General Guidelines: Books in Good condition are quite common, but still collectible. Good condition books sell for about 15 to 25 percent of Near Mint books. The most valuable titles feature popular names such as Flash Gordon, Dick Tracy, Shirley Temple or Disney characters.

Little Golden Books

The fist LGBs were produced in 1942 by Simon & Schuster's Western Print & Lithographing Co. There were 12 different LGBs produced, each 42 pages. They sold for a quarter, and the 12-book line sold 1.5 million units within the first half year of release. By the end of World War II, about 40 million LGBs were sold. LGBs continue to be printed today, by the Western Publishing Co. In 1986, Western published the billionth LGB.

General Guidelines: Most Little Golden Books sell in the $1-$5 range. First editions, books with original gold-colored bindings, books with "extras," rare titles and books by certain illustrators may command much more.

Some collectors seek specific characters, especially those by Walt Disney. Still others collect by artist (Eloise Wilken, Connie Malvern) or author (A.A. Milne).

First editions are often the most valuable. To find an edition number (on pre-1990s books), check the lower right corner of the back page; the letter found there tells you which printing and edition the book is. The first printing is noted with an "A," the second with a "B" and so on. First editions sell for the most. Subsequent editions sell for from 25 to 75 percent of the price of the "A" printing.

Little Golden Books containing "extras," such as Band-Aids, facial tissue, metal clock hands or puzzles are especially coveted but must be complete to command top price.

Books from the 1940s-1960s are the most in demand today. Top on that list are the original 12 books, along with all Disney-related books, cowboy heroes and TV- and cartoon-related books.

Big Little Book, *Popeye and the Jeep*, Whitman Publishing Co., #1405

Clubs

•Golden Book Club
19626 Ricardo Ave., Hayward, CA 94541

•Big Little Book Collector Club of America
P.O. Box 1242, Danville, CA 94526

VALUE LINE

Big Little Books

Ace Drummon, 1935, VG $32
Andy Panda All Picture Comics, 1943, G $35
Aquaman: Scourge of the Sea, 1968, VG $20
Blondie: No Dull Moments, 1948, G $25
Bobby Benson on the H-BAR-O Ranch, 1934, VG $38
Brenda Starr and the Masked Impostor, 1943, VG $45
The Buccaneer, G $20
The Buccaneers, 1958, VG $28
Buck Rogers in the War With Planet Venus, EX $75
Captain Easy, Soldier of Fortune, NM $65
Charlie Chan, 1939, G $25
Charlie Chan Solves a New Mystery, 1942, VG $35
Dan Dunn (Secret Operative 48) and the Border
    Smugglers, 1938, VG $45
Dan Dunn (Secret Operative 48) Fast Action Zeppelin
    of Doom, VG $75
David Copperfield (movie), EX $45
Dick Tracy and the Bicycle Gang, 1948, G $25
Don Winslow and the Great War Plot, VG $45
Don Winslow, USN, Lieutenant Commander, NM $55
Donald Duck Up in the Air, 1945, NM $65
Donald Duck: Silly Symphony, 1937, NM $85
Flash Gordon and the Tournaments of Mongo, 1935, G ... $45
Flash Gordon and the Red Sword Invaders, 1934, VG $33
Frank Merriwell at Yale, 1935, VG $25
Flash Gordon in the Forest Kingdom of Mongo, EX $75
Foreign Spies: Doctor Doom and the Ghost
    Submarine, VG $28
G-Man and the Gun Runners, EX $55
G-Man Breaking the Gambling Ring, EX $45
G-Man on the Crime Trail, EX $48
G-Man vs. the Red X, VG $38
The Green Hornet Strikes, NM $125
Grimm's Ghost Stories, 1976 .... $3
Guns in the Roaring West, 1937, VG $22
Gunsmoke, 1958, EX $18
Hall of Fame of the Air (Rickenbacker), VG $35
Houdini's Big Little Book of Magic, NM $75
International Spy: Doctor Doom Faces Death at Dawn,
    VG $25
In the Name of the Law: War Against Crime, VG $22
Invisible Scarlet O'Neil v. Slum King, 1946, VG $35
Jim Starr of the U.S. Border Patrol, G $10
Jimmie Allen and the Airmail Robbery, VG $35
Journey to the Center of the Earth, 1968, Near Mint $10
Junior G-Men and the Counterfeiters, NM $45
Kayo & Moon Mullins & the One Man Gang, 1939, VG . $30

Kayo in the Land of Sunshine, EX $45
Ken Maynard and the Gun Wolves of the Gila, NM $48
Lassie: Old One Eye, 1975 .... $9
The Laughing Dragon of Oz, 1934, rare, NM $195
Li'l Abner Among the Millionaires, VG $35
Little Orphan Annie and the Ghost Gang, EX $48
Little Women (featuring Katherine Hepburn), 1934, VG .. $22
Lone Star Martin of the Texas Rangers, 1939, G $15
The Lost Patrol, VG $42
Myra North Special Nurse and Foreign Spies, EX $38
Peggy Brown and the Runaway Auto Trailer, EX $35
Popeye in Quest of His Poopdeck Pappy, 1937, EX $45
Popeye's Ark, EX $120
Prairie Bill and the Covered Wagon, VG $22
Radio Patrol, 1935, VG $40
Red Barry: Undercover Man, VG $28
Red Ryder and the Squaw Tooth Rustlers, 1946, VG $25
Red Ryder and Western Border Guns, EX $45
Secret Agent X-9, 1936, VG $25
Sir Lancelot, 1958, G $15
Skippy and Sooky, 1933, G $15
Space Ghost, 1968, VG $20
Tailspin Tommy in Flying Aces, NM $75
Tarzan: The Beasts of Tarzan, VG $45

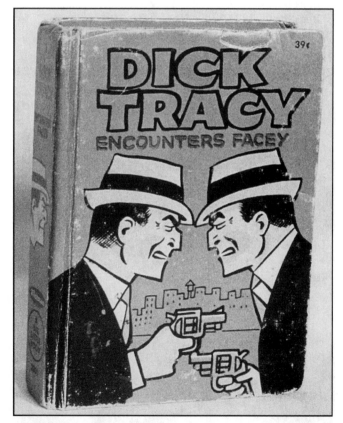

Big Little Book, Dick Tracy Encounters Facey by Paul S. Newman, Whitman Publishing Co., #2001, 1967.

Tarzan Lord of the Jungle, 1946, VG $35
Terry and the Pirates the Plantation Mystery, EX $42
The Texas Kid, EX $25
Tiny Tim and the Mechanical Men, NM $55
Treasure Island, 1934, G $10
Tweety & Sylvester: The Magic Voice, 1976 .... $7
Two-Gun Montana, EX $35
Uncle Wiggily's Adventures, NM $55
Union Pacific: Story of Railroad Building in the West,
    NM $55
Wimpy the Hamburger Eater, VG $35
The World War in Photographs, 1934, VG $25
Zip Saunders King of the Speedway, NM $35

Little Golden Books

Animal Babies, 1947, "C" printing, VG $17
Animal Daddies and My Daddy, 1968, "A" printing, VG . $12
Baby's Christmas, 1972, 4th printing, G $6
Bamm-Bamm with Pebbles Flintstone, 1963, EX $20
Barbie and the Big Splash, 1992, NM $5
Barbie and the Missing Wedding Gown, 1992, NM $12
Beany & Cecil Go to Sea, NM $28
Bedtime Stories, 1968, 11th printing, G $9
Benji, McDonald's Little Golden Book, VG $4
Betsy McCall: A Paper Doll Story Book, 1965, no
    dolls, G $10
Bobby and His Airplanes, 1949, "A" printing, G $22
Bugs Bunny, 1949, "A" printing, VG $27
Bugs Bunny, 1972, 11th printing, G $6

Little Golden Book, Walt Disney's Bambi.

Bugs Bunny and the Indians, 1951, , "C" printing, G $8
Bugs Bunny's Birthday, 1950, EX $10
Captain Kangaroo and the Panda, 1957, "D" printing, G . $12
Christmas in the Country, 1950, EX $14
Crispy Critters, "Crispy in the Birthday Band," 1987, Post
    Crispy Critters cereal premium $5
Crispy Critters, "Crispy in No Place Like Home," 1987,
    Post Crispy Critters cereal premium $5
A Day in the Jungle, 1943, "G" printing $17
The Emerald City of Oz, 1952, "A" printing, F $17
Fire Engines, 1959, EX $12
Four Puppies, 1960, "A" printing, VG $17
Gene Autry, 1955, EX $28
Gene Autry & Champion, 1956, NM $30
The Golden Book of Flowers, 1943, with dustjacket, 1st
    printing, VG $60
Good-Bye Tonsils, 1972, G $8
Hansel and Gretel, 1943, "E" printing, VG $17
Happy Birthday, 1960, EX $11
Hong Kong Phooey: Fortune Cookie Caper, 1975, NM ... $18
Hopalong Cassidy & Bar 20 Cowboy, NM $28
Howdy Doody and Santa Claus, 1955, EX $24
Howdy Doody and Clarabell, VG $15
Howdy Doody's Circus, 1950, EX $35
Lassie & The Big Clean-Up Day, 1971, VG $5
Lassie and Her Day in the Sun, 1969, G $5
Little Galoshes, 1949, EX $14
The Little Golden Book of Hymns, 1947, no dustjacket,
    "C" printing, G $17
The Lively Little Rabbit, 1943, "I" printing, VG $17
Make Way for the Thruway, 1961, EX $12
Machines, 1961, VG $7
Mickey Mouse Goes Christmas Shopping, 1953, "I"
    printing, G $7
Mickey Mouse's Picnic, 1950, VG $10
Mighty Mouse and the Scarecrow, 1954, VG $12
Mighty Mouse: Dinky Learns to Fly, 1953, EX $15
A Name for Kitty, 1948, "A" printing, VG $32
The Night Before Christmas, 1946, "C" printing, VG $17
The Night Before Christmas, 1949, "D" printing, EX $17
The Night Before Christmas, 1949, "O" printing, G $8
Ookpik the Arctic Owl, 1968, "A" printing, VG $22
Peter Rabbit, 1958, "A" printing, VG $17
Play Ball!, 1958, EX $14
The Rescuers Down Under, Disney, 1990 .... $2
Rudolph the Red-Nosed Reindeer, 1958, EX $8
Sergeant Preston & Rex, 1956, NM $25
The Seven Sneezes, 1948, "A" printing, VG $32
Shazam Circus Adventure, 1960, VG $12
The Shy Little Kitten, 1946, 1st edition, dustjacket, G $60
Steve Canyon, 1959, "A" printing, G $22
Supercar, NM $35
A Surprise for Felix the Car, 1959, NM $25
The Taxi That Hurried, 1946, 1st edition, dustjacket, G ... $60
The Three Bears, 1948, "A" printing, VG $27
The Three Little Pigs, 1948, "A" printing, VG $32
Tom Corbett Space Cadet and a Trip to the Moon, NM $28

Tom Terrific and Mighty Manfred, EX $30

Tom Terrific's Greatest Adventure, NM $30

Tootle, 1946, "F" printing, VG $20

Uncle Wiggily's Adventures, 1961, NM $25

Underdog and the Disappearing Ice Cream, 1975, EX $22

A Year in the City, 1948, "A" printing, G $27

A Year on the Farm, 1948, "B" printing, VG $20

Yogi Bear, 1960, EX $10

Walt Disney's Bambi, 1948, EX $20

Walt Disney's Bedknobs and Broomsticks, 1st edition
1971, G $10

Walt Disney's Davy Crocket: King of the Wild Frontier,
1955, NM $25

Walt Disney's Dumbo, 1955, "D" printing, VG $22

Walt Disney's Ludwig von Drake: Dog Expert, 1962,
EX $28

Walt Disney's Jungle Book, 1967, 1st edition, VG $17

Walt Disney's Mother Goose, 1952, VG $7

Walt Disney's Peter and the Wolf, 1947, "C" printing,
VG $17

Walt Disney's Santa's Toy Shop, 1950, "A" printing, EX . $33

Walt Disney's Sleeping Beauty, 1957, "A" printing, G $14

Walt Disney's Snow White, 1948, "A" printing, VG $37

Walt Disney's Snow White, 1948, "Z" printing, G $12

Walt Disney's Uncle Remus, 1969, 20th printing, VG $12

Walt Disney's Winnie the Pooh and Tigger, 1968, VG $12

Walt Disney's Winnie the Pooh Honey Tree, 1969, 4th
printing, G $6

Walt Disney's Zorro, 1958, "B" printing, VG $22

The Waltons and the Birthday Present, 1975, NM $28

We Help Mommy, 1959, VG... $8

We Like Kindergarten, 1969, G $6

Wild Animals, 1958, "A" printing, VG $17

Winky Dink, 1956, NM $25

Where is the Poky Little Puppy?, 1962, EX $10

Wyatt Earp, 1958, NM $25

Little Golden Book, The Color Kittens by Margaret Wise Brown.

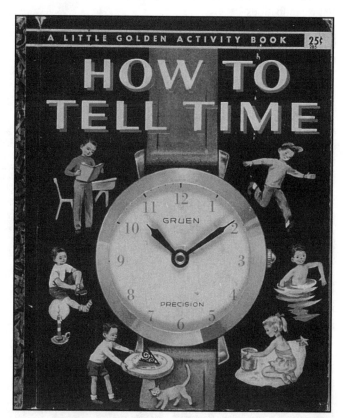

Little Golden Activity Book, How to Tell Time.

COCA-COLA

When you think of the world's most identifiable logos, Coca-Cola's script name over a red background immediately comes to mind. The company has proven what proper mass marketing can do on a worldwide scale. Coca-Cola has been around since before the turn of the century, so there are many items available to collectors.

In 1886, Dr. John Pemberton, an Atlanta pharmacist, formulated Coca-Cola. From its humble beginnings (as a beverage that purportedly cured headaches and other ailments), it eventually grew into a nationwide and worldwide phenomenon.

Today, most of the Coca-Cola items produced are made to be collected and saved, unlike vintage advertising items, which were not made as collectibles, but were saved and are highly desirable today.

New items available to Coke enthusiasts include everything from die-cast cars and trucks to magnets and trading cards. These collectibles are, with some exceptions, not likely to be of any great value in the future.

The most desirable Coca-Cola collectibles are those made originally to advertise the beverage; most preferably, those items created prior to 1960. There are plenty of reproductions on the market, however, so new collectors should learn how to spot fakes and reproductions.

1943 Coca-Cola cardboard sign, pictures woman and soldier on bicycles, 29" x 50", $750.

General Guidelines

Tin: From the early 1900s to the 1920s, small pocket mirrors were produced featuring full-color artwork of a woman, along with the Coke logo. Most of these sell for $200 to $350. Reproductions exist, most with a 1973 date; these are valued at $5 or less.

Some of the most well-known Coca-Cola items are the change and serving trays that featured beautiful women enjoying Coca-Cola. The company stuck with this mode of marketing for many years, from about 1900 to the mid-1950s.

These are interesting items for several reasons. They established in the minds of marketers that beautiful women can help sell products; they show changes in fashions and hairstyles from 1900 through the 1950s; and these colorful trays are great display items when found in top condition. The 1909, 1912, 1914 and 1917 trays were reproduced in the early 1970s; repros sell for from $8 to $15, while originals are valued at several hundred dollars each.

Bottles: The classic curved Coca-Cola bottle shape that everyone is familiar with was first designed in 1915. Prior to that, bottles were made in many different forms. Coke bottles can be dated by numbers on the bottom of the bottles. If there is one set of four digits, the last two digits indicate the year the bottle was made. Some pre-1920 bottles can be valued at $100 to $300.

Some newer 6-ounce bottles, from the 1980s and 1990s, were made to commemorate events, such as the Green Bay Packers' 1997 Super Bowl win. These new bottles are finding collectors; however, many were saved and there will likely be a better-than-average supply of Mint condition bottles well into the future. Some bottles do, however, sell for $4 to $20 or more apiece. The higher-end prices can be partially attributed to the regional nature of many of these special promotions. For example, the Packers bottles were widely distributed in Wisconsin but not in other parts of the country.

Miscellaneous: Like serving trays, Coca-Cola calendars enjoyed their heyday from just before the turn of the century through the 1950s. Similar artwork was used on the signs and the calendars — in fact, sometimes the same artwork was used. Locating a calendar in top condition, with its pad still intact, is a rare find. The earliest calendars, those from about 1890 to 1905, can fetch prices in the low- to mid- four-figure range. Even those from the 1920s and 1930s run several hundred dollars.

Coca-Cola collectors have to fight radio collectors for the several radios that carry the Coca-Cola logo. A 1930 bottle radio can have a value of more than $1,000, while a 1949 cooler radio can realize $400 to $500. On a more contemporary note, look for 1960s-1970s Coca-Cola transistor radios, in the shape of Coke machines, that are valued from $75 to $125.

Signs are another important area of Coca-Cola collecting. Made of wood, tin, porcelain, cardboard, chrome and plastic, these signs are popular as decorating items, as well as being collectibles in their own right. Many of the early signs breach the four-figure mark.

Coca-Cola sponsored drinking glass giveaways at fast-food restaurants, mostly in the 1970s and 1980s. These glasses, featuring the likes of King Kong, Star Trek, Popeye, Mickey Mouse and even Holly Hobbie, are generally inexpensive. These common items can often be found for a few dollars, but some are valued at more than $10.

Because Coca-Cola mania is a worldwide phenomenon, there is a wealth of foreign Coke advertising items available. Unfortunately, much of it is still in the foreign countries in which it was made. There are a few ways you can get your hands on these items. First, if you or someone you know travels, look for the items yourself. If not, connect with other collectors in those countries and try a little horse-trading.

Clubs
•Coca-Cola Collectors Club International
P.O. Box 49166, Atlanta, GA 30359-1166.

FAMOUS COKE SLOGANS

Proper marketing went a long way to establish Coke's success. Here are some of the advertising slogans used by Coca-Cola. This might help pinpoint the age of an item.

Ca. 1900: Delicious and Refreshing
1905: Coca-Cola Revives and Sustains
1917: Three Million a Day [number of servings of
   Coca-Cola consumed per day]
1922: Thirst Knows No Season
1925: Six Million a Day
1929: The Pause that Refreshes
1932: Ice-Cold Sunshine
1938: The Best Friend Thirst Ever Had
1942: The Only Thing Like Coca-Cola is Coca-Cola
   Itself — It's the Real Thing
1948: Where There's Coke There's Hospitality
1952: What You Want is a Coke
1956: Making Good Things Taste Better
1963: Things Go Better with Coke
1970: It's the Real Thing
1971: I'd Like to Buy the World a Coke
1976: Coke Adds Life
1979: Have a Coke and a Smile
1982: Coke is It
1986: Catch the Wave
1989: Can't Beat the Feeling
1990: Can't Beat the Real Thing
1992: Always Coca-Cola

VALUE LINE

Airline Cooler, mid-1950s, holds 18 bottles, EX $375
Animation cel, 1995, Polar Bear, MT $210
Bicycle, Huffy, 1986, 100th Anniversary, 25,000 made,
   MT $750
Bottle, 1992, Albertville Olympics $4
Bottle, 1993, Denver Broncos $4
Bottle, 1993, Florida Marlins $5

Bottle, 1993, NBA All-Star Weekend, Salt Lake City
   1993 .... $10
Bottle, 1993, World of Coca-Cola $18
Bottle holder, metal, "Enjoy Coca-Cola while you shop.
   Place bottle here," 1950, MT $75
Calendar, 1919 .... $1,750
Calendar, 1924 .... $900
Calendar, 1925 .... $750-$1,000
Calendar, 1933 .... $550
Calendar, 1936 .... $650
Calendar, 1944 .... $275
Calendar, 1958 .... $200
Camera, 35mm, shape of Coke can, made in Singapore,
   working $25
Clock, 1951, metal, maroon with red logo "Drink
   Coca-Cola" $110
Clock, 1960s, plastic, 15-inch square, "Things go Better
   with Coke" $85
Cooler, 1950s, average condition $50
Drinking glass, Holly Hobbie Merry Christmas, each $2
Drinking glass, King Kong, 1976, each $8
Drinking glass, Mickey's Christmas Carol, 1982, each $5
Drinking glass, Popeye, 1975 .... $15

Coca-Cola early 1900s glass syrup bottle, $1,250.

1950s Coca-Cola cardboard three dimensional die-cut window display, soda fountain scene with soda jerk, 24" x 36", $400.

Drinking glass, National Flag, each $8
Drinking glass, Star Trek: The Motion Picture, each $14
Drinking glasses, bell-shaped, 1960s, price for pair $12
Lithograph, "Luge" commercial, polar bear holding
    bottle of Coke, 8" by 10", matted $40
Magazine ads, 1910s, color, full page .... $12-$18
Magazine ads, 1910s, black and white, full page .... $8-$12
Napkin holder, metal $35
Neon clock, 1980s, MT $600
Pins, 1996 Olympics, various, each $6
Playing cards, 1909, Gibson girl images $2,250
Playing cards, 1915, pink parasol $1,100
Playing cards, 1928, sipping girl $350
Playing cards, 1943, nurse .... $65-$100
Playing cards, 1951, cowgirl $75
Playing cards, 1956, ice skates $85
Pushbar, porcelain enamel, 1950s average condition $135
Radio, shape of Coke machine, 1980s working $48
Serving tray, metal, 1916, woman under tree with
    flowers, EX-NM $320
Serving tray, metal, 1921, woman in blue hat, NM $1,000
Serving tray, metal, 1922, woman in white hat, EX $500

Serving tray, metal, 1925, woman in blue hat and fur,
    EX $350
Serving tray, metal, 1931, boy with dog, NM $900
Serving tray, metal, 1936, woman on couch, EX-NM ... $200
Serving tray, metal, 1937, woman in yellow bathing
    suit,   NM $350
Serving tray, metal, 1939, woman in white bathing suit,
    NM $300
Serving tray, metal, 1940, woman in sailor hat on dock,
    NM $425
Serving tray, metal, 1941, woman with ice skates, NM . $425
Serving tray, metal, 1942, two women by car, NM $425
Serving tray, metal, 1950, woman with white glove,
    EX-NM $130
Serving tray, metal, 1953, woman looking at menu, MT $110
Sign, cardboard, "Good With Food," 1951, 36" x 20",
    Niagara Litho Co., VG $250
Sign, glass, 1950s, "Drink Coca-Cola," VG-EX $100
Sign, hanging, paper, 1958, Mint $20
Sign, metal, 20" x 28", 1950, "Drink Coca-Cola Ice
    Cold," VG-EX $170
Sign, metal, 1960, "Coca-Cola A Sign of Good Taste,"
    VG-EX $160
Sign, neon, 1989, "Coca-Cola Classic: The Official
    Softdrink of Summer," Mint $2,400
Sign, plastic light-up 12" diameter $48
Sign, porcelain, double-sided, 1939, 3' x 5', EX-NM $750
Sign, porcelain, "Drink Coca-Cola," 1950s, 4' diameter,
    EX $500
Six-pack holder, metal, 1930, NM $150
Six-pack holder, metal, 1950s, NM $110
Syrup glass, 1916, Mint $200
Syrup glass, 1970s, Mint $45
Syrup jug, 1940s, EX $65
Syrup jug, 1960s, EX $30
Tip tray, metal, 1907, "Relieves Fatigue," woman in
    green dress, EX-NM $900
Vending machine, Vendo 44, EX, working $2,500

1963 Coca-Cola cardboard cut-out, Smokey Bear cubs carrying picnic basket, $475.

COCKTAIL SHAKERS/BARWARE

Primitive versions of the cocktail shaker date back as far as 7000 B.C. when liquids were mixed within the confines of a South American jar gourd. In 3500 B.C., what could be seen as the world's first cocktails were made when ancient Egyptians added spices to their grain fermentations to improve taste.

By the late 1800s, bartenders used a shaker as a standard tool of their craft. The modern cocktail shaker arrived on the scene in the 1920s with stylishly-shaped shakers made of materials such as glass, Bakelite, chrome and sterling silver. When Prohibition ended in 1933, the cocktail shaker enjoyed another surge in popularity. Cocktail shakers fell from favor with the advent of the electric blender.

General Guidelines: Most popular are stainless steel and chrome-plated designs from the 1920s-1940s. Many shakers can be found in the $30-$100 range, but scarcer pieces — like those created by designer Norman Bel Geddes — may sell for several hundred or even several thousand dollars. Bel Geddes' Manhattan Skyscraper set can command as much as $3,000.

Cocktail shakers are available in many shapes, including airplanes, animals, golf bags, skyscrapers and more. Well-made examples in unique shapes may generate more collector interest.

Glass shakers with brilliant colors are more desirable than clear shakers. Be aware, however, that cracks or chips detract from the shaker's value.

Penguin cocktail shaker, Emile A. Schuelke for The Napier Co., Meriden, Conn., 1936. (Photo courtesy of The Seagram Museum)

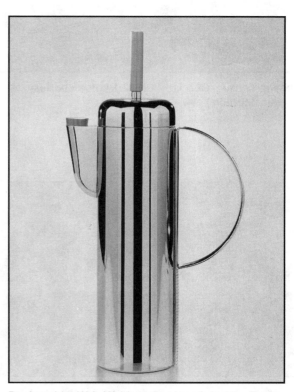

Designed by W.A. Weldon, director of design, Revere Copper & Brass Inc., Rome, N.Y., c. 1930s, chromium, Bakelite. (Photo courtesy of The Seagram Museum)

Liquor set, brass ring holds four gold banded glasses,
  1950s $18
Martini pitcher, Cambridge glass, Diane pattern,
  crystal $750
Martini set, glass, pheasants on pitcher and glasses $18
Punch bowl set, Duncan Miller, Caribbean pattern,
  crystal, 14-piece set $225
Cordial glass, Cambridge Glass, Caprice pattern, blue ... $125
Cordial glass, Cambridge Glass, Chantilly pattern,
  crystal $65
Cordial glass, Heisey Glass, Plantation pattern, crystal $90
Wine glass, Cambridge Glass, Imperial Hunt Scene
  pattern, emerald green $55
Wine glass, Cambridge Glass, Valencia pattern, crystal ... $30
Wine glass, Fostoria, Fairfax pattern, rose $30
Whiskey glass, Duncan Miller, Tear Drop pattern,
  crystal $15
Whiskey glass, Fostoria, American pattern, crystal $10
Whiskey glass, Fostoria, Kasmir pattern, yellow $25
Whiskey glass, Heisey Glass, Plantation pattern, crystal .. $50

The stunning skyscraper service, designed by Norman Bel
Geddes, 1930s.

Zeppelin shaker, German, 1930. (Photos courtesy of the
Seagram Museum)

"Aeroplane" German silver plate shaker, 1928, adaptation of
zeppelin shaker, rectangular flasks added as wings.

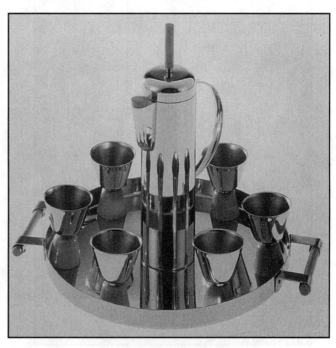

Sheridan Serving Set, 1937.

COIN-OPERATED MACHINES

Coin-operated machines have intrigued the public since their inception in the late 1800s. This category includes — among other items — jukeboxes, slot machines, gumball and candy machines and arcade and carnival games.

Arcade/Amusement/Vending Machines

These machines debuted in the 1890s. At the forefront of early enterprises to house these marvels was the aptly–named "penny arcade." Here, for one cent, the customer could listen to music, test their lung capacity, see pictures of faraway lands, maneuver iron claws to get prizes, and even have their fortunes told.

Collectors should look for patent numbers or dates on the cabinets of coin–operated machines, especially those in early vintage styles. A paper with the inspection number or date is also frequently glued to the cabinet wall. However, an early patent date doesn't necessarily mean the model was manufactured during that year, since patents might still apply to some models produced thirty or more years later. Nonetheless, this information can provide background when researching the model.

Jukeboxes

Music boxes developed in Europe during the Industrial Revolution and, as improvements were made, the coin operated mechanism was developed.

Some early upright Wheel of Fortune slot machines had a "musical attachment" where every play of the machine was accompanied by a song. In general the song was repeated until the operator changed the music roll.

Although not yet referred to as such, early jukeboxes came into being in 1889 when Louis Glass, the owner of San Francisco's Palais Royale Saloon used an Edison wax cylinder to make 24 machines, into which he ingeniously placed a coin slot. Called "Nickel and Slot," it immediately attracted attention as an entertaining, and inexpensive, diversion.

These coin operated music boxes were eventually displaced by the jukebox in the '20s and '30s. The term jukebox is attributed to the culture of the southern United States, and was in common usage in the 1930s, deriving from a term of West African origin meaning "to dance."

General Guidelines: Golden Age jukeboxes, predominately Wurlitzers of the late '40s and early '50s, are the most desirable. Silver Age jukeboxes, predominately Seeburgs of the late '50s and early '60s, sometimes called the "Fonzie type," are the second in desirability to those of the Golden Age. Jukebox prices, in general, are on a steady increase.

Especially desirable models to look for include the 1906 Gabel Automatic Entertainer, Western Electric Selectraphone, Wurlitzer models from 1941-'49, Rockola 1422 and 1426 models and the Rockola Premier.

Most jukeboxes can be purchased today in the $700 to $3,000 price range (with many of those from the 1950s and '60s available for between $1,000 and $2,000).

One-cent gumball machine, Columbus Vendor, green enamel, Columbus, Ohio.

WATCH OUT FOR REPRODUCTIONS

Reproduction slot machines are readily available as vintage-style decorations. But if you are seeking antiques, be on guard. So far only the slot machines made by the Mills Novelty Company of Chicago have been reproduced, with the Silent "War Eagle," Mystery "Blue Front," Jewel, 21, Standard and other "Hightop" models being the most prevalent.

Fantasy Mills models, such as a golfer and the Golden Nugget varieties, have been made and sold in great quantity. They work well, but they aren't antiques, and their resale value reflects this. Slot machines made by Jennings, Watling, Caille Bros., Pace and others have not yet been reproduced. But in time they probably will be. The very valuable Mr. Peanut scale has also been replicated.

Pinball Machines

General Guidelines: Only payout pinballs of the 1935-1942 period garner significant sums as they are regarded as table slot machines rather than playable pin games. Along with jukeboxes, pinballs are the only vintage coin-ops whose current models are regarded as collectibles and largely outvalue vintage machines. Pinball back glasses and playfield graphics constitute about 70 percent of the value of a game, so a degraded or broken backglass and worn playfield quickly reduce game value to a "basket case." Early 1931-1933 countertops are collectible as historical artifacts and not for their play principles. Mechanical marvels from 1933-1934 are the premier pinball collectibles, with games such as Jig Saw, World's Series and Army/Navy commanding the highest collector prices.

Although graphically interesting, the pre-flipper electromechanical games of 1935-1947 have little value. Flipper games from 1947-1975 are from the Golden Age of pinball, with Gottlieb games of the '50s and Bally celebrity games of the 1970s the most desirable collectibles. Select modern pinball games are regarded as prime collectibles and are generally valued greater than any of the vintage games.

Slot Machines

Rated as the top collectible among coin machines, slots are gambling machines that pay out in coins or tokens. If the machine doesn't physically pay out when a winner is hit, and instead makes its awards in points, scores, replays, free games or any other non-physical form of payout, it is considerably less desirable as a collectible, and greatly reduced in value.

History: The first primitive slot machines entered the world of commerce around 1885. In 1888, the first automatic payout machine was manufactured by the Eureka Box Co. of Baltimore and called the Eureka Box. The first machines to pay out a metered amount were the 3–for–1 models introduced by the John Lighton Machine Co. in the early 1890s.

The Horse Shoe and Star is credited as the first automatic payout counter-model wheel, while the three-reel Liberty Bell machine, developed in 1895 by Charlie Fey, is now considered by many experts to be the most collectible of all slot machines. Fey's machine was a counter-top model with three reels and an automatic payout, enabling the players to indulge in a roulette-style game as opposed to the "wheel of fortune" concept. Only 55 Liberty Bell models were made, making them extremely rare and valuable. These early counter machines were in the toe-footed cast-iron style, revolutionizing the industry because of their portability, which substantially increased space availability marketing potential.

It wasn't until 1915 that the modern slot machine was born. Manufactured by Mills Novelty Co., which was responsible for many popular earlier models, it boasted a wooden cabinet and large cash box, and was called the Operator Bell.

General Guidelines: Among the most collectible slot machines to look for include: Fey Liberty Bell, Watling Rol-a-Tor, Buckley Bones, Caille Bix Six Lone Star Twin, Caille Roulette, Rol-A-Top Bells, White Floor Models, Mills Double Dewey. Payout slot machines fall into four groups. (1) Wooden cabinet clockwork and simple trip mechanism models 1885–1900 tend to be rare, and valuable. (2) Floor and counter mechanical machines, including early electrical floor machines, 1895-1918 are major collectibles. (3) Post-WWI and Golden Age slots 1919-1963 are generally all mechanical in wooden cabinets with cast display fronts, although the 1930s electrical floor consoles appear in this period. (4) The electromechanical Bally of 1964, and its current slot descendents, are among the hottest slot collectibles as they offer the casino experience in the home. The more advanced solid state and all-electronic slot machines just entering the home market are not particularly desirable or collectible as there is great concern over long-term maintenance issues. Until that is resolved they are orphans.

Trade Stimulators and Counter Games

Generally regarded as smaller slot machines that don't make payouts, the saloon, country store and cigar counter trade stimulators of 1882-1919 paid off in "Free Drinks, Free Cigars" or merchandise, followed by the later counter games of 1920 to date which displayed card symbols, "points" or cigarette reels to be exchanged for cash, merchandise or packs of cigarettes over the counter. Due to their wide variety of play and game formats they are highly desirable as collectibles. The classic period of wooden and cast iron trade stimulators is 1895-1915, with the Golden Age of cast aluminum and sheet steel counter games 1933-1942.

General Guidelines: Both trade stimulators and counter games have a wide variety of play formats, including horse race games, dice toss, pointers, wheels, spinners, roulette, coin-shooting target, coin drop, single reel, multiple reel poker card, number, fruit, cigarette machines and other distinctive game principles. Modern counter games tend to be solid state poker machines which are not yet regarded as collectibles.

Vending Machines

Although many were also part of the old–time arcades, the venue for most vending machines was in small retail outlets. Generally not as complex as other arcade offerings, they remain fascinating contraptions with a unique appeal.

Contributors to this section: the late Richard M. Bueschel; Joseph Jancuska, 619 Miller St., Luzerne, PA 18709.

In Search Of Liberty Bell

The first three reel automatic payout slot machine was made by German immigrant Charlie Fey of San Francisco around the turn of the century, most likely in 1905. In honor of his newfound country he called it Liberty Bell. Only three were known, one of which went for a record auction price of $135,000 plus buyer fees and taxes in 1995. The Fey Liberty Bell became the Holy Grail of slot machines. Two showed up in the San Francisco area in 1996, and the search is on for more. The machine name became so popular that tens of thousands of adaptations and improved versions of the Liberty Bell were made by Mills Novelty, Caille Bros., Watling, Industry Novelty and even counter game maker Daval between 1907 and 1941, with the later machines valued at anywhere from $150 to $10,000 depending on the age and model. Only one, the Fey Liberty Bell, carries a value near $100,000, so don't be misled by a machine name.

Arcade/Amusement/Vending Machines

Prices listed are for complete operating machines in good condition with all award and directions paper in place as well as decals and other unique machine graphics.

Hummer, Belk, Schafer (Alton, IL), 1896 .... $3,500

Confections, Volkman, Stollwerck (Brooklyn, NY), 1897 .... $3,200

Adams Pepsin, U. S. Slot Machine (New York, NY), 1897 .... $2,800

Star Pepsin, Hollands (Detroit, MI), 1899 .... $2,000

Automatic Clerk, Automatic Clerk (New Haven, CT), 1901 .... $600

Colganis Gum, National Vending (Chicago, IL), 1902 .... $1,800

Collar Button, Price (Iowa City, IA), 1904 .... $1,500

Taffy Tolu, National Vending (Chicago, IL), 1905 ..... $1,450

Chicago, Coleman (Chicago, IL), 1905 .... $2,400

Gum Machine, Gravity vending (Chicago, IL), 1907 . $2,200

Hilo Gum Climax, Hilo Gum (Chicago, IL), 1907 .... $900

Automatic Cigar, Pope (Chicago, IL), 1908 .... $3,000

Crystalets, Crystal (Columbus, OH), 1908 .... $1,250

Penny Peanut, Griswold (Rock Island, IL), 1910 .... $900

Globe, Advance (Chicago, IL), 1911 .... $600

Columbus Model B, Columbus (Columbus, OH), 1912 $450

Climax 10, Advance (Chicago, IL), 1915 .... $900

Bluebird 1-2-3. Bluebird (Kansas City, MO), 1915 .... $300

Gold Seal, Millard (New York, NY), 1922 .... $150

Match Vender, Krema (Chicago, IL), 1922 .... $350

Rex, Hance (Columbus, OH), 1923 .... $1,000

The National, National (St. Paul, MN), 1924 .... $250

Master, Norris (Columbus, OH), 1924 .... $200

Deluxe, Rowe (Los Angeles, CA), 1928 .... $400

E-Z Baseball, Ad-Lee (Chicago, IL), 1930 .... $700

Wrigley's 5A, Hoff (New York, NY), 1931 .... $300

Empire, D. Robbins (Brooklyn, NY), 1932 .... $450

Model 33, Northwestern (Morris, IL), 1933 .... $175

Model 34, Columbus (Columbus, OH), 1934 .... $225

Merchant, Mills Automatic (Long Island City, NY), 1938 .... $250

Model 33 Penny Back Peanut, Northwestern (Morris, IL), 1937 .... $550

King Jr., Automat Games (Chicago, IL), 1940 .... $150

Sun, Los Angeles (Los Angeles, CA), 1946 .... $25

Silver King, Silver King (Chicago, IL), 1946 .... $100

New Univender, Stoner (Aurora, IL), 1949 .... $150

Park-O-Meter, Magee-Hale (Oklahoma City, OK), 1949 $30

American Postmaster, Dillon (Washington, DC), 1950 ... $65

Adams Gum, Du Grenier (New Haven, CT), 1951 .... $60

Coca-Cola Model V-81, Vendo (Kansas City, MO), 1955 .... $1,500

Acorn 300, Oak (Los Angeles, CA), 1955 .... $35

Candy Univender, Stoner (Aurora, IL), 1957 .... $160

Coca-Cola Model V-56, Vendo (Kansas City, MO), 1958 .... $1,200

Coca-Cola Model C-51, cavalier (Chattanooga, TN), 1958 .... $600

Model 74 U-Select-T, Coan (Madison, WI), 1958 .... $85

Model P, Schermack (Detroit, MI), 1960 .... $50

Duncan Meter, Duncan (Elk Grove Village, IL), 1980 ..... $25

Jukeboxes

1942 Wurlitzer 950 .... $16,000-$30,000

1941 Wurlitzer 850A .... $14,000-$25,000

1942 Rock–ola Premier .... $12,000-$25,000

1941 Wurlitzer 850 .... $12,000-$23,000

1941-42 Rock–Ola Spectravox .... $8,000-$20,000

1940-41 AMI Singing Towers .... $4,000-$14,000

1941 Wurlitzer 81 Countertop .... $6,000-$12,000

1942 Rock-Ola Commando .... $3,000-$12,000

1946-47 Wurlitzer 1015 .... $5,000-$10,000

1940 Seeburg Concert Master .... $ 4,000-$9,000

Model M, Edison Manufacturing (Orange, NY), 1896 .... $15,000

Type AS Graphophone, Columbia (New York, NY), 1897 .... $4,750

Type BS Eagle Graphophone, Columbia (New York, NY), 1898 .... $2,750

ACME, Edison Manufacturing (Orange, NY), 1906 . $12,000

Cail-O-Phone, Caille Bros. (Detroit, MI), 1908 .... $3,500

Hexaphone, Regina (Rahway, NJ), 1909 .... $7,000

Gabwel Automatic Entertainer, Gabel (Chicago, IL), 1917 .... $4,500

1929 Automatic Entertainer, Gabel (Chicago, IL), 1929 .... $3,800

Electramuse Super-Tone, Holcomb & Hoke (Indianapolis, IN), 1929 .... $3,500

Model 3 Junior, Capehart (Fort Wayne, IN), 1931 ...... $1,200

Ampliphone, Wilcox (Chicago, IL), 1932 .... $2,600

Simplex Model 10, Wurlitzer (North Tonawanda, NY), 1933 .... $2,200

Selectophone, Seeburg (Chicago, IL), 1934 .... $1,600

Dance Master, Mills (Chicago, IL), 1934 .... $450

Symphonola Model B, Seeburg (Chicago, IL), 1936 .. $2,800

Junior Elite, Gabel (Chicago, IL), 1936 .... $1,800

Zephyr, Mills (Chicago, IL), 1938 .... $850

Streamliner, AMI (Grand Rapids, MI), 1938 .... $3,400

Standard 20, Rock-Ola (Chicago, IL), 1939 .... $2,200

616 Illuminated Front, Jacobs Novelty (Stevens Point, WI) 1939, ... $2,200

1939 Singing Towers, AMI (Grand Rapids, MI), 1939 $6,000

Model 61, Wurlitzer (North Tonawanda, NY), 1939 ... $4,000

Model 700, Wurlitzer (North Tonawanda, NY), 1940 . $4,500

Model 800, Wurlitzer (North Tonawanda, NY), 1940 . $4,800

1940 Singing Towers, AMI (Grand Rapids, MI), 1940 $6,000

Symphonola Concert Master, Seeburg (Chicago, IL), 1940 .... $6,000

Model 1401 Master, Rock-Ola (Chicago, IL), 1940 ... $2,600

Model 750 Victory, Wurlitzer (North Tonawanda, NY), 1941 .... $6,500

Model 780 Colonial, Wurlitzer (North Tonawanda, NY), 1941 .... $3,500

Model 850 Super Deluxe Victory, Wurlitzer (North Tonawanda, NY), 1941 .... $9,500

Model 950 Victory, Wurlitzer (North Tonawanda, NY), 1941 .... $24,000

Model 1415 Commando, Rock-Ola (Chicago, IL), 1942 .... $8,500

Coronet, Aireon (Kansas City, KS), 1946 .... $1,400

1015, Wurlitzer (North Tonawanda, NY), 1946 .... $8,500

Constellation, Mills (Chicago, IL), 1947 .... $1,200

Fiesta, Aireon (Kansas City, KS), 1947 .... $1,000

Model 1426, Rock-Ola (Chicago, IL), 1947 .... $4,500

Model 1100, Wurlitzer (North Tonawanda, NY), 1947 .... $4,200

P-147 Symphonola, Seeburg (Chicago, IL), 1947 .... $2,400

Constellation, H.C. Evans (Chicago, IL), 1948 .... $1,000

Model C, AMI (Grand Rapids, MI), 1949 .... $2,400

S-45, Ristaucrat (Kaukauna, WI), 1951 .... $450

M-100C Select-O-Matic, Seeburg (Chicago, IL), 1952 $2,500

Model 1600 Deluxe, Wurlitzer (North Tonawanda, NY), 1953 .... $2,600

Model E, AMI (Grand Rapids, MI), 1953 .... $1,600

Model F, AMI (Grand Rapids, MI), 1954 .... $1,200

Model H, AMI (Grand Rapids, MI), 1957 .... $1,600

KD-100 SELECT-0-MATIC, Seeburg (Chicago, IL), 1957 .... $2,500

Model 2400, Wurlitzer (North Tonawanda, NY), 1960 .. $600

Model 2500 Stereo, Wurlitzer (North Tonawanda, NY), 1961 .... $1,200

LPC-1 Select-O-Matic, Seeburg (Chicago, IL), 1962 .... $750

Model 3000, Wurlitzer (North Tonawanda, NY), 1966 .. $550

Model 3100 Americana, Wurlitzer (North Tonawanda, NY), 1967 .... $450

Model 1050 Nostalgia, Wurlitzer (North Tonawanda, NY), 1973 .... $3,000

SPS2 Matador, Seeburg (Chicago, IL), 1973 .... $650

SMC-1 Disco, Seeburg (Chicago, IL), 1978 .... $650

Pinball Machines

Gottlieb Golden Arrow; 1966 .... $275-$500

Gottlieb Gold Star; oak rail; flipper; 1954 .... $275-$550

Gottlieb Big Broadcast; radio theme; 1933 .... $300-$600

Gottlieb Whizz Bang; 1932 .... $300-$600

Groetchen Pike's Peak; ballbearing climb incline; 1940 .... $150-$300

Keeney's League Leader; baseball theme; 1951 ... $275-$550

Mills Owl; slot machine style; 1942 .... $350-$700

Rockola World Series; metal ball players; 1937 . $700-$1,400

Williams King of Swat; wood trim; flipper; 1954 . $275-$550

Little Manhattan, Caille-Schiemer (Detroit, MI), 1901 .. $700

Log Cabin, Caille Bros. (Detroit, MI), 1904 .... $1,600

Whiffle, Automatic Industries (Youngstown, OH), 1931 $350

Baffle Ball, Gottlieb (Chicago, IL), 1931 .... $300

Ballyhoo, Bally (Chicago, IL), 1932 .... $350

Favorite, Buckley (Chicago, IL), 1932 .... $250

Five Star Final, Gottlieb (Chicago, IL), 1932 .... $300

Wings, Rock-Ola (Chicago, IL), 1933 .... $350

Jig Saw, Rock-Ola (Chicago, IL), 1933 .... $1,600

Base Ball, Genco (Chicago, IL), TBD 1934 .... $500

Contact, Pacific (Los Angeles, CA), 1934 .... $350

World's Series, Rock-Ola (Chicago, IL), 1934 .... $1,200

Army/Navy, Rock-Ola (Chicago, IL), 1934 .... $550

Lite-A-Line, Pacific (Chicago, IL), 1934 .... $450

Sportsman, Jennings (Chicago, IL), 1935 .... $750

Jumbo, Bally (Chicago, IL), 1935 .... $450

Cheer Leader, Genco (Chicago, IL), 1935 .... $300

Bumper, Bally (Chicago, IL), 1937 .... $375

Double Feature, Gottlieb (Chicago, IL), 1937 .... $400

Electric Scoreboard, Gottlieb (Chicago, IL), 1937 .... $500

One-Two-Three, Mills (Chicago, IL), 1938 .... $650

Fleet, Bally (Chicago, IL), 1940 .... $300

Washington, Caille Bros. (Detroit, MI), 1905 .... $8,500

Weatherproof Talking Scale, United Vending (Cleveland, OH), 1908 .... $9,000

Aristocrat, Caille Bros. (Detroit, MI), 1916 .... $1,250

1918 Accurate Scale, Mills (Chicago, IL), 1917 .... $1,600

Aristocrat (Peerless), Caille Bros. (Detroit, MI), 1919 $1,250

Aristocrat Deluxe, Caille Bros. (Detroit, MI), 1921 .... $2,500

National Model 103, National Novelty (St. Paul, MN), 1922 .... $1,600

President, Watling (Chicago, IL), 1928 .... $1,900

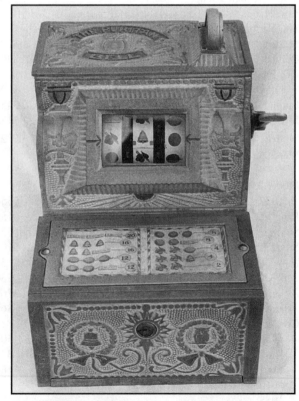

Five-cent slot machine, 9-1/8" x 7-3/8" x 10-1/4", "The Puritan Bell."

Senator, Watling (Chicago, IL), 1928 .... $1,700
Normandy Chimes, National Automatic (St. Paul,
    MN), 1929 .... $1,800
Ideal Scale, Ideal (Los Angeles, CA), 1929 .... $225
Honest Weight, Columbia Scale (New York, NY), 1930 $1,250
Moderne, Caille Motor (Detroit, MI), 1930 .... $300
Featuristic, Rock-Ola (Chicago, IL), 1930 .... $200
Little Giant, Camco (New York, NY), 1931 .... $400
Tom Thumb, Watling (Chicago, IL), 1931 .... $400
Bantam, Pace (Chicago, IL), 1931 .... $250
Modern Scale w/ Health Chart, Mills (Chicago, IL),
    1931 .... $250
Improved Tom Thumb, Watling (Chicago, IL), 1935 ..... $300
Accurate Scale, A. S. L. Sales (Dayton, OH), 1936 .... $120
Personal Weigher (P. W.), Hamilton (Toledo, OH), 1936 $125
Fortune Model 300, American Scale (Washington, DC),
    1937 .... $250
Guess-Er, Kirk (Chicago, IL), 1938 .... $800
Personal Scale, Public Scale (Chicago, IL), 1939 .... $150
Model 400, American Scale (Washington, DC), 1947 ... $100
Fortune Model 400, Watling (Chicago, IL), 1948 .... $450
Mr. Peanut, Hamilton (Toledo, OH), 1949 .... $15,000
Model 403, American Scale (Washington, DC), 1950 ... $120
Super Horoscope, Watling (Chicago, IL), 1957 .... $600
Combination Model 530, American Scale
    (Washington, DC), 1968 .... $100

Slot Machines

*Prices listed are for complete operating machines in Good
condition with all award and directions paper in place as well as
decals and other unique machine graphics.*

Slot Machine No. 4, Lighton (Syracuse, NY), 1893 ... $7,500
Nonpariel, Nonpariel Novelty (New Haven, CT), 1893 $3,500
Pyramid Banker, Maley (Cincinnati, OH), 1893 .... $3,200
Three Jackpot, Clawson (Newark, NJ), 1893 .... $2,000
3 Jackpot, Amusement Machine (New York, NY),
    1893 .... $1,800
Klondyke, Mills (Chicago, IL), 1897 .... $3,700
Columbia, Paupa & Hochriem (Chicago, IL), 1897 .... $3,500
Sun Check, Cowper (Chicago, IL), 1897 .... $3,000
Little Egypt, Mills (Chicago, IL), 1898 .... $4,200
Oregon, Cowper (Chicago, IL), 1898 .... $7,000
Owl, Mills (Chicago, IL), 1898 .... $6,000
Owl, D. N. Schall (Chicago, IL), 1899 .... $5,500
Uncle Sam, Paupa & Hochriem (Chicago, IL), 1899 .. $3,500
Judge, Mills (Chicago, IL), 1899 .... $6,000
Duplex, Mills (Chicago, IL), 1899 .... $30,000
Dewey, Mills (Chicago, IL), 1899 .... $9,000
Brownie, Mills (Chicago, IL), 1900 .... $2,750
Judge, Berger (Chicago, IL), 1900 .... $5,000
New Century Puck, Caille Bros. (Detroit, MI), 1901 $10,000
Roulette, Mills (Chicago, IL), 1901 .... $35,000
Cricket, Mills (Chicago, IL), 1904 .... $24,000
Liberty Bell, Fey (San Francisco, CA), 1905 .... $100,000
Eclipse, Caille Bros. (Detroit, MI), 1906 .... $11,000
Peerless, Caille Bros. (Detroit, MI), 1907 .... $45,000
Liberty Bell, Mills (Chicago, IL), 1907 .... $8,500

Liberty Bell, Watling (Chicago, IL), 1908 .... $8,500
Liberty Bell, Caille Bros. (Detroit, MI), 1909 .... $9,000
Jefferson, Watling (Chicago, IL), 1909 .... $3,000
1910 Liberty Bell, Mills (Chicago, IL), 1910 .... $7,000
Liberty Bell Gum Vender, Caille Bros. (Detroit, MI),
    1911 .... $11,000
Silver Cup, Caille Bros. (Detroit, MI), 1912 .... $8,500
1915 Operator Bell, Mills (Chicago, IL), 1914 .... $1,450
Operator's Bell, Watling (Chicago, IL), 1919 .... $1,250
Operator's Bell, Jennings (Chicago, IL), 1922 .... $900
1922 Operator Bell, Mills (Chicago, IL), 1922 .... $900
Automatic Counter Vendor, Jennings (Chicago, IL),
    1924 .... $1,000
1925 Operator Bell, Mills (Chicago, IL), 1925 .... $800
1927 Front, Pace (Chicago, IL), 1927 .... $1,250
Today, Jennings (Chicago, IL), 1928 .... $1,200
1928 Front, Pace (Chicago, IL), 1928 .... $1,250
1928 Operator Bell, Pace (Chicago, IL), 1928 .... $1,000
Baby Bell, Watling (Chicago, IL), 1928 .... $1,200
Superior, Caille Bros. (Detroit, MI), 1927 .... $800
Superior Jackpot, Caille Bros. (Detroit, MI), 1928 .... $900
Jackpot, Watling (Chicago, IL), 1929 .... $1,000
Baseball, Jennings (Chicago, IL), 1930 .... $2,400
Bantam Jak-Pot, Pace (Chicago, IL), 1930 .... $950
Trip-L-Jax, A.B.T. (Chicago, IL), 1930 .... $650
Four Jacks, Field (Peoria, IL), 1930 .... $550
Twin Jackpot, Watling (Chicago, IL), 1931 .... $1,100
Silent "War Eagle," Mills (Chicago, IL), 1931 .... $1,650
Silent Golden "Roman Head," Mills (Chicago, IL),
    1932 .... $1,850
Mystery "Blue Front," Mills (Chicago, IL), 1933 .... $950
Little Duke, Jennings (Chicago, IL), 1933 .... $1,400
Extraordinary, Mills (Chicago, IL), 1933 .... $800
Q.T., Mills (Chicago, IL), 1934 .... $1,000
Gooseneck Golden, Superior Confection (Columbus, OH),
    1934 .... $1,600
Escalator Golden, Superior Confection (Columbus, OH),
    1934 .... $1,750
Rol-A-Tor, Watling (Chicago, IL), 1935 .... $2,800
Rol-A-Top, Watling (Chicago, IL), 1935 .... $2,750
Dough Boy, Caille Bros. (Detroit, MI), 1935 .... $500
Races, Superior Confection (Columbus, OH), 1935 ... $5,500
Golf Ball, Jennings (Chicago, IL), 1935 .... $4,500
1935 Paces Races, Pace (Chicago, IL), 1935 .... $7,500
Grand Champion, Seeburg (Chicago, IL), 1935 .... $2,800
Multi-Bell, A. C. Novelty (Detroit, MI), 1936 .... $2,800

Columbia, Groetchen (Chicago, IL), 1936 .... $450
Chief, Jennings (Chicago, IL), 1936 .... $1,000
Rou-Lette, H. C. Evans (Chicago, IL), 1036 .... $3,500
All Star Comet, Pace (Chicago, IL), 1936 .... $1,100
Reliance, Bally (Chicago, IL), 1936 .... $5,000
Bones, Buckley (Chicago, IL), 1936 .... $4,500
Cherry, Mills (Chicago, IL), 1937 .... $1,000
Bonus, Mills (Chicago, IL), 1937 .... $2,200
Kitty, Pace (Chicago, IL), 1937 .... $2,500
Bally Bell, Bally (Chicago, IL), 1938 .... $2,400
Twin Royal, Pace (Chicago, IL), 1938 .... $5,500
Vest Pocket, Mills (Chicago, IL), 1938 .... $250
Paces Races "Red Arrow," Pace (Chicago, IL), 1939 .. $7,000
Bronze Chief, Jennings (Chicago, IL), 1940 .... $1,250
Black Cherry, Mills (Chicago, IL), 1945 .... $900
Golden Falls, Mills (Chicago, IL), 1946 .... $1,000
Standard Chief, Jennings (Chicago, IL), 1946 .... $1,000
Bonus Super Bell, Keeney (Chicago, IL), 1946 .... $600
Jewel, Mills (Chicago, IL), 1947 .... $1,000
Challenger, Jennings (Chicago, IL), 1947 .... $2,400
Deluxe Draw Bell, Bally (Chicago, IL), 1947 .... $450
Standard Chief Console, Jennings (Chicago, IL), 1947 $2,400
21 "Hightop," Mills (Chicago, IL), 1949 .... $1,000
Sun Chief, Jennings (Chicago, IL), 1950 .... $1,600
Buckaroo, Jennings (Chicago, IL), 1954 .... $2,700
Pointmaker, Buckley (Chicago, IL), 1955 .... $300
Tim-Buc-Too, Games (Chicago, IL), 1958 .... $200
Double Shot, Games (Chicago, IL), 1958 .... $250
Money Honey, Bally (Chicago, IL), 1964 .... $1,400
4-Reel, Baldecchi (Reno, NV), 1967 .... $900
Model M, Mills (Sparks, NV), 1968 .... $750
Model 400, TJM (Jennings), (Elgin, IL), 1979 .... $1,000

Trade Stimulators and Counter Games

Guessing Bank, Winchester (New York, NY), 1878 ... $5,500
Automatic Dice, Automatic Machine (New York, NY),
    1892 .... $1,200
Dice Shaker, Lighton (Syracuse, NY), 1892 .... $3,000
Improved Roulette, Western Automatic
    (Cincinnati, OH), 1894 .... $700
Little Model Card Machine, Sittman & Pitt
    (Brooklyn, NY) 1894, ... $1,800
Vector, Drobisch (Decatur, IL), 1897 .... $1,000
Fairest Wheel, Decatur (Decatur, IL), 1897 .... $650
Advertising Register, Drobisch (Decatur, IL), 1896 .... $1,200
The Bicycle, Sun (Greenfield, OH), 1898 .... $3,000
Perfection, Canda (Cincinnati, OH), 1898 .... $650
King Do-Do, Mills (Chicago, IL), 1903 .... $3,200
Wasp, Caille Bros. (Detroit, MI), 1904 .... $3,500
Draw Poker, Foley (Chicago, IL), 1904 .... $4,000
Daisy, Hamilton (Hamilton, OH), 1907 .... $250
Leader, Banner (Philadelphia, PA), 1922 .... $350
Puritan, Mills (Chicago, IL), 1926 .... $600
Try-It, Ad-Lee (Chicago, IL), 1927 .... $300
Pok-O-Reel, Groetchen (Chicago, IL), 1932 .... $400
Card Machine, Jennings (Chicago, IL), 1934 .... $350
21 Vender, Groetchen (Chicago, IL), 1934 .... $450

Cigarette, Superior Confection (Columbus, OH), 1935 . $450
Lite-A-Pax, Bally (Chicago, IL), 1937 .... $350
Target Practice, Hance (Columbus, OH), 1923 .... $1,200
Metal Stamper, Harvard (Cleveland, OH), 1923 .... $2,000
Information, Information Vending (Des Moines, IA),
    1925 .... $450
Ten Pin, Gatter (Philadelphia, PA), 1926 .... $500
Play Football, Chester Pollard (New York, NY), 1926 $1,600
Bag Puncher, Mills (Chicago, IL), 1926 .... $2,400
All Steel Mutoscope, Intl. Mutoscope (New York, NY),
    1926 .... $1,200
Target Skill, A.B.T. (Chicago, IL), 1926 .... $350
Striking Clock, Exhibit Supply (Chicago, IL), 1927 ... $2,000
Princess Doraldina, Doraldina (Rochester, NY),
    1928 .... $12,000
Grip Tester, Edwards (Fort Worth, TX), 1929 .... $200
Play Derby, Chester Pollard (New York, NY), 1929 ... $3,500
Vest Pocket Basketball, Peo (Rochester, NY), 1929 ...... $450
Baseball, Atlas (Chicago, IL), 1931 .... $500
Barn Yard Golf, Peo (Rochester, NY), 1931 .... $300
20th Century, Exhibit Supply (Chicago, IL), 1933 ...... $2,750
1937 World's Series, Rock-ola (Chicago, IL), 1937 .... $6,500
1938 Love Meter, Exhibit Supply (Chicago, IL), 1938 .. $300
Ask Me Another, Exhibit Supply (Chicago, IL), 1939 ... $300
Ten Pins, H. C. Evans (Chicago, IL), TBD $3,500
Chicken Sam, Seeburg (Chicago, IL), 1939 .... $700
Crystal Palace, Exhibit Supply (Chicago, IL), 1939 ... $1,800
Air Raider, Keeney (Chicago, IL), 1940 .... $450
Improved Deluxe Grip Scale. Gottlieb (Chicago, IL),
    1946 .... $95
1946 Challenger, A.B.T. (Chicago, IL), 1946 .... $300
Deluxe Athletic Scale, Mercury (Detroit, MI), 1947 .... $65
Bat-A-Ball Junior, Munves (New York, NY), 1947 .... $650
Slugger, Marvel (Chicago, IL), 1948 .... $450
10th Inning, United (Chicago, IL), 1949 .... $500
Bowling League, Genco (Chicago, IL), 1949 .... $250
Mercury Athletic Scale, Great Lakes (Flint, MI), 1951 .... $50
Big Broncho, Exhibit Supply (Chicago, IL), 1951 .... $350
Imperial Shuffle Alley, United (Chicago, IL), 1953 .... $250
American Eagle, Daval (Chicago, IL), 1940 .... $300
Imp, Groetchen (Chicago, IL), 1940 .... $150
Cub, Daval (Chicago, IL), 1940 .... $135

TIPS OF THE TRADE

Identifying a Cast-Iron Machine:

Cast metal cabinet trade stimulators, vending and slot machines of the 1898-1915 period are highly desirable collectibles. They can easily be confused with the bronze, cast aluminum and steel fronts made after this period, with the latter often being plated in nickel, copper or chrome. It's the metal underneath that counts. Carry a refrigerator door magnet with you to auctions, shows, flea markets or house sales so you can unobtrusively find out if a cabinet is cast iron. The magnetic attraction goes right through the plating. If the magnet falls off the material it is probably aluminum. But if it sticks it is likely cast iron, or in more modern machines, steel.

COINS

Coin collecting as a hobby probably began shortly after the first coins were produced in Asia Minor about 600-700 B.C. Popular interest in collecting didn't develop, however, until the beginning of the 20th century.

Interest in collecting U.S. coins has grown significantly since World War II. Several valuable minting varieties, such as the hub-doubled 1955 and 1972 cents (more commonly called doubled die cents, on which the dates appear to be out of focus) drew many new collectors into the hobby. They joined the ranks of true coin collectors while checking their pocket change for these rare error coins, of which only a handful were produced.

General Guidelines: If your coin is uncirculated, has very little wear or is dated before the 1960s, it is probably more valuable than newer or heavily-worn coins.

The mint mark on a coin can make a difference in its value. Each mint that strikes coins uses a letter to identify its coins – P for Philadelphia (except on the cents), S for San Francisco, D for Denver, W for West Point. Older mints included Carson City (CC), New Orleans (O), Dahlonega (D) and Charlotte (C), the latter two used only on gold coins in the 1800s.

Besides the date and mint mark, the key element that determines the value of a coin is the grade. U.S. coins are graded on a 70-point scale to indicate the amount of wear, from mint condition (MS) down to a badly worn piece with nearly unrecognizable denomination and date (G-4).

The higher the grade number, the higher the value. In the MS-60 to MS-70 range, values may jump by hundreds, even thousands, of dollars for each grade point. Many higher value coins are graded and encased (slabbed) and labeled by a certified grading service. The grade is only valid if the sealed case is intact, so don't break it unless you want to pay to have the coin regraded.

Mintage figures are another key element in determining a coin's value. In general, the fewer of a certain coin made, the more likely it is to be valuable. Mintage figures can be found in any coin periodicals or books.

Gold coins: All gold coins are worth at least the value of the bullion (raw metal) they contain. A U.S. $20 gold piece (1849-1933) contains almost an ounce of gold, currently worth about $380.

Silver coins: From 1890-1964 dimes, quarters, half-dollars and dollars were made of 90 percent silver. If they've been circulated, these silver coins are worth about three times their face value.

Dollars: Silver dollars minted between 1878 and 1935 are worth between $5 and $10 each; Eisenhower and Susan B. Anthony dollars are worth a dollar.

Kennedy halves: Like the older silver coins, 1964 Kennedy halves are 90 percent silver; those dated 1965 to 1970 are 40 percent silver and are worth about 60 to 65 cents each. Most coins in circulation today are post-1964; half dollars and quarters dated later than 1940 are worth only their bullion value.

Franklin halves: Some Franklin halves (1949-S, 1953, 1955) are worth more, but unless the coins are in exceptional condition, the silver content rules the value.

Bicentennial: Bicentennial coins (quarters, half dollars and dollars) are worth face value.

Mercury dimes: Mercury dimes have a winged liberty on the back and are worth 30 cents.

Buffalo nickels: Produced from 1913-1938, Buffalo nickels are often badly worn. A Buffalo nickel with the full date still showing is worth between 30 and 40 cents. If the date is completely worn away or only has one or two digits showing, the nickel is worth face value or can be sold for 20 cents to be used in jewelry making.

"V" nickels: Produced from 1883-1913, "V" (Roman numeral "five") nickels are usually worn flat and bring one dollar each.

Indian head cents: Indian head cents (1859-1909) run from $1 for the later dates, up to $2 or so for those dated in the 1880s and 1890s. Indian Head cents and "V" nickels with earlier dates are worth more.

Wheat-back cents: There are a few key dates of wheat-back cents worth saving, but the majority of them are worth only two cents. The 1909-S, 1914-D and 1931-S are valued at $30 and up. In all conditions, the 1909-S VDB and 1922 wheat cents are worth from $300 to $600.

Lincoln cents: In 1943 Lincoln cents were made of zinc-coated steel, giving them a silver coloring similar to a nickel. Often mistakenly thought to be valuable, they are very plentiful and often corroded, and are only worth two cents. Newer Lincoln cents with the memorial reverse (1959 to present) have only a few "keepers," which require specialized knowledge to spot.

1981 United States proof set.

Shipping envelopes and packaging for most modern U.S. coins have little or no effect on a coin's value. For some older coins — especially commemoratives — the original shipping envelopes bring a premium, but they have become collectibles in their own right, often bought and sold without the original coin.

Clubs/Associations

•American Numismatic Association
818 N. Cascade Ave., Colorado Springs, CO 80903-3279
719-632-2646

•American Numismatic Society
Broadway at 155th St., New York, NY 10052
212-234-3130

•Canadian Numismatic Association
P.O. Box 226, Barrie, Ontario, Canada L4M 4T2
705-737-0845

PROOF SETS, MINT SETS AND COMMEMORATIVE COINS

With the exception of circulating commemoratives — produced from 1892-1957 — these three types of coins are uncirculated and were made specifically for coin collectors.

Proof set: One coin of each denomination minted for a specific year, specially struck to have a sharper (sometimes frosted) image on a clearer background (which is often mirrored). Proof sets dated from 1930 to 1959 should be checked in a guide to determine the value. Proof sets from 1960 and later are worth from $5-$10.

Mint set: One uncirculated coin of each denomination from each mint (P for Philadelphia or D for Denver) for a specific year, struck to regular standards and then packaged by the mint for collectors. Mint sets from 1947 through 1958 contain two examples of each coin mounted in cardboard holders that caused the coins to tarnish. Beginning in 1959, the sets were packaged in sealed Pliofilm packets and include only one specimen of each non-commemorative coin authorized for that year. The 1965 sets were packaged in Pliofilm, the '66 and '67 sets in plastic cases. Mint sets produced prior to 1962 should be checked in a guide for value. Mint sets from 1962 on are worth $4.

Commemorative coins (non-circulating): Produced since 1982 to commemorate specific events or charities, these coins are not valid U.S. currency. Non-circulating commemoratives are not very valuable, and usually will decrease in value from issue price. They are most profitably purchased on the secondary market; check a guide to determine values.

Commemorative coins (circulating): Produced from 1892-1954, these coins were meant to be used as U.S. currency; most are very common. If the coin has been circulated, value is a very low multiple of face value. Uncirculated coins of this variety should be checked in a guide to determine value.

Bicentennial quarter.

HOT TIPS!

- Never clean your coins. Cleaning or polishing can reduce collector value by 50 percent or more. Removing loose dirt and grease with a weak solution of dish soap (not detergent) is safe for most circulated silver and nickel coins, but not for uncirculated or proof coins, especially copper alloy coins.

- Ask any dealer or shop owner you are considering doing business with if they are a member of the Professional Numismatists Guild (PNG). This will help ensure you are dealing with a reputable professional.

- Before disposing of any collection, make sure you know what each coin is worth. If you decide to become a collector, a reputable local coin dealer is a good place to get advice and guidance in getting started. Shop different dealers for the best offer on your coins.

- Don't buy coins on impulse until you are thoroughly familiar with them. While you may get a bargain, you are much more likely to pay too much for coins that may have been cleaned or are otherwise in poor condition.

- Coin prices don't correspond directly to their numerical grade. An MS-70 coin is not automatically 3-1/2 times the value of a Fine-20 coin.

VALUE LINE

Here are some typical prices for several rarer coins in grades ranging from well worn (G-4) to uncirculated and near perfect (MS-65). The amount of wear makes a substantial difference.

1877 1 Cent	$425, $6,100
1880 Nickel	$275, $4,000
1916-D Dime	$470, $11,350
1932-S Quarter	$28, $1,800
1921-D Half	$98, $11,000
1928 Peace Dollar	$65, $2,550

Commemoratives (1892-1954)
(uncirculated MS-63 condition)
Quarter

1893, Isabella	$525

Half dollars

1921, Alabama 2X2	$580
1921, Alabama	$450
1936, Albany	$210
1937, Antietam	$420
1935, Arkansas PDS set	$245
1936, Arkansas PDS set	$245
1937, Arkansas PDS set	$290
1938, Arkansas PDS set	$425
1939, Arkansas PDS set	$825
Arkansas type coin	$68
1936, Bay Bridge	$110
1934, Boone	$85
1935, Boone PDS set w/ 1934	$730

Franklin half dollar.

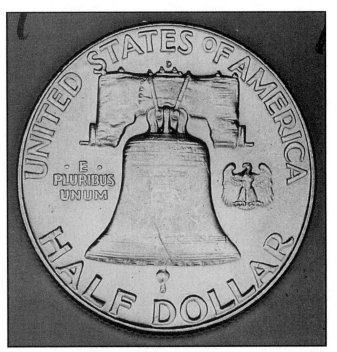

Franklin half dollar.

1935, Boone PDS set	$255
1936, Boone PDS set	$255
1937, Boone PDS set	$575
1938, Boone PDS set	$825
Boone type coin	$75
1936, Bridgeport	$110
1925S, California Jubilee	$155
1936, Cincinnati PDS set	$700
1936, Cincinnati type coin	$230
1936, Cleveland, Great Lakes	$66
1936, Columbia PDS set	$520
1936, Columbia type coin	$160
1892, Columbian Expo	$80
1893, Columbian Expo	$75
1935, Connecticut	$195
1936, Delaware	$215
1936, Elgin	$170
1936, Gettysburg	$270
1922, Grant with star	$1,450
1922, Grant	$155
1928, Hawaiian,	$1,700
1935, Hudson	$495
1924, Huguenot-Walloon	$100
1918, Lincoln-Illinois	$80

1946, Iowa	$75
1925, Lexington-Concord	$95
1936, Long Island	$68
1936, Lynchburg	$155
1920, Maine	$150
1934, Maryland	$130
1921, Missouri two-star	$870
1921, Missouri	$595
1923S, Monroe	$110
1938, New Rochelle	$275
1936, Norfolk	$350
1926, Oregon	$110
1926S, Oregon	$110
1928, Oregon	$170
1933D, Oregon	$255
1934D, Oregon	$160
1936, Oregon	$120
1936S, Oregon	$150
1937D, Oregon	$140
1938, Oregon PDS set	$600
1939, Oregon PDS set	$1,200
Oregon type coin	$110
1915S, Panama-Pacific	$610
1920, Pilgrim	$77
1921, Pilgrim	$140
1936, Rhode Island PDS set	$225
1936, Rhode Island type coin	$75
1937, Roanoke	$175
1936, Robinson-Arkansas	$80
1935S, San Diego	$58
1936D, San Diego	$66
1926, Sesquicentennial	$150
1935, Spanish Trail	$790
1925, Stone Mountain	$46
1934, Texas	$92
1935, Texas PDS set	$290
1936, Texas PDS set	$290
1937, Texas PDS set	$305
1938, Texas PDS set	$730
Texas type coins	$90
1925, Fort Vancouver	$340
1927, Vermont	$155
1946, B.T. Washington PDS set	$47
1947, B.T. Washington PDS set	$73
1948, B.T. Washington PDS set	$105
1949, B.T. Washington PDS set	$205
1950, B.T. Washington PDS set	$105
1951, B.T. Washington PDS set	$130
B.T. Washington type coin	$14
1951, Washington-Carver PDS set	$85
1952, Washington-Carver PDS set	$95
1953, Washington-Carver PDS set	$97
1954, Washington-Carver PDS set	$85
Washington-Carver type coin	$14
1936, Wisconsin	$170
1936, York County	$150

1988 United States proof set.

Silver dollar

1900, Lafayette	$1,400

Gold dollars

1903, Louisiana, Jefferson	$700
1903, Louisiana, McKinley	$650
1904, Lewis and Clark Expo	$1,850
1905, Lewis and Clark Expo	$2,750
1915S, Panama-Pacific Expo	$600
1916, McKinley Memorial	$600
1917, McKinley Memorial	$1,050
1922, Grant Memorial w/o star	$1,600
1922, Grant Memorial w/star	$1,850

Gold $2.50 piece

1915S, Panama-Pacific Expo	$2,750
1926, Philadelphia Sesquicentennial	$585

Gold $50

1915S, Panama-Pacific Expo, round	$37,500
1915S, Panama-Pacific Expo, octagon	$32,000

Proof Sets

1936	$3,800
1937	$2,350
1938	$910
1939	$940
1940	$700
1941	$570
1942 six coins	$620
1942 five coins	$570
1950	$315
1951	$265
1952	$125
1953	$100
1954	$53
1955 box	$53
1955 flat pack	$55
1956	$28
1957	$12
1958	$20
1959	$14
1960 large date	$11
1960 small date	$22
1961	$8
1962	$8
1963	$8
1964	$8
1968S	$5
1968 S no mint mark dime	$7,500
1969S	$5
1970S large date	$11
1970S small date	$59
1970S no mint mark dime	$365
1971S	$5
1971S no mint mark nickel	$645
1972S	$5
1973S	$6
1974S	$6
1075S	$7
1976S three coins	$14

1976S	$7
1977S	$6
1978S	$7
1979S Type I	$6
1979S Type II	$66
1980S	$5
1981S Type I	$6
1981S Type II	$180
1982S	$4
1983S Prestige set	$78
1983S	$5
1983S no mint mark dime	$325
1984S	$24
1984S	$9
1985S	$4
1986S Prestige set	$31
1986S	$14
1987S	$5
1987S Prestige set	$20
1988S	$6
1988S	$25
1989S	$5
1989S Prestige set	$32
1990S	$10
1990S no S 1¢	$1,250
1990S Prestige set	$22
1990S no S 1¢ Prestige set	$1,250
1991S	$18
1991S Prestige set	$57
1992S	$17
1992S Prestige set	$56
1992S Silver	$17
1992S Silver premier	$18
1993S	$24
1993S Prestige set	$53
1993S Silver	$36
1993S Silver premier	$36
1994S	$18
1994S Prestige set	$59
1994S Silver	$34
1994S Silver premier	$36
1995S	$25
1995S Silver	$29
1995S Prestige set	$113
195S Silver premier	$34
1996S	$11
1996S Silver	$22
1996S Prestige set	$135
1996S Silver premier	$35
1997S	$13
1997S Silver	$21
1997S Prestige set	$135
1997S Silver premier	$35

Mint Sets

Values listed are only for those sets packaged and marketed by the U.S. Mint. Sets were not offered in years not listed. Listings for 1965, 1966 and 1967 are for "special mint sets," which were of higher quality than regular mint sets and were prooflike. The 1970 large-date and small-date varieties are distinguished by the size of the date on the cent. The 1976 three-piece set contains the quarter, half dollar and dollar with the Bicentennial design. The 1971 and 1972 sets do not include a dollar coin; the 1979 set does not include an S-mint marked dollar.

1947	$565
1948	$3
1949	$365
1951	$350
1952	$265
1953	$215
1954	$100
1955	$73
1956	$60
1957	$94
1958	$78
1959	$13
1960	$19
1961	$14
1962	$9
1963	$9
1964	$9
1965 SMS*	$4
1966 SMS*	$4
1967 SMS*	$6
1968	$3
1969	$4
1970 large date	$11
1970 small date	$37
1971	$4
1972	$3
1973	$9
1974	$7
1975	$8
1976 3 coins	$14
1976	$8
1977	$6
1978	$6
1979	$6
1980	$7
1981	$13
1984	$5
1985	$4
1986	$9
1887	$6
1988	$4
1989	$4
1990	$4
1991	$10
1992	$11
1993	$6
1994	$10
1995	$11
1996	$10

1925 Mercury dime.

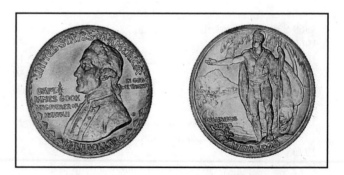

1928 Hawaiian Commemorative half dollar.

COMIC BOOKS

The comic books we know today haven't been around long, compared to many other collectibles. But in a few cases, a single copy can bring tens of thousands of dollars to the lucky owner. In many more cases, comics can bring the delights of a well-told story in an American art form.

Some collectors are only interested in a specific era of comics publishing; some only care about a favorite character, whether he's Uncle Scrooge or Superman; some collect issues with particular themes.

History: In the late 1800s, comic strips began to appear in American newspapers but modern collectors look on Richard Outcault's Yellow Kid as the first major modern comic strip character. He first appeared in 1896.

The evolution from comic strips to comic books took a bit longer. *Famous Funnies #1* (with a cover date of July) went on sale in May 1934, ran for 218 issues over the next 21 years, was the first monthly comic book and sold for 10 cents.

Ten cents was the standard cover price for comics for more than 25 years after that, and millions of children — and adults — bought them regularly. Today, any comic book with a 10-cent cover price is worth a second look, since it was distributed more than 35 years ago. Though superhero characters had appeared in popular fiction — and even comic strips — before, *Action #1* is considered to be the starting point for superhero comics. It was in that issue that Superman made his first appearance.

While many other types of comic books are collected today — and a few of them command prices of more than $1,000 — the most-collected comic books are those devoted to superheroes.

General Guidelines: Whether you're buying or selling comic books, one of the most important factors in determining value is condition. A scuffed, torn "reading copy" will bring only a fraction of the price of a copy of the same issue in the same shape in which it came from the newsstand.

On the other hand, beat-up copies can provide bargains for collectors whose primary focus is reading the story. The same goes for reprints of comics which would otherwise be hard to find. Signs of repeated use as chunks (or even pages) missing; food stains; water damage; multiple folds and wrinkles; a rolled spine (permanently bent by folding back the pages); and tape repairs all reduce the market value of comic books.

Eras: Comic book collectors divide the early history of comics into the Golden Age and the Silver Age. Golden Age indicates the first era of comic book production — which occurred in the 1930s and 1940s. It was a time of incredible creation in the field — when such characters as Superman and Batman first appeared. Silver Age indicates a period of comic book production of slightly less nostalgic luster than that of the Golden Age. It is usually considered to have begun with the publication of the first revival of a 1940s superhero — the appearance of The Flash in *Showcase #4* (Sep-Oct 1956). However, that was a lone appearance at the time, so many collectors focus on when Marvel entered the field — with the publication of *Fantastic Four #1* (1961). Both of these starred characters known today as superheroes.

That's probably the foremost genre of collectible comic book today and brings as a rule the highest prices — especially for "key issues" (in which characters are introduced, a new plot element occurs, new costuming appears and the like). But there are also "funny animal" comics, "noir" crime comics and comics based on movies and TV shows, to name three types.

Publications
Comics Buyer's Guide
700 E. State St.
Iola, WI 54990

Comic Book Checklist and Price Guide, 1961 to Present
700 E. State St.
Iola, WI 54990

Robert M. Overstreet's *The Overstreet Comic Book Price Guide* (Avon Books)

Wonder Woman, Aug. No. 124, D.C. National Comics.

ComicBase 3.0, a CD-ROM database
Human Computing
4509 Thistle Dr.
San Jose, CA 95136

COLLECTOR ALERT

Watch for forgeries and reprints. There aren't many fakes in the field, but what there are can catch the unwary hobbyist.

At this point, there have been too many pitfalls to produce a fake issue of, say, the first appearance of Superman. But given that copies of that issue (Action #1, published in June 1938) can go for more than $170,000, some people have lost money by overpaying for items which are not the original printing. Especially beware of Life magazine-sized copies of old comics; with very rare exceptions, the real originals were roughly the size of today's comics, though with more pages.

Some comic books have been reissued for promotional purposes; check to be sure there's a price printed on the cover and to see if there's no notation anywhere that the item is a later printing.

Action Comics No. 1, June 1938, marks the first appearance of Superman. Graded in Fine condition, this copy sold at a Christie's auction for $63,000.

TIPS OF THE TRADE

• Some collectibles challenge the collector because you have to be a detective to figure out what you've found. But with comic books, it's easy, because they tell you about themselves, and excellent guides are available to fill in the rest. Just look for the little print that carries the copyright information; it's usually in the first few pages of the issue. That gives you the title and issue number and/or date. Then, it's easy to look it up in reference books.

• Comics buffs love to read what they buy. But comics get damaged easily. Folding back a corner of a cover, getting food on an issue or mending a tear with tape can lower its value. If you want to preserve your comic, put it in a plastic bag to protect it when you store it. That way, you can quickly find what you've got without tearing a cover off accidentally, and you can even label the bag for fast identification without damaging the comic book.

VALUE LINE

Values listed are for comic books in Good condition.

Archie first appeared in *Pep #22* (December 1941) $900

Daredevil first appeared in *Daredevil #1* (April 1964) from Marvel $175

The original Flash first appeared in *Flash Comics #1* (January 1940) $5,000

TV character Flash first appeared in comic books in *Showcase #4* and started the so-called Silver Age of Comics (September-October 1956) $2,000

Howard the Duck first appeared in *Fear #19* from Marvel (December 1973) $2

The Hulk first appeared in *Incredible Hulk #1* (May 1962) $1,000

The Mask first appeared in *The Mask #1* from Dark Horse (August 1991) $1

The Maxx first appeared in *Darker Image* (March 1993) from Image $1

The Rocketeer first appeared in *Starslayer #2* from Pacific (April 1982) $2

The Silver Surfer first appeared in *Fantastic Four #48* (March 1966) $75

Spawn first appeared in *Spawn #1* (May 1992) $4

Spider-Man first appeared in *Amazing Fantasy #15* (August 1962) $2,600

A version of Swamp Thing first appeared in *The House of Mystery #195* (October 1971) $2

Teenage Mutant Ninja Turtles #1 was their first (Spring 1984, black and white from Mirage; counterfeits exist, so beware!) $28

Uncle Scrooge first appeared in *Dell Four-Color #178*,
Donald Duck (December 1947) "Christmas on
Bear Mountain" story $110
Wonder Woman first appeared in *All-Star #8*
(December-January 1941-1942) $2,500
The X-Men first appeared in *The X-Men #1*
(September 1963) $525

TV-Related Titles
The Adventures of Bob Hope, 1950-1951 .... $30-$60
1952-1955 .... $10-$15
1956-1961 .... $5-$9
1962-1968 .... $3-$4
The Adventures of Dean Martin & Jerry Lewis/
The Adventures of Jerry Lewis 1952-1953 .... $20-$30
1954-1956 $9- $12
1957-1958 .... $5-$6
1959-1967 .... $2-$4
1968-1971 .... $1
Beverly Hillbillies, 1964-1971 .... $3-$5
Captain Video, 1951 .... $50-$60

Car 54, Where Are You?, 1962-1965 .... $2-$3
Hogan's Heroes, 1966-1967 .... $3-$5
I Love Lucy, 1990-1991 .... $1
I Love Lucy Comics, 1954-1962 .... $10-$20
The Monkees, 1967-1969 .... $4-$6
My Little Margie, 1955-1964 .... $2-$7
Our Gang, 1942 .... $30-$45
1943 .... $25
1943-1944 .... $40-$55
1944-1947 .... $10-$25
1948-1949 .... $3-$5
Little Rascals, 1956-1962 .... $3-$7
Roy Rogers Comics, 1948-1949 .... $10-$18
1949-1951 .... $7-$9
1952-1961 .... $3-$5
Roy Rogers Western Classics, 1989-present .... 50¢
Star Trek, 1968-1969 .... $20-$30
1970-1973 .... $10-$16
1974-1975 .... $5-$8
1976-1979 .... $3

Detective Comics No. 31 is worth $15,000 or more.

A copy of "Superman No. 1" was offered at a Sotheby's sale with an estimate of $15,000.

BETTER TO BE FIRST?

Traditionally, the most pricey issue of a comic book series is the first issue. This is because the first issue customarily marks the start of a series and is, therefore, a turning point. So it is that the reigning champion of comics in terms of price is also one of the most important: Action #1, which contained the first appearance of Superman. Another reason it's high in price is that very few copies survive, since it was created when comics were routinely tossed out. (Fewer than 100 copies may exist today.)

But it's the start of a popular feature that governs the importance of an item. So Detective Comics #1 (March 1937) brings only about half the price of a later issue in its series, #27 (May 1939) — because it was in #27 that Batman made his first appearance.

Detective Comics No. 27, May 1939, sold for $68,500 at a Sotheby's auction. The scarce comic features the debut of Batman.

COLLECTING TIPS

• Learn as much about the field as you can before you invest large sums of money. Some titles do depreciate.

• If you don't enjoy reading comics — if you have no feel for this art form — chances are you'll lose money.

• Comics cost more than when you were a kid. In the 1940s, most were 10 cents. In the early 1960s, they went to 12 cents, then 15 cents, and it's been an upward trend ever since.

• If you decide to maintain a collection, it's well worth the added investment to preserve it. Buy plastic bags designed to protect comic books.

• Handle comics gently. Don't snap them open sharply; the cover may split at the spine.

• Don't fold the cover and early pages back on themselves so that you can conveniently hold the issue for reading; such handling can permanently damage the spine. Don't eat while you read. Don't write your name and address on the issue.

• Don't file copies loosely in comics boxes designed to hold dozens of comics upright because the edges will bend under the weight of the comics.

• Do not lend your comics to someone else.

COOKBOOKS

Offering more than just a glimpse into kitchens of the past, cookbooks are rare sources of information on everyday life in America. To read a cookbook from any era is to discover the varying philosophies that affected daily life; the trends, the fads, the development of scientific rules for healthy diets, even the religious beliefs that found their way into the story of American food.

History: The earliest known cookbook is contained on a group of clay tablets from before 1500 B.C., now held in the Yale University Babylonian collection. The recipes indicate that food preparation included such techniques as braising, boiling and roasting, as well as the use of seasonings and flavorings. Men were usually the head cooks in wealthy houses of the ancients, and so men wrote the cookbooks (the first known cookbook written by a woman did not appear until 1598). The books were written for the upper classes, as the average person could not afford a personal cook nor the exotic, rare ingredients called for by the writers.

American cookbooks have their culinary start in the late 18th century; by 1876 more than 1,000 cookbooks and pamphlets had been printed in the United States. Since the earliest period of white settlement in America, cookbooks have been treasured sources of family history, recipes, medical concoctions and other information important to daily living. The books were carefully handed down from mother to daughters and sometimes daughters-in-law, until generations had enjoyed the wisdom, common sense and humor found in the books' pages.

The 19th century was the first time in the history of American society when women authors dominated the cookbook world. Trends taken up by 19th century cookbooks included cleanliness, careful use of food, healthy cooking, temperance, common sense and dislike of European (particularly French) elements.

General Guidelines: Since cookbooks were used in the kitchen, damage is a common problem. Flour, grease, water, sugar and batter could stain a cookbook, and at the same time led to increased vermin and insect damage. A cookbook in Good condition has indications of use but the pages and cover are intact and the illustrations are present (the dust jacket may be worn or not present at all). Cookbooks with good dust jackets will command a higher price. Slight water stains on the book's cover may not significantly affect its value but the pages, text and illustrations should never have damage of this type.

A famous title on a book does not by itself guarantee high value; heavy emphasis is also placed upon whether a book is from an early or later edition. A first edition of Fannie Farmer's *Boston Cooking-School Cookbook,* for example, may bring 50 times what a much later edition will command.

Few, if any, American cookbooks have been faked. Many times, however, a later edition of a cookbook will be mistakenly offered as a first edition. First editions are not easily identified; modern publishers sometimes note on the copyright page the edition and number of books in print. Some 19th century cookbooks contain introductions in which the author states that a new edition was required, due to popularity. Often the determination can only be made by researching the publishing history of the book and comparing the book to a known first edition. It is sometimes simpler to look for clues that the book is a later edition than to try to prove that it is a first edition.

Many popular cookbooks were issued in a reprint at a much later date. Reprints are worth much less, but fairly easy to spot and exist as important reference books; they provide a window into the tastes of the past without the need to buy a book in poor condition at a high price or to use a rare, fragile book more than necessary. The 19th century edition of "a Boston housekeeper's" *The Cook's Own Book* may command several hundred dollars on the market; the 20th century reproduction may cost $20 or less.

19th Century Cookbooks

Covers were usually plain with embossed titles in solid color inks or gold lettering, although some books published near the turn of the twentieth century had more elaborate treatments, including printed cover designs. Illustrations were often simple line drawings.

Kerr Home Canning Book, 1943, 56 pages, very good condition, $15.

Baker's Coconut Recipes, 1922, 12 pages, VG+ condition, $20.

General Guidelines: Nineteenth century cookbooks in Good condition by popular authors such as Beecher, Hale and Farmer can command $125 or more. Many books from this period received extensive use and they may have loose or missing pages, torn hinges and spines, stains and other marks of wear; all affect a book's value. Few cookbooks, if any, were issued with dust jackets; a 19th century cookbook still in a protective wrapping of that kind would be very valuable.

Charity Cookbooks

Recipes for these books were usually gathered from a limited, specific group like a ladies' club, then printed in book form and sold to raise funds for a special cause. Charity cookbooks received a boost from the fund-raising efforts of relief agencies and ladies' clubs during the Civil War era. Often strewn among the recipes were snippets of poetry, essays on local history, household hints, personal reflections, quotations and prayers.

General Guidelines: Charity cookbooks received a lot of wear, including staining, tears, tape repairs and handwritten annotations, so prices for used books range from $2 to $3 for more recent publications, to more than $100 for rare copies of early examples in Good condition. Late 19th and early 20th century hardcover examples in Good condition can command $25-$50. A charity cookbook will be bought and sold at higher prices closer to its original location.

20th Century Cookbooks

General Guidelines: Appliance cookbooks are an underrated collectible and generally sell for $8-$10, especially the books that accompanied some of the more trendy electric kitchen items, such as hot dog steamers or crepe pans. Television and radio cookbooks were either promotional giveaways from local stations, or they could be purchased. Prices are often affected by the fame of the stars who contributed recipes, but $15 and under is a common value. Diet cookbooks are another overlooked collectible and are generally priced at $8 or less.

Clubs

•Cook Book Collectors Club of America, Inc.
Bob and Jo Ellen Allen
P.O. Box 56, Saint James, MO 65559-0056
314-265-8296

•Cookbooks 'N Things
Betty Gabbert
HCR 33 Box 58, Compton, AR 72624
501-420-3418

VALUE LINE

Alice B. Toklas Cook Book Toklas, Alice; Harper and
   Brothers, 1954 .... $55
American Cookery Simmons, Amelia; Albany, NY, 1804,
   third edition $4,000
American Heritage Cookbook and Illustrated History
   Bullock, Helen D.; American Heritage Magazine, 1964, 2
   vols., illustrated, first edition $55
*American Practical Cookery Book, A Practical
   Housekeeper* John E. Potter and Co., 1859, illustrated $65
American Soda Book, The American Soda Fountain Co.,
   1912, illustrated $45
America's Charitable Cooks Cook, Margaret; 1971,
   illustrated $50
Apicius: Cooking and Dining in Imperial Rome Vehling,
   Joseph; 1936, numbered, limited edition $500
Apples of New York Beach, S.A.; Dept. of Agriculture,
   State of New York, 1905: 2 vols., illustrated $125
Art of Confectionery J.E. Tilton and Comp., 1866, ... $200
Art of Entertaining, The Sherwood, M.E.W.; Dodd,
   Mead & Co., 1892, fine condition $35
Bachelor's Cupboard, A Phillips, A.; Luce Co., 1906 ...... $35
Baker's Coconut Recipes 1922 .... $20
Baker's Dot Chocolate four page foldout, very good
   condition $4

Ballet Cook Book, The LeClerq, Tanaquil; Stein and Day, 1966, illustrated $50

Barry's Fruit Garden Barry, P.; Orange Judd Co., 1890, illustrated $35

Belgian Relief Cook Book Belgian Relief Committee, 1915, signed recipes, celebrity recipes $45

Best in American Cooking, The Paddleford, Clementine; Charles Scribner's Sons, 1970 .... $25

Best of the Bake-Off Collection: Pillsbury's Best 1,000 Recipes Pillsbury, Ann; Consolidated Book Publishers, 1959, illustrated, signed recipes $45

Better Homes and Gardens Golden Treasury of Cooking Meredith Corp., 1973, illustrated $20

Better Homes and Gardens Good Food on a Budget Meredith Corp., 1971, illustrated $8

Better Homes and Gardens Heritage Cook Book Meredith Corp., 1975, illustrated, first edition $40

Better Homes and Gardens Junior Cook Book Meredith Corp., 1955, illustrated $15

Better Homes and Gardens New Cookbook Meredith Publishing, 1953, very good, first edition $25

Betty Crocker's Cake and Frosting Mix Cookbook Golden Press, 1966, illustrated, first edition $10

Betty Crocker's Dinner for Two Cookbook Golden Press, NY, 1973, illustrated, first edition $10

Betty Crocker's Kitchen Garden Campbell, M.; Scribner's Sons, 1971, illustrated $12.50

Betty Crocker's New Boys and Girls Cookbook Golden Press, 1965, illustrated, first edition $22.50

Betty Crocker's Picture Cook Book McGraw Hill Book Co., 1950, illustrated, first edition .... $48; 1956, illustrated $35

Bibliography of American Cookery Books, 1742-1860 Lowenstein, Eleanor; American Antiquarian Society, Worcester, MA $50

Book of Entertainments and Frolics for All Occasions Dawson, Mary, and Telford, Emma; David McKay, 1911, illustrated $15

Borden's Eagle Brand Magic Recipes, 1946, very good condition $5

Boston Cooking School Cook Book, The Farmer, Fannie Merritt; Little, Brown & Co., 1906, illustrated $25

Brown Derby Cookbook Doubleday Co., 1949, illustrated $30

Cape Cod Cook Book Gruver, Suzanne; Boston, 1936 .... $50

Carolina Housewife, The Rutledge, Sarah; Babcock & Co., 1847 .... $125

Carolina Housewife, The (1847) (Reprint) Rutledge, Sarah; Univ. of S. Carolina Press, 1987 .... $12

Child Life Cook Book Judson, Claire Ingram; Rand McNally and Co., 1926, illustrated $45

Chop Sticks State Street Methodist Episcopal Church, Troy, NY, 1883, signed recipes, local ads $35

Common Sense in the Household Harland, Marion; Scribner, Armstrong & Co., 1872 .... $70

Compleat Housewife, The (Fifth edition) Smith, Eliza; L.S. and P., London, 1732 .... $650

Compleat Housewife, The (1753) (Reprint) Smith, Eliza; L.S. and P., London, 1973 .... $25

Congressional Club Cook Book, The The Congressional Club, Wash., DC, 1965, signed by senator, ... $30; 1927, first edition $75

Cook's Guide, The Francatelli, Charles Elme; Richard Bentley and Son, London, 1877, fair condition $60

Cook's Oracle, The Kitchener, William; Monroe and Francis, 1822, first American edition $175

Cook's Own Book, The Lee, Mrs. N.K.M.; Oliver Felt, 1865, ... $165

Cook's Own Book, The (1832) (Reprint) Lee, Mrs. N.K.M.; Arno Press, 1972 .... $15

Cross Creek Cookery Rawlings, Marjorie Kinnan; Charles Scribner's Sons, 1942 .... $55

Culinary American Brown, Cora and Bob; Bobrich Library, 1961 .... $50

Daily New Food, A Ladies of St. Paul's Church, 1885, illustrated, signed recipes, local ads $45

Dr. Chase's Recipes Chase, A.W.; R.A. Beal, 1870, illustrated, 6th edition $45

Early American Inns and Taverns Lathrop, Elise; Tudor Publishing Co., 1935, illustrated, first edition in slipcase $55

Elsie's Cook Book Elsie the Cow; Wheelwright, 1952, illustrated, first edition $17.50

Encyclopedia of Practical Gastronomy Ali-Bab (E. Benson, trans.); McGraw Hill Book Co., 1974, first American edition $40

Epicurean, The Ranhofer, Charles; 1894, lavishly illustrated, first edition $275

Epicurean, The Ranhofer, Charles; John Wiley Publisher, 1920 edition $200

Experienced English Housekeeper Raffald, Elizabeth; London, 1776, illustrated $150

Famous Old Receipts Smith, Jacqueline; John Winston Co., 1908 .... $45

Fannie Farmer Junior Cook Book, The Perkins, Wilma Lord; Little, Brown and Co., 1942, first edition $15

Fifty Years in a Maryland Kitchen Howard, Mrs. B.C.; J.B. Lippincott, 1873 .... $65

Fifty Wonderful Ways to Use Cottage Cheese, American Dairy Association, fine condition $2

Fireside Cookbook, The Beard, James; Simon and Schuster, 1949, illustrated $30

First Dutch Reformed Cook Book Pompton Plains, NJ, 1889, fair condition $20

Food and Finesse: The Bride's Bible Charpentier, Henri; 1945, signed and numbered by author $125

Freezing Prepared or Precooked Foods 1954, very good condition $3

French Chef Cookbook Child, Julia; Alfred Knopf, 1968 .... $17.50

Gala Day Luncheons Burrell, Caroline B.; Dodd, Mead & Co., 1901, illustrated $35

Gastronomical Me Fisher, M.F.K.; Duell, Sloane and Pearce, 1943, first edition $40

Gems of the Household Northrop, Henry; A.B. Kuhlman and Co., 1893, illustrated $35

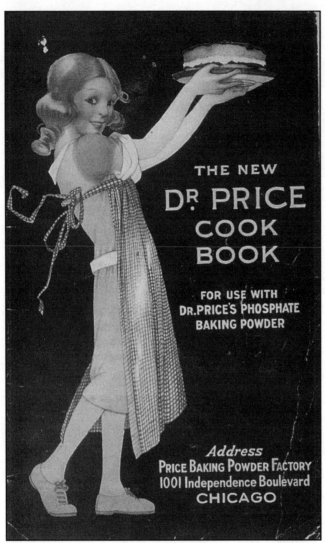

The New Dr. Price Cook Book, 1921, 49 pages, good condition, $8.

General Foods Kitchens Cookbook, The 1959, very good condition $9

Gentleman's Companion: Exotic Cookery and Drink Baker, Charles; Crown Publishers, 1946 .... $45

Gone with the Wind Cook Book Pebeco Toothpaste, ca. 1939, illustrated $35

Goodholme's Domestic Cyclopaedia of Practical Information Goodholme, Todd; Scribner's and Sons, 1889, illustrated $35

Great Dinners from Life Graves, Eleanor; Time-Life Books, 1969, illustrated $35

Hearthstone, The Holloway, Laura; L.P. Miller, 1888, very good condition, illustrated $45

History of a Mouthful of Bread Mace, Jean; Harper & Brothers, 1871 .... $65

Home Maker Magazine, Vol. 1, The Hardland, Marion, editor; 1888-89, illustrated $45

Horizon Cookbook Hale, William; American Heritage Publishing Co., 1968, illustrated $35

Hotel St. Francis Cook Book, The Hirtzler, Victor; Hotel Monthly Press, 1919, illustrated $100

House Servant's Directory Roberts, Robert; 1827 ...... $1,200

How to Win Compliments for Your Cooking—The Wesson Oil & Snowdrift Cookbook 1950, very good condition $6.50

Inside History of the White House Willets, Gilson; Christian Herald, 1908, illustrations, kitchen lore $20

It's Fun to Try New Recipes Mary Ellis Ames, Pillsbury, no. 10 in a series, three page foldout, very good condition . $2

James Beard's American Cookery Beard, James; Little, Brown and Co., 1972, first edition $35

James Beard's Theory & Practice of Good Cooking Beard, James; 1977, illustrated $20

Joy of Cooking, The Rombauer, Irma; 1931, first edition $1,000

Joy of Cooking, The Rombauer, Irma; Bobbs Merrill, 1941 .... $35

Julia Child and Company Child, Julia; Alfred Knopf, 1979, illustrated $15

Julia Child and More Company Child, Julia; Alfred Knopf, 1979, illustrated $15

Kerr Home Canning Book, 1943; very good condition $15

Knox Gelatine Salads, Desserts, Pies, Candies; 1943, very good condition $6

La Cuisine Creole Hearn, Lafcadio; F.F. Hansell and Brother, 1885, second edition $35

Ladies' Book of New Cookery Hale, Sarah J.; H. Long and Brother, 1852, illustrated $65

Lowney's Cook Book Howard, Maria; Walter M. Lowney Co., 1907, illustrated $20

Magic and Husbandry Burdick, Lewis Dayton; Otseningo Publishing Co., 1905 .... $35

Manners and Social Usages Sherwood, Mrs. J.; Harper and Brothers, 1887 .... $30

Manuscript Cookbook anonymous; ca. 1880, food and medical recipes, hardcover notebook, fair, ... $25; 1883, handwritten, hardcover notebook, contains recipes and medical suggestions $45

Marion Harland's Cookery for Beginners Harland, Marion; D. Lothrop Co., 1893, illustrated $75

Mary Margaret McBride's Harvest of American Cooking McBride, Mary Margaret; G. Putnam's Sons, 1957, fine condition $20

Medley of Meat Recipes; Hormel and National Livestock and Meat Board, very good condition $5

Memoirs of An American Lady Grant, Anne; Dodd, Mead and Co., 1909, illustrated $35

Milwaukee Cook Book, The Magie, Mrs.; Wisconsin Training School for Nurses, 1894, local ads $30

Miss Beecher's Domestic Receipt Book Beecher, Catharine; Harper & Bros., 1864, illustrated, ... $80; 1856, third edition $250

Miss Leslie's New Cookery Book Leslie, Eliza; T.B. Peterson and Brothers, 1857, fair condition $200

Mmm...in Minutes—Mouth-Watering Pies to Remember from Cool-Whip 1981, fine condition $4

Modern Cookery in All Its Branches Acton, Eliza; Longman, Brown, Green, et al, 1849, illustrated $275

Mrs. Lincoln's Boston Cook Book Lincoln, Mrs. D.A.; Roberts Brothers, 1884, first edition, ... $200; 1891 .... $85

Mrs. Rorer's Philadelphia Cook Book Rorer, Sarah Tyson; Arnold and Co., 1886, illustrated $65

My Better Homes and Gardens Cook Book Meredith Publishing Co., 1930, first edition $35

My Cookery Books Pennell, Elizabeth Robins; Holland Press Ltd., 1983, illustrated, one of a numbered series $95

Mystery Chef's Own Cook Book MacPherson, John; 1940, signed by Mystery Chef $37.50

National Cook Book, The Harland, Marion; Charles Scribner's Sons, 1896 .... $45

National Cook Book, The Hibben, Sheila; Harper & Bros., 1932 .... $25

New England Cook Book Harland, et al; Charles Brown Publishing, 1906, illustrated, local ads $45

New Dr. Price Cook Book, The; 1921, 49 pages, good condition $8

New Household Receipt Book, The Hale, Sarah Josepha; H. Long and Brother, 1853, fair condition $65

Nine Easy Recipes for Delicious Homemade Candy!; 1950, Baker's Dot Chocolate, four page foldout, very good condition $4

Now Speed Bake Without Kneading Northwestern Yeast Co., 1936, three page foldout, very good condition $2

Old Cook Books Quayle, Eric; Brandywine Press Books, 1978, illustrated, first edition $35

Our Deportment Young, John; F.B. Dickerson and Co., 1882, illustrated, fine condition $35

Pan-Pacific Cook Book McLaren, L.L.; Blair-Murdock Co., 1915, illustrated, from Panama-Pacific Exposition $65

Pear Culture for Profit Quinn, P.T.; Tribune Association, 1869, illustrated $25

Pennsylvania Grange Cook Book Pennsylvania State Grange Committee, 1925, signed recipes $40

Pillsbury Bake-Off Booklet #1 Pillsbury Co., 1950, illustrated $80

Pillsbury Bake-Off Booklets Pillsbury Co., 1951 on, illustrated .... $9 each

Pocumtuc Housewife, The Deerfield Academy, 1906, rare edition $45

Practical Cooking and Dinner Giving Henderson, Mary F.; Harper & Bros., 1878, illustrated $70

Practical Housekeeping Buckeye Publishing Co., 1883, illustrated, revised edition of *Buckeye Cookery* $45

Presbyterian Cook Book First Presbyterian Church, Dayton, OH, 1877, illustrated, local ads $45

Princess Cook Book Akerstrom, Jenny; Albert Bonnier Publishing House, 1936, illustrated, first edition $45

Quaker Oats Whole Grain Cookbook, The 1979, very good condition $7

Queen of the Household Elssworth and Brey, 1905, illustrated $22.50

Salute to American Cooking, A Longstreet, Stephen and Ethel; Hawthorn Books, 1968 .... $22

Saratoga Favorite, The Young Women's Mission Circle, Saratoga Springs, NY, 1882, signed recipes, local ads, fine condition $85

Savannah Cook Book, The Colquitt, Harriet Ross; 1933, illustrated, first edition $40

Sensible Etiquette Ward, Mrs. H.O.; Porter and Coates, 1878 .... $22.50

Settlement Cook Book, The Kander, Mrs. Simon; Settlement Cook Book Co., 1931 edition, illustrated .. $35

Settlement Cook Book, The (facsimile edition) Kander, Mrs. Simon; Scribner Book Co., 1984, illustrated $15

Shaker Recipes for Cooks and Homemakers Lassiter, William; Greenwich Books, 1959, first edition, signed by author $22.50

Short-title Catalogue of Household and Cookery Books, A Maclean, Virginia; Prospect Books, 1981 .... $95

Simply Salmon Bumble Bee, four page foldout, c. 1978, very good condition $1

Six Hundred Dollars A Year anonymous; Ticknor and Fields, 1867 .... $40

Six Hundred Receipts Worth Their Weight in Gold Marquart, John; John E. Potter and Co., 1867, very good condition $30

Social Life in New Orleans Ripley, Eliza; Appleton and Co., 1912, illustrated $30

Knox Gelatine cookbook, 1943, $6.

Something Different First Unitarian Church, Buffalo, NY, 1919, signed recipes, local ads $22.50

Soup Book, The DeGouy, Louis; Greenberg Publisher, 1949 .... $20

Sour Cream Salad Ideas, American Dairy Association of Wisconsin, four page foldout, very good condition $1

Southern Cooking Dull, Henrietta; Grosset and Dunlap, 1941, illustrated $22.50

Soyer's Paperbag Cookery Soyer, Nicolas; Sturgis and Walton Co., 1911, illustrated, first edition $25

Spice Cookbook, The Day, Avanelle, and Stuckey, Lillie; David White Co., 1964, first printing $22.50

Stag at Ease Squire, Marian; Caxton Printers Ltd., 1938 . $45

Stoy Cook Book, The; 1944, 47 pages, VG+ $8

Table Service Allen, Lucy G.; Little, Brown Co., 1915, illustrated $25

Tested Receipts Ladies of the First Baptist Church, 1913 $40

The Table: How to Buy Food, How to Cook It and How to Serve It Filippini, Alessandro; Charles L. Webster, 1891, illustrated $35

Thousand Ways to Please A Husband, A Weaver, Louise, and LeCron, Helen; A.L. Burt Co., 1917, illustrated ... $35

Yes! 100 Ways to Enjoy Bananas, 1925, 16 pages, fine condition, $6.

Three Hundred Games and Pastimes Lucas, E.; Macmillan, 1903, illustrated $45

Treatise on Adulterations of Food, A (1820) (Reprint) Accum, Fredrick; Mallinckrodt Chemical Works, 1966 .... $25

Treatise on Baking, A Wihlfahrt, Julius; Fleischmanns Co., 1928, illustrated $50

Treatise on Domestic Economy, A Beecher, Catharine; Marsh, Capen, Lyon and Webb, 1841, illustrated, first edition $80

Try These New "Balanced" Recipes Mary Ellis Ames, Pillsbury, no. 11 in a series, three page foldout, very good condition $2

Twentieth Century Book for the Baker Gienandt, F.L.; Self, 1927, illustrated $35

Twentieth Century Cook Book and Practical Housekeeping Smiley Publishing Co., 1900, illustrated $22.50

275 Tested Recipes Cook Book Ladies of Centre Bennington, Bennington, VT, 1888, signed recipes $35

209 Years of Charleston Cooking Rhett & Gay; 1931, illustrated $45

United States Regional Cook Book, The Berolzheimer, Ruth; Culinary Arts Press, 1947, illustrated, thumb tabs $25

Up to Date Waitress, The Hill, Janet McKenzie; Little, Brown, and Co., 1929, illustrated, very good $40

Virginia Housekeeper, The (1860) (Reprint) Randolph, Mary; Avenel Books, ca. 1970 .... $15

Watkins Cook Book J.R. Watkins Co., 1938 .... $49

What Can One Do With A Chafing Dish? Sawtelle, H.L.; Stilwell and Co., 1889, local ads, fair condition $35

What Salem Dames Cooked in 1700, 1800 & 1900 Esther Mack Industrial School, 1910, very good condition $65

Whistler's Mother's Cook Book MacDonald, Margaret; G.P. Putnam's, 1979, illustrated $22.50

White House Cook Book, The Ziemann, Hugo, and Gillette, Mrs. F.; The Werner Co., 1897, illustrated $65

White House Cook Book, The Ziemann, Hugo, and Gillette, Mrs. F.; The Werner Co., 1899 edition $40

With Bold Knife and Fork Fisher, M.F.K.; G.P. Putnam's Sons, 1969 .... $35

Woman's Day Encyclopedia of Cookery Tighe, Eileen; Woman's Day, 1965, illustrated $75

Women's Institute Library of Cookery Women's Institute of Domestic Arts and Sciences, PA, 1925, illustrated . $45

Yes! 100 Ways to Enjoy Bananas, 1925, fine condition $6

Young Housekeeper's Friend, The Cornelius, Mrs.; Taggard and Thompson, 1864 .... $55

Young People's Library of Entertainment and Amusements Meek, Thomas; W.E. Schull, 1903, illustrated $25

COOKIE JARS

Cookie jars came into common use in America during the early 1930s, and since they were made in hundreds of shapes and styles — at first mostly utilitarian but soon decorative, as well.

General Guidelines: Cookie jars made by particular manufacturers are especially desirable. Top names to look for (markings are often found on the bottom of the jar) include Abingdon, Brush Pottery, American Bisque, McCoy, Hull, Shawnee, Red Wing and Metlox.

Condition is essential, but remember that cookie jars were meant to be used on a daily basis, and that normal wear is a part of a jar's overall charm.

Much of the decoration found on jars was painted on top of the glaze or on the bisque itself, making this paint susceptible to flaking, chipping and marring after years of regular use. Chips and cracks, however, will greatly reduce the value of a jar, as will a poor attempt at restoration or paint job. Among the hottest cookie jars to look for include those with the following themes: Black Americana, advertising or character (Disney, Hanna-Barbera, etc.).

Trends: Most of the fluctuation in the market has been artificial, based on an event, and not reflective of the true market. The cookie jar market has remained active and strong. Many cookie jars are available for under $25, but jars in the $50, $100 and $150 range are not uncommon.

Humpty Dumpty cookie jar.

Publications

Cookie Jarrin', Joyce Roerig, RR2 Box 504, Walterboro, SC 29488-9278, 803-538-2487

Exclusively Shawnee, P.O. Box 713 , New Smyrna Beach, FL 32170-0703

Our McCoy Matters, c/o Carol Seaman, 216-526-2094

Cookie Jar Collectors Express, P.O. Box 221, Mayview, MO 64071-0221, 816-584-6309

National Cookie Jar Show / Tennessee State Fairground Walter F. Sill Jr., 557 Forest Retreat Road, Hendersonville, TN 37075-2247 615-824-4646

The Cookie Jar Museum Lucille Brombereck, 111 Stephen St., Lemont, IL 60439 708-257-5012

VALUE LINE

Abingdon

Money Sack	$40
Pumpkin	$375
Humpty Dumpty	$375
Hippo	$595
Train	$250

Advertising Cookie Jars

Keebler Tree, unmarked,	$80-$95
Ernie Keebler w/ box, Benjamin & Medwin	$50-$75
Milk Bone dog house, Roman, Thailand	$60-$80
Oreo, Dorrane of California	$40-$55
Pillsbury Doughboy, Benjamin & Medwin	$30-$45
ALF	$150
Spuds MacKenzie	$245
Walt Disney Cookie Bus, 1950	$950

American Bisque

Yarn Doll	$125-$175
Butter Churn	$20-$30
After School Cookies Bus	$60-$80
Majorette	$125-$135
Baby Elephant	$195
Bear with Hat	$75
Indian Maiden	$250
Jack in the Box	$175
Clown w/ raised arms	$80-$100
Davy Crockett	$350-$400

Cat in Basket .... $50-$65
Cookie Truck .... $50-$70
Donkey with Cart .... $75-$95
Spool of Thread $210

Brush

Covered Wagon $475
Hippopotamus $275
Humpty Dumpty $295
Little Angel $750
Panda $195

Character

Barney Rubble .... $30-$55
Donald Duck, Hoan $45
Mickey Mouse, Hoan $75
Kliban Cat .... $200-$300
Betty Boop .... $400-$500
Hello Kitty .... $30-$45
Winnie The Pooh .... $90-$110
Pinocchio, Doranne $295
Eeyore $750
Kermit the Frog, Sigma $525
Peter Rabbit, Sigma $495
Betty Boop, Vandor $650
Cookie Monster .... $70-$85

F&F Mold &Works

Black Mammy .... $625-$650

Hull

Cookies crock .... $20-$35
Little Red Riding Hood .... $125-$175
Barefoot Boy $435
Train Depot $75

McCoy

Apple, 1970s .... $30-$45
Black Stove, 1960s .... $35-$45
Chinese Lantern .... $30-$50
Clown Head, 1940s .... $50-$65
Bobby Baker, 1970s .... $55-$70
Black Potbellied Stove, 1960s .... $30-$45
Cinderella .... $75-$100
White Stove, 1960s .... $30-$50
Green Cookie Jug, 1970s .... $30-$45
Friar (Thou Shalt Not Steal) .... $30-$40
Cow w/ cat finial .... $110-$130
Cookie House .... $80-$100
Wren House $210
Raggedy Ann $70
Strawberry, white $45
Winking Pig $175
Chilly Willy $35
Grandfather Clock $85
Indian Head $350
Pineapple $60

Metlox

Barrel of Apples $45
Basset Hound $575
Ears of Corn $75
Humpty Dumpty $250

Budweiser Wagon $325
Watermelon $350
Woodpecker on Acorn $375
Grapes $195
Orange $45
Porsche $125
Rabbit on Cabbage $165
Bear on Roller Skates $100
Fido Dog $275
Penguin $100

North American Ceramics

Fire Truck .... $125-$140

Pottery Guild

Hostessware, 1930s .... $30-$45
Dutch Boy $55
Dutch Girl $75
Puppy $65
Red Riding Hood $155

Regal

Barn $275
Quaker Oats $100
Majorette, gold $400
Oriental Woman $600

Robinson Ransbottom

Peter Pumpkin Eater $145

Shawnee

Smiley Pig w/ clover bloom .... $275-$300
Jack (Boy w/ gold trim) .... $285-$300
Jill (Girl, no gold) .... $170-$185
Owl .... $115-$135
Queen Corn $75
Snowflake, yellow $65

Sigma

Dalmatian Fireman $425
Planetary Pals $275
Mrs. Tiggy Winkle $450

Treasure Craft

Humpty Dumpty $45
Coffee Pot $25
Ben Franklin $325
Farmer Pig $25
Locomotive $30
Monk $48
Granny $75
Potbellied Stove $75

Twin Winton

Mother Goose $175
Sheriff Bear $50
Dutch Girl $100
Cow $80
Ranger Bear $55
Rooster $75
Ark $145
Bambi $150
Poodle $90
Santa, black $595

COSTUME JEWELRY

An appreciation of the beauty and workmanship found in quality costume jewelry has been gaining in importance during the past several decades.

Many individuals search for pieces produced during specific time periods — like Art Deco or Victorian — while others devote their efforts to finding examples from specific manufacturers or designers. Overlapping these categories is the collector who focuses on both, covering time periods from the past, as well as collectibles of the future being made today.

History: The historical significance of costume jewelry is enhanced by a host of talented individuals and master artisans. Originally a term referring to only those pieces worn by stage actresses — in an era when acting and actresses were offered little social respect — it wasn't until the early days of renowned couturiers like Coco Chanel and Elsa Schiaparelli that it garnered the attention of affluent, fashionable women. Both recognized the possibilities for beauty, playfulness, and ingenuity of expression inherent in faux jewelry.

Meanwhile, in the world of fashion geared to the average woman of the 1920s and 1930s, the Eisenbergs of Chicago positioned themselves at the forefront of a new movement. In what would prove to be a marketing coup, they added sparkling baubles to many of their clothing. Unexpectedly, combining fashion and accessorizing in each garment proved costly, since the brooches and clips soon disappeared, while many of the clothes remained unsold. The Eisenbergs wisely concluded that concentrating solely on costume jewelry might well offer greater sales opportunities than their fashions. Thus, along with pioneers like Chanel and Schiaparelli, the term "costume jewelry" gained respectibility and was brought into the mainstream of fashion.

During the 1930s, costume jewelry appeared on famous stars of the silver screen, and women could afford to buy similar items at their local emporiums.

By the 1940s, the industry had a difficult time meeting the demands of an eager public. However, World War II saw many factories formerly devoted to the manufacture of costume pieces being converted to the production of metal parts for the defense industry. When the war ended, the interest in costume jewelry escalated, continuing the frantic pace for over three decades. The offerings of hundreds of manufacturers and designers flooding the market with costume jewelry, yet most were barely able to keep up with the demand. As a consequence, many pieces by the higher–end participants left production lines unsigned or often only one piece of a parure bore an indentification, leading to still more unsigned pieces when sets were later separated or pieces lost.

It was a boom that would continue until the late 1970s when an emergence of small gold pieces and tiny chains, all geared to modest pocketbooks, became the rage. Always eager for something new, the "gold rush" was on, leading to the unfortunate demise of many stalwarts in the costume jewelry industry. For those able to weather the bad times, a turnaround was inevitable, and by the mid–1980s, the lure of quality costume jewelry once again found a place in the hearts, and jewelry boxes, of women around the world. Although many fashion designers have chosen to

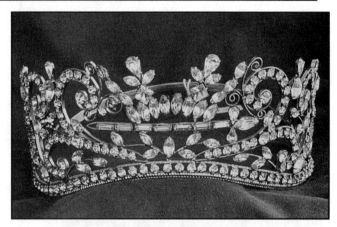
Rhinestone tiara with adjustable band.

sparsely accessorize their models on the couture runways of the 1990s, a host of smartly dressed women have chosen to reject this approach. Instead, a return to individual expression when accessorizing has led to renewed appreciation, in all age groups, of quality costume jewelry and treasures from the past.

General Guidelines: Designer names to look for in costume jewelry include Eisenberg, Chanel, Schiaparelli, Boucher, Hobe, the Mazer and Jomaz lines of the Mazer family, Schreiner, DeLillo, Polcini, Panetta, Hollycraft, Mimi d'N and others.

Of special appeal are the works of designers who used wired-on faux pearls and gems, beads, and mirrorbacks — most notably Miriam Haskell, Robert, and DeMario — as well as those bearing the names of couturiers Hattie Carnegie and Nettie Rosenstein, and the varied designs of Kenneth Jay Lane are also in demand. Particularly popular with collectors are the distinctive designs of Eugene Joseff, known as Joseff of Hollywood.

Most of the aforementioned designers and manufacturers had distinctive styles. Just as many signed pieces are by manufacturers whose offerings were generally of poor quality or of no significance in today's collectibles market, as might also be expected, not every piece of jewelry by even the higher-end and sought-after names was particularly noteworthy. Consequently, it's wise to give attractive unsigned pieces careful attention. Many of the finest and most treasured pieces in the collections of astute buyers do not bear identifying marks.

Publications

•*Costume Jewelry Collectors Showcase*
P.O. Box 656675
Fresh Meadow, NY 11365

•*Vintage Fashion and Costume Jewelry*
P.O. Box 265
Glen Oaks, NY 11004

Contributor to this section: Joanne Ball

COLLECTORS' ALERT

Beware of reproductions. Fake Eisenberg, Weiss and Trifari pieces have appeared in abundance.

Be particularly wary of "jelly bellies." Primarily featuring animals, insects, etc., the originals most often bore the names of Trifari and Coro and can be distinguished by a clear, domed "belly" that dominates whimsical figurals of fish, turtles, frogs, etc. Usually in sterling silver, these bogus pieces also bear what is purported to be the authentic manufacturer's mark. Pay attention to the bellies, which were originally made of a clear synthetic material; fraudulent ones are most often of glass. Potential buyers need only tap their teeth against them to tell the difference.

VALUE LINE

Signed items

Eisenberg sterling floral spray fur clip featuring large clear stones; scrolled "E"; 3-1/4"; 1930s ..... $800-$1,200

Eisenberg lead–backed spray brooch; red/clear stones; Marked Eisenberg (in script) Original; 4-1/2"; 1930s .... $400-$650

Hobe faux ivory Chinese figural brooch, pink robe, large headdress of pink and greet stones set in scrolled wire; 3-1/2", 1940s .... $1,000 up

Hobe sterling floral brooch; large aqua stones, engraved leaves and bow design; 4-1/4"; 1940s–'50s .... $500 up

Marked "Joseff Hollywood," double section, silver leaf brooch, center flower featuring giant faux sapphire stones; 4"; 1940s .... $1,000+

Joseff 3" dia. burnished gold brooch; angelic figural of children surrounded by openwork design of flowers and rhinestones; five 3" dangles capped with faceted crystals; 1940-'50s .... $500-$800

Nettie Rosenstein vermeil enameled fur clip; aqua and red beads encased in open–topped flower; 3-1/4"; early 1940s .... $700+

Schiaparelli bracelet, confetti and rough hewn stones in shades of green and yellow; 1950s .... $350-$500

Miriam Haskell 1/2" cuff bracelet; florentine finish, center section encasing mobe pearl encircled with seed pearls; 1950s-'60s .... $225-$275

Mimi d'N domed brooch, pave rhinestone design with faux amethysts and emeralds, emerald center; 2-3/4" dia .... $450+

Hollycraft necklace; coppery marcasite and amber stones, matching copper–colored snake chain; 1940s-1950s .... $250-$350

Robert necklace, bracelet and earrings parure; pink beads and stones, rhinestone spacers; elaborate layered center designs featuring large pink stones, wired on beaded flowers and rhinestones; 1960s .... $1,000+

Schreiner maltese cross brooch, giant clear stones; elaborate center section with jeweled sceptres at each corner; decorative prongs .... $600-$900

Schreiner bib necklace; 38 strands of multi-colored and shaped stones, edged in scalloped design; earrings of large emerald-cut stones .... $1,800+

Trifari necklace of large, high–quality double–strand faux pearls; gold beaded clasp; 28-1/2"; 1950s–60s .... $275-$375

Trifari three-dimensional green enameled frog brooch, silvertone accents, red eyes; 3"; 1950s .... $350+

Trifari sterling (vermeil) crown brooch; large blue cabochons, red, green, pave clear accent stones; 2"; 1950s .... $300-$400

Boucher reversible "night and day" brooch; one side as gold flower with pearl center, the other paved rhinestones; rare style and design; 2-1/2" dia.; 1940s-1950s .... $375 up

Weiss "apple" brooch, closely-spaced red stones set in japanned (black) backing, green enamel leaves; 2-1/2"; 1960s .... $125-$175

Coro Duette (one brooch that separates into two clips); rose-colored enameled love birds, pave and floral accents; 2-1/2"; 1940s .... $200-$350

CoroCraft Duette, sterling (vermeil) bees; multi-enamel and pave rhinestones; 2-3/4"; 1940s .... $350-$450

Hollycraft Christmas tree; rare; openwork antique finish; multi stones featuring clear candles, red stone "flames;" 1950s .... $200+

Florenza multi-colored enamel clown, head and torso; white finish; 2-3/4"; 1950s .... $50-$75

Pennino five-strand, four-sectioned faux pearl bracelet; pave rhinestone claspand section dividers; 1950s .... $175-$250

McClelland Barclay rectangular gold brooch; Deco–style with overlapping raised section of pave rhinestones featuring three large red stones; 2-3/4"; 1930, early 1940s .... $250-$350

KJL (Kenneth Jay Lane) 1-1/4" center opening, heavy gold cuff bracelet; two 1" square-cut faceted crystals; 1960s .... $225-$300

KJL 18-3/4" triple–strand, faux pearls necklace; large center section in 3D floral design encrusted with crystals; 1960s-70s .... $1,500+

Accessocraft silver finish magnifying glass pendant; Art Deco filigree pattern surrounding glass; long heavy chain .... $65-$85

Napier sterling bow brooch; 3-1/4" wide; large dangling marbleized amethyst stone; 1940s-50s .... $225-$325

Vendome paper-tagged, long-stemmed flower; 2-1/2" dia. yellow/green enamel flower; raised center stones of faux amber and citrines; long-stemmed, 4-1/2" overall length;1950s .... $175-$250

Maison Gripoux for Maggy Rouff double-strand necklace of red glass and crystal ovals, accented by large pearl drops .... $800-$1,000

Jeanne Peral jet beaded collar, French lattice work jet pendant, large black jet drop .... $600-$800

Georg Jensen sterling silver brooch; Nouveau design featuring large Chrysoprase cabochon .... $850-$950

Unsigned

Circular brooch, openwork design, layered stones in intricate design, clear and faux emerald stones; 3-1/4" dia.;1950s .... $275 up

Necktie-style brooch; multi-colored stones; sectional design with eleven strands capped with turquoise beads; 9"; 1950s-'60s .... $300-$500

Sterling jelly belly frog pin, large red eyes; 1940s $350-$450

Heavy gold florentine-finish floral brooch; faux pearl center; 2" dia.; 1960s .... $45-$60

Giant confetti and clear-colored parure; bib necklace, 3" dia. brooch, bracelet, earrings; shades of green and orange; 1960s .... $1,500+

French enamel parure; blue/ivory mosaic beads; blue beaded pendant, center lapis-colored stone; ring/earrings; 1970s .... $500+

Faux ivory cuff bracelet, center designs of raised gold; unsigned Accessocraft; 1940s-'50s .... $30-$45

Gold eagle brooch in heavy design; raised feathers; unsigned Accessocraft; 2-1/2"; 1950s .... $55-$75

Gold eliptical-sectioned necklace; pave rhinestone spacers; three teardrop faux pearl dangles; 1950s-'60s .... $50-$65

Layered brooch; intricate design of multi-shaped, blue-hued stones; prong set; heavy silver backing; 1-3/4" sq.; 1960s-70s .... $75-$95

Earrings in style similar to Eisenberg and Weiss of the period; clear paves over green/blue multi-shaped, prong-set stones; 1950s .... $45-$65

Sterling, 3D brooch featuring matador with cape and sword; signed Mexico; 1940s-'60s .... $135-$175

Floral spray of multi-layered purple/lavender hued crystals of various shapes and sizes; 4-1/2"; Marked Austria .... $400+

Shield pin, gold crown top; blue/green enamel centered with 3 raised Napoleonic bees; 2-1/4"; marked Italy; 1950s-'60s .... $55-$75

Four-layer brooch/pendant; bottom layer of six-pointed openwork "star" rimmed with rhinestones, six four-sectioned "rays" in blue/clear rhinestones above, overlaid with blue/white enamel star rimmed with silver and centered with high-set blue crystal; all prong-set stones; 4-1/2" dia. .... $450+

Silver Art Nouveau pendant with moonstone "spacers" on chain; elaborate pendant featuring large center moonstone; probably German .... $850-$950

Pendant with black onyx drop overlaid with sterling filigree; silver chain; 1920s .... $65-$95

Rhinestone pin and earrings, yellow and brown colored stones, gold covered base metal.

COWBOY COLLECTIBLES

More than any other legendary characters, cowboys have always been uniquely American heroes. From the pioneers' earliest ventures westward on trails through untamed Indian territories, generations of Americans have been reared on cowboy stories and steeped in Western folklore. In print, on radio, in big screen films and on television, cowboys have galloped their way into our hearts and collective national consciousness like no other hero before or since.

Of all the many six-gunned desperadoes and valiant horsemen who rode through weekly radio shows and movie serials, four truly epitomized the American cowboy spirit — Gene Autry, Hopalong Cassidy, Roy Rogers and The Lone Ranger. Within the genre of cowboy and Western collectibles, items bearing the names, images and likenesses of these "big four" remain the most sought-after.

History: Autry sang his way to radio and film success starting in 1927. Released seven years later, *In Old Santa Fe* propelled Autry beyond his radio and recording star status as he became a movie matinee idol. His impressive career included 89 feature-length films and more than 400 records over a forty-year span. William Boyd starred in over 60 films as Hopalong Cassidy before his NBC series began in 1949. Cassidy's cowboy character proved immensely popular with American kids — so much so that he was among the earliest fictional characters to appear on hundreds of products and toys.

Roy Rogers also began his career as a singing cowboy during the 1930s. Beginning in 1938, this cowboy king made some 80 films in addition to hosting his radio show, which ended each episode with his trademark theme song, *Happy Trails*. By the mid-1950s, Rogers was endorsing over 400 products carrying his name. The Lone Ranger rode into stateside living rooms via radio airwaves in 1933, accompanied by his white stallion Silver and faithful Indian companion Tonto. One of the most celebrated and revered characters in all of American pop culture, the Lone Ranger made his masked way from radio to television to film for the next 24 years, leaving an enduring legend.

General Guidelines: Hopalong Cassidy items remain in greatest demand, leaving Roy Rogers and Gene Autry riding in close second. Always a standout for his legendary status, Lone Ranger collectibles come next.

Movie memorabilia, especially posters and lobby cards, and toys are two biggest areas of interest. Perhaps most popular among cowboy and Western collectibles are cap pistols, either in holsters or by themselves. Items in original boxes command top dollar.

Children's book, *Roy Rogers and the Sure 'Nough Cowpoke*, authorized edition, Tell-A-Tale Books, story by Elizabeth Beecher, illus. by Randy Steffen, ©1952 by Roy Rogers Enterprises.

TIPS OF THE TRADE

- Any memorabilia associated with famous cowboys, lawmen and outlaws is highly collectible. Buffalo Bill Cody is especially desirable to collectors.

- While gunbelts and holsters used to hold little value for gun collectors, the leather "rigs" are now often considered more valuable than the guns themselves!

- Beware of reproductions and fraudulent items being passed off as vintage cowboy collectibles.

COLLECTORS' ALERT

The Topps Gum Company issued a series of Hopalong Cassidy trading cards in 1950. Today, this card set is valued at $2,500 in Mint condition.

Clubs

•Friends of Hopalong Cassidy
4613 Araby Church Road, Frederick, MD 21705

•Roy Rogers & Dale Evans Collectors
P.O. Box 1166, Portsmouth, OH 45662

•Toy Gun Collectors of America
312 Starling Way, Anaheim, CA 92807

VALUE LINE

Ranges listed are for items in Excellent to Mint condition.

Gene Autry

Adventure Comics Book, Pillsbury, 1947	$75-$190
Boston Garden Rodeo litho button, 1940	$40-$75
Bread labels with photos, 1950s	$10-$15
Carded horseshoe nail ring, 1950s	$40-$250
Cello button, 1940s	$25-$45
Columbia Records publicity photo, 1950s	$10-$18
Composition statue, 1930s	$250-$400
Dixie Ice Cream picture, 1948	$25-$50
Dell Comics U.S. flag plastic ring, 1948	$150-$200
Dell Picture Strip, 1950s	$50-$75
Dell Publishing picture strip, 1949	$50-$80
Flying A brass wings badge, 1950s	$40-$75
Flying A cardboard wrist cuffs, 1950s	$100-$200
Gene Autry & Champion cello button, 1950s	$25-$35
Gene Autry Comics English fan club badge, 1950s	$75-$125
Gene Autry ring, 1940s	$115$150
Litho tin club tab, 1950s	$30-$60
March of Comics #25, 1940s	$75-$170
March of Comics #120, 1954	$30-$70
Medal of Honor, 1950s	$200-$300
Official club badge cello button, 1940s	$25-$40
Penguin Melody Ranch cigarette lighter, 1950s	$45-$80
Plastic ring, 1950	$15-$20
Puffed Wheat/Rice Comics, Quaker, 1950	$35-$75
Republic's Singing Western Star Cello Button, 1940s	$50-$75
Republic Studio fan photo, 1940	$20-$35
Rodeo souvenir photo, 1957	$12-$20
School tablet, 1950s	$25-$50
Stroehmann's Bread trail map, 1950s	$60-$100
Sunbeam Bread cardboard gun, 1950	$40-$65
Sunbeam Bread color photo, 1950	$18-$30
Sunbeam Bread litho button, 1950	$15-$20
"The Big Show" Wheaties box back, 1937	$20-$35
Thunder Riders Club button, 1935	$400-$600
World Championship Rodeo handbill, 1940	$50-$85
Wrigley Doublemint Gum store sign, 1940s	$60-$125

Hopalong Cassidy

Adult hat, 1950	$200-$400
Aladdin steel lunch box, 1950	$125-$300
Aladdin steel Thermos bottle, 1950	$70-$150
Aluminum medal, 1950	$10-$15
Bar 20 bracelet, 1950s	$80-$160
Bar 20 chow set boxed glassware, 1950	$50-$75
Barclay Knitwear photo, 1949	$25-$40
Big Top Peanut Butter Bar 20 TV chair, 1949	$500-$1,000
Big Top Peanut Butter ID bracelet, 1950	$100-$150
Big Top Peanut Butter Junior Chow ad, 1950	$25-$50
Big Top Peanut Butter premium catalog, 1950	$100- $200
Bill Boyd/For Democracy cello button, 1942	$200-$350
Binoculars, 1950	$60-$100
Bond Bread book cover, 1950	$20-$35
Bond Bread hang-up album, 1950	$50-$80
Bond Bread label flyer, 1950	$75-$125
Bond Bread loaf end labels, 1950	$6-$12
Bond Bread store sign, 1950	$175-$250
Bond Bread postcard, 1950	$15-$25
Boxed camera, 1950	$150-$225
Burry's Cookies cut-out panel, 1950	$40-$60
Butter-Nut Bread *Troopers News* Vol #1, 1949	$150-$250
Cap gun, Wyandotte, 1950s	$100-$150
Capitol Records cardboard noisemaker gun, 1950	$60-$100
Child's hat, 1950	$75-$150
Chinese Checkers, Milton Bradley, 1950	$150-$200
Cole Brothers circus pennant, 1948	$50-$80
Compass hat ring, 1950s	$250-$300

Paladin figure, 1950s-1960s, Hartland — 1950s 9-inch figure with horse, $100 Excellent; 1960s 5-inch figure with horse, $30.

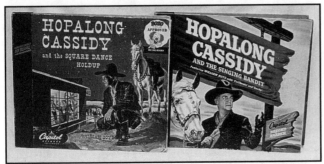

Hopalong Cassidy records, 78 rpm, Capitol, 1950.

Dairylea Ice Cream carton, 1950 .... $75-$150
Dairylea Milk class, 1950 .... $150-$300
Dairylea Milk paper poster, 1950 .... $100-$150
Dixie Ice Cream picture, 1938 .... $40-$85
Drinking straws, 1950 .... $80-$140
Fan club letter, 1946 .... $60-$100
Glass mugs, 1950 .... $18-$30
Grape-Nuts Flakes comic book, 1950 .... $35-$85
Grape-Nuts Flakes radio show handbill, 1950 .... $75-$125
Hammer Brand pocketknife, 1950 .... $65-$125
Honey Roll Sugar Cones box, 1950 .... $300-$450
Hoppy's Favorite Bond Bread cards, 1950 .... $6-$12
Hoppy's Favorite litho button, 1950 .... $25-$50
Ideal hard plastic figures, 1950 .... $60-$100
Melville Milk cardboard sign, 1950s .... $150-$250
NY Daily News cardboard clicker gun, 1950 .... $60-$125
NY Daily News cardboard poster, 1950 .... $175-$250
NY Daily News cello button, 1950 .... $30-$50
People and Places magazine, 1950s .... $60-$120
Picture gun and theatre, Stephens, 1950s .... $150-$200
Pillsbury Farina punch-out gun and targets set,
   1940 .... $80-$175
Pillsbury promotional sign, 1940, ... $400-$600
Plastic bank, 1950 .... $75-$125
Plastic wrist compass, 1950 .... $50-$75
Portrait ring, 1950 .... $40-$60
Post Cereals trading cards, 1951 .... $10-$20
Post Raisin Bran badge, 1950 .... $25-$50
Puzzle set, Milton Bradley, 1950s .... $65-$80
Radio, Arvin, 1950s .... $450-$600
Rollfast Bikes and Skates ad card, 1950 .... $60-$100
Round-Up Club Special Agent pass card, 1948 .... $30-$50
Saving Rodeo Bulldogger Litho Button, 1950 .... $25-$35
Saving Rodeo Tenderfoot Litho Button, 1950 .... $40-$60
Saving Rodeo Wrangler Litho Button, 1950 .... $18-$25
Savings Club Thrift Kit, 1950 .... $150-$300
Silvered Tin Badge, 1950 .... $40-$75
Stationery, Whitman, 1950s .... $50-$100
Stroehmann's Sunbeam Bread Ranch House Race
   Game .... $65-$100
Table utensils, 1950 .... $20-$30
Timex painted latex store display, 1950 .... $1,500-$2,500
Tin potato chips can, Kuehmann Foods, 1950 ..... $125-$200
Topper bracelet, 1950s .... $60-$120

Topps candy bag, 1950 .... $50-$75
Topps chewing gum wrapper, 1950 .... $50-$100
Troopers Club application card, 1949 .... $25-$40
US Time watch, 1950 .... $400-$600
US Time watch paper sign, 1950 .... $225-$400
Wonder Bread TV show special guest sign, 1950 . $125-$200

Roy Rogers

Alarm clock, Ingraham, 1950s .... $300-$400
Bubble gum album, 1951 .... $150-$250
Bullet tin ring, 1953 .... $30-$50
Child's ring, 1940s .... $210-$300
Coloring book, Whitman, 1975 .... $20-$30
Crayon set, Standard Toykraft, 1950s .... $50-$75
Dale Evans Fan Club cello button, 1940s .... $60-$100
Dale Evans statue, Hartland, 1950s .... $80-$200
Dale Evans tin ring, 1953 .... $35-$60
Dale Evans wristwatch, Ingraham, 1951 .... $110-$175
Dixie Ice Cream picture, 1938 .... $40-$75
Fix-It Chuck Wagon & Jeep, Ideal, 1950s .... $150-$300
March of Comics #47, 1949 .... $65-$150
March of Comics #77, 1951 .... $45-$110
Microscope ring, 1949 .... $80-$110
Microscope ring ad, 1949 .... $30-$50
Nodder, Japanese .... $165-$250
Paper dolls, Whitman, 1954 .... $55-$80
Paper pop gun, 1951 .... $30-$50
Post Cereals RR Bar Ranch Set, 1953 .... $200-$300
Quaker brass badge, 1950 .... $60-$100
Quaker Cereals branding iron/initial brass ring,
   1948 .... $160-$225
Quaker Oats contest card, 1948 .... $20-$40
Quaker Oats plastic mug, 1950 .... $18-$30
Raisin Bran rings sign, 1953 .... $400-$600
RCA Victor store sign, 1940s .... $350-$500
Republic Studios Broadway Journal, 1938 .... $135-$200
Republic Studios *My Pal Trigger* poster, 1946 ...... $150-$250
Republic Studios photo, 1940s .... $20-$30
Rodeo board game, Rogden, 1949 .... $140-$200
Rodeo souvenir cello button, 1940s .... $30-$60
Rodeo sticker fun book, Whitman, 1953 .... $55-$110
Roy Rogers and Trigger figures, Hartland,
   1950s .... $100-$175
Roy Rogers club membership card, 1948 .... $30-$50
Roy Rogers cookie box, 1951 .... $400-$600
Roy Rogers Riders Club comics, 1952 .... $35-$180
Roy Rogers Riders Club member pack, 1950 .... $450-$800
Sons of Pioneers photo card, 1935 .... $125-$200
Stagecoach, Ideal, 1950s .... $65-$90
Sterling silver saddle ring, 1948 .... $385-$525
Tattoo transfers kit, 1948 .... $70-$125
Three-gun double holster set, Classy, 1958 .... $600-$800
Thrill Circus pennant, 1950 .... $40-$75
Toy chest, 1950s .... $300-$500
Toy football, 1950s .... $40-$60
Trick lasso, 1947 .... $15-$25
Trigger tin litho ring, 1953 .... $24-$40
Trigger trotter, 1950s .... $225-$300
Truck, Marx, 1950s .... $150-$250

The Lone Ranger

Banjo figure, Gabriel, 1979 .... $30-$60
Bat-O-Ball, 1939 .... $90-$150
Bestyett Bread brass star badge, 1938 .... $75-$125
Betty Crocker Soups bandanna, 1950 .... $60-$90
Bond Bread cardboard sign, 1940 .... $200-$300
Bond Bread color cellophane picture sheet, 1939 .. $75-$125
Bond Bread color photo, 1940 .... $25-$50
Bond Bread Safety Club application postcard, 1939 $20-$35
Bond Bread Safety Club badge, 1938 .... $25-$40
Bond Bread Safety Club roundup newspaper, 1939 .$100-$150
Bond Bread poster, 1938 .... $110-$175
Bond Bread world's fair penny premium, 1939 .... $40-$60
Bond Bread wrapper, 1940 .... $40-$65
Buffalo Bill Cody figure, Gabriel, 1980 .... $18-$35
Butch Cavendish figure, Gabriel, 1980 .... $20-$40
Cheerios Comic Story of Silver, 1954 .... $45-$110
Cheerios frontier town box, 1948 .... $350-$500
Cheerios Lone Ranger deputy kit, 1980 .... $20-$35
Cheerios paper mask, 1951 .... $60-$100
Cheerios Wild West Town figure set, 1957 .... $325-$400
Cobakco Bread calendar, 1939 .... $150-$200
Cobakco Bread picture card, 1938 .... $30-$50
Cobacko Bread Safety Club badge, 1938 .... $60-$100
Coloring book, Whitman, 1975 .... $10-$15
Dr West's Toothpaste cello button, 1938 .... $65-$110
General Mills Lone Ranger standee, 1957 ...... $2,000-$3,000
General Mills movie film ring, 1950s .... $150-$300
Hand puppet, 1940s .... $90-$160
Horlick's Malted Milk picture, 1939 .... $30-$50
Kix Atomic Bomb Ring, 1947 .... $100-$150
Kix blackout kit, 1942 .... $200-$300
Kix Cereal "Name Silver's Son" contest poster,
    1941 .... $2,000-$3,000
Kix decal sheet, 1944 .... $30-$50
Kix luminous blackout belt, 1941 .... $75-$150
Lone Ranger and Silver figure set, Gabriel, 1979 ... $75-$150

Lone Ranger and Tonto target set, MultipleToymakers,
    1970s .... $35-$50
Lone Ranger cello button, 1938 .... $50-$75
Lone Ranger figure, Gabriel, 1979 .... $28-$55
Lone Ranger figure, Hartland, 1950s .... $90-$150
Lone Ranger lucky ring, 1938, ... $2,000-$4,000
Magic lasso, 1950s .... $325-$400
Merita Bread brass star badge, 1938 .... $50-$75
Merita Bread coloring book, 1955............................ $20-$35
Merita Bread photo, 1938 .... $50-$75
Merita Bread Safety Club branding booklet, 1956.... $50-$85
Meteorite ring, 1942 .... $2,400-$5,000
Movie serial ticket with Sears offer, 1938 .... $60-$100
National Defenders look-around ring, 1941 .... $115-$150
National Defenders secret portfolio manual,
    1941 .... $150-$250
New Haven Time Co. lapel watch, 1939 ... $200-$400 and up
Oke Tonto photo card, 1934 .... $25-$50
Orange Pops cardboard sign, 1940 .... $300-$500
Record player, Dekka, 1940s .... $225-$450
Sheriff jail keys, Esquire Novelty, 1945 .... $65-$125
Silver Bullet Defender leaflet with .45 silver bullet,
    1941 .... $75-$150
Silver figure, Gabriel, 1979 .... $35-$70
Silver's lucky horseshoe brass badge, 1938 .... $40-$75
Silvercup Bread Lone Ranger hunt map, 1938 ..... $100-$175
Silvercup Bread photo, 1938 .... $30-$75
Silvercup Bread radio sponsorship brochure, 1934 $100-$150
Silvercup Bread Safety Club folder, 1934 .... $65-$100
Silvercup Chief Scout brass badge, 1934 .... $200-$325
Silvercup Bread Safety Scout badge, 1934 .... $20-$50
Six-gun ring, 1947 .... $90-$125
Smoking click pistol, Marx Toys, 1950s .... $80-$150
Supplee Milk newsletter, 1940 .... $50-$75
Tonto and Scout figure set, Gabriel, 1979 .... $60-$120
Tonto figure, Gabriel, 1979..................................... $25-$45
Tonto bracelets, 1948 .... $100-$200
Tonto lucky ring, 1938 .... $1,600-$3,000
Victory Corps brass tab, 1942 .... $30-$60
Victory Corps cello button, 1942 .... $60-$100
Victory Corps club promo, 1942 .... $100-$200
Weber's White Bread victory wrapper, 1942............ $40-$60

Roy Rogers' death in 1998 created increased interest in related collectibles.

Hopalong Cassidy Radio, 1950s, Arvin, $450 Excellent.

DISNEYANA

Walt Disney is considered one of the greatest contributors to American pop culture with good reason. Cheerfully led by Mickey and Minnie Mouse, the artist's endearing characters have propelled Disney's collectibles through over 60 years of pioneering prosperity, in the process creating one of the broadest and most active toy collecting genres. From *Steamboat Mickey* to *Hercules*, Disneyana thrives.

Disneyana refers to merchandise licensed by the Walt Disney Company. Disney collecting may be divided into three major categories — dimensional ware (dolls, figurines, jewelry, toys); ephemera (printed matter including books, catalogues, periodicals and sheet music) and animation art (cels, drawings, backgrounds and such). From Mickey Mouse's 1928 debut until today, the Walt Disney Company has produced literally millions of items and issued licensing rights to thousands of other companies. However, Disneyana was not widely collected prior to the 1970s.

General Guidelines: Due to the enormity of the Disneyana field, beginning collectors should become acquainted with the field. Knowing the availability, vintage and value of desired pieces will save effort, time and money.

This celluloid Mickey Mouse whirligig, complete with original box, sold for $5,750 at a James Julia Auction. The Mickey Mouse Ingersoll Pocket Watch sold for $1,092.50.

Disneyana collectors may choose to generalize and collect everything Disney or specialize by character, group of characters (heroes, princesses, villains), by film, by date or vintage, by event (anniversaries, character birthdays, movie premieres), by type of merchandise, by artist (Carl Barks, Bill Justice and Ward Kimball are popular), by manufacturer, by limited editions or by country (German and Japanese pieces are favorites).

Tin toys, especially those made by the Louis Marx Company, are among some of the most highly-prized Disney collectibles. Puzzles, games and books — especially those made prior to World War II — are eagerly sought.

Markings: There are three types of copyright markings for Disney collectibles. The earliest pieces, from the late 1920s to early 1930s, bear the marking "Walt E Disney" or "Walter E Disney." The majority of vintage Disney items produced during the 1930s bear the marking "Walt Disney Enterprises," which is sometimes reduced to the three initials "WDE." Items produced from 1940 on carry the "Walt Disney Productions" mark. Items from 1984 and later are marked "Disney/Walt Disney Company."

Dating Disney: Often the look of a particular character can help date an item. Mickey Mouse first appeared in the animated sound cartoon *Steamboat Willie* in 1928. At that time, he had rat-like features with triangular pie-slice-shaped eyes, a longer snout and toothy grin. Donald Duck, introduced in 1934, originally had a long orange bill and feet with feathery hands. Later his bill was shortened, and his hands looked more human. Beware of reproductions, however.

Trends: Disneyana continues to be desirable since the characters and products are merchandised regularly. Their perennial appeal alone suggests that people will always collect Disney.
The Walt Disney Company continually produces numerous items associated with its characters; many are limited editions. Demand for Disney items such as videotapes usually increases every time that release is withdrawn from the marketplace, only to be re-released at a later date.

Over the years, the particular type of Disneyana in greatest demand will likely shift to reflect the changing eras, as collectors usually tend to seek out items associated with their childhood. Every Disney era has been represented on the collectible scale so far, from Mickey Mouse's pot-bellied beginnings to Annette Funicello's memorable television turn as a charter Mouseketeer on *The Mickey Mouse Club*.

Vintage Disney remains a strong force, as the merchandise manufactured prior to 1950 was produced strictly for user enjoyment and not intended as collectibles. As toys were abandoned by children after use, so too were early animation cels thrown out by the Disney company itself. For this reason, items in Excellent or Mint condition show the greatest demand.

While specifics about those future collectibles are hard to predict, demand is not. The trend is clear — the market for classic toys featuring Mickey Mouse, Donald Duck, Pinocchio and other early Disney characters is secure and will likely stay that way. We can only imagine what those first few vintage 1930s Disney toys will be worth when they become a century old, or how much today's *Toy Story* gems will escalate in value by 2098.

Clubs

•Disneyana Dreamers of San Diego County
P.O. Box 106, Escondido, CA 92033

•National Fantasy Fan Club for Disneyana (NFFC)
P.O. Box 19212, Irvine, CA 92713

•The Mouse Club
2056 Cirone Way, San Jose, CA 95124

Contributor to this section: Joel Cohen, Cohen Books and Collectibles, P.O. Box 810310, Boca Raton, FL 33481, 561-487-7888 (text only; not values).

TIPS OF THE TRADE

• Limited-edition pieces may or may not increase in value over time. It's important to understand the item's price in relation to edition size. Higher-quality pieces will most likely see values rise. But the nature of limited-edition pieces means most will be kept, which ensures a future supply (as opposed to a toy which may be discarded).

• First editions of any Disney collectible are often highly valued.

• Auction prices vary considerably from one auction to another based upon the items, their condition, and, most significantly, the competition.

• Know the prices and values of the Disney items you want. Subscribe to collector magazines, read price guides, consult other collectors, join clubs and attend auctions, antique shows and flea markets.

VALUE LINE

Ranges listed are for items in Near Mint to Mint condition.

101 Dalmatians
101 Dalmatians Snow Dome, Marx, 1961 .... $65-$100
101 Dalmatians Wind-Up, Linemar, 1959 .... $115-$375
Dalmatian Pups Figures, Enesco, 1960s .... $23-$125
Lucky Figure, Enesco, 1960s .... $65-$100
Lucky Squeeze Toy, Dell .... $10-$35

Alice in Wonderland
Adventures in Costumeland Game, Walt Disney
   World, 1980s .... $125-$200
Alice Bank, Leeds, 1950s .... $80-$125
Alice Cookie Jar, Regal .... $1,600-$2,500
Alice Cookie Jar, Leeds, 1950s .... $115-$175
Alice Costume, Ben Cooper, 1950s-70s .... $35-$50
Alice Disneykin, Marx, 1950s, unpainted .... $16-$25
Alice Doll, Duchess, 1951 .... $65-$100
Alice Doll, Gund, 1950 .... $35-$50
Alice Figure, Sears, 1980s .... $16-$25

Alice Figure, Haken-Renaker, 1956 .... $250-$400
Alice Figure, Sydney Pottery, 1950s .... $325-$500
Alice Little Golden Book #D-20, Whitman, 1951 .... $20-$50
Alice Coloring Book, Whitman, 1974 .... $7-$10
Alice Punch Out Book, Whitman, 1951 .... $80-$125
Alice Marionette, Peter Puppet, 1950s .... $65-$150
Alice Mug, Disney, 1970s .... $25-$35
Alice Wristwatch, US Time, 1950s .... $165-$250
Fan Card, Walt Disney, 1951 .... $65-$75
Looking Glass Cookie Jar, Fred Roberts Co. .... $260-$500
Mad Hatter Costume, Ben Cooper, 1950s-70s .... $35-$50
Mad Hatter Disneykin, Marx, 1950 .... $45-$75
Mad Hatter Doll, Gund, 1950s .... $35-$50
Mad Hatter Plush Doll, Gund, 1950s .... $225-$350
Mad Hatter Figure, Hagen-Renaker, 1956 .... $225-$350
Mad Hatter Figure, Shaw, 1951 .... $130-$300
Mad Hatter Figure, Marx, 1950s .... $16-$25
Mad Hatter Marionette, Peter Puppet, 1950s .... $65-$150
Mad Hatter Nodder, Marx, 1950s .... $35-$50
Mad Hatter Teapot, Regal, 1950s .... $975-$1,500
March Hare Costume, Ben Cooper, 1950s-70s .... $35-$50
March Hare Disneykin, Marx, 1950s .... $16-$25
March Hare Plush Doll, Gund, 1950s .... $325-$500
March Hare Figure, Hagen-Renaker, 1956 .... $225-$400
March Hare Figure, Shaw, 1951 .... $325-$400
March Hare Figure, Marx, 1950s .... $16-$25
March Hare Marionette, Peter Puppet, 1950s .... $65-$100
Queen of Hearts Disneykin, Marx, 1950s .... $50-$75
Queen of Hearts Doll, Gund, 1950s .... $40-$50
Queen of Hearts Figure, Sears, 1980s .... $16-$25
Queen of Hearts Figure, Disney Store, 1992 .... $13-$20
Queen of Hearts Figure, Marx, 1950s .... $16-$25
Tea Set, Banner Plastics, 1956 .... $325-$500
Tea Set, Disneyland, 1990s .... $10-$15
TweedleDee and TweedleDum Dolls, Gund, 1950s,
   each .... $35-$50
TweedleDee and TweedleDum Figures, Shaw, 1951,
   each .... $130-$200
TweedleDee and TweedleDum salt/pep shakers,
   Regal, 1950s .... $325-$500
Walrus Doll, Lars/Italy, 1950s .... $325-$500
Walrus Figure, Shaw, 1951 .... $225-$350
White Rabbit Disneykin, Marx, 1950s .... $50-$75
White Rabbit Doll, Gund, 1950s .... $35-$50
White Rabbit Plush Doll, Gund, 1950s .... $225-$350
White Rabbit Doll, Buena Vista/Disney, 1974 ...... $100-$150
White Rabbit Figure, Sears, 1980s .... $16-$25
White Rabbit Figure, Shaw, 1951 .... $130-$200
White Rabbit Figure, Marx, 1950s .... $16-$25
White Rabbit Sugar Bowl, Regal, 1950s .... $325-$500

Bambi
Bambi Book, Grosset & Dunlap, 1942 .... $25-$45
Bambi Soaky .... $20-$40
Thumper Bank, Leeds, 1950s .... $80-$150
Thumper Pull Toy, Fisher-Price, 1942 .... $75-$150
Thumper Soaky, Colgate-Palmolive, 1960s .... $30-$60

Cinderella

Cinderella & Prince Wind-Up, Irwin .... $65-$175
Cinderella Paper Dolls, Whitman, 1965 .... $45-$65
Cinderella Puzzle, Jaymar, 1960s .... $25-$35
Cinderella Soaky, 1960s .... $20-$30
Cinderella Wind-Up Toy, Irwin, 1950 .... $100-$175
Cinderella Wristwatch, US Time, 1950 .... $80-$125
Gus Doll, Gund .... $115-$175
Prince Charming Hand Puppet, Gund, 1959 .... $50-$75

Disney Miscellaneous

Disney Ferris Wheel, Chein .... $625-$1,000
Disney Rattle, Noma, 1930s .... $115-$275
Disney Shooting Gallery, Weslo Toys, 1950s .... $115-$225
Disney Treasure Chest Set, Craftman's Guild,
  1940s .... $125-$190
Disney World Globe, Rand McNally, 1950s .... $50-$175
Disney Bunnies, Fisher-Price, 1936 .... $115-$175
Disneyland Puzzle, Whitman, 1956 .... $25-$40
Disneyland View-Master Set, View-Master, 1960s ... $25-$75
Disneyland Wind-Up Roller Coaster, Chein .... $650-$750
Fantasia Bowl, Vernon Kilns, 1940 .... $210-$325
Fantasyland Puzzle, Whitman, 1957 .... $25-$35
Horace Horsecollar Hand Puppet, Gund, 1950s ...... $50-$125
Jose Carioca Figure, Marx, 1960s .... $8-$125
Pecos Bill Wind-Up Toy, Marx, 1950s .... $150-$225
Robin Hood Colorforms, Colorforms, 1973 .... $25-$40

Donald Duck

Donald Duck & Pluto Car, Sun Rubber .... $60-$150
Donald Duck Alarm Clock, Bayard, 1960s .... $150-$350
Donald Duck Bank, Crown Toy, 1938 .... $100-$425
Donald Duck Camera, Herbert-George, 1950s .... $50-$125
Donald Duck Car, Sun Rubber, 1950s .... $65-$125
Donald Duck Choo Choo Pull Toy, Fisher-Price,
  1940 .... $165-$275
Donald Duck Disney Dipsy Car, Marx, 1953 .... $650-$895
Donald Duck Doll, Knickerbocker, 1938 .... $325-$850
Donald Duck Doll, Mattel, 1976 .... $50-$75
Donald Duck Dump Truck, Linemar, 1950s .... $145-$375

Fisher-Price Mickey Mouse Safety Patrol, litho paper on wood, #733 (1956) $200.

Donald Duck Figure, Seiberling .... $80-$125
Donald Duck Figure, Dell, 1950s .... $65-$125
Donald Duck Figure, Fun-E-Flex, 1930s .... $80-$275
Donald Duck Funee Movie Set, Transogram,
  1940 .... $150-$250
Donald Duck Marionette, Peter Puppet, 1950s .... $60-$125
Donald Duck Nodder, 1960s .... $50-$125
Donald Duck Paint Box, Transogram, 1938 .... $30-$125
Donald Duck Pocket Watch, Ingersoll, 1939 .... $115-$375
Donald Duck Scooter, Marx, 1960s .... $140-$225
Donald Duck Telephone Bank, NN Hill Brass,
  1938 .... $130-$275
Donald Duck Tricycle Toy, Linemar, 1950s .... $440-$675
Donald Duck Wristwatch, US Time, 1940s .... $225-$350

Dumbo

Dumbo Figure, Dakin .... $20-$40
Dumbo Roll Over Wind-Up Toy, Marx, 1941 .... $250-$500
Dumbo Squeak Toy, Dakin .... $20-$45
Dumbo Squeeze Toy, Dell, 1950s .... $20-$45

Ferdinand The Bull

Ferdinand Doll, Knickerbocker, 1938 .... $180-$275
Ferdinand Figure, Delco, 1938 .... $65-$125
Ferdinand Figure, Seiberling, 1930s .... $50-$125
Ferdinand Figure, Disney, 1940s .... $130-$275
Ferdinand Hand Puppet, Crown Toy, 1938 .... $80-$125
Ferdinand Savings Bank, Crown Toy .... $40-$175
Ferdinand The Bull Book, Whitman, 1938 .... $35-$125
Ferdinand/Matador Wind-Up, Marx, 1938 .... $425-$750
Ferdinand Wind-Up, Marx, 1938 .... $350-$450

Goofy

Backwards Goofy Wristwatch, Helbros, 1972 ...... $490-$750
Goofy Car, Madem/Spain .... $30-$45
Goofy Figure, Arco .... $16-$25
Goofy Figure, Marx .... $35-$50
Goofy Night Light, Horsman, 1973 .... $30-$45
Goofy Rolykin, Marx .... $50-$75
Goofy Safety Scissors, Monogram, 1973 .... $7-$15
Goofy Twist'N Bend Figure, Marx, 1963 .... $20-$30

Jungle Book

Baloo Doll, plush .... $16-$25
Jungle Book Carrying Case, Ideal, 1966 .... $50-$85
Jungle Book Magic Slate, Watkins-Strathmore, 1967 $16-$30
Mowgli Figure, Holland Hill, 1967 .... $35-$65
Shere Kahn Figure, Enesco, 1965 .... $25-$35

SERIOUS ABOUT SERIES

Disney collectors are series serious when it comes to completing their collections. They may often pay more for an item in order to round out a series with a missing Big Little Book or one missing dwarf.

Lady and The Tramp

Lady and Tramp Figures, Marx, 1955 .... $45-$80
Lady Doll, Woolikin, 1955 .... $80-$150
Perri Doll, Steiff, 1950s .... $40-$80
Tramp Doll, Schuco, 1955 .... $100-$200

Little Mermaid

Ariel Doll .... $16-$25
Eric Doll .... $16-$25
Flounder Doll .... $16-$25
Little Mermaid Figures, Applause .... $4-$5
Scuttle Doll .... $20-$30
Sebastian Doll .... $16-$25

Mary Poppins

Mary Poppins Doll, Gund, 1964 .... $50-$175
Mary Poppins Paper Dolls, Whitman, 1973 .... $30-$65
Mary Poppins Tea Set, Chein, 1964 .... $60-$100

Mickey and Minnie Mouse

Mickey and Donald Alarm Clock, Jerger, 1960s ... $100-$150
Mickey and Donald Jack-in-the-Box, Lakeside,
    1966 .... $50-$145
Mickey and Minnie Dolls, Gund, 1940s .... $210-$550
Mickey and Minnie Flashlight, Usalite Co, 1930s .. $65-$100
Mickey and Minnie Sled, SL Allen, 1935 .... $260-$400
Mickey and Minnie Tea Set, Ohio Art, 1930s .... $80-$125
Mickey and Three Pigs Spinning Top, Lackawanna $65-$135
Mickey Mouse Bank, Crown Toy, 1938 .... $100-$350
Mickey Mouse Bank, Transogram, 1970s .... $25-$35
Mickey Mouse Bean Bag Game, Marks Bros,
    1930s .... $125-$200
Mickey Mouse Bump-N-Go Spaceship, Matsudaya,
    1980s .... $65-$100
Mickey Mouse Camera, Ettelson, 1960s .... $35-$50
Mickey Mouse Choo Choo Pull Toy, Fisher-Price,
    1938 .... $210-$325
Mickey Mouse Club Fun Box, Whitman, 1957 ...... $70-$110
Mickey Mouse Club Magic Kit, Mars Candy,
    1950s .... $50-$75
Mickey Mouse Club Marionette, 1950s .... $80-$225
Mickey Mouse Club Mouseketeer Doll, Horsman,
    1960s .... $45-$100
Mickey Mouse Club Mouseketeer Ears, Kohner ...... $20-$30
Mickey Mouse Club Toothbrush, Pepsodent, 1970s ... $7-$10
Mickey Mouse Colorforms Set, Colorforms, 1976 ... $16-$50
Mickey Mouse Dart Gun Target, Marks Bros,
    1930s .... $55-$225
Mickey Mouse Dinner Set, Empresa Electro,
    1930s .... $245-$375
Mickey Mouse Doll, 1930s .... $575-$875

Mickey Mouse Doll, Schuco, 1950s .... $210-$350
Mickey Mouse Doll, Knickerbocker .... $340-$525
Mickey Mouse Doll, Knickerbocker, 1935 .... $210-$325
Mickey Mouse Fireman Doll, Gund, 1960s .... $50-$75
Mickey Mouse Talking Doll, Hasbro, 1970s .... $35-$50
Mickey Mouse Drum, Ohio Art, 1930s .... $55-$175
Mickey Mouse Electric Table Radio, General
    Electric, 1960s .... $50-$125
Mickey Mouse Figure, Marx, 1970 .... $16-$35
Mickey Mouse Figure, Seiberling, 1930s .... $100-$150
Mickey Mouse Figure, Goebel, 1930s .... $65-$100
Mickey Mouse Fire Engine, Sun Rubber .... $80-$135
Mickey Mouse Fire Truck w/ figure, Sun Rubber ... $80-$125
Mickey Mouse Figure, Fun-E-Flex, 1930s .... $455-$700
Mickey Mouse Gumball Bank, Hasbro, 1968 .... $30-$45
Mickey Mouse Jack-in-the-Box, 1970s .... $45-$65
Mickey Mouse Circus Train, Lionel, 1935 ...... $1,050-$1,600
Mickey Mouse Circus Train Handcar, Lionel .... $440-$675
Mickey Mouse Magic Slate, Watkins-Strathmore,
    1950s .... $30-$45
Mickey Mouse Marbles, Monarch .... $7-$10

This top condition Mickey Mouse Slate Dancer sold at auction for $29,150.

Mickey Mouse Mechanical Robot, Gabriel .... $120-$135
Mickey Mouse Movie Projector, Keystone, 1934 . $260-$400
Mickey Mouse Music Box, Schmid .... $115-$175
Mickey Mouse Night Light, Disney, 1938 .... $165-$250
Mickey Mouse Ornament, Hallmark, 1978 .... $20-$50
Mickey Mouse Pocket Watch, Ingersoll, 1930s .... $350-$700
Mickey Mouse Print Shop Set, Fulton Specialty,
    1930s .... $130-$200
Mickey Mouse Pull Toy, Fisher-Price, 1936 .... $165-$250
Mickey Mouse Pull Toy, Toy Kraft .... $550-$850
Mickey Mouse Pull Toy, NN Hill Brass, 1935 ...... $245-$375
Mickey Mouse Puppet Forms, Colorforms, 1960s .... $20-$40
Mickey Mouse Radio, Emerson, 1934 .... $700-$3,000
Mickey Mouse Record Player, GE, 1970s .... $100-$150
Mickey Mouse Riding Toy, Mengel, 1930s .... $715-$1,100
Mickey Mouse Rolykin, Marx .... $16-$25
Mickey Mouse Sand Pail, Ohio Art, 1938 .... $80-$225
Mickey Mouse Sand Shovel, Ohio Art .... $50-$125
Mickey Mouse Sled, Flexible Flyer, 1930s .... $210-$600
Mickey Mouse Squeeze Toy, Dell, 1950s .... $60-$95
Mickey Mouse Squeeze Toy, Sun Rubber, 1950s ..... $40-$60
Mickey Mouse Steamboat, Matsudaya, 1988 .... $55-$125
Mickey Mouse Telephone Bank, NN Hill Brass,
    1938 .... $130-$275
Mickey Mouse Toy Tractor, Sun Rubber .... $55-$85
Mickey Mouse Tricycle Toy, Steiff, 1932 .... $780-$2,000
Mickey Mouse Wind-Up Toy, Gabriel, 1978 .... $15-$35
Mickey Mouse Wooden Bell Pull Toy, NN Hill
    Brass .... $225-$350
Mickey Mouse Wristwatch, Timex, 1958 .... $210-$325
Mickey Mouse Wristwatch, Bradley, 1978 .... $115-$175
Mickey Mouse Wristwatch, Ingersoll, 1939 .... $375-$575
Mickey's Air Mail Plane, Sun Rubber, 1940s .... $65-$125
Minnie Mouse Car, Matchbox, 1979 .... $10-$20
Minnie Mouse Choo-Choo Train Pull Toy, Linemar,
    1940s .... $125-$250
Minne Mouse Doll, Petz, 1940s .... $210-$325
Minnie Mouse Doll, Knickerbocker, 1930s .... $195-$475
Minnie Mouse Figure, Ingersoll, 1958 .... $55-$85
Minnie Mouse Figure, Fun-E-Flex, 1930s .... $225-$350
Minnie Mouse Hand Puppet, 1940s .... $95-$145
Minnie Mouse Music Box, Schmid, 1970s .... $20-$50
Minnie Mouse Wristwatch, Timex, 1958 .... $100-$150
Mouseketeer Cut-Outs, Whitman, 1957 .... $45-$65
Spinning Top, Chein, 1950s .... $100-$225

Peter Pan
Captain Hook Figure .... $15-$25
Captain Hook Hand Puppet, Gund, 1950s .... $60-$90
Peter Pan Baby Figure, Sun Rubber, 1950s .... $80-$125
Peter Pan Doll, Duchess Doll, 1953 .... $275-$425
Peter Pan Doll, Ideal, 1953 .... $180-$275
Peter Pan Hand Puppet, Oak Rubber, 1953 .... $80-$95
Peter Pan Nodder, 1950s .... $150-$250
Peter Pan Paper Dolls, Whitman, 1952 .... $65-$100
Peter Pan Push Puppet, Kohner, 1950s .... $50-$80
Tinkerbell Doll, Duchess Doll, 1953 .... $210-$325
Tinkerbell Figure, AD Sutton and Sons, 1960s .... $50-$75
Wendy Doll, Duchess Doll, 1953 .... $210-$325

BANKABLE MICKEY

A rare Mickey Mouse mechanical bank sold for a record $36,850 at a 1996 James Julia auction. Made in Germany in 1931, the 7-inch tall bank is described by collectors as the elusive "hands apart" version with a "pull-on-the-ear" mechanism.

Pinocchio and Jiminy Cricket
Figaro Figure, Multi-Wood Products, 1940 .... $75-$150
Figaro Figure, Knickerbocker, 1940s .... $150-$240
Figaro Friction Toy, Linemar, 1960s .... $120-$250
Figaro Wind-Up Toy, Marx, 1940 .... $225-$400
Gepetto Figure, Multi-Wood Products, 1940 .... $95-$145
Jiminy Cricket Doll, Ideal, 1940 .... $250-$450
Jiminy Cricket Doll, Knickerbocker, 1962 .... $45-$80
Jiminy Cricket Figure, Marx .... $50-$75
Jiminy Cricket Figure, Ideal, 1940s .... $200-$350
Jiminy Cricket Hand Puppet, Gund, 1950s .... $40-$75
Jiminy Cricket Marionette, Pelham Puppets,
    1950s .... $130-$275
Jiminy Cricket Ramp Walker, Marx, 1960s .... $125-$250
Jiminy Cricket Soaky .... $20-$35
Jiminy Cricket Wristwatch, US Time, 1948 .... $115-$225
Pin the Nose on Pinocchio Game, Parker Bros,
    1939 .... $75-$125
Pinocchio Doll, Knickerbocker, 1962 .... $45-$80
Pinocchio and Jiminy Hand Puppet, Marx, 1960s .. $45-$100
Pinocchio Bank, Crown Toy, 1939 .... $120-$250
Pinocchio Book Set, Whitman, 1940 .... $175-$300
Pinocchio Color Box, Transogram .... $30-$60
Pinocchio Cut-Out Book, Whitman, 1940 .... $70-$125
Pinocchio Doll, Knickerbocker, 1940 .... $350-$650
Pinocchio Doll, Ideal, 1939 .... $180-$400
Pinocchio Figure, Crown Toy .... $90-$180
Pinocchio Figure, Multi-Wood Products, 1940 .... $80-$200
Pinocchio Hand Puppet, Knickerbocker, 1962 .... $45-$75
Pinocchio Hand Puppet, Gund, 1950s .... $50-$100
Pinocchio Paint Book, Disney, 1939 .... $35-$85
Pinocchio Plastic Cup, Plastic Novelties, 1940 .... $50-$100
Pinocchio Pull Toy, Fisher-Price, 1939 .... $130-$300
Pinocchio Push Puppet, Kohner, 1960s .... $25-$65
Pinocchio Soaky .... $25-$45
Pinocchio Tea Set, Ohio Art, 1939 .... $90-$200
Pinocchio the Acrobat Wind-Up Toy, Marx, 1939 $550-$900
Pinocchio Walker, Marx, 1939 .... $400-$750
Pinocchio Wind-Up Toy, Linemar .... $175-$350

Pluto
Pluto Alarm Clock, Allied, 1955 .... $125-$250
Pluto Bank, Disney, 1940s .... $65-$110
Pluto Figure, Seiberling, 1930s .... $65-$120
Pluto Figure, Fun-E-Flex, 1930s .... $50$100
Pluto Hand Puppet, Gund, 1950s .... $35-$75
Pluto Pop-A-Part Toy, Multiple Toymakers, 1965 ..... $30-$45
Pluto Pop-Up Critter Figure, Fisher-Price, 1936 ... $145-$175
Pluto Purse, Gund, 1940s .... $50-$85
Pluto Push Toy, Fisher-Price, 1936 .... $130-$250

Pluto Rolykin, Marx .... $30-$60
Pluto Sports Car, Empire .... $16-$25
Pluto the Acrobat Trapeze Toy, Linemar .... $200-$250
Pluto the Drum Major, Linemar, 1950s .... $325-$700
Pluto Toy, Linemar .... $55-$200
Pluto Tricycle Toy, Linemar, 1950s .... $325-$650
Pluto Watch Me Roll Over, Marx, 1939 .... $275-$425

Sleeping Beauty
Fairy Godmother Hand Puppets, 1958 .... $70-$200
King Huber/King Stefan Hand Puppets, Gund,
    1956 .... $50-$125
Sleeping Beauty Alarm Clock, Phinney-Walker,
    1950s .... $75-$125
Sleeping Beauty Jack-in-the-Box, Enesco .... $60-$135
Sleeping Beauty Magic Paint Set, Whitman .... $45-$65
Sleeping Beauty Squeeze Toy, Dell, 1959 .... $45-$65
Sleeping Beauty Sticker Fun Book, Whitman, 1959 . $25-$35

Snow White and The Seven Dwarfs
Bashful Doll, Ideal, 1930s .... $100-$200
Doc and Dopey Pull Toy, Fisher-Price, 1937 .... $145-$345
Doc Doll, Ideal, 1930s .... $100-$200
Dopey Bank, Crown Toy, 1938 .... $100-$175
Dopey Doll, Ideal, 1930s .... $100-$225
Dopey Doll, Chad Valley, 1938 .... $95-$195
Dopey Doll, Krueger .... $165-$250
Dopey Doll, Knickerbocker, 1938 .... $165-$375
Dopey Rolykin, Marx .... $50-$100
Dopey Soaky, 1960s .... $20-$30
Dopey Ventriloquist Doll, Ideal, 1938 .... $210-$500
Dopey Walker, Marx, 1938 .... $525-$800
Grumpy Doll, Knickerbocker, 1938 .... $165-$350
Happy Doll, 1930s .... $65-$175
Seven Dwarfs Figures, Seiberling, 1938 .... $210-$450
Seven Dwarfs Target Game, Chad Valley, 1930s ... $210-$325
Sneezy Doll, Krueger .... $210-$325
Snow White Doll, Knickerbocker, 1940 .... $145-$350
Snow White Doll, Horsman .... $25-$75

Snow White Doll, Ideal, 1938 .... $450-$700
Snow White Marionette, Tony Sarg/Alexander,
    1930s .... $115-$225
Snow White Paper Dolls, Whitman, 1938 .... $145-$225
Snow White Soaky .... $25-$35
Snow White Tea Set, Ohio Art, 1937 .... $120-$250
Snow White Tea Set, Marx, 1960s .... $65-$145

Three Little Pigs
Big Bad Wolf Pocket Watch, Ingersoll, 1934 .... $340-$525
Three Little Pigs Sand Pail, Ohio Art, 1930s .... $80-$125
Three Little Pigs Soaky Set, Drew Chemical,
    1960s .... $115-$175
Three Little Pigs Wind-Up Toy, Schuco, 1930s .... $450-$700
Who's Afraid of the Big Bad Wolf Game, Parker Bros,
    1930s .... $115-$175

Toy Story
Flying Buzz Lightyear Figure, Thinkway, 1996 .... $4-$8
Hamm Figure, Thinkway, 1996 .... $4-$8
Karate Buzz Figure, Thinkway, 1996 .... $4-$8
Kicking Woody Figure, Thinkway, 1996 .... $4-$8
Quick-Draw Woody Figure, Thinkway, 1996 .... $4-$8
Rex Figure, Thinkway, 1996 .... $4-$8
Talking Buzz Lightyear Figure, Thinkway, 1996 ...... $15-$40
Talking Woody Figure, Thinkway, 1996 .... $15-$40

TIPS OF THE TRADE

When the great Lionel Train Company was teetering on the brink of bankruptcy in the 1930s, Mickey Mouse saved the day in his usually colorful way. Lionel's Mickey Mouse Circus Train and Mickey Mouse Hand Car were two toys which essentially brought the legendary trainmaker back on the profitable track towards prosperity. In 1933, Disney's famous mouse rescued the Ingersoll watchmakers from a similarly perilous fate.

Minnie and Mickey ceramic holders, marked copyright Disney, Japan on bottom, 4-1/2" height, 2-1/2" diameter holder, $10 each.

MODERN DOLLS

The term "modern" dolls generally refers to dolls made from 1950 to the present. Most were originally intended to be played with, rather than to be shelved as collectibles, so they often had a short lifespan. That translates into high value among collectors today.

Some collectors prefer to concentrate on dolls produced by certain manufacturers, such as Madame Alexander (Cissy), Vogue (Ginny dolls), Ideal (Chrissy, Shirley Temple) or Mattel (Chatty Cathy). Others collect dolls by decade (such as 1950s) or by medium (vinyl, composition, cloth, etc.). *(See separate "Barbie" chapter).*

General Guidelines: Dolls in original boxes command premium prices. Wigs should be original and not soiled or restyled. The skin surface should be free of marks, cracks or blemishes. Original sleep eyes must be free moving, and all mechanical parts (including voice boxes) should be operational.

To command top prices, dolls should be dressed in original clothing and have all original accessories (hats, shoes, etc.). Certain popular outfits may command extra value. Original tags and labels add a premium.

Any imperfections — like stains, missing or broken limbs, cracked bodies or cut hair — detract from a doll's value.

Be aware of the markings on dolls, often found on the doll's torso, buttocks or back of head. Most composition and modern dolls are marked with the manufacturer's name and date. Sometimes, however, the date may be a copyright date only and not the same as the date the actual doll was manufactured. A doll with a 1966 copyright date may actually have been made in the 1980s.

Collecting Terms

Here are some terms commonly used in doll collecting.

Composition. A mixture of materials including wood pulp or sawdust, flour, rags, glue and other materials. They have a distinctive appearance, often with tiny cracks called crazing. Crazing indicates the doll has been exposed to extremes in temperature and climatic conditions.

Flirty eyes. An American term applied to doll eyes that shift from side to side.

Hard plastic. A firm material used after 1948 to mold dolls.

Molded hair. The doll's head is molded to have the appearance of hair. Paint or tint is usually applied to the sculpted curls and waves.

Rooted hair. Tiny plugs of synthetic hair pierced into the doll's scalp area.

Sleep eyes. Eyes that close as the doll is laid down.

Stationary eyes. Eyes that do not move when the doll's head is turned. These may be painted on or set into the head.

Turning head. A head that can be rotated from left to right.

Vinyl. A soft plastic material commonly used in dolls made after 1950.

HOT COLLECTING CATEGORIES

- **Advertising Characters** were often offered as premiums when products were purchased. Examples include the Campbell's Kids; Kellogg's Snap, Crackle & Pop; and Cream of Wheat dolls. Cloth dolls are especially popular in this category.

- **Celebrity dolls** depict celebrities like Shirley Temple, Margaret O'Brien, Sonja Henie or Disney characters.

- **Limited-edition collector dolls** are made in limited numbers, or offered for a limited time, specifically for the collector market.

Vogue, Ginny doll with Mickey Mouse hat, eight inch, $120.

Magazines and Newsletters

Doll Castle News
PO Box 247, Washington, NJ 07882

Dolls—The Collector's Magazine
170 Fifth Ave. 12th Floor, New York, NY 10010

Antique Doll World
225 Main St., Suite 300, Northport, NY 11768

Doll Reader
6405 Flank Dr., Harrisburg, PA 17112-2750

Doll Collector's Price Guide
(also *Doll World*)
306 East Parr Road, Berne, IN 46711

National Doll & Teddy Bear Collector
PO Box 4032, Portland, OR 97208-4032

VALUE LINE

Prices listed are for dolls in Near Mint to Mint in Box condition.

Advertising Dolls

Allied Van Lines, 18" $10
Blue Bonnet, 12", 1986 mail-in premium $25
Buddy Lee, 12", hard-plastic head and body, Lee denim
    shirt, bib overalls, hat and red bandanna $350
Campbell Kid, 12", composition character head,
    Horsman $475
Clorox, Lots of Legs, 12", 1985 .... $25
Johnson Wax, Minnie Mouse, 11-1/2", Applause, 1988
    mail-in premium $20
Jolly Green Giant, 16", 1969 mail-in premium $50
Little Debbie, 12", 1985 mail-in premium $50
Lysol, 1988 mail-in premium, Fancy Fresh or Squeaky
    Clean $20
Northern Tissue, 16", 1987 mail-in premium $60
Planters Peanut, Mr. Peanut, 17", monocle on left eye,
    1960s $20
Scrubbing Bubbles, Mr. Bubble, 10", plush $20

American Character

Betsy McCall, 8", hard plastic, 1960 .... $45
Michael Landon, Little Joe, *Bonanza*, vinyl, fully
    jointed body, painted brown hair and eyes, molded
    clothing, c1965 .... $65
Toni, 10", collegiate outfit, orig. booklet $70
Tiny Toodles, 10-1/2", vinyl, molded, painted hair, 1958 $25
Tiny Tears, 12", hard-plastic head, vinyl body, curly
    rooted hair, sunsuit, wood and plastic bathinette,
    c1955 .... $2,500
Bottle Tot, 13", composition head, body mark, orig.
    tagged clothes $175
Baby, 16", composition head, cloth, 1925 .... $125
Sally, 18", composition head, cloth body $200
Sweet Sue Sophisticate, 19", vinyl head $325
Toni, 20" $365
Betsy McCall, 30", vinyl head and body, blue sleep
    eyes $275
Sandy McCall, 35", vinyl head and body, blue sleep
    eyes $530

Arranbee

Little Dear, 8", stuffed vinyl body, rooted hair, blue
    sleep eyes, c1956 .... $80
Littlest Angel, 11", vinyl head, hard plastic body,
    jointed, rooted dark brown hair, 1959 .... $40
Angel Skin, 13", soft vinyl head, magic-skin body and
    limbs $80

Horsman, 11" doll, plastic hands, head, beanbag body, mark: Horsman Dolls Inc.

Nancy Lee, 14", vinyl, blue sleep eyes $115
Baby Bunting, 15", vinylite plastic head, stuffed magic-
    skin body, molded, painted hair $60
Nanette, hard plastic, glued-on wig, sleep eyes,1952 .... $250
Judy, 19", hard plastic, nylon blond wig, braids, metal
    knob to wind hair back into head, open mouth, 1951 .$75
Nanette, hard-plastic fully jointed body, saran braided
    wig, blue sleep eyes, closed mouth,1953 .... $155
Taffy, 23", plastic, socket head, blue eyes, brunette saran
    wig, straight walker legs, 1954 .... $175

Coleco
Cabbage Patch Kids, vinyl, 1980s .... $25-$150

Cosmopolitan Doll
Ginger, 7-1/2", hard plastic, glued-on wig, walker,
    head turns, 1955, various outfits .... $35-$50
Little Miss Ginger, 8-1/2", vinyl head, hard plastic
    body, rooted ash-blond hair, 1956 .... $20
Merri, 14", plastic, rooted blond hair, high-heeled shoes,
    red gown, white fur trim, 1960 .... $20

Deluxe Reading / Topper
Dawn and Friends series, 6", vinyl .... $10-$15 each
Susie Cutie, 7", vinyl, rooted blond hair,
    battery-operated $20
Baby Party, 10", vinyl head and arms, hard-plastic body
    and legs, rooted blond hair, painted eyes, blows
    whistle and balloon $35
Luv-N-Care, 18", vinyl head, hard plastic body, rooted
    blond hair, blue sleep eyes, open mouth, battery-
    operated,1969 .... $48
Sweet Amy School Girl, 23", vinyl head, latex body $50

Eegee Doll Mfg. (Goldberger)
Dimples, 11", vinyl head, cloth beanbag type body,
    rooted blond hair, painted eyes, musical $24
Andy, 12", vinyl head and arms, plastic body and legs $18
Granny, 14", vinyl head, plastic body $65

Talking Charmin' Chatty Travels 'Round the World, Mattel, 1960s,
$175 mint in package.

Bundle of Joy, 19", vinyl head, arms, plastic legs, stuffed
    cloth body, 1964 .... $18
My Fair Lady, vinyl head and body, blond hair, black net,
    orig. costume, c1958 .... $55
Karne Ballerina, 21", hard plastic and vinyl, rooted hair,
    sleep eyes, jointed, ballet dress, 1958 .... $45
Susan Strolled, 23", vinyl head, hard plastic walker,
    1958 .... $50

Effanbee
Fluffy, 1954 .... $40
Patsy Baby, 11", composition head, ... $275
Babette, 11-1/2", composition head and hands, stuffed
    pink cloth body, molded painted brown hair, closed
    eyes and mouth, orig. tags and box, c1945 .... $100
Butterball, 12", all vinyl, molded blond hair, orig box,
    1969 .... $60
Cupcake, 1963 .... $40
Dy Dee Baby, caracal wig, orig. wardrobe and trunk $185
Patricia Walker, 14", 1952 .... $125
Alice, 15", 1958 .... $145
American Child, Barbara Ann, 16", composition head,
    green sleep eyes, human hair wig $450
Anne Shirley, 18", composition $175
Cinderella, 18", 1952 .... $200
Prince Charming, 18", 1952 .... $225
Schoolgirl Writing, 18", 1963 .... $80
Snowsuit Susan, 18", 1967 .... $85
Sugar Plum, 20", 1980 .... $65
Sweetie Pie, 21", composition head, blue flirty eyes,
    closed mouth $225

Horsman
Mary Poppins, all vinyl, c1965 .... $40
Ruthie, 12-1/2", all vinyl, rooted black hair $30
Bye-Lo, 14", vinyl head, arms and legs, cloth body,
    molded straight hair $50
Dimples Toddler, 15" $150
Pram Baby, 19", vinyl, jointed head, glass sleep eyes,
    closed mouth, coos $65

Ideal
Little Miss Revlon, 10", vinyl, rooted saran hair, sleep
    eyes, orig. clothes, c1957 .... $95
Baby Snooks, 12", composition head and hands, wood
    torso, wire limbs $200
Betsy Wetsy, 12", composition head, rubber body, jointed
    at neck, shoulders and hips, drinks, wets and cries $50
Marama, 13", brown composition head, painted brown
    eyes, grass skirt, orange lei $590
Betsy McCall, 14", vinyl head, hard-plastic body, dark
    brown curly saran wig, round brown sleep eyes,
    c1953 .... $100
Mary Hartline, 16", hard plastic, jointed neck, shoulders
    and hips, nylon wig, sleep eyes $700
Bonnie Walker, 17", hard plastic, walker, blue sleep eyes,
    open mouth $85
Thumbelina, 20", vinyl head, arms and legs, cloth body,
    rooted dark-blond hair, painted blue eyes, music box,
    1962 .... $45

Princess Mary, 21", vinyl head, plastic body, 1952 .... $150
Kissy, 22", soft vinyl head, rigid vinyl body, rooted
  hair, c1962 .... $48
Saucy Walker, 22", vinyl head, hard-plastic body, c1955 $75
Patty Playpal, 36", vinyl head and arms, plastic body,
  rooted brown hair, blue sleep eyes, closed mouth,
  orig. clothes, 1960 .... $125

Knickerbocker
Holly Hobbie, 12", cloth, 1970s .... $15-$20
Holly Hobbie, 6", cloth, 1970s .... $5-$7
Raggedy Ann and Andy, 12", cloth, 1970s-1990s,
  each .... $15-$30

Madame Alexander
Quiz-Kid, 7-1/2", hard plastic head $225
Americana Series, 8"Amish Boy, c1965 .... $450
Colonial Girl, c1962 .... $350
International Series, 8"China, 1973 .... $235
Greek Boy, jointed knees, 1968 .... $275
Morocco $225
Spanish Boy, 1964 .... $375
Thailand, 1970 .... $135
Cissette Renoir, 9-1/2", hard plastic, jointed knees $100
Brenda Starr, 12", vinyl head and arms, hard plastic
  body and legs, 1964 .... $800
Lissy Ballerina, 12", hard plastic $250
Alice in Wonderland, 14", hard plastic, blond hair,
  blue eyes, blue taffeta dress, 1950 .... $700
Binnie Walker, 14", hard plastic, blond hair, black
  striped dress, yellow pinafore and straw hat, c1950 .. $500
Goldilocks, 14", vinyl head and arms, hard plastic torso
  and legs, blond synthetic wig, 1978 .... $100
Jenny Lind and Cat, 14", vinyl head and arms, hard
  plastic torso and legs, synthetic wig, sleep eyes,
  1969 .... $300
Maggie, 14", hard plastic, walker, blond mohair wig,
  brown sleep eyes $125
Nina Ballerina, 14", hard plastic, brown wig, sleep eyes,
  closed mouth $300
Caroline, 15", vinyl head, blue sleep eyes, rooted hair
  in orig. set, ... $300
Amy, 16", cloth doll, dressed mask face, blond hair, painted
  blue eyes, flowered print dress, replaced shoes and socks,
  cloth dress tag $80
Marybel, 16", vinyl head, blond rooted hair, brown sleep
  eyes, c1959 .... $160
Elise Bridesmaid, 17", vinyl, 1966 .... $250
Polly, 17", vinyl, 1965, ball gown $195
Baby, 18", hard plastic head, vinyl arms and legs, cloth
  body, pink organdy dress $85
Cissy, 20", brown hair, blue sleep eyes, bridal gown and
  accessories $150
Goya, 21", vinyl $250
Madame, 21", vinyl $325
Melanie, 21", vinyl $275
Mary Ellen, 31", hard plastic head, blue sleep eyes,
  saran wig, hard plastic walker body $215

Mattel
Buffy, 10-1/2", vinyl head, plastic body, blond ponytails,
  painted blue eyes, painted upper teeth, pull talk string,
  holding Mrs. Beasley doll, c1969 .... $125
Cabbage Patch Kids, 1980s .... $5-$30
Donny and Marie Osmond, 10-1/2", vinyl heads, plastic
  bodies, painted eyes, pair, c1977 .... $40
Truly Scrumptious, 11-1/2", *Chitty Chitty Bang Bang*,
  vinyl, straight legs, blond hair, pink and white
  gown, matching hat, c1969 .... $90
Cheerful Tearful, 12", vinyl head and body, 1966 .... $35
Bozo the Clown, 16", vinyl head, cloth body, pullstring,
  c1962 .... $65
Chatty Cathy, 18", soft vinyl head, hard plastic body,
  c1965 .... $60
Charmin' Cathy, 25", vinyl head and arms, plastic body
  and legs, rooted blond hair, blue side-glancing sleep
  eyes, closed mouth, orig. clothes and metal trunk,
  1961 .... $100

Nancy Ann Storybook
Christening Baby, 3-1/2", all hard plastic, molded painted
  yellow hair, closed mouth, straight baby legs, 1952 .... $25
Autumn, 5" $28
Little Joan, 5" $25
Lucy Locket, 5", blue hat $25

Advertising character, Campbell Kid, 10" vinyl doll.

Bridesmaid Teen, 5-1/2", bisque $30
Southern Belle, 5-1/2", bisque $28
Valentine, 5-1/2", bisque $20
Daffidown Dilly, 5-1/2", hard plastic $30
First Communion, 5-1/2", hard plastic $25
School Days, 5-1/2", hard plastic $20
Jeannie, Moonlight and Roses, 6", hard plastic, 1952 ..... $25
Lori Ann Walker, 10", all hard plastic, head turns,
    glued-on brown wig,1953 .... $35
Debbie, 11", hard plastic $60

Sun Rubber
Happy Kappy, 7", rubber body, molded painted hair $25
SoWee, 10", bottle, booties, jacket, towel, soap $35
Tod-L-Dee, 10-1/2", rubber body, molded painted hair,
    open nurser mouth, molded diaper, shoes and socks .. $25
Betty Bows, 11", rubber, fully jointed, molded hair,
    1953 .... $35
Gerber Baby, 11", all rubber, molded, ... $45

Terri Lee Dolls
Ginger Girl Scout, 8" $100
Baby Linda, 9", all vinyl, molded painted hair, black
    eyes, c1951 .... $90
Tiny Jerri Lee, 10", hard plastic, fully jointed, blond
    curly wig, brown sleep eyes, closed mouth $175
Tiny Terri Lee, 10", hard plastic, fully jointed, blond
    wig, inset eyes, closed mouth, trunk with six tagged
    outfits $425
Jerri Lee, 16", hard plastic, jointed at neck, shoulders and
    hips, orig. curly wig, painted eyes, orig. clothing and
    accessories $225
Terri Lee, 16", hard plastic, jointed at neck, shoulders and
    hips, orig. curly wig, painted eyes $200

Vogue
Hansel and Gretel, 7", hard plastic, jointed at neck,
    shoulders and hips, blond mohair wigs $325
Ginny, 8", 1948-1950, all hard plastic, painted eyes,
    molded hair, mohair wigCinderella $150
Clown $225
Coronation Queen $1,100
Springtime $115
Valentine $125
Ginny, 8", 1950-1953, moving eyes
Catholic Nun $165
Christmas $125
Mistress Mary $135
Roller Skating $200
Ginny, 8", 1954, walking mechanism
Ballerina, poodle cut wig $100
Rainy Day $75
School Dress $75
Springtime $70
Ginny, 8", 1957, bended knees
Beach outfit $75
Davy Crockett $80
Southern Belle $90
Wee Imp $155
Jeff, 10" $35
Jill, 10", bride's dress $50

Baby Dear, 12", all composition, bent baby limbs, 1961 . $40
Welcome Home Baby, 20" $50
Hug-a-Bye Baby, 22", pink pajamas $40

Publications
The 12th Blue Book of Dolls & Values by Jan Foulke
(Hobby House Press)

Modern Collector's Dolls Identification and Value Guide
by Patricia Smith (Collector Books)

Horsman Dolls 1950-1970 by Patikii Gibbs (Collector
Books)

Twentieth Century Dolls and *More Twentieth Century Dolls*
by Johana Anderton (Trojan Press)

Shirley Temple Dolls and Fashions by Edward Pardella
(Schiffer Publishing)

Collector's Guide to Vogue Dolls by Carol Stover and
Judith Izen (Collector Books)

Ideal, Shirley Temple doll, 12", all original 1950s.

FAST FOOD TOYS

Although kids' meal toys and boxes were formerly discarded as fast as the food was eaten, these items have come into their own as collectibles.

Almost 30 restaurants currently issue toys for young and old to collect. This simple marketing inducement has given collectors an inexpensive way to acquire high quality toys representing characters from comic books, movies, sports and television. The hobby is an investment in fun, where affordability is the key driving force.

History: Burger Chef became the first restaurant to regularly promote the concept of the kid's meal in 1972. Their initial effort was called a "Funmeal," a forerunner of the now-common box in which these meals are served. The Funmeal box featured the restaurant's own cast of characters, including Burger Chef and Jeff. Like the modern fast food toy meal boxes to follow, the box itself was designed to be played with, complete with games and pictures.

Burger Chef's Funmeal concept quietly continued until their first truly recognizable promotion took the fast food industry by surprise. In 1977, the Triple-Play Funmeal baseball team box set featured one box of each of the 24 different Major League Baseball teams. The use of a nationally-known subject matter — in this case, baseball teams — was a major breakthrough. Today, a mere two decades later, this set of 24 Funmeal boxes is worth over $1,000.

The Triple-Play Funmeal success was soon followed by the introduction of the seven-box *Star Wars* Funmeal set in 1978. Burger Chef continued to issue boxes and related items until 1983, finishing with Indy 500 race cars with stickers and boxes.

Most restaurants issued toys or promotions for kids in the 1960s on an irregular and limited basis. McDonald's was primarily responsible for taking the industry to the next level with regular kids' meal toys and related box promotions. In 1978, they began tests of what are now known as Happy Meal toys. After mixed results, they hit upon a *Star Trek* promotional tie-in which gave them the same kind of success Burger Chef had enjoyed with their Triple-Play Funmeal baseball box program. By 1988, one thing seemed clear to both McDonald's and fast food toy collectors alike — recognizable characters were fun to collect.

Toy Story figures; $1 Excellent for each, 1995, Burger King.

General Guidelines: Since the typical kids' meal consumer is under age 12 — an age range known for rough play habits — this makes condition of fast food toys a critical factor. Only the rarest toys hold any value if found in less than perfect condition. Fast food toys and restaurant premiums are generally valued using two grading classifications, Mint in Package (MIP) and Mint No Package (MNP), also known as "loose." As these designations suggest, MIP toys have never been removed from their original packaging and played with. On the average, MIP toys are valued at 200 percent of MNP toys. MNP toys may show minor evidence of play, but they remain clean and intact. Loose toys in poor condition are generally of little or no value to collectors. To retain maximum potential value, older toys in package should always be left in package.

Buying older toys MIP can show dramatic price differences. Pre-1986 McDonald's and pre-1992 non-McDonald's fast food toys are considered older and more scarce in this hobby.

Rarity also has an impact on value. A toy's age, cross-collectibility and overall popularity play important roles in this. Modern movie tie-in toys, such as Disney's *Toy Story*, are frequently worth more than older toys due to the strong Disneyana collector market. The same holds true for well-known cartoon and comic character items.

Distribution also affects rarity. Some fast food toys and premiums, called "regionals," are offered only in designated geographic areas. Due to their limited distribution, regionals command higher than average prices.

Toys designed for children under age three ("under three" toys) are valued 20 percent higher than the standard toys in a promotion. Crossover categories such as Disney characters, professional sports teams, cartoon, comic book and TV characters are often most popular. They are easily recognizable by collectors in other fields, which adds to their appeal and fuels the demand for these collectibles.

A note on prices: While some toys and boxes sell for more than $25, ninety percent of all toys and boxes still sell for under two dollars.

Garfield figures; $3 Excellent for each, 1989, McDonald's.

Clubs
- •Fast Food Toy Club of Northern Illinois
  164 Larchmont Lane, Bloomingdale, IL 60108

- •McDonald's Collectors Club
  424 White Road, Fremont, OH 43420-1539

Contributor to this section: Jeff Escue, Fundamental Research, Inc., 164 Larchmont Lane, Bloomingdale, IL 60108-1412.

COLLECTING TIPS

- Loose fast food toys removed from their original packaging have relatively little value to collectors. If relatively new, most loose toys may be worth 25 cents each or less. Toys that are missing parts, scratched or worn are worthless to collectors.

- •Older boxes are emerging as some of the most valuable of the hobby's collectibles because of their great artwork and relative scarcity. Nobody kept them!

- Older Happy Meal toys may be more valuable due to their scarcity. This is especially true for regionally-produced toys and the special under-three toys, which are manufactured in smaller quantities. Loose, these toys typically sell for between $2 and $5 apiece.

- Most collectors seek toys Mint in Package. More recent MIP toys generally sell for $1. Older toys in MIP condition, however — including scarcer regionals and "under three" toys — may sell for $3 to $10 or more.

VALUE LINE

Prices listed are for toys in Near Mint to Mint in Package condition. Prices are for each toy in a set, not the entire set.

Arby's, 1981-present
Babar figures, set of four	$1-$3
Babar license plates, set of four	$1-$2
Babar puzzles, set of four	$3-$5
Babar stampers, set of three	$2-$4
Babar World Tour vehicles, set of three	$2-$4
Little Miss figures, set of seven	$2-$4
Looney Tunes Car-Tunes, set of six	$2-$4
Looney Tunes Characters, set of three	$2-$4
Looney Tunes figures, six different	$3-$6
Looney Tunes figures, six different stiff-legged	$3-$6
Looney Tunes figures, seven on oval base	$4-$8

Big Boy, 1960s-present
Action figures, set of four	$2-$5
Big Boy Bank, large, 1960s	$300
Big Boy Board Game	$75-$100
Big Boy Kite	$10-$25
Big Boy Nodder, 1960s	$1,500

Big Boy Stuffed Dolls, set of three	$30-$50
Helicopters, set of three	$1-$3
Monster In My Pocket, various packs	$2-$4

Burger Chef, 1970s
Funmeal boxes	$40

Burger King, 1984-present
Aladdin figures, set of five	$2-$4
ALF puppets, four with records	$5-$10
Alvin & The Chipmunks, set of three toys	$1-$2
Aquaman Tub Toy	$3-$5
Barnyard Commandos, set of four	$2-$3
Beauty & The Beast, set of four PVC figures	$2-$4
Beetlejuice, set of six figures	$2-$4
BK Kids Action figures, set of four	$2-$4
Bone Age Skeleton Kit, set of four dinos	$3-$6
Capitol Critters, set of four	$2-$4
Captain Planet, set of four flip-over vehicles	$2-$4
Disney 20th Anniversary figures, set of four	$3-$5
Freaky Fellas, set of four	$2-$4
Go-Go Gadget Gizmos, set of four	$2-$4
Lickety Splits	$2-$4
Matchbox cars, set of four	$3-$6
Pinocchio, set of five toys	$1-$2
Pocahontas Pop-Up Puppets	$2-$4
Purrtenders, set of four	$3-$6
Simpsons dolls, set of five	$2-$4
Simpsons figures, set of five	$2-$4
Super Heroes cups, set of five	$4-$8
Teenage Mutant Ninja Turtles badges, six different	$2-$4
Thundercats, set of four toys	$3-$8
Toy Story puppets	$5-$10
Toy Story figures	$3-$5

Chuck E. Cheese, 1980s
Chuck E. Cheese PVC figures	$4-$7

Denny's, 1990-present
Dino-Makers, set of six	$2-$4
Flintstones Dino Racers, set of six	$2-$4
Flintstones Fun Squirters, set of six	$1-$2
Flintstones Glacier Gliders, set of six	$1-$4

Pocahontas figures; $1 Excellent for each, 1995, Burger King.

Flintstones Mini Plush, four sets .... $2-$4
Flintstones Rock & Rollers, set of six .... $2-$4
Flintstones Stone-Age Cruisers, set of six .... $2-$4
Flintstones vehicles, set of eight .... $2-$4
Jetsons Game Packs, set of six .... $1-$2
Jetsons Space Balls, set of six .... $1-$2

Domino's Pizza, 1987-present
Noids, set of seven figures .... $1-$2

Hardee's, 1987-present
Beach Bunnies, set of four .... $2-$4
California Raisins .... $2-$4
California Raisins plush, set of four .... $3-$6
Days of Thunder racers, set of four .... $3-$6
Fender Bender 500 racers, set of five .... $2-$4
Flintstones First 30 Years, set of five .... $2-$4
Gremlin Adventures, set of five book/record sets .... $2-$4
Home Alone 2, set of four .... $1-$2
Pound Puppies, set of six .... $3-$6
Shirt Tales plush dolls, set of five .... $3-$6
Smurfin' Smurfs, set of four .... $2-$3
Super Heroes, set of four vehicles .... $3-$6
Waldo's Straw Buddies, set of four .... $2-$3

International House of Pancakes (IHOP), 1992
Pancake Kids, set of six .... $2-$4
Pancake Kids plush, two different .... $4-$9

Kentucky Fried Chicken, 1960s-present
Alvin & The Chipmunks, two Canadian issues .... $3-$5
Colonel Sanders figure .... $35-$50
Colonel Sanders nodder .... $75-$150
WWF Stampers, set of four Canadian issues .... $2-$4

Long John Silver's, 1989-present
Fish Cars .... $2-$4
Sea Walkers, set of four .... $3-$5
Sea Watchers kaleidoscopes, set of three .... $3-$5
Water Blasters, set of three .... $3-$5

McDonald's, 1977-present
101 Dalmatians, set of four PVC figures .... $2-$4
101 Dalmatians, under three toy .... $3-$6
Adventures of Ronald McDonald, set of seven rubber
    figures .... $5-$10
Astrosnicks, set of eight rubber creatures .... $5-$10
Back to the Future, set of four .... $2-$4
Bambi, set of four .... $2-$4
Barbie, eight different dolls .... $5-$10
Batman Returns, set of four vehicles .... $2-$4
Cabbage Patch, set of five dolls .... $2-$4
Chip 'N Dale's Rescue Rangers, set of four .... $2-$4

┌─ **FUN FACT** ─────────────────────────────┐
│   McDonald's outsells every other restaurant chain when │
│ it comes to kids' meals. In the two decades since the Happy │
│ Meal was launched, they've reaped sales of more than 3.6 │
│ billion meal-and-toy combos worldwide.   │
└──┘

Dinosaur Days, set of six .... $2-$4
Disney Masterpiece Collection figures .... $2-$5
Duck Tales, set of four toys .... $2-$4
Dukes of Hazzard, set of five vehicles .... $5-$10
Flintstone Kids, set of four .... $3-$6
Garfield, set of four figures .... $2-$4
Grimace Bank .... $10-$20
Hot Wheels, eight different cars .... $3-$6
Jungle Book, set of four wind-ups .... $2-$4
Lego Building Sets, set of four Duplo kits .... $4-$8
Little Mermaid, set of four figures .... $2-$4
Looney Tunes Quack-Up Cars, four different .... $2-$4
Mac Tonight, set of six vehicles .... $2-$4
McNugget Buddies, set of 10 figures .... $3-$5
Muppet Babies, four different .... $3-$5
My Little Pony, 1980s $80
New Archies, set of six cars .... $5-$9
Peanuts, under three toys .... $3-$6
Rescuers Down Under, set of four camera toys .... $2-$4
Sonic The Hedgehog, set of four .... $2-$4
Star Trek, set of four rings .... $4-$8
Super Mario Brothers, set of four figures .... $2-$4
Tailspin, set of four planes .... $2-$4
Tiny Toons Flip Cars, set of four .... $2-$4
Tom & Jerry Band, set of four .... $3-$5
Tonka, set of five vehicles .... $1-$2
Young Astronauts, set of four vehicles .... $2-$4

Muppet Babies; $3 Excellent for each, 1987, McDonald's.

Pizza Hut, 1988-present

    Beauty & The Beast puppets, set of four .... $3-$6

    Eureeka's Castle puppets, set of three .... $3-$6

    Land Before Time puppets, set of six .... $3-$6

    Universal Monster Cops, set of three .... $2-$5

Taco Bell

    Star Wars collection, 1997 .... $2-$5

Wendy's, 1984-present

    ALF Tales, set of six .... $2-$4

    All Dogs Go To Heaven, set of six .... $2-$4

    Fast Food Racers, set of five .... $2-$4

    Jetsons figures, set of six in ships .... $2-$4

    Mighty Mouse, set of six .... $3-$5

    Teddy Ruxpin, set of five .... $2-$4

    Wacky Wind-Ups, set of five .... $2-$3

    World Wildlife Foundation, set of four plush .... $5-$10

    Yogi Bear & Friends, set of six .... $2-$4

White Castle, 1991-present

    Castle Friends Bubble Makers, set of four .... $2-$3

    Castle Meal Friends, set of six .... $2-$4

    Cosby Kids, set of four .... $2-$3

    Godzilla Squirter .... $3-$6

    Nestle's Quik plush bunny .... $2-$7

    Silly Putty, set of three .... $2-$4

    Tootsie Roll Express, set of four .... $2-$4

Flintstones Fun Squirters; $2 Excellent for each, 1991, Denny's.

Simpsons figures; $2 Excellent for each, 1991, Burger King.

FIESTAWARE

Making its colorful debut at the 1936 Pottery and Glass Show in Pittsburgh, Fiestaware captivated the dinnerware trade — only hinting at its future reception by American families. Designed and modeled by Fredrick Rhead, Arthur Kraft, Bill Bersford and Dr. A.V. Blenininger, Fiesta was produced by Homer Laughlin, one of the world's foremost potteries.

Fiestaware's immediate acceptance by the general public was by no means accidental. Homer Laughlin had sought to win its place at dinner tables across America using a simple but effective strategy — forego formal ware in favor of a subtler everyday line. Fiesta featured two key ingredients that also set it apart — accessories that allowed families to complement and expand their table service and rich colors distinct enough to warm any setting, yet interchangable enough to mix and match with any family's personally selected, customized Fiesta arrangement.

The original Fiestaware was manufactured in five vivid colors: orange-red, cobalt blue, light green, bright yellow and ivory. Over the years, Fiestaware was made in turquoise, forest green, rose, chartreuse and gray, the latter four of which are commonly referred to by collectors as "the Fifties colors." Eleven colors would eventually permeate the line.

General Guidelines: Affordability and interchangeability translated into tremendous popularity for Fiestaware; a popularity that began in the late 1930s and continued through the 1950s. Collecting Fiestaware today is easier because of distinctive colors and unmistakable marks on nearly every piece. Demitasse cups, juice tumblers and salt and pepper shakers are among the line's few unmarked items.

While most teacups are generally unmarked, some feature an ink stamp. Ashtrays, onion soups and sweet compotes have been found both marked and unmarked. But by familiarizing themselves with Fiesta's streamlined originality, most collectors can easily identify authentic pieces.

Several factors contribute to the value of Fiestaware including color, scarcity, type of piece and condition. Mint condition pieces command top prices. Slightly scratched pieces are generally valued at 30 percent below Mint prices. Pieces marked with more apparent damage, such as dings and heavy scratches, are valued at half the Mint price or less.

While color plays a primary role in determining values, the popularity of colors has shifted throughout the years. Ivory did not catch on as a popular color among even the most enthusiastic of Fiesta collectors at first. Today, ivory pieces are as popular as other original colors.

Medium green pieces remain the exception to this rule, however. Produced in far fewer numbers than any other Fiesta colors, these pieces are highly desired by collectors and command higher premiums. Almost any piece in medium green is considered worth at least twice as much as a differently-colored corresponding piece. Made only until 1946, Fiesta carafes are difficult to find and usually sell for $200 and up.

Trends: So far, no significant trends in collecting Fiestaware have emerged. Most collectors eagerly gather any and all pieces they come across. While limiting a collection to a particular color is one way to go, the built-in interchangeability of colors — one of Fiesta's hallmarks — encourages collectors to assemble an assortment of their own design.

Like every other kind of collectible, certain pieces of Fiestaware are rarer than others. These pieces were more often than not manufactured in lower numbers than the rest of the line. Made for only one year in 1936, one collector estimates that less than 200 onion soups were produced — translating into an item on every Fiesta collector's wish list.

Clubs
•The Fiesta Club of America
 P.O. Box 15383, Love Park, IL 61132-5383

Orange carafe, $110.

TIPS OF THE TRADE

- Decals should be complete, showing well-preserved colors and otherwise little wear. Pieces featuring faded, scuffed or worn decals are worth less.

- The undersides of many pieces feature three sagger pin marks. Not to be confused with damage, these marks are a result of the stacked firing process.

VALUE LINE

Prices listed are for items in Mint condition.

Ashtray, red	$50
Ashtray, cobalt	$50
Ashtray, ivory	$50
Ashtray, yellow	$42
Ashtray, turquoise	$42
Ashtray, light green	$42
Ashtray, Fifties colors	$75
Ashtray, medium green	$140
Bowl, covered onion soup, cobalt and ivory	$550
Bowl, covered onion soup, red	$600
Bowl, covered onion soup, turquoise	$2,200
Bowl, covered onion soup, yellow and light green	$465
Bowl, cream soup, red	$55
Bowl, cream soup, cobalt	$55
Bowl, cream soup, ivory	$55
Bowl, cream soup, yellow	$40
Bowl, cream soup, turquoise	$40
Bowl, cream soup, light green	$40
Bowl, cream soup, Fifties colors	$70
Bowl, cream soup, medium green	$3,200
Bowl, 6" dessert, red	$48
Bowl, 6" dessert, cobalt	$48
Bowl, 6" dessert, ivory	$48
Bowl, 6" dessert, yellow	$35
Bowl, 6" dessert, turquoise	$35
Bowl, 6" dessert, light green	$35
Bowl, 6" dessert, Fifties colors	$48
Bowl, 6" dessert, medium green	$325
Bowl, footed salad, red	$275
Bowl, footed salad, cobalt	$275
Bowl, footed salad, ivory	$275
Bowl, footed salad, yellow	$220
Bowl, footed salad, turquoise	$220
Bowl, footed salad, light green	$220
Bowl, 11-3/4" fruit, red	$235
Bowl, 11-3/4" fruit, cobalt	$235
Bowl, 11-3/4" fruit, ivory	$235
Bowl, 11-3/4" fruit, yellow	$190
Bowl, 11-3/4" fruit, turquoise	$190
Bowl, 11-3/4" fruit, light green	$190
Bowl, 4-3/4" fruit, red	$30
Bowl, 4-3/4" fruit, cobalt	$30
Bowl, 4-3/4" fruit, ivory	$30

Bowl, 4-3/4" fruit, yellow	$24
Bowl, 4-3/4" fruit, turquoise	$24
Bowl, 4-3/4" fruit, light green	$24
Bowl, 4-3/4" fruit, Fifties colors	$32
Bowl, 4-3/4" fruit, medium green	$375
Bowl, 5-1/2" fruit, red	$32
Bowl, 5-1/2" fruit, cobalt	$32
Bowl, 5-1/2" fruit, ivory	$32
Bowl, 5-1/2" fruit, yellow	$25
Bowl, 5-1/2" fruit, turquoise	$25
Bowl, 5-1/2" fruit, light green	$25
Bowl, 5-1/2" fruit, Fifties colors	$35
Bowl, 5-1/2" fruit, medium green	$65
Bowl, 7-1/2" individual salad, red, turquoise or yellow	$75
Bowl, 7-1/2" individual salad, medium green	$95
Bowl, #1 mixing, red, cobalt or ivory	$150
Bowl, #1 mixing, yellow, turquoise or light green	$130
Bowl, #2 mixing, red, cobalt or ivory	$100
Bowl, #2 mixing, yellow, turquoise or light green	$85
Bowl, #3 mixing, red, cobalt or ivory	$110
Bowl, #3 mixing, yellow, turquoise or light green	$95
Bowl, #4 mixing, red, cobalt or ivory	$125
Bowl, #4 mixing, yellow, turquoise or light green	$110
Bowl, #5 mixing, red, cobalt or ivory	$145
Bowl, #5 mixing, yellow, turquoise or light green	$130
Bowl, #6 mixing, red, cobalt or ivory	$185
Bowl, #6 mixing, yellow, turquoise or light green	$165
Bowl, #7 mixing, red, cobalt or ivory	$260
Bowl, #7 mixing, yellow, turquoise or light green	$220
Bowl, 8-1/2" nappy, red, cobalt or ivory	$45
Bowl, 8-1/2" nappy, yellow, turquoise or light green	$35
Bowl, 8-1/2" nappy, Fifties colors	$50
Bowl, 8-1/2" nappy, medium green	$110
Bowl, 9-1/2" nappy, red, cobalt or ivory	$60
Bowl, 9-1/2" nappy, yellow, turquoise or light green	$48
Bowl, 9-1/2" nappy, red, cobalt or ivory	$60
Bowl, unlisted salad, red, cobalt or ivory	$310
Bowl, unlisted salad, yellow	$90
Candleholders, bulb, red, cobalt or ivory	$110
Candleholders, bulb, yellow, turquoise or light green	$85
Candleholders, tripod, red, cobalt or ivory	$485
Candleholders, tripod, yellow, turquoise or light green	$385
Carafe, red, cobalt or ivory	$225
Carafe, yellow, turquoise or light green	$180
Casserole, red, cobalt or ivory	$180
Casserole, yellow, turquoise or light green	$125
Casserole, Fifties colors	$265
Casserole, medium green	$500
Casserole, French, red, cobalt or ivory	$475
Casserole, French, turquoise or light green	$475
Casserole, French, yellow	$245
Casserole, promotional, any color complete	$140
Coffee pot, red, cobalt or ivory	$210
Coffee pot, yellow, turquoise or light green	$165
Coffee pot, Fifties colors	$265
Coffee pot, gray	$350
Coffee pot, demitasse, red, cobalt or ivory	$300
Coffee pot, demitasse, yellow, turquoise or light green	$250

FIESTA FINDS

The following pieces are considered true gems by experienced collectors due to limited production runs:

- Any medium green piece
- Covered onion soups (especially in medium green)
- 10-inch and 12-inch flower vases (produced only from 1936 to 1942)
- Marmalades
- Mixing bowls
- Syrup pitchers

Comport, 12" red, cobalt or ivory $165
Comport, 12" yellow, turquoise or light green $130
Comport, sweets, red, cobalt or ivory $80
Comport, sweets, yellow, turquoise or light green $68
Creamer, red, cobalt or ivory $28
Creamer, yellow, turquoise or light green $20
Creamer, Fifties colors $38
Creamer, medium green $68
Creamer, individual, red $200
Creamer, individual, turquoise $295
Creamer, individual, yellow $60
Creamer, slick-handled, red, cobalt or ivory $50
Creamer, stick-handled, yellow, turquoise or light green .. $38
Cup, demitasse, red, cobalt or ivory $62
Cup, demitasse, yellow, turquoise or light green $56
Cup, demitasse, Fifties colors $270
Egg cup, red, cobalt or ivory $60
Egg cup, yellow, turquoise or light green $50
Egg cup, Fifties colors $145
Lid for mixing bowl #1-3, any color $600
Lid for mixing bowl #4, any color $650
Marmalade, red, cobalt or ivory $225
Marmalade, yellow, turquoise or light green $190
Mug, Tom and Jerry, red, cobalt or ivory $75
Mug, Tom and Jerry, yellow, turquoise or light green $55
Mug, Tom and Jerry, Fifties colors $90
Mug, Tom and Jerry, medium green $105
Mustard, red, cobalt or ivory $220
Mustard, yellow, turquoise or light green $180
Pitcher, disk juice, gray $2,000
Pitcher, disk juice, red $345
Pitcher, disk juice, yellow $42
Pitcher, disk water, red, cobalt or ivory $145
Pitcher, disk water, yellow, turquoise or light green $105
Pitcher, disk water, Fifties colors $225
Pitcher, disk water, medium green $950
Pitcher, ice, red, cobalt or ivory $135
Pitcher, ice, yellow, turquoise or light green $110
Pitcher, 2-pt jug, red, cobalt or ivory $100
Pitcher, 2-pt jug, yellow, turquoise or light green $70
Pitcher, 2-pt jug, Fifties colors $130
Plate, cake, red, cobalt or ivory $700
Plate, cake, yellow, turquoise or light green $620
Plate, 13" red, cobalt or ivory $45

Plate, 13" chop, yellow, turquoise or light green $35
Plate, 13" chop, Fifties colors $85
Plate, 13" chop, medium green $175
Plate, 15" chop, red, cobalt or ivory $62
Plate, 15" chop, yellow, turquoise or light green $42
Plate, 15" chop, Fifties colors $100
Plate, 10-1/2" compartment, red, cobalt or ivory $38
Plate, 10-1/2" compartment, yellow, turquoise or light green $35
Plate, 10-1/2" compartment, Fifties colors $65
Plate, 12" compartment, red, cobalt or ivory $55
Plate, 12" compartment, yellow, turquoise or light green . $52
Plate, deep, red, cobalt or ivory $48
Plate, deep, yellow, turquoise or light green $38
Plate, deep, Fifties colors $50
Plate, deep, medium green $110
Plate, 6" red, cobalt or ivory $7
Plate, 6" yellow, turquoise or light green $5
Plate, 6" Fifties colors $9
Plate, 6" medium green $18
Plate, 7" red, cobalt or ivory $10
Plate, 7" yellow, turquoise or light green $9
Plate, 7" Fifties colors $13
Plate, 7" medium green $30
Plate, 9" red, cobalt or ivory $18

Syrup pourer, cobalt blue, $120.

READY OR NOT FOR RADIOACTIVE RED?

When Fiesta red was reintroduced after World War II, rumors circulated that these items might indeed prove hazardous. Concerned citizens wrote to Homer Laughlin worried about the uranium in their Fiesta red glaze. Follow-up studies proved these fears unfounded, as the uranium oxide content in Fiestaware was well below levels considered safe for human exposure.

COLLECTOR ALERT

Homer Laughlin ran a promotional campaign from 1939 to 1943 that offered several items priced at $1 each. Hard to find today, these promotionals are highly desired by Fiesta collectors. They include a casserole with pie plate; chop plate with detachable metal holder; four-piece refrigerator set; jumbo coffee cups and saucers; and salad bowl with fork and spoon.

Plate, 9" yellow, turquoise or light green	$12
Plate, 9" Fifties colors	$22
Plate, 9" medium green	$42
Plate, 10" red, cobalt or ivory	$40
Plate, 10" yellow, turquoise or light green	$30
Plate, 10" Fifties colors	$50
Plate, 10" medium green	$100
Platter, red, cobalt or ivory	$44
Platter, yellow, turquoise or light green	$32
Platter, Fifties colors	$55
Platter, medium green	$120
Salt & pepper shakers, red, cobalt or ivory	$28
Salt & pepper shakers, yellow, turquoise or light green	$20
Salt & pepper shakers, Fifties colors	$40
Salt & pepper shakers, medium green	$115
Sauce boat, red, cobalt or ivory	$60
Sauce boat, yellow, turquoise or light green	$40
Sauce boat, Fifties colors	$70
Sauce boat, medium green	$130
Saucer, red, cobalt or ivory	$5
Saucer, yellow, turquoise or light green	$4
Saucer, Fifties colors	$6
Saucer, medium green	$10
Saucer, demitasse, red, cobalt or ivory	$20
Saucer, demitasse, yellow, turquoise or light green	$16
Saucer, demitasse, Fifties colors	$85
Sugar bowl with lid, red, cobalt or ivory	$52
Sugar bowl with lid, yellow, turquoise or light green	$40
Sugar bowl with lid, Fifties colors	$65
Sugar bowl with lid, medium green	$130
Sugar bowl, individual, turquoise	$310
Sugar bowl, individual, yellow	$95
Syrup, red, cobalt or ivory	$310
Syrup, yellow, turquoise or light green	$260
Teacup, red, cobalt or ivory	$32
Teacup, yellow, turquoise or light green	$25
Teacup, Fifties colors	$35
Teacup, medium green	$55
Teapot, large, red, cobalt or ivory	$190
Teapot, large, yellow, turquoise or light green	$150
Teapot, med, red, cobalt or ivory	$165
Teapot, med, yellow, turquoise or light green	$140
Teapot, med, Fifties colors	$260
Teapot, med, medium green	$625
Tumbler, juice, red, cobalt or ivory	$40
Tumbler, juice, yellow, turquoise or light green	$35
Tumbler, water, red, cobalt or ivory	$65
Tumbler, water, yellow, turquoise or light green	$55
Vase, bud, red, cobalt or ivory	$80
Vase, bud, yellow, turquoise or light green	$62
Vase, 8" red, cobalt or ivory	$520
Vase, 8" yellow, turquoise or light green	$450
Vase, 10" red, cobalt or ivory	$680
Vase, 10" yellow, turquoise or light green	$610
Vase, 12" red, cobalt or ivory	$900
Vase, 12" yellow, turquoise or light green	$785

FIRST EDITION BOOKS

With so many printings and copies of books, it may be confusing for non-collectors to understand book collecting. For collectors, however, often the most valuable books are first editions. A first edition is *often* the same as first printing, which means the number of books produced while the printing plates are on the press for the first time. But first printing *doesn't always* mean first edition.

The key page in the identification of first editions is the back side of the title page, or copyright page. Notations on the copyright page may denote that the book is from the third, fifth or even 29th printing. Such books are rarely collectible (unless autographed by the author) and are worth no more than the price on the dust jacket.

Modern first editions by best-selling authors probably will have little increase in value in the future since initial print runs are so large.

General Guidelines: Condition is key. A prime copy is one that looks new. Writing on the endpapers or in the text, dog-eared pages, fading to the spine or covers, browning of the pages or other flaws seriously detract from a book's value.

A book's dust jacket — the paper covering that protects the binding from dirt and wear — is extremely important. Dust jackets did not routinely appear on books until the 1920s, and few books with vintage jackets have survived. Finding a book with an intact dust jacket always adds value to the book, and sometimes, the jacket itself can be worth more than the book it covers. A chipped or badly torn jacket can make an otherwise collectible title a tough sell.

Certain authors command more interest from collectors. Perennial favorites include fantasy and adventure author Edgar Rice Burroughs, beat writer Jack Kerouac, mystery writer Raymond Chandler and classics authors Ernest Hemingway, John Steinbeck, F. Scott Fitzgerald, William Faulkner and Sinclair Lewis.

Contemporary authors are not to be overlooked, however. Books by giants such as Stephen King, John Grisham, Michael Crichton and Tom Clancy can bring top prices as well. Especially collectible are first editions of hot authors' first books, before the authors became big names.

An author's autograph can add value to any book, but especially to a first edition.

Watch out for first printings of "book club" editions; they have no collector value.

VALUE LINE

Values listed are for American first editions in Near Mint condition with crisp dust jackets.

Mickey Spillane, *I, The Jury*, 1947 .... $200-$275
James M. Cain, *The Postman Always Rings Twice*,
    1934 .... $1,000-$1,500
Alice Walker, *The Color Purple*, 1982 .... $300-$500
John Steinbeck, *East of Eden*, 1952 .... $200-$400
Tony Hillerman, *Listening Woman*, 1978 .... $300-$500
James Michener, *Hawaii*, 1959 .... $125-$200

The Hunt for Red October by Tom Clancy.

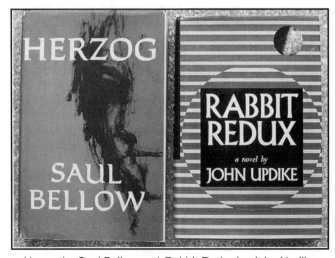

Herzog by Saul Bellow and *Rabbit Redux* by John Updike.

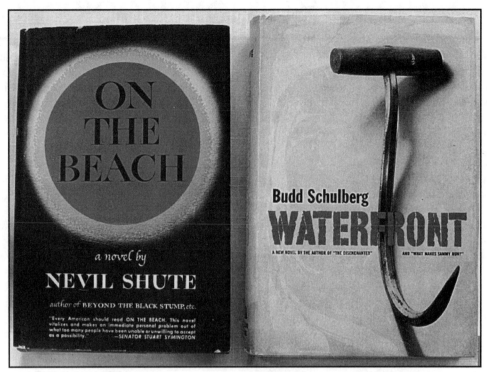

On the Beach by Nevil Shute and *Waterfront* by Budd Schulberg.

Dean Koontz, *Night Chills*, 1976 .... $150-$250

Dick Francis, *Rat Race*, 1970 .... $50-$75

Raymond Chandler, *The Big Sleep*, 1939 .... $3,000-$5,000

Jack Schaefer, *Shane*, 1949 .... $1,000-$1,500

John Updike, *Rabbit, Run*, 1960 .... $200-$300

Erle Stanley Gardner, *The Case of the Careless Hatter*,
    1942 .... $75-$125

Sara Parentsky, *Deadlock*, 1984 .... $75-$100

Ayn Rand, *Atlas Shrugged*, 1957 .... $300-$500

Ray Bradbury, *The Martian Chronicles*, 1950 ...... $500-$700

Robert Frost, *A Masque of Reason*, 1945 .... $50-$75

Richard Adams, *Watership Down*, 1974 .... $75-$100

Harper Lee, *To Kill a Mockingbird*, 1960 .... $750-$1,000

Marjorie Kinnan Rawlings, *The Yearling*, 1938 ...... $75-$150

Herman Wouk, *The Caine Mutiny*, 1951 .... $150-$250

Michael Crichton, *The Andromeda Strain*, 1969 ..... $75-$100

Truman Capote, *Breakfast at Tiffany's*, 1958 .... $100-$200

Douglas Adams, *The Hitchhiker's Guide to the Galaxy*,
    1980 .... $50-$100

John Steinbeck, *East of Eden*, 1952 .... $800-$1,200

Mario Puzo, *The Godfather*, 1969 .... $150-$250

Jack Kerouac, *On the Road*, 1957 .... $1,500-$2,000

Stephen King, *Carrie*, 1974 .... $650-$800

Stephen King, *Night Shift*, 1978 .... $250-$300

Stephen King, *The Dead Zone*, 1979 .... $45-$75

Alex Haley, *Roots*, 1976 .... $35-$50

Sue Grafton, *"A" is for Alibi*, 1982 .... $800-$1,000

Sue Grafton, *"B" is for Burglar*, 1985 .... $200-$400

Sue Grafton, *"C" is for Corpse*, 1986 .... $100-$150

Bernard Malamud, *The Natural*, 1952 .... $250-$300

Norman Mailer, *The Naked and the Dead*, 1948 ... $350-$600

Anne Tyler, *The Accidental Tourist*, 1985 .... $50-$75

Gore Vidal, *Myra Breckenridge*, 1968 .... $30-$60

J. R. R. Tolkien, *The Hobbit*, 1938 .... $1,250-$1,700

Tom Clancy, *The Hunt for Red October*, 1984 ...... $600-$750

Tom Clancy, *Patriot Games*, 1987 .... $25-$30

Willa Cather, *My Antonia*, 1918 .... $900-$1,400

Joseph Heller, *Catch-22*, 1961 .... $700-$1,000

Robert Bloch, *Psycho*, 1959 .... $300-$350

Ian Fleming, *Casino Royale*, 1954 .... $700-$1,000

Ian Fleming, *The Spy Who Loved Me*, 1962 .... $40-$60

J.D. Salinger, *The Catcher in the Rye*, 1951 .... $2,000-$3,000

John Knowles, *A Separate Peace*, 1959 .... $400-$500

Bob Dylan, *Tarantula*, 1971 .... $50-$75

FISHING COLLECTIBLES

Who would have ever dreamed that a fishing lure would be a desirable collectible, much less a valuable one? You may be able to find a hidden treasure in the bottom of that old "possum-belly" tackle box, or anywhere there might be fishing tackle, rods or reels from the '60s and earlier. Values can go quite high, even into the thousands. The norm is $5 or $10, up to $200.

History: It is most likely that the first artificial lures were fashioned when early man began to formulate ways of outwitting his prey. Whether his piscatorial pursuits were of a sporting nature, or to supplement his diet, is an academic point.

It was probably the native American who first developed the artificial lure on this continent, but the lure as we know it today has its roots in the late eighteenth century. There was little interest in fishing as a sport in early American history but much commercial fishing, and probably a little fly fishing by visiting European aristocrats. By then fly fishing as a sport was already well developed in England.

Probably the oldest manufactured ancestor of today's modern fishing lure is the "Phantom Minnow." This English lure first made its appearance in America in the early 1800s. The first of these consisted of a metal head and metal fins on either side of a soft body usually made of silk. The "Phantom Minnow" remained essentially the same for the next 75 to 80 years. It underwent a few changes with regard to hooks and leaders, but remained a staple lure into the 1940s.

The first American artificial lure listed in United States patent records (patented in 1876) incorporating a wood body—and confirmed to have been manufactured—was H.C. Brush's "Floating Spinner." There were no further innovations in artificial lures outside of metal spinners and spoons until around 1890. It is about this time that the first American-made artificial lures appeared, reflecting the look of a natural minnow.

Rods

Rod-making progressed over time, with specific makers preferring different types of wood. In the mid-1800s, the English favored greenheart wood, while Americans used hickory and ash. American rods of the Civil War era looked like the cue sticks used in billiards and sported varnished rattan handles. European varieties had butt sections of greenheart wood with bamboo tips, and early examples were mottled. Poachers' rods, made of greenheart and calcutta cane, were fashioned in four sections and hidden in walking sticks or secured in leather cases.

Best known for their resiliency, bamboo fly rods are considered the forte of 19th century American rod makers such as Samuel Phillipe, Charles Murphy and Hiram Leonard. Bamboo rods remain a favorite with many anglers and collectors.

During the 1940s, a Bakelite impregnation process was used to seal the cane fibers and contributed to the rod's durability. Considered "top of the line" among these are rods manufactured by Wright and McGill (Granger series) and the trout rod by Heddon. Gillium, Dickerson and Garrison also produced rods of high quality during the 1950s and 1960s. Heddon models generally had

hardwood handles and sported the "leaping bass" decal. American-made rods usually had two tips, whereas many British rods had only one.

Spinning rods were also made of bamboo. Considered among the best of these is the ultra-light Orvis model, including their "Rocky Mountain" series. The lighter weight preempted the heavier bamboo styles, making the bamboo spinning rod category, with certain exceptions, a less popular one with collectors.

General Guidelines: Defects like cracking, rust, bent seats, loose ferrules and replacement parts decrease the value of rods. Short or broken sections also devalue the rod, as do cracked varnish and damaged cork. Steel rods, made during the 1920-1950s, are generally considered difficult to use but interesting to collectors. On the other hand, most of the fiberglass models, which appeared after World War II, have little collector value with the exception of those by Russ Peak, Winston, the Golden Eagle series by Orvis, and Harry Wilson at Scott Pow-R-Ply. Custom bamboo bait casting models by Orvis, Thomas, Leonard and Payne are harder to find, with some commanding values in the thousands of dollars.

Reels

Called "winches," the first 18th century crank reels were made of iron or brass. Of English origin, the first geared reel was hand made around 1780, while the first American multiplying reel is attributed to Kentuckian George Snyder in 1812. Jonathan and Benjamin Meek of Kentucky improved upon this basic design. Reels specifically designed for saltwater fishing followed.

Kingfisher "Wood Minnow" lure, series 101, 3", three treble hooks, two spinners, glass eyes, green/orange/red body.

Reels from the Civil War period appeal not only to fishing collectors but to those interested in fine early American nautical pieces.

Centered in the New York area, early saltwater reel manufacturers included Conroy, Bates and Vom Hofe, followed in the early 20th century by Hofe's "big game" reels and drag models by Pflueger. During the early decades of the 20th century, large companies like Shakespeare, Horton, Heddon, Meisselbach, South Bend Tackle, Enterprise (Pflueger) and Hendryx emerged. Later, and noteworthy, are those custom made by Arthur and Oscar Kovalovsky, whose 1940s and 1950s reels are highly regarded in the auction market and among collectors.

Free spool reels followed World War II. These included the Shakespeare "President," the Pflueger "Supreme," and what is considered by many to be at the apex of this category, the "Ambassadeur" from Abu of Sweden.

General Guidelines: Some of the early German silver fishing reels ($150-$400) are good collectible items; however, most poles and reels have not attained this value level, other than the fly rods by some of the famous makers ($1,000-$3,000). The Meek reel is much in demand by today's collectors.

Fly and Spinning Reels

Called "pirns," the first fly fishing reels were of British 19th century crank design. American fly fishermen of the mid-19th century relied on either British reels or those made by hand; during the 1880s, however, American models made inroads in this market. Again, the names of Orvis, Leonard, Conroy and Vom Hafe came to the fore, Orvis with a simple spool reel, Leonard with his "raised pillar" design, and small, finely-crafted, models by Conroy and Vom Hofe that sported rubber side plates and rims of German silver. Also of note were the spool reels by Pflueger and Meisselbach that were distributed between 1895 and 1917.

Early models of spinning reels include Scotland's Mallach sidecaster, circa 1884, and the 1905 Illingwortb "Mark One." Generally left to European makers, the better reels are from Allcock, Quick, Mitchell, Luxor, Zebco and Alcedo (responsible for the 1960s Orvis models). American makers included Penn, Bache Brown, Pflueger and Fin Nor (circa 1940s-1950s).

General Guidelines: The "Medalist" by Pflueger is the most commonly available to collectors today. Their "Gem" design, circa 1950, is also noted for its reasonable price, with the latter somewhat harder to find and thus of greater value to collectors. Conversely, spring-loaded fly wheels are readily available and have little collectible value.

Lures

Known as bass plugs, the first patented lure was the Riley Haskell "Minnow" of 1859. This was followed by a floating model, circa 1876, by the H. C. Brush Co., and the "Flying Hellgrammite," patented by Harry Compstick in 1883, which boasted metal wings and a wood body, the latter becoming the most desirable among collectors worldwide.

The "modern" wood bass plug is attributed to the Heddon Company late in the 19th century, with the most renowned being their Dowagiac Minnow of 1904.

The use of metal lures preceded wooden plugs, with numerous models produced in both the United States and England in the early 1800s. Using what was close at hand, these were initially just silver dinner spoons with an attached hook. This concept led to what later became known as spinners, which could be either cast or trolled.

Most collectible in this earlier group are the pre-1900 Skinners, the Chicago Spinner and those by J.E. Pepper, Chapman and the Hendryx Company. Metal lures from the 1930s and 1940s are also high on collectors' lists. Names to look for are the "Silver Minnow" by Johnson, Arbogast's "Tin Liz," the first "Daredevles" by Eppinger and South Bend's "Tri-Oreno." Also in the metal lure category are torpedo-shaped metal devons, and those made specifically for salmon fishing.

Another lure considered to be one of the most effective is the jig. This type has a single hook, a lead head and, in its earlier form, a body and tail fashioned of wispy feathers or maribou. Some modern jigs have plastic bodies and curled tails.

General Guidelines: Original cardboard or rare jointed wooden boxes add to a lure's value, as do original company catalogs. From 1920 through 1950 many companies produced plugs, most of which are easily found today at reasonable prices.

Lately there has been a lot of attention paid to the early plastic lures—some manufacturers were still making wooden lures up into the 1960s. The plastics are still down in the five to $15 range for the most part and plenty of hunting grounds remain as of yet untouched. Many of these early plastics are interesting and make very attractive displays.

There is also rapidly growing interest in collecting ice fishing decoys and early folk art-like homemade fishing lures.

"Sunnybrook" fly reel, 2-5/8" in diameter, Union Hardware Co., Torrington, CT, line capacity not given, nickel plated brass.

Casting reel, 1-1/2" in diameter, Pennell Reel Co., Philadelphia, line capacity 40 yards, all brass.

Antique fishing lures have increased tremendously in value over the last 15 years. The wooden lures of the '20s, '30s and '40s are a must for the sporting collector. Any good wooden lure with good paint is worth $10 and some bring from $50 to several hundred dollars. The key for the beginning collector is to look at the general condition. Is the paint complete? Be sure that the original paint has age cracks. If it doesn't, it may be a repaint. Consult a long-time collector to help in your decision.

Flies

From soft to wet there are a plethora of fly types, including streamers, spinners, emergers, soft hackles and nymphs. For those who tie their own, there are fly-tying tools like vises, magnifiers, bobbins, bobbin threaders and specialty pliers. Because provenance is generally unknown, and they can be found in abundance, most collectors search only for those flies tied by specific "names," many of which command several hundred dollars or more. These renowned anglers include Syd Glasso, Preston Jennings, Ruben Cross, Harry Darbee, Carrie Stevens and Roderick Haig-Brown.

On the other hand, gut-eyed flies require no provenance. Wound on blackened hooks and often framed, they are both beautiful and collectible.

General Guidelines: Piquing the interest of serious collectors are flies that remain in their original envelopes or are embedded in the maker's card. L.L. Bean, Orvis and William Mills sold packaged flies, while Hardy, Allcocks and Pflueger provided the popular "spinner-flies," noted for their colorful graphics.

Accessories

In addition to the tools necessary for fly tying, this category includes early hooks (with their containers often generating more interest that the hooks themselves); silk worm gut leaders and lines; colorful bobbers made of cork, quill, or wood; casting or practice plugs; lead or "split" shot (along with their containers), landing nets, and creels, as well as rare and desirable Indian fish baskets. Aluminum storage boxes, which can range from simple to fancy, are also collectible, as are leather wallets, which featured wool, paper, or imitation felt pages.

General Guidelines: Hard to find in good condition—and most desirable—are the Victorian handmade styles, which are noteworthy for their parchment pages.

Books

Old Fishing Lures and Tackle — Identification and Value Guide by Carl F. Luckey (Krause Publications).

Old Fishing Tackle and Collectibles; Dan Homel; Forest-Park Publishers, Bellingham, WA; 1995

Collector's Guide to Old Fishing Reels; Dan Homel; Forest-Park Publishers, Bellingham, WA

Compleat Angler's Catalog, The; Scott Rolderer; Johnson Books, Boulder, Go.; 1985

Publications

Fishing Collectibles Magazine, P.O. Box 2797, Kennebunkport, ME 04046

The American Fly Fisher, P.O. Box 42, Manchester, VT 05254

The Splash, P.O. Box 33, Hayward, WI 54843

American Angler, 126 North St., Bennington, VT 05201

Saltwater Fly Fishing, 126 North St., Bennington, VT 05201

Old Reel Collectors Assn. Newsletter, 849 NE 70th Ave., Portland, OR 97213

Clubs and Museums

•National Fishing Lure Collectors Club
22325 B Drive South, Marshall, MI 49068

•Florida Antique Tackle Collectors Inc.
P.O. Box 420703, Kissimmee, FL 34742-0703

•American Museum of Fly Fishing
P.O. Box 42, Manchester, VT 05254

•National Fresh Water Fishing Hall of Fame
P.O. Box 33, Hayward, WI 54843

•American Fish Decoy Association
P.O. Box 252, Boulder Junction, WI 54512

Lures

Al Foss—Shimmy Wiggler .... $5-$10
Arbogast—Jitterbug .... $5-$25
Bass Seeker .... $7-$25
Bite-Em Bait Co. Lipped Wiggler lure .... $90-$135
Comstock "Flying Hellgrammite" lure .... $1,200+
Crazy Crawler .... $7-$35
Creek Chub Bait Co. "Injured Minnow" lure .... $10-$25
Creek Chub—Pikie Minnow .... $7-$35
Chapman "Allure" #1 and #2 lures .... $135-$175
Chapman "Pickerel Spinner" lure .... $60-$85
Dalton Special .... $5-$12
Dingbat .... $10-$40
Dixie Wiggler .... $7-$15
Egypt Wiggler .... $7-$15
Eppinger early "Dardevle;" boxed .... $5-$15
Florida Fishing Tackle—Dillinger .... $5-$10
Florida Shad .... $10-$15
Globe .... $10-$30
Haskell "Minnow" lure; 1859 .... $3,000+
Hastings Wilson's Six-in-One Wobbler .... $150-$200
Hastings Wilson's Winged Wobbler .... $45-$75
Hardy "Devon" lure .... $20-$50
Heddon #210 "Surface Minnow" lure .... $20-$45
Heddon "Crab Wiggler" lure .... $30-$55
Heddon "Dummy Double" lure .... $300+
Heddon—Lucky Thirteen .... $10-$40
Heddon "Punkinseed" lure .... $25-$45
Hula Popper .... $5-$15
Injured Minnow .... $6-$25
Keeling "Expert Minnow" lure; 1905-20 .... $200+
Metal devon .... $15-$30
Moonlight—99 percent Weedless .... $15-$30
Moonlight Bait .... $20-$45
Mustane Minnow .... $5-$25
Nip-I-Dippee .... $5-$15
Paw Paw—Castine Minnow .... $15-$35
Pflueger—Pal-o-mine .... $6-$25
Pikie .... $5-$15
Pup .... $5-$20
River Runt .... $15-$45
Shakespeare—Swimming Mouse .... $6-$25
South Bend—Bassoreno .... $5-$20
Surforeno .... $7-$35
Tin Liz .... $15-$45
Wiggle Diver .... $12-$30
Wottafrog .... $15-$40

Reels

Abu Ambassadeur #2600; 1958 .... $30-$50
Abu Limited Edition gold Ambassadeur .... $400-$500
Allcock brass fly reel; 1890 .... $75-$125
Alcedo micron spinning reel .... $35-$75
B.C. Milam reel .... $375+
Bristol #65 and #66 fly reels .... $10-$15
Carlton automatic fly reel; 1915 .... $50-$90

Chubb brass pirn; 1890 .... $25-$50
Farlow Saphire fly reel; 1960 .... $40-$65
Farlow brass pirn crank reel; 1880 .... $75-$125
Fin or Gold Spinning reel .... $150-$250
Fin Nor Fly reel; saltwater; "wedding cake"
    design .... $300-$500
Hardy Jock Scott casting reel .... $275-$400
Hardy brass Perfect fly reel; 1900 .... $400+
Hardy Silex reel .... $125-$300
Heddon Chief Dowagiac casting reel .... $60-$95
Heddon Model 3-25 casting reel; 1927 .... $95-$150
Heddon 335 nickel/silver .... $80-$95
Hendryx "raised pillar" brass fly reel .... $15-$30
Hendryx "raised pillar" nickel over brass .... $15-$25
J.F. Meek casting reel; 1835-1840 .... $2,500+
Kovalovsky "big game" reel .... $1,000+
Luxor spinning reel; 1950 .... $30-$50
Meek and Milam reel; 1851-1878 .... $600+
Montague nickel over brass .... $15-$25
Meisselbach Synploreel #255 casting reel .... $50-$80
Meisselbach saltwater bay reel .... $35-$70
Meisselbach #660 automatic; 1920 .... $40-$75
Malloch salmon reel; 1920 .... $100-$195
Montague Imperial 6/0 big game reel .... $95-$150
Orvis trout fly reel; walnut box; 1874 .... $400+
Pennell Tournament Casting nickel silver .... $30-$45
Pflueger Golden West fly reel; 1930 .... $100-$185
Pflueger Superex 3775 automatic fly reel; 1910 .... $40-$60
Pflueger Supreme #1573 casting reel .... $25-$40
Pflueger Everlaster bay reel .... $30-$50
Pflueger Adams big game reel .... $125+
Pflueger Summit .... $10-$25
Shakespear Standard pro .... $15-$30
Shakespeare #1847 automatic fly reel .... $10-$20
Shakespeare "Kazoo," fly reel .... $20-$35
Shakespeare Miller-Autocrat big game reel .... $135-$200
Shakespeare President #1970A; 1955 .... $15-$30
South Bend #850 surfcasting Reel; 1940 .... $10-$20
Talbot (Kansas City, Mo.) casting reel .... $175-$350
Edward Vom Hofe Perfection fly reel; 1900 .... $1,500+
Edward Vom Hofe Peerless fly reel; 1883 pat. .... $900+
Edward Vom Hofe Model #521 saltwater reel .... $165-$300
Edward Vom Hofe Model #721 "Commander Ross" ... $400+
Julius Vom Hofe all metal trout fly reel; 1889
    pat. .... $200-$300
Julius Vom Hofe "B-Ocean" big game reel;
    1911 pat. .... $150-$175
Frederich Vom Hofe brass bay reel; pre-Civil War ... $900+
Winchester 4142 casting reel .... $65-$90
Wordens Belt Reel; 1953 .... $45-$65
J. W. Youngs Beaudex fly reel .... $30-$55
Zebco Cardinal spinning reel .... $25-$50
Zebco Zero Hour Bomb spinning reel .... $15-$25

Fly Rods

Abbey & Imbrie Centennial fly rod; 9-1/2'; two tips;
    1917 .... $135-$225
Constable empress fly rod; 8'; two tips .... $150-$275
Thomas Chubb Lancewood fly rod; 10'; 1890 .... $60-$100

Thomas Chubb calcutta bamboo fly rod; 1900 ..... $100-$200

Devine bamboo fly rod; 9'; two tips .... $150-$350

Dickerson fly rod .... $1,000+

Edward spinning rods; 6-7'; two tips .... $100-$175

Farlow calcutta salmon fly rod; 1900 .... $150-$250

Granger Victory fly rod; 7'; two tips .... $400-$500

Hardy Phantom fly rod; 9'; two tips .... $150-$275

Hardy Marvel fly rod; 7-1/2'; two tips .... $300-$500

Heddon #600 bamboo casting rod .... $60-$100

Heddon #50 fly rod; 8-1/2'; two tips .... $165-$275

Leonard Tournament 8-1/2' trout fly rod; two
tips .... $350-$700

Montague (L.L. Bean label) fly rod; 9-1/2'; two
tips .... $65-$135

Montague Splitswitch casting rod; 5'; two tips .... $20-$40

Orvis Battenkill fly rod; 8-1/2'; two tips .... $295-$475

Orvis Wes Jordan fly rod; leather case .... $450-$675

Orvis Model #99 fly rod; one tip .... $175-$300

C.F. Orvis fly rod; 1 tip; 1900 .... $180-$375

Shakespeare Spring Brook fly rod; 8-1/2'; two tips;
1950 .... $40-$85

South Bend #77 bamboo fly rod; 9'; two tips .... $65-$125

South Bend #25 Sport Oreno fly rod; 7-1/2';
two tips .... $125-$190

F.E. Thomas salmon fly rod; 10'; two tips .... $195-$350

Vom Hofe Big Game bamboo boat rod .... $125-$250

Vom Hofe antique wood boat rod .... $100-$195

Winchester Armax fly rod; 9'; two tips .... $125-$225

"Cue Stick" hickory rod; ring guides; Civil
War period .... $65-$175

Winston Lew Stoner; 9'; one tip .... $295-$425

Nets

Hardwood Net; 1950s .... $20-$30

Hardy Royde landing net .... $150-$200

Richardson "Harrimac" net; trout size .... $10-$15

Richardson "Harrimac" net; salmon size .... $30+

Flies

Hardy Spinner fly; original card .... $10-$15

Orvis single fly; orig. wrapper .... $5-$10

Gut-eyed fly; blackened hook .... $15+

Miscellaneous

Fly box; imitation tortoise shell; 1930s .... $50+

Fly box; blackened aluminum; pre-1910 .... $75+

Hardy sectioned bag .... $100-$150

Ideal bobber; red/green; 6"; 1920s .... $20-$30

Spooled silk line (good condition) .... $8+

Antique creel; leather closure .... $40-$80+

Indian fish basket; woven twig .... $200+

Lawrence western creel .... $100+

Catalogs

Charles F. Orvis (1900) .... $100+

Meek (reels) .... $100+

Early Winchester .... $100+

Julius Vom Hofe (1900) .... $100+

Hardy Anglers Guide (pre-1928) .... $100+

Hardy Anglers Guide (1928-1940) .... $50-$100

Creek Chub Bait (1930) .... $50-$100

Folsom Arms (1930) .... $50-$100

Pflueger (1920-1940) .... $25-$50

South Bend Bait (pre-1940) .... $25-$50

South Bend Bait (1940-1950s) .... $15-$25

Heddon Pocket Catalogs .... $15-$25

L.L. Bean (1950-1960s) .... $15-$25

Orvis (1950-1960s) .... $15-$25

Casting reel, 2", "Sturdi-Bilt/
Ezy-2-Part/4 multiple,"
unknown maker, line capacity,
80 yards, nickel-plated brass,
jeweled bearings.

FOUNTAIN PENS

In the past 10 to 15 years, collectors have been turning their attention to writing instruments, especially fountain pens. Baby boomers may remember fountain pens from penmanship class in grade school — the unfamiliar feel of a thick barrel between the fingers, the struggle to form cursive letters and the unmistakable ink-stained fingers after class. Fond memories often lead collectors to the quest for the ultimate specimen.

Vintage writing instruments from the early 20th century can bear price tags up to $10,000! Fortunately, many others are readily available for under $100.

History: Since the early 1700s, the challenge of finding an alternative to the dipping pen nagged at manufacturers and inventors. It wasn't until the late 1820s a practical solution was developed. Early pens didn't work very well since the nib (point) wore out quickly with repeated use, and none of the methods for storing and dispensing ink worked properly.

Nevertheless, manufacturers persisted and by the 1870s were producing beautiful pens of expert craftsmanship and complicated, if not successful, methods of feeding ink onto paper. Creative minds continued to apply themselves to the problem, and by the 1880s, several inventors had developed practical systems for commercial fountain pens.

In 1884, Lewis E. Waterman was granted a patent for a workable fountain pen. The new system involved a channel under the nib through which air would travel to the ink reservoir. This prevented the vacuum that had caused trouble for so many years. The result was an even flow of ink to the paper.

Early fountain pens all had hollow barrels filled with ink by means of an eye dropper. This was slightly messy, but still a considerable improvement over previous fountain pens.

By the early 1900s, several manufacturing companies had patented self-filling models in their product line. Self-filling included lever-fillers, blow-fillers, button-fillers, matchstick and pump-fillers. Other innovations included threaded caps and retractable nibs. The lever-filling pen became the most popular system of filling the pen for the next four decades.

Later methods of filling the pen with ink included the suction-filler (mid 1920s), the piston-filler (1930s-1940s), piston-shaft fillers and the snorkel (1940s-1950s). During the 1950s, a removable transparent plastic ink cartridge was developed. Cartridge pens are not as popular with today's collectors as their self-filling cousins.

Hard black rubber was the earliest material used to make fountain pens; red, green, and black mottled hard rubber were used infrequently. By World War I, a hard rubber with a complicated woodgrain and hard rubber with a ripple pattern had been developed. Some companies attempted to use celluloid, casein and other plastic precursors. Plastics were finally introduced in a wide variety of colors in the mid-1920s. Combinations, such as mother-of-pearl and black, became popular. Pens became a status symbol of the educated in the 1900s. The larger and brighter or more detailed, the more sophisticated.

With the onset of the Depression in the 1930s, pen manufacturers searched for cost-effective methods of mass production. Competition was keen, with each company searching for a gimmick to capture consumers' attention. The no-nonsense tenor of the political times was reflected in the sleek, utilitarian designs of pens with little embellishment.

General Guidelines: Mint in Box pens are hard to find, but are most desirable. Especially valuable are pens from 1900-1936. Ornate pens with lots of detail will be more expensive than a pen of the same vintage with little or no detailing. Metal filigree detailing over hard rubber is especially desirable. Pens with pierced or engraved metal details are even more valuable than those with filigree.

Pens by major manufacturers are preferable to those by unknown manufacturers.

Generally speaking, the larger the pen the more expensive.

Examine the pen's color. Brightly colored pens are often more expensive than a comparable pen in muted tones.

Repairs do not affect price negatively, as long as they are completed with original parts. A pen in need of repair is not worthless, but some repairs are expensive and the price should be adjusted accordingly.

Pen Manufacturers

Aurora: 1919 to present, Italy. Originally produced hard-rubber fountain pens, expanded to include celluloid by 1925.

De La Rue: 1881-1957, United Kingdom. Produced pens under the brand names Pelican and Onoto.

Dunn: 1921-1924, United States. Famous for two very large pens, the Super Giant and the Super Dreadnought.

LeBoeuf: 1918-1936, United States. Made barrels and caps out of tubing rather than having to drill them out of rod. It was thus able to use different, usually more beautiful, materials than its competitors.

Montblanc: 1910-present, Germany. Among the most famous of all fountain pen manufacturers, the name Montblanc is known to collectors and non-collectors alike.

Sheaffer's pen and pencil set, white dot "Triumph" pen, 14K point.

Parker: 1891-present, United States. This company was owned by a firm in the United Kingdom in the 1970s, but returned to American ownership around 1973. Parker's Duofold 1927 Mandarin Yellow Senior, which originally sold for $7 is now a classic collector's choice at $750 or more. Parker also introduced a reproduction of the classic model in 1995, which listed at $850.

Arthur A. Waterman: 1895-1920s, United States.

L. E. Waterman: 1882-1940s, United States; 1940-present, French-owned.

HOT TIPS

Ladies' pens are not considered as collectible as men's pens. Consequently, some very lovely pens of superior quality are available at reasonable prices.

Dipping pens are another overlooked category. It is not unusual to find a beautiful dipping pen with mother-of-pearl stem, gold nib, and in the original velvet box for around $50!

Clubs
•Pen Collectors of America
The PENnant (newsletter)
P.O. Box 821449, Houston, TX 77282-1449

Publications
Pen World International
P.O. Box 6007
Kingwood, TX 77339

Penfinder Quarterly
928 Broadway, Suite 805
New York, NY 10010

The Book of Fountain Pens and Pencils
By Stuart Schneider and George Fischler
(Schiffer Publishing)

Fountain Pens and Pencils — The Gold Age of Writing Instruments
By Stuart Schneider and George Fischler
(Schiffer Publishing)

The Illustrated Guide to Antique Writing Instruments
By Stuart Schneider and George Fischler
(Schiffer)

Contributor to this section: Stuart Schneider, P.O. Box 64, Teaneck, NJ 07666.

VALUE LINE

Parker USA, #47, 1905, mother-of-pearl and abalone handle, gold-over brass barrel and cap .... $6,000-$7,000

Parker USA, #180, made between 1976-1983, feed/over-feed nib .... $125-$150

Parker USA, 1927 Duofold senior, Mandarin yellow .... $750-$800

Parker USA, 1936, vacumatic .... $300-$325

Parker USA, #61, 1957, first edition, turquoise w/rainbow cap .... $325-$350

Pullworks, 1890s, early filigree, no markings, identified by unusual feed; long, tapering cap; both cap and barrel have filigree .... $1,800-$2,000

Swan, 1920-1930s, etched sterling silver barrel and cap .... $450-$500

Moore USA, 1930, L-96, oversize, midnight blue plastic .... $500-$525

LeBeouf, USA #90, 1927, black-and-bronze plastic, level fill .... $1,100-$1,150

Pioneer USA, 1934, pioneer pen, green-and-black marbled plastic .... $150-$165

Pelikan Germany, 1939, #100, green-and-black plastic, piston-fill .... $275-$300

Conklin USA, Nozac, olive herringbone plastic, piston fill .... $400-$425

Conklin, Endura Model, desk set, black marble base, two pens, side-lever fill, double narrow gold-colored bands, "Patent Nov. 17, 1925," on pen barrel, black-brown overlay color $125

Conklin, Model 20, 5-5/16", #2 Conklin pint-nib, black crescent filler #20, gold clip, narrow gold band on cap, pat date May 28, 1918, stamped on clip $75

Conklin, Model 25P, pen, ladies filigree cap ribbon, black, crescent filler, 1923 .... $70

Conklin, Model 30, pen, black hard rubber, 1903 .... $75

Dunn, black, red barrel, gold-plated trim, c1920 .... $40

Epenco, black case, gold-plated trim $25

Eversharp, CA Model, ball-point pen, black, gold-filled cap, 1946 .... $42

Doric, desk pen, gold seal, green marble cover, lever fill, large adjustable nib, c1935 .... $55

Doric, fountain pen, amber threading, restored $225

Marvel, black chased hard rubber, eyedropper, 1906 .... $75

Moore, desk set, gray and black marble base, black pen, 12k nib, side-lever fill $75

Moore, pen, rose color, fancy band around cap, warranted nib, side-lever filler $65

Moore, ribbon pen, lady's, black, three narrow gold bands on cap, lever fill, pat nib #2 .... $70

Onoto, Ink Pencil Stylographic pen, black chased hard rubber, eyedropper, 1924 .... $40

Parker, Blue-Diamond-51, pen, black, gold-plated cap, button filled, 1942 .... $70

Parker, Duofold Deluxe, pen and pencil set, black and pearl, three narrow gold-colored bands on cap, push-button fill, 1929 .... $575

Parker, Senior, Flashing Black, 1923 .... $185

Parker, Streamline, burgundy and black, double narrow band on cap, 1932 .... $125

Parker, Model 48, ring top, gold-filled barrel and cap, button filled, 1915 .... $150

Parker, Model 51, maroon, stainless steel cap, chrome-plated trim, aeromatic filler, 1950 .... $50

Parker, Vacumatic, gray-black, arrow clip, arrow design engraved on nib, silver-colored clip and band on cap, oversized model, 1932 .... $125

Reynolds, Model 2, pen, orig ball-point, c1945 .... $75

Security, pen, check protector, red hard rubber, gold-filled trim, 1923 .... $85

Sheaffer Junior pen-and-pencil set, blue and black with white veins .... $350-$375/set

Sheaffer, 1937 Lifetime demi, roseglow radite, lever fill) .... $200-$250

Sheaffer, Strato Writer, ball-point pen, gold-filled metal mountings, 1948 .... $65

Sheaffer, Triumph Lifetime, desk set, green marble base, two black snorkel-design pens, c1940 .... $95

Sheaffer, White Dot, pen, green jade, gold-plated trim, lever filled, 1923 .... $95

Sheaffer, White Dot Lifetime, classic torpedo design cap and body, lever filler on side, 1930 .... $115

Wahl, Lady's, ribbon pen, double narrow band on cap, 14k #2 nib, lever fill, 1928 .... $75

Wahl, USA, 1940, Skyline, First year, black plastic .... $100-$125

Wahl, Tempoint No. 305A, pen, gold-filled metal mounted, eyedropper, 1919 .... $145

Wahl, Eversharp, gold seal, black, gold-filled trim, lever filled, 1930 .... $125

Waterman #26, 1895, semi-flexible nib, eyedropper-fill .... $855-$875

Waterman #94,1926, olive ripple, lever-fill, near mint .... $360-$380

Waterman #94, 1935, blue-and-yellow marbled plastic set .... $325-$350

Waterman #12, pen, mottled brow, 14k gold bands, 1886 .... $125

Waterman #42-1/2V, Safety Pen, gold filigree, retractable screw-action nib, 1906 .... $135

Waterman #71, pen, ripple red, hard rubber case, gold-plated trim, white clip, lever filled, 1925 .... $150

Waterman, Taperite, pen, black, gold-filled metal mounted cap, gold-filled trim, lever filled, c1949 .... $75

G.I. JOE

Hasbro introduced the first 12-inch G.I. Joe action figures in 1964 — the Action Sailor, Action Soldier, Action Marine and Action Pilot.

Hasbro officials, fearful boys wouldn't play with a doll, invented the term "action figure" for its new figures, traditionally dressed in wartime garb (from soldiers to a G.I. Nurse). The ploy must have worked because over 250 million G.I. Joes have been sold worldwide since their inception. Smaller (3-3/4-inch) Joes were introduced in the 1980s, but a new wave of traditional 12-inch figures was introduced in the late 1990s.

General Guidelines: Condition is vital. Because they've long been popular playthings for boys, G.I. Joes are hard to find in Mint condition. Finding the boxes is even harder, especially for 1960s Joes.

It's doubtful a collector will be interested in a figure that saw lots of action on front lines, but a figure in Mint condition can be worth hundreds or even thousands of dollars. While figures and sets from the 1960s and 1970s tend to bring the highest prices, newer G.I. Joe items from the 1980s and 1990s can also bring prices ranging anywhere from $10 for an easy-to-find item to over $300 for certain sets.

Boxes can add 50 percent or more to a G.I. Joe's value. For instance, a Russian Infantry figure from 1966 is valued at $400 in Mint condition without its original package, but the same figure in Mint condition with its original package could sell for $2,000.

Boxes also aid in identification. Without the box, it is difficult to identify a G.I. Joe. The date found on a figure's buttocks is a patent date and often not the same as the actual year it was produced.

Unclothed G.I Joes of unknown date (in Good or better condition) may have some collector value, especially for parts. Check with a reputable dealer or consult a book to identify the figure and its era.

Rarity also affects prices, and the hard-to-find G.I. Nurse, Action Soldiers of the World, Aquanaut and Talking Astronaut command some of the highest prices today.

Rarity can pertain to an unusual variation as well as a specific figure. For example, while most G.I. Joes contain a trademark scar on faces, scars were rare on the Action Soldiers of the World figures. A scar-faced Action Soldier of the World can bring $1,000 more than the same figure without a scar.

Talking figures and African-American figures are also popular with collectors and may command slightly higher prices. Recent (1990s) editions of classic G.I. Joes are also collectible and have seen prices increase in just a few years for figures still in the box.

Australian Jungle Fighter, Action Soldiers of the World, 1966, $350 loose.

Amphibious Personnel Carrier, 3-3/4" Series #2, 1983, $25 loose.

Accessories — like weapons, footlockers and uniforms — are collectible and some can even sell for higher prices than a figure itself. Sets are often found with accessories missing, and collectors seek individual items to complete sets.

Accessories increase value. For instance, A Russian Infantry figure dressed only in a basic uniform is worth $1,600 Mint in Box, but the same figure with additional, original equipment is valued at $2,700 MIB.

Some sets featured equipment only, some came with a figure, while still others were vehicle sets. Some 1960s vehicles alone are worth close to $1,000.

Clubs
- •G.I. Joe Collectors Club
  225 Cattle Baron Parc Dr., Fort Worth, TX 76108

- •G.I. Joe Collectors Club
  150 S. Glenoaks Blvd., Burbank, CA 91510

VALUE LINE

*With several exceptions (Irwin made some 1960s vehicles), G.I. Joe figures and accessories are manufactured by Hasbro. Prices listed are for figures and accessories in Mint condition **without** the box.*

Figure Sets

Action Marine, 1964 .... $130
Action Pilot, 1964 .... $125
Action Sailor, 1964 .... $200
Action Soldier, 1964 .... $100
Action Soldiers of the World Series, 1966 .... $300-$750
Australian Jungle Fighter, standard set $350
Australian Jungle Fighter, deluxe set (additional
   equipment) $400
British Commando, standard set $350
British Commando, deluxe set $425
Foreign Soldiers of the World, Talking Adventure Pack $750
French Resistance Fighter, standard set $275
French Resistance Fighter, deluxe set $350
German Storm Trooper, standard set $300
German Storm Trooper, deluxe set $400
Japanese Imperial Soldier, standard set $500
Japanese Imperial Soldier, deluxe set $600
Russian Infantry Man, standard set $300
Russian Infantry Man, deluxe set $400
Adventures of G.I. Joe Series, 1969 .... $150-$600

Sea Adventurer, Adventure Team, 1970, $175 loose.

Ad for Adventure Team Headquarters Set #7490, 1972, $125 loose.

Aquanaut	$350
Negro Adventurer	$600
Shark's Surprise Set with Frogman	$300
Talking Astronaut	$150
Adventure Team, 1970s	$75-$150
Air Adventurer, 1970	$135
Air Adventurer with Kung Fu grip, 1974	$75
Black Adventurer, 1970	$100
Black Adventurer with Kung Fu grip, 1976	$75
Canadian Mountie Set, Canadian Sears exclusive, 1967	$450
G.I. Nurse, 1967	$2,000
Talking Action Marine, 1967	$225
Talking Action Pilot, 1967	$165
Talking Action Sailor, 1967	$350
Talking Action Soldier, 1967	$135
3-3/4-inch Series, 1982-1986	$5-$75
Airborne, Series #2, G.I. Joe, 1983	$25
Big Boa, Series #6, Cobra, 1986	$7
Breaker, Series #1, G.I. Joe, 1982	$30
Lady Jaye (female figure), Series #4, G.I. Joe, 1984	$15
Scarlett (female figure), Series #1, G.I. Joe, 1982	$75

Accessories

Air/Sea Rescue, Action Pilot Series, 1968	$400
Aqua Locker, Adventures of G.I. Joe, 1969	$180
Beachhead Mess Kit, Action Marine Series, 1964	$210
Dress Parade Adventure Pack, Action Soldier Series, 1968	$900
Landing Signal Officer, Action Sailor Series, 1966	$200
Military Police Uniform, Action Soldier Series, 1967	$900
Search for the Abominable Snowman, Adventure Team, 1973	$200
Tactical Battle Platform, 3-3/4-inch Series #4, G.I. Joe, 1984	$20

Vehicle Sets

Amphibious Duck, Action Soldier Series, 1967	$425
Amphibious Personnel Carrier, 3-3/4-inch Series #2, G.I. Joe, 1983	$25
Armored Car, Action Soldier Series, 1967	$300
Dreadnok Cycle, 3-3/4-inch Series #6, Cobra, 1986	$10
Fantastic Sea Wolf Submarine, Adventure Team, 1975	$100
Spacewalk Mystery Set without Spaceman, Adventures of G.I. Joe, 1969	$275
Spacewalk Mystery Set with Spaceman, Adventure Team, 1970	$300
U.S.S. Flagg (aircraft carrier), 3-3/4-inch Series #4, G.I. Joe, 1984	$100

Black Action Soldier, 1965, $800 loose. All G.I. Joe figures and accessories by Hasbro.

Action Soldier, 1964, $100 loose.

GLASS

When you think about it, it's amazing how much glassware has survived over the years. There's a lot of glassware that's 50, 75 or even more than 100 years old still in top shape. Much of this glassware was used for years in people's daily lives, and it's surprising that more of it hasn't broken. The glassware of years' past, however, was higher quality and made to withstand more punishment.

Since so much good glassware has remained intact, it's no surprise that fine quality glassware is one of the largest collecting fields in antiques. Akro Agate, cut, Depression and carnival glass are four of the most popular collecting areas for hobbyists.

Akro Agate

Around 1910, the Akro Agate Company was formed with the intention of making marbles. This business was successful, but around 1930, with stiff competition from other marble makers, the firm decided to diversify. It began creating floralware lines, bottles for perfume companies and children's dishes. This strategy worked well until after World War II when cheap imports forced the company to halt its operations in 1951. What Akro Agate left collectors is a rich line of collectible glassware that employed distinctive and beautiful marbleized color combinations.

Akro Agate items are marked "Made in USA" and many times have a mold number. Some have a small crow flying through the "A" mark. Pieces are currently being reproduced with no markings.

Because Akro Agate was so popular and because it is such thick glass, much survived in Mint condition. Look for children's dish sets in original boxes. The box adds 25 to 50 percent more

Depression, pretzel creamer, 4", clear.

value to the set. Some of the different patterns available are Chiquita, Concentric Rib, Concentric Ring, Interior Panel, Miss America, Octagonal, Stacked Disc and Stippled Band.

Carnival Glass

For those who couldn't afford the more expensive art glass, carnival glass carried a reasonable price. Carnival glass, made from the early 1900s through the 1920s, was simply pressed glass that was coated with a sodium solution and fired to display an exterior luster.

The most common colors are blue, green, marigold and purple. Holding the glass to light will determine the color of the glass. Major manufacturers of carnival glass include Dugan, Fenton, Northwood and Imperial. There are more than 1,000 known patterns; reproductions do exist.

Cut Glass

American brilliant cut glass is some of the most striking and sought-after glassware available. It's heavy and shines like diamonds. It's expensive, and many pieces run into the hundreds, even thousands, of dollars. There are, however, many that are priced at less than $100.

While cut glass has been made in the United States for more than 200 years, glassware from the late 19th century to the early part of the 20th century (1880-1917) is the best. What makes American cut glass from the Brilliant period so good is the amount of lead used in the crystal and the purity of the crystal. Because of the amount of lead, etchers were able to make deeper cuts in the glass, giving the glass a higher shine. Glassware made after the Brilliant period was of lower quality.

Here are some clues about the quality of cut glass.
- •Hand-polished pieces are better than acid-polished pieces. The polishing was done to lessen the harshness of the cuts. The acid-polished pieces are less brilliant.
- •The more complex the pattern, the better the glass. Patterns with a swirls and pointed loops are more highly prized. Arabian, Imperial, Lattice and Parisian are examples of highly desirable patterns.
- •Large items, such as punch bowls and ice cream trays, and unusual items, such as hinged boxes and inkwells, are premium items.
- •Cut glass with color etched to the crystal are especially in demand.
- •Artist-signed pieces can carry premium values, but generally the quality of the item rules. Watch for faked signatures, however, along with some forgeries of patterns and repaired pieces.

Depression Glass

Most Depression glass was made from the 1920s to 1940. It was cheap glassware that was often given away as premiums through gas stations or grocery stores. However, some patterns were made in the 1940s and even through the 1960s. This post-1940 glass is considered by most to be Depression glass and collected as such.

There are 150 or more different Depression glass patterns that are actively collected. The best advice is to pick a pattern and collect it (some people collect glass by color). Actually, the first thing a new collector should do, after finding a pattern, is to learn if the pattern has been reproduced. Many original pieces have been reproduced, and price guides offer photos and other information that will alert collectors to the telltale signs of reproductions.

Collectors should also be aware of "fantasy" pieces — pieces not originally produced in those patterns. Other fantasy pieces are those that are made in entirely new colors than originally produced. Look for reproductions/fantasy items in the following patterns: Adam, Avocado, Cameo, Cherry Blossom, Madrid, Mayfair, Miss America and Sharon.

The biggest producers of vintage Depression glass were Anchor Hocking, MacBeth-Evans, Jeannette, Hazel Atlas, Indiana Glass, U.S. Glass, Federal Glass, Paden City and Imperial Glass. Prices vary widely between patterns and colors. While pink, yellow and green are the most common colors, black, blue, amethyst, red and white items were also made. Crystal is almost always the cheapest; it's not as exciting as the colored pieces, but it is affordable and a good starting point for many collectors.

One pattern that appeals to many hobbyists is Royal Ruby from Anchor Hocking. This glassware (available in many patterns) is still reasonable, but has definitely risen in value over the past five years and appears to be getting more popular. Distinctive and readily found, this glassware is the darkest and richest of any company's ruby red glass (the addition of copper gave Royal Ruby its deep color). Made from the late 1930s through the 1960s, this was the first ruby glass on the market to be machine made (earlier ruby glass was handblown). Because of it beauty and affordability, this glassware is highly sough today and the prices are reasonable.

Clubs

•Akro Agate Art Association
  Box 758, Salem, NH 03079

•Akro Agate Collector's Club
  10 Bailey St., Clarksburg, WV 26301-2524

•American Cut Glass Association
  P.O. Box 482, Ramona, CA 92065-0482

•Canadian Depression Glass Club
  P.O. Box 104, Mississaugua, Ontario L53 2K1 Canada

•National Depression Glass Association
  P.O. Box 8264, Wichita, KS 67208

•National Westmoreland Glass Collectors Club
  P.O. Box 372, Westmoreland City, PA 15692

Contributors to this section: Akro Agate: Roger Hardy, 10 Bailey St., Clarkburg, WV 26301-2524; Cut Glass: Martha Louise Swan, Portland, OR.

Depression, plate, beaded block, 7-3/4" square, vaseline.

VALUE LINE

Akro Agate

Ashtray, square, 4" x 2-7/8", red marble $8
Cereal Bowl, Concentric Ring, children's, blue, large $25
Cereal Bowl, Interior Panel, children's, green,
    transparent, large $15
Cigarette Holder, Octagonal, 2-5/8", blue and white $12
Creamer, Interior Panel, children's, blue, opaque, large ... $40
Creamer, Stacked Disc, children's, green, opaque $6
Creamer and Sugar, Chiquita, children's, cobalt blue $20
Creamer and Sugar, Interior Panel, children's, turquoise . $50
Creamer and Sugar, Stacked Disc Interior Panel,
    children's, turquoise $50
Cup, Chiquita, children's, cobalt blue $7
Cup, Chiquita, children's, green, opaque $4
Cup, Concentric Ring, children's, green, opaque $7
Cup, Concentric Ring, children's, rose, large $35
Cup, Interior Panel, children's, blue $6
Cup, Octagonal, children's, green, large $10
Cup, Stacked Disc, children's, green, opaque $5
Cup, Stacked Disc Interior Panel, children's, blue,
    transparent, large $40
Cup, Stippled Band, children's, green, large $20
Cup and Saucer, Chiquita, cobalt blue, transparent $18
Cup and Saucer, Interior Panel, children's, green and
    white marble $35
Cup and Saucer, Stacked Disc Interior Panel, children's,
    green and white marble $35
Cup and Saucer, Stippled Band, children's, cobalt Blue,
    large $35
Flowerpot, 2-1/4" h, ribbed, green and white $9
Flowerpot, Stacked Disc, 2-1/2", green and white $10
Flowerpot, Stacked Disc, 2-1/2", orange and white $15

Flowerpot, Stacked Disc, 4", green and white $22
Pitcher, Interior Panel, children's, green, transparent $30
Pitcher, Octagonal, 2-3/4", blue $22
Pitcher, Stacked Disc, children's, green, opaque $10
Pitcher, Stippled Band, children's, green, transparent $15
Plate, Concentric Rib, children's, green, opaque $3
Plate, Concentric Rib, children's, yellow, opaque $3
Plate, Concentric Ring, children's, dark blue $5
Plate, Octagonal, children's, blue, large $10
Plate, Octagonal, children's, green, opaque, large $4
Plate, Stacked Disc Interior Panel, children's, blue,
    transparent, large $18
Plate, Stippled Band, children's, green, transparent,
    4-1/4" $6
Powder Jar, Colonial Lady, white $60
Sugar, white $11
Saucer, Concentric Rib, children's, yellow $3
Saucer, Concentric Ring, children's, green, opaque $3
Saucer, Interior Panel, children's, green $3
Saucer, Octagonal, children's, pink, dark $6
Saucer, Stacked Disc Interior Panel, children's, blue,
    transparent, large $15
Saucer, Stippled Band, children's, green, transparent,
    2-3/4" d $3
Teapot, cover, Interior Panel, children's, blue marble $45
Teapot, cover, Stippled Band, children's, amber $10
Teapot, no lid, Chiquita, children's, green opaque $8
Teapot, no lid, Concentric Rib, children's, light blue
    opaque $8
Teapot, no lid, Interior Panel, children's, oxblood marble $28
Teapot, no lid, Stacked Disc, blue and white $16
Teapot, no lid, Stacked Disc, green and white $10
Tea Set, Interior Panel, "The Little American Maid Tea
    Set," 21 pieces, with box, blue and white $350

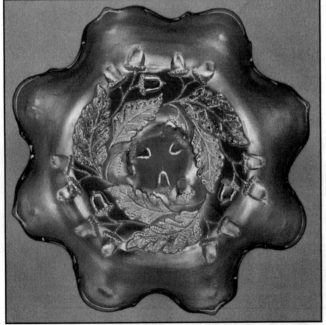

Carnival, Acorn design by Fenton, found on bowls and plates in a wide range of colors.

Tumbler, Stacked Disc, white $9
Tumbler, 2" h, Stacked Disc, children's, white $6
Vase, cornucopia, multicolored, 3-1/4" $15

Carnival Glass

Blackberry
Basket, open edge ruffled, green $110
Compote, ruffled, purple $55
Spray, candy ribbon edge, amber $75
Spray, red $300

Blackberry Wreath
Bowl, 7", six ruffles, amethyst $90
Bowl, 8", ice cream shape, green $75
Bowl, 8-3/8", round flared, amethyst $90
Bowl, 10", six ruffles, amethyst $180
3-in-1 edge bowl, 6", green $65

Butterfly
Bon Bon, green $155
Bon Bon, plain exterior, marigold $50
Bon Bon, smooth back, purple $55

Corn
Bottle, smoke $250
Bottle, marigold $200
Vase, flower base, green $475
Vase, marigold $850
Vase, plain base, marigold $1,550
Vase, purple $500
Vase, white $175

Flute & Cane
Milk pitcher, marigold $130
Milk pitcher, small, marigold $65
Water goblet, marigold $40
Water pitcher, marigold $145

Good Luck
Bowl, pie-crust edge, blue $400
Bowl, pie-crust edge, basketweave exterior, green $375
Bowl, ruffled, ribbed exterior, blue $185
Bowl, ruffled, ribbed exterior, marigold $230
Bowl, ruffled, ribbed exterior, purple $225
Plate, 9" $800

Grape & Cable
Banana boat, ice green $375
Banana boat, ice blue $400
Banana boat, marigold $175
Banana boat, purple $220
Banana boat, white $425
Bon Bon, amethyst $75
Bon Bon, green $90
Bon Bon, electric blue $170
Bowl, 8-3/4", smooth exterior, green $170
Bowl, master berry, amethyst $85
Bowl, pie-crust edge, basketweave exterior, marigold ... $110
Bowls, master and five small bowls, thumbprint, purple $325
Butter dish with lid, tiny base nick, amethyst $105
Candlesticks, pair, amethyst $400
Compote, covered, marigold $1,350
Cup and saucer, purple $165

Orange bowl, 11", amethyst $145
Perfume bottle, purple $350
Plate, 6-1/4", basketweave exterior, amethyst $125
Plate, 7", basketweave exterior, amethyst $165
Plate, 8", hand grip, basketweave exterior, amethyst $145
Plate, 9", basketweave exterior, amethyst $175
Punch bowl and base, ruffled, purple $350
Punch cup, purple $27
Ruffled fruit bowl, amethyst $325
Ruffled sauces, amethyst $55
Sherbet, amethyst $30
Tankard tumbler, amethyst $55
Tumbler, amethyst $42
Water pitcher, purple $350
Water set, green $575
Whiskey shot glass, amethyst $210

Heavy Grape

Bowl, 10", ruffled, purple $85
Chop plate, amber $75
Chop plate, green $85
Chop plate, purple $125

Lustre Rose

Fruit bowl, footed, marigold $85
Spooner, purple $125
Tumbler, purple $60
Water pitcher, purple $145
Water set, seven pieces, marigold $130

Memphis

Berry set, seven pieces, marigold $200
Fruit bowl, two pieces with four cups, marigold $350

Orange Tree

Bowl, fruit, marigold $85
Cream/sugar set, breakfast, blue $100
Hatpin holder, blue $400
Hatpin holder, marigold $350
Loving cup, blue $200
Loving cup, marigold $185
Mug, shaving size, blue $35
Mug, shaving size, marigold $25
Mug, small, blue $70
Plate, 9", blue $500
Plate, 9", clambroth $300
Plate, 9", marigold $325
Plate, 9", white $200
Powder jar, marigold $75
Tumbler, blue $55

Pansy

Bowl, 9-1/4", lavender $125
Bowl, 9", ruffled, purple $210
Pickle dish, oval, amber $50
Pickle dish, ruffled, amber $45
Pickle dish, ruffled, purple $70
Nappy, handled, purple $55

Persian Medallion

Bowl, 7", ruffled, green $55
Bowl, 8", candy ribbon edge, marigold $100
Bowl, 10", footed, ruffled, marigold $170
Bowl, 10", ruffled, blue $300

Bowl, ice cream shape with plain back, green $140
Chop plate, 10", small flake on back, blue $400
Chop plate, 10-1/4", blue $500
Compote, crimped edge, large, blue $195
Compote, crimped edge, ruffled, large, marigold $175
Compote, ruffled, small, marigold $105
Hair receiver, marigold $115
Plate, 9", blue $1,300
Sauce, round, red $550

Ripple

Vase, 7", purple $105
Vase, 12", 4-1/4" top, purple $90
Vase, 12", 5-1/4" top, purple $95

Rooster

Hat pin, electric blue $50
Hat pin, lavender $175
Hat pin, teal $100
Hat pin, white $80

Cut Glass

Basket, Quaker City Glass, twisted handle, three-step
    pedestal base, 5-1/2" x 8" $375
Berry bowl, pinwheel cut, scalloped edge, 8" d $250
Berry bowl, Hawkes, hobstar and fan cut, 9" d $250
Bowl, Marseilles pattern, hobstar and star, 8" d $225
Bowl, Adonis pattern, cane, fan, hobstar and strawberry,
    signed Clark, 9" d $245
Box, covered, C.F. Monroe, 3-1/2" d $400
Butter dish with underplate, hobstar and floral, domed
    lid, 7-1/2" d $225
Candy dish, divided, intaglio floral, twin handles, 8" d ... $85
Celery tray, geometric and floral cut, 10" x 5" $65
Centerpiece, hobstar pattern, 19" l, c1870 .... $2,200
Cologne, square, Dorflinger, Colonial Pattern $295
Cologne, Dorflinger, Renaissance Pattern, c1900 .... $160
Cordials, Dorflinger, set of four, Renaissance Pattern ... $340
Decanter, Dorflinger, Heavy Flute Pattern $365
Goblet, Diamond $60
Goblet, Silva $40
Humidor, notched prisms, large hobstar lid, 8-1/2" h $425
Mint tray, hobstars and nailhead, sawtooth and
    scalloped edge, 6" d $120
Mustard jar, Maple City Glass Co., c1900 .... $225
Nappy, Iris, Hawkes, 8" d $120
Pitcher, Harvard Palter, c1890 .... $450
Pitcher, Dorflinger, Brilliant Pattern, c1880 .... $695
Pitcher, Libbey, Marcella Pattern, 11-3/4" h $2,800
Punch bowl, pedestal and bowl, signed Maple City,
    c1890, 16" h $2,100
Punch cup, Russian pattern, hobstar foot $75
Sugar and creamer, Dorflinger, Old Colony pattern $395

Depression Glass

Adam

Ashtray, 4-1/2", green $28
Cake plate, footed, 10", pink $41
Plate, grille, 9", green $26
Plate, sherbet, 6", pink $14

Plate, square dinner, 9", green $37
Plate, square dinner, 9", pink $41
Plate, square salad, 7-3/4", green $26
Platter, 11-3/4", pink $45
Sherbet, 3", pink $41

American Sweetheart
Bowl, berry, round, 9", pink $70
Cup and saucer, pink $34
Plate, salver, 12", pink $25
Platter, oval, 13", pink $70
Sherbet, footed, 3-3/4", pink $20

Block Optic
Candy jar and cover, 6-1/4", green $110
Cup and saucer, pink $19
Cup, square handle, green $11
Pitcher, 54 oz, 7-5/8", green $70
Plate, luncheon, 8", green $11
Plate, dinner, 9", green $26
Plate, sherbet, 6", green $6
Salt/pepper shakers, footed, green $45
Salt/pepper shakers, footed, yellow $80
Saucer, 6-1/8", crystal $4
Sherbet, 3-1/4", green $6

Bubble
Berry bowl, 8-3/8", crystal $7
Bread plate, crystal $2
Dinner plate, 9-3/8", crystal $6
Serving plate, 10", crystal $7
Tumbler, 12 oz., 4-1/2", Royal Ruby $10

Cameo
Bowl, cereal, 5-1/2", yellow $30
Sugar, 3-1/4", green $20
Tumbler, footed, 3 oz., 3-1/4", green $55

Candlewick
Sauce bowl, deep, 5-1/2", crystal $37
Bowl, handled, two-part, 7", crystal $25

Cherry Blossom
Bowl, berry, 4-3/4", green $17
Pitcher, 6-3/4", green $85

Chinex Classic
Creamer, footed, ivory $7
Cup, ivory $7
Plate, cake, 12", ivory $9
Plate, dinner, 9-3/4", ivory $6
Plate, sherbet, 6-1/4", ivory $4
Saucer, ivory $4

Cloverleaf
Salt/pepper shakers, black $75
Salt/pepper shakers, yellow $110
Saucer, green $4

Cubist or Cube
Bowl, dessert, 4-1/2" deep, pink $7
Candy jar cover, green $20
Creamer, crystal $3
Coaster, 3-1/4", green $7.50
Plate, luncheon 8", pink $6
Powder jar, crystal $30
Saucer, pink $3

Sugar bowl, 2-3/8", pink $3
Sugar and creamer, crystal $4

Dogwood
Bowl, berry, 8-1/2", pink $79
Cake plate, 13", pink $120
Creamer, thick footed, pink $20
Cup and saucer, pink $28
Plate, bread and butter, 6", pink $8
Plate, grille, border design, 10-1/2", pink $20
Saucer, pink $7
Sugar, thin flat, 2-1/2", pink $18

English Hobnail
Cocktail, stem, 3 oz., crystal $8
Mayonnaise, 6", crystal $10
Salt/pepper shakers, crystal $40
Salt/pepper shakers, crystal $120

Fire King "Jane Ray"
Bowl, soup plate, 7-5/8" $14
Cup and saucer $5
Plate, dinner, 9-1/8" $8
Plate, salad, 7-3/4" $6
Sugar with cover $15

Florentine #1
Cup, yellow $10
Pitcher, footed, 6-1/2", 36 oz, yellow $45
Plate, salad, 8-1/2", pink $11
Plate, sherbet, 6", green $7
Sherbet, footed, green $11
Sugar, pink $14
Tumbler, 5 oz., green $16

Florentine #2
Bowl, berry, 4-1/2", yellow $20
Bowl, cereal, 6", yellow $38
Bowl, cream soup, crystal $14
Candlestick, single, yellow $30
Candy dish and cover, yellow $150
Coaster, yellow $21
Cup, yellow $10
Gravy boat and platter, yellow $100
Plate, sherbet, 6", crystal $4
Plate, sherbet, 6", yellow $6
Saucer, crystal $4
Pitcher, cone footed, 7-1/2", yellow $30
Plate, salad, 8-1/2", crystal $10
Plate, salad, 8-1/2", yellow $9
Plate, dinner, 10", yellow $14
Plate, dinner, 10", crystal $15
Salt/pepper shakers, yellow $65
Saucer, yellow $5
Sherbet, yellow $11
Tumbler, footed, 4", yellow $17
Tumbler, juice, 3-3/8", 5 oz., yellow $23
Tumbler, 4", yellow $21
Tumbler, 4-1/2", 9 oz. footed, green $26

Fruits
Bowl, berry, crystal $13
Cup, green $8
Plate, luncheon, 8" green $7
Saucer, green $6

Horseshoe No. 612

Creamer, footed, green $17
Tumbler, footed, 9 oz., yellow $25

Madrid

Bowl, low console, 11", amber $25
Bowl, oval vegetable, 10", amber $18
Bowl, sauce, 5", amber $6
Bowl, soup 7", amber $16
Candlesticks, 2-1/4", amber $26
Cookie jar, no lid, amber $22
Creamer, amber $14
Creamer, crystal $9
Cup, amber $8
Plate, grill, 10-1/2", amber $14
Plate, luncheon, 8-7/8", amber $15
Plate, sherbet, 6", amber $5
Platter, oval, 11-1/2", amber $18
Salt/pepper shakers, flat, amber $47
Salt/pepper shakers, flat, green $100
Salt/pepper shakers, footed, green $140
Saucer, amber $5
Sherbet, amber $8
Sherbet, green $12
Sugar, amber $14
Tumbler, 4-1/4", 9 oz., amber $16

Mayfair

Bowl, low, flat, 11-3/4", green $40
Bowl, oval vegetable, 10", yellow $30
Bowl, scalloped, fruit, 12" deep, green $40
Platter, oval, 12", yellow $27
Sandwich server with center handle, green $37

Miss America

Bowl, berry, 4-1/2", green $12
Bowl, cereal, 6-1/4", crystal $10
Bowl, oblong celery, 10-1/2", pink $30
Bowl, oval vegetable, 10", pink $25
Celery dish, oblong, 10-1/2", pink $40
Coaster, 5-3/4", crystal $15
Pitcher, 65 oz., crystal $120
Plate, dinner, 10-1/4", pink $27
Platter, oval, 12-1/4", pink $26
Plate, sherbet, 5-3/4", pink $7
Relish, four-part, 8-3/4", crystal $11
Relish, four-part, 8-3/4", pink $24
Salt/pepper shakers, crystal $45
Sherbet, crystal $8

Moderntone

Creamer, footed, cobalt $11
Cup, cobalt $19
Plate, sherbet, 5-7/8", amethyst $6
Salt/pepper shakers, cobalt $40
Salt/pepper shakers, Platonite White $26
Saucer, cobalt $9
Sherbet, Platonite White $5
Sugar, cobalt $16
Tumbler, 9 oz., Platonite White $9

New Century

Cup and saucer, crystal $11

Sherbet, footed, 3", crystal $10
Tumbler, 9 oz., 4-1/4", crystal $16

Ovide

Creamer, Art Deco $75
Sherbet, footed, green $3

Patrician

Cup, crystal $8
Sherbet, crystal $13
Creamer and sugar, crystal $19
Plate, dinner, 10-1/2", yellow $10
Plate, salad, 7-1/2" crystal $15
Platter, oval, 11-1/2", crystal $30
Sherbet, yellow $13

Petalware

Bowl, cream soup, 4-1/2", Cremax $14
Creamer, footed, Monax $6
Cup, gold trim, Cremax $10
Lamp Shade, Monax $25
Plate, salad, 8", Monax $10
Salver 11", Cremax $18
Saucer, Cremax $3.50
Sherbet, low footed, floral, 4-1/2", Monax $35
Sugar bowl, footed, open, Monax $6

Depression, vase, pink.

Pineapple and Floral
Platter, divided relish, 11-1/2", crystal $19
Cup, crystal $10
Cream soup, yellow $20
Tumbler, 4-1/4", 8 oz, crystal $18

Pretzel
Bowl, soup, 7-1/2", crystal $10
Bowl, berry, 9-1/2", crystal $18
Plate, salad, 8-3/8", crystal $6
Plate, sandwich 11-1/2", crystal $11

Princess
Ashtray, inner rim roughness, green $70
Bowl, berry, 4-1/2", green, inner rim roughness $20
Bowl, cereal, 5", green, inner rim roughness $25
Bowl, hat-shape, 9-1/2", green $45
Bowl, oval vegetable, 10", green $28
Butter dish with cover, tiny nick, green $100
Cake stand, 10", green $25
Cup and saucer, green, for set $22
Cup, pink $12
Pitcher, 6", 37 oz., green $53
Pitcher, 8", 60 oz., green $58
Plate, grille, closed handle, 10-1/2", green $12
Plate, salad, 8", green $14
Plate, sherbet, green $10
Salt/pepper shakers, 5-1/2", green $40
Sherbet, footed, green $22
Sugar, bottom frosted, pink $12
Tumbler, 4", 9 oz, green $28

Roulette
Cup and saucer, green $10
Plate, luncheon, 8-1/2", green $6
Plate, sherbet, 6" $5

Royal Ruby
Ashtray, 4-1/2", leaf $5
Beer Bottles, various sizes, each .... $25-$30
Cup and saucer, round or square, each set $6
Goblet, 9 oz. $9
Goblet, 9-1/2 oz $14
Ice bucket $45
Pitcher, tilted, 3 qt $40

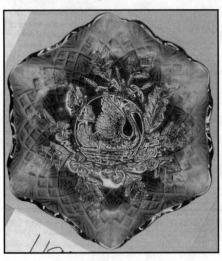

Carnival, Millersburg bowl in the Nesting Swan pattern.

Pitcher, upright 3 qt $35
Plate, dinner, 9-1/8" $12
Plate, luncheon, square, 8-3/8" $9
Plate, salad, 7" d $3
Tumbler, 3-1/2" h $4
Tumbler, 9 oz. $4
Tumbler, cocktail, 3-1/2 oz. $8
Tumbler, juice, 4 oz. $4
Tumbler, juice, 5-1/2 oz. $6
Sherbet, stem, 6-1/2 oz. $8
Sugar and creamer, flat or footed, each set $14
Vase, 3-3/4" h $5
Vase, 6-3/8" h $8
Vase, 6-5/8" h $10
Vase, 9" h $13
Vase, 10" h, fluted $35

Sandwich-Hocking
Bowl, oval, 8-1/4", crystal $9
Bowl, salad, 9", crystal $25
Bowl, scalloped, 6-1/2", crystal $10
Creamer, crystal $10
Pitcher, 1/2-gallon, crystal $90
Plate, 8", crystal $8
Sugar, crystal $10

Sandwich-Indiana
Cup, crystal $4
Plate, dinner, 10-1/2", crystal $9
Plate, luncheon, 8-3/8", crystal $7
Plate, sherbet, 6", crystal $4
Sherbet, 3-1/4", crystal $7
Sugar, crystal $10

Sharon
Bowl, berry, 5", pink $13
Bowl, fruit, 10-1/2", pink $50
Bowl, large berry, 8-1/2", amber $9
Bowl, soup, flat, 7-3/4", amber $50
Bowl, oval vegetable, 9-1/2", amber $20
Cake plate, footed, crystal $30
Cup and saucer, amber $16
Cup and saucer, pink $30
Plate, bread and butter, 6", pink $11
Plate, dinner, 9", amber $12
Plate, dinner, 9-1/2", amber $11
Plate, dinner, 9-1/2", pink $25
Platter, oval, 12-1/2", amber $17
Platter, oval, 12-1/2", pink $35
Sherbet, 2-1/4", amber $12
Sherbet, footed, pink $20

Twisted Optic
Candy, covered, low, flat, green $35
Console bowl, rolled edge, 10-1/2", green $20
Vase, 8", two handles, straight edge, pink $30

Windsor
Plate, chop, 13-5/8", pink $40
Plate, dinner, 9", green $25
Plate, sherbet, 6", pink $6
Sugar and cover, pink $30
Tumbler, 4", 9 oz., pink $20

GOLF COLLECTIBLES

About 500 years ago, golf was played along the eastern coast of Scotland, where the land — called links land — was non-aerable and mostly sandy, as its primary purpose was for grazing sheep. Early golfers used long whippy shafted wooden head clubs to propel a leather jacketed ball filled with goose feathers. The delicate wooden head clubs, usually made by bow makers — Play Club (Driver), Brassie, Long and Short Spoons — were used to sweep the ball from sheep mown grass lies. The Baffie was used to loft the ball over an obstacle or stream from a grass lie.

As a misplayed stroke would damage the delicate feather ball, few iron head clubs were used. Clubs with deep, broad concave faces were forged by the local blacksmith for playing the ball from the sandy lies and were called Bunker or Sand clubs. A small rounded cupped face club was made to extract the ball from the deep hoof and cart tracks and accordingly called a Rut or Track club. A long shallow blade club with very little loft was used to hit the ball from bare hard ground or to hit a low running shot in windy weather. An Approaching Putter and/or Holing Out Putter, usually made from wood, rounded out the set.

Wood-shaft golf clubs

Feather ball-era clubs were usually made by carpenters, bow makers, barrel makers, wheelwrights and other craftsmen with woodworking backgrounds. The irons were forged by the local armor maker or blacksmith.

A "play club" was used from the teeing ground, a "brassie" was used to strike long, low shots from the fairway, and the "long spoon" and "mid-spoons" were used to hit moderately long-lofted shots. The "short spoon" (sometimes also called a baffie) was used to hit short-lofted shots around the green or over trouble.

General Guidelines: Fewer than five percent of all wood shafted clubs are valuable. Metal shafted clubs that have been painted or "wood-grained" to look like wood have no collectible value to the "wood shaft collector." Likewise, a club that has been restored or cleaned, is warped or cracked, has heavy rusting and pitting or bad or missing grips will drop substantially in value.

Tens of millions of low grade clubs were made and sold from 1915 to 1935. Spalding, MacGregor, Burke, Kroydon, Hillerich & Bradsby, Wilson, Wright & Ditson and scores of others made clubs with line, dot, hyphen and other face markings. Most of these are common and have little value beyond their conversational, decorative or playable worth.

Some tipoffs that a club is common:
• No manufacturer's name, or a common name like Biltmore, Hollywood, Thistle, Bonnie, Metropolitan, Columbia, Ace, Majestic
• Metal caps at the end of the grip
• Yardage ranges stamped on the back (ie. 145-155 yds)
• Chromed, chromium or stainless steel heads
• Numbered irons from sets, or "matched set" irons
• Iron faces scored with dots, hyphens or lines

Characteristics of an uncommon, valuable club:
• Irons with no face markings, or unusual face markings
• Irons or putters with unusual head shapes; wood head putters
• Woods with a thick, curved, oval neck covered with four or five inches of string "whipping"
• Smooth face irons with the following names: Anderson, Park, Army & Navy, Ayres, Carrick, Forgan, Gray and Morris
• Certain Spalding, MacGregor, Condie, Nicoll, Stewart, Gibson and Wright & Ditson clubs with smooth faces

Golf balls

Clubs were affordable, however only the very wealthy could afford the feather balls of this pre-1850 era. A skilled ball maker could make only three or four balls a day, which resulted in the very high cost. In the late 1840s, gutta-percha — a rubbery compound commonly used to line wooden shipping boxes containing fragile items — was molded into golf balls. The gutta-percha balls were far less expensive and, as a result, golf became more affordable.

As more people took up the game of golf, refinements of courses, clubs and balls were made. During the late 1800s, many patents were taken out on all forms of golfing artifacts. One of the most significant was the Haskell patent. Working for Goodyear Rubber Company, Coburn Haskell and Bertram Works developed a process of winding thin rubber strips around a central core, then covered these windings with gutta-percha. The "Haskell" ball was the leading factor in the development and refinement of golf clubs and the game as we know it today.

General Guidelines: As with clubs, pre-1800s balls are scarce. Pre-1860 gutta-percha balls are scarcer than featheries. Named maker balls of both types are even scarcer. Balls with markings on them from this period are among the rarest. There are also a few balls painted for winter play that are highly sought after. While most are red or orange, there have been blue, yellow and black balls noted.

Common mesh pattern golf balls — circa 1930 from Worthington, Dunlop or Spalding — in above average condition sell for about $75. An identical ball, but with a cover cut or other damage, will bring only $10 to $15.

Faroid or Park Royal balls are so rare and seldom offered, even damaged examples are highly sought after and bring premium prices.

SIGNATURE BALLS

With the prices of odd pattern balls, gutta-perchas, brambles and wrapped balls escalating at a brisk pace, many collectors cannot afford to purchase top quality examples. For those who want to collect balls in top quality, signature balls may be the answer. Signature balls are golf balls that were imprinted, at the time of manufacturing, with a professional's name. At present they are plentiful, most are priced under $50 and can be acquired in top condition.

Tees

Tees are a highly collectible area of golf. The first tees were a small mound of sand formed into a cone to accommodate the feather ball. Shortly before the turn of the century metal cone-shaped molds, mostly made of brass, were in vogue. Many golf courses provided a "Sand Box" with a pail of water at each tee and the player or his caddy used the mold to shape the wet sand for a tee.

During the 1920s, the wooden tee and some wire, plastic, rubber and zinc tees were introduced. Tees have been made of aluminum, paper, plastic, steel, wire, zinc, rubber—anything that would raise the ball from the turf. Shapes and forms were stars, triangles, domes, tethers, spinners, molds and just about anything else imaginable.

In the early 1900s, packaging to promote the merchandising of tees became an industry in itself. Tees were packaged in large and small boxes with very ornate designs. Another packaging concept was cloth tee bags, similar to a tobacco pouch, which held 50 or 100 tees. Paper bags were also used to hold 15 to 25 tees. Most bags were white with the printed advertisement of the golf companies.

Tee packets similar to matchbooks are also collectibles and have been produced since the early 1920s.
Bags or boxes of tees are less valuable if they are only partially full.

Autographs

The autograph hobby dates back about 1,000 years, and with the first British Open Championship in 1860, golf began to establish itself as a sport. As a result, autographs of golf's greatest players did not escape interest of collectors. Autographed photographs, trading cards, books, golf balls, letters and other items are highly sought after by collectors.

Books

Golf books cover many categories including instruction, architecture, history, rules, anthologies and fiction. Some reference books generally acquired for information and pricing are highly collectible as well.

In 1457 Scotland's King James II issued a decree outlawing golf because his soldiers were golfing more than practicing their archery skills. This decree became the first printed reference to the game of golf. It wasn't until the golf boom of the 1890s that books on golf were published in great quantities. The most prominent one of this period was *Golf: The Badminton Library* by Horace Hutchinson (1890).

Richard E. Donovan and Joseph S. F. Murdoch collaborated to publish *The Game of Golf and the Printed Word* (1988) which is a bibliography of golf literature in the English language. This is a highly regarded and collectible reference book.

General Guidelines: Prices of books are determined by condition, edition, scarcity and desirability. First printings of first editions command higher prices than later printings.

Books in poor condition (missing pages, broken cover or contents damaged, badly soiled or stained) or library books are generally useful for information only. Underlining, margin notes, repair or rebinding all reduce the value of a book.

Metal golf collectibles

The wealthy golfer from 1875 to 1930 spared no expense when it came to displaying the game he loved. Collectibles came in the form of trophies, tees, medals, dining utensils, jewelry, smoking paraphernalia, whiskey flasks, music boxes, watches, ink wells and more.

Trophies were made of gold and silver. There were sterling silver toast racks, tea pots, knives, forks, and especially spoons with golf motifs, as well as any other dining table items. Whiskey flasks were also made of sterling silver. The businessman had in his den or on his office desk golf-affiliated paperweights, ink wells, pens, clocks, humidors, ashtrays, letter openers and scores of other knickknacks.

Smoking had not yet been demonized and pipe, cigar, and cigarette cases, match safes, humidors, ashtrays and other tobacco related items were made of gold, silver and bronze.

Clubs
•Golf Collectors Society
P.O. Box 20546, Dayton, OH 45420
513-256-2474

•British Golf Collectors Society
Box13704, North Berwick, Wast Lothian
EH39 4ZB, Scotland, U.K.

VALUE LINE

Autographed items

Harry Vardon signed photo, circa 1910-1920 .... $650
Tom Morris signed photo, circa 1900 .... $1,500
Ben Hogan signed photo, circa 1960-1980 .... $300
Ben Hogan signed photo, circa 1940-1950. Vintage ink
    pen signature $450
Robert T. Jones, Jr. signed photo, circa 1955-1970.
    Shaky ball point pen signature $650
Robert T. Jones, Jr. signed photo, circa 1930-1950.
    Black fountain pen signature $2,250
Arnold Palmer signed photo, circa 1975 .... $40
Byron Nelson signed photo, circa 1960-1990s $40
Gene Sarazen signed photo, circa 1960s-'90s $40
Gene Sarazen signed photo, circa 1925-1950. Fountain
    pen vintage signature $90
Jack Nicklaus signed photo, circa 1980 .... $75
Byron Nelson signed photo, circa 1935-1950. Fountain
    pen vintage signature $100

Books

Golf Course Mystery by C.K. Steel, fiction, 1919 .... $125
History of Golf in Britain by Bernard Darwin, history,
    1952 .... $300
Golf; Badminton Library by Horace Hutchinson,
    anthology, 1890 .... $325
Scotland's Gift; Golf by C.B. MacDonald, architecture,
    1928(Reprints $35) $700
This Game of Golf by Henry Cotton, instructional, 1948 $60

The Bobby Jones Story by G. Rice and O.B. Keeler, biography, 1953 .... $65

Life of Tom Morris by W.W. Tulloch, biography, 1908 .... $1,200

Power Golf by Ben Hogan, instructional, 1948 .... $30

Walter Hagen Story by Hagen and M. Heck, biography, 1956 .... $125

Encyclopedia of Golf by Steel, Ryde and Wind, reference, 1975 .... $35

Golf in the Making by Henderson and Stirk, reference, history, 1979 .... $150

Clubs

Prices are for items in Excellent condition.

Schenectady putter, Lee, Harry C, New York, circa 1903-1915. Patent date March 24, 1903 on back $300

Mills 'K' model, Standard Golf Co., circa 1900-1910, very long head $400

Long nose putters, Ayres, FH, London, England, circa 1885-1895. Long Nose Putter. Beech head $1,250

Long nose putters, Morris, Tom, St. Andrews, circa 1860-1880. Beech head stamped "T Morris." Long head with large lead back weight $2,500

Long nose putters, Forgan, Robert, St. Andrews, circa 1860-1880. Beech head. "R Forgan" large block letters mark. Long head, large lead back weight $2,500

Down-it 486 putter, MacGregor, Dayton, OH, circa 1915-1920 wooden head mallet putter. Brass face plate with hatched scoring $375

Corrugated deep groove, various makers, circa 1915-1922. Mashie, Mashie Niblick and Niblicks $125

Slot deep groove irons, various makers, circa 1915-1922. Wide slot deep grooves. Mashie, Mashie-niblick and Niblick $150

Rotary illegal irons, Burke Mfg. Co., Newark, OH, circa 1920. All clubs. Half waffle pattern, half slot deep groove. Monel Metal $425

Waterfall irons, Spalding, USA, circa 1920. Single Waterfall "F" Series $500

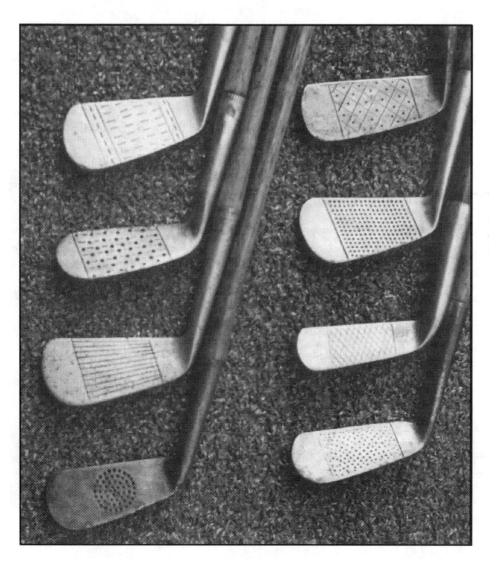

Common iron face markings. Some are a bit less common, like the "ball dot," most often found on c1915 Spalding irons, and the "crisscross" and "crisscross with dots," rarely found on clubs other than pre-World War I British clubs.

Cran irons, Spalding, USA, circa 1897-1915 with wood face insert. "The Spalding," "Crescent" and "Gold Medal" marks $950

Anti-shank irons, various makers, circa 1900-1925. Both Smith and Fairlie's Patent irons $200

Concave sand wedge, Walter Hagen & La Young, circa 1930. Smooth concave face. Large Flange $500

Rut iron, blacksmith made, circa 1840-1860. Small cupped face. Long thick hosel with heavy nicking $3,500

Smooth face cleek, blacksmith made, circa 1840-1860. Five inch long hosel with crude heavy nicking $2,700

Bunker or sand iron, blacksmith made, circa 1840-1860. Very thick long hosel with crude heavy nicking. Usually with a concave face $4,500

Holing out putter, blacksmith made, circa 1840-1860. Very thick long hosel with crude heavy nicking..... $3,000

Rake irons, Winton, W & Co., Ltd., circa 1905. The Major. Seven pointed tines $6,000

Long nose woods, Philp, Hugh, St. Andrews, circa 1840-1856. "H Philp" in block letters, thorn head $10,000

Pretty face woods, various makers, circa 1920s. Various pretty face inserts $125

Aluminum head woods, Braddell, Belfast, Ireland, circa 1894-1900. "Braddell Patent 1112," leather face insert $650

One-piece wood, Bridgeport Gun & Implement, circa 1898-1902. Driver or Brassie one-piece hickory head and shaft. Has a leather face insert $2,000

Long nose woods Ayres, F.H., London, England, circa 1885-1895. Play Club, Brassie or Spoon. "FH Ayres" on Beech head $1,650

Long nose woods, Simpson, Robert, circa 1883-1890. Play Club, Brassie or Spoon. "R Simpson" on a Beech head. Many have leather face inserts $2,250

Long nose woods, McEwan, Musselburgh, circa 1870-1880. Play Club or Brassie. Long head, large lead back weight. "McEwan" mark $2,750

Golf Balls

Feather ball, no maker's name, circa 1840-1860 .... $5,000

Feather ball, Gourlay, John Musselburgh, circa 1840-1860. "J Gourlay" and size number $9,000

Feather ball, Morris, Tom, St. Andrews, circa 1840-1860. "T Morris" and size number $15,000

Smooth gutta-percha, no maker's name, circa 1850-1860. White, brown or black usually with a "test" mark $3,000

Hand hammered gutta, no maker's name, circa 1850-1880 .... $2,000

Hand hammered gutta, Forgan, Robert, St. Andrews, circa 1865-1880. Stamped "R Forgan", usually with size number $2,500

Line cut gutta-percha, remade, no name, circa 1880-1905 .... $300

Line cut gutta-percha, various makers, circa 1880-1905 .... $500

Bramble gutta-percha, remade, no name, circa 1895-1905 .... $250

Bramble gutta-percha, various makers, circa 1895-1905 .... $450

Bramble gutta-percha, Spalding, Vardon Flyer, circa 1900. "Vardon Flyer" at both poles $950

Bramble rubber core, various makers, circa 1905-1920, celluloid or rubber cover $275

Bramble rubber core, various makers, circa 1900. Gutta-percha cover $325

Bramble rubber core, Haskell, circa 1900. "Haskell Bramble" at one pole, "Pat Apr. 11, 99" at other pole $500

Mesh cover, various makers, circa 1910-1940. Square markings $75

Dimple cover, Spalding, USA, circa 1908-1920. Baby Dimple, Domino, Dot, Glory Dimple, and others $125

Diamond cover, Spalding, USA, circa 1920-1930. Entire cover with diamonds. "Spalding" at poles $150

Warwick, Dunlop, Birmingham, Eng., circa 1925-1935. Alternating rows of square and dimple markings $175

Metal Collectibles

Sterling silver spoons, circa 1900-1930, golfers on handle $80

Sterling tee infuser, Watrous, Wallingford, CT, circa 1910-1915, shaped like a driver $300

Toast rack, Derby Silver Co., circa 1900-1910, four slice rack $500

Silver plate ink well, Birmingham, England, circa 1900. 6" x 11" size, two golf ball inkwells $500

Sterling cigarette case, circa 1900-1920, golfing scene on cover $575

Spalding diamond cover golf ball, circa 1920-1930.

Sterling match safe, Unger, Newark, NJ, circa 1900-1910, caddy with bag $650

Sterling whiskey flask, Kerr & Co., Newark, NJ, circa 1920s, 4" x 8" pint size, knickered golfers on front .. $800

Gold golf ball cuff links, Dunlop, New York, circa 1920, nickel size 10k gold mesh golf ball cuff links $175

Pottery

Stoneware pitcher, Doulton, Lambeth, England, circa early 1900s. Golfers in white relief $1,400

Porcelain spill vases, Doulton, Lambeth, England, circa early 1900s $750

Stoneware pitcher, Copeland spode, circa 1900. Golfers in relief, white on blue or green background $650

Stoneware jardiniere, Copeland Spode, circa 1900. Golfers in relief, white on blue or green background $650

Stoneware ewer, Copeland Spode, circa 1900. Golfers in relief, white on blue or green background $650

Silver rim tankard, Lenox, Lawrenceville, NJ, circa 1905. Lady and gentleman golfers on a green background $1,300

Silver lid tankard, Lenox, Lawrenceville, NJ, circa 1905. Lady and gentleman golfers on a blue background $1,500

Creamer, Wedgewood, Burslem, circa early 1900s. Golfers in white relief $650

Sugar bowl with lid, Wedgewood, Burslem, circa early 1900s. Golfers in white relief $750

Tees

Prices listed are for full boxes or bags.

The Reddy Tee, Nieblo Mfg. Co., circa 1930. Wooden tees in green, white and red box $70

The Scot-tee, circa late 1920s, box of 18 wood tees $100

Perfect Golf Tee, patented 1927. Molded rubber tee secured in the ground by a nail $100

Novel-tees, Spurgin Mfg., Chicago, circa late 1920s. A book of 18 paper tees $75

Pryde's Orange Tee, Orange Mfg. Co., circa late 1920s. Carrot shaped wood tees. Blue and orange box $100

K-D sand tee mold, K-D Mfg., Lancaster, PA, circa 1920s. Polished aluminum with spring plunger $475

Sand tee mold, circa 1890-1920. Brass with spring plunger $650

Rex zinc tees, The Rex Co., Chicago, circa 1930. Red box, zinc tees $100

Tees in bags, various makers, circa 1930s-'40s. Draw string bags of fifty and one hundred wooden tees $50

Rubber Manhattan tee, circa 1920. Five inch long rubber tee with round weight at one end, tee at other $100

Keystone sand tee mold, circa 1920-1930. Bakelite plastic with spring plunger $350

Contributor to this section:
Chuck Furjanic, P.O. Box 165892, Irving, TX 75016

An assortment of collectible golf tees.

Halloween Collectibles

Running a close second after Christmas as the holiday with the most collectibles, Halloween enjoys a resurgence of new interest each fall.

Ghosts, black cats, and jack-o-lanterns are some of the most visible images related to this spooky holiday. But collectors seek almost anything associated with the bewitching October 31.

The holiday became popular in the United States in the late 1800s, and paper items like postcards, decorations and invitations are among the earliest Halloween collectibles. Because of their colorful display potential, 20th century items generating high interest are boxed costumes, tin noisemakers, trick-or-treat bags and intricate crepe paper decorations.

General Guidelines: Anything Halloween-related is collectible, but pre-1960s items are most valuable. Victorian paper items from the 1890s sell for $10-$30 each, with some rarer or more elaborate examples commanding $50-$150. Boxed costumes were manufactured as early as 1910; character costumes from the 1960s-70s by manufacturers Ben Cooper and Collegeville are most popular with collectors as are more generic 1940s-'50s examples. Masks from all eras are highly collectible. Papier-mache jack-o-lanterns are highly prized by collectors and can be worth from $25-$80 or more. Tin noisemakers can sell for $5-$20 for small generic pieces up to $100 for older, more elaborate examples.

Prices listed are for items in Excellent condition.

Boxed costumes, w/mask, 1940s-50s .... $35-$65
Candy containers, figural, composition, 1920s ..... $100-$400
Candy container, black cat, head, 3" h, pressed cardboard, cut-out eyes and mouth, wire handle, Germany $60
Candy container, pumpkin, glass, painted, 4" h, scary face, wire handle, metal screw-on lid $120
Crepe paper rolls, early 1900s .... $40-$75
Fan, foldout, wooden stick, tissue paper, witch riding broom, black and orange, 1920s, Germany $25
Figure, black cat, 9" h, cardboard, flat, movable legs and tail, Beistle $18
Ghost, 9-1/2" h, cardboard standup $15
Green Hornet costume, Ben Cooper, 1960s $150
Howdy Doody costume, Collegeville, 1950s $85
Witch, roly poly, 3" h, celluloid, orange and black, Japanese $180
Horn, 4" h, wood, black and orange, painted cat face, marked "Czecho-Slavakia" $24
Horn, 8" h, paper, orange and black, wood mouthpiece, Germany $10
Jack-o-lantern, papier-mache, 1940s $45

Illustrated by artist Winsch Schumucker, this early 1900s postcard is worth from $100 to $125.

Postcard, published by Tuck, $15-$20.

Lanterns, figural, paperboard, 1920s .... $100-$500

Lantern, pumpkin, 4" h, papier-mache, paper eyes and mouth, wire handle, candleholder in base, Germany .. $60

Lantern, 6" h, glass and metal, battery operated, Hong Kong, 1960s $35

Magazine cover, *The Farmer's Wife*, October 1925, costumed boy, holding pumpkin on pole, black cat $16

Mask, boy, papier-mache, painted face, cloth ties, stamped "Germany" $35

Mask, devil, rubber, red, black and white, rubber ties...... $15

Mask, duck, buckram, molded bill, cloth ties $28

Mask, man, wire mesh, painted feature, cloth ties $75

Noisemakers, tin, 1920s .... $25-$45

Noisemakers, tin clickers .... $10-$25

Noisemaker, clicker, tin, frying pan shape, litho, orange and black, Chein $25

Noisemaker, wood with papier-mache witch, Germany $250

Paper decorations, 1920s .... $50-$75

Paper decorations, 1930s-50s .... $25-$50

Paper decorations, modern .... $3-$10

Party napkins, package,1930s $30

PEZ dispenser, Jack-o-lantern, skull or witch, 1990 ..... $1-$3

PEZ dispenser, three-piece witch, no feet $30

Postcards, 1908-1914, Tuck, each .... $15-$20

Postcard, "The Magic Halloween," Winsch Schumacker illustration, pumpkins looking down at woman draped in sheet .... $100-$125

Postcard, "A Joyous Halloween," kids looking at black cat on jack-o-lantern, published by PFB ..... $50-$60

Postcard, "An Upsetting Situation," modern Halloween, 1950s, boys pushing over outhouse .... $12-$15

Sheet music .... $5-$30+

Tambourine, litho tin, cat face, orange and black, T. Cohn $20

Trick-or-treat bags, paper, 1940s-1960s .... $15-$35+

Wall decorations, paper, 1930s-40s .... $10-$50

Zorro costume, Ben Cooper, 1950s $75

Published by PFB, this postcard from the early 1900s, is valued at $50-$60.

Postcards are one of the most common Halloween collectibles.

HUMMELS

Often imitated, the endearing figurines of children known as Hummels are valuable collectibles.

Collectors are familiar with the charming three-dimensional interpretations of the art of the German nun Sister Maria Innocentia (Berta) Hummel. Many people, however, mistakenly call any cute figurines of children Hummels. Legitimate Hummels, however, are products of the German firm W. Goebel Porzellanfabrik, GmbH (Goebel) or a company licensed to produce Hummel items. The words "M.I. Hummel" and "M.I. Hummel Club" in signature and/or block forms are registered trademarks of W. Goebel Porzellanfabrik, Germany.

History: By the early 1930s, Goebel had gained considerable experience and expertise in fashioning products of porcelain and fine earthenware. Sister Maria Innocentia's art came to their attention in 1933 in Munich as religious note cards for Christmas and New Year's.

Upon seeing the cards, Goebel conceived of depicting the children on the cards as figurines with Sister Maria Innocentia's permission. They presented the first models at the Leipzig Trade Fair in 1934.

There have been many different versions of Wayside Harmony since its introduction in the late 1930s, none with significant changes. They may be valued at $200 or more.

Production of Hummel figurines and practically everything else in the Goebel lines dwindled during World War II, and by the end of the war, production had ceased altogether. When Goebel resumed production, figurines became quite popular among U.S. servicemen who purchased them as gifts, creating a new popularity for Hummel figurines.

The figurines, all handmade, have been continuously produced since, and many new ones have been added to the line.

General Guidelines: The two most important things to look for in identifying authentic Hummels are the signature and the trademarks. Authentic pieces bear a facsimile of the M.I. Hummel signature, usually incised or impressed into the item. It is most often found on the base of figurines, but can be elsewhere.

Various Goebel trademarks are also found on figurines. These and other markings are sometimes known as backstamps. Goebel used the same trademarks on virtually all products before and during the Hummel production years, so just because a piece bears a trademark does not mean it is a Hummel item. In 1991, Goebel finally instituted a special trademark to be used exclusively on Hummel pieces. The following are trademarks found on Hummels and the years they were used.

Crown Mark (™1): 1934-1950
Full Bee Mark(™2): 1940-1959
Stylized Bee Mark(™3): 1960-1972
Three Line Mark(™4): 1964-1971
Goebel Bee or Last Bee Mark(™5): 1972-1979
Missing Bee(™6): 1979-1991
Hummel Mark or Current Mark(™7): 1991-present

Clubs
•M.I. Hummel Club
Goebel Plaza, Rte. 31, P.O. Box 11
Pennington, NJ 08534
800-666-2582

•Hummel Collector's Club
P.O. Box 257, Yardley, PA 19067-2857
888-5-HUMMEL

Contributor to this section: Carl Luckey

VALUE LINE

Anniversary Plates
1975, Stormy Weather, #280	$165
1980, Spring Dance, #281	$135
1985, Auf Wiedersehen	$160

Ashtrays
Boy with Bird, #166	$80
Joyful, #33	$75
Let's Sing, #114	$75
Bank, Little Thrifty, c1972	$50

Bells

Knit One $85
Let's Sing $140
Mountaineer $85
Sing Along $80
Thoughtful $80
Calendar, 1955. .... $15
Candlestick, Girl with Fir Tree, 1956 .... $35

Christmas Plates

1971, Heavenly Angel, #264 .... $725
1972, Hear Ye, Hear Ye, #265 .... $125
1973, Globetrotter, #266 .... $70
1974, Goose Girl, #267 .... $100
1975, Ride into Christmas, #268 .... $90
1976, Apple Tree Girl, #269 .... $880
1977, Apple Tree Boy, #270 .... $95
1978, Happy Pastime, #271 .... $75
1979, Singing Lesson, #272 .... $85
1980, School Girl, #273 .... $100
1981, Umbrella Boy, #274 .... $100
1983, Postman, #276 .... $110
1984, A Gift from Heaven, #277 .... $105
1985, Chick Girl, #278 .... $110
1986, Playmates, #279 .... $135
1987, Feeding Time, #283 .... $135
1988, Little Goat Herder, #284 .... $135
1989, Farm Boy $115

Dolls

Carnival, porcelain $190
Chimney Sweep $80
Easter Greetings, porcelain $200
Gretel $60
Hansel $60
Little Knitter $65
Postman, porcelain $200
Rose, pink $50

Figures

Adoration, #23/111, 7-1/8", ™ 5 .... $375
Angelic Song, #144, ™ 6 .... $65
Apple Tree Girl, #141/1, ™ 5 .... $145
Artist, #304, ™6 .... $90
Barnyard Hero, #195/2/0, ™ 2 .... $115
Be Patient, 6", ™3 .... $145
Bookworm, #8, ™5 .... $75
Boots, #143/1, ™3 .... $175
Builder, #305, ™4 .... $82
Carnival, #328, ™6 .... $80
Cinderella, #337, ™6 .... $110
Culprits, #56, ™3 .... $200
Doll Bath, #319, ™5 .... $75
Duet, #130, ™1 .... $300
Eventide, ™3 .... $135
Farewell, ™2 .... $275
Feeding Time, #199/l, ™2 .... $215
Follow The Leader, ™5 .... $425
Gay Adventure, #356, ™6 .... $75
Girl with Doll, #239, ™6 .... $25

Good Hunting, #307, ™4 .... $130
Goose Girl, #47/0, ™2, 4-1/4" $200
Hear Ye, #15/0, ™1 .... $300
Herald Angels, #37, ™2 .... $80
Just Resting, #112/I, ™1 .... $300
Kiss Me, #311, ™4 .... $145
Little Fiddler, #4, ™1 .... $250
Little Gardener, #72, ™2 .... $60
Little Scholar, #80, ™3 .... $55
Lost Sheep, #68/0, ™3 .... $72
Mountaineer, #315, ™4 .... $145
Out of Danger, #56/B, ™3 .... $110
Photographer, ™2 .... $225
Puppy Love, #1, ™3 .... $75
Retreat to Safety, #201/2/0, ™4 .... $90
School Girl, #81/2/0, ™3 .... $60
Sensitive Hunter, #6/0, ™1 .... $275
Sister, #98/0, ™6 .... $65
Soloist, #135, ™2 .... $80
Spring Cheer, #72, ™3 .... $80
Sweet Music, #186, ™1 .... $125
Telling Her Secret, #196/0, ™2 .... $235
Tuneful Angel, #359, ™6 .... $45
Village Boy, #51/2/0, ™1 .... $115

Newly released in 1987, Sing Along (#433) can have either ™6 or ™7 and is valued at around $275.

Waiter, #154/0, ™2 .... $1,309
Wash Day, #321, ™4 .... $80
Weary Wanderer, #204, ™6 .... $80
Worship, #84/0, ™1 .... $250

Fonts

Angel Cloud, #206, ™4 .... $25
Angel Sitting, #167, ™4 .... $40
Angel with Birds, #22/0,™6 .... $18
Angels at Prayer, #91B, ™3 .... $70
Child with Flowers, #36/0, ™2 .... $48
Good Shepherd, #35/0, ™6 .... $25
Madonna and Child, #243, ™6 .... $25
Worship, #164, ™2 .... $120
Inkwell, With Loving Greetings, blue $135

Lamps

Apple Tree Boy, #M/230, ™5 .... $165
Birthday Serenade, #M/231/I, ™2, reverse mold $900

Good Friends, #M/228, ™5 .... $165
Just Resting, #M/225/II, ™5 .... $175
Loves Me, Loves Me Not, #M/227, ™2 .... $180
Out of Danger, ™2 .... $275

Music Boxes

Chick Girl $235
Ride Into Christmas $240

Nativity Figures

Angel Serenade, #214/D/II $40
Donkey, #214/J/II $35
Infant Jesus, #260 .... $80
King, kneeling on one knee, #214/M/II $100
Lamb, #214/O/II $15
Little Tooter, #214/H/II $65
Madonna, #214/A/M/II $110
Stable, three pieces, #214/S/II $35
Print, Moonlight Return, litho $500

Although early samples of Smiling Through were larger, the piece's final size of 4-3/4" (#408/0, ™6), is worth around $200.

HUNTING COLLECTIBLES

North America's first settlers brought with them old country hunting tools — like guns, traps and decoys — to harvest the teeming game of this vast and unsettled wilderness *(see also Fishing chapter)*. These items were the essentials of early settlers. Antique hunting items have become collectible mainly within the last 25 years.

Decoys

The origin of bird decoys is sketchy, but records seem to indicate wood decoys were in use as early as the 1770s. Collected primarily as handmade folk art, decoys of geese, shorebirds (plovers, curlews) and ducks command much collector interest.

General Guidelines: The carver of a decoy (individual or factory) greatly influences value. Most carvers' markings are found on the bottom of a decoy. Carvers from certain schools of design or regions may bring higher prices than others. Factory-made decoys by Mason are especially valuable.

Condition, of course, is a top consideration. Decoys with much original paint are preferable. Poor repainting, cracks, termites and breaks can detract from a decoy's value. Professional repainting and restoration, however, can improve an otherwise worthless decoy.

Certain species of birds (and, in some cases, even the duck's gender) are more valuable than others. Merganser and teal decoys are widely popular, while wood duck decoys are rarer. Drake (male) decoys are more common than hens (females).

Guns

The American settlers brought with them one of their most prized possessions — the black powder musket (or muzzle loader). These early tools also had a companion collectible — black powder. Old muzzle loaders can sell for $150 up to thousands of dollars.

Early waterfowling punt guns are rare and worth more than black powder muskets. They generally command $2,000 to $5,000. Those of unusual length or size may sell for more.

One box of 12 shells for these large guns recently sold for $3,000. The shoulder punt guns in the four-gauge range bring from $4,000 to $10,000 depending on the maker. Many large-bore muzzle loaders with twist steel barrels have been sold for between $500 and $2,000. Rust detracts from a gun's value, and to command top dollar, a gun should still be operational.

Powder Cans

Powder cans, often used as decorations, are highly collectible, especially if the graphics are clean and clear. Tin containers with clean graphics can sell for $50 to $300. Containers shaped like wooden barrels are often worth $200 to $400. Cans with paper or printed end labels in Good or better condition command premiums.

Shell Boxes

The first shell boxes were introduced in the late 1800s. The two-piece cardboard boxes were printed with beautiful labels of hunting scenes or color graphics usually on the top and sides of the box. Some had game scenes on the labels and some only had the name of the company. Boxes by U.M.C., Remington, Winchester and Eastern Cartage are especially desirable. Two-piece boxes sell in the $20-$50 range; those with especially clean graphics may command more. After the turn of the century, the one-piece box debuted, but they are not as collectible as two-piece boxes.

Traps

Bear traps are valued between $150 and $500. Small wooden and wire traps cost from $10 to $150, depending on their condition. Rabbit, fox, mink and beaver traps generally sell for less than $100. Trapper permit buttons, game and fish permits may sell from $30 to $100.

Contributors to this section: Howard Harlan, 4920 Franklin Rd., Nashville, TN 37220, 615-832-0564; Carl Luckey.

Decoy, Mallard, hen, Wildfowler Decoy Co., Quoque, Long Island, 1960s.

Decoy, Bluebill drake, E. end of Lake Ontario, hollow, carved, c. 1920.

VALUE LINE

Values listed are for decoys in Good to Excellent condition by carvers from various regions listed.

Decoys

Long Island
Thomas Gelston Duck Decoys	$250-$1,000
Obediah Verity	$1,500-$6,000
Al Ketchum	$1,000-$1,500

Maine
George Huey	$500-$2,500
Gus Wilson Mergansers, Black Ducks	$1,000-$5,000
Gus Wilson (others)	$700-$3,500
Other Maine carvers	$250-$750

Mason's Decoy Factory
Black Duck	$300-$1,000
Canada Goose	$500-$2,000
Green Wing Teal	$600-$2,000
Mallard	$300-$1,500

Massachusetts
Joe Lincoln	$1,000-$6,000
Elmer Crowell	$600-$6,000
Benjamin Smith	$500-$2,000

New York State
Sam Denny	$250-$1,000
Chauncy Wheeler	$500-$3,000
Frank Lewis	$50-$250

North Carolina
Lem and Lee Dudley	$2,000-$10,000
Alvira Wright	$4,000-$10,000
Mitchell Fulcher	$2,000-$10,000

Pacific Coast
Richard Ludwing Jantzen	$750-$5,000
Horace Crandall	$750-$2,000

St. Clair Flats
Thomas Chambers	$750-$3,500
Ralph Reghi	$200-$500
George Warin	$750-$1,500

Stratford (Connecticut)
Ben Holmes	$500-$2,000
Roswell Bliss	$500-$1,200

Decoy, Pintail—Delaware River; Bordentown, N.S. by Black.

Albert Laing	$1,000-$5,000

Susquehanna Flats
Sam Barnes	$200-$600
R. Madison Mitchell	$150-$500
R. Madison Mitchell swan decoys	$1,000-$3,000
Ben Dye	$150-$500

Wisconsin
August "Gus" Moak	$500-$1,000
Frank Strey	$200-$600

Shot Guns

Values listed are for guns in Good condition.
Parker shot gun 12-gauge	$350-$700
Fox shot gun 12-gauge	$350-$400
L.C. Smith 12-gauge	$350-$400
Browning 12-gauge automatic	$150-$250
Lefever 12-gauge	$150-$250
Stevens / Savage 12-gauge	$50-$150
Winchester Lever Action 12-gauge	$75-$150
Springfield Armory Musket	$150-$200

Shot Shell Boxes
Winchester Super X	$20-$25
Peters single piece box	$15-$25
Remington UMC two-piece	$50-$75
Winchester Sunburst	$40-$50
Winchester Ranger (Dog on Point)	$25-$40
Montgomery Ward two piece Flying Goose	$40-$55
Leader 200 round box	$65-$75
Remington Game Load	$50-$75
Montgomery Ward two-piece Mallard	$50-$65
Winchester two-piece all brass (empty)	$75-$100

Traps
Fly traps	$50
Minnow Glass Trap	$75
Wire trap	$10-$15
Beaver traps, Triumph #315	$50
Newhouse #4	$25
Wolf traps, Newhouse 4-1/2"	$100
Wolf traps, Hawley and Norton	$150
Fish Traps,	
Underwood	$200
Evans	$300
Gabriel	$200
Leg hold traps, Newhouse, small	$10
large	$25
Sargent & Co. small	$20
Sargent & Co. large	$35
Triumph small	$4-$5
Triumph large	$20
Bird Traps, common cage type	$10
Gibbs Hawl trap	$75
Mole traps, Nash, Kalamazoo, MI	$7
Reddick mole traps	$10
Gibbs mole trap	$35
Mouse traps, Oneida and Lovel wooden four-hole Choker	$10
Mouse trap, all metal Victor	$25
Live wire traps, "Qurouze" type	$20
Bear Traps, Newhouse, Blake and Lamb	$300-$1,000

INSULATORS

Insulators are glass domes placed on the top of electric poles to prevent the leakage of current. Insulators began with the invention of the telegraph by Samuel F.B. Morse in 1844. Morse initially attempted to install his transmission wire underground. Unfortunately, the wire became grounded after a short distance, the electrical current dissipated, and the signal could not be transmitted. His first demonstration was delayed until overhead wires were installed.

Morse's first insulator consisted of a wire, which was wrapped in cloth and sandwiched between two plates of glass, installed in notches cut in cross arms attached to a pole. This application was unsatisfactory. As a result, a race to develop adequate insulators began and would continue for more than 100 years.

Insulated telephone cables replaced insulators in communications lines. By 1972, all major U.S. glass insulator manufacturers had ceased production. It took more than 125 years, but Morse's original idea finally came to fruition. Communications lines could be laid underground, and the overhead insulator was no longer needed.

The principal manufacturing era was from 1850 to the mid-1900s. Leading companies include Armstrong (1938-1969), Brookfield (1865-1922), California (1912-1916), Gayner (1920-1922), Hemingray (1871-1919), Lynchburg (1923-1925), Maydwell (1935-1940), McLaughlin (1923-1925) and Whitall Tatum (1920-1938).

General Guidelines: Most insulators are made of glass or porcelain with a variety of insulating materials. Later, wood, Bakelite, asbestos compositions, Teflon-silica compounds, plastic and petroleum-based rubber were used to make insulators.

Most glass insulators are aquamarine colored due to the small amount of iron present in the sand used in the glass manufacturing process. Other colors resulted from the introduction of different elements into the raw materials. Many shades came from the use of refuse glass, and many colors were created to color code circuits, since a single pole may have contained up to 200 separate wires. Contrary to popular belief, insulators, except for the light purple ones, do not change color when exposed to sunlight.

Legitimate insulator colors include wide ranges of greens, blues, ambers, purples, yellows and oranges. Carnival and milk glass were also used. Most porcelain insulators are brown or white, but many specimens are available in ranges of blues, greens, yellows, oranges, and tans. Purple, red and pink porcelain specimens have also been found.

The value of better insulators has risen in recent years. In 1996, a single insulator sold at auction for $30,800. However, most insulators are valued at less than $100, and hundreds of the most common are sold for only a few dollars each.

There are about 500 styles of glass insulators. Each style has been given a CD (consolidated design) number, found in N.R. Woodward's *The Glass Insulator in America*. Colors and names of the makers and all lettering found on the same style insulator have nothing to do with the CD number. The style of insulator is the key to the number.

Publications
Crown Jewels of the Wire, P.O. Box 1003, St. Charles, IL 60174.

Clubs
•National Insulator Association
1315 Old Mill Path, Broadview Heights, OH 44147

Contributor to this section: Michael Guthrie, 1209 W. Menlo, Fresno, CA 93711-1477.

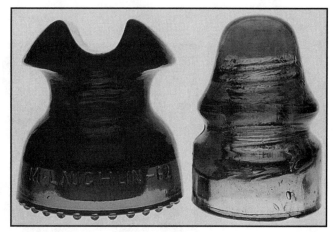

Left: McLaughlin cable top, emerald green. Right: Brookfield signal, yellow green.

VALUE LINE

102, Bar/Bar, dark purple	$18
102, Diamond, royal purple	$25
102, Star, aqua	$2
106.1, Duquesne, cornflower	$75
112, Star, blue	$4
115, McLaughlin #10, light green	$7
115, Whitall Tatum #3, peach	$4
121, Agee, amethyst	$25
121, AM Tel & Tel, jade milk	$8
121, CD&P Tel Co., light blue	$20
121, McLaughlin 16, dark green	$12
121, WFG Denver, steel/cornflower	$125
122, McLaughlin 16, light citron	$100
124, Hemingray 4, aqua-jade swirl	$135
126.4, WE Mfg. Co., lime green	$45
133, BGM Co., sun-colored amethyst	$75
133, No name #20, green	$3
133.1, Electric Supply Chicago, aqua	$25
134, WGM, sun-colored amethyst	$65

142, Hemingray TS-2, carnival $25
145, American, light grass green $60
145, HG Co., petticoat, emerald $175
147, Patent Oct. 8, 1907, aqua $5
152, Diamond, light green $8
154, Whitall Tatum, purple $20
154, Whitall Tatum, straw $3
160, McLaughlin 14, dark olive $25
161, California, light yellow $125
162, Hamilton Glass Co., light blue-aqua $25
162.4, No name, dark purple $75
164, HG Co., green milk $30
164, McLaughlin, emerald, with drips $8
164, Star, aqua $3
165.1, Whitall Tatum, aqua $5
168, Hemingray D510, gold carnival $30

168, Hemingray D510, ice blue $5
168, Hemingray D510, olive amber $15
168, Hemingray D510, red amber $25
168, Hemingray D510, silver carnival $20
178, Cal Santa Ana, purple $110
190/191, B, blue $35
208, Brookfield, aqua, large olive streak $20
214, Nacionales, red amber $75
218, Hemingray 660, clear $7
280, Prism, aqua $30
296, #20, dark aqua $6
326, Pyrex#453, dark carnival $125
326, Pyrex #453, light carnival $75
422, Agee, dark amethyst $30
575, L'Electro Verre, emerald $125
734, McMicking, aqua $50
735, Mulford, bright aqua $275

Top and bottom: Various sizes, designs and colors of insulators.

KITCHEN COLLECTIBLES

Vintage kitchenware, including pots, pans, skillets, utensils, bowls, appliances, coffeemakers and tins are popular collectibles today, and Americans are reaching back to their past for kitchen items to collect and display. Most hobbyists show off their kitchen collectibles in the kitchen; some actually use the items daily.

Popular single items to amass include ice cream scoops, flour sifters, rolling pins, egg beaters, churns, pie birds, peelers, cookie cutters and coffee pots.

Collecting kitchenware has a long history in the antiques world, with a group of loyal and hard-core collectors leading the charge. Most pre-1900s items are already pricey. Post-1900 items are generally priced from $2 to $50 and are not difficult to locate. Here are some inexpensive items that have the potential to increase in value.

Pyrex. This durable glassware that is present in 75 percent of American homes was in its creative heyday in the mid-1950s to mid-1960s. Look for casserole dishes, refrigerator dishes and bowls in such striking patterns as Snowflake, Butterprint, Gooseberry, Town & Country and Gold Acorn. Solid colors are, however, even more popular than patterns. Pyrex is abundant, so hold out for pieces in Near Mint or better condition. Most collectible Pyrex is in the $5 to $12 range.

Ice Cream Scoops. Older wood-handled scoops are the most popular and expensive (especially those with unusual-shaped scoops), but newer plastic-handled scoops and solid aluminum scoops are still available for $4 to $10.

Utensils. Wood-handled utensils, usually painted green or red, have been popular for many years. Those with paint still on the handle are worth more. Collectors have also started paying attention to utensils with handles made of Bakelite and other plastics.

Appliances. Art Deco-inspired appliances, such as juice squeezers, waffle irons and toasters, may be the sleepers in this category. Deco seems to have currently been supplanted by other styles, but Deco will be back in style again soon.

Coffee Pots. Aluminum coffee pots from Wear Ever and Mirro are beginning to catch collectors' eyes. They display well, come in a variety of shapes and sizes and are affordable now (anywhere from a few dollars to $15).

Cast-Iron Skillets. Wagner and Griswold are the two big names in cast-iron skillets, griddles, pans, Dutch ovens and other cookware. Some of the more unusual items cost $100 or more, but most are $25 to $60.

Rolling Pins. Some rolling pins, especially glass pins and those that are highly decorated, are costly. But run-of-the-mill pins can still be found for $8-$15.

Enamelware. Enamel-covered pots and kettles have moved slowly the last few years, but 10 to 15 years ago enamelware was really hot. There appear to be some good buys in this area now. Look for pieces in the best condition with no chipped paint.

See also Cookbooks and Cast Iron chapters.

Publications
Kitchen Antiques & Collectibles News, 4645 Laurel Ridge Dr., Harrisburg, PA 17110.

Clubs
•Association of Coffee Mill Enthusiasts
 5941 Wilkerson Rd., Rex, GA 30273

•Cookie Cutter Collectors Club
 1167 Teal Rd., SWDellroy, OH 44620

•Corn Items Collectors Association
 613 N. Long St., Shelbyville, IL 62565

•Eggcup Collectors' Corner
 67 Stevens Ave., Old Bridge, NJ 08857

•Griswold & Cast Iron Cookware Association
 54 Macon Ave., Asheville, NC 28801

•International Society for Apple Parer Enthusiasts
 3911 Morgan Center Rd., Utica, OH 43080

•Jelly Jammers Club
 110 White Oak Dr., Butler, PA 16001

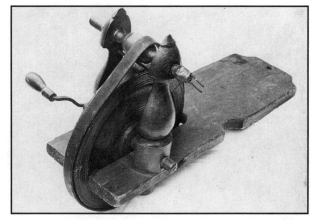

Wooden apple corer, 22" x 13-1/2", made around Harrisburg, PA.

Gilchrist's No. 31 wood-handled ice cream scoop, bronze plated mechanism, stainless steel bowl and dislodger, 11".

Apple corer, White Mountain, orig box $30
Apple peeler, Turntable No. 98 .... $85
Apple parer, C.E. Hudson, 1884 .... $75
Apple parer, Reading, 1878, original green paint $75
Biscuit cutter, Calumet $2
Biscuit cutter, Rumford, 2-1/2" dia., 1" deep, 2-1/2"
   handle, metal $10
Blender, Androck dough blender, orange handle $3
Blender, Androck wood handle $5
Blender, Oster 471 Classic Blender, chrome $60
Blender, Oster 403 Deluxe Blender, chrome $68
Bowl, Hazel Atlas, cobalt blue, 7-5/8" $30
Bowl, vegetable, flow blue, W.H. Grindley & Co., 10"
   dia., small rim chips repaired $78
Bowls, Yellow Ware, nesting, 14", 12", 9" $245
Box, Hill Country Butter, paper $5
Butcher block table, 29" dia., single-piece top, turned
   legs, 36" high $275
Butter churn, Dazy, No. 40, wood paddles $125
Butter pats, set of eight, flow blue, by W.H. Grindley &
   Co., rim chips $60
Canisters, chef decoration, 7" tall and 6-1/2" tall,
   "Parmeco, Baltimore, MD" on bottom, for pair $44
Canisters, Hall Red Poppy design, 6" tall, 6-3/4" tall,
   Decoware $45

Graniteware coffee pot, $20.

Canister, Jadite, 4" x 4" x 5" $40
Can opener, cast iron, fish figure, c1865 .... $140
Cherry stoner, Enterprise Mfg. Co., No. 16 .... $38
Chopper, primitive, hand-made, mid 1800s $35
Clothesline dispenser $26
Coffee bin, signed by maker, Henry Troemer,
   Philadelphia $395
Coffee maker, Guardian Service, 8 cup, 6" x 8" with
   matching percolator and glass lid $75
Coffee mill, Nonesuch, early 1900s $65
Coffee pot, cobalt and white enamel, L&G Mfg. $75
Coffee pot, Guardian, glass top $35
Coffee pot, small, graniteware $65
Coffee grinder, cast iron, wall mount $85
Colander, black and white enamel $35
Corkscrew, Jolly Old Topper, Steele & Johnson
   Mfg. Co. $55
Corkscrew, wall-mount corkscrew/cap lifter, Starr
   Brown, 1925 .... $18
Corn grinder, 16" tall, red paint $125
Corn mold, Wear Ever $5
Cracker Box, James McClurg $65
Creamer, Majolica, 3" $110
Creamer, Majolica, 5-1/4" $85
Crock, Norton, decorated, Worcester, Mass. $195
Crock, Union Stoneware Co., Red Wing, five gallon,
   red Red Wing logo, Dec. 21, 1915 .... $67
Crock, Western Stoneware, two gallon crock, Western
   emblem on one side and plants on other $32
Cupboard, traces of original red paint, 56" high, 36"
   wide $495
Dough box, replaced base, refinished $175
Dutch oven, Griswold, Tite-Top, No. 8, lid, bail and
   trivet, patent date Mar. 16, 1920 .... $120
Eggcup, baby bird $45
Eggcup, Pluto, 1930s $125
Eggcup, Popeye, 1930s, multicolored $110
Egg Timer, chef $50
Egg Timer, girl on phone $50
Egg Timer, winking chef, timer on back $195

Toaster, Universal, Landers, Frary & Clark, New Britain, CT.

Flour bag, Southern Flour Mills, 50 lb., cut-out and sew sailor pattern on back of bag $28

Flour bag, Southern Flour Mills, 50 lb., cut-out and sew doll pattern on back of bag $38

Gas/oil burner, 1923, unused, complete $65

Glasses, juice size, Sweet Cherry, set of six $40

Grape mold, Yellow Ware, 6-1/2" x 5-1/2" $95

Grater, Bluffton slaw cutter $4

Grater, tin, 5" x 10" $18

Ironing board, sleeve ironing board, patent date 1903 ...... $35

Jelly cupboard, grain paint, 62" high, 48" wide $795

Kettle, Griswold, No. 9, Pattern No. 812, flat bottom, with bail, lid missing $90

Kettle, Guardian Service, 12" dia., 8" deep, with bail, lid missing $80

Kettle, copper, 36" x 30", hand-forged steel handle $320

Kitchen table, oak, Eastlake, 40" square, 29" high $375

Kitchen cupboard, oak, zinc top, 40" wide, Ideal Furniture Co. $595

Lard press, Griswold $135

Match holder, cast iron, 4-1/4" high $40

Match holder, cast iron, 6-1/4" high $45

Matchsafe, angel kissing woman, with lid, 6-1/2" tall $38

Milk measure, 1/16 pint, metal $15

Mold, corn, tin $45

Mold, melon, 6" $43

Mold, melon, 8" $32

Mold, pudding/cake $62

Mold, pudding, 7" $35

Mold, Santa, Nordicware $35

Nut chopper, clear bottom, red tin top, 1950s $15

Pan, Griswold, No. 273, 930, Crispy Corn Stick $20

Pan, Griswold, No. 11, 950A, French roll $85

Pan, Griswold/Wagner, muffin, 11 openings $36

Pan, Guardian Service, 9-3/4" dia., 4-1/2" deep, double handle, no lid $25

Pan, Guardian Service, triangular 9" dia., 4" deep, no lid $12

Pan, Guardian Service, triangular 10" dia., 2-1/2" deep, no lid $20

Pan, R&E Manufacturing, muffin, eight openings $100

Pan, Super Cookware, cast aluminum, 9" x 15" x 5" deep, with lid $22

Pan, Wagner, cornstick, 13" x 5-3/4", patent date July 6, 1920 .... $25

Pan, Wagner, Magnalite, 3-1/2 quart, 9" x 3-1/2", no lid .. $15

Pan, Wagner, Magnalite, 10" x 4", with lid $30

Pan, Wagner, Magnalite 4265P, roaster, cast aluminum, 10" x 13" x 5" with lid and aluminum rack $85

Pie bird, blue and gray, long neck $90

Pie bird, yellow and brown, long neck $90

Pie safe, factory-made, 1900-1920, green paint $395

Pie safe, hanging, old gray paint, single board shelves, 37" high, 43" wide, 25" deep $225

Pie safe, primitive, screened hanging, gray paint, 39" high, 31" wide, turned legs $325

Pitcher, Purinton, 5" $38

Pot, blue graniteware, hole in bottom $70

Pot, Guardian Service, straight-sided, 9" dia., 4-1/2" deep, no lid $35

Pot, Superior Foundary, cast-iron tripod pot, 3-1/2" x 3" high $10

Pot, unknown maker, cast iron with white enamel interior, 8" dia., 4-1/4" deep, bail, handle and spout ... $20

Pyrex, blue covered refrigerator dish, 7" square, 4" deep . $15

Pyrex, set of four graduated nesting bowls, solid colors ... $45

Reamer, Hazel Atlas crisscross $18

Refrigerator dish, Federal, pink, 8" x 8" $45

Refrigerator dish with cover, Hazel Atlas, square $11

Refrigerator jar with cover, Fire King, sapphire blue, 5-1/8" by 9-1/8" $32

Rolling pin, wooden, 17" l, red handles $35

Salt and pepper range shakers, milk glass, primrose pattern $25

Salt and pepper shakers, Hull, Little Red Riding Hood, 3-1/2" $130

Salt and pepper shakers, Vitrock, decals, for pair $40

Salt box, Shawnee, Fern pattern, light green $140

Saucers, set of eight, flow blue, by W.H. Grindley & Co. $70

Scale with removable metal round pan on top, cream paint, kilos $45

Skillet, Erie, No. 7 .... $20

Skillet, Erie, No. 8, 704A $24

Skillet, Erie, No. 8, 704T $24

Skillet, Favorite, No. 3 .... $16

Skillet, Griswold, No. 4, 702C, red/white porcelain coated, with lid $40

Waffle Iron, General Electric, catalog #119W4, chrome plated, Bakelite handles, cast aluminum interior, 12"w handle to handle, 4"h.

Skillet, Prizer-Ware, SP 1020, 8-1/2", turquoise
  porcelain coated, matching lid and trivet $65
Skillet, Prizer-Ware, SS 1090, 5-1/2" square, red/white
  porcelain coated $45
Skillet, unknown maker, three-legged, 10" $60
Skillet, Wagner, No. 3, 1053B $12
Skillet, Wagner, No. 3, 1053T $12
Skillet, Wagner, No. 3, 1053H $12
Soup pail, tin, Campbell's Tomato Soup, Cheinco
  Housewares, 5-3/4" tall $48
Spice jars/shakers, aluminum, set of 11 .... $55
Stacking bowl, Federal, yellow, 6-1/2" $11
Stacking bowl, Federal, yellow, 7-1/2" $11
Stacking bowl, Federal, yellow, 8-1/2" $14
Strainer, yellow wood handle $2
Sugar and creamer, McCoy, Pinecone, 1945 .... $35
Sugar and creamer, Purinton $38
Sugar nippers, primitive $295
Swankyswig, glass Chrysanthemum $7
Swankyswig, glass, Red/Black Band No. 2, 3-3/8" $7
Swankyswig, glass, Tulip No. 1, 3-1/2" $7
Table, drop-leaf, walnut, mid 1800s, single board top,
  leaves $695
Tea pot, Purinton, 4" $25
Tin, Battle Creek Lacto Dextrin, 9-1/4" x 5" x 5",
  some wear $48

Tin, Bon Ami $17
Tin, Chase & Sanborn's Tea, 4-3/4" x 3-3/4" x 3-3/4" $15
Tin, coconut, Snowdrift Brand, 14" high $38
Tin, coffee, Golden Rule Coffee, 10" high $68
Tin, Mackintosh's Toffee de Luxe, 3-1/4" by 4-1/2",
  oval, worn, surface rust $18
Tin, peanut butter, Red & White Brand, 9" high $65
Tin, Rose Marie Tea, 5" x 3-1/2" x 3-1/2", worn finish $22
Toaster, Kenmore 344-6330 .... $35
Toaster, Toastmaster IA5, single slice $44
Toaster, Toastmaster IB14 .... $39
Toaster, Toastmaster IB24, 1940s/1950s $37
Toaster, Westinghouse 501B, Deco design $48
Tobacco cutter, Griswold, Star Model 2498, 7" tall by
  18" long by 5" wide $250
Trivet, 1800-1820, forged $95
Trivet, unknown maker, cast-iron horseshoe trivet,
  7" long w/three feet $36
Trivet, Wilton, cast iron, brooms and plants, 5" x 8" $22
Waffle iron, Griswold, No. 8 .... $180
Waffle iron, Wagner, steel wire handles, with stand $60
Waffle iron, Wagner, wooden handles, with stand $80
Waffle iron, Wear Ever, aluminum with cast-iron
  holder, 8" $60
Water carrier, graniteware $125
Water cooler, 1800s, decorated, no cover or bottle $75
Whisk, wire handle $4

Graniteware Kettle, $95

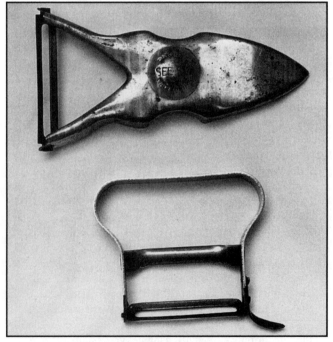

Peelers, top: See Saw, made in USA; bottom: DeVault Peeler, Chicago.

KNIVES

Fixed blades dominated the early-to-late 19th century, from grand bowies and hunting knives by England's George Wostenholm and America's Will & Finck, to the hunting knives of J. Russell & Co. and others. Knife blades were made from cast steel and stag (antler), bone, ivory and wood were among the other knife materials. With the dawn of the 20th century such makers as Marble's, Union Cutlery (now known as Ka-Bar), Remington, Case and Western entered the fixed-blade, hunting-knife arena, and the era of the mass-produced blade and stacked-leather handle kicked into high gear.

It was also in the late 19th and early 20th centuries that the American pocketknife industry came of age, with such companies as Cattaraugus, Camillus, Winchester and Remington leading the way. Cast and carbon steels, bone, stag and celluloid were seen on factory knife grips (handles). Stainless steel appeared in 1914 but was not used on most pocketknives until the 1930s.

General Guidelines: Blades produced by factories in large numbers from the late 19th to mid-20th centuries are the most collected today, in large part because they are plentiful and very well made. Mint condition draws top dollar on all knife collectibles. This means the knife should never have been sharpened, used or carried extensively and should be free of rust, pitting, scratches, nicks and other imperfections. Any defects decrease value. Knives with rare or unusual markings can also be valuable. Original boxes, wrappers or sheaths increase value.

Antique Knives

The most famous name in antique knives is Case, with Remington a close second. Case pocketknives, produced until 1970, were well made and plentiful enough to accommodate many collectors. Case pocketknives also have a numbering system that makes them easy to identify.

Remington pocketknives were made from 1920 to 1940. The master blade of each of the very rare knives is etched REMINGTON TRADE MARK. Many Remington pocketknives were etched REMINGTON MASTER KNIFE on the master blade. Many Remington pocketknives were deeply stamped on the front of the master blade. In most cases, the stamp was a circle, inside of which was stamped REMINGTON UMC (Union Metallic Cartridge).

General Guidelines: The most desirable Remingtons are the Bullets, so named for their handle shields shaped like a bullet. There were 13 different bullet patterns, and a full set is almost impossible to find. In 1982, Remington began an annual series of bullet reproductions. The first of these, the R1123 made in 1982, was bringing over 10 times its value less than a decade after it was made. In most cases, however, reproductions made after 1983 are worth less than originals.

Though extremely well made, Remington antique fixed blades don't command the higher prices of the vintage Remington pocketknives.

A Remington sheath knife in Mint condition complete with original sheath is rare.

A recent trend in antique collectibles is that of vintage fixed-blade hunting and fishing knives. Among the names to watch for are Remington, Marble's and Western.

Military Knives

Military knives (produced specifically for use by servicemen) dating from World War I to present are highly collectible. Probably the most famous example is the USMC fighting/utility knife, also known as a kabar.

The kabar is just one of many collectible military knives which were employed not only for use in combat, but also as a tool to be used in daily life. The pieces date from the Hicks knife of the 1840s to today's Buck M9 fighting/utility knife and include all kinds of different patterns — from Swiss army-type pocketknives to the handmade knives of World War II and beyond.

Some specific military collectibles include vintage World War II V-42s, Fairbairn-Sykes stilettos, John Ek knives, various handmades, survival bowies/machetes (mistakenly called V-44s by some) and Vietnam SOG knives. Knives and other blades used by the Nazis during World War II are valuable.

Clubs

- National Knife Collectors Association
  P.O. Box 21070, Chattanooga, TN 37424
  423-899-9456

- International Blade Collectors Association
  700 E. State St., Iola, WI 54945
  715-445-2214

- Buck Collectors Club
  P.O. Box 1267El, Cajon, CA 92022
  619-448-2721

- Case Collector's Club
  P.O. Box 4000, Bradford, PA 16701

- International Fight'n Rooster Club
  P.O. Box 936, Lebanon, TN 37087

- Ka-Bar Knife Collectors Club
  35-A North Chillicothe, Aurora, OH 44202
  216-562-8422

Contributor to this section: Steve Shackleford, editor, Blade Magazine, 700 E. State St., Iola, WI 54990.

VALUE LINE

Antique Knives

All values are for original antique knives in Mint condition.

Boker folding hunter (bone) $180
Boker toothpick (bone) $165
Boker canoe (bone) $600
Boker reverse peanut (celluloid) $75
Boker doctor's knife (pearl) $290
Camillus toothpick (celluloid) $150
Camillus easy opener (bone) $65
Camillus fish knife (celluloid) $45
Case 5111 1/2 L SSP Cheetah 4" (Bradford) $700
Case C61050L Tested (greenbone) $2,650
Case 5165SAB $500
Case 61093 Tested (greenbone) $500
Case 9240SP Tested (imitation pearl) $1,000
Case 6250 XX (greenbone) $750
Case 928R Tested (cracked ice) $350
Case 5391 Tested (red stag) $2,000
Cattaraugus 22359 swell-end jack (bone) $210
Cattaraugus 22759 doctor's knife (bone) $455
Cattaraugus 3239-H bartender's (bone) $275
Diamond Edge/Keen Kutter B307 barlow (bone) $255
Diamond Edge/Keen Kutter B609 trapper (bone) $675
Diamond Edge/Keen Kutter S319 cattle (bone) $500
Imperial M277 punch jack (bone) $110
Ka-Bar 62191 dogshead trapper (bone) $1,450
LF&C 0255 congress (rubber) $130
LF&C 02617 lobster (rubber) $80
LF&C 42301 dogleg jack (celluloid) $130
LF&C 0352 whittler (rubber) $200
Maher & Grosh 157 one-blade trapper (bone) $245
Maher & Grosh 95 serpentine pen (wood) $200
Maher & Grosh 14 boy's knife (wood) $175
Maher & Grosh 214 swell-center pen (pearl) $130
Miller Bros. 714 senator (bone) $260
New York Knife 142 hawkbill (wood) $150
New York Knife 20 office (celluloid) $165
New York Knife 251 rooster comb (celluloid) $305
New York Knife 233 sowbelly (bone) $470
New York Knife 2077 peanut (pearl) $270
New York Knife 2515 cigar (wood) $760
O.V.B. 1480P slim jack (celluloid) $80
O.V.B. 2693P fruit sampler (bone) $110
John Primble C1-5019S bowtie (bone) $255
John Primble C1-4987S moose (bone) $160
John Primble C1-931S serpentine (bone) $80
Remington R303 one-blade trapper (bone) $400
Remington R1303 Bullet trapper (bone) $2,320
Remington R1253 Bullet lockback hunter (bone) $2,610
Remington R181 teardrop jack (wood) $255
Remington R315 two-blade trapper (celluloid) $435
Remington R718 hawkbill (wood) $220
Remington R945-M toothpick (celluloid) $520
Remington R982 peanut (rubber) $320
Robeson 511168 barlow (bone) $290

Robeson 622105 equal-end pen (bone) $80
Robeson 62130 chain boy's (bone) $145
Robeson 62237 cigar jack (bone) $565
Robeson 622306 senator (bone) $100
Robeson 623343 lobster (bone) $200
John Russell 7354 whittler (ivory) $900
Schatt & Morgan 1096 equal-end jack (bone) $325
Schatt & Morgan 200 tool knife (nickel silver) $145
Schrade 196 pruner (Delrin) $45
Schrade SSD2084PO fish (celluloid) $75
Henry Sears 3472 senator (celluloid) $80
Henry Sears 4287 doctor's (bone) $325
Henry Sears 7216 peanut (celluloid) $130
Ulster B.B. barlow (bone) $190
Ulster U2320 swell-end jack (stag) $225
Ulster 21317 senator (pearl) $85
Ulster U3321 whittler (bone) $255
Utica 22563 moose (bone) $260
Utica 22315 dogleg jack (bone) $230
Utica 42401-A sleeveboard pen (celluloid) $75
Winchester 1613 speying (wood) $115
Winchester 2078 serpentine pen (celluloid) $200
Winchester 2363 congress (pearl) $230
Winchester 2380 doctor's knife (pearl) $515
Winchester 2879 jumbo sleeveboard $515
Wostenholm 5010A plumber's (wood) $75
Wostenholm 3B art nouveau (bronze) $100
Wostenholm B181X stock (imitation ivory) $100
Wostenholm B133 premium stock (bone) $180

Military Knives

Values are for knives in Near Mint condition.

Vietnam CIA knives .... $2,500-$3,000
Vietnam 5th Special Forces stiletto $1,000
Vietnam Lagana tomahawk $1,000
Vietnam Parson knuckle knives .... $200-$300
Vietnam SOG knives .... $1,200-$1,400
WWII Fairbairn-Sykes (knurled handle) .... $200-$225
WWI Henry Disston & Sons brass-handle knuckle
    knives $600
WWI Oneida Community Ltd. brass-handle knuckle
    knives $1,200
WWI Henry Disston & Sons wood-handle knuckle
    knives $600
WWI Oneida Community Ltd. wood-handle knuckle
    knives $300
WWII Case V-42 stiletto $3,000
WWII Collins No. 18 machete (horn) .... $300-$350
WWII Fairbairn-Sykes (ridged handle) .... $85-$95
WWII 5- to 6-inch utility/fighting knives .... $75-$150
WWII Taylor Huff knuckle knives .... $1,200-$1,300
WWII M-3 trench knife .... $125-$325
WWII Marine Corps Mark II .... $75-$150
WWII Navy Mark I .... $75-$150
WWII Navy Mark II .... $75-$150
WWII Frank Richtig knuckle knives .... $1,200-$1,300
WWII E.W. Stone knuckle knives .... $1,200-$1,300
WWII Western parachute knives $1,500

LABELS

Since the late 1800s, labels on everything from cigar boxes to fruit crates have been a flattering art form. Their colorful designs, lithography and nostalgia make them popular collectibles.

The golden age of lithography (1870-1920) came about as a result of the fierce competition between manufacturers. The result was some of the most spectacular pieces of work ever to appear in the art world.

Ephemeral by design, many labels never survived, but hundreds of others have languished in dusty warehouses until they were discovered decades later.

General Guidelines: A label's condition is a prime factor in value and collectibility.

Since many labels were stored in bundles, most of them (excluding those at the top and bottom of the bundles) survived in Mint condition.

Many were printed on rag paper with a clay coating which makes them look almost new. Some originals, therefore, are often mistaken as reproductions. Examination with a magnifying glass will identify the stipple method of stone lithography which is impossible to reproduce.

In addition to the condition of the label itself, the condition of *the image* on the label is paramount. A label with some glue stains, small tears or rough corners will be valued less than a pristine label, but a collector will gobble up any label new to his collection regardless of condition until a better one comes along.

Can Labels

Collectors seek labels from canned goods such as tomatoes, salmon and other products. Can labels printed by stone lithography prior to the 1930s are beautiful examples of the lithographer's craft, with the top-of-the-line labels made by Calvert Litho in Detroit, Michigan (1861-1968).

The average label size is 4" x 12".

The most highly-collected labels were made from 1918 through 1930, when labels were elaborately embossed and decorated.

Clubs
•American Antique Graphics Society
P.O. Box 924, Medina, OH 44258

Cigar Labels

Cigar labels are unquestionably the most desired labels for several reasons. Foremost is the quality of workmanship. The booming Victorian era cigar industry provided unlimited funds to lithographers to produce the most spectacular images on the inside lid of the box. In fact, illiterate consumers often bought cigars based on the box labels.

By 1890, labels were extremely colorful and elaborate; many featured embossing and gold leaf.

Labels featured popular themes of the turn of the century. Cuban cigar makers adopted Spanish themes, but in keeping with the times, American cigar makers illustrated themes including cow-

boys, Native Americans, African-Americans, sports, transportation, animals, children, beautiful women and others.

For many years, cigar labels were not considered important collectibles. Today, they are collected as pieces of art. By 1978, however, art dealers, knowledgeable in Victorian era lithography, began to realize cigar labels were superior in quality and workmanship to anything that existed in their own inventories from the same period.

Size, subject matter and method of printing all affect the value of a label.

Clubs
•Cigar Label Collectors International
P.O. Box 66, Sharon Center, OH 44274-0066

Cut Plug (Caddy) Labels

Caddy labels were affixed to the outside of a wooden boxes holding plugs of chewing tobacco.

Produced during the early stages of stone lithography done for advertising purposes (1870-1890), the artwork and colors (many

Vegetable crate, full figure of lion, red, blue and black background, white letters, 7" x 9".

times up to 16 colors) are striking and equal in beauty to many cigar labels. The few that survived are highly coveted by collectors of antique advertising and tobacco art.

The most common sizes for caddy labels are 11-1/2" square and 7-1/2" x 14-1/2".

Fruit and Vegetable Crate Labels

Until World War II, produce was packed in wooden crates, and growers needed to attract the attention of the wholesalers and grocers with unique and attractive labels on the ends of the boxes. Earlier images depicted orchards, fields and mountains, but many buyers were immigrant entrepreneurs who could not read English, so labels also depicted pretty girls, children, cowboys and Indians.

Soon after the war, wood crates were abandoned for less expensive cardboard, and by the early 1950s, wooden crates, with few exceptions, had virtually disappeared, and so did crate labels. Since the transition occurred almost overnight, packing houses were full of unused labels, some of which have survived today.

Most of the fruit and vegetable labels that survived were of poorer quality than cigar labels. Some early images, however, were stone lithography and are coveted by collectors.

California citrus labels top the list of most collectible labels

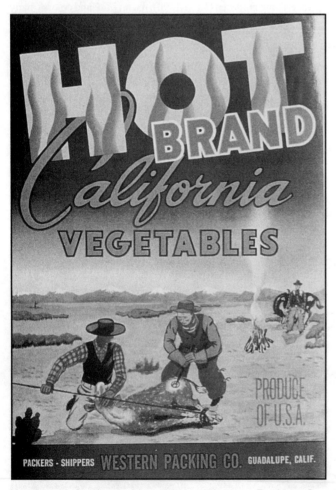

Hot brand California Vegetables, Western Packing Co., Guadalupe, Calif.

because they feature some of the best lithography.

Basic Sizes of Fruit and Vegetable Labels

California Orange, Grapefruit 11" x 10"
California Lemon, 11" x 9"
California and Washington Apples 10-1/4" x 9"
Florida Citrus 9" x 9" and 6" x 6"
West Coast Pears 10-1/2 x 7-1/2"
Vegetables 7" x 9"
Asparagus 10" x 9" (trapezoid)
Grapes 13" x 4"

Clubs

•Citrus Label Society in Southern California
800-248-8057

•The Ephemera Society of America, Inc.
Membership Secretary
P.O. Box 95, Cazenovia, NY 13035

Contributor to this section: Joe Davidson, 5185 Windfall Rd., Medina, OH 44256-8703.

Can Labels

Barefoot Boy Tomatoes, young boy	$10-$15
Butterfly Brand, large butterfly	$10-$15
Circus, clown and dog	$95-$110
Defender Brand, sailing ship	$5-$8
Defy the World, house	$3-$5
Electric Brand, girl and light bulb	$15-$25
Elkay Brand, Heavily embossed	$8-$10
Faultless Brand, Mad Anthony Wayne	$1-$5
Forest Pride, large elk	$50-$60
Frontier, hunter and fallen deer	$125-$150
Little Kernel, girl in military costume	$75-$85
Little Quaker, Quaker girl	$25-$35
Marvel Brand, waterfall	$8-$10
Maryland Chief, Indian chief	$2-$4
Mephisto, devil	$25-$35
Motor Club, early car scene	$75-$85

Polly, parrot	$8-$10
Pony Express, express rider	$45-$50
Powhaten, Indian	$5-$10
Rusk Brand, log cabin	$10-$15
Squaw Peas, squaw and papoose	$3-$5
Strong Heart, Indian brave	$75-$95
Supreme Court, courthouse bldg.	$2-$4
Thanksgiving, large turkey	$25-$35
Wayne Brand, Mad Anthony Wayne	$1-$3

Cigar Labels

Adam & Eve, in garden	$3-$5
American League, large baseball	$18-$20
Aristocrat, Cuban patron	$8-$10
Arthur Donaldson, actor	$8-$10
Aspallo, girl, horse, chariot	$45-$65
Bacchante, goddess of love & partying	$12-$15
Bleriot, aviator & plane	$75-$95
Blue Ribbon, For men who know	$3-$5
Canadian Club, Maple leaf	$2-$4
Cigarros Primeros, girls on bicycles	$65-$85
Clipper, sailing ship	$45-$65
DaVinci, artist & inventor	$30-$35
El Gaurdo, bulldog	$25-$35
First National, bank scene, cars, trolley	$18-$24
Flor del Arte, gold Pegasus, artists	$45-$65
Francis Marbois, Napoleon's finance minister	$35-$45
Gettysberg Commanders, heroes pictured	$75-$85
Irvin Cobb, writer, lecturer	$3-$5
Jewelo, French lovers	$5-$7
La Belle Creole, Actress Fanny Davenport	$40-$50
Little Quaker, Quaker girl	$35-$45
Maradas, Indians, train, ship	$45-$65
Marca Preferida, Island of Cuba	45-55
Mephisto, the devil	$35-$45
Monroe Doctrine, President James Monroe	$65-$75
National League, large baseball1	$8-$20
Nebraska Girl, lady on horse	$100-$125
Our Kitties, black & white cats	$15-$18
Paid in Full, money	$75-$90
Prima Lucia, pretty girl	$5-$7

Professor Morse	$12-$15
Record Bond, hand with money	$3-$5
Red Cloud, Chief of Sioux nation on horse	$25-$35
Red Stockings, Boston baseball players, 1874	$10,000
Red Swan, red swans	$25-$30
Rosa de Santos, girl lighting cigar	$45-$65
Tampa Life, hotel, tennis, golf scene	$125-$145
Three Twins, babies in basket	$5-$7
Uncle Sam, dumping cigars on globe	$45-$50
Victory, ornate title, gladiators	$3-$5
Wizard	$35-$45

Cut Plug (Caddy) Labels

Ascot, 1891	$100
Belinda,1874	$75
Belle of Virginia	$15
Black Bird, 1886	$25
Britannia	$30
Captain Cook	$300
Columbia	$50
Cornucopia	$250
Courage	$45
Crusader	$25
Derby, horse race	$75
Eight Bells, ship	$25
El Minero, miner	$40
Enchanter, lover playing flute	$25
Golden Eagle, eagle on flag	$35
Gypsy	$40
Harlequin	$90
Havelock Brand	$40
Juno	$20
La Caricia, lovers	$40
Lucky Hit, lady with arrows	$30
Nosegay	$20
Octoroon	$45
Ojbwa, Indian	$1,250
Old Sport, dog	$35

Fruit crate label, La Patera (The Pond), Santa Barbara County Lemons, black background, green, red and blue letters, scene in center.

Osceola Brand	$95
Red lion, Reid Tobacco	$250
Royal Delight Disraeli and Victoria	$100
Sailor's Hope lady on dock	$35
The Queen, Victoria	$225
Tough Chew, Reid Tobacco	$325
Welcome Nugget, rectangle	$35

Fruit and Vegetable Crate Labels

Athlete Oranges & Lemons	$25-$35
Best Strike Apples, baseball pitcher	$75-$95
Black Joe Grapes, old black man	$3-$5
Bronco Oranges, cowboy on horse	$10-$12
Cousin Elmer Vegetables, farmer	$3-$5
Cupid Oranges, cherub with wings	$50-$65
Dixie Boy Grapefruit, Black boy	$15-$18
Dixie Delite, FL Citrus, Art deco dancers	$5-$8
Don't Worry Apples, boy and apple	$5-$10
Exposition Lemons, Alaska Yukon	$5-$10
Gay Cock Grapes, rooster with top hat	$15-$20
Gay Johnny Vegetable, young boy	$8-$10
Goleta Lemons, sailing ship	$1-$3
Homer Oranges, homing pigeon	$15-$18
Hustler Pears, newsboy	$10-$15
King Cadets Asparagus, marching	$18-$20

Lincoln Oranges, Old Abe portrait	$12-$15
Mallard Cranberries, duck	$5-$8
Miracle Oranges, genie	$15-$25
Pala Brave Oranges, Indian chief	$7-$10
Pet Lemons, Girl and St. Bernard	$65-$75
Piggy Pears, pig with basket	$7-$10
Plenti Grand Vegetable, sexy girl	$5-$8
Rubaiyat Oranges, Arabs, tent	$8-$10
Santa Lemons, Santa and bag	$10-$15
Shamrock Oranges	$2-$3
Statue Pears, Statue of Liberty	$10-$12
Sunflower Oranges, large flower	$15-$18
Uncle Sam Apples, Sam holding hat	$25-$35
Victoria Oranges, queen	$15-$25

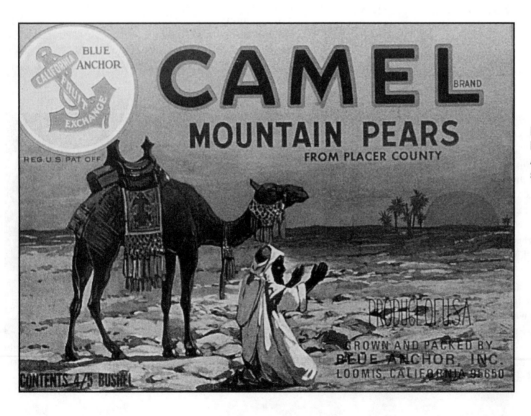

Fruit crate label, Camel Mountain Pears, Blue Anchor, Inc., desert scene.

LIMITED-EDITION FIGURINES

Figurines comprise the largest and most popular segment of the limited-edition collectibles market today. Whether it's a tiny ceramic bear wearing a sweater or a pewter Navajo chief in formal headdress, figurines run the gamut in subjects, materials and styles.

What does limited edition mean? Editions may be limited by the number of firing days, by a predetermined number of pieces or by a length of time. Many manufacturers produce both limited and open (non-limited) editions.

Figurines may be retired, which means a company will cease production of a piece. They may also be sold out or closed which means the item could go into production again at the discretion of the manufacturer. "Sold out" applies to both numbered and time-limited editions.

Some of the most well-known limited-edition figurines produced in modern times are those fashioned after Sister Maria Innocentia Hummel's delightful renderings of young children and produced by Goebel of Germany. Simply called Hummels, these endearing figurines have attracted collectors since they first appeared on the market in Germany around the mid 1930s. Their popularity rose in the United States following World War II and surged in the late 1970s. The simple, earth-toned figurines still attract collectors (See "Hummels" chapter for more information). The Precious Moments collection of teardrop-eyed children is another popular line. These figurines burst on the scene in the mid-1970s and haven't slowed down in terms of collectibility—they remain one of the strongholds in the figurine market today.

Other highly collectible lines include Dreamsicles, Cherished Teddies and Boyds Bears, all figurines that are produced primarily as open editions, with a few limited-edition pieces thrown into the mix.

Other mainstays in the figurine arena include the elegant figures by Lladro of Spain, the beautiful female figures by G. Armani of Italy, wood carvings by ANRI of Italy and ceramic children from Royal Doulton of England.

Other top manufacturers of figurines include Armani/Miller Import, Bing & Grondahl, Boyds Collection, Cast Art Industries, Enesco, Kurt S. Adler, Roman, Royal Copenhagen, Swarovski America Limited and the Walt Disney Classics Collection. Figurines are made of a number of different mediums — porcelain, crystal, wood, ceramic, resin or metal. They are often hand-painted, numbered and accompanied by certificates of authenticity. Some are signed by the artist.

During the last 20 years, decorative ornamental crystal figurines by manufacturers such as Swarovski, Iris Arc, Crystal World and others have grown to become one of the hottest types of limited edition figurines.

General Guidelines: Know a figurine and its markings. Thoroughly check each piece before you buy it, using a magnifying glass if necessary. Inspect the item for cracks or chips. If the item is crystal, use a magnifying glass to inspect the sides of facets for chips and nicks.

Look for markings. Limited-edition collectibles are usually, but not always, marked on the base or bottom of each piece. These are called backstamps or bottom stamps and often incorporate a company logo as well as a line logo. The information on the bottom of a figurine may give the piece's name, series, edition number, issue year, manufacturer, and it may identify the piece as part of a limited edition.

Backstamps are important because they are proof of authenticity. Buying a figurine without a backstamp would be like buying an autographed letter without the signature. Older figurines usually sport a tiny symbol or logo, but today's producers of limited editions have created elaborate backstamps and logos to set their figurines apart from others.

A number is usually present on the bottom of each limited-edition figurine, signifying where that particular piece fell in a predetermined number of pieces. An item may or may not be sequentially numbered, but a serially-numbered item must contain its serial number. However, whether a piece is numbered 5 or 500 in a limit of 500 does not affect the value of a piece.

Sometimes the artist who designed a figurine has embellished it with his signature. But until an artist is deceased, an artist's signature usually does not affect the value of a figurine.

The fewer pieces in circulation and the more difficult they are to find, the more a collector is generally willing to pay. Besides rarity, other factors that affect value include condition, backstamp, mold changes, paint and finish changes, and popularity.

These five Precious Moments figurines (and one ornament), produced by Enesco, have all increased in value since their 1991 retirement. Clockwise from top left: Dropping Over for Christmas, I'm So Glad You Fluttered Into My Life, the ornament Rejoice O Earth, The Spirit Is Willing But the Flesh Is Weak, Scent From Above and Smile Along the Way.

Price guides and books that list secondary market prices generally track selling prices from a geographical cross-section of dealers, "swap and sell" event results and auction results. But in the end the collectors who actually purchase figurines on the secondary market determine their secondary market values.

Clubs/Associations
•Collector's Information Bureau
5065 Shoreline Rd., Ste. 200, Barrington, IL 60010
708-842-2200

Publications
Price Guide to Limited Edition Collectibles
Krause Publications
700 E. State St., Iola, WI 54990-0001
800-258-0929

VALUE LINE

ANRI
J. Ferrandiz Woodcarvings (closed edition)
1969 Angel Sugar Heart, 6" $2,525
1970 Artist, 6" $355
1971 Good Shepherd, The, 10" $95
1971 Quintet, The, 10" $605
1974 Spring Outing, 6" $910
1975 Holy Family, 6" $670

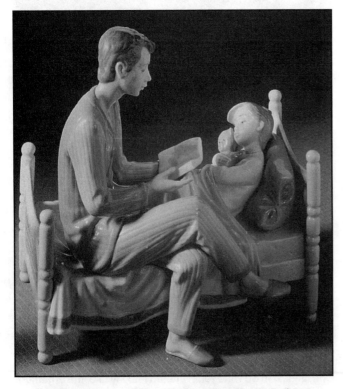

Lladro figurine, Just One More (L5899G), 1992, $450.

1977 Hurdy Gurdy, 6" $395
1978 Spreading the Word, 6" $500
1983 Cowboy, 20" $2,125
1983 Golden Blossom, 20" $5,160
1984 Bird's Eye View, 6" $705
1987 Black Forest Boy, 6" $300

Sarah Kay six-inch figurines (closed edition)
1983 Bedtime, closed $440
1985 A Special Day, closed $330
1987 Cuddles, closed $470
1989 Take Me Along, limited to 1,000 .... $530
1990 Holiday Cheer, limited to 1,000 .... $615
1991 Season's Joy, limited to 1,000 .... $625
1994 Bubbles & Bows, limited to 1,000 .... $605

Armani
Capodimonte
1976 Country Girl (Little Shepherdess) #3153, retired .. $140
191977 Napoleon #464C, retired $500
1978 Organ Grinder #3323, retired $350
1980 Old Drunk (Richard's Night Out) #3243, retired .. $240
Garden Series
1991 Lady with Cornucopia 870C, limited to 10,000 .... $600
1991 Lady with Harp 874C, limited to 10,000 .... $500
1991 Lady with Peacock 871C, limited to 10,000 .... $585
1991 Lady with Violin 872C $560
My Fair Ladies
1987 Lady with Peacock 385C, retired $2,290
1987 Lady with Peacock 385F, retired $290
1987 Lady with Peacock 385P, retired $400
1989 Two Can-Can Dancers 516C, retired $1,720
1990 Can-Can Dancer 589P, retired $465
1993 Mahogany 194C, retired $1,075
1993 Morning Rose 193C, limited to 5,000 .... $515

Artists of the World
deGrazia figurines
1984 Flower Boy, open $110
1984 Sunflower Boy, closed $300
1985 Jesus, open $55
1987 Wee Three, closed $195

Boyds Collection Ltd.
Bearstone Collection
1993 Arthur with Green Scarf, retired $95
1993 Arthur with Red Scarf 2003, retired $100
1993 Father Chrisbear and Son 2008, retired $350
1993 Wilson With Love Sonnet 2007, open $500
1994 Agatha and Shelly Scaredy Cat 2245, closed $75
1994 Bailey & Emily Forever Friends 2018, retired $120
1994 Celeste the Angel Rabbit 2230, open $295
1994 Elgin the Elf Bear 2236, closed $75
1994 Wilson at the Beach 2020-06, open $100
1995 Bailey the Honeybear 2260, closed $90
1995 Wilson the Wonderful Wizard of Wuz 2261, closed $50
1996 Grenville & Beatrice True Love 2274, open $36

Cast Art Industries

Dreamsicles (retired editions)

Most Dreamsicles produced from 1991 on are worth face value. Some exceptions are:

1992 The 1995 Ice Commemorative (Cherubs) $150
1996 Bundles of Love (Heavenly Classics) $558

Cybis

Animal Kingdom

1961 Horse, limited edition of 100 .... $4,500
1965 Raccoon, Raffles, closed $365
1968 Snail, Sir Escargot, closed $290
1970 Deer Mouse in Clover, closed $160
1971 Nashua, limited edition of 100 .... $3,000
1976 Prairie Dog, closed $345
1980 Squirrel, Highrise, limited edition of 400 .... $525
1984 Chantilly, Kitten, open $210
1985 Elephant, Willoughby, open $245
1986 Mick, the Melodious Mutt, open $275

Norman Rockwell Collection (retired editions)

1973 Back to School NR-02 .... $35
1973 Doctor & Doll NR-12 .... $150
1973 Leapfrog NR-09 .... $550
1974 Take Your Medicine NR-18 .... $95
1978 At the Doctor NR-29 .... $160
1979 Back From Camp NR-33 .... $110
1984 Scotty's Home Plate NR-46 .... $40

Department 56

Dickens' Village

1984 Original Carolers, set of three white posts, retired .. $95
1986 Christmas Carol Characters, 6501-3 .... $100
1988 Poulterer 5926-9, retired $50
1993 Chelsea Lane Shoppers 5816-5 (set of four), open . $30

Snowbabies

1986 Best Friends 7958-8, retired $115
1986 Hold on Tight 7956-1, open $14
1987 Don't Fall Off 7968-5, retired $90
1987 Down the Hill We Go 7960-0, open $22
1990 I Will Put Up the Tree 6800-4 retired $24
1991 Fishing For Dreams 6809-8, open $33

Enesco

Cherished Teddies

1992 Benji, retired $40
1992 Beth, retired $40
1992 Camille, retired $30
1992 Jasmine, suspended $40
1992 Jeremy, retired $50
1992 Katie, retired $40
1992 Mandy, retired $50
1992 Nathaniel and Nellie $40
1992 Theadore, Samantha, Tyler, retired $20
1992 Theadore, Samantha, Tyler (nine inch) $140
1992 Zachary, retired $45

Cherished Teddies Christmas

1992 Bear on Rocking Reindeer/musical, suspended $80
1992 Charlie, Spirit of Friends, retired $45
1992 Douglas, retired $65
1993 Alice, limited to one year $100
1993 Hans, suspended $80
1994 Nils, open $30

Cherished Teddies Club

1995 Cub E. Bear, limited to one year $35
1995 Hilary Hugabear, limited to one year $40
1995 Mayor Wilson T. Beary, limited to one year $60

Cherished Teddies Easter

1993 Abigail, suspended $35
1993 Charity, retired $100
1993 Chelsea, retired $250
1993 Daisy, retired $800
1993 Heidi and David, suspended $45
1993 Henrietta, suspended $85
1993 Molly, retired $40

Precious Moments

1976 He Careth For You E1377B, suspended $125
1976 Praise the Lord Anyhow E1374B, retired $100
1977 O How I Love Jesus E1380B, retired $110
1979 Christmas is a Time to Share E2802, suspended ... $100
1979 Eggs Over Easy E3118, retired $105
1979 God Loveth a Cheerful Giver E1378, retired........ $900

Susanna was inspired by the art of Maud Humphrey Bogart and produced by Hamilton Gifts.

1980 God Is Love E5213, suspended $75
1980 Thank You For Coming to My Aide E5202,
    suspended $150
1981 Bless This House E7164, suspended $200
1981 There Is Joy in Serving Jesus E7157, retired $60
1982 Dropping Over for Christmas E2375, retired $100
1982 Taste and See That the Lord is Good E9274,
    retired $160
1983 Praise the Lord Anyhow E9254, retired $90
1984 Love is Kind E5377, retired $85
1985 Brotherly Love 100544, suspended $80
1986 Sharing Our Christmas Together 102490, suspended
    .... $75
1986 Smile Along the Way 101842, retired $155
1986 The Spirit Is Willing, But the Flesh Is Weak 100196,
    retired $75
1988 Jesus Loves Me 104531, limited to 1,000 .... $1,550
1989 I'll Never Stop Loving You 521418, retired $42
1989 I'm So Glad You Fluttered Into My Life 520640,
    retired $325

Hamilton Gifts
Maud Humphrey Bogart figurines
1988 A Pleasure to Meet You H1310, retired $80
1988 Bride, The H1313 .... $90

From Armani's Florentine Gardens collection, The Embrace is a retired figurine and has increased in value from its original $1,450 to around $1,600.

1988 Cleaning House H1303, retired $70
1988 Little Chickadees H1306, retired $70
1988 Magic Kitten, The H1308, retired $85
1988 My First Dance H1311, retired $200
1988 Sarah H1312, retired $275
1988 Seamstress H1309 .... $250
1988 Susanna H1305, retired $250
1988 Tea and Gossip H1301, retired $110
1990 A Flower for You, H5596, collector's club figurine . $65
1991 Friends for Life MH911, collector's club figurine $140

Lladro
1969 Bird L1054, retired $140
1969 Shepherdess with Dog L1034, retired $250
1977 Little Red Riding Hood L4965, retired $560
1980 Samson and Delilah L5051, retired $1,500
1982 Little Boy Bullfighter L5115, retired $400
1984 Swan with Wings Spread L5231, open $140
1987 Great Horned Owl L5420, retired $310
1990 Concertina L5695G, retired $350
1990 Mommy, It's Cold L5715G, retired $400
1991 Dance of Love L5820G, retired $630
1991 On Her Toes L5818G/M, retired $525
1992 Free Spirit L2220M, retired $235
1992 Just One More L5899G, open $450
1993 Autumn Glow, limited edition of 1,500 .... $900

Miss Martha Originals
All God's Children by Martha Root
1985 Abe 1357, retired $1,200
1985 Tom 1353, retired $400
1986 Becky 1402W, open $55
1986 Grandma 1323, retired $3,400
1987 Ben 1504, retired $300
1987 Tat 1801, retired $65
1987 Tiffany 1511, open $32
1988 Maya 1520, retired $380
1989 Bo 1530, retired $70
1990 Jerome 1532, open $32
1990 Thaliyah 778, retired $1,300
1991 Samantha 1542, retired $125
1992 Caitlin 1554, retired $75
1994 Justin 1576, open $37

PenDelfin
Retired figurines
1955 Margo $450
1956 Timber Stand $175
1959 Uncle Soames $350
1960 Shiner with Black Eye $400
1964 Bandstand $80
1965 Picnic Stand $160
1966 Cake Stand $350
1967 Robert with Lollipop $175
1971 Totty $200
1988 Humphrey Go Kart $110

Possible Dreams
Saturday Evening Post retired figurines
1991 Doctor & Doll 12-1/2" $210
1991 Gone Fishing 11-3/4" $275

1992 Santa's Helpers 11" $180
1992 Self Portrait 14" $255

Roman Inc.
A Child's World 1st Edition (limited to 15,000)
1980 Beach Buddies, signed $600
1980 Beach Buddies, unsigned $500
1980 Helping Hands $75
1980 Kiss Me Good Night $50
1980 My Big Brother $200
1980 Nighttime Thoughts $75
1980 Sounds of the Sea $150

Sarah's Attic
1988 Sunshine Doll, retired $700
1989 Long Journey, retired $35
1991 Silent Night, retired $44
Black Heritage Collection
1989 Quilting Ladies, closed $285
1990 Hattie, retired $85
1991 Black Baby Tansy, closed $45
1991 Corporal Pervis, retired $110
1992 Music Masters, closed $350
1996 Mary Eliza Mahoney/4501, sold out $50
Santas of the Month
1988 Santas (black, January-December) $250
1988 Santas (white, January-December) $125
1988 Mini Santas (January-December), closed $30
Sarah's Gang
1986 Original Katie, closed $20
1986 Original Willie, closed $28

1987 Sitting Katie, closed $21
1987 Willie on Heart, closed $21
1988 Katie, closed $21
1988 Willie, closed $21
1989 Americana Katie, closed $24
1990 Clown Willie, closed $45
1995 Katie/4344, open $28

WACO Products Corp.
Melody In Motion
1986 Santa Claus, retired $225
1987 Santa Claus, retired $175
1988 Madame figurines, open $130
1989 Spotlight Clowns, retired $120
1993 South of the Border, open $190
1994 Caroler Boy, The, limited edition of 10,000 .... $180

Walt Disney Classics Collection
1992 Bambi, wheel, closed $240
1992 Bambi & Flower, wheel, limited to 10,000 .... $450
1992 Cinderella, clef, retired $375
1992 Field Mouse, hands not touching, retired $1,400
1992 Field Mouse, hands touching, retired $1,100
1992 Sorcerer Mickey, retired $245
1993 Clarabelle, wheel, closed $244
1993 Goofy, wheel, closed $2,700
1993 Peter Pan, clef, closed $225
1994 Snow White, flower, retired $200
1996 Donald and Daisy, clef, retired $575
1996 Pinocchio, open $125
1996 Pocahontas, retired $240

These six Cherished Teddies have increased in value since their 1995 retirement. Top row: Chelsea, Jeremy, Benji. Bottom row: Mandy, Beth and Douglas. With an issue price in 1993 of $15, Chelsea is the most valuable of the six today, worth $250 on the secondary market.

LUNCH BOXES

The once utilitarian lunch boxes every child carried are now highly-collected remnants of pop culture. Their colorful designs make them popular display pieces.

Steel boxes featuring prominent characters of the day began in the 1950s with a Hopalong Cassidy box. Aladdin and Thermos were, and still are, the two main manufacturers of lunch kits. Production of steel boxes ended in the mid-1980s, and plastic boxes became the norm. Vinyl lunch bags first appeared in the 1960s and continue today.

General Guidelines: Boxes and Thermos bottles are often found separately; both items are collectible. Steel boxes (especially dome or barn-shaped) are worth more than plastic. But vinyl kits, harder to find in premium condition, run a close second in value. Boxes featuring popular TV, movie, space, Western, Disney, Barbie or cartoon characters are most collectible.

Most older steel boxes will have some rust or chipped paint, but such damage decreases value, as do dents, scratches, and missing latch or handles. Likewise, plastic boxes and vinyl bags will be worth the most if they are free of scratches, punctures, stains or worn labels or other imperfections. Be aware that plastic and vinyl boxes and bags are susceptible to heat or exposure to the sun and may exhibit signs of melting.

Even without a matching box, most Thermos bottles are collectible, especially steel and glass bottles with characters like Roy Rogers or Howdy Doody. Plastic bottles featuring characters are less collectible than steel ones. Plain, undecorated plastic bottles have no collector value.

Mork & Mindy steel box, 1979, American Thermos, $25 Near Mint.

VALUE LINE

Plastic Boxes
Prices listed are for boxes (no bottle) in Near Mint condition.

101 Dalmatians, Aladdin, 1990	$15
Batman, light blue, Thermos, 1989	$40
Beauty and the Beast, Aladdin, 1991	$20
Care Bears, Aladdin, 1986	$10
Civil War, Universal, 1961	$200
Dukes of Hazzard, Aladdin, 1981	$45
Ewoks, Thermos, 1983	$20
Flash Gordon Dome, Aladdin, 1979	$60
GI Joe Live the Adventure, Aladdin, 1986	$25
Garfield, food fight scene, Thermos, 1979	$25
Gumby, Thermos, 1986	$60
Incredible Hulk Dome, Aladdin, 1980	$30
Jetsons 3-D, Servo, 1987	$75
Jetsons, The Movie, Aladdin, 1990	$30
Kool-Aid Man, Thermos, 1986	$20
Marvel Super Heroes, Thermos, 1990	$20
Pee Wee's Playhouse, Thermos, 1987	$20
Popeye & Son, Servo, 1987	$60
Raggedy Ann & Andy, Aladdin, 1988	$45
Rocketeer, Aladdin, 1990	$10
Shirt Tales, Thermos, 1981	$10
Smurfs, Thermos, 1984	$15
Sport Goofy, Aladdin, 1986	$30
Teenage Mutant Ninja Turtles, Thermos, 1990	$35
Tom & Jerry, Aladdin, 1989	$30
Wayne Gretzky Dome, Aladdin, 1980	$120
Wizard of Oz 50th Anniversary, Aladdin, 1989	$60
Woody Woodpecker, Aladdin, 1972	$60
Wuzzles, Aladdin, 1985	$10
Yogi's Treasure Hunt, Servo, 1987	$25

Steel Boxes
Prices listed are for boxes (no bottle) in Near Mint condition.

Atom Ant/Secret Squirrel, King Seeley Thermos, 1966	$200
Bonanza, green rim, Aladdin, 1963	$120
Brady Bunch, King Seeley Thermos, 1970	$250
Buck Rogers, Aladdin, 1979	$35
Bullwinkle & Rocky, Universal, 1962	$800
Care Bears, Aladdin, 1984	$7
Cracker Jack, Aladdin, 1969	$55
Disney School Bus Dome, Aladdin, 1968	$60
Disney's Magic Kingdom, Aladdin, 1960	$15
Dr. Seuss, World of, Aladdin, 1970	$100
Family Affair, King Seeley Thermos, 1969	$60
Flintstones, yellow, Aladdin, 1963	$160
Get Smart, King Seeley Thermos, 1966	$175
Happy Days, American Thermos, 1977	$40
He-Man & Masters of the Universe, Aladdin, 1984	$5

Holly Hobbie, Aladdin, 1979 .... $10

Hopalong Cassidy, Aladdin, 1950 .... $175

Hot Wheels, King Seeley Thermos, 1969 .... $70

Howdy Doody, Adco Liberty, 1954 .... $450

Jetsons Dome, Aladdin, 1963 .... $675

Little Red Riding Hood, Ohio Art, 1982 .... $25

Munsters, King Seeley Thermos, 1965 .... $370

Muppet Babies, King Seeley Thermos, 1985 .... $10

Peanuts, King Seeley Thermos, many variations ...... $20-$50

Planet of the Apes, Aladdin, 1974 .... $175

Raggedy Ann & Andy, Aladdin, 1973 .... $25

Rambo, King Seeley Thermos, 1985 .... $10

Roy Rogers Chow Wagon Dome, King Seeley Thermos,
1958 .... $230

Sesame Street, Aladdin, 1983 .... $10

Sleeping Beauty, General Steel Ware, 1960 .... $450

Smurfs, King Seeley Thermos, 1983 .... $140

Snow White, Aladdin, 1975 .... $55

Star Trek Dome, Aladdin, 1968 .... $700

Star Wars, King Seeley Thermos, 1978 .... $40

Strawberry Shortcake, Aladdin, 1980 .... $10

Superman, Universal, 1954 .... $60

Tom Corbett Space Cadet, Aladdin, paper decal,1952 ... $200

U.S. Mail Dome, Aladdin, 1969 .... $60

Underdog, Okay Industries, 1974 .... $800

Wagon Train, King Seeley Thermos, 1964 .... $740

Waltons, Aladdin, 1973 .... $50

Yankee Doodles, King Seeley Thermos, 1975 .... $45

Yellow Submarine, King Seeley Thermos, 1968 .... $350

Zorro, Aladdin, 1966 .... $200

Vinyl Boxes

Prices listed are for boxes (no bottle) in Near Mint condition.

Alice in Wonderland, Aladdin, 1972 .... $200

Alvin & the Chipmunks, King Seeley Thermos,
1963 .... $400

Ballerina, Universal, 1960s $800

Barbie, World of, pink box, King Seeley Thermos, 1971 . $75

Barbie and Midge Dome, King Seeley Thermos,1964 ... $525

Beany & Cecil, King Seeley Thermos, 1963 .... $550

Beatles Brunch Bag, Aladdin, 1966 .... $625

Casper the Friendly Ghost, King Seeley Thermos,
1966 .... $550

Deputy Dawg, King Seeley Thermos, 1960s $550

GI Joe, King Seeley Thermos, 1989 .... $175

Highway Signs Snap Pack, Avon, 1988 .... $30

Lassie, Universal, 1960s $120

Liddle Kiddles, King Seeley Thermos, 1969 .... $250

Monkees, King Seeley Thermos, 1967 .... $380

Pink Panther, Aladdin, 1980 .... $95

Psychedelic, Aladdin, 1969 .... $150

Roy Rogers Saddlebag, brown, King Seeley Thermos,
1960 .... $225

Sleeping Beauty, Aladdin, 1970 .... $240

Snoopy Softy, King Seeley Thermos, 1988 .... $20

Soupy Sales, King Seeley Thermos, 1966 .... $600

Strawberry Shortcake, Aladdin, 1980 .... $40

Tinkerbell, Aladdin, 1969 .... $260

Wonder Woman, yellow box, Aladdin, 1978 .... $200

Yosemite Sam, King Seeley Thermos, 1971 .... $560

Thermos Bottles

Prices listed are for bottles in Near Mint condition.

Action Jackson, steel, Okay Industries, 1973 .... $200

Addams Family, plastic, King Seeley Thermos,1974 ...... $25

Archies, plastic, Aladdin, 1969 .... $30

Beatles, steel, Aladdin, 1966 .... $150

Bedknobs & Broomsticks, plastic, Aladdin, 1972 .... $40

Blondie, steel, King Seeley Thermos, 1969 .... $75

Disney Express, plastic, Aladdin, 1979 .... $5

Disneyland Monorail, steel, Aladdin, 1968 .... $115

Fall Guy, plastic, Aladdin, 1981 .... $15

Fonz, The, plastic, King Seeley Thermos, 1978 .... $20

Gentle Ben, plastic, Aladdin, 1968 .... $30

Gomer Pyle, steel, Aladdin, 1966 .... $90

Get Smart steel box, 1966, King Seeley Thermos, $175 Near
Mint, steel/glass Thermos bottle, $85 Near Mint.

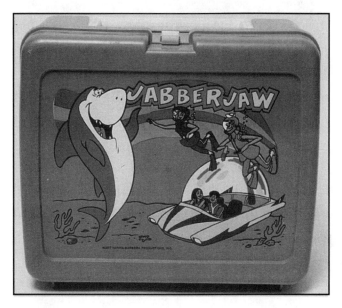

Jabber Jaw plastic box, 1977, Thermos, $60 Near Mint.

Green Hornet, steel, King Seeley Thermos, 1967 .... $175
H.R. Pufnstuf, plastic, Aladdin, 1970 .... $50
Hector Heathcote, steel, Aladdin, 1964 .... $90
Holly Hobbie, plastic, Aladdin, 1970s $7
James Bond 007, steel, Aladdin, 1966 .... $135
Land of the Lost, plastic, Aladdin, 1975 .... $35
Little Friends, plastic, Aladdin, 1982 .... $260
Little House on the Prairie, plastic, King Seeley
    Thermos, 1978 .... $35
Lost in Space, steel, King Seeley Thermos, 1967 .... $60
Munsters, steel, King Seeley Thermos, 1965 .... $125
Muppet Babies, plastic, King Seeley Thermos,
    1985 .... $5
Pac-Man, plastic, Aladdin, 1980 .... $5
Planet of the Apes, plastic, Aladdin, 1974 .... $45
Popeye, steel, Universal, 1962 .... $300
Six Million Dollar Man, plastic, Aladdin, 1974 .... $25
Star Wars: Empire Strikes Back, plastic, King Seeley
    Thermos, 1980 .... $10
Twiggy, steel, Aladdin, 1967 .... $80
Underdog, plastic, Okay Industries, 1974 .... $350
Winnie the Pooh, steel, Aladdin $110
Winnie the Pooh, plastic, Aladdin, 1976 .... $70

Porky's Lunch Wagon Dome, 1959, King Seeley Thermos, $350 Near Mint.

Hong Kong Phooey steel box, 1975, King Seeley Thermos, $40 Near Mint.

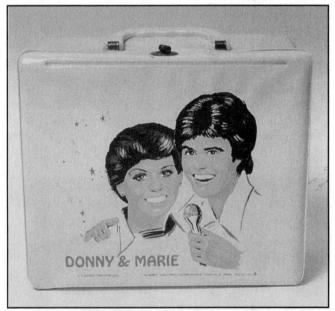

Donny & Marie vinyl box, 1978, Aladdin, $120 Near Mint.

MAGAZINES

People collect magazines for the beauty of the covers, the advertisements and historical articles and photos. The personality or event featured on the cover, however, is the most important factor.

General Guidelines: Magazines that feature the likes of Joe DiMaggio, Marilyn Monroe, Elizabeth Taylor, Michael Jordan and Lucille Ball are some of the most collectible.

Magazines with long track records, such as *Sports Illustrated*, *Life*, *Playboy* and *TV Guide* are popular with collectors. Monster magazines from the 1960s and 1970s are especially hot, along with sci-fi and some music magazines (most notably, early *Rolling Stone*). Pre-1960 movie magazines have traditionally been popular and are still so today. And there never seems to be a shortage of collectors for all types of 1950s and 1960s adult magazines, especially those with notable actresses or models in various states of undress.

Pulp magazines—covering themes like crime, detectives, love, horror and romance—from the first half of the 20th century are also popular. Pulp covers were colorful and lurid, making them attractive to buyers. Because these were printed on cheap paper, they are often found in Poor condition today.

People collect magazines in several ways—by celebrity pictured, by event (covers featuring the lunar landing), by cover illustrator. Covers illustrated by Norman Rockwell are especially desirable.

Contributor to this section: Denis Jackson, The Illustrator Collector's News, P.O. Box 1958, Sequim, WA 98382

CONDITION FACTORS

What collector wants a magazine with a coffee cup stain, a major tear or missing pages? The condition of magazines is of paramount importance to values. Understand magazine grading and how it affects values before you buy.

Newer magazines (from 1960 to the present) have little value in lower grades, since there is a good supply available in prime condition.

Older magazines (pre-1960s) are still collectible in lesser conditions since there are relatively few available in top condition. Even an older magazine in Good condition will likely find buyers.

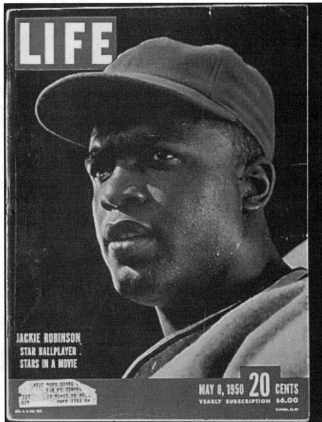 

Life, 5/8/50 Jackie Robinson; 8/1/49 Joe DiMaggio.

Life

5/3/37, Jean Harlow	$60
11/8/37, Greta Garbo	$40
1/23/38, Bette Davis	$40
5/23/38, Errol Flynn	$25
6/20/38, Rudolph Valentino	$35
10/17/38, Carole Lombard	$35
5/1/39, Joe DiMaggio	$150
11/13/39, Claudette Colbert	$25
12/11/39, Betty Grable	$30
1/29/40, Lana Turner	$25
7/15/40, Rita Hayworth	$25
12/9/40, Ginger Rogers	$35
9/1/41, Ted Williams	$100
3/30/42, Shirley Temple	$45
6/1/42, Hedy Lamarr	$30
10/16/44, Lauren Bacall	$25
11/12/45, Ingrid Bergman	$15
6/10/46, Donna Reed	$20
7/14/47, Elizabeth Taylor	$35
8/9/48, Marlene Dietrich	$25
8/1/49, Joe DiMaggio	$60
5/8/50, Jackie Robinson	$60
6/12/50, Hopalong Cassidy	$25
4/7/52, Marilyn Monroe	$75

The Saturday Evening Post, May 24, 1958; Rockwell cover.

GRADING GUIDELINES

The following are general guidelines for grading magazines:

Mint: Perfect — a magazine that is still in its shrink-wrap or mailing envelope. Older magazines are rarely, if ever, found in Mint condition.

Near Mint: An uncirculated magazine with no noticeable flaws. No mailing label or any type of damage. Again, older magazines are very difficult to locate in this condition, and the ones that are in this condition command premium prices.

Excellent: Essentially an unblemished magazine with slight imperfections. At first glance, it might appear to be in Near Mint condition. Issues may have a mailing label, slight fading, finger marks on the cover, minimal spine wear, has its cover gloss, tight staples, no folded or bent pages, no tears or significant spots or stains. Valued at about 75 percent of a Near Mint magazine.

Very Good: Shows one or two of the following problems: wear or cracking of spine, small chips or spots, some loss of cover gloss, small corner bends, creases from handling, yellowed pages on older copies (because of improper storage). Valued at about 50 percent of a Near Mint magazine.

Good: Shows three to five of the imperfections listed under Very Good condition. Valued at about 35 percent of a Near Mint magazine.

Fair: A complete magazine with several defects: tape on spine, missing part of the spine, writing on cover, heavily faded cover, tears or scratches on cover, spots, stains, minor warping due to moisture, loose staples and any number of other defects. Valued at about 20 percent of a Near Mint magazine.

Poor: Incomplete magazine with many defects. Valued at less than 10 percent of a Near Mint magazine.

5/25/53, Marilyn Monroe/Jane Russell	$60
7/20/53, John Kennedy	$20
4/26/54, Grace Kelly	$25
8/8/55, Ben Hogan	$50
4/23/56, Jayne Mansfield	$30
6/25/56, Mickey Mantle	$100
3/11/57, John Kennedy	$15
4/20/59, Marilyn Monroe	$35
11/9/59, Marilyn Monroe	$35
1/27/61, Kennedy Inauguration	$10
8/18/61, Mickey Mantle/Roger Maris	$75
4/13/62, Taylor/Burton (w/ baseball cards)	$200
6/22/62, Marilyn Monroe	$25
8/17/62, Marilyn Monroe	$25
8/23/63, Sandy Koufax	$35
11/29/63, Kennedy assassination	$20
12/6/63, Kennedy funeral	$10
3/6/64, Cassius Clay	$45
8/28/64, The Beatles	$30
5/7/65, John Wayne	$10
7/30/65, Mickey Mantle	$50
1/7/66, Sean Connery	$10
7/23/71, Clint Eastwood	$10

LIFE MAGAZINE

Life, published weekly from Nov. 23, 1936, to Dec. 29, 1972, is one of the most collected magazines. The fact that there is a better-than-average supply of Life, compared to other magazines of the same period, adds to its collectibility.

Life featured a variety of Hollywood stars, sports heroes, war heroes, villains, famous politicians and other characters; issues with such covers are valued from $10 to $75. Generic issues (with no big celebrity or event on the cover) sell for the following prices: 1930s issues ($8 to $12), 1940s ($5 to $8), 1950s ($3 to $6), 1960s-70s ($1 to $3).

The most expensive issue of *Life* is the April 13, 1962, issue with Elizabeth Taylor and Richard Burton on the cover. It featured an insert of Mickey Mantle and Roger Maris baseball cards. This issue retails from $150 to $200 with the cards intact. Often, this magazine will be found without the cards; such issues sell for from $10 to $15. Likewise, the cards, if torn out, are worth far less than if they were still in the magazine.

Playboy

12/53, Marilyn Monroe $2,500

Sports Illustrated

2/49, Ralph Beard $125
3/49, Marcel Cerdan $100
4/49, Lou Boudreau $100
5/49, Joe DiMaggio $200
6/49, Rex Barney $100
12/53, Dummy Issue No. 1 (Stadium Fans) $300
4/19/54, Dummy Issue No. 2 (Pebble Beach) $350
8/16/54, Eddie Mathews, baseball card inserts $400
8/23/54, Golf Bags, baseball card inserts $450
4/4/55, Ben Hogan $55
4/11/55, Willie Mays, etc., baseball card inserts $195
4/18/55, Al Rosen, baseball card inserts $125
7/11/55, Yogi Berra $45
8/1/55, Ted Williams $115
1/9/56, Bob Cousy $45
5/14/56, Al Kaline $45
6/11/56, Sam Snead $45
6/18/56, Mickey Mantle $150
7/9/56, Mickey Mantle/Ernie Banks/Stan Musial $85
9/10/56, Whitey Ford $55
10/1/56, Mickey Mantle $75
3/3/57, Mickey Mantle $85
4/18/57, Gordie Howe $45
7/8/57, Ted Williams/Stan Musial $95
6/2/58, Eddie Mathews $55
7/7/58, All-Star Game $65
4/15/59, Willie Mays $45
9/12/60, Jack Nicklaus $65
10/2/61, Roger Maris/Mickey Mantle $85
7/2/62, Mickey Mantle $75

6/10/63, Cassius Clay $95
1/20/64, Swimsuit $95
12/7/64, Bill Bradley $50
1/18/65, Swimsuit $65
4/6/65, Arnold Palmer/Jack Nicklaus $55
6/21/65, Mickey Mantle $65
1/17/66, Swimsuit $55
8/21/67, Carl Yastrzemski $45
12/25/67, Carl Yastrzemski $45
11/28/83, Michael Jordan $65
7/23/84, Michael Jordan $40
12/10/84, Michael Jordan $40

TV Guide

#1 Lucy's $50,000,000 Baby $800
#10 Dean Martin and Jerry Lewis $100
#12 Ed Sullivan $50
#16 Lucy and Desi $375
#17 Groucho Marx $150
#27 Red Skelton $50
#38 Bob Hope $75
#56 Lucille Ball $100
#59 Frank Sinatra $50
#72 Dean Martin and Jerry Lewis $75
#82 Walt Disney & Friends $200
#103 Art Carney of *The Honeymooners* $50

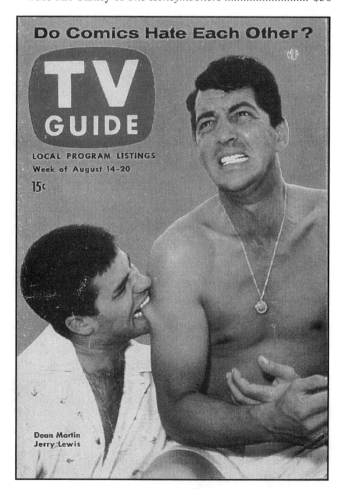

TV Guide, Dean Martin and Jerry Lewis on cover.

STORAGE AND CARE

Proper care is a must since humidity, heat and light can wreak havoc with magazines. Magazines should be stored in individual plastic sleeves with an acid-free cardboard backing for support. The issues should then be placed in specially-designed boxes and stored in a humidity-controlled environment. The sleeves, backing and boxes can be purchased through any number of places, including magazine and comic book dealers.

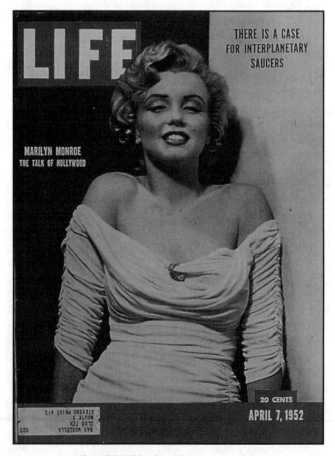

Life, 1/27/61 The Kennedy Inauguration.

Life, 4/7/52 Marilyn Monroe on cover.

MAJOLICA

Majolica is a ceramic art form that best illustrates the decorative exuberance of the Victorian era. It is a brilliantly glazed, dramatically sculpted and whimsically soft earthenware dedicated to the conservatories and dining rooms of Victorian society.

The porous ceramicware is molded in relief, fired with an opaque tin-oxide glaze and painted with pigments in metallic-oxide bases. Strictly speaking it is a 19th-century revival of "maiolica," a pottery popular in the 15th century, which also featured an opaque tin-oxide glaze. Majolica's design philosophy of "fitness for purpose" illustrated the function of each piece, be it an oyster server, lobster platter, strawberry server or game-pie dish.

History: Majolica mania began in 1851 at the Crystal Palace in London, which housed the first Great Exhibition of the Works of Industry of all Nations. The appeal of these Victorian decorative pieces expanded to the United States after its introduction at the Philadelphia Centennial Exhibition in 1876.

Soon well-appointed parlors and dining rooms across America were filled with elegant Majolica pieces, from cheese bells and candlesticks to cuspidors and more. Competition among the English, German, French, Italian, Portuguese, Scottish and American manufacturers was keen. Each strived to develop a signature style. The result was elaborate relief in molding, complex coloration and distinctive patterns. This competition also led to the imitation of successful patterns, frequently in blatant copyright violation.

Majolica, with its rich textures and warm colors, was a welcome relief from the proliferation of blue-and-white and white ironstone which had been the staple of middle class families for so long. Adding to its popularity was that it was considerably less expensive than English bone china or porcelains from Italy, France or Germany.

During the early 20th century, as the opulent detail of the Victorian era began to be viewed as excessive and pretentious, Majolica, too, fell into disfavor. As a result the height of popularity and manufacture of Victorian Majolica fell between 1851 and 1899.

Revival in the interest of Victorian Majolica in the United States has only begun in the last two decades. A major exhibit of English Majolica in America was held at New York City's Cooper-Hewitt Museum of the Smithsonian Institute in 1982. This exhibit helped once again spark public interest in collecting this colorful form of ceramics. The organization of the Majolica International Society in 1989 and a proliferation of auctions dealing exclusively in Majolica further increased public enthusiasm.

General Guidelines: Manufacturer's marks increase the value of the piece. Correct identification of potters' marks, unfortunately, can be difficult. A good reference guide will help identify marks. Collectors can also become familiar with the works of different manufacturers by observing as much as possible from frequent visits to antique shows and auctions.

The best Majolica usually has an undersurface of pink, blue, green and occasionally white, or exhibits a fine mottled blue/black or blue/brown.

Glazing that is dull, that does not conform to the outline of the design or that looks "heavy" and overpainted, is not as desirable. Also watch for dullness and lack of translucency or shine. These can indicate a repair, which would devalue the piece considerably. Chips, cracks that go through the piece and crazing (cracking on the glazed surface) also decrease value.

French Majolica, or barbotine — very much in the style of Minton or later Art Nouveau design — has always had its devotees and has greatly increased in popularity. French Majolica interiors are often deep red, teal blue or occasionally brown, while English and American Majolica interiors are more often pink, blue and occasionally green.

Many English pieces with well-glazed yellow undersurfaces are thought to be from Thomas Forester, but pieces with yellow undersurfaces that are not glazed as well may be American. Grossly mottled undersurfaces may indicate that the piece is American.

Japanese Majolica is considerably less expensive than other makes.

Majolica pitcher; 10" Clifton signed.

MINTON TEAPOTS

The venerable, and venerated, Minton & Co. celebrated its bicentennial in 1993 with the reproduction of a Majolica teapot and will continue to reproduce an additional Majolica teapot each year. Production is limited, and each teapot is fully marked to inform the buyer of its origin.

Majolica collectors who are lucky enough to own both the original teapot and the modern reproduction of the same design can enjoy the contrast between the original Majolica and the present-day, fine china version.

Common Collecting Terms

Agate Ware: Pottery made to look like agate.

Barbotine: French Majolica, with or without raised flowers. Also refers to raised flowers on English or American Majolica made in the French style of molded slip.

Bone China: English porcelain made by adding bone ash to clay to produce a very white surface. It is softer than some hard-clay porcelains and harder than some soft-clay porcelains.

Brubensul Ware: Light-brown to dark-brown highly glazed Majolica.

Crackle: Decorative cracks deliberately created in the body and glaze during firing.

Crazing: Unintentional cracks due to errors in heating and cooling during firing or due to decomposition of the glaze with age.

Earthenware: Porous pottery (unless glazed) softer than stoneware or porcelain.

Ewer: A wide-mouth pitcher or jug, often intended to hold wine or water.

Graniteware: Stoneware sprayed with lead glaze to produce a speckled finish to imitate granite.

Ironstone: Stoneware hardened with the addition of glassy ironstone slag to resemble porcelain.

Lead glaze: Hard, glassy, transparent coating made of silica and alumina fused with lead oxide. Used to seal porous clay surfaces.

Pip: A pimple or blemish on a ceramic piece caused by contact with kiln parts during firing.

Porcelain: Hard, non-porous white ceramic ware fired at high temperatures.

Registry Mark: English mark required on goods manufactured between 1842 and 1883.

Sanded Majolica: Majolica coated with a gritty glaze.

Stoneware: Hard, white pottery made from a blend of clay and fusible stone. Fired at temperatures halfway between earthenware and porcelain. Additional glaze is unnecessary.

Winslow Ware: Type of Majolica made by Portland Stone Ware Company, Portland, Maine, between 1878 and 1886. The company changed its name to Winslow and Co. in 1882.

COLLECTORS' ALERT

Beware of marks that have been partially obliterated so as to appear older than they actually are.

Also beware of copies. For the most part, copies are lighter than authentic pieces, and the glaze does not have the richness of true Majolica. Imitation Majolica often features an undersurface that is not glazed; true Majolica is almost always glazed. In recent years, there has been an onslaught of cobalt pitchers on the market that have fooled many knowledgeable collectors and even dealers.

As for modern reproductions, a reputable manufacturer operating today will mark its Majolica with its own factory name and, many times, the date of production.

English Manufacturers

Minton. Minton & Co. designed the eclectic mix of art revival styles that became, over the next four decades, the reference book for other Majolica manufacturers. Minton's earliest Majolica, on display at the 1851 Crystal Palace Exhibition, was in deeply sculpted Italian Renaissance style.

George Jones and Sons. George Jones worked for Minton for a decade before establishing his own factory in the early 1860s. The company later became George Jones and Sons.

Pieces in the naturalistic style are sometimes hard to distinguish between Minton and Jones, except for the maker's marks on the undersurface. Some collectors regard Jones' work as the quintessential example of Majolica's humor, whimsy and brilliant color.

Josiah Wedgwood and Sons. Josiah Wedgwood and Sons joined in the production of Majolica in 1861. This manufacturer is noted for more serious pieces, excellent modeling and resilient glazes.

Griffen, Smith and Hill, also known as Etruscan. Griffen, Smith and Hill of Phoenixville, Pa., had family ties with potters in Stoke-on-Trent, England. The company is believed to have produced the best examples of American Majolica. Their most famous pattern is Shell and Seaweed, modeled after Wedgwood patterns.

Among the most valued pieces are those where swan finials appear atop a cheese bell, a sardine box and a small paperweight.

TIPS FOR IDENTIFYING MANUFACTURER'S MARKS:

- Almost all Etruscan Majolica is clearly marked, with an English-style monogram in the center of two concentric circles.

- Markings on English Majolica may include the name of the factory and the English registry mark. The lozenge-shaped registry mark indicates the date of the patent registration, there to protect the design for three years.

- Minton, George Jones and Wedgwood marks include a three- or four-digit number corresponding to the number of the piece in the pattern books.

- Minton and Wedgwood also have date-code symbols to indicate the exact date of manufacture of each piece, even if it was a repetition of an earlier piece.

- Majolica from James Carr's New York City Pottery was unmarked, but for identification purposes there is a photograph of his display from the 1876 Centennial.

- The great ceramists also may have signed their pieces, such as Paul Comolera on the Minton peacock.

- Because some artists worked for several firms, (such as Hughes Protat, who did work for Minton, Wedgwood and T.C. Brown-Westhead Moore), identification of the firm cannot be made by the name of the artist alone.

Clubs

•Majolica International Society
1275 First Ave., Suite 103, New York, NY 10021-5601

Publications

Majolica: A Complete History and Illustrated Survey by Marilyn G. Karmason with Joan B. Stacke (Harry N. Abrams, 1989)

Majolica by Nicholas M. Dawes (Crown Publishing, 1990)

Majolica Pottery: An Identification and Value Guide by Mariann Katz-Marks (Collector Books, 1986)

The Collector's Encyclopedia of Majolica by Mariann Katz-Marks (Collector Books, 1992)

Victorian Majolica by Leslie Bockol (Schiffer Publishing, 1996)

Maiolica: American & European Wares by Jeffrey B. Snyder and Leslie Bockol (Schiffer Publishing, 1994)

Contributor to this section: Marilyn Karmason, 449 East 68th St., New York, NY 10021.

Cabbage-shaped mayonnaise bowl, 5", underplate 6-3/4", green.

MARBLES

Small, spherical marbles have been played with as early as ancient Egypt. Today, collectors avidly seek colorful marbles, both handmade and machine-made.

Handmade marbles are individually made by craftsmen. Those most sought by collectors are those produced in Germany during the late 19th century and early 20th century. German-made marbles represented the bulk of the marble market until the early 1920s. Handmade marbles can be distinguished by a pontil — a rough spot at the bottom of the marble where it was sheared off its glass cane.

Handmade marbles are generally more valuable than machine-made marbles.

Machine-made marbles are considered collectible; some of the major manufacturers include Akro Agate, Marble King, Peltier and Christensen Glass.

General Guidelines: Marbles still in original packaging (box, bag, etc.) are most valuable. Also collectible are marble-related items like tournament award pins, instruction sheets or contest cards.

Especially collectible are marbles depicting cartoon characters like Popeye, Betty Boop or Little Orphan Annie.

Four major factors determine the value of a marble — type, size, condition and visual appeal. Marbles are characterized by many colorful names, such as Latticinio, Lutz, Mica, Onionskin and Clambroth. Each identifies a distinct design. One example is a sulfide — a clear glass marble with a tiny figure inside.

Any damage to the surface of a marble will decrease its value. Bigger marbles aren't necessarily more valuable than smaller ones. But generally, larger handmade marbles are better than smaller ones. Machine-made marbles are usually under one inch in diameter. Particular types of marbles may be rare in larger sizes and, therefore, command a premium price.

Brightly-colored marbles or those with symmetrical or intricate designs generally command higher prices.

Clubs
•Marble Collectors Society of America (MCSA)
 P.O. Box 222, Trumbull, CT 06611

Publications
Marbles: Identification and Price Guide by Robert Block (MCSA, 1996)

Monkey sulphide.

Swirl-ribbon marble, red, white, blue, yellow swirl on outside interior; 2-1/2" in diameter.

VALUE LINE

Ranges listed are for individual marbles in Good to Mint condition.

Comic character picture marbles, Peltier Glass .... $25-$100

Corkscrews, Akro Agate .... $5-$25

Peppermint swirls .... $30-$100

World's Best Guineas, boxed set, Christensen
    Agate $10,000

Sulphides .... $30-$100

Clambroths (opaque base w/colored swirls) .... $30+

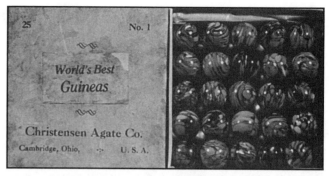

Christensen Agate was a popular marble manufacturer during the 1920s. This boxed set of colorful World's Best Guineas is valued at $11,000.

Original box of tri-color Agates, Akro Agate Co.

A variety of collectible marbles.

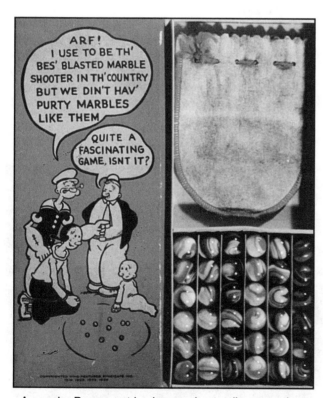

A popular Popeye set is always a best seller at auction.

Sulphide marble.

MARX PLAY SETS

For many dedicated collectors, the words "Marx" and "play set" go together. If you ask any American youngster who grew up during the 1950s or 1960s, play sets may have very well been invented by Louis Marx. His modern version of an age-old toy — and the success it enjoyed — still stands as a fitting tribute to the incredible marketing and manufacturing talents the toy king possessed, along with his whimsical genius.

Typical Marx play sets include small-scale buildings (usually made of lithographed tin), plastic figures and small realistic accessories, all of which combine to help bring these miniature worlds — from a farm to the Alamo to Roy Rogers' ranch — to life. Deft use of mass production and mass marketing through chain stores kept Marx toys affordable while maintaining high standards of quality. A master at producing new toys utilizing the same basic components, Marx knew that existing parts could be slightly modified to accompany whatever newly lithographed buildings were created from their standard stock. Part of his successful strategy also included using popular TV and movie tie-ins to breathe new life into existing products.

General Guidelines: A Mint in Box play set is one that is untouched and unassembled in its original box. Excellent condition means a complete set, but the buildings are assembled and the box may be worn or damaged. Good condition means the play set exhibits wear and may have a few minor pieces missing. Play sets command the most money in Mint in Box condition, but collectors also look for individual pieces and even empty boxes to complete sets. To command top value, boxes should be in prime condition with clean graphics and no defects like tears, creases or fading.

VALUE LINE

Values listed are for sets in Excellent condition in original box. Since sets were made in many variations (number of pieces, etc.), price ranges are listed for some sets.

Miniature Sets
101 Dalmatians, 1961	$300
Fairykins TV Scenes	$150
Ludwig Von Drake, 1962	$100
Quick Draw McGraw	$115
Sleeping Beauty, 1961	$175

Regular Play Sets
Battle of Iwo Jima, 1964, large set	$240
Battle of the Blue & Gray, centennial edition	$700
Battleground sets	$90-$250
Ben Hur sets, 1959	$500-$1,000
Cape Canaveral Missile Center, 1959	$100-$250
Daniel Boone Wilderness Scout, 1964	$225

Modern Service Station. 1966, Marx, $105 Excellent.

I.G.Y. Arctic Satellite Base, 1959, Marx, $700 Excellent.

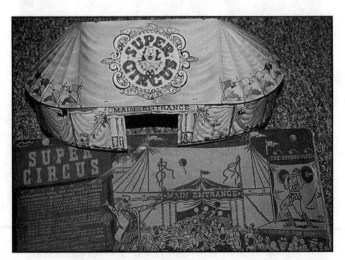

Super Circus, 1952, Marx, $290 Excellent.

Fort Apache sets .... $50-$400
Gunsmoke Dodge City, 1960 .... $1,200
Johnny Ringo Western Frontier $1,800
Johnny Tremain Revolutionary War $1,200
Medieval Castle .... $95-$300
Prehistoric Times .... $75-$200
Prince Valiant Castle, 1955 .... $300
Revolutionary War .... $300-$500
Rin Tin Tin at Fort Apache .... $500-$700
Roy Rogers Rodeo Ranch .... $100-$700
Roy Rogers Western Town .... $100-$500
Sears Store $1,200
Tales of Wells Fargo .... $100-$450
U.S. Armed Forces Training Center .... $150-$300
Walt Disney's Zorro .... $500-$700
Western Town .... $200-$800
White House and Presidents $40
Wyatt Earp Dodge City $450

Medieval Castle Set.

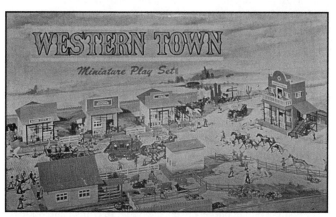

Western Town, miniature set.

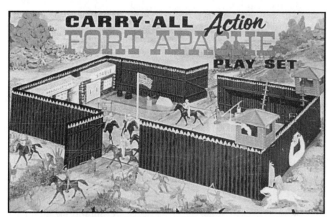

This Fort Apache set came in a metal carry case.

MATCHBOOK COVERS

For almost half a century (1920s-1960s), matchbooks were the single most widely used form of American advertising. They were inexpensive, easy to produce and, best of all, free. Matchbooks were given away at tobacco counters and in vending machines. Advertisers could have their own design on a matchcover or merely rent space.

History: Although the discovery and use of fire dates back to the dawn of humankind, it wasn't until 1827 that it was conveniently captured and packaged in the form of matches and matchbooks. That year, English druggist John Walker marketed a sulphur-tipped splint called a "Congreves." Explosive in nature, these first matches were dangerous to handle.

Joshua Pusey is credited with making the first matchbook in 1894. Originally for his personal use, the Philadelphia-based lawyer sold the patent rights to the Diamond Match Company for $4,000 two years later.

The first commercial matchbook owes its existence to the Mendelson Opera Company which, in 1895, hand-decorated some 100 blank matchbooks for one evening's performance.

Soon after this, Diamond salesman Harry Traute sold the commercial advertising idea to three major companies including Pabst beer and Bull Durham tobacco. Sensing a future for this new kind of advertising, chewing gum magnat William Wrigley placed an order for one billion matchbooks. And with a flash akin to those explosive first matches, matchbook covers ignited American advertising.

Political, Nixon for President, $5-$8.

General Guidelines: Matchbook covers come in many different sizes and are commonly named for the number of matchsticks they contain. The standard vending machine size, which contains 20 matches, is called a "20-strike." Other common sizes include a 10-strike, 30-strike and 40-strike. Special match sizes made for specific purposes include the Midget (a reduced standard 20-strike with 14 sticks), the 24-strike, the Giant (an oversized flat-stick matchbook) and popular souvenir attraction matchbooks including the 100-strike, 200-strike and 240-strike.

As with any paper collectibles, condition is the most important factor. Matchcovers are collected whether they are used or unused. Mint condition means no edge dings, creases, nicks or blemishes of any kind. A single scratch mark on an otherwise pristine full matchbook can reduce its value by 50 to 75 percent. Watch out for glue or adhesive marks on the insides of matchbook covers, as well as faded corner marks.

Most matchbook covers now considered valuable were made prior to 1960, featuring a striker on the front. Three broad areas of matchbook covers include pictorial covers (celebrities, colleges, city views, souvenir views, etc.), advertising covers or general covers (clubs, associations, public agencies, anniversaries, etc.).

Colorful or graphically-pleasing covers are most desirable to collectors. Early matchbook covers were printed with four- and five-color processes, a printing art form which has been lost in today's collector market.

Generally, values of matchbook covers do not suffer considerably when the matchsticks are removed. The one major exception are covers which feature printing or pictures on the matches themselves. These should always be left intact to retain maximum collectibility and value.

Flattened matchbook covers are easier to collect and trade by mail. For the fire-protection minded, this is probably a safer storage method as well. But purists abound, and many collectors would not even consider removing a single match stick.

Most matchbook covers are worth mere pennies, but serious collectors' categories can sell for from $1 to $50 each and include patriotic, sports, WWII, railroads, airlines, beer, girlie pictures and national political themes.

Rare matchbook covers command hundreds of dollars. A copy of the 1927 Charles A. Lindbergh matchbook, used at a commemorative dinner upon Lindy's return, once brought $4,000 at auction.

Clubs

•The American Matchcover Collecting Club
P.O. Box 18481, Asheville, NC 28814
704-254-4487

Contributors to this section: Bill Retskin & John Williams, P.O. Box 18481, Asheville, NC 28814.

Abbreviations

10S: 10-Strike
12S: 12-Strike
20S: 20-Strike
24S: 24-Strike
30S: 30-Strike
40S: 40-Strike
100S: 100-Strike
240S: 240-Strike
1B: One Box
F: Front
B: Back
F/B: Front and back
FB: Full Book
FS: Front Striker
BS: Back Striker
FT: Flat (Salesman's sample)
MS: Mixed Strikers
U: Used or Struck
WS: Wooden Sticks (Book match)

VALUE LINE

Values listed are for matchcovers in Excellent to Mint condition. Most of the matchcovers shown are standard 20-strike; 30-strike examples are indicated by "30S."

Airlines

Alaska Airlines w/4-engine plane, "25 Years Serving Alaska,"30S ....$8-$12
Allegheny w/jet Custom Class, "We have a lot more going" ....$4-$7
Braniff Air, one from set of 12, 1963, "World's Finest" 30S ....$10-$15
British Caledonian Airways, lion shield ....$5-$8
Pan American, one of 15, 1957, '57-'58 calendar, 30S ....$12-$20
United Airlines w/logo, "Red Carpet Club," 30S ....$3-$6

Automobiles

Pontiac, one from set of 15, 1961 30S ....$3-$6
Dodge, one of four, 1967, trucks, 30S ....$6-$9
Brown & Bigelow Antique Cars, 1965, one of four (1910 Brush,1911 Stanley, 1915 Brewster, 1923 Haynes) ....$3-$6
The 1956 Chevrolet, Stauffer Chevrolet, Scranton, Pa. ..$5-$8

Beer

Canada's Finest Black Horse Ale w/logo ....$6-$9
Buckeye Beer, Toledo, Ohio, "It's Kraeusened" ....$6-$9
Falstaff, Cavalier w/stein ....$7-$10
Hamm's Beer, w/busty blonde holding tray ....$12-$16
Kingsbury Pale Beer w/logo, "Jim's Bar, Jefferson, Wis. ....$8-$12
Schmidt's City Club Beer, Jacob Schmidt Brewing Co., St. Paul ....$15-$20
White Crown Beer and Ale, Akron, Ohio ....$7-$9

Black-Themed

Connie's Inn, 48th & Broadway, two black entertainers ....$17-$22
Mammy's Shanty, Restaurant & Lounge, Atlanta ....$5-$8
Piccadilly, "We Win Their Favor ..." shows black child ....$25-$30
Uncle Remus Restaurant, Eatonton, Ga. ....$8-$12

Buses

Aztec Bus Lines for Charter ....$3-$6
Bowen Motor Coaches ....$8-$12
Lincoln Transit Co. ....$5-$8
Ride Mo-Ark Trailways ....$8-$12

Casinos

Atlantic City Claridge Casino, 30S ....$3-$6
Dunes Hotel and Country Club ....$4-$7
Royal Casino, 30S ....$4-$7
Showboat Hotel-Casino Bar & Restaurant, paddle-wheel boat, 30S ....$10-$15

Country Clubs

Bahia Corinthian Yacht Club, Corona Del Mar, yacht flag ....$3-$6
Club House, Corinthian Island, Tiburon, Calif., yacht flag ....$3-$6
Fairview CC, Elmswood, N.Y., crossed golf clubs & ball ....$4-$7
La Jolla Beach & Tennis Club, flag with seahorse logo $4-$7

Colleges/Universities

Bates College, Lewiston, Maine, w/crest Condita, " Oft times at night I light my pipe and dream of dear old Bates" ....$4-$7
Colby Junior College, New London, N.H. ....$3-$6
Long Beach State College, 1949 crest ....$4-$7
The University of New Hampshire, 1923 crest ....$4-$7
Colorado A&M Book Shop, dressed ram ....$5-$8

Diners

Caesar's Wind Gap Diner, Wind Gap, Pa., "Gateway to the Poconos," with dinner & mountains ....$8-$12
East Haven Diner, East Haven, Conn., with diner, clock ....$8-$12
Max Diner, Mansfield, Ohio, "3 Good Places to Eat" ..$5-$7
Paul's Diner, Secaucus, N.J. "Gateway to N.J. Turnpike" ....$8-$12
Triple XXX, Seattle, Wash., "Curb Service," photo of diner ....$8-$12

Features

The Airline Showbar, Chicago, airliner on each match stick .... $6-$9

Bell's Sea Food, Steaks, Norfolk, Va., produce on sticks .... $9-$14

Bradley's Covered Wagon, Great Neck, waitress on each bottle-shaped stick .... $15-$20

Cliff House at Seal Rocks, San Francisco, Seal Rocks across match sticks .... $12-$16

Sam Costanizo Shoe Repair, Cleveland, hat and shoes across match sticks .... $7-$10

Holmes Mens Wear, Ft. Wayne, Ind., style names on sticks .... $5-$8

The Italian Village, Los Angeles, nude across sticks $15-$20

Youngwear, New York, child on each stick .... $7-$10

Pin-up Girls

Atlas Set, one of five, 1975, 40S .... $10-$15

Brown & Bigelow Hilda Fat Girls, series of seven ... $27-$35

Mad Cap Maids Set #9, set of five, 1955 .... $7-$10

Maryland Merlin Girlie Set #2, set of five .... $15-$20

Superior Petty Set #3, set of five .... $10-$15

Starline Eng Set #3, set of six, 30S .... $4-$7

Superior Live Models Set #9A, set of four, 1976 .... $5-$8

Superior Thompson Set #3, set of five, 1955 .... $10-$15

Universal Titanoxer Set #1, 1953, set of six .... $15-$20

Native Americans

Apache Hotel, Las Vegas, "Gateway to Boulder Dam" $6-$9

The Chief Motel, Pocahontas, Iowa, "34 All-New Units" .... $4-$7

Devoe & Raynolds Co., Inc., Louisville, w/Indian in logo .... $4-$7

The Mohawk National Bank, Schenectady, N.Y., two feathered Indians .... $5-$8

Seneca Cocktail Lounge, Hotel Seneca, Rochester, N.Y. .... $5-$8

The Wal-A-Pai Courts, Kingman, Ariz., w/chief .... $8-$12

Military

Edwards Air Force Base NCO Club, w/wings .... $5-$8

Sandia Base Officers Open Mess, nuclear symbol .... $5-$8

Officers' Open Mess, Hickham AF Base, Hawaii ..... $15-$20

Ft. Sam Houston Officers' Open Mess .... $5-$8

Spokane Army Air Depot Exchange .... $5-$8

American Battles 1st Series, 1942 .... $3-$6

Clearfield Naval Supply Depot .... $3-$6

US Marine Corps, w/crest, "This match is for your cigarette/There is no match for a marine" .... $4-$7

Naval Training Center, Great Lakes, Ill., crest .... $4-$7

U.S.S. Fulton, w/ship's crest, "Service to Submarines .. $4-$7

U.S.S. Wharton, w/flag, U.S. Navy w/crest .... $4-$7

US Naval Operating Base, Norfolk, large "V" w/"Remember Pearl Harbor!" .... $7-$10

Miscellaneous

Lindbergh Cover, Lion Safety, Hotel Astor, (Type 1) .... $2,800-$4,000

Bullitt Jeans, matchcover, shaped like a bullet .... $8-$12

Kewpee Hamburg Shops, Grand Rapids, Mich., Kewpee baby holding match, "Strike up an acquaintance" $12-$16

Ex-Lax jingles, one of 12, 1936 .... $20-$25

Los Angeles Times, 1943, "Everybody's newspaper .. $8-$12

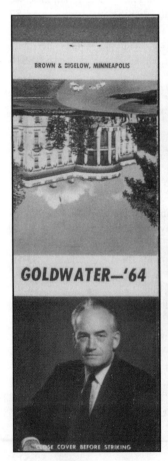

Political, Barry Goldwater campaign.

Sports, Detroit Tigers, $10-$15.

GOT A LIGHT?

Matchbooks weren't always given away. After the Depression, company advertising revenues plummeted, causing matchbook makers to feel the pinch. Attempting to remedy the situation, the Diamond Match Company (the world's largest matchbook manufacturer) produced matchbooks that did not feature advertising. Called Group 1, this category featured sports personalities and entertainers.

Issued in twos, fours, eights and packages of 16, these matchbooks were sold at dime stores, small grocery stores and souvenir shops. Baseball, football and hockey stars appeared on the sports series, which averaged a penny per book.

Early movie stars, along with NBC and CBS radio greats, comprised the entertainment series. Produced between 1933 and 1938, Group 1 matchbooks helped pull Diamond through Depression-era woes. Today, covers in the sports series sell for from $5 to $75; those in the entertainment series are valued at from $3 to $25.

Mennen for Men, 1953, one of six .... $3-$6

Reed's Butter Scotch, "Famous for Purity" .... $5-$8

Tootsie Rolls, "America's favorite chewy. . . ," with
boy and girl riding roll .... $6-$10

Parks and Recreation

Boystown, Father Flanagan's, Nebraska, w/monument $5-$8

Chequaga Falls, Montour Falls, N.Y., w/Indian
smoking pipe .... $4-$7

Our National Parks, Set of 12, Diamond Match .... $5-$8

The National Zoo Park Restaurant, Washington D.C. ... $3-$6

Patriotic

Bond Bread Set #2, 1943, set of 12 war planes ..... $130-$150

Bundles for Britain, 1941 .... $6-$9

Gold's Drug Stores, soldier, w/"He stands with
MacArthur, You stand behind him .... $4-$7

MacArthur, 1944, "I Shall Return" .... $125-$175

Political

Kennedy-Johnson Inauguration, 1961, Diamond
Match Co, 30S .... $8-$12

Nixon-Agnew Inauguration, 1969, Diamond, 30S ..... $7-$10

Bush for President, 1988, photo,30S .... $3-$6

Jimmy Carter, presidential seal30S .... $4-$7

I Like Ike, Sunflower Hotel, Abilene, Kansas .... $8-$12

JFK Presidential Museum & Library, 30S .... $12-$16

LBJ for the USA .... $8-$12

Nixon for President, "The Matchless Man," AFL-CIO . $5-$8

McGovern for President, 1972 .... $7-$10

Railroads

Bangor and Aroostook RR, 30S .... $7-$10

The Chessie Route, sleeping kitten .... $15-$20

Blue Streak Service, St. Louis Southwestern Railway .. $5-$8

MKT Katy RR, logo, Katy Lines Southwest, w/train ... $4-$7

Missouri Pacific Lines, "Route of the Eagles,"
"Dependable Freight Service" .... $5-$8

Norfolk & Western, "The Scenic Route" .... $4-$7

Rio Grande, "The Direct Central Transcontinental
Route" .... $5-$8

Southern Pacific Streamlined Daylights, colorful
Deco-type train .... $5-$8

Union Pacific RR, "Be Specific/Say Union Pacific"..... $5-$8

Western Maryland Railway, logo .... $5-$7

Ship Lines

American President Lines, flag w/"New York, California,
Orient Round the World via The Sunshine Route" . $5-$7

Carnival Cruise Lines, "The Fun Ships" .... $3-$6

Delta Line, w/ship & flag, "South America West
Africa via Delta Lines" .... $5-$8

Furness Lines, set of 6, 1964 .... $7-$10

Herreshof, Bristol, R.I., photo of torpedo boat .... $10-$15

NY and Cuba Mail Steamship Co., "All Expense
Cruises to Havana and Mexico/ Weekly Sailings" ... $5-$8

Shinnihon Line, w/flag .... $5-$8

Soda

7-Up, "Nothing Does It Like 7-Up/So Pure, So Good,
So Wholesome, " square 7-up logo .... $6-$9

A&W Root Beer, 5-cent logo, "This coupon good
for. . ." .... $5-$8

Blossom Brand Fruit Syrups, Brooklyn, w/fountain
and girl drinking, "Served at Better Fountains" ... $10-$15

Canada Dry, "Handy King Size Bottles, True Fruit
Flavors" .... $6-$9

Coca-Cola Bottling Works, Havre de Grace, Md., "Over
the River and Through the Woods," winter scene,
30S .... $7-$10

Drink Coca-Cola, w/round red logo, Santo Coca-Cola
Bottling, Japanese .... $10-$15

Hippo Size Carbonated Beverages, Alamo Bottling
Works, San Antonio, w/hippo .... $8-$12

Mr. Nibbs, World's Finest Mixers, Heinz Beverages,
Pittsburgh .... $4-$7

Girlie and advertising themes are popular with collectors.

COLLECTORS' ALERT

Reproductions are practically nonexistent since billions were made and given away free. Some fake matchbook covers (ones that were never produced) do exist, however. Conceived as a gag for Gaslight Productions, a real 30-strike matchbook cover was made for Presidential candidate Al Smith. But Smith's campaign ran long before 30-strike matchbook covers were ever invented.

Orange Crush, "Feel Fresh, Drink Orange-Crush"
Legion Community Hall, Forestville, Wis. .... $6-$9
Pepsi-Cola, logo, modern .... $3-$6
Drink Poland Water, w/fat bottle, South Poland,
Maine .... $6-$9
Saratoga Geyser Water, w/geyser .... $8-$12

Space
Apollo 12, Conrad, Gordon Bean, 30S .... $6-$9
Apollo 16, Young, Mattingly, Duke, April 16-27, 1972,
30Ss .... $8-$11
Neil Armstrong, "First Man on the Moon" set of 8,
40S .... $20-$25

Sports
Chicago White Sox 1955 .... $5-$8
Dean Chance, LA Dodgers, b/w photo .... $9-$14
Carl Hubbell, NY Giants .... $45-$60
Washington Senators, set of 10, 1960 .... $100-$145
Manny Almeida's Ringside Tap, Providence, R.I. ..... $12-$16
Jack Dempsey's on Broadway, 30S .... $4-$7
Abe Kaplan Sportsmen Cafe, Yermo, Calif. .... $10-$15
Papke's Rhythm Nite Club, Los Angeles .... $15-$20

Jack Sharkey's Ringside Bar, Boston .... $9-$14
Gene's Ringside Tavern, Trenton .... $8-$12
Sam Taub's Ringside Personalities .... $4-$7
Famous Redskins, 1st Federal Set .... $15-$20
Canadian Olympics, 1976, 30S .... $25-$30
Rose Parade, 1959, ABC TV, Quaker Oats, 30S .... $13-$16
Don Drysdale's Dug Out Whaler's Pub .... $25-$30
Stan Musial & Biggies Hotel, Resort and Restaurant . $8-$12
Johnny Unitas' Colt Lanes .... $8-$12
Detroit Tigers, 1952 .... $10-$15
Minnesota Twins Baseball Club, 1973 .... $10-$15
Oakland Raiders, 1973 .... $12-$16

Theater / Film
Gone with The Wind, 1967, 40S .... $9-$14
How The West Was Won .... $6-$9
Fabian Theatres, "The Best Show in Town" .... $6-$9
BS Odeon, "The finest in theater entertainment" .... $4-$7
Universal City Studios, "The Entertainment Center of the
World w/logo .... $4-$7

World's Fairs
1933 Century of Progress .... $35-$50
1935-36 California-Pacific Exposition .... $12-$16
1936 Texas Centennial .... $14-$17
1939-40 Golden Gate Int'l Expo .... $4-$7
1939 New York World's Fair .... $4-$7
1940 New York World's Fair .... $3-$6
1964 New York World's Fair .... $4-$7
1967 Montreal Expo .... $5-$8
1968 Hemisfair, set of eight .... $3-$6

Sports, Jack Dempsey's
on Broadway, $4-$7.

MILITARIA

The practice of collecting militaria is centuries old—as old as the first Crusaders who returned with a Saracen sword to hang on the castle wall. Every war has more finely-honed the time-honored soldier's tradition of souvenir hunting.

Some souvenir hunters and collectors have taken a mass-market approach to collecting, helping themselves to anything that was not nailed down—as well as many things that were—providing yet another interpretation of the phrase "the spoils of war." Militaria collecting is not confined to enemy souvenirs; it also represents the perpetuation of a historical record of items used by American, as well as allied, forces.

History: During and after every war, there has been a brisk trade in militaria not only among the participants, but civilian collectors as well. For instance, the aftermath of the Revolutionary War found almost every household with a flintlock rifle and powder horn hanging over the mantel.

Following the Civil War, Scotsman Francis Bannerman, who had recently emigrated to the U.S., founded a war-surplus empire by purchasing at auction all the Union and captured Confederate war materials he could find. Bannerman also opened a retail/warehouse facility at 505 Broadway in New York City. Long a mecca for the militaria collector, many items were available for what amounted to "small change," opening the field to to many collectors.

General Guidelines: As in most fields of collecting, original condition is of paramount importance, especially in the case of uniforms, headgear and firearms. Those pieces that are in excellent, working condition, with the fewest marks, blemishes or moth holes will command the highest prices.

Firearms: In firearms collecting, weapons must bear matching numbers, show little wear or use, and retain all original markings and parts, such as cleaning rods, slings, etc. Beware of rarer pieces that have been repaired or reconstructed by a competent gunsmith. Look for specimens that were made in lesser numbers; these will command the highest prices.

Publications
Gun List, 700 E. State St., Iola, WI, 54990

The Shotgun News, Box 669, Hastings, NE, 68902

CADA Gun Journal, Blue Book Pub., 1 Appletree Sq., Minneapolis, MN, 55425

Man at Arms, P.O. Box 460, Lincoln, RI, 02865

Headgear: Make sure all parts, especially straps, helmet plates, liners and trim, are original to the piece. German spike-top helmets are particularly collectible, and, for the more exotic specimens, command outstanding prices. These helmets are difficult to find in original condition, with most lacking one or more of the original components, such as strap or trim.

Steel helmets, developed during World War I by the warring nations, are highly collectible due to the many different styles and experimental models. The French Adrian helmet of 1915 was used by many countries and individualized by differing helmet plates. German steel helmets from World War I through World War II offer a field of collecting unto themselves, with numerous design variations over the life of the helmet's use. Many helmets have been repainted by dealers or collectors to make them look original.

Collectors can still find headgear from the Revolutionary War, the Napoleanic Wars and earlier campaigns. As always, condition and scarcity determine the selling price. It stands to reason that not many cloth and fabric items have survived 200 to 300 years.

Publications
The History of the German Steel Helmet, 1916-1945 Ludwig Baer. R. James Bender Publications, San Jose CA. 1985.

Pickelhauben (Spiked Helmets), Erik Johansson. H.S.M. Publications, Independence, MO. 1982.

Militaria, Jan K. Kube. Schiffer Military History, Atglen, PA. 1987.

Uniforms: Over the years uniforms have been personalized with patches, swatches, epaulettes and insignia for reasons of accomplishment and self pride. Uniforms from all time periods are collectible.

Uniforms, however, suffer damage from wear, storage and moths. Seams and bindings should be intact for highest value.

Clubs
•The Company of Military Historians
Westbrook, CT 06498

•Military and Police Uniform Association
Louis Wendruck
P.O. Box 69A04, West Hollywood, CA 90069

Medals and Decorations

Military medals, orders and decorations have been eagerly sought by collectors for hundreds of years. In many cases, these awards are outstanding examples of the jeweler's art, designed to exemplify the devotion of soldiers to a higher duty. Campaign medals are usually designed to represent a particular battle, or campaign, covering a particular period in time. Usually such medals will bear a representation that will readily identify the campaign involved.

Orders and decorations for bravery, long service and military merit are usually of a higher quality than campaign medals, with the more rarely awarded medals often surpassing the quality of fine jewelry. Enamels, diamonds, brilliants and other precious gems are to be found in the orders of some countries.

Most collectors prefer to limit their area of collecting to a particular country or group of countries involved in the same conflict; some become so finite as to collect only those medals that were awarded to members of a particular regiment.

It is important to build a reference library covering the subjects of one's interest. An important source of information for the collector is the Orders and Medals Society of America, a group of collectors who have succeeded in maintaining high standards of professionalism and honesty amongst dealers and collectors.

Military insignia and badge collectors have proliferated over the last 50 years, with scarcity driving up prices that were quite modest after World War II. The American Society of Military Insignia Collectors (ASMIC) was formed as a focus point for these collectors, and its ranks have steadily grown over the years.

Publications

Military Medals, Orders, and Decorations to the beginning of World War Two, Ball and Peters, Schiffer Publishing, 1995.

Orders and Decorations, Werlich, 3rd edition, Quaker Press, 1973.

British Army Campaign Medals, Robert Ball, Antiques and Collectibles Books, 1996.

Orders, Decorations, Medals and Badges of the Third Reich, Littlejohn and Dodkins. Bender Publishing, 1968.

American War Medals and Decorations, Kerrigan, Viking Press, 1963.

Equipment

This category includes webbed equipment, footgear, survival equipment and load carrying equipment, as well as the personal kit that made life bearable for the fighting man. This equipment differed from country to country, and from war to war.

As perishable as this type of equipment tends to be, specimens from the Revolutionary War and every war since can still be found, in relatively good condition.

Vehicles

Collectors also seek original and restored military vehicles, including everything from jeeps and Crossley tenders to deactivated armored fighting vehicles and tanks.

One of the larger organizations devoted to maintaining interest in old fighting vehicles is the Military Vehicle Preservation Association of Independence, Mo.

Foreign military vehicles appear on the U.S. market with regular frequency, including German half-tracks, British Ferret and Saracen Armoured Cars, as well as general utility vehicles, command cars, ambulances and many others.

Contributor to this section: Robert Ball

VALUE LINE

Firearms

Values shown are for weapons in Excellent condition.

M1795 Type I US Springfield Flintlock Musket, dated 1799	$2,600-$4,500
M1816 French Charleville Flintlock Musket	$1,800
British Land Pattern Musket	$1,800
British Brunswick P1837 Musket	$900
US M1842 Musket	$900
French M1853 Musket	$500
US M1855 Rifled Carbine	$2,700
British Pattern P1861 Sergeant's Rifle (Confederate)	$1,000
US M1870 Rolling Block Standard Navy Rifle	$700
Turkish Peabody-Martini Rifle	$700
German M1871 Mauser Rifle	$400
US M1873 Trapdoor Carbine	$2,200
US M1884 Trapdoor Rifle	$500
German M1871/84 Mauser Rifle	$600
German M1888 Mauser and Commission Rifle	$150
US M1896 Krag-Jorgensen Rifle	$400
US M1898 Krag-Jorgensen Rifle	$400
US M1898 Krag-Jorgensen Carbine, 26" barrel	$2,200
German M1898 Mauser Rifle	$300
British SMLE Mk.III Rifle	$125
US M1903 Springfield Rifle	$400
US M1903 A3 Springfield Rifle	$350
US M1917 Rifle (Enfield)	$175
German K98k Carbine	$350
US MI Garand Rifle, rebuilt, any manufacturer	$400

Headgear

Prices listed are for pieces in Very Good original condition, with original removable parts, such as chin straps, helmet plates and buttons.

French M1915 Adrian Steel Helmet, Russian plate	$400
French M1915 Adrian Steel Helmet, Engineer's plate	$50
Italian WWI Adrian-style Steel Helmet, Bersaglieri	$75
British WWI Steel Helmet	$25
German leather Uhlan Helmet	$1,500
German M1916 Steel Helmet, plain	$60
German Prussian EM Spike-top Helmet	$275
German M1916 Camouflaged Steel Helmet	$125
Siamese M1915 Adrian Steel Helmet	$75
Mexican M1926 Adrian Steel Helmet	$100
Spanish M1926 Steel Helmet	$25
M1821 Pattern Bell Crown Shako, "Massachusetts Militia"	$1,200
Civil War period Infantry Kepi	$400
Indian Wars Cavalry Kepi, c.1883	$500
WWI US Aviator's overseas cap, French made	$200
WWI US 90th Div. Steel Helmet	$125
German Waffen SS EM Visored Hat	$1,700
German M35 Steel Helmet, Army	$300
German Allgemeine SS Parade Helmet	$1,600
German M42 Steel Helmet, Army	$300
WWII US Steel Helmet	$20
US Kevlar "Fritz"-style Helmet	$75

Insignia, Metal and Cloth

US Civil War Infantry Sergeant's stripes, pair	$50
US Civil War Massachusetts Militia Shako Plate	$40
US Indian Wars Farrier's cloth insignia	$20
US Spanish American War period Medical Department collar devices, bronze, pair	$15
US WWI Air Service Collar device, Officer, bronze, with silver propeller	$40
US WWI Tank Corps Collar Device, 1st pattern	$90

US WWI 32nd Division Shoulder Patch $20
US WWI GHQ Shoulder Patch $30
US WWII AAF Pilot's Winged badge, "Sterling" $50
US WWII CBI Patch, siver bullion, hand embroidered.... $70
US c.1980 Mixed lot, 20 pieces Army Shoulder patch
    insignia $50
Prussian Infantry Lt.'s shoulder insignia, c.1890, pair $60
Prussian WWI Machine Gunner's Sleeve Insignia $90
Japanese WWII Superior Private collar insignia $15
German WWII "RLB" Sleeve Insignia $50
German WWII Army "Afrika Korps" cuff title $200

Medals, Insignia, Badges

Prices listed are for items in Fine condition, with original ribbons and no repairs.

US Civil War Medal, Army, boxed $175
US Indian Wars Medal, named $250
US Sampson Medal, named to Marine $700
US Cuban Pacification Medal $35
US First Haitian Campaign Medal, named $90
US WWI Victory Medal, bar "FRANCE" $35
US WWII Purple heart, named to KIA, Tarawa $700
US WWII European Theater of Operations Medal $10
US WWII Bronze Star $15
US WWII Distinguished Flying Cross $20
US Korean War Service Medal $10
US Vietnam Service Medal $10
US Gulf War Service Medal $15
Imperial German WWI Iron Cross, II Cl $25
Imperial Baden War Service Medal $25
Imperial Bavarian Order of St. Michael, silver and blue
    enamel $300
Imperial Hesse WWI Bronze Bravery Medal $60
Imperial Black Army Wound Badge $25
German WWII Iron Cross I Cl., PB $60
German WWII "East Front" Medal $25
German WWII War Service Cross, II Cl $25
Serbian WWI Obolitch Gold Bravery Medal $125
Japanese WWII Red Cross Medal $40
Italian WWII Campaign of Liberation Medal, 1943-45 ... $25
French Legion of Honor, Knight's Grade $90
French WWII Croix de Guerre, bronze, w/star $35

Military Vehicles

Prices listed are for vehicles in restored, operating condition.

US Renault FT17 Tank $30,000
US WWII Jeep $5,000
US WWII M3A2 Half-Track $9,000
US M1941 Chevrolet Staff Car $6,000
US Stuart "Honey" Light Tank $18,000
German WWII Volkswagen $6,000
German Post-WWII Czech-built Sd Kfz 251 Half
    Track $12,000
British 1951 Ferret MkII Armored Car $8,000
British Saracen Armored Command Car $8,000

Swords, Knives

Prices listed are based on items in Excellent original condition.

Civil War Union Presentation Staff and Field Officer's
    Sword, German, inscribed $6,000

Civil War Union Non-regulation German engraved
    Officer's Sword $600
Civil War Bowie Knife, believed Confederate $500
Civil War Bowie Knife, Union, elliptical crossguard $600
C.1880 Militia Officer's Sword, Knight's head pommel $125
US M1902 Army Officer's Sword $200
US M1904 Hospital Corps Knife $250
US WWI Trench Fighting Knife, knuckle bow,
    triangular blade $100
US WWI Trench Fighting Knife, Mk II, knuckle duster
    grip $175
US WWII Marine Corps Fighting Knife, "K-Bar" $175
WWII MI Carbine Bayonet, "Camillus" $50
French WWI field-made Trench Fighting Knife $75
Imperial German Infantry Hanger, c.1850 .... $100
Imperial Saxon Infantry Officer's Sword, engraved and
    inscribed. $750
Imperial M98/05 Sawtooth Bayonet $75
Hitler Youth Knife $60
SA Dagger $225
Labor Corps Hewer $250
Engraved Dress Bayonet $200
First Model Luftwaffe Dress Sword $700
Italian WWII Air Force Officer's Sword $200
Japanese WWII Cavalry Sword $200
Russian Imperial Shaska $600
British c.1880 Socket Bayonet $75
Austrian M95 Bayonet $35
Spanish M1913 Simpson Bayonet $25

Uniforms

Prices listed are for uniforms free of moth holes, repairs and/or replaced insignia.

US Revolutionary War Period Tail Coat, Private
    Soldier $4,000
US War of 1812 Naval Officer's Uniform set,
    complete $4,000
US Mexican War period Officer's undress jacket $2,500
British Officer's Mess Jacket, Indian Mutiny $1,600
German Hussar Officer's Dress Jacket, c.1870s $900
French Lancer's Tunic, Mexican Expedition, c.1867 ..... $800
US Civil War Period Artillery Officer's Mess Jacket $600
US Spanish-American War Rough Rider's Tunic, EM... $400
German SW Africa Schutz-Trupp Tunic $700
WWI French Poilu Uniform, complete $500
WWI German Infantry Tunic, EM $300
WWI US Officer Complete Uniform, North Russia
    Expedition $800
WWII Paratroop Uniform, 101st AB, complete field
    outfit $1,000
WWII US Officer Class A Uniform $150
German WWII 1st Sgt. Infantry, Field Tunic $400
Polish WWII Infantry Uniform, complete $800
Japanese WWII Naval Landing Force Field Uniform,
    complete $500

MODEL KITS

Model kits, usually plastic or resin kits that require assembly, have long been popular toys, particularly for boys. They have recently gained a new following among older collectors seeking to recapture a treasured part of their youth.

Vehicles of every kind have been reproduced in kit form and are sought by collectors. But 1960s kits featuring monsters and other popular movie, TV and science fiction characters bring top dollar.

History: Prior to the figural kit (kits based on popular characters) boom in the 1960s, most model kits were fashioned after vehicles. The first plastic model kits were produced just before the start of World War II. But it wasn't until after the war ended that plastic kit building really began to take hold as a serious hobby. Various automobiles, aircraft and ships all became subject matter for the miniature replicas made popular by such companies as Aurora, AMT, Revell, Monogram, MPC and Lindberg.

Scale for vehicles — ranging from cars to boats to airplanes — varied from one manufacturer to another and from line to line. But models generally fell into several popular scales, with 1:43 (1/43 of the vehicle's actual size) being the smallest and 1:8 the largest.

During the 1980s, figure kits enjoyed a resurgence as new large-scale kits of rather limited production runs were being made in vinyl and resin. Often called "garage kits," these kits bear watching as their limited-run nature will likely translate into future collectibility.

Trends: Trends in model kit collecting follow cultural trends. Figural kits of characters have seen their popularity rise and wane with the changing times as well. Collectors are intent on owning a miniature piece of pop culture representing their favorite personalities, from the ever-popular mop-topped Beatles to the menacing *Star Wars* bounty hunter Boba Fett.

Vehicles of every kind have been reproduced in kit form for over 40 years and are still sought by collectors. Model car kits in particular have seen some price increases during the last few years.

While most collectors would not recommend speculating in car models as an investment vehicle, even relatively recent kits are appreciating in value. Eager engines are revving at the gate as many collectors are realizing the worth of unassembled, Mint in Box kits.

Due to the high premiums and prices placed on unbuilt car kits, a significant market has been developing for built-up cars. If an older model car kit is built well, not painted and not otherwise customized, it can fetch as much as $150.

General Guidelines: The most sought-after kits today are figure and character kits produced in the 1960s. The most valuable kits are those based on Universal Monsters like Frankenstein and the Mummy, Godzilla and science fiction characters. The key to model kit collectibility is the box. Without the box, kits are virtually worthless, except for some very rare titles. The attractively illustrated boxes are so vital, in fact, that even empty boxes have sold for hundreds of dollars.

To command top prices, kits should remain unassembled, sealed in interior bags, and still have instruction sheets. But assembled kits may have some value — Universal monsters, science fiction and superhero characters are sure bets.

Clubs
- International Figure Kit Club
  Box 201, Sharon Center, OH 44274

- Model Car Collectors Association
  5113 Sugar Loaf Drive, S.W. Roanoke, VA 24018

- Dinosaur Toy & Model Collecting Club
  145 Bayline Circle, Folsom, CA 95630

Angel Fink, 1965, Revell, $100 Near Mint.

COLLECTOR ALERT

Watch for reissues. Many reissued kits are packaged in original boxes, complete with an original copyright date, but may be clearly marked with an updated copyright. While the basic kit remains the same, the box art often changes with other reissues.

Beware of box art reproduced with color laser printers! It may look brighter or grainier than originals.

VALUE LINE

Price ranges listed are for model kits in Near Mint to Mint condition in original box.

Addar

Caesar, Planet of the Apes, 1974	$40-$45
Cornelius, Planet of the Apes, 1974	$30-$35
Dr. Zaius, Planet of the Apes, 1974	$25-$30
Dr. Zira, Planet of the Apes, 1974	$25-$30
General Aldo, Planet of the Apes	$25-$30
General Ursus, Planet of the Apes	$30-$35
Jailwagon, Planet of the Apes, 1975	$40-$45
Jaws diorama	$50-$60
Stallion & Soldier, Planet of the Apes, 1974	$75-$100
Treehouse, Planet of the Apes, 1975	$40-$45

Airfix

Anne Boleyn, 1974	$15-$20
Black Prince, 1973	$25-$30
Boy Scout, 1965	$15-$20
Charles I, 1965	$20-$25
Henry VIII, 1973	$8-$10
James Bond and Odd Job	$65-$100
James Bond's Aston Martin DB-5	$200-$225
Julius Caesar, 1973	$25-$30
Monkeemobile, 1967	$240-$275
Queen Elizabeth I, 1980	$15-$20
Queen Victoria, 1976	$15-$20
Richard I, 1965	$25-$30
Yeoman of the Guard, 1978	$8-$10

AMT

Bigfoot, 1978	$60-$75
Cliff Hanger, 1960s	$10-$15
Drag-U-La, Munsters, 1965	$200-$225
Flinstones Rock Crusher, 1974	$50-$60
Flintstones Sports Car, 1974	$55-$65
Girl from U.N.C.L.E. Car, 1974	$250-$300
Graveyard Ghoul Duo, Munsters, 1970	$100-$125
KISS Custom Chevy Van, 1977	$50-$60
Laurel & Hardy '27 T Roadster, 1976	$50-$60
Laurel & Hardy '27 T Touring Car, 1976	$50-$60
Man from U.N.C.L.E. Car, 1966	$175-$200
Monkeemobile	$55-$65
Mr. Spock, 1973	$125-$150
Munsters Koach, 1964	$150-$175
My Mother The Car, 1965	$35-$40
Sonny & Cher Mustang	$250-$300
Threw'd Dude, 1960s	$10-$15
Touchdown?, 1960s	$10-$15
UFO Mystery Ship	$60-$75
USS Enterprise Bridge, Star Trek, 1975	$25-$30
USS Enterprise, Star Trek, 1966	$125-$150
USS Enterprise w/lights, Star Trek, 1967	$200-$250

Aurora

Addams Family Haunted House, 1964	$750-$800
American Astronaut, 1967	$60-$75
American Buffalo, 1964	$20-$25
American Buffalo, reissue, 1972	$12-$15
Apache Warrior on Horse, 1960	$300-$450
Aramis, The Three Musketeers, 1958	$75-$100
Aston Martin Super Spy Car	$150-$200
Athos, The Three Musketeers, 1958	$75-$100
Banana Splits Banana Buggy, 1969	$400-$500
Batboat, 1968	$400-$450
Batcycle, 1967	$350-$400
Batman, 1964	$200-$250
Batman, Comic Scenes, 1974	$40-$60
Batmobile, 1966	$275-$325
Batplane, 1967	$200-$250
Black Bear and Cubs, 1962	$30-$40
Black Bear and Cubs, reissue, 1969	$20-$25
Black Fury, 1958	$25-$30
Black Fury, reissue, 1969	$13-$15
Black Knight, 1956	$30-$35
Black Knight, reissue, 1963	$13-$15
Blackbeard, 1965	$200-$225
Blue Knight, 1956	$35-$50

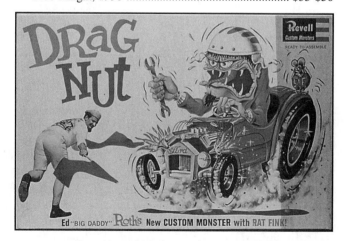

Drag Nut, 1963, Revell, $50 Near Mint.

Frankenstein, 1983, Monogram, $30 Near Mint.

Blue Knight, reissue, 1963	$17-$20
Bond, James, 1966	$325-$450
Bride of Frankenstein, 1965	$650-$750
Brown, Jimmy, 1965	$150-$175
Canyon, Steve, 1958	$175-$250
Captain Action, 1966	$275-$300
Captain America, 1966	$250-$300
Captain America, Comic Scenes, 1974	$100-$125
Captain Kidd, 1965	$70-$80
Cave Bear, 1971	$35-$40
Chinese Girl, 1957	$20-$25
Chinese Mandarin, 1957	$25-$30
Chinese Mandarin & Girl, 1957	$200-$300
Chitty Chitty Bang Bang, 1968	$85-$100
Confederate Raider, 1959	$300-$350
Creature From The Black Lagoon, 1963	$325-$400
Creature From The Black Lagoon, Glow Kit, 1969	$175-$200
Creature From The Black Lagoon, Glow Kit, 1972	$100-$125
Creature, Monsters of Movies, 1975	$200-$225
Cro-Magnon Man, 1971	$30-$45
Cro-Magnon Woman, 1971	$25-$35
Crusader, 1959	$150-$200
D'Artagnan, The Three Musketeers, 1966	$150-$175
Dr. Deadly, 1971	$70-$80
Dr. Deadly's Daughter, 1971	$65-$75

Dr. Jekyll as Mr. Hyde, 1964	$250-$350
Dr. Jekyll, Glow Kit, 1969	$100-$150
Dr. Jekyll, Glow Kit, 1972	$65-$80
Dr. Jekyll, Monster Scenes, 1971	$100-$125
Dr. Jekyll, Monsters of Movies, 1975	$60-$70
Dracula, 1962	$225-$300
Dracula's Dragster, 1966	$350-$400
Dracula, Glow Kit, 1969	$100-$150
Dracula, Glow Kit, 1972	$60-$75
Dracula, Monster Scenes, 1971	$150-$200
Dracula, Monsters of Movies, 1975	$200-$250
Dutch Boy, 1957	$25-$30
Dutch Boy & Girl, 1957	$200-$300
Dutch Girl, 1957	$20-$25
Flying Sub, 1968	$175-$200
Flying Sub, reissue, 1975	$85-$100
Forgotten Prisoner, 1966	$350-$400
Forgotten Prisoner, Frightning Lightning, 1969	$325-$450
Forgotten Prisoner, Glow Kit, 1969	$175-$200
Forgotten Prisoner, Glow Kit, 1972	$150-$175
Frankenstein, 1969	$210-$250
Frankenstein, Frightning Lightning, 1969	$375-$400
Frankenstein, Gigantic 1/5 scale, 1964	$1,000-$1,200
Frankenstein, Glow Kit, 1969	$65-$150
Frankenstein, Glow Kit, 1972	$50-$75
Frankenstein, Monster Scenes, 1971	$75-$100
Frankenstein, Monsters of Movies, 1975	$200-$250
Frankie's Flivver, 1964	$350-$400
Frog, Castle Creatures, 1966	$200-$250
Ghidrah, 1975	$260-$300
Giant Insect, Monster Scenes, 1971	$350-$400
Godzilla, 1964	$425-$500
Godzilla's Go-Cart, 1966	$2,500-$3,000
Godzilla, Glow-Kit, 1969	$250-$300
Godzilla, Glow Kit, 1972	$150-$175
Gold Knight on Horse, 1957	$250-$300
Gold Knight on Horse, 1965	$250-$275
Green Beret, 1966	$150-$175
Green Hornet "Black Beauty," 1966	$350-$450
Gruesome Goodies, 1971	$80-$100
Guillotine, 1964	$350-$400
Hanging Cage, 1971	$80-$100
Hercules, 1965	$250-$275
Hulk, Comic Scenes, 1974	$75-$85
Hulk, Original, 1966	$250-$300
Hunchback of Notre Dame, 1964	$250-$300
Hunchback of Notre Dame, Glow Kit, 1969	$100-$150
Hunchback of Notre Dame, Glow Kit, 1972	$65-$75
Indian Chief, 1957	$90-$100
Indian Chief & Squaw, 1957	$125-$150
Indian Squaw, 1957	$38-$45
Infantryman, 1957	$75-$100
Invaders UFO, 1968	$85-$100
Invaders UFO, 1975	$65-$75
Iwo Jima, 1966	$175-$200
Jesse James, 1966	$175-$200
Kennedy, John F., 1965	$100-$150
King Arthur, 1973	$125-$200

King Arthur of Camelot, 1967 .... $65-$75
King Kong, 1964 .... $350-$400
King Kong's Thronester, 1966 .... $850-$1,000
King Kong, Glow Kit, 1969 .... $200-$250
King Kong, Glow Kit, 1972 .... $150-$175
Land of the Giants Space Ship, 1968 .... $300-$350
Land of the Giants Diorama, 1968 .... $360-$400
Lone Ranger, 1967 .... $150-$175
Lone Ranger, Comic Scenes, 1974 .... $45-$50
Lost In Space, large kit w/chariot, 1966 .... $1,100-$1,300
Lost In Space, small kit, 1966 .... $800-$900
Lost In Space, The Robot, 1968 .... $600-$700
Mad Barber, 1972 .... $125-$150
Mad Dentist, 1972 .... $125-$150
Mad Doctor, 1972 .... $125-$150
Man From U.N.C.L.E., Illya Kurakin, 1966 .... $150- $175
Man From U.N.C.L.E., Napoleon Solo, 1966 .... $225-$250
Marine, 1959 .... $80-$100
Mays, Willie, 1965 .... $250-$300
Mexican Caballero, 1957 .... $100-$150
Mexican Senorita, 1957 .... $100-$150
Mod Squad Wagon, 1970 .... $125-$150
Monster Customizing Kit #1, 1964 .... $110-$125
Monster Customizing Kit #2, 1964 .... $150-$175
Moon Bus from 2001, 1968 .... $275-$300
Mr. Hyde, Monsters of Movies, 1975 .... $65-$75
Mr. Spock, 1972 .... $100-$125
Mummy, 1963 .... $275-$300
Mummy's Chariot, 1965 .... $400-$450
Mummy, Frightning Lightning, 1969 .... $300-$350
Mummy, Glow Kit, 1969 .... $100-$150
Mummy, Glow Kit, 1972 .... $50-$60
Munsters Living Room, 1964 .... $900-$1,200
Neanderthal Man, 1971 .... $40-$50
Neuman, Alfred E. (MAD Magazine), 1965 .... $250-$300
Nutty Nose Nipper, 1965 .... $175-$200
Odd Job, 1966 .... $350-$400
Pain Parlor, 1971 .... $100-$125
Pendulum, 1971 .... $65-$75
Penguin, 1967 .... $450-$500
Phantom of the Opera, 1963 .... $275-$300
Phantom of the Opera, Frightning Lightning,
    1969 .... $300-$350
Phantom of the Opera, Glow Kit, 1969 .... $100-$150
Phantom of the Opera, Glow Kit, 1972 .... $70-$80
Pilot USAF, 1957 .... $150-$175
Porthos, The Three Musketeers, 1958 .... $75-$100
Pushmi-Pullyu, Dr. Doolittle, 1968 .... $75-$85
Rat Patrol, 1967 .... $75-$90
Red Knight, 1957 .... $75-$100
Red Knight, 1963 .... $40-$50
Robin, 1966 .... $75-$90
Robin, Comic Scenes, 1974 .... $70-$85
Rodan, 1975 .... $300-$350
Roman Gladiator with sword, 1959 .... $150-$175
Roman Gladiator with trident, 1964 .... $150-$175
Roman Gladiators, 1959 .... $225-$250
Ruth, Babe, 1965 .... $250-$300

Sailor, U.S., 1957 .... $25-$30
Scotch Lad, 1957 .... $25-$30
Scotch Lad & Lassie, 1957 .... $85-$100
Scotch Lassie, 1957 .... $20-$25
Seaview, Voyage to the Bottom of the Sea, 1966 .. $250-$300
Seaview, Voyage to the Bottom of the Sea, 1975 .. $175-$200
Silver Knight, 1956 .... $45-$50
Silver Knight, 1963 .... $20-$25
Sir Galahad, 1973 .... $45-$50
Sir Galahad of Camelot, 1967 .... $100-$175
Sir Kay, 1973 .... $45-$50
Sir Lancelot, 1973 .... $45-$50
Sir Lancelot of Camelot, 1973 .... $100-$125
Sir Percival, 1973 .... $45-$50
Spartacus (Gladiator/sword reissue), 1964 .... $200-$250
Spider-Man, 1966 .... $250-$300
Spider-Man, Comic Scenes, 1974 .... $75-$85
Star Trek, Klingon Cruiser, 1972 .... $65-$75
Star Trek, USS Enterprise, 1972 .... $85-$100
Superboy, 1964 .... $225-$250
Superboy, Comic Scenes, 1974 .... $50-$60
Superman, 1963 .... $275-$300
Superman, Comic Scenes, 1974 .... $45-$50
Tarpit, 1972 .... $100-$125
Tarzan, 1967 .... $175-$200
Tarzan, Comic Scenes, 1974 .... $30-$35

USS Enterprise (with dome lights), Star Trek, 1966, AMT, $125 Near Mint.

Three Knights Set, 1959 .... $150-$175
Three Musketeers Set, 1958 .... $300-$350
Tonto, 1967 .... $175-$200
Tonto, Comic Scenes, 1974 .... $20-$25
Tracy, Dick, 1968 .... $200-$250
Tracy, Dick Space Coupe, 1968 .... $125-$150
U.S. Marshal, 1958 .... $90-$100
Unitas, Johnny, 1965 .... $150-$175
Vampire, Castle Creatures, 1966 .... $200-$250
Vampirella, 1971 .... $125-$150
Victim, 1971 .... $65-$75
Viking, 1959 .... $200-$250
Voyager, Fantastic Voyage, 1969 .... $400-$450
Wacky Back Whacker, 1965 .... $200-$250
Washington, George, 1965 .... $65-$75
West, Jerry, 1965 .... $125-$150
White Stallion, 1964 .... $25-$30
White Stallion, reissue, 1969 .... $17-$20
White-tailed Deer, 1962 .... $25-$30
White-tailed Deer, reissue, 1969 .... $17-$20
Whoozis kits, 1965-66, each .... $65-$75
Witch, 1965 .... $250-$300
Witch, Glow Kit, 1969 .... $150-$200
Witch, Glow Kit, 1972 .... $100-$125
Wolfman, 1962 .... $250-$300
Wolfman's Wagon, 1965 .... $350-$400
Wolfman, Frightning Lightning, 1969 ..... $350-$400
Wolfman, Glow Kit, 1969 .... $100-$150
Wolfman, Glow Kit, 1972 .... $65-$75
Wolfman, Monsters of Movies, 1975 ...... $200-$250
Wonder Woman, 1965 .... $450-$500
Zorro, 1965 .... $275-$300

Billiken

Bride of Frankenstein .... $200-$225
Colossal Beast, 1986 .... $35-$40
Creature From Black Lagoon, 1991 .... $90-$100
Cyclops .... $150-$200
Dracula .... $135-$150
Frankenstein .... $100-$125
Joker, 1989 .... $100-$125
Mummy, 1990 .... $135-$150
Phantom of the Opera .... $225-$250
Predator .... $60-$65
Saucer Man .... $35-$40
She-Creature .... $ 45-$50
Syngenor .... $200-$225
The Thing .... $275-$300
Ultraman .... $35-$40

Hawk

Beach Bunny, 1964 .... $65-$75
Daddy the Way-Out Suburbanite, 1963 ..... $75-$85
Davy the Way-Out Cyclist, 1963 .... $75-$85
Digger and Dragster, 1963 .... $75-$85
Drag Hag, 1963 .... $75-$85
Endsville Eddie, 1963 .... $50-$60
Francis The Foul, 1963 .... $35-$40
Frantic Banana, 1965 .... $80-$100
Frantic Cats, 1965 .... $70-$75

Frantics Steel Pluckers, 1965 .... $70-$75
Frantics Totally Fab, 1965 .... $80-$100
Freddy Flameout, 1963 .... $65-$75
Hidad Silly Surfer, 1964 .... $65-$75
Hot Dogger Hangin' Ten, 1964 .... $65-$75
Huey's Hot Rod, 1963 .... $45-$50
Killer McBash, 1963 .... $125-$150
Leaky Boat Louie, 1963 .... $80-$90
Riding Tandem .... $65-$75
Sling Rave Curvette, 1964 .... $25-$30
Steel Pluckers, 1965 .... $65-$85
Totally Fab, 1965 .... $75-$100
Wade A Minute, 1963 .... $25-$30
Weird-Oh Customizing Kit, 1964 .... $250-$300
Wild Woodie Car .... $50-$55
Woodie On A Surfari, 1964 .... $85-$100

Lindberg

Bert's Bucket, 1971 .... $80-$90
Big Wheeler, 1964 .... $80-$90
Blurp, 1964 .... $20-$45
Creeping Crusher, 1965 .... $40-$55
Fat Max, 1964 .... $80-$90
Glob, 1964 .... $20-$45
Green Ghoul, 1965 .... $35-$50
Krimson Terror, 1965 .... $40-$55
Mad Mangler, 1965 .... $40-$55
Road Hog, 1964 .... $80-$90
Satan's Crate, 1964 .... $125-$150
Scuttle Bucket, 1964 .... $80-$90
Sick Cycle, 1971 .... $80-$90
Voop, 1964 .... $20-$45
Zopp, 1964 .... $20-$45

Monogram

Battlestar Galactica, 1979 .... $35-$40
Dracula, 1983 .... $25-$30
Flip Out, 1965 .... $150-$175
Frankenstein, 1983 .... $30-$35
Godzilla, 1978 .... $65-$75
Mummy, 1983 .... $30-$35
Snoopy & Motorcyle, 1971 .... $25-$30
Snoopy & Sopwith Camel, 1971 .... $30-$35
Snoopy as Joe Cool, 1971 .... $50-$100
Speed Shift, 1965 .... $175-$200
Super Fuzz, 1965 .... $200-$225
Superman, 1978 .... $30-$35
UFO, The Invaders, 1979 .... $35-$40
Wolfman, 1983 .... $30-$35

MPC

Alien, 1979 .... $75-$100
AT-AT, Empire Strikes Back, 1980 .... $30-$35
Barnabas Vampire Van .... $200-$225
Barnabas, Dark Shadows, 1968 .... $300-$350
Batman, 1984 .... $30-$35
Beverly Hillbillies Truck, 1968 .... $175-$200
Bionic Bustout, Six Million Dollar Man, 1975 .... $25-$30
Bionic Repair, Bionic Woman, 1976 .... $25-$30
Condemned to Chains Forever, 1974 .... $45-$50
Curl's Gurl, 1960s .... $65-$75

Darth Vader Bust, 1977 .... $45-$50
Darth Vader with Lightsaber, 1977 .... $35-$40
Dead Man's Raft, 1974 .... $90-$100
Dead Men Tell No Tales, 1974 .... $45-$50
Encounter With Yoda Diorama, 1981 .... $30-$35
Escape From The Crypt, 1974 .... $45-$50
Evil Rider, Six Million Dollar Man, 1975 .... $20-$35
Fate of the Mutineers, 1974 .... $45-$50
Fight for Survival, Six Million Dollar Man, 1975 ..... $20-$35
Fonzie & Dream Rod, 1976 .... $30-$35
Fonzie & Motorcycle .... $15-$20
Freed in the Nick of Time, 1974 .... $70-$75
Ghost of the Treasure Guard, 1974 .... $45-$50
Grave Robber's Reward, 1974 .... $45-$50
Hogan's Heroes Jeep, 1968 .... $85-$100
Hoist High The Jolly Roger, 1974 .... $45-$50
Hot Curl, 1960s .... $45-$50
Hot Shot .... $45-$50
Hulk, 1978 .... $30-$35
Jabba's Throne Room, 1983 .... $35-$40
Jaws of Doom, Six Million Dollar Man, 1975 .... $20-$35
Milennium Falcon with light, 1977 .... $85-$100
Monkeemobile, 1967 .... $170-$200
Muldowney, Shirley Drag Kit .... $55-$65
Night Crawler Wolfman Car, 1971 .... $100-$125
Paul Revere & The Raiders Coach, 1970 .... $100-$125
Play It Again Sam, 1974 .... $90-$100
Raiders of the Lost Ark chase scene, 1982 .... $35-$40
Road Runner Beep Beep .... $65-$75
Spider-Man, 1978 .... $30-$35
Strange Changing Mummy, 1974 .... $35-$40
Strange Changing Time Machine, 1974 .... $45-$50
Strange Changing Vampire, 1974 .... $45-$50
Stroker McGurk & Surf Rod, 1960s .... $85-$100
Stroker McGurk Tall .... $85-$100
Superman, 1984 .... $20-$25
Sweathog Dream Machine, 1976 .... $15-$20
Vampire's Midnight Madness, 1974 .... $45-$50
Werewolf, Dark Shadows, 1969 .... $200-$225
Wile E. Coyote .... $55-$65
Yellow Submarine, 1968 .... $170-$200

Multiple Toymakers
Iron Maiden, 1966 .... $100-$150
Painless Tooth Extractor, 1965 .... $65-$75
Signal for Shipwrecked Sailors, 1965 .... $65-$75
Torture Chair, 1966 .... $100-$150
Torture Wheel, 1966 .... $100-$150

Park Plastics
Born Losers series, 1965, Castro, Hitler, Napoleon,
    each .... $65-$75

Precision
Cap'n Kidd the Pirate, 1959 .... $65-$75
Crucifix .... $45-$50

Pyro
Der Baron, 1958 .... $75-$100
Gladiator Show Cycle .... $40-$50
Indian Chief .... $50-$60

Indian Medicine Man .... $50-$60
Indian Warrior, 1960 .... $50-$60
Li'l Corporal, 1970 .... $65-$75
Rawhide, Gil Favor, 1958 .... $50-$60
Restless Gun Deputy, 1959 .... $50-$60
Surf's Up, 1970 .... $35-$40
U.S. Marshal .... $50-$60
Wyatt Earp .... $50-$60

Remco
Flintstones Paddy Wagon, 1961 .... $90-$150
Flintstones Sports Car & Trailer, 1961 .... $75-$125
Flintstones Yacht, 1961 .... $75-$125

Revell
Angel Fink, 1965 .... $100-$125
Beatles, George Harrison, 1965 .... $200-$250
Beatles, John Lennon, 1965 .... $200-$250
Beatles, Paul McCartney, 1965 .... $175-$200
Beatles, Ringo Starr, 1965 .... $150-$165
Bonanza, 1965 .... $125-$150
Brother Rat Fink, 1963 .... $50-$55
Cat in the Hat, 1960 .... $100-$130
Charlie's Angels Van, 1977 .... $20-$25
Drag Nut, 1963 .... $50-$60
Fink-Eliminator, 1965 .... $175-$200
Flash Gordon & Alien, 1965 .... $125-$150
Flipper, 1965 .... $125-$150
Horton the Elephant, 1960 .... $85-$100
McHale's Navy PT-73, 1965 .... $65-$75
Mother's Worry, 1963 .... $60-$75
Mr. Gasser, 1963 .... $75-$90
Mr. Gasser BMR Racer, 1964 .... $75-$90
Phantom & Witch Doctor, 1965 .... $175-$200
Rat Fink, 1963 .... $60-$70
Rat Fink Lotus Racer, 1964 .... $65-$75
Robbin' Hood Fink, 1965 .... $350-$400
Roscoe the Many Footed Lion, 1960s .... $50-$100
Scuz-Fink with Dingbat, 1965 .... $400-$450
Superfink, 1964 .... $300-$350
Surfink, 1965 .... $85-$100
Tweedy Pie with Boss-Fink, 1965 .... $350-$400

Spock model kit, Star Trek, 1973, AMT, $130 Excellent.

MOVIE POSTERS

Lights, camera, action! Action is what movie posters have experienced lately. What was once a hobby for the few is quickly becoming a favored hobby of the masses. In other words, movie posters have moved from the small art-house cinema to the multiplex.

Movie posters first became a popular collectible in the 1960s. Posters used to be produced in limited quantities — enough to advertise a movie at all the theaters that would show the movie. In fact, in earlier times, theater owners were required to return the posters to the movie studios, where the posters were destroyed. That's one reason few older posters have survived. But theater owners began to ignore this rule; posters were saved and eventually bought and sold. Thus, a market was born.

In the 1980s, movie studios discovered there was an outlet for posters. So began the era of large printings for most wide-release films. Finding top examples of newer titles isn't too difficult, and this is reflected by the prices for recent posters (usually $10 to $20). Don't expect most new posters to appreciate greatly in the near future.

There are exceptions, however, including Disney posters and advance posters. Disney limits the number of posters it prints, and advance posters are also printed in limited quantities.

Reprints are also made for popular movies, such as *Star Wars* and *Citizen Kane*. Reprints, especially of recent films, can be difficult to distinguish from originals. The size, color and/or thickness of paper is usually slightly different on reprints than originals. Original movie posters are considerably more valuable than reprints.

Don't confuse reprints with reissues. Reissues are posters made when a movie is re-released. For instance, an original *Raiders of the Lost Ark* poster from 1981 sells for about $85, while a 1982 reissue poster is valued at $35 to $40, and a 1991 10th anniversary reissue poster sells from $25 to $30.

General Guidelines: With major auction houses entering the poster picture, seemingly outlandish prices have been noted for several classic movie posters. A few years ago, an original *Dracula* poster sold for $250,000, making it the highest price ever paid for a movie poster. Others have breached the $100,000 mark. But even without the auction houses helping out, the prices for original posters have skyrocketed in the past decade (posters with only a few known copies to exist are difficult to value).

Generally, movie poster prices increase over time, especially for popular stars and pre-1940 items. But even more recent posters from the 1950s through the 1970s are escalating in value. Particularly desirable posters are those from science fiction, Western, Disney and horror/monster movies, as well as posters featuring stars such as Audrey Hepburn, James Dean, Marilyn Monroe and Elvis Presley. Posters from cult status movies, such as those by director Ed Wood or those featuring Bruce Lee, are also very hot. Certain short-run posters from recent cult films as *Pulp Fiction* and *The Usual Suspects* are gaining in value and popularity, too.

Perhaps undervalued and underappreciated are foreign posters of U.S. films. Several foreign countries make their own posters for U.S. films. These foreign posters feature different art and are not mass produced, as they are in the United States. Many U.S. collectors, however, don't like the foreign posters, and so the posters sell for about the same or less than their U.S. counterparts despite the fact that the foreign posters are produced in smaller quantities and are often of higher quality.

Condition plays a role in the value of a poster (see sidebar). Almost all older posters have damage such as pinholes, tears or fading. For the majority of newer posters to be collectible, only top condition is acceptable. A poster in top condition can fetch 10 percent to 25 percent more than those in average condition. Posters in less-than-average or worn condition only achieve 25 percent to 75 percent of the top value.

Condition of Posters

Mint: Never used. Some signs of aging could be noted, but condition would be like new.

Near Mint: Never used or very carefully used. Minor storage damage, such as a minor tear or pinholes in corners.

Excellent: Few signs of use. No fading, clean, no major defects.

Very Good: Could have slight browning of paper but no flaking or brittleness. Might have a small amount of writing in some subtle place. May have small tears, stains, minor border repair or signs of average use. The image area should be appealing.

Good: Below average, but still collectible. Worn and used, with obvious signs of use that affect the visual appeal. Small pieces could be missing from borders. May have tape, writing, tears, numerous pinholes.

Poor: Worn, torn, damaged, crumpled, worn or missing corners. Evidence of tape, pinholes, stains, writing and crumbling.

PRESERVATION AND RESTORATION OF POSTERS

Movie posters were never intended to be kept or collected. Being made of paper — often, cheap paper — makes them susceptible to damage. To keep posters in top condition, they must be carefully preserved. A properly protected poster will be more attractive and less vulnerable to damage in the years to come. Two popular ways of preserving posters are adding a linen backing and encapsulation. There are experts who specialize in preservation, as well as restoration. As with any field, some of these experts are more adept at their craft than others. Ask experienced dealers and collectors who they most trust in doing a quality job.

An additional concern for the preservation of posters is sunlight and florescent lighting which can quickly fade a poster's colors.

IDENTIFYING AND DATING POSTERS

Generally, identifying and dating posters is simple. The title of a poster is usually prominently displayed across the front of the poster.

The date can most likely be found in the copyright information in the bottom border of the poster. Sometimes, this information is found in the bottom corner of the poster. For example: "51/109" would tell you that the poster was released in 1951 and 109 would be an internal reference to the printer of the poster (perhaps the number poster printed in that year).

This 1925 poster, offered at a 1994 Christie's sale, carried a $50,000-$75,000 estimate.

VALUE LINE

Abyss, 1989, Ed Harris, one-sheet	$25
African Queen, 1960s, Humphrey Bogart, Katharine Hepburn, 22" x 31"	$150
Aladdin, 1992, advance one-sheet	$75
Aladdin, 1992, one-sheetv	$45
Aliens, 1986, one-sheet, Ripley/Newt	$45
Aliens, 1986, one-sheet, logo	$20
Badlands, 1939, fine	$225
Batman, 1989, Michael Keaton, one-sheet	$25
Beetlejuice, 1988, Michael Keaton, one-sheet	$25
Black Fury, 1935, Paul Muni, 23" x 43"	$175
Birdman of Alcatraz, 1962, one-sheet	$125
Buck Rogers in the 25th Century, 1979, Gil Gerard, one-sheet	$45
Camille, 1936, Greta Garbo, Robert Taylor, one-sheet	$425
Casino, 1995, Robert DeNiro, one-sheet	$20
Covered Wagon, 1923, one-sheet, fine	$1,200
Dangerous Coward, 1924, one-sheet, near mint	$700
Dawn of the Dead, 1979, one-sheet, folded	$85
Day Mars Invaded Earth, 1963, one-sheet, excellent	$90
Devil's Own, 1997, Harrison Ford, one-sheet	$18
Dial M for Murder, 1954, on linen	$300
Diamonds Are Forever, 1971, foreign, folded three-sheet	$175
Dirty Dozen, Lee Marvin, one-sheet	$15
Edward Scissorhands, 1990, Johnny Depp, one-sheet	$20
Empire Strikes Back, 1980, Mark Hamill, one-sheet, style B	$65
Empire Strikes Back, 1981, one-sheet, reissue	$35
Empire Strikes Back, 1982, one-sheet, reissue	$35
Empire Strikes Back, 1990, 10th anniversary, one-sheet	$25
E.T., 1982, one-sheet	$45
E.T., 1985, reissue, one-sheet	$20
Fargo, 1996, Frances McDormand, one-sheet	$15
A Few Good Men, 1992, Jack Nicholson, one-sheet	$20
Firm, The, 1993, Tom Cruise, one-sheet	$20
Forrest Gump, 1994, Tom Hanks, one-sheet	$25
48 Hours, 1982, Eddie Murphy, one-sheet	$15
For Your Eyes Only, 1981, Roger Moore, one-sheet	$25
Frenzy, 1972, Alfred Hitchcock, one-sheet	$45
Funny Face, 1956, Audrey Hepburn, on linen	$450
Gauntlet, 1979, Clint Eastwood, one-sheet	$20
Get Shorty, 1995, John Travolta, one-sheet	$15
Ghostbusters, 1984, Bill Murray, one-sheet	$25
Godfather III, 1990, Al Pacino, one-sheet	$18
Goodfellas, 1990, Robert DeNiro, one-sheet	$25
Green Hornet, 1974, Bruce Lee, one-sheet	$150
Hard Day's Night, 1964, Beatles, three-sheet	$450
Hard Day's Night, 1964, Beatles, one-sheet	$325
Heavy Metal, 1981, one-sheet	$25
Hellcats of the Navy, 1957, Ronald Reagan, Nancy Davis, one-sheet	$200
High and Mighty, John Wayne, one-sheet	$75

I'll Be Seeing You, 1945, Ginger Rogers, Joseph Cotton,
Shirley Temple $150
Indiana Jones and the Last Crusade, 1989, Harrison
Ford, one-sheet $18
Indiana Jones and the Temple of Doom, 1984, Harrison
Ford, one-sheet, style A $35
Journey to the Seventh Planet, 1964, one-sheet,
excellent $100
Lawrence of Arabia, 39" x 55", folded, Italian $1,000
League of Their Own, 1992, Geena Davis, Madonna,
one-sheet $20
Leaving Las Vegas, 1996, Nicholas Cage $20
Leech Woman, 1960, 41" x 81" $250
Legends of the Fall, 1995, Brad Pitt, one-sheet $30
Let's Make Love, average condition $325
Lethal Weapon 2, 1989, Mel Gibson, one-sheet $20
Lethal Weapon 3, 1992, Mel Gibson, one-sheet $15
Let's Spend The Night Together, 1983, The Rolling
Stones, one-sheet $25
Licence to Kill, 1989, Timothy Dalton, one-sheet $18
Live and Let Die, 1973, Roger Moore, folded
one-sheet $85
Lords of Flatbush, 1974, folded, one-sheet $22
Mad Max, 1980, Mel Gibson, one-sheet, near mint $75
Mad Max Beyond Thunderdome, 1985, Mel Gibson,
one-sheet advance $40
Magic Christian, 1970, Ringo Starr, one-sheet $65
Maverick, 1994, Mel Gibson, one-sheet $15
Mrs. Doubtfire, 1993, Robin Williams, one-sheet $18
My Favorite Spy, 1951, Bob Hope, Hedy Lamarr,
one-sheet $100
My Fair Lady, 39" x 55", Audrey Hepburn, Italian, on
linen, restored $1,100
My Own Private Idaho, 1991, River Phoenix,
one-sheet $30
Mystery Science Theater 3000, 1996, Michael J. Nelson,
one-sheet $18
Night Walker, 1964, excellent $150
Notorious Mr. Monks, 1958, one-sheet, excellent $75
Omen, 1976, Gregory Peck, 40" by 60" $50
Pale Rider, 1985, Clint Eastwood, one-sheet $15
Patriot Games, 1992, Harrison Ford, one-sheet $15
Persona, 39" x 55", Italian $225
Phantom, 1996, Billy Zane, one-sheet advance $15
Philadelphia, 1993, Tom Hanks, one-sheet $20
Pink Floyd: The Wall, 1982, one-sheet international $20
Planes, Trains and Automobiles, 1987, Steve Martin,
one-sheet $25
Predator, 1987, Arnold Schwarzenegger, one-sheet $24
Pulp Fiction, 1994, John Travolta, one-sheet $25
Purple Rain, 1984, Prince, one-sheet $25
Raiders of the Lost Ark, 1981, Harrison Ford, one-sheet $85
Raiders of the Lost Ark, 1982, reissue, one-sheet $40
Raiders of the Lost Ark, 1991, 10th anniversary,
one-sheet $25
Rain Man, 1988, Dustin Hoffman, one-sheet $20

Return of the Jedi, 1983, Mark Hamill, one-sheet,
style A $25
Return of the Jedi, 1983, one-sheet, style B $70
Return of the Jedi, 1985, one-sheet, reissue $25
Return of the Jedi, 1993, one-sheet, 10th anniversary ... $20
Rhapsody In Blue, 1946, Robert Alda, one-sheet $110
Rocketeer, 1991, Bill Campbell, one-sheet $30
Rocky III, 1982, Sylvester Stallone, one-sheet $48
Rodan, U.S., 1957, one-sheet, excellent $350
Santa Clause, 1994, Tim Allen, one-sheet, style B $20
Scanners, 1981, Michael Ironside, one-sheet $30
Schindler's List, 1993, Liam Neeson, one-sheet $20
Seven, 1995, Brad Pitt, one-sheet $20
She Went to the Races, 1945, James Craig, Ava Gardner,
one-sheet $75
Shine On Harvest Moon, 1943, Ann Sheridan,
27" x 40" $100
Silence of the Lambs, 1990, Jodie Foster, one-sheet
international $20
Son of Paleface, 1952, one-sheet, very good $100
Star Trek III: The Search for Spock, 1984, Leonard
Nimoy, one-sheet $35
Star Trek V: The Final Frontier, 1989, William Shatner,
one-sheet advance $20
Terminator, 1984, Arnold Schwarzenegger, one-sheet ... $42
Terminator 2: Judgment Day, 1991, Arnold
Schwarzenegger, one-sheet $20
That's the Way It Is, 1970, Elvis, Spanish, 28" by 42" ... $65
This Woman Is Dangerous, 1952, Joan Crawford,
one-sheet $75
Three Musketeers, 1974, Oliver Reed, one-sheet $25
Time Bandits, 1981, one-sheet $30
Tootsie, 1982, Dustin Hoffman, one-sheet $15
To Have and Have Not, Humphrey Bogart, 22" x 28" .. $225
Top Gun, 1986, Tom Cruise, one-sheet international $20
Toy Story, 1995, one-sheet $35
Trainspotting, 1996, one-sheet $30
Triple Justice, 1940, three-sheet, very good $125
12 Monkeys, 1995, Bruce Willis, Brad Pitt, one-sheet ... $18
Twilight Zone: The Movie, 1983, John Lithgow,
one-sheet $20
Unforgiven, 1992, Clint Eastwood, one-sheet $30
Usual Suspects, 1995, Gabriel Byrne, one-sheet British . $20
View to a Kill, 1985, Roger Moore, one-sheet advance ... $25
Who Framed Roger Rabbit?, 1988, Bob Hoskins,
one-sheet, style A $45
Who Framed Roger Rabbit?, 1988, one-sheet, style C ... $25
Wild Geese Calling, 1941, Henry Fonda, Joan Bennett,
one-sheet $175
Wizard of Oz, 1989, 50th anniversary, one-sheet $35

NEWSPAPERS

The collecting of antiquarian newspapers is a small hobby compared to others. Still, most people have set aside a newspaper on occasion as a memento of some event significant to their lives, the nation or the world.

History: Although their ancestors date back to ancient Rome, newspapers are essentially a product of the early 17th century. The first English language newspaper appeared in Amsterdam in 1620 and in England the following year.

The first American newspaper, *Public Occurrences both Forreign and Domestick*, appeared in Boston in 1690, but was abruptly stopped by the Crown after just one issue. On April 24, 1704, the first successful American newspaper appeared, *The Boston News-Letter*.

At the time newspapers were about 7" x 10" and 2-4 pages long. Published weekly, they had no pictures except an occasional woodcut in the masthead (the newspaper's title at the top of the front page) or in advertisements.

In 1817, the first paper-making machine in America appeared, paving the way for the soft white sheet prevalent throughout most of the 19th century.

In the 1830s, *The Sun* appeared in New York as the first American penny daily. Using the new high-speed cylinder presses, the penny sheets depended upon huge sales to justify their price, and they got those huge circulations figures by giving the people what they wanted — sensationalism. Although two generations would pass before the term "yellow journalism" became commonplace, papers like the *New York Sun* and the *New York Herald* paved the way.

Over the years a cheap and plentiful substitute was sought to replace the scarce and expensive rag paper. In 1863, the first newspaper appeared on newsprint (wood pulp paper). During the 1870s most papers gradually changed to newsprint, although some were still printed on rag paper well into the 20th century.

Newspapers going back to the early days of the United States are fairly easy to find. During the past 40 or 50 years, enormous quantities of early American newspapers have been replaced by microfilm in libraries and universities. Many of these newspapers were scrapped or recycled, but large numbers ended up in the hands of various book or antique dealers and collectors.

Probably 90 percent of newspapers over 100 years old were previously in a bound volume in a library. Because of this, the majority of earlier newspapers show traces of binding along the spine, in the form of remnants of glue or cord holes. If the disbinding was done neatly it does not detract from the value of the paper. Neither do library rubber stamps, when neatly applied.

Newspapers are susceptible to damage such as foxing (brown spots of varying sizes), tears, stains and those two poxes of newspaper collecting — close trimming around the edges and cut-outs. The former was often done when a volume was being bound by a careless hand, while the latter is nothing but vandalism. Any of these faults detracts from the value, depending on the damage done and the distraction it plays upon the eye.

The greatest scourge in newspaper collecting was undoubtedly the use of newsprint or wood pulp paper, which became popular following the Civil War. As a cheap and plentiful substitute to rag paper, newsprint unfortunately is made with the use of acid. No matter how much the paper was rinsed afterward, some of that acid remains today, eating away at the paper, turning it brown and brittle.

Newspapers can be deacidified (neutralized) to stop this process, but it's fairly expensive, and the current value of many newspapers doesn't justify the cost. The deacidification process doesn't reverse the browning and brittleness that has already taken place, but, so long as some common sense precautions are taken, will prevent it from getting worse.

General Guidelines: Newspapers reporting the assassinations of John F. and Robert Kennedy are common, except for those few newspapers issued when John F. Kennedy was not known to be dead. With headlines such as "Kennedy Shot, Wounded," or "President Shot Critically," these are very scarce and weren't generally known to exist by newspaper collectors until recently.

Papers reporting the assassination of Martin Luther King, Jr. are quite scarce, especially those with large headlines and large photos of him.

Moon landing newspapers are quite common because, like the Kennedy assassination, everybody saved them. Newspapers of the 1957 launching of Sputnik, however, weren't commonly saved and aren't as plentiful.

Japan Declares War After Attacking U.S., *The Post Standard*, Syracuse, N.Y., Dec. 8, 1941, volume 113, No. 84.

While a lot of newspapers reporting Elvis's death have been saved, papers in Good condition announcing the death of Marilyn Monroe are very scarce and in great demand.

Exceptionally popular are newspapers containing reports on major criminals such as John Dillinger, Bonnie and Clyde, Jesse James and Billy the Kid.

Newspapers from large cities are preferred (*The New York Times* is usually most desired), with reports in small town newspapers commanding slightly lower prices.

Look for big banner headlines and big pictures when collecting newspapers issued in the past 100 years — the more sensational, the better. "Yellow journalism," a term first popular just a century ago, still sells.

Probably 90 percent of newspapers are "atmosphere" newspapers, or newspapers without a specific article, picture or headline which makes them valuable today. These are full of the typical news of the day and tell what the world was like at that time and place. Most dealers will have a large number of these for sale at $2 to $3 each.

This won't, however, include any newspaper which can be sold as a collectible in itself, such as $2 Confederate, territorial, Gold Rush or 18th century newspapers, although each category has its own atmosphere papers which sell at a certain base price. Association papers are those which had some connection to a prominent person, such as papers delivered to US presidents Jefferson, John Quincy Adams, Polk, Fillmore, Buchanan, Andrew Johnson, Hayes and Hoover.

Contributors to this section: Jim Lyons; Timothy Hughes, P.O. Box 3636, Williamsport, PA 17701, 717-326-1045, fax:717-326-7606

PRESERVATION TIPS

Newspapers, like all collectibles, need attention paid to their care and preservation.

- Store newsprint in a polyethylene bag. Replace the bag every several years.
- Store newspapers in a cool, dry, dark place, such as a lower closet shelf, cabinet or dresser drawer.
- Frame newspapers using acid free or museum framing supplies. Don't let the paper come in direct contact with the glass.
- Keep newspapers out of direct sunlight.
- Use incandescent, not fluorescent, lights for reading or displaying newspapers.

VALUE LINE

Prices listed are for complete, American newspapers in Good condition. Minor flaws such as margin tears and light discoloration would be expected, however more noticeable flaws will decrease value. Dates listed are when the event happened; actual reports in newspapers may be several days later. Large banner headlines can command a premium above the prices noted.

1778; Average Revolutionary War newspaper $250
1795; Typical late 18th century newspaper $25
1813; Typical War of 1812 newspaper $15
March 6, 1836; Battle of the Alamo $240
April 12, 1861; Civil War begins $170
March 9, 1862; Battle of the Monitor vs. Merrimac $135
1863; Typical Civil War newspaper $14
July 4, 1863; The Battle of Gettysburg $185
April 14, 1865; Lincoln is assassinated at Ford's
        Theater $600
June 25, 1876; Custer's Massacre (not reported in
        newspapers until July 7 and later) $175
1880; Typical late 19th century newspaper $7
April 3, 1882; Jesse James killed $240
Feb. 15, 1898; The battleship Maine sunk $55
Sept. 6, 1901; President McKinley shot $45
Dec. 17, 1903; The Wright Bros. first flight $325
April 18, 1906; San Francisco earthquake $60
Feb. 14, 1912; Arizona joins the Union $25
April 15, 1912; The Titanic sinks $500
April 6, 1917; War is declared: the U.S. enters WWI $35
1918; Typical World War I newspaper $7
Nov. 11, 1918; The Armistice is signed, ending WWI $58
Jan. 16, 1920; Prohibition goes in effect $27
Nov. 2, 1920; Harding elected $21
Sept. 23, 1926; Tunney-Dempsey fight $26
May 21, 1927; Lindbergh successfully lands in Paris $75
June 18, 1928; Amelia Earhart crosses the Atlantic $78
Nov. 6, 1928; Hoover elected $21
Feb. 14, 1929; St. Valentine's Day massacre $170
Oct. 24, 1929; Stock market crash begins $125
June 5, 1931; Al Capone prosecuted for tax evasion........ $33
Jan. 14, 1932; Babe Ruth refuses $70,000 for 1932........ $35
March 1, 1932; Lindbergh baby is kidnapped $57
Jan. 31, 1933; Hitler becomes chancellor of Germany $25
March 4, 1933; Franklin D. Roosevelt is inaugurated...... $25
March 23, 1933; Hitler becomes dictator $27
April 7, 1933; End of Prohibition $38
July 6, 1933; First All-Star game $30
May 23, 1934; Bonnie and Clyde killed in Louisiana.... $210
Aug. 2, 1934; Hitler proclaims himself Fuehrer and
        Reich Chancellor $23
Feb. 13, 1935; Hauptmann is convicted/Lindbergh case .. $25
May 26, 1935; Babe Ruth hits home run #714 .... $40
Aug. 16, 1935; Will Rogers and Wiley Post killed $35

Aug. 3, 1936; Jesse Owens captures the 100-meter gold at the Berlin Olympics $25

May 6, 1937; The Hindenburg disaster at Lakehurst, New Jersey $95

July 3, 1937; Amelia Earhart disappears $70

June 2, 1941; Lou Gehrig dies $58

Dec. 7, 1941; Pearl Harbor attack $37

June 5, 1942; Battle of Midway $17

1943; Typical World War II newspaper $4

June 6, 1944; D-Day invasion of France $35

Aug. 25, 1944; Allies enter Paris $12

Dec. 16, 1944; Battle of the Bulge begins, continuing through Dec. 26 .... $15

April 12, 1945; President Franklin D. Roosevelt dies $25

May 8, 1945; Germany surrenders: V-E Day $36

Aug. 6, 1945; Atom bomb is dropped on Hiroshima $38

Aug. 16, 1948; Babe Ruth dies $70

June 28, 1950; Korean War begins $22

Oct. 5, 1953; Yankees win the World Series $24

March 13, 1959; Hawaii joins Union $21

April 20, 1961; The Bay of Pigs invasion $22

Feb. 21, 1962; John Glenn orbits Earth $20

Aug. 6, 1962; Marilyn Monroe dies $72

Aug. 28, 1963; Civil Rights march on Washington: "I have a dream..." speech by Martin Luther King, Jr. $37

Nov. 22, 1963; John F. Kennedy assassinated $25

Feb. 21, 1965; Malcolm X assassinated in New York City $70

Sept. 9, 1965; Sandy Koufax pitches a perfect game $26

Jan. 16, 1967; First Super Bowl, Green Bay Packers defeat Kansas City Chiefs $20

April 15, 1968; Martin Luther King, Jr. is assassinated ... $43

July 21, 1969; Man walks on the moon $26

April 15, 1970; Beginning of the Apollo 13 flight $13

May 4, 1970; Kent State shooting by the National Guard $22

Nov. 5, 1972; Nixon is re-elected $14

Aug. 17, 1977; Elvis Presley dies in Memphis $23

DETECTING REPRINTS

Hundreds of newspapers have been reprinted or copied over the years, usually to promote the anniversary of a newspaper or local historical event. While many of the "legitimate" copies were marked as a reprint, quite a few weren't and can be deceiving.

If the newspaper was printed using raised type (each letter was printed by a piece of type coated with ink), then the type will have indented the paper of an original. To check this, put a lamp opposite the edge of the paper so that it casts the shadow of the type, as tiny as it may be. Look on the back side of the page for the slight shadow cast by the indented type. A paper can be authenticated if just a few of its letters can be found to have type indents.

Most modern newspaper reprints were done by the offset method — a photographic process — so no type was used. Every fault from the original, however, will appear on the copy in black ink. Tape and stains will appear on the copy in black ink, and creases and wrinkles will appear as jagged lines of black ink. A hole in the original will appear as a black outlined circle of paper on the copy. Any close cutting along the edges and missing type or cutouts will also appear as blank paper.

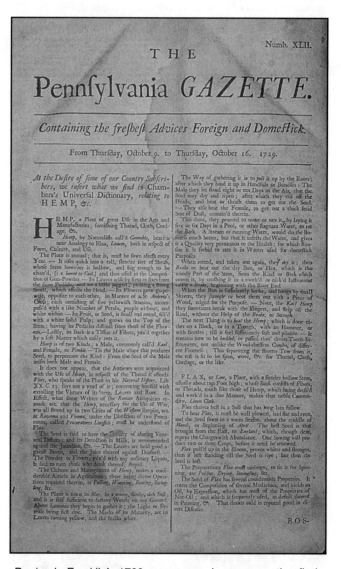

Benjamin Franklin's 1700s newspaper is a rare auction find.

OCCUPIED JAPAN

After World War II, the United States occupied Japan to help rebuild the country's infrastructure. Japan responded and became a world economic power over the next several decades.

From 1945-1952, items made in Japan for export to other countries were marked "Occupied Japan." Little did anyone think at the time that the addition of the word "occupied" on Japanese ware would spawn an entire collecting area that has drawn thousands of die-hard hobbyists.

The same items made for sale *within* Japan in these occupation years were *not* marked with the "occupied" moniker. Also, not all exported items were marked "Occupied Japan." Unmarked Occupied Japan pieces — which were exactly like the marked versions — are generally valued at about 50 percent to 75 percent of the marked pieces. As a final aside, items made during the U.S. occupation of post-World War II Germany were marked "U.S. Zone Germany." These U.S. Zone Germany items are not, for the most part, high sought-after or highly collected.

With more people collecting Occupied Japan than ever before, more people are chasing the same items, which, in turn, has driven the prices up. Sticking to an economic theme, this is a matter of supply and demand.

Figurines

Figurines are some of the more common Occupied Japan items. They include glazed and unglazed ceramics, as well as bisque and celluloid figures. There is a great variance in quality of the figurines. Some were finely detailed, while others were somewhat shoddy and sloppy. It appeared they were made hurriedly.

General Guidelines: Generally, the larger the figurines, the higher the value. Chips, dings and cracks make figurines almost worthless. Often seen are Hummel-style boys and girls of a lesser quality than original Hummels. Since they are so recognizable, expect to pay $20 to $30 for Occupied Japan versions. American-style children were also made in great quantities and variety. Highly popular, they retail for $20-$30.

Figures of Asian children and adults can be readily found for $8 to $20. Other Occupied Japan figures to look for include colonial-style people, animals, angels, elves, clowns, pixies, Cinderella coaches and shelf-sitters (figurines that can sit on a shelf). Figurines were often produced in sets or pairs.

Salt and Pepper Shakers

Themes to look for include Native Americans, animals, fruits and vegetables. All sell in the $10 to $20 range.

Toby creamer; black hat, yellow coat, green vest, brown pants.

Child's tea set made in Occupied Japan; pink ground, red flowers, gold handles, Maruyama.

Planters

Figural ceramic planters were all the rage in the United States in the 1940s and 1950s, with U.S. companies such as McCoy, Royal Copley and Shawnee providing a steady stream of planters. Not to be outdone, Japan also made figural ceramic planters during the occupation years. They are usually thinner and lighter than the American-made planters. And the Japanese were producing the planters (as well as all other items), more cheaply than U.S. companies.

General Guidelines: Occupied Japan planters aren't as popular as figurines, priced mainly between $8 and $20, so this is an area that beginning collectors might want to consider as a starting point. Animals and children are the staple of the planter group.

Toys

Some of the most expensive Occupied Japan items are toys. Made from metal, tin, celluloid or a combination of materials, many toys have survived over the years, some even with original boxes. Collectors surmise that many have survived because the Japanese toys were considered a cheap gift not worth playing with so the toy often stayed in its box.

That may or may not be true, but the fact remains that Occupied Japan toys are costly. Wind-up toys start at around $50, routinely cost $100 to $200 and can skyrocket to $400 or more. There are several wind-up Santas that both Occupied Japan collectors and Santa collectors vie for.

Clubs
•The Occupied Japan Club
29 Freeborn St., Newport, RI 02840

COLLECTOR'S ALERT

Be on the lookout for a rubber-stamped "Occupied Japan" mark on glazed ceramic pieces which may denote a reproduction. Some people have applied an Occupied Japan mark on unmarked glazed items to make them appear to be legitimate. The test to see if a fake mark was applied is simple — if fingernail polish remover removes the mark, the piece is fake, since the original marks are under the glaze. Don't try this test, however, on an unglazed item.

VALUE LINE

Ashtray, brass	$25
Basket with flower decoration, ceramic, 2-1/2" wide by 1-3/4" long	$15
Binoculars, opera-size, pink	$12
Bowl, Blue Willow pattern, 5-1/4"	$10
Bowl, rice, Iris pattern, 10" diameter	$20
Candy container, dog, 3-1/2", celluloid	$35
Celluloid pin, flower basket, 2" by 1-1/2"	$12
Celluloid pin, Scotty dog, 3" by 2"	$15
Crumb tray, lacquerware on metal base	$100
Cup and saucer, Blue Willow pattern	$15
Cup and saucer, demitasse, "Maruka China"	$15
Cup and saucer, demitasse, "Regal China"	$25
Cup and saucer, demitasse, "Ucagco China"	$25
Dinner set, 12 pieces	$800
Doll, celluloid, 7"	$28
Doll, green celluloid, 6"	$38
Figure, Santa, cloth and composition, 5-1/2"	$95
Figure, Santa, cloth and composition, 7"	$135
Figurine, ballerina in pink skirt, 3-1/2"	$45
Figurine, ballerina in white skirt, 3"	$45
Figurine, boy climbing onto shell	$35
Figurine, boy laying down with tennis racket	$25
Figurine, boy sitting with bird on toes	$25
Figurine, cherub musician, 6"	$35
Figurine, Colonial couple, 4"	$20
Figurine, Colonial couple, 4-1/2"	$25
Figurine, Colonial man holding jacket open, 3"	$15
Figurine, Colonial woman playing cello, 3-1/4"	$15
Figurine, Hummel-type boy and girl gardening, 6"	$23
Figurine, Hummel-type boy and girl with basket, 5-1/2"	$28
Figurine, Hummel-type boy and girl with boats, 6"	$28
Figurine, Hummel-type boy, 4-1/2"	$20
Figurine, Hummel-type girl, 4-1/2"	$20
Figurine, man in colonial dress, 9"	$90
Figurine, Oriental musicians, 3", pair	$25
Figurine, Oriental, set of six, 4"	$100
Figurine, peasant boy, 7"	$30
Figurine, reindeer, celluloid, various sizes, each	$10-$18
Figurine, Rudolph the reindeer, celluloid	$28
Figurine, terrier	$20
Figurine, woman in colonial dress, 9"	$90
Figurine, woman with a basket, 9"	$90
Figurine, zebras, 3", pair	$25
Fold-out fans, party favors	$5
Lamps, Wedgwood-style, 10"	$150

Colonial dancers figurine, 4".

Pitcher, parrot, small $15
Planter, cat, 4" $20
Planter, dog, 4" $20
Planter, girl with flowered hat, pink, 4-1/2" $30
Planter, mouse 4" $20
Planter, donkey pulling cart $12
Planter, duckling, 4-1/2" $20
Plate, 8" square, floral, "Merit" $30
Purse, white beads $40
Saki cups, each $15
Salt and pepper shaker, birds $20
Souvenir plate, small, Niagara Falls $12
Teapot, brown $18
Toby mug, Gen. McArthur, 4-1/2" $65
Toby mug, Indian head, 3" $35
Toby mug, medieval man $25

Toby mug, man with mustache $25
Toy, bunny on tin tricycle, celluloid $375
Toy, circus tricycle, tin and celluloid, in original box $145
Toy, "Hurricane Racer," tin and celluloid, with original
    box $325
Toy, "Lucky Car" in original box, 4-1/2" $115
Toy, Mickey Mouse crib toy, composition, 3" $175
Toy, Mickey Mouse trapeze toy, celluloid and meal,
    8" high, rare $1,000
Toy, nodder, donkey, celluloid, 6" $55
Toy, nodder, wind-up Santa, celluloid, 3-1/2" $150
Toy, remote-control car in original box, tin $125
Toy, squirt gun, metal, 4" by 3" $24
Toy, wind-up boy on trike, celluloid $65
Toy, wind-up bus, tin, original box, 4" $115
Toy, wind-up crawling baby, celluloid $65
Toy, wind-up dancing couple, celluloid $145
Toy, wind-up itchy dog, celluloid $65
Toy, wind-up monkey, 4" $100
Toy, wind-up penguin, tin, original box, 3-1/2" $65
Toy, wind-up Santa on sled with reindeer, celluloid and
    tin $225
Toy, wind-up Santa on sled, bell, celluloid and tin $95
Toy, wind-up Santa on sled, bell, celluloid and tin $125
Toy, wind-up skier, celluloid body and tin skis $395
Trophy cup, silver metal, 3" $8
Wall plaques, bust of man and woman in Renaissance-
    style dress $75

Female figurine, 7-1/4", rose dress, brown base, marked.

Colonial couple pair of figurines, 5-1/2", woman has yellow skirt, blue bussel and rose blouse; man has tan coat, blue vest and brown pants.

PAPER TOYS

Coloring Books

The earliest coloring books, often called paint books, date back to the 1880s with books by McLoughlin Bros. The children's book giant continued to publish this type of book through the 1920s. As early as 1894, coloring and painting books were used as merchant giveaways, and in the early 1900s, the Stokes Co. issued Buster's Paint Book and the Buster Brown Stocking paint box by Richard Outcault, famous for his Yellow Kid comic strip.

Major publishers of vintage coloring books include Saalfield, Whitman (now Western Publishing) and Merrill.

The 1960s are considered the golden age of coloring books featuring characters from television shows, comic strips, even politics.

General Guidelines: Few remain in pristine, unused condition today. Most valuable are those in unused or Mint condition without any creases, tears, marks or missing pages. Books with neatly colored pages are generally acceptable to collectors.

Older (usually pre-1950s) coloring books bring the highest prices. The 1933 Tarzan Coloring Book, published by Saalfield, has sold for $250 at auction. Expect 1950s books in Good condition to bring $50-$100 if they are of popular subjects such as Leave it to Beaver, Hopalong Cassidy, Family Affair or Walt Disney subjects. Books from the 1960s in Good condition can sell for $10-$25, depending on the subject.

Generic coloring books are worth little. Generally, the more colorful and dynamic the artwork, the more valuable the book, especially those featuring superheroes (Superman, Green Hornet) and Disney characters. The highest valued books are ones that include paper dolls with the coloring pages.

Paper Dolls

Paper dolls sold for play use were first published in the early 1900s. Movie and radio personalities were the earliest subjects, including actresses Judy Garland, Carmen Miranda and Elizabeth Taylor. Paper dolls can be found in books, folders or boxes.

General Guidelines: To command top value, paper dolls and clothing should be uncut (or unpunched) and in original packaging. Generic paper dolls books are not worth much, but books or sets featuring popular celebrities may command over $50. Top subjects include Shirley Temple, Vivien Leigh, Elizabeth Taylor and other movie stars. Sets featuring Mattel's Barbie doll are collected by Barbie doll collectors as well.

Dolls cut from the book and dolls with tape, tears or other imperfections have little collector value.

Esther Williams cutouts and coloring, Merrill Co., 1953.

Leave It To Beaver coloring book, Saalfield.

Superman coloring book, Saalfield.

Clubs
•Original Paper Doll Artists Guild (OPDAG)
Judy Johnson
P.O. Box 14, Kingfield, ME 04947

VALUE LINE

Prices are for coloring books in Excellent condition.

Coloring Books

101 Dalmatians, Watkins-Strathmore, 1960	$15
Addams Family, The, Artcraft	$65
Adventures of Batman, Whitman, 1966	$30
Astro Boy, Saalfield	$80
Banana Splits, Whitman	$50
Beverly Hillbillies, Watkins-Strathmore, 1964	$30
Beverly Hillbillies, Whitman, 1963	$30
Bewitched Fun and Activity Book, Treasure	$50
Bugs Bunny, Whitman	$30
Bugs Bunny's Big Busy Color & Fun, Whitman	$30
Bullwinkle the Moose, Whitman, 1960	$45
Captain America, Whitman, 1966	$30
Captain Kangaroo, Lowe, 1977	$20
Captain Kangaroo Trace and Color, Whitman, 1960	$15
Car 54, Where Are You?, Whitman, 1962	$40

Carmen Miranda, Saalfield	$50
Charlie Chaplin Up in the Air, M.A. Donahue & Co., 1914	$85
Clutch Cargo, Artcraft	$60
Clutch Cargo, Whitman, 1965	$90
Courageous Cat and Minute Mouse, Artcraft	$140
Dick Van Dyke, Artcraft	$75
Donald Duck, Whitman, 1959,	$20
Draw & Paint Tom Mix, Whitman, 1935	$80
Elizabeth Taylor, Whitman, 1950	$60
Felix the Cat, Saalfield, 1959	$35
Funny Company, Whitman, 1966	$125
Garrison's Gorillas, Whitman, 1968	$20
Gene Autry Cowboy Adventures to Color, Merrill, 1941	$60
George of the Jungle, Whitman, 1967	$50
Gone with the Wind Paint Book, Merrill, 1940	$50
Grace Kelly, Whitman, 1956	$60
Green Acres, Whitman	$45
Green Hornet, Watkins, 1966	$20
Green Hornet, Whitman, 1966	$35
Gunsmoke, Whitman, 1958	$30
H.R. Pufnstuf, Whitman, 1970	$20
Hopalong Cassidy, Abbott	$50
Hopalong Cassidy Starring William Boyd, Lowe, 1950	$55
Hot Wheels, Whitman, 1969	$30
I Love Lucy Coloring Book, Whitman, 1954	$50
I Love Lucy, Lucille Ball, Desi Arnaz, Little Ricky, Western/Dell, 1955	$45
Jimmy Durante, Funtime	$60
Jimmy Durante Cut-Out Coloring Book, Pocket Books, 1952	$40
John Wayne, Saalfield, 1951	$100
Jonny Quest, Whitman, #1091	$50
Jonny Quest, Whitman, #1111	$50
Josie and the Pussycats, Saalfield	$30
Kimba the White Lion, Saalfield	$60
King Kong, Whitman	$60
Lady and the Tramp, Whitman, 1954	$15
Land of the Lost, Whitman, 1975	$25
Leave It To Beaver, Saalfield/Artcraft, 1958	$50
Leave It To Beaver: A Book to Color, Saalfield, 1963	$30
Li'l Abner & Daisy Mae, Saalfield, 1942	$60
Li'l Abner, Saalfield, 1941	$50
Little Annie Rooney Paint Book, Whitman, 1930s	$40
Little Lulu & Tubby, Whitman, 1959	$30
Little Lulu, Watking-Strathmore, 1950s	$25
Little Orphan Annie, Saalfield, 1974	$30
Munsters, The, Whitman, #1149	$40
Munsters, The, Whitman, #1648	$65
Our Gang Coloring Book, Saalfield, 1933	$20
Ozzie & Harriet, David & Ricky, Saalfield	$40
Petticoat Junction, Whitman	$40
Popeye, Lowe, 1958	$35
Raggedy Ann & Andy, Saalfield, 1944	$40
Rita Hayworth, Merrill, 1942	$60
Sgt. Bilko, Treasure, 1959	$35
Shari Lewis and Her Puppets, Saalfield	$25
Shirley Temple Crosses the Country, Saalfield, 1939	$110

Shirley Temple Drawing & Coloring Book, Saalfield, 1936 .... $60
Sonja Henie Coloring Book, Merrill, 1939 .... $50
Space Angel, Artcraft $50
Superman, Whitman, 1964 .... $35
Tennessee Tuxedo, Whitman $40
Three Stooges, The, Lowe $50
Three Stooges, The, Whitman $20
Touche Turtle, Whitman $50
Voyage to the Bottom of the Sea, Whitman, 1965 .... $30
Wally Gator, Whitman $50
Walt Disney's Alice in Wonderland Paint Book, Whitman, 1951 .... $50
Walt Disney's Mickey Mouse Paint Book, Whitman, 1937 .... $60
Walt Disney's Snow White and the Seven Dwarfs Paint Book, Whitman, 1938 .... $50
Walt Disney's Zorro, Whitman $30
Wyatt Earp Coloring Book, Whitman, 1958 .... $35

Paper Dolls

Unless noted, valued listed are for original Mint paper dolls in uncut book or sheet form.

Alice Faye $95
Arlene Dahl, Saalfield, five dolls, 8 pgs, 1953 .... $60
Baby Sandy, Merrill Publishing Co., 1941 .... $185
Barbie's Boutique, Whitman, 1973 .... $10
Bedknobs and Broomsticks, 1971 .... $40
Betsy McCall, Biggest Paper Doll, Samuel Gabriel & Sons, 1955 .... $24
Cinderella, Saalfield Publishing Co., four dolls, 4 pgs $18
Dainty Dollies and Their Dresses, E.P. Dutton $48
Dean & Son, Dolly's Wardrobe, cloth folder, c1910, ... $85
Deanna Durbin, Merrill, 1940, ... $245
Dennison's Doll & Dresses No. 34, three sizes of dolls and patterns for dresses, crepe paper, orig instructions $65
Dotty and Danny on Parade, Burton Playthings, #875, 1935 .... $35
Fairliner Paper Doll Book, Merrill, two dolls, eight pgs, 1953 .... $10
Forest, Sally, Debby Reynolds and Monica Lewis, double cover, heavy statuette dolls, 1951 .... $295
Gone with the Wind, Merrill, c1940, uncut $265
Haley Mills That Darn Cat, 1965, CPC, cut $55
Jack & Jill, Folk Festival, Philadelphia Mummers, Jan, 1951, Janet Smalley, artist, uncut sheet $12
Julia, Artcraft #5140, five dolls, four pgs, 1971 .... $25
Lennon Sisters, Whitman, 1957, cut $55
Let's Play Paper Dolls, McLoughlin, 1938 .... $25
Lizzie, McLoughlin, one doll, c1870 .... $165
Lucille Ball & Desi Arnez, Whitman, 1953 .... $80
Mamie, three outfits, hats, orig paper envelope, late 1800s... $40
Margy & Mildred, American Colortype Co., 1927 .... $25
Mary's Trousseau, Saalfield, c1918, neatly cut $10
Mary Poppins, 1973, partially cut $35
Mickey and Minnie, partially cut $20
Miss America Magic Doll, Parker Bros., 1953 .... $20

Moving Eye Dolly, Toddling Tom, Samuel Gabriel & Sons, 1920 .... $24
Nanny and the Professor, Artcraft, #5114, six dolls, four pgs, 1971 .... $24
Natalie Wood, Whitman, 1957, cut $80
Oliver, Artcraft, #4330, four pgs, 1968 .... $12
Our Gang, Whitman, 1931, clothes $60
Our Happy Family, Samuel Gabriel & Sons $24
Playtime Fashions, Stephens Publishing Co., 1946 .... $10
Pony Tail, Samuel Gabriel & Sons................................... $20
Roy Rogers and Dale Evans, Whitman, two dolls, 1956 .. $35
Sally Dimple, Burton Playthings, 1935 .... $25
Sparkle Plenty $55
This Is Margie, Whitman, 1939 .... $45
Triplet Dolls, Stephens Publishing Co., c1950 .... $10
The Waltons $35
The Wedding Party, Samuel Gabriel & Sons $35
Your Own Quintuplets, Burton Playthings, 1935 .... $40

Tricia Paper Doll, Artcraft, 8-1/4" x 12-1/4", six pages, 1970.

PAPERBACK BOOKS

Paperback books were a revolutionary marketing concept when they were introduced in the United States in the late 1930s. They allowed publishers to create cheap books for those who couldn't afford higher-priced hardcover books. Pocket Books was one of the first companies to publish paperbacks; about 1939, the company printed 10 titles that cost a dime each.

These first 10 books, which featured authors such as James Hilton, William Shakespeare, Agatha Christie and Emily Bronte, are true collector classics, valued from $30 to more than $100 in top condition. Estimates of the print run of these first 10 books ranges from 2,000 to 10,000. Either way, there are few on the market in collectible condition.

Actually, collecting vintage paperbacks from the 1930s to the 1950s (even some from the 1960s and 1970s) is an inexpensive hobby. The previously mentioned books are some of the more pricey paperbacks; most paperbacks are priced from $1-$10 with many examples in the $3-$6 range.

Vintage paperbacks are often found for less than $1. However, serious collectors network with dealers, since they will have the nicest books available. Consider trading with dealers. This is often a good way to build a collection.

General Guidelines: Condition is everything. Most paperbacks aren't in collectible condition, but collectors may buy those books just to read. Collectors may own two copies of a title — one to read and one to collect.

By their very nature, paperbacks, often made from cheap paper, deteriorate over time, even with the best care. Pages yellow and cover colors fade. Also, paperbacks were not meant to be saved with great care, as were their hardcover cousins. Paperbacks were often treated roughly.

General Guidelines: Many collectors concentrate on themes — including science fiction, horror, Westerns, mysteries/crime, Beat writers, counterculture writers, sports, romance and war. Particularly collectible authors include Edgar Rice Burroughs, Dashiell Hammett, Louis L'Amour, Raymond Chandler, Mickey Spillane, Zane Grey and Jack Kerouac.

Others collect by publisher, assembling runs of early Pocket Books, Avon, Dell, Graphic, Gold Medal, Handi-Books and Popular Library paperbacks.

Cover art is a popular area of collecting. The lurid and racy (and sometimes racist) covers of the 1940s and 1950s are the most popular area for collectors.

Books that were made into movies are a growing area of interest. These books appeal to movie memorabilia collectors as well as paperback collectors. Even more current books are collectibles, especially *Star Wars* and *Star Trek* paperbacks from the 1970s and 1980s. These books, like the movie tie-in books, are sought by sci-fi paperback collectors and collectors of *Star Trek* and *Star Wars* memorabilia.

First editions are valued more highly than subsequent prints. Values for non-first editions are usually 50 percent less than for first editions.

JUDGING A PAPERBACK'S CONDITION

It is difficult to find paperbacks, especially older ones, in Mint or unused condition. And since condition directly relates to value, it is important to grade books appropriately. Listed below are some general guidelines to follow.

Mint: Perfect in every regard. Never been cracked open. Very few of these books are available.

Very Fine: Nearly new. It may have been read, but it has no cover creases, markings or imprints.

Fine: No tears or creases, retains its luster on the laminated cover, pages little or no signs of yellowing, only slight wear from reading, may have slight cover crease that does not detract from appearance.

Very Good: Shows some signs of wear such as minor creases, yellowing of pages, spine creases and obvious creases on cover.

Good: Shows considerable wear, but not falling apart. May have been taped, the spine may be loose, the cover may have heavy creases and the pages may be yellowing. This condition book is not collectible (unless it's a rare book) and is used only as a reading copy.

Fair: Much damage, including loose or missing pages, torn cover, writing on the pages, etc.

The Boomerang Clue, Agatha Christie, Dell; and *Sherlock Holmes—The Hound of the Baskervilles*, Sir Arthur Conan Doyle, Bantam.

VALUE LINE

Edgar Rice Burroughs

At the Earth's Core, Ace F156, F $6
Back to the Stone Age, Ace 04631, VG $1.25
Beasts of Tarzan, Ballantine 24161, VG $2
The Chessmen of Mars, Ace F170, VG $3
The Gods of Mars, Ballantine 23579, F $2
John Carter of Mars, Ballantine U2041 1st, VG $2
Jungle Tales of Tarzan, Ballantine U2006, VG $2
Land That Time Forgot, Ace F213, VG $2
Llana of Gathol, Ballantine 23587, VG $2
The Moon Men, Ace G748, VF $3
Pirates of Venus, Ace 66504, F $2
A Princess of Mars, Ballantine 23578, F $2
The Return of Tarzan, Ballantine 22702, VG $2
Savage Pellucidar, Ace F280, F $4
The Son of Tarzan, Ballantine F748, 1st, VG $2
Swords of Mars, Ballantine 23585, F $2
Synthetic Men of Mars, Ballantine 23586,
    VF $2
Tanar of Pellucidar, Ace F171, F $4
Tarzan & the Golden Lion, Ballantine 24168, VG $2
Tarzan & the Jewels of Opar, Ace F204, VG $2
Tarzan & the Lost Empire, Ace, F169, F $5
Tarzan & the Madman, Ballantine 29813, F $2
Tarzan of the Apes, Ballantine F745 1st, G $2
Tarzan Triumphant, Ballantine U2015, 1st, VG $2
Thuvia, Maid of Mars, Ace F168, VG $4
The Warlord of Mars, Ballantine F711, F $4

Agatha Christie

A Murder is Announced, Pocket 820, VF $5
Death on the Nile, Avon #46, VG $18
Hickory Dickory Death, Pocket 1151, VF $4
Peril at End House, Pocket 167 F $6
Towards Zero, Pocket 398, VF $6

Carter Dickson

He Wouldn't Kill Patience, Dell 370, F............................. $5
My Late Wives, Pocket 633, VF $8
Plague Court Murders, Avon, F $12
She Died A Lady, Pocket 507, VF $8

Zane Grey

Nevada, Bantam 3 .... $5
Western Award Stories, Dell 523, F $4
Fugitive Trail, Pocket 50658, F $4

Ian Fleming

Goldfinger, Signet D2052, F $3
Casino Royale, Signet D1997, VF....................................... $12
Thunderbolt, Signet D2126, VF $4
For Your Eyes Only, Signet S1948, VF $13

Mickey Spillane

Big Kill, Signet 915, F $5
Bloody Sunrise, Signet D2718, VF...................................... $3
Bypass Control, Signet P3077, 1st, VF $5
Kiss Me Deadly, Signet 1000, VF....................................... $8
Last Cop Out, Signet Y5626, VF $4
One Lonely Night, Signet 888, VF $9

Ellery Queen

Dragon's Teeth, Pocket 459, VF $9
Tragedy of Y, Pocket 313, F.. $4
Calamity Town, Pocket 283, VF $6

Other Titles

A Clockwork Orange, Anthony Burgess, Ballantine
    U5032, VF $3
Adventures of Dr. Thorndike, Austin Freeman, Popular
    122, VF $10
Against the Mob, Oscar Fraley, Popular G512, VF $6
All the Ships at Sea, William Lederer, Pocket 763, VF $5
Anatomy of a Murder, Robert Traver, Dell F75, F............. $6
Animal Farm, George Orwell, Signet 1289 .... $6
Apache Devil, Edwin Corle, Pyramid 63, VF $9
Awakening of Judy, Lillian Colter, Gold Medal 109, VF $5
Baa, Baa, Black Sheep, Gregory Boyington, Dell F88, VF $3
Beat Generation and the Angry Young Men, Gene
    Feldman (ed.), Dell F84, VG $12
Behind That Curtain (Charlie Chan), Earl Derr Biggers,
    Pocket 191, VF $9
Bengal Fire, Lawrence Blockman, Dell 311, F $6
Beyond This Horizon, Robert A. Heinlein, Signet 1891 ..... $5
Big Corral, Al Cody, Popular 353, VF $9
Big Sleep, Raymond Chandler, Pocket 696, VF $18
Black Rose, Thomas Costain, Bantam A818, VF $8
Blood and Sand, Vincente Blasco Ibanez Dell 500, VF $8

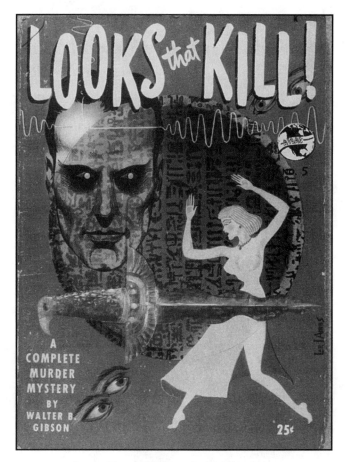

Looks That Kill, Walter B. Gibson, Atlas.

It Aint Hay, David Dodge, Dell, $50

Duke, Hal Ellson, Popular Library and *Death on Scurvy Street*, Ben Ames Williams, Popular Library.

PAPERWEIGHTS

Often considered far too beautiful to just hold down papers, these delicate glass treasures have been locked in the vaults of kings and collected by some of the world's most famous personalities. Antique paperweights are still increasing in value, despite the turbulent economic times of the past few decades.

History: Although paperweights originated in ancient Egypt, their zenith came in the early 1840s in France. From 1845-60, artists at the great French glasshouses of Clichy, Baccarat and Saint Louis produced the finest pieces by painstakingly crafting flowers, birds, butterflies and fragile designs comprised of millefiori — tiny colored glass canes used to make complex patterns — and encasing them in clear crystal. In 1851, when nations of the world were invited to display their finest accomplishments at London's Great Exhibition, the French exhibit included a display of paperweights.

In the early 1850s the New England Glass Co. in Cambridge, Mass., and the Boston and Sandwich Glass Co. in Sandwich, Mass., became the first American factories to make paperweights.

Popularity peaked during the classic period and faded toward the end of the 19th century. In 1953, exporter and avid paperweight collector Paul Jokelson encouraged the famous French factories of Baccarat and Saint Louis to revive the lost art, and in recent years paperweight-making has enjoyed something of a renaissance, both in France and America. Contemporary weights are still made by Baccarat, Saint Louis, Perthshire and many studio craftsmen in the United States and Europe.

General Guidelines: The value of a paperweight depends on design, workmanship, condition and rarity. Major cracks, bruises or scratches, and dirt or other "cullet" in the glass, all decrease value. The glass should be clear (free of a yellow tinge) and colors should be bright and vibrant, not washed out. The design should be well-centered and create an overall pleasing effect.

The most valuable and desirable weights are those made between 1845 and 1860 by Baccarat, Clichy and Saint Louis. "Simple millefiori" or "garland" and "patterned" weights are generally the least expensive of the antique weights. Likewise miniature paperweights — those under two inches in diameter — are also worth less. Becoming increasingly popular are paperweights from the New England Glass Company, located in Cambridge, Mass.

Modern paperweights — some created within the past few decades — are beginning to bring prices rivaling the antique paperweights. Among the top producers of modern paperweights are Rick Ayotte, Paul Stankard, Chris Buzzini, Randall Grubb and Parabelle Glass. While most antique paperweights are not signed in any way, almost all modern weights are signed and dated in some fashion.

COLLECTORS' ALERT!

Valuable American paperweights still turn up every once in a while, considerably underpriced, at antique shops—especially in the New England area. Be on the lookout, however, for "junk weights" being sold at high prices. To help determine whether it's old or new, look for vibrant colors in the glass; modern glassmakers are still unable to replicate many of the colors produced during earlier periods.

Clichy, red and white flower, $4,900.

Antique Baccarat, silhouette canes on lace, $2,900.

Clubs

•International Paperweight Society
761 Chestnut St., Santa Cruz, CA 95060

•Paperweight Collectors Assoc. Inc.
P.O. Box 1059, Easthampton, MA 01027

VALUE LINE

Antique

Baccarat, 3-1/16" diameter, double overlay, six circlets of coral red, cobalt blue, white and leaf green arrow canes and six-pointed stars, central circlet of yellow, blue, green and white canes with florets and arrow canes, blue over white double overlay with six and one faceting $6,600

Bohemian, 3-1/8" diameter, patterned millefiori, blue, white, green and red stardust canes, clear ground $330

Clichy, swirled, 2-5/8" diameter, alternating purple and white pinwheels emanating from white, green and pink pastry mold cane, minor bubbles $2,090

Degenhart, John, 3-3/16" x 2-1/4" x 2-1/4", window, red crystal cube with yellow and orange upright lily set in center, one top window, four side window, bubble in center of flower's stamens $1,210

Gillinder, 3-1/8" diameter, orange turtle with moving appendages in hollow center, pale orange ground, molded dome $413

Millville, 3-1/8" diameter, 3-3/8" height, umbrella pedestal, red, white, green, blue and yellow int. umbrella design, bubble in sphere center directly above umbrella $770

Nailsea, 6-9/16" height, bottle, bullet-shaped green glass dome with teardrop shaped bubbles, minor chip on top $220

New England Glass Co., 2-3/4" diameter, crown, red, white, blue and green twists interspersed with white latticinio emanating from a central pink, white and green complex floret/cog cane, minor bubbles in glass ... $2,200

North Bohemian, 2-13/16" diameter, 4-1/8" height, memorial, child's photograph on colored glass ground, allover geometric faceting $187

Pinchbeck, 3-3/16" diameter, pastoral dancing scene, man and woman dancing before a group of onlookers, two minor chips in side $523

Ruby Flash Overlay, 3-1/2" diameter, circular top facet, four side windows, elaborate cutting $523

Saint Louis, 3-1/16" diameter, close concentric millefiori, central silhouette with man and woman dancing, chartreuse, cadmium green, white, opaque pink, mauve, salmon, peach, powder blue and ruby florets, cross canes, cogs, and bull's-eye canes $5,500

Sandwich Glass Company, 3" diameter, double poinsettia, red flower with double tier of petals, green and white Lutz rose, green stem and leaves, bubbles between petals $1,100

Val St Lambert, 3-1/2" diameter, patterned millefiori, four red, white, blue, pistachio and turquoise complex canes circlets spaced around central pink, turquoise and cadmium green canes circlet, canes set on strips of lace encircled by spiraling red and blue torsade, minor blocking crease $825

Whitefriars, 3-5/8" diameter, close concentric millefiori, pink, blue, purple, green, white and yellow cog canes, 1848 date cane, minor bubble in dome $880

D'Albret, double overlay astronauts, $500-$800.

Antique St. Louis, concentric rings of canes, $1,400.

Modern

Ayotte, Rick, 2-3/16" diameter, yellow finch with yellow breast and head, black and white wings, perched on branch, faceted, signed and dated, limited edition of 25, 1979 .... $550

Baccarat, 3" diameter, yellow carpet, 12 zodiac silhouette canes, tiny yellow florets ground, date/signature cane, limited edition of 300, 1972 .... $303

DiNardo, Leonard, 3-9/16" diameter, Hopi Indian, burgundy over white double overlay, traditional Indian pattern cutting, signed and dated, 1984 .... $330

Charles Kaziun, double overlay rose, $2,000-$3,000.

Kaziun, Charles, 2-1/16" diameter, concentric millefiori, heart, turtle silhouette, shamrocks, six pointed stars and floret canes encircled by purple and white torsade, turquoise ground flecked with goldstone, K signature cane $990

Manson, William, 3-1/16" diameter, compound triple butterfly, three pink, white, powder blue, green and gold aventurine, and yellow millefiori butterflies, approaching pink double clematis on bed of green leaves, encircled by garland of pink and white complex canes, date/signature cane, 1981 .... $330

Perthshire, 3" diameter, crown, central complex cane with projecting red and blue twisted ribbons alternating with latticinio ribbons, date/signature cane, limited edition of 268, 1969 .... $770

Saint Louis, 3-3/8" length, 2-1/8" width, 2-5/16" height, basket of fruit, six pears, three plums and three red cherries, bed of green leaves, swirling latticinio basket, handle with encased lace twist, limited edition of 250, date/signature cane, 1985 .... $1,430

Stankard, Paul, 3" diameter, bouquet, yellow meadowreath, blue forget-me-nots, red St. Anthony's fire, white bellflowers, and white chokeberry blossoms and buds, 1977 .... $2,200

Tarsitano, Delmo, 3-1/4" diameter, wasp with translucent yellow wings and striped brown and yellow abdomen, beige and amber millefiori field made to resemble wasp's nest, six and one faceting, DT signature cane $1,320

Whitefriars, 3-1/16" diameter, five rows of green, yellow, aqua and red complex canes around central quail portrait, five and one faceting, date/signature cane, 1978 .... $495

Whittemore, Francis, 2-3/8" diameter, two green and brown acorns on branch with three brown and yellow oak leaves, translucent cobalt blue ground, circular top facet, five oval punties on sides $275

Ysart, Paul, 2-3/4" diameter, pink fish with translucent red fins, sandy ground encircled by ring of spaced bubbles $440

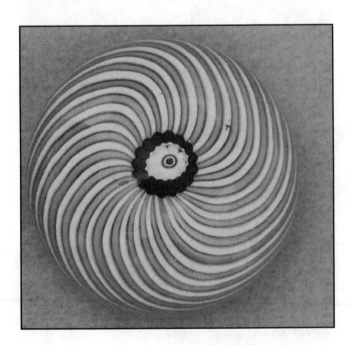

Clichy, antique swirl weight, $1,000-$2,000.

Baccarat, antique garlanded primrose, $2,000-$3,500.

PEDAL CARS

Originally designed for children, pedal cars first emerged during the 1920s. Due to their expense, however, only a few fortunate individuals can recall owning one as a child. Far more adults remember lucky friends who had one or recall yearning for a shiny new model to call their own while earnestly window shopping. A pedal car is a child's toy vehicle which features axles, body, pedals, steering assembly and tires. Intended for outdoors play, many pedal cars underwent rigorous travels at the hands of their tiny owners and left in backyards — the most significant reasons why today most examples are in less than Mint condition.

Before 1940, most pedal car owners were children of affluent families. But just as the majority of our country's population was far from wealthy at that time, many current pedal car collectors never owned one during their childhood. What was formerly a child's own American dream, to have his or her very own pedal car, has now evolved into an enthusiasm pursued by many adults. Perhaps a pedal car's innate attraction lies in its link to the automobile, a mode of transportation which continues to hold our fascination to this day.

While pedal cars have often been found abandoned or stored in attics, basements and garages, many more were probably discarded by their owners' parents after some use. Holding a powerful appeal both emotional and sentimental, pedal cars are desirable collectibles. Some individuals purchase, restore and resell them, gleefully pedaling their way to profits.

Leading pedal car manufacturers include AMF, Garton, Gendron, Jetliner, Murray, Steelcraft and Toledo Wheel.

Many vintage pedal cars remain rare for good reasons. Expense may be the chief among them, as the actual numbers of early pedal cars manufactured and sold might well have been relatively low when compared with other more affordable toys. While featured as stock items in catalogs, many deluxe pedal cars of the 1930s and 1940s may have been produced as special orders only. An ordinary tricycle may have cost $6 compared to a late 1920s model pedal car's price of $60!

The short lifespan of several early pedal car companies factors into today's scarcity, as does the fact that many examples simply wore out from heavy play. Scrap metal drives to support war efforts also led to the disappearance of these precious toys, as many likely fell prey to these government-sponsored collections.

General Guidelines: Condition plays a vital role in grading and valuing pedal cars. A well-preserved pedal car features original paint and exhibits only minor scuffs, scratches and oxidation. To command the highest price, the car should be complete with all parts and trim intact.

Well-restored pedal cars are highly valued and can command $1,000 or more depending on worksmanship, style and manufacturer.

Rare and unusual Garton Pursuit Pedal Airplane, 1940s, painted silver, red and black. Very Good condition, with some overall rust pitting, its presale estimate was $800-$1,200.

TIPS FOR BUYING PEDAL CARS

- Age, availability, condition and demand are the primary factors in determining a pedal car's value.

- A pedal car's demand is the most important element when determining price.

- A pedal car in excellent original condition is generally preferred over a restored model. Unrestored examples in excellent original condition realize the highest prices.

- Buy and collect the makes and models which appeal to you. Personal preference should drive selection.

- Complete pedal cars are better finds than incomplete ones. When a model's parts are damaged or missing, it's best to determine if these parts are available before purchasing.

- Buyers should beware of the risks involved where authenticity and restorability are concerned. Old pedal cars come with no warranties.

VALUE LINE

Values listed are for unrestored pedal cars in Excellent original condition. Professionally restored vehicles may command much more.

Apperson Roadster, Am National, 1925	$3,500
Atomic Missile, Murray, 1950s	$1,500
Auburn Roadster, Am National, 1927	$4,300
BMC Station Wagon, Jetliner, 1950s	$1,000
Buick Roadster, Am National, 1927	$5,200
Buick Roadster, Toledo, 1933	$3,100

Buick Five-Wheel Roadster, Steelcraft, 1928 .... $4,500
Cadillac, Am National, 1920 .... $7,500
Cadillac, Steelcraft, 1924 .... $3,500
Cadillac Roadster, Am National, 1928 .... $4,300
Car, Keystone, 1915 .... $550
Chrysler Airflow, Am National, 1935 .... $9,500
Chrysler, Steelcraft, 1933 .... $3,000
Chrysler, Toledo Wheel Co., 1930 .... $3,000
Cord Roadster, Gendron, 1931 .... $5,000
Custer Electric Car, 1924 .... $750
Dan Patch Car, 1920 .... $1,250
Delahaye, Eureka $750
Dodge Roadster, Am National, 1926 .... $4,500
Fast Mail Locomotive, Toledo Wheel Goods $1,700
Federal Dump Truck, Toledo, 1925 .... $1,800
Fire Chief's Car, Gendron, 1927 .... $2,500
Fire Pumper #6, Toledo, 1924 .... $2,500
Fire Truck, Am National, 1930 .... $7,500
Fire Truck #2, Am National $1,700
Hi-Speed Gas Dump Truck, Steelcraft, 1929 .... $3,000
Jordan Roadster, Gendron, 1927 .... $3,850
Kidillac, Garton $1,500
Lincoln, Gendron, 1928 .... $2,500
Lincoln Tandem, Am National, 1935 .... $7,500
Lincoln Zephyr, Garton, 1937 .... $4,000
Little Joe, Steelcraft, 1950s $750
Mack Dump Truck, Steelcraft $1,250
Mack 2.5 Ton Dump Truck, Steelcraft, 1930 .... $1,800
Murray Skipper Motor Boat, Murray, 1960s $1,500
National Pedal Car, Am National, 1928 .... $2,500
Packard, Am National, 1928 .... $5,500
Packard Electric Car, Am National, 1927 .... $2,750
Packard Roadster, Gendron, 1928 .... $5,500
Packard Roadster, Steelcraft, 1924 .... $3,900
Paige Roadster, Am National, 1925 .... $4,200
Pierce Arrow, Am National $4,300

Pierce Arrow, Steelcraft, 1935 .... $3,300
Pioneer Air Express Plane, Marx, 1920s $250
R&S Special Race Car, Triang, 1950s $575
Race Car #6, Gendron, 1924 .... $3,800
Red Bird Roadster, Am National, 1924 .... $2,800
Red Wing Airplane, Am National, 1930s $2,000
Roadster, Steelcraft, 1932 .... $3,500
Roadster, Torck $275
Roamer, Am National, 1927 .... $3,750
Roamer Shaft-Drive, Am National, 1927 .... $4,800
Shaft Drive Car, Am National, 1928 .... $3,500
Skippy Chrysler Airflow, Am National, 1935 .... $4,500
Skippy Chrysler Airflow, Gendron, 1935 .... $3,000
Skippy Fire Truck, Gendron, 1940 .... $4,200
Skippy Pontiac, Gendron, 1935 .... $3,500
Skippy Roadster, Gendron, 1939 .... $1,800
Skippy Shark-Nose Graham, Am National, 1938 .... $4,300
Skippy Speedster, Gendron, 1935 .... $2,800
Skylark Airplane, Am National, 1928 .... $2,800
Spirit of America Airplane, Steelcraft, 1926 .... $3,200
Spirit of St Louis, Am National, 1932 .... $4,500
Studebaker Roadster, Steelcraft, 1935 .... $3,000
Stutz Roadster, Garton, 1924 .... $3,600
Stutz Roadster, Steelcraft, 1929 .... $4,200
Sunbeam Racer #8, Gendron, 1932 .... $3,800
Super Charger Deluxe, Steelcraft, 1941 .... $4,400
T-Bird, Murray, 1960s $1,800
Torpedo, Murray, 1950s $3,750
Tractor Junior, BMC Mfg $650
Velie Roadster, Am National $3,550
White Dump Truck, Am National, 1924 .... $2,200
Zephyr Deluxe, Steelcraft, 1941 .... $2,800

Murray Deluxe Fire Chief, 1960s, Excellent condition, $250.

PETROLIANA

From the early days, cars ran on gasoline, and companies that sold gasoline competed for motorists' dollars by establishing and heavily promoting strong brand identities.

Gas stations usually had a distinctive look to identify them as part of a chain, and everything from advertising signs to oil cans carried the company's easy-to-spot color scheme and corporate logo. From the red star labels on Texaco lubricants to blue-and-yellow Sunoco gas pumps and the red Mobil Pegasus horse, the oil industry's products and equipment were colorful symbols of life on wheels.

Gas station artifacts are known as petroliana. Some examples include antique gasoline pumps and the ornate globes that sat atop them, porcelain signs from vintage gas stations, oil cans and other packaging, advertising and promotional items created by oil companies and even obsolete service station equipment.

Many old-car hobbyists enjoy collecting and displaying petroliana.

General Guidelines: Petroliana is hot in today's old-car hobby. Along with the increased interest, prices are escalating, although there may be some degree of overkill and market saturation setting in. Watch for reproduction items which are plentiful and extremely authentic looking.

Items in most demand today include products of service station suppliers that did not stay in business long; porcelain signs from the 1930s to 1950s; glass oil containers; metal quart oil cans; marine and racing petroliana; oil can banks given away as service station premiums; gas pump globes with aircraft graphics; vintage road maps; air machines with globes; and globes with ethyl or premium incorporated into their graphics.

EVER SEEN A FLYING HORSE?

Perhaps the most famous is the Pegasus used to represent Mobilgas.

Large enamel signs featuring the red horse decorated many vintage gas stations. And while few people may have room to display such a collectible, those large signs have recently skyrocketed in popularity. A large Mobilgas Pegasus sign is valued at $800 or more in Excellent condition today.

Clubs/Associations

•International Petroliana Collectors Association
Jerry Keiser
P.O. Box 937, Powell, OH 43065-0937
614-848-5038

•Iowa Gas Swap Meet
John Logsdon
2417 Linda Dr., Des Moines, IA 50322
515-251-8811

People's Choice Supply Co. globe, 16", $150.

VALUE LINE

Visible Gasoline Pumps
Fry, early "Mae West" 5-gal. model .... $1,950-$3,000
Fry, early "Mae West" 10-gal. model $1,625-2,500
Hays, early model .... $975-$1,500
Gilbert & Barker, early "lighthouse" model .... $1,300-$2,000
American, "slab-side" model .... $520-$800

Gasoline Pumps
Erie pump, Gulf gasoline, 72", no globe .... $1,000-$1,400
Frye pump, Atlantic gasoline, 73", glass
    globe .... $1,125-$1,500
Tokheim pump, Sky Chief gasoline, 57-1/2", no
    globe .... $1,200-$1,600
Tokheim Volumeter pump (model 950), Gulf gasoline, clock-
    face, c. 1932, glass globe .... $1,125-$1,500
Wayne pump, clock face, 78", no globe .... $495-$600
1970s Gulf dual digital computing gas pump (No-nox and
    Gulftane brands) .... $500-$800

Gasoline Pump Globes
America, metal body .... $225-$300
American Liberty, plastic body .... $300-$600
Amoco, metal body .... $115-$175
Atlantic Capital, metal body .... $275-$400
Badger 60-62, glass body .... $350-$500

Baron, glass body .... $195-$300
Beeline, plastic body .... $275-$400
Blue Streak, metal body .... $450-$800
Blue Sunoco, metal body .... $300-$600
Bolivar, glass body .... $425-$600
Browder 76 Regular, plastic body .... $175-$325
Champlin Presto, glass body .... $200-$300
Col-Tex 70 Octane, plastic body .... $100-$250
Conoco, plastic body .... $125-$175
Crown Ethyl, Red Crown, glass body .... $340-$525
Crown Ethyl, Gold Crown, glass body .... $310-$475
CrownZol, gill body .... $200-$350
Crystal Flash Anti-Knock, metal body .... $280-$450
Delco, one-piece glass body .... $900-$1300
Dino Supreme, plastic body .... $100-$150
Dixcel, metal body .... $585-$900
Dixie Ethyl, glass body with rippled edge .... $1,500-$2,000
(Roar with) Gilmore, metal body .... $1,600-$2,300
Gulf No-Nox Motor Fuel, one-piece glass
    body .... $1,300-$1,800
Hudson Regular, plastic body .... $250-$400
Husky, glass body .... $2,350-$3,200
Indian (Havoline), one-piece glass body .... $1,600-$2,300
Indiana Ethyl, plastic body .... $100-$200
Indiana Premium, plastic body .... $100-$200
Lion, glass body .... $450-$600
Me-tee-or High Test, metal body .... $450-$600
Mobilgas, metal body .... $165-$300
Mustang, glass body .... $230-$350
Noc-Les, metal body .... $600-$800
Omar Ethyl, glass body .... $300-$400
Penco, metal body .... $230-$350
Phillips Unique, plastic body .... $450-$800
Red Feather, plastic body .... $110-$225
Rock Island, plastic body .... $450-$600
Save More System Regular, glass body .... $210-$300
Security, metal body .... $450-$800
Skelly Premium, glass body .... $350-$400
Shell, one-piece glass, shaped like shell .... $350-$425
Sinclair, one-piece glass body .... $550-$750
Sinclair H.C., glass body .... $195-$300
Sinclair H.C., plastic body .... $115-$175
Sunoco Dynafuel, metal body .... $550-$750
Texaco, metal body .... $700-$1,000
Texaco, milkglass body shaped like a star,
    1930s .... $6,000-$8,000
Texaco Ethyl, one-piece glass body .... $1,125-$1,500
Texan Ethyl, gill body .... $1,100-$1,400
Tydol Ethyl, gill body .... $450-$600
Tydol Flying A (company in transition), metal
    body .... $330-$500
White Rose, metal body .... $555-$850
White Eagle, glass body .... $650-$1000
Wolf's Head, glass body .... $575-$800
Zephyr Ethyl, glass body .... $250-$400

Tire Valve Caps
Red Crown (original; set of 4) .... $10-$15
Gold Crown (original; set of 4) .... $13-$20

Harley-Davidson Motorcycle Items
1940 Silver Heat Resistant Finish, pint, full .... $20-$50
1958 touch-up paint, glass jar, full .... $20-$50
Gunk motorcycle cleaner, full, 4-1/2" .... $125-$200
Pre-Luxe motorcycle oil tin can, quart, full, 5-1/2". $90-$125
AMF Pre-Luxe motorcycle oil cardboard can, quart, full,
    5-1/2" .... $55-$75
Two-Cycle motor oil cone top tin can, full, 5-3/4" .. $90-$125

Car Care Products/Parts/Tools
Americo Grease, 10-pound tin can, full .... $19-$25
Benford's Monarch Golden Giant spark plug, 24-k gold
    plated, in box .... $35-$55
Cadillac Chromium Cleaner, quart tin can, full .... $15-$30
Camel Tube Gum tire tube repair kit, 3-3/4"x 6-5/8" card-
    board can, contents complete .... $40-$70
Champion (Commercial) Spark Plug (part J-10),
    in box .... $7-$15
Conoco Transmission Grease (c. 1920), 10-pound tin
    can .... $110-$225
Delco Hydraulic Shock Absorber Fluid, quart tin
    can .... $18-$35
Fiebing's Auto Mohair Dye, 3-1/2" x 7-1/2" tin can with
    paper label .... $40-$75
Film-Fyter Windshield Wash service station cabinet, tin, in
    box .... $35-$75
Firestone tire tube repair kit, 3-1/2" x 9-1/4" tin can, contents
    complete .... $40-$70
Ford Body Polish (M-230-F), 32 oz. .... $40-$75
Huffman one-quart oil jar with baked-on logo,
    13-1/2" .... $30-$45
Huffman embossed one-quart oil jar, 13-1/2" .... $18-$30
Peak Anti-Freeze, one gallon tin can .... $15-$25
Sears Premium gasoline can, two-gallon tin can,
    empty .... $20-$30
Shell embossed one-quart oil jar, 14-1/2" .... $75-$120
Sinclair bulk oil dispenser .... $195-$250
Tagolene (Skelly) Pressure Gun Grease, 25 lb. tin
    can .... $16-$35
Thermo Anti-Freeze, 1945, quart tin can .... $7-$15
Whiz Motor Rythm engine tuning fluid, one-gallon tin
    can .... $14-$25
Wonder Mist Cleanser Polisher, quart tin can .... $30-$45

Motor Oil, Quart Cans
Ace High .... $35-$45
Cen-Pe-Co Super Racing Oil .... $18-$28
D-A Speed-Sport, cardboard can .... $18-$28
Exceloyl .... $6-$12
Indian Premium Motorcycle Oil .... $180-$210
Oilzum Special, cardboard can .... $35-$45
Texaco Marine .... $35-$50
Wanda Paraffin .... $15-$25

Motor Oil, One-Gallon Tin Cans
Agalion .... $175-$210
Bull Dog .... $90-$125

Dearco .... $75-$100
Excelsior .... $185-$220
Gold Crest .... $30-$60
Mona .... $290-$335
Opaline (Sinclair), 1921 .... $90-$125
Pioneer .... $75-$100
Pure as Gold SAE 40 .... $25-$50
Russolene .... $30-$60
Sterling, 1925 .... $75-$100
Sun Ray Heavy .... $65-$85
Tiolene .... $30-$60
Veedol .... $25-$50

Motor Oil, Two-Gallon Tin Cans
Bonded .... $90-$115
Booster .... $35-$45
Bull Dog .... $175-$225
Defender .... $90-$115
Golden Flash .... $35-$45
Grand Champion .... $105-$135
Lord Calvert Auto Oil .... $35-$45
Lucky Star .... $28-$38
Many Miles .... $160-$210
Marathon .... $90-$115
Penn Stag .... $28-$38
Polarine .... $35-$45
Ravenoyl .... $60-$75
Red Bell .... $28-$38
Road Boss .... $35-$45
Rocket .... $35-$45
Silver Shell .... $105-$135
Sturdy .... $45-$55
Tomahawk Hi-Speed .... $90-$115
Traffic .... $35-$45
Your Friend .... $35-$45

Motor Oil, Other Sizes
Ace High, five-quart tin can .... $30-$50
Admiral Penn, five-quart tin can .... $35-$50
Bolivar, five-quart tin can .... $50-$75
En-ar-co National, five-gallon tin can .... $50-$75
Freedom Perfect, five-quart tin can .... $50-$75
Invader, five-quart tin can .... $35-$50
Jay-Bee, 1915, half-gallon tin can .... $55-$75
Keystone Condensed Oil, 10-pound tin can .... $40-$65
Parapride, five-quart tin can .... $50-$75
Quaker State Medium Oil, five-gallon tin can .... $50-$75
Trop-Arctic, 1917, half-gallon tin can .... $150-$250
Veedol, five-quart tin can .... $35-$50

Advertising Signs
Atlantic White Flash gasoline sign, porcelain, 13" x 17",
    1949, red/white/blue .... $120-$150
Authorized United Motors Service/Harrison Radiators
    combination sign, tin, 1920s .... $350-$575
Auto-Lite Spark Plug sign, tin, 12" x 30" .... $250-$475
Carburetor Specialists Hygrade System sign, tin, round,
    yellow/blue .... $200-$250
Champion Spark Plug sign, tin, white/red .... $150-$225

400 Pacer with Ethyl gasoline sign, porcelain, 8-1/2" x 14",
    black/red/yellow/white .... $200-$375
Havoline sign, tin; red/white/blue .... $50-$75
Humble Gasoline sign, porcelain .... $50-$75
India Gasoline sign, porcelain .... $50-$75
Mobilgas Pegasus sign, red, 1930s, 30" x 45" ...... $520-$800
Oilzum building mount sign, tin, 20" x 12", oval . $110-$180
Royal Triton (Union 76) 10-30 sign, tin,
    oil-can-shaped .... $90-$165
Sinclair gasoline sign, tin, white/red/black/green .. $200-$375
Sinclair H-C Gasoline sign, porcelain,
    green/red/white .... $375-$575
Standard Oil Co. sign, porcelain, with Donald Duck "Knock-
    outs for Winners" sales promotion .... $195-$300
Texaco Diesel Chief sign, porcelain, 12" x 18", 1966, red/
    white/black/green .... $90-$115
Texaco distributor sign, porcelain, black on white
    background .... $125-$250
Texaco "Fire Chief" gasoline pump sign, 1930s .... $50-$75
Vico/Pep 88 Gasoline, black/orange, porcelain .... $70-$95
Willard Batteries sign, tin, 1930s .... $33-$50

Paper/Cardboard/Cloth Memorabilia
Clason's Touring Atlas of U.S. and Canada, 1930,
    softcover .... $40-$65
Derby Anti-Freeze wall banner, cloth with stitched edges,
    blue .... $130-$180
Goodyear hose and belt sign, cardboard, 1930s, with logoed
    brown paper storage wrapper .... $75-$100
Gulf "Check Up Today" lubrication reminder card, 4" x 3"
    inches .... $2-$3

Bell glass globe.

Personal Budget Book from The Cities Service, 1930,
softcover .... $4-$8
Pure road map of Michigan, 1956 .... $7-$15
Quaker State wall banner, paper, white/green .... $35-$55
Richfield road map of New Jersey, 1934 .... $40-$70
Standard Oil Eastern U.S. Interstate Map, 1957 .... $28-$55
Standard Oil Co. Stanolind Almanac, 1928-29,
red/blue .... $30-$60
Sunoco road map of Ohio-Indiana, 1950 .... $25-$45
Texaco Dealers Profit Computer, cardboard sleeve with paper
insert, 1956 .... $15-$35
Texaco Premium Type Anti-Freeze wall banner, cloth with
stitched edges, aqua .... $55-$75
Wadhams road map of Wisconsin, 1920s .... $15-$35
Tropic-Aire (in-car heating system) product brochure, 1930,
8-page fold-out .... $20-$40

Service Station Premiums

Atlantic Premium gas pump bank, tin litho, 2-1/4" x 5",
red/white/blue .... $40-$65
Blue Sunoco cigarette lighter, 1-1/2", chrome-plated
metal .... $25-$35
Cities Service bottle opener, 6-1/2", plastic handle, white and
green .... $7-$10
Esso salt & pepper shaker set, 1" x 2-1/2", plastic,
red/white/blue .... $20-$30
Mobil flying horse tie clip, metal with red enameled
horse .... $50-$75
Skelly playing cards, two decks in plastic display
case .... $30-$50
Standard Oil Checkers game with checkerboard, cardboard
base with wood checkers .... $75-$100
Sunoco gas pump AM/FM portable radio, 2-1/2" x 4-1/8",
plastic, blue and yellow .... $30-$50
Texaco serving tray with picture of 1910 Ford Torpedo,
1940s, tin, black edge .... $40-$65

Assorted motor oil tin cans.

COLLECTOR PLATES

Like other new, limited-edition collectibles, collector plates are enjoying steady, lasting popularity. Not to be confused with dinnerware, collector plates are created as decorative pieces to be displayed. Most are issued in limited editions and are relatively inexpensive. Many do, however, over time, increase in value.

General Guidelines: The back of the plates usually contains information such as manufacturer, year of production, company or line backstamp, artist's name, plate name, series name and number of pieces in the edition.

Many plates produced in the last 30 years also tell where in the production run that particular plate fell — for example, #5231 in 10,000. Lower numbers, however, have no impact on value.

Plates produced in smaller editions will likely be more valuable than those in larger editions. This is especially true of older plates. However, if too few plates were issued, they generate little interest because too few people know of them.

Plates by well known and respected manufacturers will hold value better than ones produced by short-term manufacturers. Plates by recognized and popular artists will appeal to more buyers. Artists like Norman Rockwell and Sister M.I. Hummel will always be in demand. Whether an artist is still living doesn't affect the value of the plate, and individually-signed plates aren't worth much more than unsigned ones.

If the subject or theme of the plate is broad, the market will also be broader. Popular plate themes include holidays, cartoons, animals, flora, children, dolls, movies, sports, television, fairy tales, ethnic, historical, transportation, science fiction, fantasy and music. Plates commemorating an important or historical event are likely to have timeless appeal.

Complete sets of plates aren't automatically worth more than the individual ones combined. Often more individual plates are sold because collectors are looking to fill gaps in their collections. Many plates are produced as editions in a series. For example, a manufacturer may produce a four-plate series, issuing one plate at a time. Collectors like to own an entire series and will tend to buy all four plates even if they don't like one of the editions. As a general rule, the first plate in a series is the most valuable.

The material the plate is made from also affects its value. Quality ceramic plates are made from durable hardpaste porcelain which will 'ping' when the edge is tapped with a pencil. The finest metal plates are pure, not plated, and the best glass plates are 24 percent lead.

Any visible flaws — such as cracks, chips, splotches, blisters, off-center images, fading paint or warping — will diminish the value of a plate. Plates in Mint condition with original box and packaging are worth more, but don't let the absence of a box stop you from purchasing a plate you like. The difference in price isn't likely to exceed 15 percent.

Many plates can sell for more than original issue price; however, some values decrease.

Trends: The plate market experienced a downturn in the early 1980s because of too much supply, too little demand. Plate fever had gripped the United States for almost 10 years, with manufacturers frantically trying to produce new plates for eager buyers. New manufacturers entered the market and existing manufacturers increased the number of offerings so much that collectors couldn't keep up. There were too many choices, and collectors could no longer afford to buy all the plates being produced in their areas of interest.

The market for these plates today, however, has recovered. Manufacturers produce enough plates to profit, but not too many to glut the market.

Is now the right time to invest in limited edition plates? It's a logical assumption, but as with anything, it could go either way. Recognizing a bargain plate or one likely to appreciate is conjecture even for knowledgeable dealers, and all but impossible for uninformed buyers.

Publications
The Price Guide to Limited Edition Collectibles (Krause Publications, 1996)

Clubs
•International Plate Collectors Guild
  P.O. Box 487, Artesia, CA 90702-0467

"Harmony" by Bessie Pease Gutmann from the Magical Moments series, released originally for $29.95 and produced by Artaffects, is estimated at $70.

"The Lord's Candle" by Ted DeGrazia (Artists of the World), originally released for $39.50, is now estimated at $100.

WHAT DOES LIMITED EDITION REALLY MEAN?

The term "limited edition" can mean different things to different manufacturers.

There are four ways to limit an edition, and three of them don't disclose the specific number produced.

- Plates may be limited to the year of issue. For example, some plates will be limited to a 1992 issue date. This doesn't tell you the total number of plates produced, but it does tell you that no more were made after the end of that year.

- Some manufacturers limit production to match the number of orders received. This method is the least used and least popular with collectors because there is no definite end to production.

- Production may be limited to a certain number of firing days. This doesn't tell you much unless you know how many plates can be produced in one day, and that varies with each manufacturer. This is the most commonly used method and has gained acceptance with collectors. At least they know there is a finite time, which is usually pretty short. Firing day limits are almost always shorter than a year, with some being restricted to as little as five firing days, although the most common seem to be 30 and 60 days.

- Production may be limited to a fixed number determined before production begins.

Plates limited by any of these methods may or may not be numbered and may or may not include a certificate of authenticity.

THE COLLECTOR PLATE IS BORN

Harald Bing of Denmark, director of the Bing & Grondahl porcelain house, commissioned artist Frans August Hallin to design a special plate for the 1895 holiday season. The result was Behind the Frozen Window with an inscription which read "Jule Aften 1895" (Christmas Eve 1895).

When enough plates had been produced to satisfy his needs (the best guess is about 500), Bing ordered the mold destroyed. That order created the first ever limited-edition plate and the first commemorative plate with the date and occasion fired into the porcelain. When, in 1896, another Christmas plate titled Jule Aften 1896 was created, the continuing series tradition began.

VALUE LINE

Anna-Perenna Porcelain
   American Silhouettes Family Series, P. Buckley Moss
1981, Family Outing $100
1982, Homemakers Quilting $140
1982, John and Mary $100
1984, Leisure Time $90
   Annual Christmas Plates, P. Buckley Moss
1984, Noel, Noel $210
1985, Helping Hands $100
1986, Night Before Christmas $100
1987, Christmas Sleigh $100
1988, Christmas Joy $100
1989, Christmas Carol $130
1990, Christmas Eve $140
1991, The Snowman $140
1992, Christmas Warmth $125
1993, Joy to the World $125
1994, Christmas Night $125
1995, Christmas at Home $125
1996, Under the Mistletoe $85
Artaffects
   Magical Moment collection, Bessie Pease Gutmann
1981, Happy Dreams $65
1981, Harmony $70
1982, His Majesty $60
1982, Thank You God $50
1982, Waiting for Daddy $50
1983, The Lullaby $75
   Masterpieces of Rockwell, N. Rockwell
1980, After the Prom $90
1980, The Challenger $75
1982, Girl at the Mirror $75
1982, Missing Tooth $75

Rockwell Americana Collection, N. Rockwell

1981, Shuffleton's Barbershop	$125
1982, Breaking Home Ties	$125
1983, Walking to Church	$125

Rockwell Trilogy, N. Rockwell

1981, Stockbridge in Winter1	$60
1982, Stockbridge in Winter 2	$60
1982, Stockbridge in Winter 3	$65

Tribute Series, various artists

1982, Gee, I Wish (H.C. Christy)	$50
1982, I Want You (J.M. Flagg)	$50
1983, Soldier's Farewell (N. Rockwell)	$50

Artists of the World

Celebration collection, Ted DeGrazia

1993, Caroling	$100
1993, Holiday Lullaby	$100
1993, The Lord's Candle	$100
1993, Pinata Party	$100

Children, Ted DeGrazia

1976, Los Ninos	$785
1977, White Dove	$90
1978, Flower Girl	$70
1978, Flower Girl, signed	$455
1978, Los Ninos, signed	$905
1978, White Dove, signed	$455
1979, Flower Boy	$55
1979, Flower Boy, signed	$455
1980, Little Cocopah	$70
1980, Little Cocopah Girl, signed	$325
1981, Beautiful Burden	$55
1981, Beautiful Burden, signed	$325
1981, Merry Little Indian, signed	$455
1982, Merry Little Indian	$55
1983, Wondering	$50
1984, Pink Papoose	$45
1985, Sunflower Boy	$65

Children mini-plates, Ted DeGrazia

1980, Los Ninos	$305
1981, White Dove	$40
1982, Flower Boy	$40
1982, Flower Girl	$40
1983, Beautiful Burden	$55
1983, Little Cocopah Indian Girl	$30
1984, Merry Little Indian	$30
1984, Wondering	$30
1985, Pink Papoose	$30
1985, Sunflower Boy	$30

Bing & Grondahl

Centennial Collection, various artists

1992, Copenhagen Christmas (H. Vlugenring)	$60
1992, Crows Enjoying Christmas (D. Jensen)	$75
1993, Christmas Elf (H. Thelander)	$80
1994, Christmas in Church (H. Thelander)	$80
1995, Behind the Frozen Window (A. Hallin)	$85

Christmas plates, various artists

1895, Behind the Frozen Window (F. Hallin)	$7,000
1896, New Moon (F. Hallin)	$2,400
1897, Sparrows (F. Hallin)	$1,400
1898, Roses and Star (F. Garde)	$978
1899, Crows (F. Garde)	$2000
1900, Church Bells (F. Garde)	$1,600
1900, Angels and Shepherds (H. Moltke)	$79
1900, Expectant Children (M. Hyldahl)	$290
1900, St. Petri Church (P. Jorgensen)	$80
1900, Three Wise Men (S. Sabra)	$450
1902, Going to Church (E. Hansen)	$99
1902, Gothic Church Interior (D. Jensen)	$437
1904, Fredericksberg Hill (C. Olsen)	$179
1905, Christmas Night (D. Jensen)	$179
1906, Sleighing to Church (D. Jensen)	$110
1907, Little Match Girl (F. Plockross)	$133
1910, The Old Organist (C. Ersgaard)	$110
1913, Bringing Home the Tree (T. Larsen)	$49
1914, Amalieborg Castle (T. Larsen)	$25
1915, Dog Outside Window (D. Jensen)	$139
1916, Sparrows at Christmas (P. Jorgensen)	$65
1917, Christmas Boat (A. Friis)	$90
1918, Fishing Boat (A. Friis)	$90
1919, Outside Lighted Window (A. Friis)	$89
1920, Hare in the Snow (A. Friis)	$82
1921, Pigeons (A. Friis)	$82
1922, Star of Bethlehem (A. Friis)	$55
1923, The Ermitage (A. Friis)	$79
1924, Lighthouse (A. Friis)	$79
1925, Child's Christmas (A. Friis)	$79
1926, Churchgoers (A. Friis)	$79
1927, Skating Couple (A. Friis)	$95
1928, Eskimos (A. Friis)	$59

HOT TIP!

Here are some of the top plate manufacturers and most collectible artists to look for in limited-edition collector plates:

Manufacturers

Danbury Mint
Franklin Mint
Bing & Grondahl/Royal Copenhagen
Goebel
Reed & Barton
Lenox
Royal Doulton
Lalique

Artists

Norman Rockwell
Bessie Pease Gutmann
Sam Butcher
Terry Redlin
P. Buckley Moss
Thomas Kinkade
Sister M.I. Hummel
Charles Wysocki

1929, Fox Outside Farm (A. Friis) $89
1930, Yule Tree (A. Arestrup) $99
1931, Christmas Train (A. Friis) $87
1931, Town Hall Square (H. Flugenring) $90
1932, Life Boat (H. Flugenring) $95
1933, Korsor-Nyborg Ferry (H. Flugenring) $77
1934, Church Bell in Tower (H. Flugenring) $77
1935, Lillebelt Bridge (O. Larson) $77
1936, Royal Guard (O. Larson) $77
1937, Arrival of Christmas Guests (O. Larson) $80
1938, Lighting the Candles (I. Tjerne) $109
1939, Old Lock-Eye, the Sandman (I. Tjerne) $49
1940, Christmas Letters (O. Larson) $149
1941, Horses Enjoying Meal (O. Larson) $243
1942, Danish Farm (O. Larson) $174
1943, Ribe Cathedral (O. Larson) $174
1944, Sorgenfri Castle (O. Larson)............................... $99
1945, The Old Water Mill (O. Larson) $119
1946, Commemoration Cross (M. Hyldahl) $79
1947, Dybbol Mill (M. Hyldahl) $99
1948, Watchman (M. Hyldahl) $65
1949, Landsoldaten (M. Hyldahl) $73
1950, Kronborg Castle (M. Hyldahl) $109
1951, Jens Bang (M. Hyldahl) $95
1952, Thorsvaldsen Museum (B. Pramvig) $70
1953, Snowman (B. Pramvig) $79
1954, Royal Boat (K. Bonfils) $89
1955, Kaulundorg Church (K. Bonfils) $123
1956, Christmas in Copenhagen (K. Bonfils) $123
1957, Christmas Candles (K. Bonfils) $139
1958, Santa Claus (K. Bonfils) $115
1959, Christmas Eve (K. Bonfils) $129
1960, Village Church (K. Bonfils) $170

1961, Winter Harmony (K. Bonfils) $80
1962, Winter Night (K. Bonfils) $79
1963, Christmas Elf (H. Thelander) $127
1964, The Fir Tree and Hare (H. Thelander) $47
1965, Bringing Home the Tree (H. Thelander) $49
1966, Home for Christmas (H. Thelander) $47
1967, Sharing the Joy (H. Thelander) $65
1968, Christmas in Church (H. Thelander) $39
1969, Arrival of Guests (H. Thelander) $80
1970, Pheasants in Snow (H. Thelander) $25
1971, Christmas at Home (H. Thelander) $25
1972, Christmas in Greenland (H. Thelander) $25
1973, Country Christmas (H. Thelander) $25
1974, Christmas in the Village (H. Thelander) $25
1975, Old Water Mill (H. Thelander) $39
1976, Christmas Welcome (H. Thelander) $39
1977, Copenhagen Christmas (H. Thelander) $39
1978, Christmas Tale (H. Thelander) $49
1979, White Christmas (H. Thelander) $20
1980, Christmas in Woods (H. Thelander) $49
1981, Christmas Peace (H. Thelander) $49
1982, Christmas Tree (H. Thelander) $83
1983, Christmas in Old Town (H. Thelander) $75
1984, Christmas Letter, The (D. Jensen) $75
1985, Christmas Eve at the Farmhouse (D. Jensen) $77
1986, Silent Night, Holy Night (D. Jensen) $75
1987, The Snowman's Christmas Eve (D. Jensen) $77
1988, In the Kings Garden (D. Jensen) $77
1989, Christmas Anchorage (D. Jensen) $71
1990, Changing of the Guards (D. Jensen) $71
1991, Copenhagen Stock Exchange (D. Jensen) $55
1992, Christmas at the Rectory (J. Steensen) $79
1993, Father Christmas in Copenhagen (J. Steensen) $72

Bradford Exchange
Peppercricket Grove, Charles Wysocki
1993, Black Crow Antique Shoppe $40
1993, Budzen's Fruit & Vegetables $40
1993, Gingernut Valley Inn $40
1993, Liberty Star Farms $40
1993, Overflow Antique Market $40
1993, Peppercricket Farms $40
1993, Pumpkin Hollow Emporium $40
1993, Virginia's Market $40
Danbury Mint
1973-79, Bicentennial plate series .... $195 each
1993, Boys Will Be Boys series (Jim Daly) .... $46 each
1991, Little Companions series (M.I. Hummel) ...... $51 each
Enesco Corp.
Precious Moments Christmas Blessings series, Sam Butcher
1990, Wishing You a Yummy Christmas 523801 .... $75
1991, Blessing From Me to Thee 523860 .... $65
1992, But the Greatest/Love 527742 .... $55
Precious Moments Christmas Love series, Sam Butcher
1986, I'm Sending You a White Christmas 101834 .... $60
1987, My Peace I Give to Thee 102954 .... $95
1988, Merry Christmas Deer 520284 .... $85
1989, May Your Christmas Be/Happy Home 523003 ...... $60

"Winter Birds," the 1987 release in Royal Copenhagen's "Christmas" series, is estimated at $100.

Precious Moments Joy of Christmas series, Sam Butcher

1982, I'll Play My Drum for Him E2357 .... $75

1983, Christmastime is for Sharing E-0505 .... $100

1984, Tell Me the Story of Jesus 15237 .... $100

1984, The Wonder of Christmas E-5396 .... $85

Precious Moments the Four Seasons series, Sam Butcher

1985, Summer's Joy 12114 .... $60

1985, The Voice of Spring 12106 .... $75

1986, Autumn's Praise 12122 .... $50

1986, Winter's Song 12130 .... $60

Goebel

M.I. Hummel Annual Collectible Plates, Sister M.I. Hummel

1971, Heavenly Angel HUM-264 .... $600

1972, Hear Ye, Hear Ye HUM-265 .... $40

1973, Globe Trotter HUM-266 .... $75

1974, Goose Girl HUM-267 .... $50

1975, Ride Into Christmas HUM-268 .... $40

1976, Apple Tree Girl HUM-269 .... $50

1977, Apple Tree Boy HUM-270 .... $80

1978, Happy Pastime HUM-271 .... $40

1979, Singing Lesson HUM-272 .... $30

1980, School Girl HUM-273 .... $44

1981, Umbrella Boy HUM-274 .... $45

1982, Umbrella Girl HUM-275 .... $125

1983, Postman HUM-276 .... $193

1984, Little Helper HUM-277 .... $83

1985, Chick Girl HUM-278 .... $94

1986, Playmates HUM-279 .... $165

1987, Feeding Time HUM-283 .... $400

1988, Little Goat Herder HUM-284 .... $100

1989, Farm Boy HUM-285 .... $130

1990, Shepherd's Boy HUM-286 .... $250

1991, Just Resting HUM-287 .... $149

1992, Wayside Harmony HUM-288 .... $268

1993, Doll Bath HUM-289 .... $320

1994, Doctor HUM-290 .... $250

1995, Come Back Soon $250

M.I. Hummel Christmas Plates

1987, Celestial Musician $69

1988, Angel Duet $50

1989, Guiding Light $75

1990, Tender Watch $75

Lalique

Annual series, M. Lalique

1965, Deux Oiseaux (Two Birds) $1,200

1966, Rose de Songerie (Dream Rose) $125

1967, Ballet de Poisson (Fish Ballet) $100

1968, Gazelle Fantaisie (Gazelle Fantasy) $65

1969, Papillon (Butterfly) $40

1970, Paon (Peacock) $60

1971, Hibou (Owl) $70

1972, Coquillage (Shell) $65

1973, Petit Geai (Jayling) $100

1974, Sous D'Argent (Silver Pennies) $100

1975, Duo de Poisson (Fish Duet) $140

1976, Aigle (Eagle) $75

Lenox China

American Wildlife series, N. Adams

1982, Black Bears $70

1982, Buffalo $70

1982, Dall Sheep $80

1982, Jack Rabbits $70

1982, Mountain Lions $70

1982, Ocelots $80

1982, Otters $70

1982, Polar Bears $70

1982, Raccoons $70

1982, Red Foxes $70

1982, Sea Lions $80

1982, White Tailed Deer $70

Reed & Barton

Audobon

1970, Pine Siskin $175

1971, Red-Shouldered Hawk $100

1972, Stilt Sandpiper $100

1973, Red Cardinal $100

1974, Boreal Chickadee $100

1975, Yellow-Breasted Chat $100

1976, Bay-Breasted Warbler $100

1977, Purple Finch $100

Twas the Night Before Christmas (J. Downing)

1989, 'Twas the Night Before Christmas $85

1990, Visions of Sugarplums $85

1991, Away to the Window $79

HOT PLATE!

This 1895 Christmas Plate by Bing & Grondahl—the first annual Christmas plate ever issued, at an original cost of 50 cents—is now worth around $7,000!

"Peppercricket Farms" by Charles Wysocki for the Bradford Exchange, was released in 1993 for $24.90 and is now estimated at $40.

Royal Copenhagen
Christmas plates (varied artists)
1908, Madonna and Child (C. Thomsen) $4,900
1909, Danish Landscape (S. Ussing) $243
1910, The Magi (C. Thomsen) $179
1911, Danish Landscape (O. Jensen) $210
1912, Christmas Tree (C. Thomsen) $210
1913, Frederik Church Spire (A. Boesen) $163
1914, Holy Spirit Church (A. Boesen) $210
1915, Danish Landscape (A. Krog) $210
1916, Shepherd at Christmas (R. Bocher) $129
1917, Our Savior Church (O. Jensen) $129
1918, Sheep and Shepherds (O. Jensen) $129
1919, In the Park (O. Jensen) $115
1920, Mary and Child Jesus (G. Rode) $115
1921, Aabenraa Marketplace (O. Jensen) $115
1922, Three Singing Angels (E. Selschau) $97
1923, Danish Landscape (O. Jensen) $97
1924, Sailing Ship (B. Olsen) $129
1925, Christianshavn (O. Jensen) $115
1926, Christianshavn Canal (R. Bocher) $145
1927, Ship's Boy at Tiller (B. Olsen) $173
1928, Vicar's Family (G. Rode) $145
1929, Grundtvig Church (O. Jensen) $113
1930, Fishing Boats (B. Olsen) $145
1931, Mother and Child (G. Rode) $145
1932, Frederiksberg Gardens (O. Jensen) $129
1933, Ferry and the Great Belt (B. Olsen) $195
1934, The Hermitage Castle (O. Jensen) $210
1935, Kronborg Castle (B. Olsen) $309
1936, Roskilde Cathedral (R. Bocher) $243
1937, Main Street Copenhagen (N. Thorsson) $339

1938, Round Church in Osterlars (H. Nielsen) $439
1939, Greenland Pack-Ice (H. Nielsen) $597
1940, The Good Shepherd (K. Lang) $597
1941, Danish Village Church (T. Kjolner) $499
1942, Bell Tower (N. Thorsson) $565
1943, Flight into Egypt (N. Thorsson) $759
1944, Danish Village Scene (V. Olson) $405
1945, A Peaceful Motif (R. Bocher) $599
1946, Zealand Village Church (N. Thorsson) $275
1947, The Good Shepherd (K. Lang) $339
1948, Nodebo Church (T. Kjolner) $309
1949, Our Lady's Cathedral (H. Hansen) $339
1950, Boeslunde Church (V. Olson) $399
1951, Christmas Angel (R. Bocher) $439
1952, Christmas in the Forest (K. Lang) $163
1953, Frederiksberg Castle (T. Kjolner) $163
1954, Amalienborg Palace (K. Lang) $195
1955, Fano Girl (K. Lang) $243
1956, Rosenborg Castle (K. Lang) $210
1957, The Good Shepherd (H. Hansen) $163
1958, Sunshine Over Greenland (H. Hansen) $163
1959, Christmas Night (H. Hansen) $163
1960, The Stag (H. Hansen) $195
1961, Training Ship (K. Lange) $195
1962, The Little Mermaid $309
1963, Hojsager Mill (K. Lange) $109
1964, Fetching the Tree (K. Lange) $69
1965, Little Skaters (K. Lange) $746
1966, Blackbird (K. Lange) $38
1967, The Royal Oak (K. Lange) $38
1968, The Last Umiak (K. Lange) $38
1969, The Old Farmland (K. Lange) $38
1970, Christmas Rose and Cat (K. Lange) $38
1971, Hare in Winter (K. Lange) $25
1972, In the Desert (K. Lange) $27
1973, Train Homeward Bound (K. Lange) $27
1974, Winter Twilight (K. Lange) $30
1975, Queen's Palace (K. Lange) $25
1976, Danish Watermill (S. Vestergaard) $27
1977, Immervad Bridge (K. Lange) $27
1978, Greenland Scenery (K. Lange) $27
1979, Choosing Christmas Tree (K. Lange) $82
1980, Bringing Home the Tree (K. Lange) $35
1981, Admiring Christmas Tree (K. Lange) $82
1982, Waiting for Christmas (K. Lange) $82
1983 Merry Christmas (K. Lange) $82
1984, Jingle Bells (K. Lange) $82
1985, Snowman (K. Lange) $95
1986, Christmas Vacation (K. Lange) $83
1987, Winter Birds (S. Vestergaard) $98
1988, Christmas Eve in Copenhagen (S. Vestergaard) $98
1989, The Old Skating Pond (S. Vestergaard) $113
1990, Christmas at Tivoli (S. Vestergaard) $210
1991, The Festival of Santa Lucia (S. Vestergaard) $113
1992, Queen's Carriage (S. Vestergaard) $83
1993, Christmas Guests (S. Vestergaard) $113
1994, Christmas Shopping (S. Vestergaard) $83
1995, Christmas at the Manor House (S. Vestergaard) $75

POLITICAL MEMORABILIA

Political memorabilia is often associated with the election of candidates for public office, but non-campaign items—such as mourning ribbons worn for Abraham Lincoln's death, inaugural materials, and buttons protesting Prohibition—are collectible as well.

History: Each campaign throughout history has tempted the public with yet another gimmick, usually with considerable success. This has created a collector's bonanza, including a range of items like the ever-popular buttons and pins, paper memorabilia (including prints and cartoon depictions of the candidates) and a plethora of novelty items. An increase in the scope of campaign items occurred around the time of the 1840 William Henry Harrison campaign and escalated thereafter. By the beginning of the 20th century, the influx of immigrants even necessitated that some of the written materials be offered in native languages.

General Guidelines: Items generally have greater value if they relate to figures who played dominant roles during significant periods of U.S. history, or if they relate to those who were merely notable for their colorful speech or behavior.

Pins, Buttons, Lapel Devices and Medals

Pins and buttons are commonly associated with political campaigns. Although rare buttons command high prices, campaign buttons are the most popular collectible due to their availability and general low cost.

The period between 1896 and 1920 is considered the "golden age" of campaign buttons, with hundreds of companies contributing to their manufacture. They are noteworthy for innovative designs and unusual graphics.

Buttons and pins offer the collector a multitude of choices, from early clothing styles commemorating the inauguration of George Washington to colorful rhinestone pins bolstering the candidacy of General Dwight Eisenhower. Jugate buttons pictured the two candidates (president and vice president). Coattail buttons featured the presidential candidate and a Senate or similar candidate, although in some cases even two or more candidates rode the coattails of the presidential contender on the campaign "button" trail.

The graphics and mechanical devices found on many early pins and buttons make them particularly collectible. Mechanical pins were especially ingenious; when opened, they revealed the candidate's picture. Medalets are also of interest to collectors, such as the trio produced for the 1824 Jackson campaign, featuring either the Battle of New Orleans or the Congressional Medal that honored him.

There were beautiful porcelain studs, as well as celluloid buttons. Although invented in 1839, celluloid did not reach general usage until the mid-19th century. Its first appearance in the political arena was as both a lapel stud and bookmark in the campaign of 1888. Celluloid advanced in popularity during the 1896 campaign of William McKinley, which also ushered in the mass production of pinback buttons.

Popular during the mid-19th century were two-piece buttons, lapel studs and brooches, all of which are included in a wide variety of lapel items. Brooches often featured cameos, most of which were French made and fashioned on a small one-inch scale. On a colorful enameled base, the candidate's face appeared in cameo form. Both surfaces were enclosed in glass and mounted in a pinbacked brass frame.

Small lapel studs for the buttonhole were produced in large quantities in the late 19th century. Some of the most interesting were in eye-catching shapes like drums, flags and hats. Over 500 types were produced during this period, making it a fertile field for collectors. Brass lapel pins from more recent campaigns, like those in the outline of various states with the candidate's name inside the "boundaries," are particularly colorful and appealing.

General Guidelines: For avid button collectors design generally takes precedence, as do unusual themes, such as those calling attention to Teddy Roosevelt's association with the Rough Riders. Picture buttons that show both the Presidential and Vice Presidential contenders are also more desirable than single candidate buttons.

Condition is important, although minor defects can be overlooked in rare items. Scarcity, of course, adds to the collectibility and value of any button. Dents, rust, scratches and tears detract from value. Campaign budget restrictions and buttons for local and state campaigns translate into less distribution—hence, fewer buttons.

Buttons used to promote a "non-running" candidate during the party nominating convention are generally of little value.

Buttons from the 1920 Cox-Roosevelt campaign are rare. Although not exciting in design, few exist in the varying styles produced, making these among the rarest. Also scarce are pins from the campaigns of James Davis in 1924.

Third party items are also worthy of consideration in rounding out any serious collection. Silk screen designs on cloth from modern campaigns are rare and desirable. Beginning around 1972, psychedelic designs also contributed to colorful presentations.

Ribbons, Ribbon Badges, Silks

Campaign ribbon badges from early campaigns (1800-1864) are less limited for the collector than others in the textile category, like banners and early silks. Although many fall into the rarer category, some campaigns, like William Henry Harrison's, inundated the voters with over 150 designs, making this series a coup for the specialized collector.

Ribbon badges had a medal or celluloid button or sheet on the fabric or suspended from it. Some overly-large ribbons, referred to as fringes and tassels, sported fringes of metallic threads featuring elaborate symbols and inscriptions.

The majority of ribbons from this period were lithographed in black. Rarely in dark colors, background shades were generally white, cream or other pale hues. Most emphasized symbols or issues pertinent to the voter, such as ribbons for the "Know Nothing" party covering a variety of subjects in about 25 different designs. Many of these were imprinted with the names of cities, towns and villages, even specific wards.

Bar clasps on other ribbons featured items exclusively associated with a given candidate. Until 1932, select individuals traveled to the home of the presidential candidate and formally notified him of his victory, making ribbons worn by the 50 to 100 members of these now defunct notification committees of historical and political interest.

General Guidelines: Silks are more rare. Card-mounted portrait silks made by the Thomas Stevens Company of Coventry, England, are extremely limited, with only five concerning American subjects—Washington, Harrison, Grant and Mr. and Mrs. Cleveland—plus two variants, now known to exist. The one picturing President and Mrs. Cleveland has a cigarette advertisement on the card mount. There were also silks for the Confederacy, although only a few styles are known. These include the Stars and Bars with the names of President Jefferson Davis and his Vice President Alexander Stephens, and possibly one other designed for the inauguration. Embroidered ribbons manufactured by the aforementioned Stevens Company remain the most desirable in this category. Called Stevengraphs, they appeared as bookmarks and portrait silks.

Multi-color ribbon designs for candidate Henry Clay; ribbons for Martin Van Buren; Franklin Pierce; Andrew Jackson; Winfield Scott; John Quincy Adams; Lewis Cass; and the majority of those produced for the "Know Nothing" Party are rare.

Ferrotypes

Unlike voters today who view their candidates almost daily on television, during the mid to late 19th century ferrotypes, or tintypes, were one of the few ways for the public to see a likeness of the candidate. Framed in brass of varying shapes and, more rarely, made of plush cloth, the candidate's face usually appeared on one side with his running mate on the reverse. Less often, both candidates were shown together, with a pin on the back.

By placing a hole at the top, ferrotypes could then be displayed by hanging them from the lapel. This style first appeared during the campaigns of 1860, with over 300 different types known to have existed.

In 1864, a variation of the earlier ferrotype was offered, with the pictures framed in thin sheets of metal that were stamped in elaborate designs in raised relief. Called shell badges, they were usually of copper or brass.

This time period also introduced the albumin print. Simply a paper photograph, it was understandably popular because of its lower production cost and eventually replaced its predecessors. Although shell models continued until about 1904, by the 1880s ferrotypes were rarely seen on the campaign circuit, replaced instead by cardboard photo badges.

General Guidelines: The scarce survival of ferrotypes from the 1860-1864 period makes them more valuable, as does the interest of Lincoln collectors for these campaign lapel items. For example, a Lincoln/Johnson ferrotype in elaborate brass frame can command upwards of $20,000.

Textiles/Fabric/Banners

Information on political textiles is limited, making this an often overlooked category for collectors. Parade banners and campaign ribbons, for instance, were common to early campaigns, but they remain more obscure and less understood than other political collectibles.

Some of these textiles are referred to as campaign chintzes but, for the most part, they were simply swatches of fabric in varying sizes that featured the candidate and/or his campaign. They ranged from simple depictions to elaborate illustrations appropriate to the period or the candidate. Campaign chintzes were introduced for George Washington's inauguration in 1789 and continued through the Civil War. With the exception of the 1872 and 1880 campaigns, few were seen after that time. Also of interest are the small quilts called "crazy quilts" that were a product of the 1840 and 1880 campaigns.

Early campaign and parade banners, and those that hung in the candidate's headquarters, also fall into the textile category. These were often of expensive fabrics and hand-painted, not only with simple slogans but also in unique designs and pictures. Many are now considered fine examples of early American folk art. Although some command attention for their skillful graphics, by the end of the 19th century banners were produced commercially and lost much of their individuality. Nonetheless, these later styles remain of interest to collectors who focus on particular campaigns. By the 1930s and 1940s, however, headquarter banners had become a thing of the past.

From a later time period are the tiny banners that hung in the front windows of dwellings during World War II. These featured a star or stars to indicate the number of persons from that family in the Armed Forces; blue stars were for the living, gold stars for those who had died in service.

Made of cloth, bandannas and kerchiefs fall into the textile category. Although most popular during the 19th century, especially from 1840 on, they nonetheless continued to appear throughout the 20th century. Ranging from large squares to handkerchief sizes, they were of linen, cotton and silk.

General Guidelines: Rarely found today are the large canvas banners from 1876-1928 that were often suspended across streets. Smaller versions were intended for hanging in the windows of homes; printed on both sides, these same rare miniatures might well have been used as salesmen's samples.

Paper and Art

Cartoons and drawings have been an ongoing source of amusement to the public. Many were found in newspapers and periodicals, some appeared on postcards and sheet music, and still others were displayed on trade cards. Many advertisements can also be found depicting candidates touting everything from beer to sewing machines.

Political cartoons are exaggerations of figures and topics and are intended more to ridicule than to evoke laughter. An offshoot of cartoons is found in the caricature—exaggerated but less direct and more irreverent depictions of candidates.

Paintings of political figures by renowned artists of the day were frequently converted to prints. Purchased primarily by wealthy individuals, engravings were also prevalent during this country's early history, and all now fall into the political collectible category. Stone lithographs, which were introduced in 1820, brought prints into the realm of the general public. Along with cartoons and broadsides, they filled a need, providing information about the candidates, however questionable their accuracy. Patriotic and overblown, they became an entirely separate art form.

Certain series present a challenge to collectors, like those by Currier and Ives from 1851 to 1868 portraying all the presidents from Washington to Lincoln in front of a draped background of either red or green. Here the goal is to find the entire series in the same background color.

Lithographs were also made for presidential birthplaces, deathbed scenes, inaugurations, etc. In addition to Currier and Ives, the chief publishers of these lithographs were Buford, Prang, Kellog, Endicott, Baille, Sarony and Robinson. Today, even small book prints of political figures from later periods comprise part of this collecting genre.

More formal entries in the paper category are items like invitations to inaugural balls and personal papers and letters. Not to be overlooked were postcards touting individual candidates. The early 1900s brought many postcard designs that are particularly creative, including mechanicals, and thus desirable to collectors. Here too are paper posters and banners, campaign and anti-campaign biographies and brochures, paper ballots and electoral tickets. Prior to the advent of machines, voting was accomplished by ballots or electoral tickets, and during the 1920s and 1930s these were often as large as newspaper sheets. While some simply listed the candidates, others were complete with pictures. The smaller electoral tickets first appeared around 1824 and were used as voter reminders, listing candidates for a particular party and sometimes featuring portraits and patriotic symbols. Tickets showing the candidates, or those for third party candidates, are generally most desirable.

General Guidelines: Although the genre began in the mid-1700s, collectibles from that period are rare and costly. The presidency of Andrew Jackson, however, occurred at the beginning of the stone lithography period, making cartoons about the Jackson presidency more widespread. During the 1860s, dual colors came into prominence, with cartoon lithographs from this period being particularly noteworthy. Soon, weekly publications were brimming with cartoons, and by the time of the Civil War most daily newspapers carried them. Even foreign publications featured cartoons about American political figures.

Several early American cartoonists dominated the field including David Claypool Johnson, Doolittle, Charles, Tinsdale, Clay, and Thomas Nast has a vast body of work.

Surprisingly, cartoons before the 1870s are often easier to obtain. Not only did later ones from newspapers and magazines require only one master copy, but when wood pulp replaced rag in newspapers their deterioration was much more rapid.

Parade Canes and Walking Sticks

Parade canes were used from about 1868 to 1912, although others appeared infrequently after that, including a few for the campaigns of 1928 and 1932. Often the head of the cane was a likeness of the favored candidate. Usually hollow, these heads were made of silver, brass, tin, lead or other metals.

Other canes were fashioned strictly as novelty items. Some were horns that honked, others were used as torchlights, replete with fuel holders and wicks. The latter usually had paper labels with the candidate's image.

General Guidelines: More common styles included the always-popular elephants and donkeys, and even some shaped like peanuts. Most parade canes are valued in the $200-$800 range.

Especially rare is the Franklin D. Roosevelt cane from the 1932 campaign.

Tobacco Products

Snuff boxes made of pewter or tin are popular collectibles; early models were made of papier mache, enameled, lacquered and decorated with political pictures.

While most snuff boxes enjoyed popularity from the 1820s until around 1880, some are known to feature George Washington. One of these is made of tortoiseshell, with Washington's picture encased in its glass top.

Cigar cases also appeared, but their popularity lasted from 1840-1850. Dating from 1904, some candidates' pictures decorated cigar bands.

Replete with ingenious designs, political pipes are very popular in today's market. The bowls of some are carved into busts in the likeness of favored candidates. Others feature items like eagles and shields and are often inscribed with political slogans. Most were made of white clay or briar.

Match boxes also feature political candidates. Some were made of cast iron.

Lighters and cigarette packages first appeared in the 1930s. The campaign of 1956 sported particularly attractive designs featuring styles for running mates Dwight D. Eisenhower and Richard Nixon, and others for their opponents Adlai Stevenson and Estes Kefauver. In 1964, presidential opponents Barry Goldwater and Lyndon Johnson both offered small lighters with their pictures on brass medalets. Other lighters sported campaign slogans and, of course, the elephant or donkey. Cigarette boxes were also used to promote the opposing candidacies of Richard Nixon and George McGovern.

General Guidelines: Rare tobacco-related collectibles include McKinley and and Bryan merschaum pipes, French-made briar pipe with bust of FDR, 1880 Winfield Hancock rebus puzzle pipe and a double-covered cigar box with framed lithographic portraits of Blaine and Logan.

Hats

As seen on the floor of every political convention, hats have always promoted a favorite candidate. Fragile, they are hard to find, since most were unwearable by the time convention week had ended.

In earlier days, however, the hat assumed a place of honor and was treated accordingly, making those prime collectibles today. In some instances, the adornments attached to the hat garner more attention than the hat itself. One example is the early tricorn with colorful cockades that were worn for the Thomas Jefferson/John Adams political duel. The lines were clearly drawn, with Jefferson supporters attaching red, white and blue rosettes and Adams supporters favoring brown and black.

There were also parade hats, beach hats, cowboy hats, beanies, baseball caps, straw skimmers, yarmulkes, coonskin varieties, ski caps, even painters' caps. One 1896 model was fashioned from a Boston newspaper, which folded one way to promote the candidacy of William Jennings Bryan and another to favor William McKinley. After 1948, some campaigns made assembling even easier, providing cardboard models with instructions.

Toys/Banks

Often manufactured in limited quantities, political toys are hard to find; however, due to a general lack of interest, their cost to the collector remains fairly low.

Mechanical and still banks are the main items in this category, but everything from dolls and marbles to battery-operated figures and board games depicted politics.

Political Causes; Splinter Parties

Apart from the usual political campaigns involving but a few parties, items for particular causes also fall into the venue of political memorabilia. These would include such diverse groups as the National Women's Party, the Native American Party, the Know Nothings, and early labor movements like the Wobblies (Industrial Workers of the World). Prior to 1900, materials pertaining to such groups were most often of paper, with the category later dominated by buttons. With movements like those involving civil rights, abortion, nuclear power, and the Black Panthers, this category has become especially active since 1960.

Founded in 1869, the Prohibition Party has participated in every campaign since, as well as promoting its cause in the interim. The movement spawned a host of other groups, like the Women's Christian Temperance Union, the Anti Saloon League, the Washington Temperance Society (Washingtonians) and the Cold Water Army (a children's temperance group).

Suffragette materials ran the gamut from parade sashes, tote bags and broadsides to china and tin window hangers.

Anti-prohibition and anti-suffrage items were equally popular. These included decals, bar items, beer schooners, and canes with beer barrel tops from the 1933 Chicago World's Fair.

An early advocate for women's rights and outspoken nonconformist was Victoria Claflin Woodhull, who ran for president in 1872 and was a prime target for cartoonists like Thomas Nast. Also prominent in the movement was Belva Ann Lockwood, nominated for president by the National Equal Rights Party in 1884. Materials relating to both Woodhull and Lockwood are rare.

In addition to a 1872 campaign poster, only three items are known for the latter—the paper *Equal Rights*, a campaign rebus puzzle ribbon and a card featuring Lockwood with a movable paper skirt.

General Guidelines: Especially rare are all items for Victoria C. Woodhill, Prohibition Party lapel pins/buttons from the campaigns of 1872, 1876 and 1880, as well as Wobblie literature.

Clocks and Watches

The earliest political timepiece is from the Harrison 1840 campaign. Watch fobs also conveyed political themes. Although most were of brass, there were also celluloid models, some with fiber-board or leather backings. One of the earliest wristwatches is from the Woodrow Wilson campaign, with others following in more contemporary campaigns, many in caricature stylings.

General Guidelines: All 19th century clocks and pocket watches are rare. Especially noteworthy are the 1888 pocket watch with a Harrison/Morton jugate and the 1896 one featuring a McKinley portrait. Considered quite rare is a 1920 pocket watch with Cox/Roosevelt on the dial.

Publications
Collecting Political Americana by Edmund B. Sullivan (Christopher Publishing House, 1991)

Hake's Guide to Presidential Campaign Collectibles by Ted Hake (Wallace-Homestead)

Political Button Books by Theodore Hake (Hake's Americana and Collectibles, 1985)

Collectors Guide to Presidential Inaugural Medals and Memorabilia by R. Joseph Levine (Johnson and Jensen, 1981)

Collecting Political Buttons by Marc Sigoloff (Chicago Review Press, 1988)

American Political Ribbons and Ribbon Badges by Edmund B. Sullivan and Roger A. Fischer (Quarterman Publications, 1985)

Clubs
•The American Political Items Collectors
 P.O. Box 340339, San Antonio, TX 78234

•The Political Collector
 P.O. Box 5171, York, PA 17405

•The Political Bandwagon
 P.O. Box 348, Leola, PA 17540

•American Locals Political Items
 1111 W. Whiteside, Springfield, MO 65807

•The Thomas Nast Society
 Morristown/Morris Township Library
 Miller Road, Morristown, NJ 07960

Contributor to this section: Robert Ball

Pins, Buttons, Lapel Devices and Medals

Roosevelt/Johnson jugate; 1912 .... $1,000+

Cox/Roosevelt jugate (Americanize America);
1920 .... $40,000+

Harding/Coolidge jugate; sepia/cream; 1920 .. $1,800-$2,200

Davis/Bryan jugate; 1924 .... $900-$1,200

Taft and Wilhelm II jugate; "Sixth Annual German Day, Aug.
8, 1910" .... $175-$225

Washington inaugural button; inscribed "March the Fourth
1789 Memorable Era;" brass .... $1,500+

Pre-1872 large medalets .... $150+

Warren Harding/Calvin Coolidge jugate; 1920 .... $1,000+

Bryan/Sewell jugate; "Victory 1896" .... $200+

Kennedy brass inaugural medal; 1961 .... $40-$60

Parker/Davis jugate "Shure Mike,"1904 .... $650-$750

Van Buren clothing button; brass; 1840 .... $175-$225

Cleveland/Hendricks button; brass; 1884 .... $20-$40

T. Roosevelt "Welcome" button; 1904 .... $1,800-$2,200

"Win with Wilson," 1916 .... $30-$45

"For Vice President Franklin D. Roosevelt,"
1920 .... $1,800-$2,200

"Landon on the New Deal,"1936 .... $2,200-$2,800

"Every 'Buddy' for Wilkie," 1940 .... $325-$375

Blaine stickpin; plumed knight; 1884 .... $175-$225

Lincoln/Hamlin ferreotype; lapel device; 1860 ..... $425-$475

Hoover and wife clothing buttons; celluloid cover; brass
rims; 1932 .... $100-$125/pr

"U.S. for Ike,"1952 .... $75-$95

"Youth for Kennedy,"1960 .... $225-$250

"On the Right Track with Jack,"1960 .... $25-$35

Inauguration badge; brass hanger/pink ribbon;
1949 .... $40-$60

"Teddy's Terrors" (L.A. Rough Riders convention); early
1900s .... $425-$475

McKinley/Atlanta Peace Jubilee; 1898 .... $100-$150

Taft The Gunnison Tunnel Opening/Montrose, CO; elliptical
design; 1910 .... $275-$325

Al Smith Day (button and ribbons); 1928 .... $275-$325

"Be Safe with Hoover,"1932 .... $35-$50

"Me for Al" (Smith campaign); 1928 .... $45-$65

"No Oil on Al," 1928 .... $225-$265

Landon/Knox; felt sunflower w/elephant; 1936 .... $15-$25

Truman Minnesota Club; brown/gold; 1948 .... $150-$175

"Truman Fights for Human Rights," 1948 .... $175-$200

"Make the White House the Dwight House,"1952 .... $10-$15

"Veterans for Ike," blue/white; 1952 .... $15-$20

"Come Clean Geraldine" (Reagan campaign) 1984 ... $5-$10

Coattail Buttons

"Roosevelt-Lehman American Labor Party,"1936 .... $10-$15

"Wilkie/Vanderbilt," r/w/b; 1940 .... $125-$145

"Vote Harriman/Roosevelt/CIO," litho; 1944 .... $10-$15

"Work and Wages/Roosevelt/Curley,"1932 .... $275-$325

Hoover/Allen/Young; 1928 .... $55-$75

Carter/Mondale/Moynihan; 1976 .... $3-$8

Ribbons, Ribbon Badges, Silks

Ribbon, Garfield/Arthur; colorful design; dual photos;
1880 .... $175-$250

Ribbon, Blaine/Logan pictures; red/gold; 1884 .... $45-$65

Ribbon; Cleveland; r/w/b/gold; paper photo; 1888 . $85-$125

Ribbon-shaped bookmark; Harrison/Reid; celluloid; paper
photos; 1892 .... $120-$145

Ribbon; "I Am for Bryan and American Manhood,"
1908 .... $35-$50

Ribbon; Wm. Jennings Bryan; "The Commoner,"
1908 .... $55-$75

Ribbon badge; "McKinley and Hobart," celluloid jugate;
1896 .... $150-$175

Ribbon badge; Harrison; celluloid sheet w/portrait;
1892 .... $85-$125

Ribbon badge; Wm. Jennings Bryan; tin frame; cardboard
photo; metal bell; 1908 .... $55-$75

Ribbon badge; "Henry Clay Pride of America,"
1844 .... $150-$200

Ribbon badge; "Grant and Colfax," 1872 .... $475-$525

Ferrotypes

Stephen A. Douglas ferrotype; doughnut-style; silvered
brass; Hershel Johnson on reverse; 1860 ... $2,400-$2,600

"John C. Breckenridge" ferrotype; brass rim; Lane on
reverse; 1860 .... $375-$425

McClelland/Pendleton jugate ferrotype; 1864 .... $9,000+

"Abraham Lincoln" ferrotype; velvet-covered rim; Hamlin on
reverse; 1860 .... $400-$500

"John C. Breckenridge" ferrotype; brass rim; Lane on
reverse; 1860 .... $350-$450

Lincoln ferrotype; brass shell frame; reverse paper label;
1864 .... $600-$700

Lincoln ferrotype; brass rim/stickpin; 1864 .... $375-$450

Grant ferrotype; fabric rim; stickpin; 1868 .... $200-$300

"Grant/Colfax" jugate; pictures on front; brass shell frame;
pin back; 1868 .... $450-$550

"Grant/Wilson" jugate ferrotype; brass shell frame; pin on
reverse; 1872 .... $1,000-$1,200

Greeley/Brown jugate front; shell frame; reverse pin/Greeley
portrait on back; 1872 .... $1,650-$1,850

Hayes/Wheeler jugate ferrotype; stickpin reverse;
1876 .... $500-$700

Textiles/Fabric/Banners

Campaign flags .... $150+

Hoover blue/orange fabric banner; 1932 .... $225-$275

Smith canvas banner; 1928 .... $375-$425

Roosevelt fabric banner; yellow fringe; 1940 .... $45-$65

"Tippicanoe and Morton Too" bandanna; Harrison/Morton;
r/w/b; 1888 .... $150-$200

Harrison/Morton kerchief; black/white; wide dotted border;
1888 .... $125-$175

Harrison bandanna; elaborate black/white/red design;
1888 .... $325-$375

Cleveland/Thurman bandanna; black/white;
1888 .... $175-$225

"We Want Wilkie" kerchief; r/w/b; 1940 .... $45-$65

"Win With Ike for President" bandanna; 1956 .... $50-$70

"Win with Ike" bandanna; rwb; 1952 .... $50-$70

"I Like Ike" bandanna; 1952 .... $20-$40

"McGovern for President" bandanna; 1972 .... $35-$50

William Howard Taft kerchief; 1908 .... $225-$275

Wm. Henry Harison bandanna; 1888 .... $325-$375

Parker/Davis bandanna; 1904 .... $325-$375

Teddy Roosevelt bandanna; r/w/brown; 1912 .... $125-$175

Handkerchief "G.O.P. Republican Party;" elephant; r/w/b;
1964 .... $10-$20

Paper and Art

Pre-1872 cartoons and black/white prints .... $200-$800

Currier and Ives print "Abraham Lincoln/Andrew Johnson,"
1864 .... $900-$1,200

Colorful pre-1880 sheet music .... $175-$800

Political almanacs .... $100-$600

Early presidential documents and autographs .... $150+

"Who is James Buchanan?" paper; b/w portrait;
1856 .... $325-$375

Campaign biography "The Heroic Life of William
McKinley;" 48 pp.; 1902 .... $15-$25

"Official Program 43rd Inauguration 1957," 48 pp. Rockwell
cover Eisenhower/Nixon; 1957 .... $30-$45

Trade card; Garfield/Hancock; swivel cover; b/w/pink
metamorphic; Springfield, MA shoe store .... $65-$85

Trade card; Cleveland/Stevenson; 1892; "Ale & Beef
Co." .... $20-$40

Greeley Liberal Republican Ticket; 1872 .... $65-$85

Levering/Hale Natl. Prohibition Ticket; 1896 .... $65-$85

1920 Presidental ballot with party electors .... $65-$85

Truman inauguration ticket; 1949 .... $20-$25

Roosevelt framed inauguration jugate photo; 1933 ... $65-$85

Wilson inauguration program; 1917 .... $65-$85

Program; 1948 Republican Natl. Convention .... $25-$40

Democratic Natl. Convention Guest ticket; 1940 .... $5-$10

Republican party platform booklet; 24 pages; jugate cover;
1932 .... $20-$25

"Roosevelt and Johnson," b/w paper poster;
1912 .... $120-$150

"Forward with Roosevelt," b/w; cardboard; 1936 ..... $65-$85

"James M. Cox" b/w paper poster; 1920 .... $175-$225

"Warren G. Harding" brown/white paper poster;
1920 .... $75-$100

Postcard, "TR, Coming Home, Glad tidings," Taft/elephant/
Uncle Sam dancing; 1910 .... $35-$50

Postcard, "Taft," caricature; fabric clothing/brass buttons;
1908 .... $40-$60

Postcard; "Give us Roosevelt or Give us Taft,"
1908 .... $20-$35

Postcard, "Pull my Tail and See the Next President,"
elephant/Taft photo .... $45-$60

Postcard; "For President, Woodrow Wilson," 1916 ... $10-$20

Postcard; "Dewey-Warren The Way Ahead," 1948 ... $10-$20

Postcard; "Vote for John P. Kennedy,"1960 .... $10-$20

Window poster; "Keep Pennsylvania Liberal, Forward with
Roosevelt: b/w; 1936 .... $65-$85

Poster; "Calvin Coolidge;" sepia; 1924 .... $30-$50

Cardboard poster; "Elect Congressman Nixon U.S. Senator;"
Nixon portrait; 1950 .... $30-$40

Cardboard poster; "Goldwater and Miller," r/w/b;
1964 .... $20-$35

Paper poster; "Johnson/Humphrey for the USA,"
1964 .... $10-$15

Paper poster; "For Vice President Spiro T. Agnew,"
1968 .... $35-$45

"The Goldwater Cartoon Book," 1964 .... $10-$15

Parade Canes and Walking Sticks

Walking stick; Cleveland bust in white metal;
1888 .... $185-$225

Cane head; white metal bust of FDR; bronze finish; reads
"Roosevelt/Century of Progress," 1933 .... $30-$45

Tobacco Products

Papier mache snuffboxes .... $150+

Hand-painted cigar/card cases .... $350-$650

Clay pipe without stem; "Henry Clay," 1844 .... $175-$225

Clay pipe; Bryan; no stem; 3908 .... $65-$100

"Bryan and Sewall-16-1" cigar box; wooden;
1896 .... $65-$100

"Square Deal" Roosevelt cigar box; wooden;
1904 .... $65-$100

Match holder; Greeley; cast iron; 1872 .... $225-$275

McKinley silver ashtray; silver bug/brass nail;
1896 .... $225-$275

Bryan matchsafe; Bryan; silvered brass; 1896 ...... $125-$175

Carved portrait pipe; Al Smith; celluloid stem;
1928 .... $175-$225

Jumbo cigar; Al Smith on colorful label; 1928 .... $35-$50

"Presidents-Roosevelt and Garner" cigar box; white/wooden;
jugate paper label; 1932 .... $75-$100

Boxed bubble gum cigars; "I Like Adlai" on inside lid;
1952 .... $20-$40

Johnson/Humphrey match pack; jugate photos; 1964 ... $3-$5

China ashtray; Ford photo; b/w; 1974 .... $10-$15

Hats

Harrison campaign hat; beige; Harrison/Morton on inside
label; 1888 .... $225-$300

Beaver hat; felt; paper label of Cleveland/Harrison w/running
mates inside; 1892 .... $200-$350

Inscribed miniature china/glass hats .... $125-$250

Inscribed miniature terra cotta hats .... $75-$175

Unmarked miniature styles (dependent on
materials) .... $75-$175

Kennedy plastic hat; r/w/b paper band; 1960 .... $35-$45

Styrofoam hat; "Goldwater in '64," white w/black/gold band
with Goldwater pictures; 1964 .... $20-$30

Western hat; "L.B.J. for the U.S.A."; orange felt;
1964 .... $15-$20

Toys/Banks

Tammany bank; cast iron; movable politician,
1872 .... $375-$425

Harrison/Cleveland scales, bisque figures;
1888 .... $1,100-$1,300

McKinley cast-iron cap bomb w/signature;
1896 .... $275-$325

Playing Possum with Taft jigsaw puzzle w/box;
1909 .... $115-$135

Roosevelt at San Juan card game, 1899 .... $135-$175

Marble; sulphide bust of Teddy Roosevelt .... $135-$175
Al Smith celluloid dime bank; r/w/b; 1928 .... $135-$175
Roosevelt/Garner inaugural jigsaw puzzle; jugate pictures/
    Capitol; 1932 .... $30-$45
FDR bank; metal/bronze finish; 1940 .... $35-$50
Anti-Kennedy New Frontier/The Game Nobody Can Win,
    1962 .... $35-$50
Bluff board game; Kennedy/Khrushchev; 1963 .... $45-$65
Goldwater bank, 1964 .... $20-$30
Johnson donkey hand puppet, 1964 .... $8-$15
Anti-Agnew dart board; "Et tu Spiro," 1972 .... $25-$35
Jimmy the Walking Peanut wind-up toy; 1980 .... $20-$30
Miniature plastic football; "Win One More for the Gipper
    Reagan-Bush" (N.Y. Republicans); 1984 .... $10-$18

Political Causes; Splinter Parties

Mr. Dry bar set; coffin-shaped .... $150 or less
Mantel clock; cast iron; cocktail party figures; moveable
    arms under $200
Anti-Prohibition decal; donkey/elephant/beer keg
    under $100
Women's suffrage periodicals .... $75-$250
Anti-Saloon League postcard .... $10-$15
WCTU button, white ribbon, 1928, inscribed "WCTU/Vote
    for Hoover" .... $60+
Any Cold Water Army material $125
Washingtonian ribbons .... $30-$75
Carry Nation brass/mother of pearl hatchet pin; pearl/
    rhinestone .... $100+
Carry Nation iron hatchet pin .... $25-$75
"Vote for My Sake" (child); Prohibition button .... $15-$20
"Socialist Candidates 1912/Debs-Seidel" jugate .. $175-$225

Clocks and Watches

Pocket watch; Cox/Roosevelt on dial; 1920 .... $25,000
Roosevelt and Fairbanks watch fob; brass; 1904 ...... $20-$30
William J. Bryan watch fob; celluloid/leather; 1908 . $45-$60
Woodrow Wilson watch fob; celluloid; 1912 .... $75-$95
Taft watch fob; celluloid/fiberboard; 1908 .... $125-$175
Roosevelt watch fob; high relief portrait; copper;
    1904 .... $20-$35
Rough Rider clock; brass; 1904 .... $225-$275
F.D.R. The Man of the Hour metal clock; 1936 .... $125-$175
Carter/Mondale in '76 pocket watch; silver case ...... $40-$50
Nixon-Agnew wristwatch "Watch them Doing Time for You,"
    1974 .... $85-$125
Electric clock picturing all presidents from Washington thru
    LBJ; 1964 .... $35-$45
Electric clock; plastic; r/w/b figure of Agnew;
    1973 .... $45-$60

Miscellaneous Items

Wood box; Jackson inauguration; litho portrait; 1829 $3,000
Pocket mirror; Taylor campaign; pewter; French; 1848 . $500
Bryan/Stevenson tray .... $625-$675
Garfield white ceramic pitcher; raised portrait and banner;
    1880 .... $375-$425
Sheet music, *Hail, Brave Garfield*, 1880 .... $30-$40
Pressed clear glass mourning plate; bust of Garfield; "We
    Mourn our Nation's Loss," 1881 .... $25-$35
Ceramic tile; McKinley profile; light blue; 1896 ...... $35-$50

Tin horn; McKinley; "Patriotism/Protection/Prosperity,"
    1896 .... $65-$85
Umbrella, McKinley handle; 1896 .... $450+
Jugate glass; portraits of McKinley/Roosevelt in frosted
    white; "Integrity, Inspiration, Industry," 1900 ...... $65-$85
Lantern; lunch bucket style; black tin; "McKinley and
    Roosevelt" one side, "4 Years More of Full Dinner Pail"
    on other; 1900 .... $650-$750
Noisemaker; "Roosevelt/Fairbanks," wood slats/gear wheel;
    1904 .... $125-$175
W.H. Taft/J.S. Sherman oval platter; portraits; 1908 . $35-$45
Fan; "The Roosevelt Creed" picturing Teddy Roosevelt;
    advertisement on back; 1916 .... $25-$40
Sheet music, *Never Swap Horses When You're Crossing a
    Stream*, 1916 .... $20-$30
Teddy Roosevelt tray .... $475-$525
Figural bottle busts .... $150+
NRA bust of FDR; metal/gold finish; r/w/b eagle ... $85-$125
Fan; FDR, Garner, and Cabinet; 1933 .... $45-$55
Pocket mirror; "It's an Elephant's Job No Time for Donkey
    Business," 1936 .... $100-$150
That Grand Old Party sheet music; 1948 .... $10-$15
Eisenhower tie; Ike/yellow lightning/Capitol .... $40-$50
Pitcher shaped like bust of Eisenhower in military uniform;
    1952 .... $65-$85
Sunglasses; "I Like Ike," plastic/blue ribbons; 1952 . $30-$40
Sheet music, *March on with Adlai and John*, 1952 ... $35-$50
I Like Ike! ceramic elephant ashtray; 1952 .... $25-$35
Vest; "Vote Nixon Lodge Experience Counts," r/w/b stripes;
    1960 .... $30-$40
Bow tie; "I'm for Kennedy," white/embroidery;
    1960 .... $65-$85
Salt and pepper shakers; "President John F. Kennedy/Mrs.
    John F. Kennedy; 1961 .... $25-$35
Fan; "Goldwater Fan Club," cardboard; 1964 .... $25-$35

POSTCARDS

U.S. postal regulations first allowed postcards in 1872. Prior to this, early souvenir cards were produced, depicting tourist attractions and special events around the world. These early postcards were called "pioneer" cards. Most of these were illustrations on government-printed postal cards or privately-printed souvenir cards. Writing was allowed on one side of these cards with only the address on the other side.

From 1898 to 1918, many cards were printed by European publishers, especially English and German. In 1898, private printers were granted permission by the U.S. Congress to sell cards inscribed "Private Mailing Card" (PMC). In 1901, Congress granted permission to use the word "postcard." At this time, the message was still only allowed on one side of the card and the address on the other.

In 1907, divided backs were allowed, permitting the sender to write a note on the left side of the card and place the address on the right. Linen postcards became popular in the 1940s and chrome cards in the 1950s.

General Guidelines: The two general collecting categories of postcards are views and topics.

Views are pictures or photographs of places like cities, states and monuments. Views of small towns are usually more rare than those of large cities. Some of these postcards are made from actual photographs and are called "real-photo" postcards. Real-photo postcards are highly sought-after.

Topics are postcards centering around a particular theme such as holidays, advertising or Black Americana. It's easy to find many vintage topic postcards. Some of the major publishers were Tuck, Paul Finkenrath, Detroit, Whitney and Winsch. Many postcard publishers used a different logo or style for printing the words "Post Card," so by checking the back of a card, you may be able to determine the publisher.

Among the most collectible postcards are those that feature advertising, artist signatures, Black Americana, characters, hold-to-light, holidays, paper toys, political themes, sets and installments, and souvenir postcards.

Advertising postcards promoted products. Some popular advertising postcards are Bull Durham, Campbell's Soup, Coca-Cola and Cracker Jack. Political postcards promoted a particular candidate or political party. And souvenir postcards depict tourist attractions or special events. Black Americana cards portray African-Americans, often in an early racist stereotypes.

Artist-signed postcards are cards in which the artist signed the original artwork used to print the postcard. Sometimes, the signature gets cropped or completely lost from the printed postcard. A missing or cropped signature does not necessarily render the card uncollectible, especially if the artist has an identifiable style. Some popular postcard artists include Frances Brundage, Ellen Clapsaddle, H.B.G. (Griggs) and Rose O'Neill.

Characters were frequently depicted on postcards, from favorite TV show personalities to comic characters. Some popular postcard characters are Felix the Cat, Mickey Mouse and Kewpie.

Artist signed by Xavier Sager.

PRESERVATION

Because postcards are made of paper, proper preservation is essential to maintaining their value and visual appeal. Cards should be kept in a cool, dry and dark place. Sunlight and humidity can damage cards. Plastic storage sleeves should be free of PVC which will damage paper with extended exposure. If storing postcards in albums, use one with acid-free paper.

When held to light, hold-to-light postcards result in a changed image. There are two categories of hold-to-light cards. The first, and more common, are transparencies. Transparencies have a hidden inner layer that contains an image only seen when the card is held to light. The second type are die-cut cards. The top layer has small die-cut shapes that shine with illuminated color when they are held against the light. All hold-to-light cards require a significant amount of light to enjoy their full effect. These hold-to-light cards can have values into the hundreds of dollars.

Paper toy postcards often are paper dolls to cut out that have changes of outfits on other postcards. Books of paper doll postcards were also produced. Another popular postcard toy is the mechanical paper doll. The body is separate from the arms and legs of the doll; when cut out, they can be assembled with paper fasteners or strings, resulting in a mechanical doll. Unused cards carry a premium.

Some collectors look for sets, or a group of postcards that center around one theme, for instance, days of the week or the zodiac. Installments are sets that consist of three or more cards that, when pieced together, form the entire picture. These are sometimes called puzzle cards.

Condition is essential when grading a postcard. Collectors look for those in Near Mint to Mint condition. Rounded corners, tears, creasing, dirt and fading decrease a card's value.

Clubs

- Bay State Post Card Club
  P.O. Box 334, Lexington, MA 02173

- Borderland Post Card Club
  1024 Oneida, El Paso, TX 79912

- Cape Cod Post Card Club
  Short Neck Rd., South Dennis, MA 02173

- Hawaii Postcard Club
  P.O. Box 15273, Honolulu, HI 96830

- Illinois State Post Card Club
  Corn Belt Philatelic Society Postcard Division
  Janice Jenkins
  Box 625, Bloomington, IL 61702-0625

POSTCARD TERMS

The following are some terms used in postcard collecting.

appr pl: appropriate place
b&w or b/w: black and white
c: chrome
clr: color
cof: cancel (postmark) on front
cr or crs: crease
cnr or crn: corner
d/b: divided back
emb: embossed
l: linen
lt: light
m/t: margin tear
o/w: otherwise
p/ or pub: publisher
pm: postmark
rp: real photo
s/ or sgn: artist-signed
s/m: stamp missing
slt: slight
u: used
und/b or u/b: undivided back
unu: unused
wb: white border
wob: writing on back
wof: writing on front

Santa Claus, printed in Germany, postmarked 1908.

• Orange County Post Card Club
  10601 Ketch Ave., Garden Grove, CA 92643

• Tucson Post Card Exchange Club
  820 Via Lucitas, Tucson, AZ 85718

• Webfooters Post Card Club
  4838 N. Lombard St., Portland, OR 97236-1072

Contributor to this section: Susan Brown Nicholson, P.O. Box 595, Lisle, IL 60532.

POSTCARD VS. POSTAL CARD?

The biggest difference between a postcard and a postal card is that a postcard needs a stamp; a postal card does not. A postal card, printed by the U.S. Post Office, already has postage printed on it. Since 1873, postal cards have been printed in the United States.

Santa Claus, Tuck, England, card #1822 from "Oilette" series, dated 1907.

President Franklin D. Roosevelt (in auto) at Little
   White House, Warm Springs, GA $25
Rudolph Valentino playing chess $20
Russia Military Uniform "One of the Palace Grenadiers" .. $4
San Francisco souvenir book w/25 detachable cards $9
Snowman, children, Nash Children Series No. 1 .... $5
Spain, large crowd, shows Queen Ena & King Alfonso
   leaving church after their wedding $12
Tolstoy, Russian author, with daughter at typewriter $15
Uncle Sam says to Kaiser "My Hat's in the Ring" $10
Valentine's Day, Cupid "A Token of Love," $3
Valentine's Day, "The Cook" $9

World's Columbian Exposition souvenir postcard.

Official Souvenir, World's Fair—St. Louis, 1904.

Halloween is celebrated through postcards.

PUZZLES

Wooden jigsaw puzzles existed prior to the 19th century. Like board games of the time, puzzles often came in colorfully-lithographed boxes and illustrated popular characters or advertising slogans of the day.

Before the 1930s, puzzles were primarily made of wood. Those were later replaced with die-cut cardboard. Popular early manufacturers included McLoughlin Bros., Jaymar, Saalfield, Hood and Tuco.

Puzzle collectors often specialize in a particular time period, theme, or medium. Popular collecting areas include advertising puzzles, pre-World War I children's wood puzzles and puzzle blocks, and character-related puzzles.

General Guidelines: One missing piece detracts substantially from the value of a jigsaw puzzle, as much as 25 to 75 percent. The only way to make sure a puzzle is complete is to assemble it. Collectors often place a premium on the original box, since the graphics are so attractive. Boxes are also important since the picture on the cover is often essential to completing the puzzle.

Puzzles featuring advertising slogans; military themes; Black Americana; or popular TV, movie, or music characters are the most desirable. Generic landscapes have little collectors' value.

Frame tray puzzles are wood, plastic or cardboard puzzles in which the pieces are housed on a flat backing. They usually have few (less than 20) pieces and feature cartoon or television characters. Those from the 1940s-1960s featuring Western heroes, Disney characters or popular TV show themes are the most collectible. Many sell in the $5-$25 range, but popular themes can command much more.

Arthur G. Grinnell, Christmas Eve, 6 1/4" x 13 3/4", c. 1906, litho on wood, cardboard box reads "Superior picture puzzles for grown-ups, shut-ins and others."

VALUE LINE

Prices listed are for complete puzzles in Excellent condition.

Advertising Puzzles

Advertising jigsaw puzzles, 1946-present	$10-$30
Advertising jigsaw puzzles, early 1800s	$100-$300
Black Cat Hosiery, 60 pcs, c1909	$25
Chevrolet School Bus, 35 pcs, 1932	$50
Cream of Wheat, cowboy's mailbox, c1909	$35
Foiled by Essolube, 1933, Dr. Seuss illustration	$85
Folger's Coffee, c1965, cardboard, metal container	$5
Hood Farm Puzzle Box, c1905, set of three	$50
Jap Rose Soap, Kirk Co., 1910	$14
Old Fashioned New England Country Store, Chase & Sanborn, c1909	$16
Sparkalong Burgess, Burgess Battery Co., 1952	$18
The Everett Piano, 16 pcs, cardboard folder	$60
Use Coe's Fertilizer, c1909	$30

Animal Puzzles

Boston Terrier, Hobby Jig Saws series, 300 pcs, Jaymar, 1944	$5
Circus Puzzle, Milton Bradley	$75
Cut-Up Animals Spelling Slips, 27 pcs, McLoughlin Brothers, c1900	$90
Domestic Animals, Parker Brothers, 1930	$40
Farm Friends, Zig Zag Puzzle Co., 1933	$20
Thoroughbred, CC Stevens, 1930	$30

Biblical Puzzles

Temple of Knowledge, 86 pcs, double-sided, c1890	$65
The Ark Puzzle, c1880	$175
The Tower of Babel, 1870s	$50

Character Puzzles

Aladdin and His Lamp, cardboard, metal canister, c1970	$3
Atom Ant, tile, black and white, c1960	$50
Bambi, frame tray, Jaymar, 1950s	$20
Barbie & The Rockers, Golden, 1987	$5

"A Bully Time in Spain," SOHIO radio jigsaw puzzle, No. 3, complete, copyright 1933

Beatles Yellow Submarine: Beatles in Pepperland, 1970, Jaymar $110
Bullwinkle, 1971 .... $25
Captain Kangaroo, frame tray, 1977 .... $8
Dukes of Hazzard, 200 pcs, 1982 .... $10
Fairy Tales Puzzles, c1963, set of four $8
Flipper, frame tray, Whitman, 1966 .... $12
Ghostbusters, 49 pcs, floor puzzle $20
Howdy Doody, cardboard, Milton Bradley $75
Little Black Sambo, masonite pcs, 1963 .... $10
Mickey Mouse, "On the Way," Jaymar, 1962 .... $15
Mother Goose Scroll Puzzles, set of two $75
Munsters, 1965, Whitman $60
Our Gang, 80 pcs, 11" by 14" envelope $100
The Wizard Of Oz, Jaymar, 1960 .... $25
Wee Willie Winkie, 30 pcs, Milton Bradley, 1930s $14

History and Geography Puzzles

Dissected Map of the United States, with colored guide map, 1854 .... $100
Gen. John J. Pershing, 420 pcs, 1920s $35
Highlander, Girl and Tommy, England, 1915 .... $35
John Glenn, plastic envelope, Japan, 1960s $5
Nelson at Trafalgar, plywood, cardboard box $40
Our Battleships, Milton Bradley, 1917 .... $100
Reading of the Declaration, Milton Bradley, 1930 .... $75
Spiro Agnew, Friend of the Silent Majority, 500 pcs, 1970 .... $8
Tank Busters and Jeeps on The Job, Victory series, 365 pcs, J. Pressman & Co., c1943-45 .... $14
The Conquerors, 1933 .... $7

World's Columbian Exposition Puzzle, cardboard, 49 pcs, 1891 .... $125

Miscellaneous

Frame tray puzzles, cardboard, featuring TV/cartoon characters .... $5-$50
Little Golden Books w/puzzles intact, 1950s .... $20-$30
Military jigsaw puzzles, post-WWII .... $20-$50

Postcard Puzzles

Custom House, Boston, Mass, c1933 .... $6
Head House and Beach City Point, South Boston, Mass, c1909 .... $8
Jig Saw Greetings, girl holding dog, Hallmark Cards, c1940 .... $8

Puzzle Books

Case of the Duplicate Door, Mystery Puzzle of the Month #2, with 16-pg booklet, Pearl Publishing Co., 1940s $10
Murder By the Stars, Mystery-Jig series, 300 pcs, with eight-pg booklet $14

The Mayflower Compact Picture Puzzle (above), Madmar, double sided, hunting scene on reverse (below), 10" x 8".

McLoughlin Bros. was a popular early 1900s manufacturer of lithographed toys, especially puzzles and games.

RADIOS

While the first radio broadcast can be traced back to 1892, the public wasn't widely exposed to radio until 1920.

One of radio's early pioneers was Frank Conrad, a Westinghouse engineer, who transmitted amateur radio signals in 1920. A wartime hiatus had given him an opportunity to further his work, including extensive research on vacuum tubes. Conrad began his musical transmissions via phonograph records. As might be expected, interest was soon at a fever pitch, mushrooming into hundreds of broadcasting stations and the need for thousands of receivers. Manufacturers during those early days of radio included RCA Victor, Westinghouse, Atwater Kent, Crosley and Fada.

Crystal sets operated on the simple premise of an electrical reaction taking place within a mineral. Crystals could not control the volume of the signal, thus necessitating a large antenna and good grounding. Although most operators were limited to signals available within a very confined radius, large antennas and considerable patience enabled some to pick up stations hundreds of miles away. Even with the continuing advances in radio transmissions, many purists enjoyed the magic of crystal sets well into the 1930s and 1940s.

The 1930s ushered in the golden age of radio, honing an already popular form of entertainment into one that few American homes could do without. Joining the early manufacturing pioneers in this burgeoning enterprise were Zenith, Philco, Motorola, Majestic, Emerson, Arvin, Howard, Sparton and Grunow. In addition, companies like Sears, Montgomery Ward, Spiegel, Western Auto, Firestone, Goodyear, Goodrich and Walgreen's quickly recognized the sales and advertising potential in placing their own names on the cabinets.

General Guidelines: Rare and historically significant is the Atwater Kent Breadboard, which has all parts mounted on a board, with no cabinet. Others of special note are mirrored glass examples, popular during 1935–1936, as well as federal battery radios. There are, nevertheless, a bounty of collectible radios to accommodate every taste and pocketbook, with the bulk of those found in most current collections costing less than $250.

RCA Victor radio, Model 65X1, red plastic case, electric, 11" x 7" x 6 1/2".

Contributors to this section: Floyd A. Paul, 1545 Raymond Ave., Glendale, CA 91201; James Fred, 5355 S. 275W, Cutler, IN 46920.

Composition Radios

Early composition radios (1920s and 1930s) were most often made of Bakelite or Catalin plastics. Bakelite radios were brown or black; those made of Catalin were more colorful and often marbelized. Catalin radios change color with age; most shades darken or change color completely. Molding Catalin was a labor-intensive process, which made its production increasingly cost prohibitive following World War II. Catalin was also fragile, making these models scarce in today's collectible market. This, coupled with their colorful appearance, explains their generally higher values.

Plaskon was similar to Bakelite. Available in ivory and opaque colors, many of brilliant hues, it was subject to fine stress lines. Also of note, and referred to as beetle plastic, was a white marbelized composition swirled with color and manufactured under the Plaskon name during the late 1930s-early 1940s. Tenite, used most often in grilles and accessory pieces like knobs and handles, warped when exposed to heat.

International Kadette manufactured the first molded plastic radio cabinet, noteworthy for their design and color. Just one Catalin radio, the Clockette, carried the Kadette name. Kadette did, however, manufacture important models, like he Topper and the Classic, made of Plaskon, Bakelite and beetle compositions.

One of the finest plastic radios is the Bullet, made by Frank Angelo D'Andrea (Fada). The radio was called the 115 Streamliner when introduced in 1941, then redesigned in 1945 as the Model 1000.

Emerson Catalin and Bakelite radios rank equally high among collectors, as do Motorola models from this period. One of Emerson's best known stylings was the Tombstone. Also high on collectors' lists is Emersons Patriot (or Aristocrat) model. The design for this 1940 radio was the work of famed industrial designer Norman Bel Geddes.

If the radio in these vintage sets works, the heat generated will most likely crack the plastic. For this reason, many collectors choose not to operate vintage radios. Non-working models aren't necessarily worth less than working ones. Old plastic casings are also subject to shrinkage and cracking, making removal of the case risky when considering repairs.

Although their appearance is suggestive of the Art Deco period, many collectors prefer the plastic radios manufactured in the late 1940s-early '50s.

Some of the most collectible radios to look for include Fada Bullets and Temples in yellow; radios with contrasting color trims; plastic insert grilles with speaker behind; and Catalin models.

Wood Radios (Consoles/Table Models)

Standard wood radios were made as table or console (floor) models. Highboy consoles have four to six legs that encompass at least one half of the overall height; lowboys also have four to six legs, but these comprise less than half the overall height. These were popular during radio's Golden Age.

Particularly collectible are radios featuring celebrities/characters (Mae West, Mickey Mouse, Dionne Quintuplets); early models with chrome, aluminum or lacquer trims; early Stromberg-Carlson and Atwater Kent models

Transistor Radios

Models by Raytheon, Hoffman, Bulova, Regency and Zenith are the most popular; however, particular styles (such as the Emerson 888 and Regency TR-1) by a variety of other manufacturers also command attention among collectors. Any solar- powered model also ranks high. With these exceptions, other American made sets are only collectible if they meet the above criteria and are in Mint in Box condition.

Color is also important in determining desirability and value. Red and white models by Regency are fairly common; gray models and marbelized variations are not.

Except for the very first Sony and Toshiba models, sought for historical significance, most Japanese radios are not as popular as American models.

Among transistor radios, the most popular are those from 1954-1963, which, for Civil Defense purposes, carry "Conelrad" marking on their turning dials. Look for small symbols (dots, stars, arrows, triangles) or the letters "CD" (for Civil Defense) on the dial.

Sets made after 1963 have little collector interest or value. Original box, case and other accessories add a premium to a radio's value.

Clubs
•Antique Wireless Association
Box E, Breesport, NY 14816

•California Antique Radio Society
Robert Schoenbeck
9301 Texhoma Ave., Northridge, CA 91325-2330

Publications
Antique Radio Classified
P.O. Box 802
Carlisle, MA 01741

Radio Age
P.O. Box 1362
Washington Grove, MD 20880

Radio Bygones
Wise Owl Worldwide Publications
4314 W. 238th St., Dept. MACR
Torrance, CA 90505

Guide to Old Radios by David and Betty Johnson (Wallace-Homestead, 1995)

Machine Age to Jet Age; Radiomanias Guide to Tabletop Radios, 1933-1959 by Mark V. Stein (Radiomania Publishing, 1994)

Philco Radio: 1928-1942 by Ron Ramirez (Schiffer Publishing)

Radio Collector's Guide by Morgan E. McMahon (Antique Electronic Supply, Tempe, AZ)

Radios: The Golden Age by Philip Collins (Chronicle Books, 1987)

Transistor Radios, A Collector's Encyclopedia and Price Guide by David and Robert Lane (Wallace-Homestead, 1994)

VALUE LINE

Prices listed are for radios in Excellent to Near Mint condition. Radios with cracked cases, rusty chassis and missing parts are worth 10 to 50 percent less. Models are listed by manufacturer.

Tube Radios
AC Dayton (all battery)
XL-5 Bakelite panel, 3 large dials $70
XL-10 Bakelite panel, 3 large dials $75
XL-20 Bakelite panel, 5 tubes $80
XL-30 Bakelite panel, 6 tubes $90
Admiral
4Yl2 Metal, flip up handle $30
5A32 Clock radio $20
5S21 Concentric grill circles $20
5X21 Clock radio $20
6A22 Large grill $15
6C22 Oversized dial $25
6J21 Plastic portable $50
7C65 Console with phonograph $30
7C73 Console, AM/FM $35
935 11 tubes, console $50
Air King
A-410 (Camera), 1948 .... $100
Airline
15GHM Portable $20
84-WG-1060 Portable $20
American Bosch
16 "Amberola," 6 tube, battery $85
28 3 knobs, wide metal dial $100
Arvin
152T Plastic $30
242T Ivory, 1948 .... $30
250P Metal, 1942 .... $20
402 Brown bakelite $35
442 Plastic, 4 tube $35
Atwater Kent (1st six sets are battery)
5 Breadboard, one dial, 5 tubes $4,000
9 Breadboard, 1923, 2 dials, 4 tubes $1,200
10 Breadboard, 1923, 5 tubes $900
10C Breadboard, 1924, 3 dials, 5 tubes $800
12 Breadboard, 1924, 6 tubes $1,200
20C 3 dial, cabinet $120

32 1926, 2 controls	$60		NR-5 1923, 3 dials	$70

32 1926, 2 controls $60
35 1926, 2 controls $65
37 Metal, 2 controls $60
38 Metal, 2 controls $60
42 1928. metal $60
46 1929, table, metal, center gold $55
52 Console, metal, legs, ac $80

Clapp-Eastham (all battery)
HR Bakelite panel, 1 tube $200
Radak DD 1925, 2 large dials $200
RZ Radak 1922, table model, wood $500

Crosley (1st three are battery)
4-29 4 tube, 1926 .... $100
5-38 5 tube, lid lifts $65
6-60 Wood, 1927 .... $70
9-113 Brown plastic $20
9-212M 6 tube $35
52 5 tubes, 3 tubes, battery $100
66TA Bakelite $65
515 1935, table, upright $120
704 "Jewelbox" $55
Harko, Sr. 1922, Bakelite panel, battery $400
Pup 1925, metal box, 1 tube, battery $250
RFL-60 5 tube, 1960, battery $130
Trirdyne 3 tubes, 1925, battery $85
XJ 2 large dials, 4 small dials, battery $175

De Forest (all battery)
D-7 4 knobs, antenna on top $700
D-10 Portable, doors $500
D-12 1924, antenna on top $250
DT-600 Crystal set (no battery) $250
F-5M Mahogany, 1925 .... $100

Emerson
107 5 tube, 3 bands $65
410 "Mickey Mouse," 1933, black paint $2,000
520 Catalin, 2 knobs, 1946 .... $150
536 Cloth, portable $15
543 Plastic, white or black $25
559 Alligator portable $25
602 "Conqueror," FM only $40
610 AM only, maroon with gold $30
645 Maroon, tan or beige $20
652 Bakelite, circular grill $30
659 AM/FM, 1951 .... $20
747 1953, 4 sub miniature tubes $50
801 Two tone plastic, portable $30
825B Rectangular, clock radio $20
400 "Patriot," 1940, catalin $1,000

FADA
115 Catalin, 1941, various colors .... $500-$2,000
192A 3 knobs, bakelite and wood $100
254 1937, brown, black or red .... $100-$300
652 1946, different colors, catalin .... $400-$1,500

Freed-Eisemann (all battery)
30 1926, 5 knobs $80
50 3 dial, 1925 .... $70
FE-15 5 dials, wood top $90

NR-5 1923, 3 dials $70
NR-6 Similar to NR-5 .... $80
NR-20 3 large dials, 1925 .... $125

General Electric
60 1947, clock $20
65 White paint $15
160 1949, plastic, portable $15
408 1959, plastic, AM/FM $30
422 1951, AM, 2 knobs $20
555 1953, plastic, clock $20
R-6 1931, cathedral $250

Gilfillan (all battery)
10 1926, 4 tube, slanted front $100
GN-1 1924, wood, 5 tube $150
GN-2 1924, wood, 3 dial $120
GN-3 1925, 3 knobs, 4 tube $180
GN-5 1925, 3 knobs, 5 tube $150

Grebe (all battery)
CR-5 1922, 3 knobs $375
CR-8 1921, 3 knobs $400
CR-9 Similar to CR-8 .... $350
CR-12 4 tubes, 1923 .... $400
CR-18 Wood, 5 knobs $550
MU-1 "Synchrophase," wood, 1925 .... $215

Hallicrafters
S-53 1948, 5 knobs $50
S-55 1949, 4 knobs $45
S-58 1949 .... $55
SX-42 1948 .... $100
TW-2000 1954 .... $80

Jackson-Bell
60 .... $125
62 .... $200

Kennedy (all battery)
V 1923, 3 protruding tubes $350
VI 1923, 2 knobs $300
X 1923, 3 protruding tubes $400
XV 1924, 5 protruding tube $350
110 1922, 4 knobs $900
220 1921 .... $600
281 1921, 2 tube amplifier $550

Magnavox (all battery)
TRF-5 1924, doors $150
TRF-50 1924, built in speaker $200

Majestic
Charlie McCarthy, white or brown $1,000
50 Cathedral, 1931 .... $200
92 Highboy, 1924 .... $150
130 Portable, leatherette $50
Melody Cruiser Sailing ship $300

Motorola
3A5 Plastic, portable $30
5H11 1950, brown, plastic $35
5J1 "Jewel box," lid lifts $80
5M1 "Playmate," portable $50
6L1 "Town and Country," 1950 .... $25
8FM21 Console, 1951 .... $50

51X16 Catalin, yellow and green $3,000
58L11 1948, portable $25
65T21 1946, 4 knobs $35
67F21 1946, console $50
68L11 1948, portable $60
78FM22 1948, wood, phonograph $50

Packard Bell

5R1 1950, plastic $30
100 1949, plastic $30
631 1954, plastic, 2 knobs $30
682 1949, AC/DC, 3 knobs $40

Philco

15DX 11 tubes, 1932, doors $200
16B 1933, cathedral $300
16B 1933, tombstone $275
20 1930, cathedral $250
21 1930, cathedral $350
37-34 1937, cathedral $80
37-61 1937, cathedral $140
37-84 1937, cathedral $125
37-89 1937, cathedral $165
37-93 1937, cathedral $130
37-620 1937, tombstone $100
37-650 1937, console $120
38-7 1938, chairside $120
38-10 1938, BC and SW $140
38-23 1938, table, wood $100
38-34 1938, 5 tubes, battery $85
38-38 1938, table, 4 knobs $70
38-690 1938, console $500
39-70 1939, tombstone $90
39-116 1939, console $200
40-130 1940, upright, table $80
40-150 1940, wood, 8 push buttons $80
41-285 1941, console $120
42-390 1942, console $160
48-1264 1948, console, phonograph $70
50 1931, cathedral $200
60B 1935, cathedral $160
70 1932, cathedral $400
90B 1931, cathedral $450
91 1934, cathedral $300
96H 1930, console $160
511 1928, metal, brown $150
511 1928, metal, colors $300
PT-25 "Transitone," table $35

RCA

3BX671 "Strato-World," 1954 .... $80
3RF91 1952, plastic $35
4T 1935, cathedral $150
5T 1936, tombstone $120
8R71 1949, plastic, AM and FM $40
8X71 1949, plastic $30
9X11 1939, catalin $800
T60 1940, wood, push buttons $50
U111 1939, wood, phonograph $30
V101 1940, wood, phonograph $30

X551 1947, plastic $45
1 Crystal set, Radiola $500

(all of the following RCA sets are Radiola models and are battery unless marked with AC)

II 2 tube $300
III 2 tube $150
IIIA 1924, 4 tube, wood $150
IV 1923, mahogany $400
V 1923, metal $500
VI 1923, metal $500
VII 1923, wood, 5 tubes $1,500
VIII 1924, 6 tubes $550
X 1924 4 tubes $400
16 1927, 6 tubes $100
17 1927, 7 tubes, AC $100
18 1927, 7 tubes, AC $100
20 1925, 4 knobs $150
24 1925, portable $300
25 1925, loop antenna $200
26 1925, portable $325
30 1925, console $225
Grand 1922, 4 tubes $550
RA/DA 1921 .... $150

Setchell-Carlson

416 1946, plastic, AC/DC $50
447 1948, portable, leatherette $40
488 1939, two-tone wood $40

Silvertone

132.881 1951, plastic 2 knobs $20
2001 1950, brown, metal $45
2080 1953, wood, battery $30
3040A 1955, plastic $35
4500 1936, plastic, black, bakelite $70
6050 1947, wood $50
8003 1949, metal, midget $60
808-0 1948, plastic, 4 knobs $35
9005 1949, plastic 2 knobs $20

Stewart-Warner

03-5CI-WT 1939, wood $30
5IT56 1948, wood $25
300 1925, wood, 5 tubes, battery $100
325 1925, wood 3 dial, battery $120
9160-AU 1952, plastic $20

Stromberg-Carlson

1A 1924, 5 tubes, battery $160
68 1934, 10 tubes, 4 knobs $150
130-J 1937, wood, table $100
1105 1942, portable $35
1400 1949, plastic, slide rule dial $45
1500 1951, plastic, 2 knobs $60

Thermiodyne

TF6 1925, 6 tubes, battery $150

Westinghouse

Aeriola Sr. 1922, 1 tube, battery $225
H-130 1946, wood $40
H-147 1948, plastic $35

H-161 1948, wood, AM/FM $40
H-171 1948, console, phonograph $100
H-188 1948, plastic, (Oriental) $100
WR-8-R Columnaire, grandfather clock $300
WR-15 1931, grandfather clock $250
WR-22 1934, tombstone $125

Zenith
3R 1925, 1 dial, battery $500
4G800 1948, portable $40
4-K-422 1939, bakelite $70
4R 1923, battery $400
4-D-611 1942, brown, plastic $40
5-S-29 1935, tombstone $150
5-S-127 1936, tombstone $160
5-S-228 1937 .... $170
6-G-601M 1941, portable $55
6-R-886 1948, phonograph, push button $35
6-S-321 1937, 4 knobs $100
7-G-605 Transoceanic, 1941, portable $200
Stratosphere 1934, console, 23 tube $3,000
Pre–1919 Marconi Wireless $50,000
Atwater Kent (VR73) "Breadbox" Battery; 1921 .. $5,000 up
Atwater Kent (VR75) "Breadbox" Battery; 3 dials;
   1924 .... $700-$1,000
Sparton 506 "Bluebird"; large mirror/chrome trim;
   1935 .... $3,000 up

Crystal Sets
Beaver Baby Grand .... $175-$200
DeForest DT600 Everyman .... $250-$300
Gecophone (England); model BC1501 .... $400 up
RCA Radiola I (VR–109) .... $300-$500

Composition Radios

Arvin butterscotch Catalin; 1941 .... $1,000 up
Bendix 526C; Catalin; 1946 .... $625
Bendix 114; swirled plastic; 1947 .... $300
Bendix 55P3U; Bakelite with metal grille; 1949 .... $60
Bendix 953A; plastic; 1953 .... $30

Art Deco FADA radio (made in USA), Catalin, yellow with red trim, 1934.

DeWald A-501 "Harp," Catalin; 1946 .... $500 up
Emerson "Mini-Tombstone," Bakelite; 1936 .... $225-$300
Emerson AU-190; butterscotch/green Catalin; 1938 . $2,000+
Emerson 157 "Clockette," Bakelite/Plaskon;
   1937 .... $110 -$160
Emerson 190 "Mini-Tombstone"; Catalin; 1938 .... $1,200 up
Emerson 258 "Big Miracle," Catalin; 1939 .... $600+
Emerson 400 "Patriot," Catalin; 1942 .... $500 up
Emerson 561 (Loewy design); Bakelite; 1948 .... $70
Fada 260G; ivory Plaskon/gold overlay; 1936 .... $250
Fada 260G; Plaskon; black/chrome; 1936 .... $300
Fada 260G; Plaskon; red/gold; 1936 .... $500
Fada 115 prewar "Bullet," Catalin; 1940 .... $500+
Fada 252 "Temple," Catalin; 1941 .... $500+
Fada 1000 "Bullet," Catalin; 1946 .... $650-$2,000
Fada 830; swirled plastic; 1950 .... $85
International Kadette; beetle; 1932 .... $350+
International Kadette "Classic," Plaskon; 1936 .... $750+
International Kadette "Topper," Bakelite/Plaskon;
   1940 .... $300
Majestic 51; brown Bakelite; 1937 .... $125
Majestic "Charlie" (Charlie McCarthy); ivory Plaskon;
   1938 .... $900+
Majestic 5LA5 "Zephyr,"Bakelite; 1939 .... $110
Majestic 104; ivory Plaskon; Pa. Dutch designs;
   1951 .... $500+
Philco TP7 "College," Bakelite grille/trim; 1939 .... $200
Philco PT43; Tenite grille/trim; 1939 .... $125
Philco 501 Bakelite "Boomerang," 1949 .... $275
Pilot "Junior" ivory Plaskon; black grille inserts; 1940 . $350
RCA 95X; Plaskon with "beetle" grille; 1934 .... $750+
RCA onyx Catalin; maroon dials/knobs; 1939 .... $700+
RCA 9X-3; onyx/green Catalin; 1939 .... $750+
Stewart Warner 07-7130 "Dionne Quintuplets," plastic;
   1939 .... $800-$1,000
Zenith 511W; oval, white plastic; "Console-Tone,"
   1954 .... $35-$60

Wood Radios (Consoles/Table Models)
Table Models
Bulova 600s "clock-style" cathedral radio; 1933 .. $200-$250
Emerson 197 "Mae West," conical speakers .... $1,250 up
Emerson with inlaid brass; Ingraham cabinet; 1937 ...... $225
Emerson 410 "Mickey Mouse," wood/chrome; 1934 $1,800+
Grunow 500; chrome grille; 1934 .... $200+
Intl. Kadette; silver/black paint; 1933 .... $250
Intl. Kadette 21 "Moderne Clockette," lacquer trim;
   1937 .... $150
Majestic 59 "Studio," aluminum grille/lacquer trim;
   1933 .... $425
Majestic "Duo Chief" 44; aluminum grill/trim; 1933 .... $110
Philco 41-221C; swirled plastic grille; 1941 .... $40-50
Philco 42-KR5 "Refrigerator," 1942 .... $175
Philco 53-706 radio lamp; 1953 .... $150
RCA 8T-10; chrome stand/trim; black lacquer;
   1936 .... $1,000+

Stromberg-Carlson 240H; black lacquer trim; 1937 ...... $225
Stewart Warner 01-6G1; push button; 1939 .... $150-200

Consoles

Atwater Kent 700; oriental style .... $1,000+
Crosley lowboy with doors; 1929 .... $100-150
Crosley "grandfather clock" style; 1932 .... $200-$300
Fada 185/90A Neutrola Grand lowboy; drop front;
    1925 .... $150-$250
Fada 35B; highboy with doors; 1929 .... $100-$150
GE L-916; oversized, with pushbuttons; 1941 ...... $100-$150
Grunow "Teledial 12,"1936 .... $200-$300
Majestic 103 lowboy; 1930 .... $100-$150
Majestic 7FM-888; blonde wood radio/phono; 1949 $40-$50
Magnavox "Imperial" breakfront radio/phono; 1946 $1,000+
Philco 38-7; slant front; inlaid veneer; 1938 .... $125-$150
RCA Victor 811K; automatic tuning; 1937 .... $100-$150
Stromberg-Carlson Model 240R; semi-circular
    with doors; pushbuttons; 1937 .... $300-$500
Zenith Super X; horizontal highboy; concealed
    speakers; (battery or AC); 1925 .... $150-$250

Transistor Radios

Admiral 703; white plastic; 1960 .... $25
Admiral 4P21, 1957, handle $40
Arvin 8584; oversized; red; 1958 .... $50
Arvin 61R13, 1961, six transistors $25
Arvin 9562, 1957, two knobs $70
Bulova 792, 1962 .... $20
Bulova 670; metal panel; 1961 .... $40
Crosley JM8; book style; 1956 .... $110
Crown TR-333, 1959, metal grill .... $40-$80
DeWald K-701A, 1955, flexible handle $150
Emerson 888; pink; British made; 1958-1962 .... $1,000
General Electric 675, 1955, black plastic $180
Hitachi TH-621, 1958, six transistors .... $60-$80
Hoffman 706 Solar; six transistors; 1958 .... $225
Lafayette FS112, 1953, six transistors $80
Magnavox AM-2, 1957 .... $125
Motorola 6X39, 1958, AM/weather $100
Motorola 7X25, 1959, handle $20
Motorola X11, 1959, perforated grill $30
Motorola X17B; blue; large grille; 1961 .... $20-$25

Atwater Kent table model dome radio, #318.

Philco T-9, 1958, several bands $100
RCA 1-BT-58, 1958, globetrotter $15
RCA 8-BT-7, 1956 .... $50
Raytheon 8TP2; portable; 1955 .... $100-$150
Regency TR–1, 1954, ivory or black $300
Silvertone 208, 1960, "500," five transistors $10
Silvertone 2208, 1962, medalist $15
Sony TR 55 .... $150-$300
Sony TR-630; 1963 .... $40-460
Toshiba 67TP-309A; white; 1959- .... $70-$80
Toshiba "lace" .... $75-$125
Zenith Royal 500H; oval grille; 1962 .... $100-$150
Zenith Royal 3000 "Transoceanic,"1964 .... $100-$150
Zenith Royal 20, in box; 1967 .... $50-$60

RAILROAD COLLECTIBLES

The foundation for collecting railroad artifacts was laid in the 1830s when Elijah Rickard stamped "B & O RR" on the screw key locks he sold to the Baltimore & Ohio Railroad.

In the 1850s, Joseph Nock made fancy embossed brass lever locks for the Lehigh Valley Railroad. Since then, countless items were custom made by manufacturers for railroads. Variations in style, design, marking, pattern and manufacturer are prevalent.

Knowing more about manufacturers helps determine the age, scarcity and value of railroad items. One of the mysteries in railroad collecting is the dearth of artifacts available from most of the railroads.

For example, the Kansas & Pacific Railroad traveled from Kansas City to Denver, but the location of only two stamped locks and one lantern is known. Some "feeder" railroads used locks and other items from the main lines. The Pleasant Valley Railroad in Utah had its own lanterns; however, no locks, keys, or other artifacts have surfaced. The Pleasant Valley Railroad evidently used locks and keys from its main line, the Rio Grande Western.

Also collectible are items from express companies associated with the railroads, such as Wells Fargo, Adams Express and Pacific Express.

Northern Pacific, scenic four-part foldout, "Through the American Rockies on the Northern Pacific," black and red Yellowstone Park line logo, black and white photos, 1920s, 8" x 11".

Beginning collectors may collect all railroad items, but others specialize in particular types of items (like lanterns) or train lines (like Milwaukee Road).

General Guidelines: The most important factors in determining the value of an item are the railroad name, condition of the item and type of item.

Items from short line railroads, especially those that are defunct, are highly desirable. Nevertheless, items used by the larger railroads in their early years can be valuable.

Another factor that affects value is historical significance of the railroad, which was evidently achieved by its popularity with the artists, photographers and journalists of the time.

Condition is critical. Check closely for cracks, especially on china items. Holloware pieces should be dent-free and free of blemishes on silver plating. Both china and holloware serving pieces must have lids.

Lanterns are highly collectible and can be bent slightly, but corrosion pitting would be acceptable only on rare examples. Lanterns with cracked globes have no value.

Paper items, such as passes and schedules, should be free of creases, water stains, glue, tape and other marks to command top prices.

For railroad collectibles, original packaging is rarely significant. The significance of railroad artifacts is that they were actually used by railroads and represent much of our history. The most expensive categories are locks, lanterns, china and holloware.

China & Silver Holloware

Railroad china and silver holloware have long enjoyed a premier position among railroad collectibles. The price of a piece of china depends on many factors, including the railroad, the pattern, the condition and the particular setting piece. China with chips or cracks has little value. Certain setting pieces—such as butter pats, egg cups, gravy boats and demitasse sets—are particularly desirable.

Beware of counterfeits, however. Some are crude with "over glaze" decals, but higher-quality counterfeits may be difficult to detect. Expertly-restored pieces, fraudulently sold as undamaged, can fool even experienced collectors.

Train Hardware & Fixtures

Hardware and fixtures include items used on the engine, cars and caboose. Items such as builder's plates or bells have a secondary interest for most collectors; however, almost any collector would like to have a big brass bell or embossed step stool. Embossed markings are highly desirable, but many train items were not marked. Beware of fake cuspidors, especially those embossed with the Union Pacific Railroad initials, full name or logo.

Station Items

Baggage tags, telegraph items and other station items are popular, but scarce. Brass baggage tags can be a challenge to collect. Many stations had their own shape. Original tags consisted of the station tag with strap and the claim tag carried by the passenger. Finding the tags and strap together is rare, so collectors often seek just the brass station tags.

Station signs can be painted wood, painted steel or porcelain enameled steel. Values depend mostly on the railroad and the condition.

Lanterns

There were many manufacturers of lanterns from the 1850s to the 1960s. Lanterns made before 1880, however, are extremely rare.

The glass globes and thin steel and wire tie frames were fragile, so few premium examples of old lanterns exist.

The least valuable lanterns have short globes (3-1/2 to 4-1/2 inches tall) and come from a large railroad. These were made after 1910.

The most valuable lanterns have tall globes (5-3/8- to 6-inch) and come from defunct short lines, with the railroad name embossed on both the frame and the globe.

Colored globes are more valuable than clear globes. Red is the most common color. Cast globes (with the railroad name embossed in raised letters) are considerably more valuable than etched ones. A lantern with an unmarked globe is considered a "frame," and the globe has no value except for display.

Avoid fakes by learning about the markings on authentic globes.

Assuming the same railroad marking, the "bell bottom" and the brass top lanterns are more valuable than those with the wire bottom or the steel top. The value of a lantern is based on the railroad, the condition, the type of frame, the type and color of the globe and its marking, and the lantern manufacturer.

Locks

The most desirable locks are those from defunct short lines that are embossed. The most favored types are the large brass lever switch or car locks, the round lever push key type, or the E.C. Simmons Hardware locks embossed "KeenKutter" on the front with the railroad name on the back. Stamped brass locks have greater value than steel locks, but the criteria for value is about the same. The name of a manufacturer who went out of business in the mid-1800s can add appreciable value to a lock.

Almost 50 lock manufacturers have been identified on the old railroad locks. One of the favorite locks, the KeenKutter, is identified only with the jobber's name and logo. Many railroad locks were sold to the railroads through jobbers, but the jobber's name was not usually marked on the lock. E.C. Simmons was the most common. The name "E.H. Linley" (a St. Louis jobber for Wilson Bohannan locks) also appeared on locks.

Paper Items

Annual passes and public timetables are the most popular and valuable. The most desirable paper items have attractive color artwork, such as scenic views. The most valuable annual passes, however, are not made of paper, but rather sterling silver and leather. Playing cards must be complete decks and in their original box; frayed or creased corners reduce the value.

Organizations

•Railroadiana Collectors Association Inc. (RCAI)
795 Aspen, Buffalo Grove, IL, 60089

•Key, Lock & Lantern
P.O. Box 65, Demarest, NJ, 07627

Contributor to this section: Frank Arnall, P.O. Box 253, Claremont, CA 91711.

VALUE LINE

Abbreviations:
TM: Top mark or logo
BS: Bottom stamp or logo
NBS: No bottom stamp or logo

Dining Car Items

China

Dinner plate, Union Pacific, "Challenger," sometimes BS	$30
Dinner plate, Santa Fe, "Adobe"	$70
Dinner plate, Southern Pacific, "Prairie Mountain Wildflowers," BS	$60
Cereal bowl, C M St P & P, "Traveler,"BS	$30
Cereal bowl, C B & Q, "Violets and Daisies," NBS	$20
Cereal bowl, Union Pacific, "Harriman Blue," ES	$20
Cup and saucer, C & 0, "Chessie," NBS	$150
Cup and saucer, Southern Pacific, "Prairie Mountain Wildflowers," BS	$70
Cup, Santa Fe, "California Poppy," sometimes BS	$10
Demitasse cup and saucer, D & R G W, "Prospector," NBS	$250
Demitasse cup and saucer, C M St P & P, "Traveler," BS	$140
Demitasse cup and saucer, Union Pacific, "Winged Streamliner," BS	$45
Demitasse cup and saucer, Missouri Pacific, "The Eagle"	$125
Bouillon cup and saucer, Kansas City Southern, Foxbury pattern, NBS	$22
Bread plate, Florida East Coast, Seahorse pattern, NBS	$6
Dinner plate, Denver & Rio Grande, "Blue Adam," NBS	$24
Oval platter, 8", B & O, "Centenary"	$90
State Capitals plate, Missouri Pacific, "Diesel Service"	$275
Butter pat, B & O, "Centenary," BS	$15
Gravy boat, Santa Fe, "California Poppy," sometimes BS	$150

Silver Holloware

Cereal bowl, top marked "FEC"	$25
Coffee pot, individual, CB & Q	$65
Coffee pot, individual, Illinois Central	$200
Coffee pot, individual, C & NWRY	$45
Sugar bowl, covered, D & RG RR, "Curecanti"	$350
Syrup pitcher, D & RG RR, "Curecanti" logo	$250
Butter pat, Southern Pacific	$25
Creamer, individual, NYNH&H RR, "New Haven"	$45
Creamer, Baltimore & Ohio, BS	$45
Sugar bowl, Missouri Pacific, top marked "The Eagle"	$35

Celery plate, Rio Grande Western, BS $110
Individual teapot, Florida East Coast, "Royal Poincianna"
   BS FEC H Co $18

Flatware, silver plated

Fork, "FEC" in circle $9
Serving spoon, marked "D & RG" $75
Knife marked "NYC" $10
Fork, Santa Fe $12
Spoon, Southern Pacific $10
Sugar tongs, marked "UPRR" $45

Miscellaneous

Water glass, NYC, "20th Century Limited" $10
Water glass, Union Pacific $8
Table cloth, white, Burlington Route $15
Table cloth, white, Baltimore & Ohio $12
Table cloth, white, Pullman $12
Napkin, C.R.I. & P. $8
Napkin, Denver & Rio Grande, "Curecanti" logo $125

Train Hardware & Fixtures

Builders plate, American Locomotive Co., 1912 .... $165
Builders plate, Baldwin Locomotive Works, 1923 .... $175
Builders plate, General Electric, oval shape $35
Brass locomotive bell, 18" dia. $600
Locomotive whistle, 16" tall, heavy brass $250
Locomotive pressure gauge, 6" dia. $20
Step stool, B & O emb. on side $175
Smoking stand, D & RGW, brass $250
Light fixture, caboose, iron $30
Caboose coal stove $275
Luggage rack, Pullman, 36" $80
Berth ladder, Pullman $55
Coal shovel, wood handle, M.P. RR $5
Oiler can, long spout, NYC System $35
Ticket punch, P RR $15
Cuspidor, Pullman, nickel plated $85
Box car seal, O.S.L. RR $2
Door knobs, pair, emb L&N $100

Station Items

Door lock, brass, insc. UP $20
Telegraph key $15
Steel sign, painted white on black, Western Pacific,
   Feather River Route, 23" x 26" $150
Porcelain enameled sign, Railway Express Agency,
   12" x 72" $175
Steel sign, painted steel, Naegale (Colorado), 9" x 50" . $140
Fire extinguisher, RY EX AGY, wall mount $40
Cast iron stove $250
Wall clock, Santa Fe $275

Locks

Abbreviations:
Emb: Railroad name or initials cast in raised letters.
FB: Railroad name or initials emb in large letters across
the back.
E: Railroad name or initials embossed in vertical panel on
back
BL: Brass lever type
PT: Pin tumbler type
LPK: Lever push key type, 2-1/4" dia.

V G N Ry, FB, BL $390
N & W R'Y, FB, BL, Fraim $40
A & I P, E, BL $450
P RR, FB, BL $165
D & I G RR, FB, BL $1,000
Tex & Pac RY, E, BL $900
So Pacific Co., CS-44, Switch, E, BL $60
U S Y & T Co. , E, BL $80
Union Pacific, Switch, E, BL $60
L & N RR, E, BL $100
St.J. & G.I. Ry., E, BL $900
ERIE R.R., E, BL $150
Frisco, stamped, steel, Adlake $20
A.T.& S.F. Ry, stamped, steel, Adlake $5
C S & C C RR, stamped, steel, Adlake $150
N Y O S RR, stamped, iron, J.A. Goewey $250
A L & S, PT, Best $25
C & A RR, stamped, BL, Union Brass $60
U.P. RR, stamped, BL, Adlake $15
CR RR, stamped, BL, H.C. Jones $275
MO. PAC. Ry, Men Toilet Lock, LPK, emb $800
I.C RR, LPK, emb $80
N & W Ry, LPK, emb $150
A.T & S.F., stamped, RACO $5
S.P. Co., stamped, steel, Fraim $10
New Jersey Central, stamped, PT, Corbin $30
C & O, Emb, PT, Yale $25

Railroad Switch Keys

NYC $12
B & O $15
P RR (knobby) $35
C W R $65
I C RR $12
B & A P $70
Frisco $22
C C C & St L $25
D R G RR $65
T & P $25
Soo $22
B & M $20
WABASH $28
S RI $28
S S W $14
O S L $45
C & NW $20
P E Ry $55
G T W $10
S P Co $12

Paper Items

Playing cards, Amtrak $4
Playing cards, Western Pacific $10
Playing cards, Rio Grande with logo $25
Playing cards, D & RG, multiple scenes $35
Playing cards, Santa Fe, two deck set $10
Playing cards, Southern Pacific, Sunset logo, multiple
   scenes $20
Playing cards, Florida East Coast, multiple scenes $27
Stock certificate, Erie Railroad, 1955 .... $15

Stock certificate, Chicago, Rock Island & Pacific, recent.. $2
Wells Fargo Receipt, 1890 .... $35
Folding picture book, Santa Fe, California, 1931 .... $20
Timetable, Northern Pacific, 1883, ornate $250
Timetable, St. Louis & San Francisco, Frisco $2
Timetable, Rio Grande, 1961, Moffat Tunnel Route $3
Timetable, D & R G, 1887, Curecanti Logo $100
Timetable, B & O, 1957 .... $3
Timetable, Burlington Route, 1956 .... $2.50
Timetable, Washington Sunset Route, 1915 .... $30
Timetable, employee, A.T.& S.F. Ry. Co., 1981 .... $2
Timetable, Santa Fe, 1963 .... $2
Timetable, Western Pacific, California Zephyr, 1966 .... $2
Timetable, Washington Sunset Route, 1915 .... $30
Timetable, NYC, 1935 .... $14
Rules book, O.R. & N. Co., 1912 .... $20
Annual pass, Denver & Rio Grande, 1892 .... $200
Annual pass, Denver & Rio Grande Western, 1932 .... $25
Annual pass, Southern Pacific, 1947 .... $7
Annual pass, Baltimore & Ohio, 1952 .... $4
Annual pass, New York Central, 1938 .... $12
Annual pass, Illinois Central, 1928 .... $10
Annual pass, A.T.& S.F., 1894 .... $75
Matchbooks, most railroads $2
Large map of system, Missouri Pacific $35
Large map of system, Southern Pacific $40

Miscellaneous

Cold chisel, 8", B & O RR $5
Adjustable wrench, 18", S P Co $20
Cigarette lighter, Great Northern, cl950 .... $40
Smoking stand, D.& R.G.W., brass, bottom marked $350
Wool blanket, Union Pacific logo $250
Brass baggage tag, P RR Co (one part) $20
Brass baggage tags, A.T. & S.F. RR (two parts, station &
    claim) $100
Brass baggage tag, Sierra Ry. Co. of Cal (ore part) $170
Baggage sticker, Santa Fe logo $4
Watch fob, Iowa Route—Burlington $150
Lapel pin, ACL logo $15
Tie bar, A.T. & S.F. $4
Man's tie, D & R G $20
Paperweight, P C RR, white metal $6
Paperweight, U.P. RR shield design, brass $25
Gold keystone pin, P RR $25
Ticket punch, 1930s $20
Brakeman's hat and badge, New York Central System .. $135
Brakeman's hat and badge, NYC RR $95
Cap badge, PORTER $22
Conductor badge, Conrail $70
Cap badge, TRAINMAN, Erie (RR) $95
Badge, SP RR Railroad Police $190
Badge, UP RR Police $225
Badge, Patrolman, Reading Railway Co. $150
Cigar box, Burlington Route $50
First aid box, C N RR $15
Pencil, Railway Express Agency $1.50
Large map of system, Missouri Pacific $35
Large map of system, Southern Pacific $40

Badges

AMTRAK attendant silver hat badge $18
AMTRAK trainman gold hat badge $20
Australian Station assistant hat badge with number $26
BCE Railway Co., motorman badge, red with white
    letters, #1725, missing back pin $32
British Columbia police, set of two hat badges $110
Canadian Northern breast badge $10
Canadian Northern conductor hat badge, gold with black
    lettering $58
Canadian Northern lapel pin, silver with black lettering $8
Canadian Northern police hat badge, gold trim with
    cobalt blue inlay $45
Canadian Pacific police hat badge, old, copper shield
    with beaver on top $100
Canadian Pacific brass shoulder badge, worn by CPR
    police $20
Canadian Pacific hat badge $14
Canadian Pacific Hotels waiter breast badge, silver and
    blue, with number $28
LIRR trainman hat badge $28
NYNH & HRR trainman hat badge $52
Sleeping car porter badge, silver with black lettering $18

Railroad Books

The American Heritage History of Railroads in America,
    Oliver Jensen, 1975, hardcover, 320 pages, VG $30
The American West, Lucius Beebe and Charles Clegg,
    Bonanza Books, 1955, 511 pages, hardcover, dust
    jacket, MT $18
*The Crookedest Railroad in the World: A History of the
    Mt. Tamalpais and Muir Woods Railroad of California,*
    Theodore G. Wurm and Alvin C. Graves, Howell-North,
    1960 2nd ed., 123 pages, hardcover, dust jacket, EX .. $22
The Electric Railway in Theory and Practice, Oscar T.
    Crosby and Louis Bell, W.J. Johnson Co., 1893,
    2nd ed., 416 pages, hardcover, VG $25

Mug NYC, cream and rust colored, stamp mark: Shenango, China; New Castle, PA; Rim Rol Wel Rec.

Advertising mirror, The Travelers Insurance Co., The Railroad Men's Reliance, Hartford, Conn., 2 3/4" x 1 5/8", multicolored night scene.

General Motors Engine Maintenance Manual Model 567B Locomotive Engine, 3rd ed., 1,221 pages, softcover, EX $28

High Iron: A Book of Trains, Lucius Beebe, Bonanza Books, 1938, 225 pages, hardcover, dust jacket, EX .. $18

Instructions for Operation of Diesel Electric Road Locomotives: All Classes and Examination Question and Answers for Engineers and Firemen, softcover, VG $15

Mansions on Rails, Lucius Beebe, 1959, hardcover, 382 pages, dustjacket, VG $80

NP Sketches of Wonderland, published by Northern Pacific RR, 1895, 110 pages, EX $95

O&W: The Long Life and Slow Death of the New York, Ontario and Western Railway, William F. Helmer, Howell-North, 1959, 211 pages, hardcover, dust jacket, EX $30

Pacific Slope Railroads—Steam on the Rails, Mexico to Canada, George B. Abdill, Bonanza Books, 1959, 182 pages, hardcover, dust jacket, EX $18

Rails West, George B. Abdill, 1960, hardcover, 191 pages, VG $32

Redwood Railways: A History of the Northwestern Pacific Railroad and Predecessor Lines, Gilbert H. Kneiss, 1956, Howell-North, fourth printing 1960, 165 pages, hardcover, dust jacket, EX $22

Trains in Transition, Lucius Beebe, Bonanza Books, 1941, 210 pages, hardcover, dust jacket, EX $18

The Twilight of Steam Locomotives, Ron Ziel, 1963, hardcover, 208 pages, dust jacket, VG $35

Railroad China

Ashtray/pencil holder, Missouri Pacific, 6" tall $65

Baked potato dish, Delta Line, pre-1950 .... $25

Bread plate, UP Desert Flower, 5-1/2", Syracuse, 1962, MT $32

Bullion cup, SP Prairie Mountain Wildflower, Syracuse, NM $48

Butter pat, ATSF, California Poppy, no maker mark, NM $15

Butter pat, CB&Q, Violets and Daisies, 3-3/8", Buffalo, NM $95

Butter pat, FEC Carolina, Sterling, 1949, "Florida East Coast Railway," VG $28

Candlestick holder, Wabash Meridale, 9-1/2", Syracuse 1934, MT $45

Celery dish, Erie Akron, 10" long, Shenango, MT $34

Celery dish, NYC Vanderbilt, 10-1/2", Ohio Pottery, NM $48

Cereal bowl, CN Queen Elizabeth, Royal Doulton, 7-1/2", MT $24

Coffee cup, Mimbreno, 2-3/4", Syracuse, 1963 .... $100

Compartment plate, C&O Car Ferry, 9-1/2", Syracuse, 1958, MT $175

Covered sugar, KCS Roxbury, 2-3/4" high, Syracuse, 1952, MT $18

Cup and saucer, demitasse, CN Queen Elizabeth, Royal Doulton, MT $48

Cup and saucer, demitasse, KCS Roxbury, Syracuse, 1938, MT $22

Cup and saucer, Missouri Pacific Eagle, NM $165

Cup and saucer, N&W Dogwood, Syracuse 1956, NM ... $15

Cup and saucer, SP Prairie Mountain Wildflower, 1945, NM $70

Dessert plate, ATSF, California Poppy, 1970s, MT $15

Dessert plate, SP Prairie Mountain Wildflower, 7-1/4", Syracuse, NM $28

Dessert plate, UP Desert Flower, 6-1/2", Syracuse, 1954, NM $15

Dinner plate, Adobe Econorim, 1954, Syracuse China 9-1/2", EX $125

Dinner plate, Centenary, Harper's Ferry in food well, Lamberton, 1927, NM $155

Dinner plate, CN Queen Elizabeth, Royal Doulton, 8-5/8", MT $25

Dinner plate, SP Prairie Mountain Wildflower, 9-1/2", Syracuse, EX $58

Dinner plate, Wabash Meridale, 9-1/2", Syracuse 1954, EX $25

Double egg cup, UP Desert Flower, Syracuse, 1958, MT $75

Gravy boat, D&RGW Blue Adam, 3-1/4" high $45

Oatmeal bowl, UP Desert Flower, 6-1/4", Syracuse, 1955, MT $35

Plate, UP Circus Series, 8-1/4", Syracuse, 1952, MT $85

Platter, oval, NYC Dewitt Clinton, 6-1/2" by 9-1/4", Syracuse, 1943, EX $40

Platter, oval, SP Sunset, 12-1/2" by 8-1/2", Syracuse 1924, VG $210

Sauce dish, SP Prairie Mountain Wildflower, Syracuse, NM $15

Service plate, IC Pirate VG $125

Service plate, KCS Roxbury, Syracuse, 10-1/2", 1968, NM $12

Soup plate, CN Queen Elizabeth, Royal Doulton, 9-1/2", MT $28

Railroad Ephemera

Booklet, B&O Century of Progress Chicago World's
Fair, 24 pages, 1934, NM $24

Booklet, Grand Trunk Railway System, Oct. 13, 1904,
59 pages, VG $50

Brochure, Pullman 1939 World's Fair Exhibit, Art Deco,
19 pages, 1939, VG $18

Brochure, SP/CRI&P Golden State Limited, 12 pages,
1931, VG... $8

Check, Michigan Indiana & Illinois Line RR, Aug. 21,
1909 .... $4

Check, National Car Line Co., Aug. 8, 1912...................... $3

Check, National Transportation & Terminal Co., March 10,
1913 .... $3

Check, Minneapolis & St. Louis Railroad Co., Feb. 10,
1913 .... $4

Investigation report, The Bussey Bridge Train Disaster,
March 14, 1887.. $35

Schedule, The Chicago and NorthWestern Railway, The
Short Line to Chicago and all points East, fold-out, 52
panels, Oct. 1, 1885, VG $55

Time schedule, LTR&T Tahoe Tavern, Lake Tahoe CA,
ca. 1900-10, eight pages, VG.. $7

Tourist brochure, ATSF Santa Fe California Picture Book,
47 pages, 1940, 8" by 9", EX $8

Tourist brochure, ATSF Santa Fe Off the Beaten Path in
New Mexico and Arizona, 31 pages, 1925, 8" x 9",
VG $18

Tourist brochure, Boston and Main Where to Stay in
Vacationland, 16-1/2" square, 75 pages, 1917,
9" x 4-1/4", VG $45

Tourist brochure, CB&Q Burlington Escorted Tours, 44
pages, 1926, 6" x 9", EX $15

Tourist brochure, CB&Q From Wagon Wheel to Stainless
Steel, 20 pages, 1947, 8" x 9", VG $7

Tourist brochure, C&NW Summer Tours under Escort,
Dept. of Tours, 56 pages, 1931, EX................................. $18

Tourist brochure, CRI&P Rock Island: Colorado under the
Turquois Sky, 32 pages, 1924, EX................................... $15

Tourist brochure, DL&W Lackawanna Railroad: Mountain
and Lake Resorts, 111 pages, 1909, 6-1/2" x 9-1/4",
EX $85

Tourist brochure, MILW Yellowstone via Gallatin Gateway,
MT, 26 pages, 1953, 8" x 9", VG $12

Tourist brochure, NP Burlington Escourted Tours, 11
pages, 1941, 8" x 9", MT $6

Tourist brochure, UP/C&NW The Challenger, tri-fold,
24" x 9", ca. late 1930s/early 1940s), MT $14

Railroad Lanterns

Canadian Northern H.L. Piper, bamboo wood handle,
minor rust, short red globe, dated 1/44 .... $48

Canadian Northern H.L. Piper, small dent on dome, short
clear globe, dated 1/56.. $40

Canadian Northern H.L. Piper small dent on dome,
etched CNR, clear globe, dated 4/51 .... $45

Canadian Northern Caboose marker lamp, H.L. Piper,
complete, G $175

CPRY E.T. Wright, tall globe lantern, cast CPR clear
globe, chromed $150

Canadian Northern wall lamp, CNR embossed on pot,
two-piece wall mount $160

GNRY Armspear, 1925, short red globe $58

Union Pacific RR switch lamp, Adlake, two green/two
lenses, MT $195

Railroad Lapel Pins

Amalgamated Transit Union... $7

B of RT, 10 or 20 years, each $15

B of RT, 25 or 30 years, each $20

British Columbia, CROR Training $6

British Columbia Ski Train.. $8

British Columbia Telecommunications $8

Canadian Association of Train Dispatchers, 5, 10, 15 or
20 years, each $10

Canadian Northern, Expo 86 IMAX logo $9

Canadian Northern, Super Train $9

Canadian Pacific, Alberta Division..................................... $6

Canadian Pacific, award pin $8

Canadian Pacific, 100 years $8

Canadian Pacific, Rogers Pass Project $10

Canadian Pacific, Vancouver Division, 1994 .... $6

Conrail $9

Quebec North Shore, safety award $14

Southern British Columbia, CROR, 1990 .... $10

Southern British Columbia, 1-Year No Injury $12

UTU, 40 years $12

Railroad Menus

Baltimore & Ohio Railroad George Washington
Bicentennial menu, 1932, 7" x 10", VG $32

CP Canadian luncheon menu, A La Carte and Table
D' Hotel selections, 1961, 8-1/2" x 11", G................... $6

GN Empire Builder Indian lunch menu, Aug. 28, 1939,
6-1/2" x 10", NM.. $32

Great Lakes Transit Corporation dinner menu, 1928,
5-1/2" x 8-3/4", EX $15

Harvey House in Chicago Union Station lunch menu,
1962, 5-3/4" x 11-3/4", tri-fold, EX $14

NP Breakfast menu, June 1962, 8-1/2" x 11", EX $8

NP North Coast Limited Traveler's Rest, 7-1/2" x 11-1/2"
1962, VG $8

Santa Fe Dining Car Service menu, pictures Ranchos de
Taos, by E.L. Blumenschein from the Santa Fe collection
of famous paintings of the Southwest, 7" x 9-1/2",
1972, mint.. $12

Railroad Miscellaneous

Coat hanger, Canadian Northern $8

Clock, Canadian Northern, black metal casing, battery-
operated, CN logo on face $60

First Aid Kit, Canadian Northern, metal, new $28

Matches, British Columbia, pack of four $4

Matches, Frisco, 25 packages in a box car $12

Matches, Rock Island, pack of six..................................... $3

Matches, Union Pacific, pack of six $3

Membership pin, Brotherhood of Railroad Trainmen,
10-year pin, 1/2" dia., 10K gold-filled, EX $10

Portable telephone for caboose, gray metal case, 7" x 5"
by 9-1/2" $46
Step stool, Canadian Pacific, aluminum, G $195
Telegraph insulator, white ceramic, "CPR" on dome,
minor chips $5
Telegraph insulator, beehive shape, "Canadian Pacific Rly.
Co." embossed on bottom $5
Torch, B&O, 9-1/2" fabricated from sheet metal, marked
"B&O RR" on bottom $60
Torch, PRR, 9" cast iron, marked "PRR Dayton
Malleable Iron Co. 189" on side $60
Uniform buttons, each .... $1.50-$2.50
Watering can, marked PRR, watering can, 12" x 10",
EX $45

Railroad Postcards

Alford Station, train leaving for Montrose, PA, Herald Post,
used, #739, VG $4
Baltimore and Ohio Building, Baltimore, #657, MT $4
Broad Street Station, Pennsylvania RR, Philadelphia, used,
#736, EX $2
Buffalo, Rochester and Pittsburgh Depot, Rochester, NY,
GB&S, used, #T971, EX $9
CPR Depot and Mount Rundle, real photo, hand-colored,
#33, MT $4
CPR Station, Durham, Ontario, used, #549, VG $3
CRI&P Passenger Station, Davenport, IA, Rock Island
Post Card Co., #618, NM $6
Dickinson House and NYC Station, Corning, NY, Curteich,
#432, EX $5
Donner Pass Railroad Snowsheds on U.S. Highway 40,
Norden, CA, Frashers Photos, NM $1
East 26th Street Car overturned at 18th and Frank,
Aug. 3rd, 1915, Erie, PA, used, #400, NM $15

Conductor hat, LIRR, current production.

Electric Engine and Power House of Detroit River Tunnel,
Detroit, #743, MT $8
Electric Locomotive in Underground Tunnel, Chicago,
VO Hammon, #494, NM $4
Electric Train Arriving at Venice, CA, Ed. H. Mitchell,
used, #259 .... $6
Erie Depot, Elmira, NY, Rubin Bros., #427, NM $6
General View of the Bridge at Nicholson, PA, A.
Campbell, real photo, used, #742, NM $10
High Bridge, Georgetown Loop, mountains, trains and
trestle embossed, #717, NM $5
Illinois Central Depot, Chicago, VO Hammon. #131, EX . $3
Lackawanna's new passenger station, Hallstead, PA, used,
#740, G $2
New Lackawanna Station, Scranton, PA, used, #735,
VG $4.50
New Santa Fe Depot, Colorado Springs, CO, HHT unused,
#612, VG $5
New York Central Station, Utica, NY, Curteich, #443, EX $5
Olympian descending eastern slope of the Rockies,
Curteich, #313, MT $7
Oriental Limited, Great Northern RR, Scenic Hot Springs,
WA, used, #710, NM $7.50
Railroad Station, NYNH&HRR Co., Brockton, MA,
printed in Germany, used, #315, NM $3
Rock Island Depot, Topeka, KS, #196, MT $4
Santa Fe Roundhouse, Albuquerque, NM, #570, EX $3
Scene on Youngstown/Southern Electric Line, Youngstown,
OH, AC Besselman, used, #661, EX $2
Southern Pacific Company Compound Malet Engine,
Souvenir Publishing, #704, MT $8
Tarrucca Viaduct at Susquehanna, PA, Baker Bros., #741,
EX $4
Sunset Express at Yuma, AZ, Souvenir Publishing, #621,
NM $6
Tunnel in Cow Creek Canon, Shasta Route, Southern
Pacific RR, HHT, unused, #25, EX $2
Union Depot, Grand Junction, Colo., used, #545, VG $3
Union Depot, 3rd and Douglas, Sioux City, IA, Hornick
Hess & More, #452, EX $4
Union Station, Pennsylvania RR, Baltimore, #725, EX $2
Union Station, Salt Lake City, #448, EX $5
U.S. Naval Academy, Washington, Baltimore and
Annapolis Electric Railroad Co., #701, EX $3

Railroad Silverware

PRR Kings pattern broth spoon, keystone logo, 4-7/8",
International Silver Co., NM $28
PRR Kings pattern spoon, 6", Reed and Barton, NM $28
NYC Century fork (7-1/2") and spoon (6"), Century
pattern, Internatinal Silver Co., EX, each $12
NYC New York Central cake server, marked "NYC Lines"
on back of handle, 12-1/2" Reed and Barton, bend on
end of server, moderate scratches, few dings $48

Railroad Stocks

Beech Creek RR, steam engine $8
Boston and Albany Railroad Co., Indian between city
pictures, 1950s $10

Bush Terminal Company, seated allegorical female $8
Canada Southern, smoking funnel train leaving station ... $10
Central of Georgia, man with hammer $8
Chesapeake & Ohio, C&O logo with two men $10
Chesapeake & Ohio Railway Co., oncoming steam engine,
    1905, vertical $40
Chesapeake & Ohio Railway Co., man on horseback
    watching train, 1906, vertical $30
City Railway, Dayton, electric trolley with 19th century
    passengers $30
Erie-Lackawanna RR, man, woman and company logo $6
Erie RR Co., male/female around Erie logo $6
Hudson and Manhattan Railroad Co., train going through
    tunnel $10
Lionel, orange/blue, small boy playing with two toy
    trains $75
Missouri Pacific two men flanking train, oil well $6
Mohawk and Malone Railway Co., green horizontal
    format bond, buck with antlers, 1960s $15
New York Central bond, vignette of engine 3404 pulling
    passenger train $20
New York, Chicago and St. Louis Railroad Co., male and
    female flanking famous logo, 1950s $7
Norfolk & Western, no vignette, fancy green border,
    beige background, 1880s $30
Pennsylvania RR, state seal with two horses, orange/green
    .... $5
Pennsylvania RR, picture of train in famous horseshoe
    curve $7
Philadelphia Traction Co., horse drawn carriage and
    streetcars $10
Pittsburgh & Lake Erie Railroad Co., train, ship and city
    scene, 1950s $6
Pittsburgh, Youngstown and Ashtabula Railway Co., man
    on horseback watching train, 1970s $10
Reading Co., Monopoly stock, train with two allegorical
    females $7
Seatrain Lines, man with navigational instruments and
    globe $6
Southern Railway, two men flanking an industrial scene ... $8
St. Louis-San Francisco Railway, man in front of city
    scene, vertical $15
Union Pacific Corp., vignette of three men $6
Ware River RR, oval picture of a man $25
West Shore RR, river scene, ships, train $20
Western Pacific RR, man and woman flanking
    streamlined train $8
Western Maryland Railway, Mercury in front of diesel loco
    .... $6
Western Maryland Railway, uncommon issue, steam
    train in station $40

Railroad Switch Keys
Baltimore & Ohio RR Co., pocket wear, F.S. Hardware .. $15
Belt RR of Chicago Route, light pocket wear $16
British Columbia Railway, Adlake $14
Burlington Northern, pocket wear, Adlake $11
Burlington Route, pocket wear, Adlake $16

Canadian National, embossed marks, R.M. Co. $12
Canadian Pacific, embossed marks, R.M. Co. $12
Chesapeake & Ohio, pocket wear $13
Chicago & North Western, light pocket wear, Adlake...... $16
Chicago Rock Island & Pacific, pocket wear, Adlake $16
Cleveland, Cincinnati & St. Louis, pocket wear $18
Denver & Rio Grande, light pocket wear, Adlake $19
Duluth Missabee & Iron Range, light pocket wear,
    Adlake $18
Grand Trunk Western, pocket wear $18
Gulf Mobile & Ohio, near new $16
Illinois Central Gulf, crinkle, Adlake $13
Indiana Harbor Belt, pocket wear $16
International Great Northern, pocket wear $22
Kansas City Southern, Adlake, near new $16
Louisville & Nashville, small key, pocket wear $14
Missouri Pacific, near new $12
New York Central, pocket wear $14
Pacific Great Eastern, pocket wear, Adlake $36
Penn Central, Adlake, pocket wear $16
Southern Pacific, pocket wear, Adlake $16
St. Louis & San Francisco, pocket wear, Adlake $14
Western Pacific, pocket wear, Adlake $22

Railroad Timetables
Atlantic Coast Line, 1960 .... $6
ATSF Santa Fe Railway, Aug. 5, 1945, 64 pages, VG $7
ATSF Santa Fe Railway, Feb. 29, 1948, 6 pages,
    wallet-size, NM $5
Burlington Route, 1964 .... $7
C&O Passenger Train, Michigan Lines, April 26, 1964,
    six pages, NM $6
Colorado and Southern Railroad, Feb. 20, 1938, 12
    pages, MT $16
CRI&P Rock Island, July 27, 1930, 20 pages, EX $18
Delaware and Hudson, Dec. 7, 1947, 10 pages, NM $12
DRG Rio Grande, April 16, 1961, 6-page double
    fold-out, NM $4
Erie Railroad System, May 20, 1943, 20 pages, NM $11
Grand Trunk Railway System, May 1, 1906, 24 pages,
    F $15
Illinois Central, October-December 1942, 36 pages,
    EX $10
Illinois Central, 1964 .... $6
Illinois Terminal, April 26, 1953, 6-page fold-out, EX $8
Milwaukee Road, June 6, 1948, 44 pages, NM $6
New York Central, Jan. 16, 1921, F $6
New York Central, Sept. 24, 1944, accordion fold, EX $4
New York Central West Shore, Sept. 21, 1909, folds to
    9-1/4" by 31", G $18
Northern Pacific Railway Company, June 1, 1967, eight
    pages, EX $3
Pennsylvania Railroad, Nov. 5, 1944, 16 pages, EX $5
Reading Railway System, 1947, 12 pages NM $5
Rock Island, 1962 .... $8
SCL, 1969 .... $7
Seaboard Air Line Railroad, June 15, 1950, 24 pages,
    EX $10

Seaboard, 1955 .... $8
SL&SF Frisco Lines, October 1944, 28 pages, G $8
Southern Pacific, March-April 1941, 56 pages, EX $9
Southern Pacific, 1955 .... $12
Southern Railway, 1964 .... $6
Union Pacific, 1966 .... $7
Western Pacific California Zephyr, Sept. 27, 1953, eight
    pages, EX $6
Western Pacific, California Zephyr, 1962 .... $10

Railroad Watches

American Waltham Watch Co., 18S, 15J, ca. 1917 .... $135
American Watch Co., 18S, ca. 1867 .... $250
Ball Hamilton, 16S, 21J, Model 333, ca. 1920 .... $450
Ball Hamilton, 16S, 21J, ca. 1929 .... $475
Elgin, 16S, 15J Hunter Case, 1904 .... $225
Elgin, 16S, 17J Hunter Case with handpainted train on
    dial, ca. 1916 .... $325
Hamilton, 16S, 23J, model 950, ca. 1940s $750
Hamilton, 16S, 21J, model 992, ca. 1907 .... $225
Hamilton, 16S, 21J, model 992B, ca. 1950s $425

Hampden, 18S, 17J, Special Railway, ca. 1897 .... $195
Illinois, 16S, 21J, Bunn Special Model 14, 1916 .... $375
Illinois, 16S, 21J, Bunn Special, 1924 .... $350
Illinois, 16S, 23J, Bunn Special 163, ca. 1930 .... $1195
Illinois, 16S, 21J, Bunn Special 161A Type IIB, 1,700
    made, ca. 1932 .... $895
Illinois, 16S, 21J, Elinvar Type IIE, 4,234 made, ca.
    1932 .... $1100
Illinois, 16S, 21J, Burlington, 1920 .... $300
Illinois, 16S, 21J, Burlington, 1923 .... $300
Illinois, 16S, 19J, Roosevelt, ca. 1923 .... $170
Illinois, 16S, 23J, Sangamo, ca. 1902 .... $545
Illinois, 16S, 21J, Sangamo Getty Model 5, 1901 .... $625
Illinois, 16S, 23J, Sangamo, 1910 .... $800
Illinois, 16S, 23J, Sangamo Special Model 10, 3,400
    made, ca. 1920 .... $800
Illinois, 18S, 15J, C. Wheaton Keywind, ca. 1882 .... $250
South Bend, 16S, 19J, Model 219, 1916 .... $365
South Bend, 16S, 17J, Model 223, 1910 .... $950
South Bend, 16S, 21J, Model 227, ca. 1927 .... $250
Waltham Keywind, 18S, 11J, Wm. Ellery Model, ca.
    1883 .... $250

Railroad lamp, Stationmaster and Pennsylvania RR.

RECORDS

Vinyl records have fallen victim to compact discs and cassette tapes, but despite that, records continue to be manufactured, and the rarest ones continue to escalate in price.

History: The earliest records, known as 78s, were either 10 inches or 12 inches in diameter. In the late 1940s, the 33-1/3 rpm and 45 rpm records were introduced.

The success and popularity of Elvis Presley and The Beatles spawned a great interest in record collecting. With the advent of the compact disc (CD) in 1983, the record's days as the pre-eminent format for music were numbered. New titles are still issued on vinyl, and many of these could become hot collectibles because they are manufactured in very small quantities.

General Guidelines: Condition is everything! The better a record plays and looks, the more it is worth. A nearly perfect record, with no visible signs of wear, will command from four to 10 times what an average record will.

To command top value, records should included any inserts that came with them. Singles (45s and 78s) should be protected by a sleeve.

No record is completely worthless unless it can no longer be played. Many collectors will accept less-than-perfect copies of records, but such examples won't bring top dollar.

Colorful album covers are also seeing a surge in collectibility, with people seeking covers in the best condition.
As a general rule, the less popular a record was, the more collectible it will be.

Clubs

•Keystone Record Collectors
P.O. Box 1516, Lancaster, PA 17608

•International Association of Jazz Record Collectors
P.O. Box 75155, Tampa, FL 33675

Publications

Goldmine, Krause Publications, 700 E. State St., Iola, WI 54990

Goldmine Price Guide to 45 RPM Records (Krause Publications)

Goldmine Price Guide to Collectible Record Albums (Krause Publications)

78s

General Guidelines: In general, the less popular a record was, the more collectible. The most collectible 78s include country and Western, blues, jazz and early rock and roll.

The most collectible artists are blues stars of the 1920s and 1930s; early Gene Autry and Hank Williams; Louis Armstrong and other pre-swing band leaders; Charlie Parker, Miles Davis and other post-World War II jazz greats; Elvis Presley; and almost any rock and roll 78 made after 1957.

Most 78s, however, bring only a few dollars.

45s

The 7-inch 45 rpm single — the small record with the big hole — was introduced in 1949. Many are very collectible today, but condition is critical. In general, the most valuable 45s fall into the following categories.

General Guidelines: Contrary to what might make sense, often the more popular a record was, the more valuable it is in pristine shape.

Picture sleeves, featuring a photo of the artist, will, at least, double the value of the record, and often will increase it many times. Often, picture sleeves without the record are collectible and, sometimes, valuable.

Promotional records, given to radio stations, are always worth at least as much as their regular counterparts.

Many early RCA Victor records featuring colored wax are especially collectible.

In general, the most valuable 45s fall into the following categories:

• Near Mint and Mint examples of hit singles — especially from the 1950s and 1960s.
• Original label recordings of songs that were later hits on major national labels (for example, *At the Hop* by Danny and the Juniors is more valuable on the original Singular label than it is on ABC-Paramount).
• Hit songs by obscure artists or one-hit wonders — in top condition.
• Obscure recordings and lesser-known songs by major artists.

Any Elvis Presley 45 rpm record on the Sun label is worth at least $1,000 in Near Mint condition.

Classical

Look for classical recordings on the RCA Red Seal Living Stereo and Mercury Living Presence labels, both made from about 1958-62.

General Guidelines: Condition is even more important with classical than with most other forms of music.

Country & Western

General Guidelines: For two years in the early 1990s, both the BMG Music Service and Columbia House, the two major record clubs, made records of titles only available to the general public on compact discs and cassettes. Most of these were done in pressings of 5,000 or fewer, and most of these were country titles. As these become better known to collectors, their value should increase. Among those artists otherwise unavailable on LP records are Billy Ray Cyrus, Wynonna Judd (as a solo artist) and Trisha Yearwood.

Doo-Wop (Vocal Groups)

General Guidelines: Doo-wop records are nearly impossible to find in general circulation.

The lesser-known the record, the more valuable it is.

Jazz

General Guidelines: Small label 78s from the 1920s and 1930s are especially desirable, including artists such as King Oliver, and the New Orleans Rhythm Kings.

Original pressings of performances by the acknowledged legends — Charlie Parker, Miles Davis, Glenn Miller, John Coltrane — are highly sought-after. Also in demand are 1950s multi-record collections.

Novelty/Comedy

The most important are "break-in" records, a simulated interview in which the answers are excerpts from current hit songs.

Buchanan and Goodman, who invented break-in records in 1956, are the most sought-after, along with Dickie Goodman as a solo act.

Other collectible novelty records are those relating to fads, TV shows, politics, or particular artists (such as Elvis and The Beatles).

Also collectible are albums by stand-up comedians. Among the most collectible in this field are Bob Newhart, Bill Cosby, George Carlin and Redd Foxx.

Children's

Most generic children's albums aren't collectible, unless they have a celebrity tie-in. Collectors of Disney memorabilia also highly value records (and the colorful cover sleeves) of Walt Disney movies or television shows.

Rock and Pop

The Beatles

General Guidelines: Anything by the Beatles as a band is collectible; but values vary greatly.

Most collectible are mono copies of Sgt. Pepper's Lonely Hearts Club Band and Magical Mystery Tour; 45 rpm picture sleeves; and late-1960s pressings of Capitol albums with a lime-green label. In general, for the Beatles as solo artists, the less popular something was, the more valuable it is.

Elvis Presley

Any record with Elvis Presley's name in the title is collectible. Tribute records that came out after Presley's death are collected as well. While anything Elvis is collectible, it is not necessarily valuable.

General Guidelines: The more unusual an item is, the more valuable it is. The most sought-after Elvis items are his first five albums, released on Sun Records.

Common 45s and albums are inexpensive and unlikely to increase in value, unless they are in Near Mint condition. Especially those from the 1950s, however, are nearly impossible to find in prime condition.

Elvis collectibles with enduring value include 45 rpm picture sleeves; photos enclosed with original 1960s albums; any promotional item; and mono versions of Presley's late 1960s albums.

Rock and Pop

Aside from The Beatles and Elvis, the most collectible rock is by performers from the British Invasion, such as The Rolling Stones, the Animals, the Who and the Hollies.

American performers with collecting potential include Bob Dylan, The Lovin' Spoonful, and The Mamas and the Papas.

Other commonly-collected rock is the pop/garage material of the period, such as Paul Revere and the Raiders; late '60s album rock, such as Jimi Hendrix, The Doors, Love, Cream and Buffalo Springfield; 1970s classic rock, such as Jethro Tull, Pink Floyd and David Bowie; and heavy metal, including Black Sabbath, KISS, Motley Crue and Metallica.

General Guidelines: Albums by 1960s rock artists in mono or quadrophonic sound are collectible.

Also eagerly sought are early singles by Chuck Berry and Buddy Holly; girl groups, such as the Shirelles, the Crystals and the Ronettes; teen idols such as Ricky Nelson, Paul Anka, Frankie Avalon and Fabian; surf music including The Beach Boys; and other popular early 1960s performers such as Chubby Checker, Roy Orbison and The Four Seasons.

Any record with the involvement of Phil Spector or Brian Wilson — as performer, writer or producer — is highly sought after.

Since popular music was primarily a singles medium until the late 1960s, albums by rock artists released during their heyday are among the most collectible of all records. This is especially true of those records in true stereo.

Alternative

General Guidelines: Early records on local labels by "alternative" performers who became famous later — such as R.E.M., Nirvana and Soundgarden — are the ones that hold their value best.

Soul and Rhythm & Blues

General Guidelines: Blues 78s are among the rarest and most sought after. Robert Johnson 78s routinely sell for hundreds of dollars, and into four figures for discs in better shape.

Early 1950s 45s by blues and R&B artists also are hard to find in any condition.

Easily, the most collectible soul records are those recorded by Motown Records, including artists like The Supremes, Temptations, Miracles, Marvin Gaye and Stevie Wonder.

In many cases, soul records are more sought-after overseas than in the United States. Albums by soul artists are hard to find, and even albums that topped the charts are increasing in value. Early Motown 45s are difficult to find in Near Mint condition. Picture sleeves from the 1960s are extremely scarce.

Soundtracks

Soundtrack albums of everything from Broadway plays to TV shows are eagerly sought by many collectors.

General Guidelines: While albums are the most collected, there is some interest in multi-record 45 rpm sets from the early to mid 1950s and in 45s of TV theme songs. The 45 sets must have their original box or sleeves to be of significant value.

Original pressings of soundtracks from the 1950s are worth more than their counterparts in the 1960s, which are worth more than those in the 1970s and 1980s. Any soundtrack with music by Elvis Presley or The Beatles commands a premium.

Check the fine print if you encounter local cast recordings — someone famous might be lurking in the credits, and those can be worth hundreds once they become known to the collecting community.

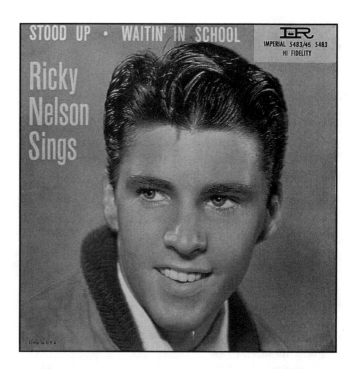

Often the attractive picture sleeves are more valuable than the record inside.

COLLECTOR ALERT

Beware of counterfeits. Almost every rare record has been counterfeited at some point. This is especially true of Beatles, Elvis Presley and 1950s material. A counterfeit is an unauthorized reproduction of a prior release by someone other than the original record company, in many cases using a replica of the original label. This is as opposed to a bootleg, which is the unauthorized release of previously unreleased material, such as live recordings or outtakes. These two should not be used interchangeably.

Spotting a counterfeit can be difficult, but not impossible. Here are some tips.

• Do the type, cover photos, etc. seem blurry?

• Is the label too glossy for the time period the record is supposed to be from?

• How about the size and color of type? If possible, compare the type to a confirmed original or to a more common record on the same label.

• Is the vinyl too thin? Most 1950s and 1960s records used a thicker vinyl than later ones.

• Is the number in the "dead wax" (the blank area on the record between the groove and the label) handwritten or machine-stamped? Machine-stamped ones almost always are originals, but a handwritten one isn't necessarily a counterfeit. It depends on the record.

• Does it look too new?

When in doubt, consult a reputable dealer before plunking down your money.

VALUE LINE

Picture Sleeves

*Prices listed are for 45 rpm picture sleeves in Very Good condition only, with **no record**. Sleeves in Near Mint or better condition can sell for several times the Very Good prices.*

Ann-Margret, 1960s	$4-$6
Louis Armstrong, 1960s	$1-$2
Beach Boys, 1980s	$1-$3
Beach Boys, 1960s	$6-$10
Beatles, 1960s	$5-$30
Harry Belafonte, 1950s	$2-$3
David Bowie, 1980s	$1-$5
Carpenters, 1970s	$1-$2
Nat King Cole, 1950s-1960s	$2-$5
Bing Crosby, 1950s-1960s	$3-$10
Bobby Darin, 1960s	$3-$5
Dion, 1960s	$3-$8
Doors, The, 1960s	$3-$10
Bob Dylan, 1980s	$1-$2
Bob Dylan, 1960s	$5-$20
Everly Brothers, 1950s	$10
Everly Brothers, 1960s	$5-$7
Fleetwood Mac, 1980s	$1-$2
Four Seasons, 1960s	$5-$7
Jan & Dean, 1960s	$5-$15
Brenda Lee, 1960s	$2-$5
Johnny Mathis, 1950s, 1960s	$2-$5
Paul McCartney, 1970s	$3-$7
Monkees, 1960s	$4-$6
Rick Nelson, 1960s	$1-$7
Pink Floyd, 1980s	$1-$2
Elvis Presley, 1950s	$7-$25
Elvis Presley, 1970s	$1-$7
Rolling Stones, 1960s	$6-$40
Mary Wells, 1960s	$6-$20

45-rpm Records

Values listed are for 45 rpm records in Very Good condition without the picture sleeve.

Animals, 1960s	$2-$6
Frankie Avalon, 1960s	$2-$7
Beach Boys, 1960s	$2-10
Beatles, 1960s	$2-$15
James Brown	$2-$7
Johnny Cash	$2-$10
Patsy Cline	$3-$7
Bo Diddley, 1950s-1960s	$2-$7
Bob Dylan, 1960s	$4-$40+
Everly Brothers, 1960s	$3-$12
Four Tops, 1960s	$2-$15
Herman's Hermits, 1960s	$2-$4
Honeys, 1960s	$30-$100
Jacksons, 1970s	$2-$7
Monkees, 1960s	$2-$8
Ricky Nelson, 1960s	$3-$25+
Partridge Family, 1970s	$2-$3
Elvis Presley, 1970s	$2-$10

Elvis Presley, any 45 on Sun label	$250-$500
R.E.M., 1980s	$2-$18
Frank Sinatra, 1950s	$3-$6

Record Albums

Values listed are for albums in Very Good condition.

Frankie Avalon, Chancellor label	$12-$30
Bachman-Turner Overdrive, Mercury	$1
Beach Boys, Capitol	$2-$25
Beatles (too much variance; consult detailed price guide)	
Carpenters, A & M	$1-$6
David Cassidy	$6-$10
Ray Charles, Atlantic	$4-$20
Chubby Checker, Parkway	$6-$12
The Clovers, Atlantic	$80-$400
Bob Dylan (too much variance; consult detailed price guide)	
Four Tops, Motown	$6-$12
Aretha Franklin, Columbia	$6-$10
Herman's Hermits, MGM	$4-$8
Madonna, Sire	$1-$12
Mamas & the Papas, Dunhill	$3-$20
Monkees, Rhino	$1-$10
Monkees, Colgems	$4-$30
Roy Orbison, Monument	$5-$200+
Platters, Muercury	$8-$40
Elvis Presley (too much variance; consult detailed price guide)	
Jimmy Reed, Vee Jay	$16-$80
Rolling Stones (too much variance; consult detailed price guide)	
Strawberry Alarm Clock, Uni	$16-$20
Styx, RCA Victor	$1-$2
Supremes, Motown	$4-$20
Ventures, Dolton	$6-$30
ZZ Top, Warner Bros.	$1

TIPS OF THE TRADE

Have you ever seen an album with a hole punched in the upper left or right corner, a slit through its spine or a corner sliced off it? Those are known as cut-outs.

The mutilation is done by record companies to indicate to a store that this record cannot be returned for full credit. Cut-out markings, which were rare before the 1970s, symbolize one of two things — the record is meant for promotional use or the record is being discontinued. To get rid of excess stock, these mutilated records are sold at reduced prices.

For obvious reasons, no cut-out is worth more, or even the same amount, as a record that hasn't been damaged with a cut-out marking. But these records are still highly playable and are often an affordable way to add hard-to-find pieces to your collection. They are worth, at most, 75 percent of a record that hasn't been cut out.

SALT AND PEPPER SHAKERS

The Victorian era saw the advent of the elaborate glass and fine china salt and pepper shakers. Prior to 1900, salt was set on the table in tiny glass bowls called salt cellars or open salts.

The first novelty shaker was patented near the turn of the century, and by 1920, novelty shakers were the popular choice for holding spices for the table. The advent of the family road trip during the mid to late 1940s caused a boom in sales of salt and pepper shakers as small, inexpensive souvenirs. Interest in novelty shakers manufactured today is just as strong as those made prior to 1960.

Novelty shakers made between 1940 and the present are extremely popular collectibles. Made of ceramic, metal, glass, plastic or wood in interesting shapes, they are quite affordable ($10-$50 per pair).

Finding shakers with manufacturer's marks is the exception, rather than the rule. The base of the shakers were often quite small and, after the plug had been added, left little space for a mark. Occasionally, a paper sticker bearing the manufacturer's name will be found intact. More often, the shakers will bear no mark at all. For more accurate identification, a price guide with photographs may be helpful.

General Guidelines: Sets will command higher prices than individual pieces. Shakers featuring Disney characters, advertising characters or Black figures are especially popular.

Collecting Terms

Art glass. Shakers made by famous glass companies, usually in patterns to match stemware. These are not considered novelty shakers and can have surprisingly high prices.

Souvenir or Landmark. Shakers made in a shape of a state, building or monument such as the Statue of Liberty or the Empire State Building. Usually sold on site or at a nearby roadside shop.

Nodders. Shakers with small bobbing heads.

Carriers. A three-piece set consisting of a holder and two shakers.

Hangers. A three-piece set consisting of a holder and two shakers hanging from the holder.

Nesters. A set in which the holder itself may be one of the shakers.

Two-sided. These shakers have faces on the front and back of both shakers.

Bench-sitters. Two shakers perched on a small wooden bench, often kissing.

Huggers. Patented in 1949 by Ruth van Tellingen, this type of shaker has arms (or necks) which entwine making the figures appear to be hugging.

Miniatures. Tiny, not full-sized, shakers.

Key Manufacturers

Bill's Novelty and Premium Company. Milwaukee, Wisc. manufacturer of miniature beer shakers.

Borough. American manufacturer of Bakelite shakers during the 1940s and 1950s.

Ceramic Arts Studio. Madison, Wisc. producer of animal shakers.

Chadwick-Miller. Boston, Mass. Contracted the production of glass light-bulb shakers in Japan.

Edward A. Muth & Sons. Buffalo, New York manufacturer of miniature beer shakers between 1933 and 1963.

Enesco. Modern manufacturer.

F & F Mold and Die Works. Manufacturer of Aunt Jemima shakers beginning in the 1950s.

Goebel. Germany manufacturer known for its Hummel figures. Produced several animal shakers between 1940 and 1956. The mark is a blue "V" with a tiny bee inside.

Heather House. Burlington, Iowa manufacturer made shakers in the shape of the 50 United States with a state product. (Ex. Vermont and syrup bucket, Massachusetts and bean pot, etc.).

Osuga. Japanese manufacturer of hand-painted ceramic shakers during the late 1940s.

Shawnee. Pottery company also known for cookie jars.

Wade. Also manufactured small animal figures with distinctive glazes.

Clubs

•Salt & Pepper Novelty Shakers Club
  P.O. Box 3617, Lantana, FL 33465

Salt and pepper refrigerators, made of milk glass, 3-1/4" in height.

Hot Collecting Categories

- Black Americana. Shakers featuring Mammy, Aunt Jemima and other stereotypical African-American characters are highly collectible and often hard to find today.

- Native American. Often depict politically incorrect versions of Native Americans.

- Art Deco. Early plastics and ceramics in a variety of bold colors and the geometric shapes of the 1930s and 1940s.

- Lustreware. Painted ceramic shakers from the 1930s and 1940s characterized by a glistening peach colored glaze. Most often made in Japan and featured hand-painted scenes with cottages, florals and fruits.

- Advertising. Shakers depicting advertising characters were often offered as premiums for buying certain products. Characters may include Borden's Elsie the Cow, Big Boy and RCA Victor's Nipper the Dog.

- Character. Cartoon characters, in any shape or form, are always collectible, especially characters from Walt Disney, Warner Bros., DC Comics or others.

VALUE LINE

Tappan chefs .... $25-$30
Budweiser bottles (in box) $10
Mr. Peanut (3" plastic) $39

Animals

Badgers $14
Poodles in hats $12
Rabbit and carrot $14
Cobalt blue glass bears $22
Dogs in a tea pot $10
Dog w/barrels $12
Giraffes w/entwined necks $12
Bird and house on a tree stump $15
Whales with wiggle eyes $10
Fish nodders $58
Green dinosaurs $34
Bunny huggers $16
Mice in Swiss cheese nodder $295
Kangaroo and baby nodders $95
Lions, Fitz & Floyd $35
Blue kissing animals, Coventryware $24
Bear holding a cookie $18
Gray hippos $10

Art Deco

Lustreware w/floral $15
Lustreware w/floral, Nippon $24
Lustreware S&P w/sugar in a dish $38
Lustreware basket of fruit $14

Black Americana

Mr. and Mrs. $25
Black chef/white chef $48

Mountain Washington, satin glass shakers; painted and enameled daisies, dated 1889.

Fish, one green, one brown, red trim, ceramic glaze, Japan, 2-1/2".

Miscellaneous

Donald Duck $40
Senor and cactus $14
Yellow roses in a leaf dish $15
Pink flamingo nodders $68
Oriental couple on bench $12
Dutch nodders $45
Green glass roses $42
Mr. & Mrs. Teapot $18
Elves $25
Toaster and toast (ceramic) $20
Matador and bull $45
Two golf clubs in a bag (ceramic) $28
Hip boots and fishing creel $12
Plastic washer and dryer .... $20-$25
Brown flat irons w/flowers $6
Plastic toaster with toast $18

Goebel

Pigs w/shamrocks on a plate $39
Bears $35
Dutch boy and girl $58

Miniature

Birthday cake and package $26
Thread and thimble $28

Shawnee

Owls $28
Mugsy $52
Mr. & Mrs. Pig w/ green clover $48

Souvenir

Deep Creek Lake (Black Americana) $68
New Orleans (black Americana) $65
Luray Caverns golf balls on a green (dish) $24
Saratoga Spring, NY Nodders $85

Vallona Starr Ceramics

Man in dog house w/angry wife $125
Flowers $35
Duck huggers $36

Cat shaker, $25.

Amber shaker, hobnail glass, $25.

SPACE/SCIENCE FICTION TOYS

Beginning with Buck Rogers and Flash Gordon in the 1930s, continuing with 1960s television hits like *Lost in Space* onto the 1980s *Star Wars* and *Star Trek* phase, collectors have many decades to choose from. The powerful draw of these films and characters has made space/science fiction collecting one of the fastest growing areas.

History: Coming at the public via newspapers and syndicated radio airwaves during the late 1920s, Buck Rogers did more than explore worlds in his 25th century — he paved the way for all kinds of sci-fi toy merchandising to follow his impressive lead. Flash Gordon soon appeared on the scene to try and win over some of Buck's devotees in comic strips and on the silver screen. A great galaxy of sci-fi characters would soon come forth from this genesis, each one eager to launch a successful mission into fan notoriety.

As radio would swiftly surrender its entertainment throne to the dawn of television during the 1950s, heroes like Captain Video (1949) and Tom Corbett (1950) took their adventures into American homes with stunning results. But none of these early forays could equal the singular trajectory taken by Gene Roddenberry's *Star Trek*, which originally aired from 1966-1969 and subsequently gained a phenomenal following in syndication and beyond. No other sci-fi TV series has spawned so many films and spin-off series, not to mention the astonishing array of toys and collectibles ranging from action figures to starships.

When it comes to space adventure, however, George Lucas' epic *Star Wars* (1977) remains unparalleled for its sheer all-around success. The top-grossing film of all time during its first theatrical release, *Star Wars* sparked a merchandising frenzy unlike any other before it; over 500 licensees issued related products, in the process setting new standards for licensing. *Star Wars* sequels *The Empire Strikes Back* (1980) and *Return of the Jedi* (1983) only strengthened its domination of the science fiction genre and collectibles market. Toys in this category range from ray guns and board games to robots, action figures and play sets. Virtually every manufacturer has capitalized on these valuable licenses.

General Guidelines: As essential to the genre as six-shooters are to cowboy westerns, ray guns are perhaps the epitome of science fiction toys. Louis Marx produced a significant number of space guns both generic and character-related. Daisy, Hubley and Wyandotte made memorable space gun contributions as well.

Ray guns have since given way to action figures, which seem to have become the most popular kind of science fiction toys on today's collectible market. Figures in original boxes and on original cards are the most valuable.

Star Wars toys lead the pack. The first *Star Wars* action figures were marketed in 1977 by Kenner. They are truly the holy grail for collectors and may sell for $100 or more each in original packaging. Toys featuring the 1960s science fiction sensations *Land of the Giants* and *Lost in Space* are highly collectible, particularly robots, premiums and model kits.

Robots from many eras, especially Japanese examples from the 1960s and earlier, are highly collectible.

Flash Gordon and Buck Rogers are among the most collectible early (pre-World War II) science fiction characters. Vintage Buck Rogers 1930s-1940s toys top collectors' lists, even in less than Excellent condition.

The fastest growing areas are *Star Wars* and *Star Trek*, with some figures and play sets from 1977 and later selling for hundreds of dollars.

Any space/science fiction toy is collectible, but not necessarily valuable. Don't pass on nondescript spaceships and figures, although those associated with a hit TV show or movie are often worth more.

Clubs

•Lost in Space Fan Club
550 Trinity A Club, Westfield, NJ 07090

•Star Trek: The Official Fan Club
P.O. Box 111000, Aurora, CO 80011

•Star Wars Collectors Club
20201 Burnt Tree Lane, Walnut, CA 91789

Robot Control, 1950s, Masudaya, $400-$500 Mint.

VALUE LINE

Values listed are for items in Excellent condition.

Alien/Aliens
Alien Blaster Target Set, HG Toys $170
Alien Chase Target Set, HG Toys $165
Alien Costume, Ben Cooper $65
Alien Figure, Kenner, 1979 .... $300
Alien Model Kit, Tsukuda, 1980s $350
Alien Warrior Model Kit, Halcyon $30
Aliens Colorforms Set $15

Battlestar Galactica
Apollo Figure, Mattel, 1978 .... $15
Batlar Figure, Mattel, 1978 .... $35
Battlestar Galactica Model Kit, Monogram $25
Boray Figure, Mattel, 1978 .... $15
Colonial Scarab, Mattel, 1978 .... $30
Colonial Stellar Probe, Mattel, 1978 .... $30
Colonial Viper, Mattel, 1978 .... $30
Colonial Viper Model Kit, Monogram $25
Colonial Warrior 12" Figure, Mattel, 1978 .... $25
Colorforms Adventure Set, 1978 .... $20
Commander Adama Figure, Mattel, 1978 .... $15
Cylon Centurian Figure, Mattel, 1978 .... $15
Cylon Centurian 12" Figure, Mattel, 1978 .... $40
Cylon Raider, Mattel, 1978 .... $30
Cylon Raider Model Kit, Monogram $25
Daggit Figure, Mattel, 1978 .... $10
Imperious Leader Figure, Mattel, 1978 .... $8
Lasermatic Pistol, Mattel, 1978 .... $30
Lasermatic Rifle, Mattel, 1978 .... $40
Lt. Starbuck Figure, Mattel, 1978 .... $10
Lucifer Figure, Mattel, 1978 .... $10

Buck Rogers
25th Century Police Patrol Rocket, Marx, 1935 .... $295
Atomic Pistol U-235, Daisy, 1945 .... $145
Atomic Pistol U-238, Daisy, 1946 .... $145
Battle Cruiser Rocket, Tootsietoy, 1937 .... $180
Buck/Wilma Paper Masks, Einson-Freeman, 1933 .... $195
Buck Rogers 25th Century Pop Gun, Daisy, 1930s $225
Buck Rogers Figure, Tootsietoy, 1937 .... $145
Buck Rogers Wristwatch, Huckleberry Time, 1970s $100
Character Figures, Cocomalt, 1934 .... $130
Chemistry Set, Grooper, 1937 .... $475
Chief Explorer Badge, 1936 .... $145
Colorforms Set, 1979 .... $15
Combat Set, Daisy, 1934 .... $425
Disintegrator Pistol XZ-38, Daisy, 1935 .... $145
Electric Caster Rocket, Marx, 1930s $210
Helmet XZ-34, Daisy, 1935 .... $475
Holster XZ-36, Daisy, 1935 .... $100
Liquid Helium Water Pistol XZ-44, Daisy, 1936 .... $260
Official Utility Belt, Remco, 1970s $25
Punching Bag, Morton Salt, 1942 .... $65
Repeller Ray Ring $600
Rocket Pistol XZ-31, Daisy, 1934 .... $180
Rocket Ship, Marx, 1934 .... $400

Rubber Band Gun, 1930s $50
Saturn Ring, Post Corn Toasties, 1944 .... $210
Sonic Ray Gun, Norton-Honer $65
Space Ranger Halolight Ring, Sylvania, 1952 .... $80
Twiki Figure, Mego, 1979 .... $15
Venus Duo-Destroyer, Tootsietoy, 1937 .... $165
Wilma Deering Figure, Tootsietoy, 1937 .... $115

Captain Video
Captain Video Game, Milton Bradley, 1952 .... $125
Flying Saucer Ring, 1950s $210
Mysto-Coder, 1950s $100
Rocket Tank, Lido, 1952 .... $95
Secret Seal Ring, 1950s $130
Troop Transport, Lido, 1950s $95

Defenders of the Universe
Battling Black Lion Voltron, LJN, 1986 .... $13
Doom Blaster Voltron, LJN, 1986 .... $13
Doom Commander, Matchbox, 1985 .... $7
Hagar Figure, Matchbox, 1985 .... $7
Hunk Figure, Matchbox, 1985 .... $7
Keith Figure, Matchbox, 1985 .... $7
King Zarkon Figure, Matchbox, 1985 .... $7
Lance Figure, Matchbox, 1985 .... $7
Pidge Figure, Matchbox, 1985 .... $7
Prince Lothar Figure, Matchbox, 1985 .... $7
Princess Allura Figure, Matchbox, 1985 .... $7
Robeast Mutilor Figure, Matchbox, 1985 .... $7
Robest Scorpious Figure, Matchbox, 1985 .... $7
Voltron Motorized Giant Commander, LJN, 1984 .... $25
Zarkon Zapper Voltron Vehicle, LJN, 1986 .... $16

Doctor Who
Ace Figure, Dapol, 1986 .... $16
Cyberman, Dapol, 1986 .... $16
Cyberman Robot Doll, Denys Fisher, 1970s $350
Dalek Bagatelle, Denys Fisher, 1976 .... $100
Dalek Shooting Game, Marx, 1965 .... $325
Davros Figure, Dapol, 1986 .... $16
Doctor Who Card Set, Denys Fisher, 1976 .... $26
Doctor Who Doll, Denys Fisher, 1976 .... $130
Ice Warrior, Dapol, 1986 .... $13
K-9, Dapol, 1986 .... $10
Tardis Transporter, Denys Fisher, 1976 .... $325

COLLECTORS' ALERT

The third *Star Wars* movie, *Return of the Jedi*, was originally titled *Revenge of the Jedi*. Some early promotional material and merchandise was even produced displaying that name. But before the film's final cut was edited, George Lucas reasoned that his legendary Jedi knights would by their very nature never seek revenge, making the title inappropriate. Despite recall efforts, some *Revenge* pieces found their way into the collector market and command high premiums today.

Uni-Tred & Space Bubble, Major Matt Mason series, 1967-1970, Mattel, $50 MNB.

Flash Gordon

Adventure on the Moons of Mongo Game $25
Air Ray Gun, Budson, 1950s $350
Arak Figure, Mattel, 1979 .... $30
Arresting Ray Gun, Marx, 1939 .... $295
Beastman Figure, Mattel, 1979 .... $30
Captain Action Outfit, Ideal, 1966 .... $275
Dr. Zarkov Figure, Mattel, 1979 .... $25
Flash Figure, Galoob, 1986 .... $10
Flash Figure, Mattel, 1979 .... $16
Flash Costume, Esquire Novelty, 1951 .... $145
Hand Puppet, 1950s $145
Lizard Woman Figure, Mattel, 1979 .... $25
Ming Figure, Mattel, 1979 .... $20
Ming's Space Shuttle, Mattel $25
Puzzle, Milton Bradley, 1951 .... $80
Radio Repeater Clicker Pistol, Marx $350
Rocket Fighter, Marx, 1939 .... $295
Rocket Ship, Mattel, 1979 .... $35
Signal Pistol, Marx, 1930s $325
Solar Commando Set, Premier Products, 1950s $105
Space Compass, 1950s $40
Space Water Gun, Nasta, 1976 .... $10
Three-Color Ray Gun, Nasta, 1976 .... $13
Two-Way Telephone, Marx, 1940s $100
View Master Set, 1963 .... $35
Water Pistol, Marx, 1940s $130
Wristwatch, Bradley, 1979 .... $115

Land of the Giants

Colorforms Set, 1968 .... $50
Coloring Book, Whitman, 1968 .... $35
Comic Book #1, Gold Key, 1968 .... $15
Costumes, Ben Cooper, 1968 .... $100
Flying Saucer, Remco, 1968 .... $100
Game, Ideal, 1968 .... $105
Motorized Flying Rocket, Remco, 1968 .... $130
Movie Viewer, Acme, 1968 .... $45
Painting Set, Hasbro, 1969 .... $65

Rub-Ons, Hasbro, 1969 .... $50
Signal Ray Gun, Remco, 1968 .... $115
Space Sled, Remco, 1968 .... $325
Spaceship Control Panel, Remco, 1968 .... $325
Spindrift Model Kit, Aurora, 1968 .... $450
Target Rifle Set, Remco, 1968 .... $145
Walkie Talkies, Remco, 1968 .... $130

Lost in Space

3-D Fun Set, Remco, 1966 .... $775
Chariot Model Kit, Lunar Models, 1987 .... $50
Costume, Ben Cooper, 1965 .... $130
Diorama Model Kit, Aurora, 1966 .... $650
Helmet/Gun Set, Remco, 1967 .... $525
Jupiter Model Kit, Marusan, 1966 .... $650
Robot, Remco, 1965 .... $310
Roto-Jet Gun Set, Mattel, 1966 .... $1,300
Saucer Gun, AHI, 1977 .... $50
Switch-and-Go Set, Mattel, 1966 .... $1,500
Trading Cards, Topps, 1966 .... $260
View-Master Set, GAF, 1967 .... $40
Walkie Talkies, AHI, 1977 .... $50

Planet of the Apes

Activity Book, Saalfield, 1974 .... $30
Astronaut Figure, Mego, 1974 .... $85
Burke Figure, Mego, 1974 .... $75
Coloring Book, Saalfield, 1974 .... $30
Cornelius Figure, Mego, 1974 .... $30
Dr. Zaius Figure, Mego, 1974 .... $40
Fortress, Mego, 1974 .... $115
Galen Figure, Mego, 1974 .... $50
General Urko Figure, Mego, 1974 .... $150
Village Playset, Mego, 1974 .... $120
Zira Figure, Mego, 1974 .... $40

Robots

Attacking Martian, SH, 1960s $65
Big Max, Remco $70
Captain Astro, 1970 .... $55
Chief Robotman, KO, 1965 .... $850
Countdown-Y, Cragstan, 1960s $145
Cragstan's Mr. Robot, 1960s $400
Forbidden Planet Robby, Masudaya $115
Laughing Robot, Marx $70
Magnor, Cragstan, 1975 .... $35
Robot YM-3, Masudaya, 1985 .... $20
Sparky Robot, 1960 .... $65
Zerak the Blue Destroyer, Ideal, 1968 .... $65

Space Patrol

Atomic Pistol Flashlight Gun, Marx, 1950s $130
Cadet Membership Card, 1950s $35
Commander Helmet, 1950s $225
Cosmic Cap, 1950s $195
Cosmic Rocket Launcher Set, 1950s $475
Cosmic Smoke Gun, 1950s $165
Hydrogen Ray Gun Ring, 1950s $115
Jet Glow Code Belt, 1950s $180
Lunar Fleet Base, 1950s $325
Outer Space Helmet Mask, 1950s $165
Periscope, 1950s $100

Rocket Gun and Holster Set, 1950s $295
Space Binoculars, 1950s $115
Space Patrol Badge, 1950s $100

Space: 1999

Adventure Play Set, Amsco/Milton Bradley, 1976 .... $50
Astro Popper Gun, 1976 .... $10
Colorforms Adventure Set, 1975 .... $16
Commander Koenig Figure, Mattel, 1976 .... $30
Dr. Russell Figure, Mattel, 1976 .... $30
Eagle Freighter, Dinky, 1975 .... $30
Eagle One Model Kit, MPC, 1976 .... $20
Eagle One Spaceship, Mattel, 1976 .... $100
Eagle Transport, Dinky, 1975 .... $30
Moonbase Alpha Play Set, Mattel, 1976 .... $50
Professor Bergman Figure, Mattel, 1976 .... $30
Talking View-Master Set, 1975 .... $10
Utility Belt Set, Remco, 1976 .... $20
Zython Figure, Mattel, 1976 .... $35

Spaceships

Eagle Lunar Module, 1960s $115
Friendship 7 .... $50
Moon-Rider, Marx, 1930s $200
Rocket Fighter, Marx, 1950s $375
Satellite X-107, Cragstan, 1965 .... $130
Sky Patrol Jet, TN/Japan, 1960s $425
Space Bus $500
Space Train $35
X-3 Rocket Gyro, 1950s $35

Star Trek

Colorforms Set, 1975 .... $20
Command Bridge Model Kit, AMT, 1975 .... $50
Communicators, Mego, 1976 .... $100
Communicators, *Star Trek: The Motion Picture*, Mego, 1980 .... $130
Controlled Space Flight, Remco, 1976 .... $115
Enterprise Model Kit, AMT, 1966 .... $350
Ferengi Costume, ST:TNG, Ben Cooper, 1988 .... $10
Figurine Paint Set, Milton Bradley, 1979 .... $20
Galileo Shuttle Model Kit, AMT, 1974 .... $95
Helmet, Remco, 1976 .... $80
Kirk Costume, Ben Cooper, 1975 .... $15
Kirk Doll, ST:TMP, Knickerbocker, 1979 .... $25
Klingon Bird of Prey, Ertl, 1984 .... $10

Klingon Costume, Ben Cooper, 1975 .... $13
Phaser, Remco, 1975 .... $50
Phaser Battle Game, Mego, 1976 .... $275
Phaser Gun, Remco, 1967 .... $115
Phaser Gun, ST III, Daisy, 1984 .... $50
Pinball Game, ST:TMP, Bally, 1979 .... $295
Spock Costume, Ben Cooper, 1973 .... $16
Spock Doll, ST:TMP, Knickerbocker, 1979 .... $25
Spock Ears, ST:TMP, Aviva, 1979 .... $10
Spock Model Kit, AMT, 1973 .... $130
Tricorder, Mego, 1976 .... $100
USS Enterprise Action Play Set, Mego, 1975 .... $180
Utility Belt, Remco, 1975 .... $65
View-Master Set, GAF, 1968 .... $10

Star Wars

Boba Fett Figure, Towle/Sigma, 1983 .... $65
Burger Chef Fun Book, Kenner, 1978 .... $8
C-3PO Bank, Roman Ceramics, 1977 .... $35
C-3PO Cookie Jar, Roman Ceramics, 1977 .... $115
Chewbacca Bank, Sigma, 1983 .... $35
Darth Vader Bank, Roman Ceramics, 1977 .... $35
Darth Vader Cookie Jar, Roman Ceramics, 1977 .... $115
Darth Vader Figure, Towle/Sigma, 1983 .... $45
Darth Vader Speaker Phone, ATC, 1983 .... $80
Darth Vader Wristwatch, Bradley, 1970s $45
Empire Strikes Back Sketchbook, Ballantine, 1980 .... $20
Han Solo Figure, Towle/Sigma, 1983 .... $65
Inflatable Lightsaber, Kenner, 1977 .... $60
Jawa Punching Bag, Kenner, 1977 .... $65
Leia Figurine Paint Set, Craft Master $16
Luke Skywalker Figure, Towle/Sigma, 1983 .... $45
R2-D2 Cookie Jar, Roman Ceramics, 1977 .... $130
Return of the Jedi Sketchbook, Ballantine, 1983 .... $16
Star Wars Sketchbook, Ballantine, 1977 .... $20

Sky Patrol Jet spaceship, 1960s, TN/Japan, $425 Excellent.

SHEET MUSIC

Sheet music may very well be the most familiar, yet least understood, of all collectibles. Nearly everyone has seen some old music, whether on the antique circuit or tucked among a family's belongings. The extreme variety and abundance of this collectible makes the task of setting firm values unrealistic. Consider that there are more than five million songs involved plus many different issues and cover variations for tens of thousands of them. Private publishings often went undocumented or unregistered for copyrights, therefore a listing of all sheet music is an impossibility.

History: Most sheet music being pulled from attics, music cabinets and piano benches today dates from the mid-1800s to present. Songsheets prior to 1850 are in short supply and are often found only in institutions' archives or in the hands of private collectors. The majority of what is most frequently seen today are popular tunes from the 1920s to the 1940s. Sheet music from those decades — an era when music publishing was at an all-time high — has survived in good condition.

General Guidelines: The most collectible topics are sports (especially baseball), political, Black Americana, cartoon (including Disney), transportation (trains, planes and automobiles), important events (such as the Titanic disaster), social issues and movements (including Ku Klux Klan, women's suffrage and the like), Civil War, and famous artists (Rose O'Neill, Norman Rockwell, Nathaniel Currier, Winslow Homer). Vivid lithographed sheet music covers issued by the E.T. Paull Publishing Co. are extremely desirable.

Certain music styles are coveted by musicians who collect for the music content. Some of these are ragtime, blues, cakewalks and jazz. Another major area of collecting is movie or show music. Still others seek songs written by certain composers; especially collectible are Irving Berlin, George Gershwin, Cole Porter, Jerome Kern, Rodgers & Hart, Harold Arlen, Vernon Duke and Vincent Youmans, not to mention many earlier and later songwriters.

Lastly, a large number of collectors fancy sheet music picturing favorite movie stars, singers or performers. At the top of the list are John Wayne, the Marx Brothers, Marlene Dietrich, Marilyn Monroe, Laurel and Hardy, Mae West, Shirley Temple, Judy Garland and Fred Astaire.

Old isn't necessarily better when it comes to the value of sheet music. Many music sheets from the 1950s are worth more than many from the 1850s. Strong topical songs with bold or colorful graphics from the last century can have considerable value, but routine love songs or plain non-topical editions are worth only a few dollars.

In general, the more familiar the song, the less valuable. Although there are exceptions, most well-known songs were printed in huge quantities and are easily obtainable.

Demographics play a role in the value of sheet music. In certain areas of the country — the Deep South for one — sheet music was difficult to store and therefore is often scarce. However, in the Northeast, where many music publishers were originally located, a large amount of music is still readily available. Also, collectors from particular parts of the country value different types of music differently. California residents, for example, would attach higher price tags to music about their state than would someone who lives in the East; or, someone out West might hanker for songs about cowboys and Indians more so than would a New Yorker.

Comic titles, bold graphics or outrageous themes may substantially raise values of a piece of sheet music.

Although illustrations by famous artists can raise values, there is not a marked increase in interest or value based on artwork done by sheet music artists who never gained national fame or recognition for their work. Among those artists' names most frequently seen on sheet music covers are E.H. Pfeiffer, Barbelle, Starmer, deTakacs, Frew and Manning. The topics depicted and the quality of artwork will influence values but rarely will the simple fact that a cover was designed by these artists.

A cover "signed" by a sheet music artist (not autographed, but signed as part of the print process) has nothing to do with a sheet that's been truly autographed by a composer or performer. If the signature is from someone important, the value is greater. How-

They Made It Twice As Nice As Paradise and They Called It Dixieland; 1916, Jerome H. Remick & Co.

ever, many obscure composers or stars signed sheet music, but the sheet's worth will not be significantly affected.

Two of the most misrepresented sheets are *Always* by Irving Berlin and *Dancing With Tears in My Eyes* picturing Rudy Vallee. Replicated signatures of Berlin and Vallee appear authentic on these covers which are often touted as "autographed" with high price tags. Either of these common sheets is worth $2-$5.

Condition is especially critical to the value of sheet music. Older large-size music (pre-1920) is apt to be a little ragged. When piano manufacturers switched from piano stools to benches, the larger sheets didn't fit inside the benches and many of the edges became frayed.

Mint is a term that hardly ever applies to sheet music; Excellent might be more appropriate, allowing for very minor flaws. Music termed Good could have some tiny tears or a little wear. Any rips, taping, holes, trimming, water-damage, large writing or other major defacements will decrease value. A small signature is acceptable on older music but diminishes the value on movie covers or other later sheets.

Trends: Sheet music prices have skyrocketed in the last five years. A wise novice will observe the market and purchase ordinary music where prices are within reason. Sellers sometimes suffer from inflated values finding it impossible to locate a buyer who is willing to pay such high figures. In many areas of the country, there are still plenty of "dollar boxes" at flea markets where both buyer and seller come away happy with the transaction. Since sheet music offers hundreds of areas in which to collect, there is literally something for everyone.

As Generation X collectors filter into the hobby, collecting trends will shift toward later issues of sheet music. Baby boomers are hot on the trail of classic rock and roll from the 1950s and rock tunes of the 1960s. Television theme music is already hot and should increase in value during the next decade. Science fiction and space oriented music is also gaining in popularity, and sheet music picturing today's movie stars and entertainers will soon become tomorrow's collectibles.

Clubs

•National Sheet Music Society
 1597 Fair Park Ave. , Los Angeles, CA 90041

•New York Sheet Music Society
 P.O. 354, Hewlett, NY 11557

•Remember That Song
 5623 N. 64th Ave., Glendale, AZ 85301

•City of Roses Sheet Music Collectors Club
 912 NE 113th Ave., Portland, OR 97220

Publications

Sheet Music Exchange
P.O. Box 2114, Key West, FL 33045

The Rag Times
15222 Ricky Ct., Grass Valley, CA 95949

The Little Ford Rambled Right Along, published by C.R. Foster.

High & Mighty, John Wayne, 1954 .... $20
I Got Stung, Elvis Presley $20
I'll Sing You a Thousand Love Songs, Clark Gable and
    Marion Davies cov, 1936 .... $12
I Love You California, 1913 .... $7
I've Got the Profiteering Blues, Al Wilson and Irving
    Bibo, 1920 .... $10
Laugh Clown Laugh, Lon Chaney, 1928 .... $30
Little Orphan Annie $15
Melody Time, Blue Shadows on the Trail, Disney, 1948 . $30
Mona Lisa, Nat King Cole $5
My Buddy, Al Jolson, c1922 .... $10
Nothing More to Say, Big Slim, 1946 .... $5

Oh Susanna, 1923 .... $45
Over The Rainbow, Judy Garland $15
Popeye the Sailor Man, Irving Berlin, 1931 .... $75
Rum & Coca-Cola, Andrews Sisters, 1944 .... $13
Silver Sleigh Bells, 1906 .... $30
Some Enchanted Evening, Richard Rodgers and Oscar
    Hammerstein II, from musical South Pacific, sgd
    Ezzio Pinza cov, 1949 .... $10
Tales My Mother Told to Me, 1911 .... $18
The Grandpappy Polka, Johnny Giacoma, Gordon
    Jennings, 1947 .... $5
The Mary Pickford Waltz, Art Craft Pictures, 1917 .... $10
When I Dream About the Wabash, Roy Rogers, 1945 ..... $10
You, the Great Ziegfeld, 1936 .... $5

March of the Boy Scouts, Oliver Ditson Co., 1913-1915.

Jazzin' the Cotton Town Blues, M. Witmark & Sons, 1917.

TEDDY BEARS

When the *Washington Post* published Clifford K. Berryman's political cartoon in November of 1902, no one could have imagined the impact it would have. The cartoon depicted President Theodore (Teddy) Roosevelt on a hunting trip in Mississippi, refusing to kill a bear caught by members of his entourage.

The cartoon and variations of it were soon familiar to most Americans, including Morris and Rose Michtom, who made a stuffed, jointed toy bear cub. According to folklore, the Michtoms contacted Roosevelt and requested permission to call it a "Teddy" bear. The president reportedly gave his permission. The Michtoms' venture developed into the Ideal Novelty and Toy Company.

About the same time, in Germany, Marguerite Steiff began designing and producing toy bears.

Regardless of which company began producing the bears first, their introduction began a relationship between bears and their owners that has lasted almost 100 years and shows no sign of diminishing.

General Guidelines: Teddy bears were intended to be loved, hugged and played with by children, so some of the most-loved teddies did not survive. Those that did often bore the marks of their owners' affections forever.

This wear and tear contributes to the decreased supply of early bears on the market today. The availability of bears manufactured before WWII is limited, and examples found, even in poor condition, can be extremely pricey.

Condition is the most significant factor in determining the value of a teddy bear. To command top prices, fur covering should be in Excellent or better condition. Foot pads, however, can be tolerated in a worn or slightly worn condition.

Bears with the manufacturer's original identification mark (be it a button, label or tag) command higher prices. Early Steiff bears are the most coveted of all bears because of their rarity and value. Identifying a bear's manufacturer can be difficult with older bears since many were not marked or lost the original manufacturer's identification marks over time. Just looking at the bear, however, can give clues to its origin. Distinguishing features of an old Steiff bear are an elongated muzzle, arms, feet and hump.

Distinguishing features of early Ideal bears are short mohair, a wide and triangularly-shaped head, an elongated slim body, wide-apart eyes and ears, and pointed pads on the feet. Ideal bears from the 1950s and '60s are commonly found with the features painted onto a molded vinyl face, and with large sleep eyes. They were often unjointed with bodies of rayon plush.

In some cases, repair or restoration can increase the value of a bear. Normally a bear obviously repaired and dressed in inappropriate clothing would be of lesser value. If it could be documented, however, that the repair was done by a child in a long-ago decade, the value could actually increase.

Miniature bears take up less space, but are not proportionally cheaper than large bears. In fact, a miniature bear in Good condition can be more expensive than its full-size counterpart! With all bears, facial appeal and rare color variations can increase value.

Bears manufactured in the 1960s and 1970s are still abundant and can be found at very reasonable prices — even at yard sales and second-hand stores.

HOT TIP

Keep a photograph of each of your bears, a copy of the original sale's receipt, and a card with a description, including any label details or marks, for easy reference and insurance purposes. Ideally, these should be stored away from the location of the collection (such as in a safety deposit box) in case of fire.

Ideal, brown mohair, felt pads, 24", c. 1920.

WHAT TO WATCH FOR

Manufacturer: Popular manufacturers to look for include Steiff, Ideal, Knickerbocker, Schuco, Chad Valley, Gund and Dakin.

Fabric: Wool mohair was commonly used before WWI, artificial silk plush around 1930, cotton plush after WWII and synthetic plush after the early 1950s.

Label: Is there a fabric label? Original cardboard hang tags are usually missing, but fabric labels sewn into a seam may still be present.

Condition: Some wear and tear is typical and many signs of distress can be repaired, but thin, rotting plush or fabric is difficult to salvage.

Body proportions: Long, thin arms and muzzle or a hump on the back generally indicate the bear was made before WWII, but variations between manufacturers make it important to consult a good reference book.

Articulation: Many old bears are jointed, but during the 1960s production costs made it popular to produce unjointed bears.

Ears: Original ear positions are important in manufacturer identification and dating. Check around the seam of the bear's head for any holes to indicate the ears may have been replaced.

Eyes: Plastic eyes generally indicate the bear was made after 1950, while glass eyes indicate the bear was manufactured after 1920. Boot-button eyes were used before WWI.

Paws: Felt was commonly used for paw pads in early bears; velvet was popular in the 1930s, while trimmed plush or leather (real or synthetic) was used later. Ultrasuede paw pads were made after 1970s.

Clubs

•Good Bears of the World Club
Terri Stong
P.O. Box 13097, Toledo, OH 43613-0097

•Teddy Bear Boosters Club
Ann Miller
19750 S.W. Peavine Mtn. Rd, .McMinnville, OR 97128

•B.E.A.R.
Bear Enthusiasts All-Round
313 Glenoaks Blvd., Glendale, CA 91207

•Steiff Clubs USA225 Fifth Ave.Suite 1022New York, NY 10010

•National Doll & Teddy Bear Collector
Rose Morgan, Ed.
PO Box 4032, Portland, OR 97208-4032

Publications

Teddy Bear Review
170 Fifth Ave.
New York, NY 10010

The Teddy Tribune
Barbara Wolters
254 W. Sidney
St. Paul, MN 55107-3494

This White Center Seam Bear, circa 1920s, 24" long, had a presale estimate of $3,000-$4,000 at a 1996 Christie's auction.

This rare white Steiff teddy bear had a presale estimate of $5,000-$7,000 at a 1994 Christie's auction.

Teddy Bear & Friends
6405 Flank Dr.
Harrisburg, PA 17112-2750

VALUE LINE

Lt. brown mohair bear, fully jointed, stuffed with excelsior and cotton, 22" tall, has a growler but no eyes, possibly English, c1930 .... $225

1920s Schuco yes-no bear $225

Steiff white miniature bear from the 1950s, in very good condition $250

3-1/2", golden mohair, metal frame, tummy opens to reveal oval mirror and powder puff tray, Schuco $325

5" h, Teddy Threesome, mohair, swivel head, stationary legs, collar with bell, felt paws, Steiff $65

5" h, white mohair, plastic brads, Schuco $65

6" h, Bedtime Bear, brown mohair, straw stuffed, glass eyes, sewn nose and mouth, jointed, Steiff, 1900s $150

6" h, Pouting Bear, brown plush, foam stuffing, molded face, sitting, Knickerbocker, 1950s $10

6-1/2" h, Berg Bear, gold plush, straw stuffed, Austria $85

7" h, Bear-at-Brunch, gold mohair, straw stuffed, stickpin eyes, sewn nose and mouth, jointed, swivel head, Germany $150

7" h, Scooter Bear, plush, windup, on wheels $150

10" h, Cocoa Bear, white felt, stuffed, button eyes, 1940s $25

11" h, Riding Bear, stuffed, blue and white checked, metal tricycle, red wood wheels $125

11" h, Brown Mohair, swivel head, gold muzzle, glass eyes, Zotty $130

11" h, Gold Mohair, glass eyes, Knickerbocker $250

11" h, Playmate Bear, gold mohair, stuffed, sewn nose and mouth, jointed, 1950s $65

12" h, Smokey the Bear, Ideal, 1953 .... $25

13" h, gold mohair, swivel head, glass eyes, Hermann $95

16" h, Gentle Ben, black plush, plastic eyes, pink mouth, red felt tongue, pull string, Mattel, 1967 .... $35

16" h, The Original Ideal Teddy Bear, 75th anniversary commemorative, brown plush, label, special-edition box, Ideal, 1978 .... $50

16" h, Yogi Bear, brown plush, stuffed, molded face, yellow paws, green felt tie, Knickerbocker, 1959 .... $85

These Steiff bears sold for $2,300 and $2,600 each at a Theriault's sale.

Jackie Bear, from the mid-1950s, was made to celebrate the 50th anniversary of Steiff.

TELEPHONES

Even though modern technology has revolutionized the telephone, collectors still long for the old-fashioned charm of early telephones.

History: Alexander Graham Bell developed and patented the first working phone in 1876; the Bell Telephone Company was established in 1877. Throughout the early 1900s, improvements continued to be made in telephones, and work began on the first pay telephones. Most telephones in the 1880s and 1890s were wood, crank wall phones with separate boxes for batteries and other components.

Early non-dial upright desk phones, known today as candlesticks, came into general use from 1900-1920. Candlestick phones with dials originated from 1920-1930.

Cradle phones came into general use from 1930-1940.

In the 1940s, metal cases were substituted with plastic, making phones lighter and allowing for more colors, and technology continued throughout the decades until today.

General Guidelines: Most telephones collected today are from the 1920s to the 1950s. Models from the 1920s and 1930s are most in demand. Phones by the following manufacturers are especially popular — Kellogg, Stromberg Carlson, Western Electric, Automatic Electric, Strowger and others. Also in demand are antique phones by European makers displaying names such as Ericsson, Aristocrat, Oslo and Regal.

Among the earliest telephones collected are wood crank wall phones used in the late 1800s and very early 1900s.

The dial candlestick phone, first used in the 1920s, is especially collectible since it was only used for a few years. Nice examples can command $400 or more.

Among the top selling phones today are stylishly-streamlined Art Deco cradle phones from the 1930s, which generally sell in the $175-$275 price range.

Pay phones are also collectible; many are available for $250-$400.

Novelty telephones — many from the 1970s and 1980s — were made in the shapes of popular characters and even products like ketchup bottles or bars of soap. Such items sell for $25-$60 depending on subject.

Telephone-related items—such as advertisements, old directories, signs and even phone booths—are also highly collectible.

Clubs
•Antique Telephone Collectors Association
P.O. Box 94
Abilene, KS 67410

•Telephone Collectors International, Inc.
19 N. Cherry Dr.
Oswego, IL 60543

Telephones

Desk, upright, Eiffel Tower, L.M. Ericsson & Co., c1890	$150
Emergency, Western Electric	$100
Intercom, Stromberg-Carlson	$75
Pay, 23J, metal, Gray Manufacturing	$150
Wall, Connecticut Telephone & Electric, watch case receiver	$25
Toy, figural, Bart Simpson, MIB	$35
Toy, figural, Beetle Bailey	$65
Toy, figural, Budweiser Beer Can	$25
Toy, figural, Garfield, 1980s	$35
Toy, figural, Pizza Hut Pete, 1980s	$50

Brass candlestick telephone, 11-1/4", West Elec. Co. Pat. Aug. 26, 1904; non-dial, 1900-1913 pat. on speaker.

Other

Almanac, Bell Systems Telephone, 58th anniversary issue,
1934 .... $14

Booklet, biography, Alexander Graham Bell,
Bell Telephone, 32 pgs, Bell portrait cover, 1951 .... $6

Broadside, Atlantic Telegraph, Triumph of Science $20

Calendar, Tri-State Telephone Co., December 1916 .... $25

Fan, Bell System, logo, blue and white $12

Magazine, General Telephone Co., of
Wisconsin News Lines, July 1956 .... $8

Paperweight, Bell System, New York Telephone Co.,
figural glass bell, dark blue, gold lettering,
c1920, 3-1/4" h $70

Pen, Bell Telephone, Esterbrook $45

Pencil, Bell Telephone, Auto Point $25

Pin, Bell System, die-cut celluloid bell-shape hanger,
blue, white lettering, "Local Long Distance
Telephone" on front, reverse with "When in Doubt,
Telephone and Find Out, Use the Bell,"
Whitehead & Hoag patent, 1905, 1" $12

Pin, New England Telephone & Telegraph, service award,
octagonal, 10k gold, raised Bell System logo
above faux ruby, 1930s, 1/2" $15

Pinback Button, Bell Telephone System, blue lettering
and logo, white ground, "3 Sale Club" on center
bell logo, "Plant Employee Sales, Go Get 'Em,
Eastern Division" on rim, 1906-07, 7/8" d $25

Pinback Button, Chicago Telephones, red ground,
white lettering, 2-1/4" d $25

Pinback Button, New England Telephone &
Telegraph Co., Bell System, blue and white $25

Playing Cards, Telephone Pioneers of America,
blue and white, Bell logo $3

Pocket Mirror, Missouri and Kansas Telephone Co.,
Bell System, American Telephone & Telegraph,
celluloid, blue and white, early 1900s, 2-1/2" l $65

Sheet Music, Call Me Up Some Rainy Afternoon,
cover with woman making phone call and man
walking in rain, 1910 .... $10

Sign, Indiana Telephone Co., Indiana Telephone
Corporation, Local & Distance Service,
18" by 18", two-sided, porcelain enamel,
black and white, late 1940s $65

Stock Certificate, American Telegraphone Co.,
District of Columbia, 1907 .... $13

Valentine, Love's Telephone, mechanical $40

Pillsbury Doughboy character phone.

Televisions

Early television sets can be divided into three distinct eras. The mechanical era was from 1925 to 1932. Sets often were known as "radiovisors" since they were visual attachments to radios. Many mechanical television sets did not have cabinets and resembled an electric fan with a round metal disk in place of the blades. These units were most prevalent in the New York City and Chicago areas. Mechanical sets from the 1920s typically have a motorized 12-

Philco "Barber-pole" set, 21" console with flat front, rounded back supports swivel screen, 1958, blonde finish.

inch diameter metal disc with a "glow tube" in back and a magnifier in front. Starting in 1938 sets used picture tubes, as they do today. Generally, the earlier the set, the smaller the screen.

Manufacturers of mechanical sets included Jenkins, Baird, Western Television, Insuline Corp. of America, Short-Wave and Television Corp., Daven, See-All, Rawls, Pioneer and Travler Radio & Television Corp. A complete mechanical set is worth several thousand dollars.

The pre-World War II era includes sets made between 1938 and 1941. By the 1939 World's Fair, RCA, DuMont, General Electric and other manufacturers had started producing electronic TV sets. These featured long picture tubes and electronics inside and a screen and controls on the front.

These prewar sets featured 1 to 5 channels with 5-inch, 9-inch or 12-inch screens.

Televisions made during this period were the first all-electronic sets and usually were combined with a multi-band radio in a fancy cabinet. A favorite design of the era was a mirror-in-the-lid arrangement, in which a mirror in the underside of a lift lid reflected the picture tube, which was pointed straight up. Production, which totaled no more than 2,000 sets, was concentrated in those areas with prewar television stations — New York City, Philadelphia, Chicago and Los Angeles. Depending on model and condition, these sets usually start at $1,000 and can exceed $5,000 on the secondary market.

As World War II approached, TV production was put on hold until after the war. Hundreds of manufacturers produced wood or Bakelite sets ranging in size from 3 inches to 12 inches. These sets were attractive, with complicated lines, contours and veneers to match any decor.

By the late 1940s, RCA, DuMont and others were producing sets with up to 20-inch screens. By the early 1950s, most mass-produced sets were very squared off with most cabinets simply wood or metal boxes.

The late 1950s and early 1960s brought a flair to the sets. Color TV was first mass-produced in 1954 and 1955.

In the 1970s and 1980s, television sets became smaller, with some portable sets sporting 2-inch screens.

General Guidelines: The easiest way to gauge the age of a television set is by the numbers found on the channel selector. Pre-1946 television sets will tune a maximum of five stations, usually channels 1 to 5. In 1946 channels 7 to 13 were added, thus sets made between 1946 and 1948 will show channels 1 to 13 on the station selector.

In 1949, channel 1 was dropped, leaving all 1949 and newer sets with VHF channels 2 to 13, as we have them today. The UHF band was added in 1953.

Brand and model number are essential in determining a set's worth. However, physical condition of the cabinet is much more important than the operating condition of the set. Even a prewar set in Poor condition is often valuable.

Early (1938-1941) electronic sets, depending on condition and model, can sell for $500-$5,000. Manufacturers to look for include RCA, General Electric, DuMont and Stromberg-Carlson.

Post-1946 sets can sell for $100 and up. Those with unusual or elaborate wood cabinets can command more. Experimental color TVs made before 1954 with 9-inch or smaller tubes or spinning color discs are rare and valuable, often worth several thousand dollars.

Few sets after 1949 have collectible value. Some notable exceptions include the first color wheel sets (1951), the giant DuMont 30-inch screen sets (1953) and limited production or oddball sets. Sets from the 1950s and 1960s are usually worth less than $100. Televisions from the 1970s and 1980s with micro-screens or space age designs most sell in the $50-$200 range.

Publications

Classic TVs, Pre-War thru 1950s (L-W Book Sales, 1997)
Poster's Guide to Collectible Radios and Televisions, (Krause Publications).

Contributor to this section: Harry Poster, P.O. Box 1883, South Hackensack, NJ 07606.

COLLECTOR'S ALERT

If a set has been in storage for more than 30 years, do not plug it in without first having it inspected by a qualified serviceman. Components can go bad and short-circuit, causing a fire. Many early sets had no fuses for protection.

VALUE LINE

1925-1932, Mechanical

Daven, kit of parts	$500
Scanning disc sets, 1920s	$500-$1,500
Insuline Corp of America (ICA), Bakelite cabinet model	$3,000
See-All, open frame	$1,500
Short-Wave and Television Corp., drum scanner	$3,000
Western Television Corp., "Ship's Wheel" cabinet type	$2,200

1938-1941, Electronic

Andrea 1-F-5	$4,000
Andrea KTE-5, 5"	$1,000-$2,500
DuMont, 180	$2,000
General Electric (GE) HM-171	$2,500
GE HM-225	$4,000
GE HM-275	$5,000
RCA TRK-5	$4,000
RCA TRK-12, Deco console	$5,000
RCA TRK-120	$3,500

1946 and Later

CBS/Columbia, 12CC2, color-wheel set	$5,000
DuMont, RA-119, 30" screen	$1,000
Motorola, VT-71	$225
Philco Predicta, table model	$225
Philco Safari	$250
Pilot, TV-37, magnifier	$200
Zenith Porthole, round screen, 10"	$75-$150
RCA 630TS	$250
RCA 648PTK	$200
RCA 8TS30	$100
RCA CT-100, first RCA color set	$200-$500
Epson Elf, micro-screen, 1984	$50-$100
JVC Videosphere, ball-shaped, 1971	$50-$75

THERMOMETERS

Galileo invented the thermometer over 400 years ago in 1593. A diagram suggesting what the first thermometer looked like sits in a Roman museum today — a slender tube, perhaps two feet long, sealed at the top and sitting in a vessel of water which moved up and down to signal a temperature change. Not as portable as modern-day versions, Galileo's thermometer evolved in 1640, featuring a sealed tube bottom with liquid inside.

The Celsius and Fahrenheit scales are derived from two early thermometer inventors. The Fahrenheit system can be traced to 1851, when the Taylor Company of Rochester, N.Y. began mass-producing inexpensive models for hardware stores. Despite the popularity of Celsius and Fahrenheit, there may have been as many as 18 different temperature scales used in the United States during that era.

Many types of thermometers have been invented since Galileo's discovery including bi-metallic (first introduced in 1860), liquid crystal or heat sensitive (1888), thermocouples, infrareds and T-sticks. As long as weather continues to change, however, we can expect even newer, more sophisticated thermometers to enhance our lives. Collecting thermometers goes way beyond our simple need to understand weather conditions.

General Guidelines: The most important question to ask when collecting thermometers is "Does it work?" In most cases, a thermometer cannot be adjusted, except by moving the tube, most of which are held in place by adhesive or brackets. However, broken thermometers sometimes can have their tubes successfully replaced, rendering them workable and therefore more valuable.

The size and shape of the glass tube, its bore and the bulb dictate a thermometer's worth. In general, the larger the glass tube and its bore, the higher its value. Mercury-filled thermometers are more valuable than those filled with alcohol. Green- or blue-tinted alcohol brings a greater price than the more common red-colored alcohol. Thermometers featuring faded alcohol are also less valuable than those featuring brighter colors.

Hires Root Beer thermometer, $65.

Backing plate materials like glass, porcelain and red clay — which weather better than metal, plastic or wood — are more collectible. Porcelain and glass examples, in particular, without chips command the best prices, especially those of older vintage. Flaws including scratches, dents, fading and rust significantly reduce the value of a thermometer. Repairs are available for some damaged examples, but not always possible depending on the problem.

Some of the leading U.S. thermometer manufacturers include Cooper, Kessler, Hartley Gove & Sons, Maximum, PSG Industries, Taylor, Wahl and Weksler.

Thermometers needn't have their original boxes to be valuable. Many are sold without boxes.

Thermometers fall into six broad categories — advertising, antique, "cute," ordinary, souvenir and unusual.

Advertising thermometers feature designs and logos for products and businesses. Ranging from auto products to soft drinks to funeral homes, older thermometers free of flaws command higher prices. Famous national trade names, multi-colored versions, fascinating captions, clever graphics and designs all add to a piece's overall worth.

While **antique thermometers** don't outnumber advertising versions, they do outclass them for their sheer value. Two examples of antique thermometers have reportedly carried asking prices in excess of $5,000 each. Both are circa mid-1800s, in Excellent condition, with carved wood inlays.

Art deco in style, **"cute" thermometers** appeal to art lovers and children alike, as they represent a unique fashion of Americana.

Souvenir thermometers often cross over into other categories such as cute, advertising or even unusual. But they can be found representing places all over the globe from Boy's Town to the San Diego Zoo. Hard to date and value, these thermometers are quickly disappearing from souvenir shops as fast as eager tourists can grab them.

Unusual thermometers are rare and present great difficulty when trying to estimate their age and values. By contrast, **ordinary thermometers** are the remainder, a broad category featuring everyday examples commonly used by chefs, doctors and others for daily measurements.

Prices have also risen to reflect increasing interest. The law of supply and demand — in many cases, old supply and new demand — dictates this. One way to grow a collection is to ask friends, relatives and people you meet to send you one or two. Diehard thermometer collectors report that the Eastern United States is generally a better hunting ground than either the Midwest or the West. Similarly, the Midwest is better than the West, as older, more rare thermometer availability seems to diminish the further West you travel. This may be due to the fact that many thermometers were broken or lost by early settlers on the Westward trails. Many dealers stock up in New England and travel South or West during the winter, providing a boon for eager thermometer collectors.

The last (or worst) place to collect thermometers is in hot climates such as the islands in the Gulf of Mexico. Thermometers are rarely seen and are considered unneccessary when the temperature is always hot. In the continental U.S., Arizona, Florida and other retirement communities have little need of thermometers, although the Northern snowbirds are marked by their habit of transporting them back and forth between homes.

Thermometers are harder to find than even a decade ago. In many cases, this has doubled or tripled their values. An accurate read of their temperature would place them as rising by degrees slowly but surely on the collectibility scale.

Clubs
•The Thermometer Collectors Club of America (TCCOA) P.O. Box 94449, Zarahelma Road, Onset, MA 02558

Contributor to this section: Richard T. Porter, Porter Thermometer Museum, Box 944, Onset, MA, 02558-0944, 508-295-5504.

VALUE LINE

Values listed are for items in Near Mint condition.

Advertising thermometers

Pedestal, metal or wood with hinged base, 1950s to present	$10
Bar of soap, floating, for baby bath disguise, 1919, 20s-40s	$25
Pictures in frame with T, 1913 to present	$19
Zipper pull (glass tube or liquid crystal), 1950s to present	$10
Porcelain backing plate, 1913 to 1960s	$30
Wood backing plate, 1900s to present	$40
Bathtub floaters (Dr. Forbes formula w/ad), 1900s to present	$24
Metal backing plate	$35
Tripod, plastic or metal	$20
Ship's steering wheel, 1920s-70s	$35
Heat-sensitive crystal type, including rulers, 1960s-70s	$10
Desk calendars, metal or plastic frame, 1920s to present	$8
Refrigerator magnet, 1960s to present	$8
Large round garden bi-metals, 1950s to present	$30
Cardboard backing plate, 1950s to present	$25

Gas Station Models

Ex-Lax, 39"	$180+
Pepsi, 26", 1940s	$150
Raybestos Fan Belts, 30"	$80
Coca-Cola, bottle shape, 18-30"	$95
Prestone, 36"	$70+
Mail Pouch Chew Tobacco, 39"	$70+
Purolator Filters, 28"	$60+
Orange Crush, 28"	$60
Hires Root Beer	$65
Mail Pouch, 6', 1930	$400+
Ed Pinaud's Hair Tonic, 27", 1915, auction price	$3,700

Antique thermometers

Wet/Dry Bulb, Taylor Co., 1880s	$175+
Chandelier, Taylor Co., 1887	$150+
Tin case, Late 1800s	$150
Wood Bath Floaters, 1900	$50
Boyce (Trademark) Motometer Radiator Caps, 1910	$300
Cottage Barometer, 1910 to present	$50
Enameled Metal Case, 1880	$50+
Black Ebonized Wood wall hanger, 1900-1950s	$150
Vertical V-grooved Backing Plate, 1850-1900s	$80+
Wood Backing Plate, 1800s to presentv	$40+
Doctor's Pocket Bi-metal Fever, 1900	$100+
German Silver Pocket, 1900	$90+
Show thermometers, 1890s-1930s	$300

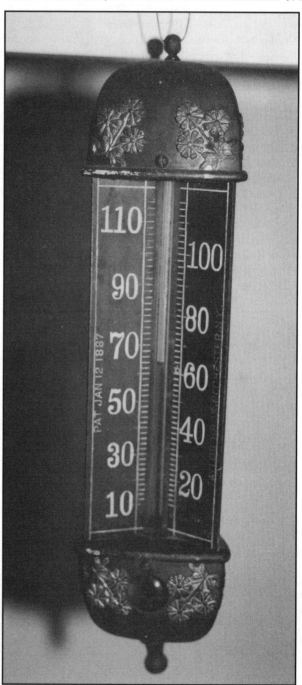

The very famous and rare Taylor thermometer, known as a "Chandelier," is valued at $200.

Ivory and Jeweled, 1900 to present	$2,000
Whiskey Stirrers, 1910	$80
Champagne Bowl Floater	$60+
Bi-metals, 1880s	$90

Cute thermometers

Canary on a perch, bi-metal	$20
Swiss Weather House, 1913 to present	$15
Skis and ski poles w/ thermometer, 1960s to present	$10
Miniature frying pan, bi-metal, 1950	$25
Plywood animals with and w/o woodburning, 1950 to present	$18
Tie-clasp, 1970 to present	$15
Pins w/ thermometers, 1970s to present	$12
Cracker Jack prizes, c. 1920s	$50
Nautical wheels, metal or wood, 1940s to present	$24
Tower or obelisk made of U.S. currency, 1950s to present	$40
Shells, 1800s to present	$18
Fountain or ballpoint pens, 1940s to present	$25
Pocket watch or wristwatch, 1970-1990	$24

Ordinary thermometers

Chef's	$10
Microwave	$15+
Medical/Clinical	$5
Oven, glass or bi-metal	$6
Lab, bright red alcohol or mercury	$8
Refrigerator, bi-metal or crystal	$6
Dairy floaters	$10
Photo lab	$8
Candy/confectioners	$20

Swimming pool floaters	$15
Auto/dashboard	$6
Yogurt maker, plastic	$4
Boiler, bi-metal	$25
Antifreeze tester, glass tube	$5
Incubating, glass tube w/narrow range	$12
Hot/Cold alarm	$15+
Evaporating	$10+
Maximum/minimum, magnet or gravity setting	$15+
Thermostats, bi-metal/mercury drop	$5+
Double and triple scale	$20+
Beehive, uncommon	$30
Brewers'	$50+
Grain Silo	$25
Terrestrial, for gardening	$15
Aquarium or Reptile	$8
Tank or cup	$5+
Key holder racks, multi-purpose	$5+
Turkey breast	$20
Stove Pipe safety	$10

Souvenir thermometers

Florida ceramic animals, glass tube or bi-metal, 1950s to present	$15
Keys to cities or attractions, 1930	$20
Anchors, 1930s	$20
Sailing vessels, ship's wheels, horses, horseshoes, 1930s	$15
Molded, free-standing, wall hangers or electric outlet cover	$25
Fairs, 1900s to present	$100+
National monuments and battlefields, 1930s to present	$30
Set-ins (coal, shells, plastic, minerals), 1940s	$10+
Windmills and Dutch shoes, 1940s	$10+
Pine slab, 1930s	$25
Electrical switchplate covers	$5+
Towers or obelisks, 1890s to present	$20+
Animals on pedestals and pine slabs, 1920s to present	$18

Mid-1880s bi-metal thermometer.

FUN FACT

The largest thermometer ever recorded was displayed at the 1933 World's Exposition in Chicago. Built by Texaco's Halvoline division, it featured three miles of red neon tubing, but not a single drop of mercury. Standing at 218 feet high, the three-sided thermometer dominated the skyline, only to be dismanted after the fair.

Today, the world's largest known thermometer stands 134 feet high in the Mojave Desert. Featuring a whopping 5,000 thermostatically-controlled spotlights, the thermolith cost one million dollars to build. It can be seen from 10 miles away and read by commuters on nearby I-15 in Baker, CA. Interested visitors can call 1-800-204-TEMP for more details.

Mother of Pearl, 1940s .... $50+
Plastic embedded $12

Unusual thermometers
St. Labre's Fish Skeleton, late 1960s-early 1980s $12
Silver mounted standing, mid-1900s .... $20+
Tin lithographed, 1930s to present $50
Railroad track laying, 1890s .... $50+
French soldier's hat paperweight, 1900s $40
Muffler or windshield shape, 1930s to present $45
Recording thermometers, drum or disk, 1930s to
    present $100
Termomento Lento, 1950 .... $150+
Postcard, heat sensitive or liquid crystal, 1980s-1990s $4
Ear fever-detecting thermometers, 1990 .... $70
Mirror type, with or w/out advertising, 1930s .... $15+
Pipe holder or pen holder, 1940s-80s $20
Plum Bob, 1940 .... $40+
Bearing and Motor burnout detectors, liquid crystal,
    1970s .... $2+
Cranberry, for crop damage control, 1940s .... $25+

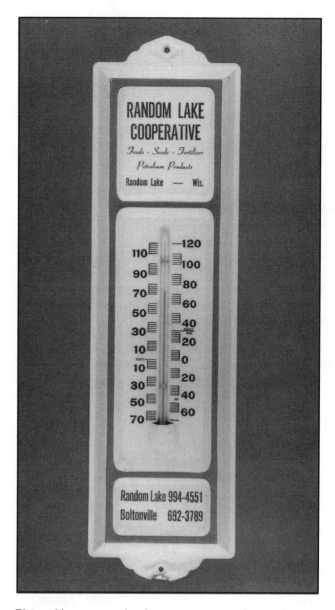

Pictured is an example of a common enamel advertising thermometer. Many reproductions exist.

TIPS OF THE TRADE

• Thermometer prices depend on overall size, mercury versus alcohol content, tube and bulb size.

• Examples featuring exotic woods (mahogany, rosewood, oak, ebony) and/or carvings command premiums.

• Larger thermometers are generally worth more than smaller ones.

• Ship steering wheel thermometers with broken or missing spoke handles, which are hard to replace, are worth much less than similar Good or Excellent examples.

• Variations with cardboard backings are extremely collectible but equally fragile due to their composition. This type of thermometer is more susceptible to deterioration, stains and water damage.

• Filling station models generally depict oil products, medicines, liquors, tobacco products and a bevy of advertising. Among the most popular of thermometers, their steep prices may be too hot for novice collectors to handle unless stumbled upon at a yard sale.

• Chandelier thermometers are very rare; only 30 of them have been documented to exist in the past decade. Originally used on railroad parlor cars and in mansions, these examples are hard to appraise by dealers due to their rarity.

• Antique thermometers featuring enameled metal casings are relatively scarce; those in perfect condition are even rarer.

VINTAGE TOOLS

Today's antique and collectible tools encompass a broad time period, ranging from those handmade prior to the Civil War to later factory-made items from the latter part of the 1800s and into the early 20th century. Pre-Civil War models were fashioned individually in small shops and, consequently, were most often of superior workmanship and had more decorative interest than their later counterparts.

Axes and Hatchets

These "edge tools" were second in importance only to rifles among early settlers on the American frontier. Chief among carpenters' tools from this period was the axe. Hand-forged with wooden handles, they were often decorated with distinctive patterns, the design of which were passed down from generation to generation. The axe, or hatchet, was also a necessary tool for latheing, shingling and barrel-making.

The single-edge felling axe took a variety of shapes and, except for those with a desirable maker's name stamped into the head, are quite inexpensive. The broad axe was used for hewing tree trunks into squared timbers and had a longer cutting edge, a one-sided bevel and a canted handle.

Planes

Wood and metal planes to smooth and cut designs can be traced to ancient Rome. Records indicate that the wood plane industry started to develop toward the end of the 18th century, peaking about 1860. By 1945, only a few makers remained. The metal plane industry, on the other hand, began around 1830; however, by 1940 electrical-powered equipment had dominated the industry.

Carpenters' planes are of special importance, commanding attention for their beauty, versatility of design and size variations. Wooden planes have been used for over 2,000 years. Those seen by collectors today most likely date from the first 75 years of the 19th century. Appearing in England just prior to the 19th century, the work of professional planemakers was authenticated by the stamping of their names near the top of the front face of their products. From that point on, the majority of British and American wooden planes carried their maker's name.

Stanley Tools provide the broadest area for collecting metal planes. Stanley began production of metal planes in 1869, which increased in popularity during the last quarter of the 19th century, almost totally replacing the earlier wooden varieties. Almost all Stanley tools carry a model number and are easily identified.

The maker's imprint is a major factor in determining the value of a wooden plane. The imprint is a stamped impression embossed near the top of the front face of the tool. A common imprint increases the value slightly, but the stamp of several early 18th century New England makers (Nicholson, Chelor, for example) can increase the value by $1,000 or more.

Measuring and Layout Tools

Early carpenters used a folding rule for measurements. Before the advent of the "zig-zag" folding six-foot rule, the two-foot "four-fold" rule was most often used, although there were also two-fold and six-fold models. The four-fold type consisted of four six-inch strips, usually of boxwood (ivory in premium grades), held together by brass or nickel silver hinges. Because graduations on the outside of these strips suffered from pocket wear, they are often unreadable, making those with clear markings highly prized. Maker's names can increase values, with the rarest Stanley ivory rules commanding hundreds of dollars.

Plumb bobs were suspended from a string to make certain that work was truly vertical. Made in a variety of shapes, they were usually of brass, although lead, steel, ivory, and even wood were also used. Of particular interest to collectors are those by Stanley with an integral reel to hold the string. Older styles with ornate shapes can command hundreds of dollars, while those of museum quality are often valued at well over a thousand.

Wood levels are made of cherry, mahogany, rosewood, ebony or boxwood. The smaller sizes are rarer, especially the Stanley 6" and Stratton 6-1/2". Premium levels had all edges protected by inlaid brass strips, while cast-iron levels, with elaborate filigree designs between top and bottom surfaces, are generally brittle. Inclinometer levels, which were used to measure the slope of a surface by means of a dial indicator, are valuable with original, unbroken glass level vials.

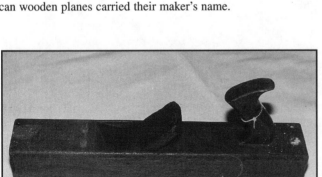
Large wood plane.

Publications

Guide to the Makers of American Wooden Planes, 3rd edition; Emil and Martyl Pollak; Astragal Press, Mendham, NJ; 1994

Collecting Antique Tools; Herbert Kean and Emil Pollak; Astragal Press, Menddham, NJ; 1990

A Price Guide to Antique Tools; Herbert Kean and Emil Pollak; Astragal Press, Mendham NJ.; Revised Ed. 1998

Antique and Collectible Stanley Tools; John Walter; The Tool Merchant, Marietta, OH; Second Ed. 1996

Clubs

•Midwest Tool Collectors Association
Rt. 2 Box 152, Wartrace, TN 37183

•Early Trades & Craft Society
11 Blythe PlaceEast, Northport, NY 11731

•L.I. Antique Tool Collector's Assn.
31 Wildwood Dr., Smithtown, NY 11787

•Early American Industries Assn.
167 Bakersville Rd.South, Dartmouth, MA 02748

•Collectors of Rare and Familiar Tools Society (CRAFTS)
38 Colony Court, Murray Hill, NJ 07974

Contributors to this section: John Whelan, 38 Colony Ct., Murray Hill, NJ, 07974; Bill Rigler, Route 2 Box 152, Wartrace, TN 37183.

VALUE LINE

Special Purpose Planes

#9 Cabinet Maker's Block Plane	$800-$2445
#10 Cabinet Maker's Rabbet	$75-$175
#10 1/4 Cabinet Maker's Rabbet	$325-$1,800
#11 Beltmaker's	$65-$250
#12 Veneer Scraper	$46-93
#13 Circular	$40-$116
#20 1/2 Circular	$93
#39 Dado	$55-$140
#40 Scrub	$50-$59
#41 Miller's Patent Plow	$425-$1,054
#43 Miller's Patent Plow	$120-$310
#45 Combination Plow	$45-$230
#46 Skew	$75-$270
#48 Tongue & Groove	$20-90
#50 Combination	$85-194
#52 Chute Board and Plane	$1,418
#55 Combination Plow	$125-$636

#56 Corebox	$800
#60 Block	$225
#62 Low Angle	$250-$512
#65 Block	$40-70
#66 Hand Beader	$60-$147
#69	$372-$550
#70 Box Scraper	$40
#75 Bull Nose Rabbet	$18-$56
#78 Duplex	$15-$55
#79 Side Rabbet	$23-$55
#80 Cabinet Scraper	$10-$31
#80 Steel Case Rebate	$250
#81 Cabinet Scraper	$10-$43;
#82	$31;
#83	$85
#85 Cabinet Scraper Plane	$525
#90 Steel Cased Rabbet	$170
#92 Cabinet Maker's Rabbet	$90
#95 Edge Trim	$119-$171
#96 Chisel Gauge	$93-$119
#97 Edge Plane	$225-$450
#98 Side Rabbet	$54
#112 Cabinet Scraper	$80-$140
#113 Circular Plane	$75-$155
#141 Bullnose Plow	$325
#144 Corner Rounding	$279
#146 Tongue & Groove Match	$132
#148 Tongue & Groove Match	$95
#164 Low Angle (low knob)	$50-$53
#171 Door Trim	$395
#180 through #192 Rabbets	$10-$53
#193 Fibre Board Plane	$35-$105
#194 Fibre Board Beveler	$22-$85
#196 Curve Rabbet Plane	$620-$1,240
#278 Rabbet & Filletster	$130-$294
#289 Filletster & Rabbet	$125-$217
#340 Furring Plane	$913
#444 Dovetail	$528-$850
#602 Bedrock Smooth	$440-$490
#602 Bedrock Smooth	$80-$140

A Miller Falls breast drill.

#604 Bedrock Smooth	$55-85:
#604-1/2	$186-$200
#605 Bedrock Jack	$35-100:
#605-1/2	$100-$140
#606 Bedrock Fore	$50-$125
#607 Bedrock Jointer	$105-$200

Wood Planes

Common makers or unmarked beech bench planes	$10-$25
Applewood planes	$20-$40
Exotic woods	$50+
Compass Planes	$40-65
T.Napier planes	$115
Coachmaker's boxwood planes	$15-$120

Boring Tools

Erlandsen Bow drill	$300
Bow drill, brass & ebony	$60:
boxwood & ebony	$150
ivory handle	$538
blackwood handle	$489
Bear "eggbeater" drills	$5-$55
Iron Braces	$10-$65
Primitive wooden braces	$85-$800
Sheffield unplated braces	$55-$175
plated	$95-$700
Ultimatum braces	$300-$600:
beech filled long form	$1,440
French 16th Century decorated iron brace	$2,400
English shipwright's brace, 17th Century	$5,440
Cherry or mahogany levels, common makers, 20" or longer	$10-$45
Rosewood, brass bound levels, common makers 20" or longer	$50-$200

Axes

Common felling	$10-$20
Rare names like Fordham & Hedges	$110
Broad axes	$50-$80
Cooper's axes, W. Greaves	$100
Continental	$200-$375
Goosewing axes	$170
Pennsylvania	$260
Beatty	$600
Continental Goosewing	$675
decorated	$1,025
Continental decorated bearded side axe	$,1700
Marbles Safety Axe	$100-$175

Chisels and Gouges

Paring chisels	$5-$20
Mortise chisels	$10-$30
Lock Mortise	$11-$30
Carving chisel sets	$15-$20 per piece

Saws

Common,	$5-$20
Brass backed saws	$45+
Early Shaw & Marshall 18"	$200
Disston D15	$128
D23	$192
240: Stair saw	$50
Fret saws, rosewood Shaker pattern	$280-$290

Wrenches

Common wrenches	$1-$5
Bemis & Call Monkey wrench	$90
Coes (early 4")	$40
Key wrench, 32"	$125
Eifel Plierwrench	$29
John Deere wrench	$95
Planet Jr. wrench	$17
Winchester S wrench	$24
Unusual adjustable Alligator wrench	$250

Tool Boxes

Common carpenter's boxes	$5-$20
Cabinetmakers chests	$400-$1,250

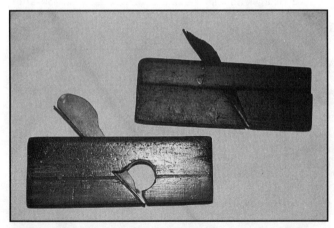

Wood planes are available in dozens of shapes and sizes. Those pictured are valued around $12-$15.

TOYS

For years, toys have fascinated collectors seeking to regain a part of their childhoods. Once discarded dolls, trains, cars, cap guns and other toys take on a more significant meaning and value the second time around.

While some collectors specialize in a particular era (1960s), others seek toys of a particular type (such as die cast vehicles or vintage tin toys), or a particular character (Popeye, Mickey Mouse, etc.).

History: American cast-iron toys were among the earliest playthings, produced in the late 1800s by companies such as Arcade and Hubley. By the 1920s, tin toys, from companies such as Marx, Lehmann and Chein appeared, featuring colorful lithography, intricate moving parts and licensed characters.

Wooden toys, by manufacturers such as Schoenhut and Fisher-Price, emerged in the early to mid-1900s.

Plastic came into regular use in the late 1950s, and by the 1960s was generally the medium of choice for toys. Model kits, space/science fiction and action figures began their heydays in the 1960s and have not slowed down since.

Today, even toys made in the 1970s and later are sought by collectors, who often buy new toys and stash them away immediately—hoping for future profits.

General Guidelines: Condition is key in any collecting area, but especially with toys.

Working condition is also important. Toys commanding the highest prices should walk, talk, spin, or operate in their original manner.

To bring top dollar, toys should be free of rust, rips, breaks, scratches, dents or other flaws.

Character Toys

Character toys are dolls, figures, books, games and other toys that depict a famous cartoon, celebrity, comic or other character.

General Guidelines: Among the most popular characters are all Disney characters (especially Mickey Mouse), comics characters like Superman and Batman and Green Hornet and Western characters like Roy Rogers or the Lone Ranger. Television characters from the 1950s-1970s are especially desirable now.

Vintage toys and memorabilia from the time period of the character's heyday are most treasured; later items issued as "collectibles" generally aren't as valuable.

Most valuable are premiums (like pinback buttons, whistles and rings) and paper items (club membership cards, etc.). Many of these items were only issued for a limited time, and few have survived over the years. Superman premiums from the 1940s typically top auction lists; some items have sold for more than $25,000. Items in their original boxes or with original mailing envelopes command top dollar.

Beware of reproductions. Many newer items are made to look like vintage character toys.

Erector Sets

Erector is a brand name coined by A.C. Gilbert in 1913 to refer to his metal girder construction sets. The numbered sets, which often included a motor, were packaged in cardboard, wood or metal boxes. Sets are still manufactured today by the Meccano Erector Company in New York.

General Guidelines: Without a box, sets are virtually worthless.

The value of Erector sets is based on three factors of condition — corrosion, cleanliness and completeness. Sets should be free of rust and corrosion; boxes should be free of damage and have complete decals; and sets should include all pieces (including motor) and instruction sheets. Inventory lists on the box help determine completeness.

Tin wind-up, "Unique Artie in Person," Unique Art Mfg. Co.,$850.

The older the set, the higher the value. Wooden boxes command higher prices than metal boxes, particularly the largest sets made from 1924-1932 which can sell for several thousand dollars in Near Mint condition. Bigger sets are usually worth more than smaller ones.

Sets from 1913-1915 bearing the Mysto Manufacturing name are also prized because they were Gilbert's first sets.

After 1966, Gabriel Industries manufactured sets using the Gilbert name. These are usually found in plastic boxes and are generally not valued by collectors.

Clubs
•A.C. Gilbert Heritage Society
594 Front St., Marion, MA 02738

•Southern California Meccano and
Erector Collectors Club
P.O. Box 7653
Porter Ranch Station, Northridge, CA 91327-7653

Fisher-Price

These wooden pull toys with colorful paper lithography originated in 1930 at the Fisher-Price company in East Aurora, N.Y. Many of the toys replicated Disney characters and featured carts, bells, xylophones or wind-up musical features.

In the late 1950s, the company introduced its Little People line, which continues in popularity today. The toys today, however, are made of plastic.

General Guidelines: Because 1930s-1950s toys are difficult to find with present, clean and unfaded paper, vintage pieces can sell for from $100-$500 up to $2,000 for Dr. Doodle, the company's first toy. Most Fisher-Price toys, especially prior to the 1960s, are found without boxes.

Fisher-Price pull toy, Donald Duck Drum Major, $300 EX.

Musical wind-up radios and televisions from the later 1950s to early 1960s are gaining popularity, selling for $5-$30.

Be aware of common reissues. Some toys, like the Chatter Telephone and Corn Popper, have been made for so many years that only the first issues have collectors' value.

Don't overlook plastic toys from the 1960s and later. While most of these play sets and individual pieces run in the $5-$40 range, those in Near Mint condition with boxes are sure to hold their value.

Clubs
•Fisher-Price Collectors Club
1442 N. Ogden, Mesa, AZ 85205

Toy Guns

Collectors generally seek several major types of toy guns — space, Western and police/spy.

Cap pistols date back to 1860 with cast iron and tin being the metals of choice. Die cast metal guns dominated the 1950s and 1960s, but plastic was also available. Major manufacturers include Kilgore, Marx, Hubley, Nichols and Classy. Post-World War II Japanese makes of ray guns and pop guns abound as well.

Western styles associated with Gene Autry, Hopalong Cassidy, Roy Rogers or the Lone Ranger top most collectors' lists. Space guns are just as popular, especially those with ties to science fiction shows like Buck Rogers and Lost in Space.

Man from U.N.C.L.E. and James Bond weapons reap the highest premiums in the spy/detective category.

General Guidelines: Guns in original boxes are preferred but hard to find, especially those from the 1930s-1940s. Sets including accessories, such as caps and holsters, should be complete.

Metal guns should have a clean, unscratched finish, and plastic should not be cracked.

Character-related guns generally are worth more than generic versions.

Clubs
•Toy Gun Collectors of America
175 Cornell St., Windsor, CA 95492-8743

Tin

Colorfully-lithographed tin toys became prominent in the 1920s, manufactured by American companies such as Marx, Chein, Unique Art and Wolverine; Marx subsidiary Linemar from Japan; and Lehmann and Strauss from Germany. Mechanical wind-up toys were often based on popular characters such as Mickey Mouse, Amos 'n Andy, Superman and Li'l Abner. Banks and spinning tops were also popular formats for tin toys.

Very old tin (1920s-1930s) can sell for thousands of dollars due to the scarcity of examples in premium condition.

General Guidelines: Best bet here is character-related toys. Mechanical (battery-operated or wind-up) pieces still in operation, and still in the original box, command the most money. Look for the cleanest tin, free of rust and "spidering" (cracks in the lithography).

See also: Banks; Barbie Dolls; Coloring Books / Paper Dolls; Disneyana; Fast Food Toys; Dolls, Modern; Games; GI Joe; Lunch Boxes; Marbles; Marx Play Sets; Model Kits; Puzzles; Space / Science Fiction Toys; Teddy Bears; TV Toys; Vehicle Toys.

Publications
1999 Toys & Prices (Krause Publications, 1998)
Collecting Toys, 8th ed. (Krause Publications, 1997)

VALUE LINE

Character Toys
Values listed are for items in Excellent condition without original box.

Fred Flintstone vinyl doll, Knickerbocker, 1960s	$70
Dick Tracy Target Set, Larami, 1969	$35
Beany & Cecil frame tray puzzle, 1960s	$55
Betty Boop composition doll, 1930s	$200
Brady Bunch Paper Dolls, Whitman, 1970s	$50
Howdy Doody Marionette, Peter Puppet, 1950s	$200
Gumby hand puppet, Lakeside, 1960s	$25
Mickey Mouse jack-in-the-box, Mattel, 1970s	$45
Underdog costume, Ben Cooper, 1969	$80
Smokey Bear soaky bottle, 1960s	$20
Porky Pig doll, Mattel, 1960s	$35
Popeye Ring Toss Game, Transogram, 1957	$50
Peanuts plastic dolls, Hungerford Plastics, 1950s, each	$70
Man from U.N.C.L.E. Counterspy Outfit, Marx, 1966	$225
Flipper Halloween costume, Collegeville, 1964	$40
Walt Disney's Television Car, Marx	$200
Superman wood-jointed doll, Ideal, 1940s	$1,500
Doctor Doolittle coloring book, Watkins-Strathmore	$15
Green Hornet coloring book, 1960s	$35
Bullwinkle Cartoon Kit, Colorforms, 1962	$50
Munsters dolls, Remco, 1964, each	$300
Magilla Gorilla Push Puppet, Kohner, 1960s	$40
California Raisins Chalkboard, Rose Art, 1988	$10
Captain Marvel Paint Set, 1940s	$300

Erector Sets
Prices are for A. C. Gilbert sets in box in Good condition.

Any set #10, oak box, 1920-1931	$4,200
Any sets from 1960-61 in tube	$50-$100
Set #8-1/2, 1931, wood box	$1,800
Set #6-1/2, 1935-1957, metal box	$45
Set #12-1/2, Walking Robot	$700
Set #10092, 1958, metal box	$750
Set #10351, 1965-66, cardboard box	$20

Fisher-Price Toys
Prices are for toys in Good condition. Boxes can add 50 to 100 percent to value. Note: Many Fisher-Price toys have been made for numerous years; modern issues of vintage toys do not command as much.

1960s wind-up nursery rhyme radios	$2-$6
1960s musical clocks, televisions	$4-$25
Individual "Little People" figures, plastic	$1-$2
Individual "Little People" figures, all wood	$2-$3
Bunny Egg Cart, 1950	$150
Buzzy Bee, 1950	$40
Cash Register, 1960	$35
Chatter Telephone, modern issue	$2-$5
Chatter Telephone, 1962	$30
Corn Popper, modern issue	$2-$5
Corn Popper, 1957	$30
Dr. Doodle, 1931	$600
Dr. Doodle, 1940 reissue	$150
Donald Duck Choo Choo, 1940	$300
Donald Duck Drum Major, 1940s	$150
Humpty Dumpty, 1957	$165
Mickey Mouse Band, 1935	$750
Mickey Mouse Choo Choo, 1938	$450
Mickey Mouse Xylophone, 1930s	$300
Musical Sweeper, 1953	$40
Play Family Hospital, 1976	$75
Pull-A-Tune Xylophone, 1957	$30
Quacky Family, 1946	$30
Safety School Bus, 1962	$50
Snoopy Sniffer, 1938	$65
Teddy Bear Zilo, 1950	$35
Ten Little Indians TV Radio, 1961	$25
Winky Blinky Fire Truck, 1954	$45

Guns
Prices are for toys in Good condition.

Atomic Disintegrator, 1954, Hubley	$165
Buck Rogers Sonic Ray Flashlight Gun, 1955, Norton-Honer	$70
Buffalo Bill Cap Pistol, 1940, Stevens	$110
Daisy Zooka Pop Pistol, 1954, Daisy	$130
Dick Tracy Shootin' Shell Snub Nose, 1960s, Mattel	$75
Dick Tracy Tommy Burst Machine Gun, 1960s, Mattel	$175
Fanner 50 Cap Pistol, 1960s, Mattel	$75
Flash Gordon Water Pistol, 1940s, Marx	$80

Happy Hooligan nodder, early 1900s, Kenton, $1,300.

Green Beret Tommy Gun, 1960s, Marx $55
Jet Plane Missile Gun, 1968, Hasbro $60
Johnny Ringo Gun and Holster, 1960, Esquire $200
Lost in Space Roto-Jet Gun, 1966, Mattel $775
Man from U.N.C.L.E. THRUSH Rifle, 1966, Ideal $875
Red Ranger Jr. Cap Pistol, 1950s, Wyandotte $55
Roy Rogers Double Holster Set, 1950s, Classy $250
Sheriff's Derringer Pocket Pistol, 1960s, Ohio Art $25
Space Navigator Gun, 1953, Asahitoy $60
Spud Gun, 1950s, Ambrit $35
Stallion .22 Cap Pistol, 1950s, Nichols $55
Star Wars, Han Solo Laser Pistol, 1978, Kenner $50
Strato Gun, 1950s, Futuristic $75
Texan Cap Pistol, 1940s, Harvel-Kilgore $85
Tom Corbett Space Cadet Gun, 1952, Marx $125

Tin

Prices are for toys in Excellent condition.
Alabama Jigger, 1920s, Lehmann $825
Amos 'N Andy wind-up walkers, 1930, Marx, each ... $1,075
Casper the Friendly Ghost wind-up, 1950s, Linemar.... $150
Cat in the Hat jack-in-the-box, 1969, Mattel $100

Dancing Monkey with Mouse, 1950s, Schuco $210
Dopey walker, 1938, Marx $525
Felix the Cat on a Scooter wind-up toy, 1924, Nifty $350
Honeymoon Express, 1920s-1940s, many
    variations, Marx .... $200-$500
Howdy Doody at the Piano, Unique Art $1,375
Huckleberry Hound Go-Cart, 1960s, Linemar $150
Jazzbo Jim Roof Dancer, 1920s, Marx $625
Li'l Abner and his Dogpatch Band, Unique Art $700
Mary Poppins Tea Set, 1964, Chein $55
Merry Go Round, Wolverine $390
Mortimer Snerd's Tricky Auto, 1939, Marx $600
Musical Man on the Flying Trapeze, Mattel $100
Mystery Taxi, 1938, Marx $250
Pluto Tricycle Toy, 1950s, Linemar $325
Popeye the Heavy Hitter, Chein $4,225
Snoopy in the Music Box jack-in-the-box, 1969,
    Mattel $50
Spinning tops, 1960s, generic designs .... $5-$20
Spinning tops, 1940s, w/Disney characters .... $50-$250
Talking Peanuts Bus, 1960s, Chein $400
Zilotone, 1920s, Wolverine $750

Ring-A-Ling Circus, 1925, Marx.

TRADING CARDS

Bubble gum cards. That's what trading cards used to be called when they were used as inserts to help sell other products. Today, and for the last 10 to 15 years, trading cards have been mostly sold by themselves. In essence, the cards have become the product.

History: Sports trading cards have been around a long time. The first baseball cards were issued in the late 1800s. In the early 1900s came tobacco cards, which were inserted into packs of cigarettes and are very scarce today, especially in top condition.

In the 1930s, bubble gum cards came into existence, with Goudey and Play Ball cards available for a short time. In the 1940s, Bowman entered the card market, but was eventually overtaken by Topps, which issued its first large set of cards in 1952. That classic set contains the famous Mickey Mantle card that sells for more than $15,000 today.

In 1957, Topps set the standard for size as we know it today — 2-1/2 inches by 3-1/2 inches. Throughout the 1950s until 1980, Topps maintained a virtual monopoly on the card market. In 1981, a court ruling allowed other companies to compete. Fleer and Donruss each issued baseball card sets. This ushered in a new era in card collecting. Almost overnight a new market sprang up, and the price of baseball cards soared. Conventions popped up everywhere, as did sports card shops and publications.

In the early 1990s, the market for newer cards took a tumble. Companies were producing too many cards and speculators were hoarding them, hoping to cash in later on. Once people figured this out, the cards were dumped into the hobby and the prices for many newer cards took a nosedive. (The player's strike that forced the cancellation of the World Series didn't help either.) Those cards, produced mainly from 1987 to 1992, are still being sold at rock-bottom prices. In the years since, companies have cut production of their cards but produced more card sets.

General Guidelines: Any pre-World War II card in Good condition is a very collectible card, regardless of whether the player is a star or a common. From the 1950s and 1960s, players like Mickey Mantle, Willie Mays, Roberto Clemente, Sandy Koufax, Hank Aaron and Brooks Robinson are most collectible.

From the 1970s and 1980s, Mike Schmidt, George Brett, Nolan Ryan, Tom Seaver, Robin Yount, Cal Ripken and Roger Clemens are the top choices. Younger players like Ken Griffey Jr. and Frank Thomas seem destined for future popularity.

Trends: The sports trading card hobby has changed greatly in the last five to 10 years. Gone are the days when "rookie cards" and "star cards" were the hot topic. Today, the hobby (at least for new products) is geared toward hard-to-find insert cards, also known as "chase" cards. These insert cards can be worth from $5 to more than $200, right out of the pack!

Collectors of today's cards don't seem too concerned with buying packs and completing their sets as was the case 15 years ago. The only complete sets that interest collectors are those that are produced in such small numbers that they are very expensive. The market for pre-1975 baseball cards is steady and solid. The market for classic cards is also strong for football, hockey and basketball. But the market today for these old cards is mostly concentrated on top condition cards. Lower condition old cards, unless very scarce or in high demand, are slow sellers and not considered investment quality.

MOST VALUABLE

The most famous tobacco card is the 1909-1911 T-206 Honus Wagner card. It has been estimated that only 50 to 100 are in circulation. There are two stories as to why this Wagner card is so rare. The first is that Wagner disapproved of the use of tobacco and that his likeness was used to help sell that product. The second is that Wagner received no payment to appear on the card. Either way, this card is the most valuable in existence and has sold for more than $400,000 at auction.

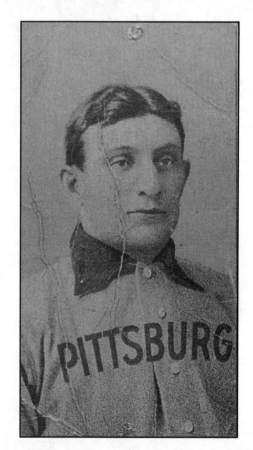

Basketball

Basketball cards are the least represented of the four major sports, with few sets produced from the 1940s through the 1960s.

Topps issued sets from 1969 to 1982, but stopped because the cards weren't moneymakers. Even the appearance of Larry Bird and Magic Johnson in the 1980-81 set wasn't enough to encourage collectors.

Fleer picked up the ball in 1986. This limited-run set featured the rookie cards of Michael Jordan ($1,000), Patrick Ewing, Akeem Olajuwon, Clyde Drexler, Karl Malone and Charles Barkley. This is a very popular and hard-to-find set, as are the 1987 and 1988 sets which contain many hot rookie cards (John Stockton, Dennis Rodman and Scottie Pippen).

General Guidelines: Today there is a myriad of cards to choose from. Most collectors seem to concentrate on just a few sets, as it is very expensive to collect too many cards. The hottest

new cards are those of the sure Hall of Famers (Jordan and many others from the 1986 Fleer set), along with exciting players like Shaquille O'Neal, Kevin Garnett, Kobe Bryant, Stephon Marbury, Antoine Walker, Vin Baker, Gary Payton and Grant Hill.

Older cards are also good sellers, with the early cards of Lew Alcindor / Kareem Abdul-Jabbar, Wilt Chamberlain, Bob Cousy, Bill Russell, Julius Erving, Oscar Robertson, Bill Bradley and Jerry West always in demand.

Football

When baseball cards became hot it took a few years for football cards to follow suit.

Bowman issued several sets in the 1940s and 1950s, but Topps again took over with sets from the 1950s until today. Philadelphia and Fleer are two other big card makers from the 1960s.

Topps had control of the market in the 1970s. Unfortunately, many of these sets had airbrushed team logos, so they are not the most delightful-looking sets. Topps continued to monopolize the football card market into the late 1980s, when Score and Pro Set began making cards. The new card makers brought a lot of excitement into football cards. Since then, many card makers produce scores of sets each year.

General Guidelines: Topps cards from the 1950s and 1960s sell extremely well today, with the cards of Bart Starr, Joe Namath, Jack Kemp, Jim Brown, Johnny Unitas, Alex Karras, Frank Gifford, Fran Tarkenton and other Hall of Fame players still at the top of many collectors' want lists. There are many good rookie cards from the 1970s, including Terry Bradshaw, O.J. Simpson, Franco Harris, Roger Staubach, Walter Payton, Tony Dorsett, Steve Largent and James Lofton. Several key rookie cards from the 1980s are Joe Montana, Jerry Rice, Dan Marino, John Elway and Reggie White, Steve Young and Jim Kelly (in Topps 1984 USFL set). Of the cards from 1989 to present, Brett Favre, Barry Sanders, Deion Sanders, Troy Aikman and Emmitt Smith are the hottest. Again, insert cards are the dominant force in this hobby.

Hockey

The Canadian-based company O-Pee-Chee, as well as Topps, were the major hockey card makers from the 1950s through the late 1980s. Parkhurst was another major card maker, with great sets from 1951-1964.

In the 1970s, the top cards included Wayne Gretzky, Guy Lafleur, Ken Dryden and Mike Bossy. The 1980s saw many big stars emerge such as Mario Lemieux, Brett Hull, Ray Bourque, Patrick Roy, Mark Messier, Grant Fuhr and Joe Sakic. In the 1990s, again there was an explosion of card makers and card sets, with big stars such as Eric Lindros, Jaromir Jagr, Pavel Bure and Teemu Selanne taking center stage.

General Guidelines: Top names from the 1950s and 1960s include Maurice Richard, Terry Sawchuk, Gordie Howe, Jacques Plante, Bobby Hull, Bobby Orr, Stan Mikita and Phil Esposito. The 1951-52 Parkhurst Howe rookie card sells for about $3,000 and the 1966-67 Topps Bobby Orr rookie is worth more than $1,500.

TOM GRIFFITH
OUTFIELD, BROOKLYN NATIONALS

American Carmel Co., Tom Griffith, outfield, Brooklyn Nationals.

CARD CONDITION

The following are general guidelines for card grading:

Mint: Perfect in all respects, including centering and gloss. Most cards before 1980 are not in Mint condition. Cards from 1980 to the present must be (in almost all cases) in at least Near Mint condition to be considered collectible.

Near Mint: May be slightly off-center. Three of its four corners must be sharp. One corner may have very slight wear. Priced at 85 percent of Mint condition.

Excellent: May have slight wear on its corners and a minor wax or gum stain. Front may show some wear. No creases. Priced at 50 percent of Mint condition.

Very Good: Corners may be rounded, may have minor creases. Many older cards fit into this condition category. Priced at 40 percent of Mint condition.

Good: A card that was heavily played with, but is still a complete card with no intentional damage, such as tape marks, pinholes or writing. Priced at 25 percent of Mint condition.

Fair: A card that has major damage, such as tape marks, pinholes or writing. Priced at 10 percent of Mint condition.

VALUE LINE

Baseball Cards

1948 Bowman Yogi Berra	$475
1948 Bowman Stan Musial	$650
1950 Bowman Jackie Robinson	$600
1950 Bowman Ted Williams	$700
1951 Bowman Mickey Mantle	$5,500
1952 Bowman Duke Snider	$150
1952 Topps Willie Mays	$2,400
1952 Topps Mickey Mantle	$17,500
1953 Topps Mickey Mantle	$2,400
1954 Topps Henry Aaron	$1,300
1955 Topps, Roberto Clemente	$1,800
1956 Topps Mickey Mantle	$1,100
1957 Topps Frank Robinson	$175
1957 Topps Brooks Robinson	$175
1958 Topps Roger Maris	$500
1959 Topps Stan Musial	$120
1960 Topps Sandy Koufax	$100
1963 Topps Pete Rose	$800
1964 Topps Roberto Clemente	$200
1965 Topps Steve Carlton	$275
1965 Topps Joe Morgan	$65
1967 Topps Tom Seaver	$750
1968 Topps Nolan Ryan	$800
1969 Topps Reggie Jackson	$350
1970 Topps Nolan Ryan	$400
1972 Topps Carlton Fisk	$70
1973 Topps Mike Schmidt	$350
1974 Topps Dave Winfield	$150
1975 Topps Robin Yount	$120
1975 Topps George Brett	$120
1978 Topps Eddie Murray	$100
1978 Topps Paul Molitor	$100
1979 Topps Ozzie Smith	$80
1980 Topps Rickey Henderson	$60
1982 Donruss Cal Ripken	$50
1982 Fleer Cal Ripken	$50
1982 Topps Cal Ripken	$80
1982 Topps Traded Cal Ripken	$275

Basketball Cards

1948 Bowman George Mikan	$4,500
1957-58 Topps Bob Cousy	$500
1957-58 Topps Bill Russell	$2,000
1961-62 Fleer Wilt Chamberlain	$1,300
1961-62 Fleer Oscar Robertson	$500
1961-62 Fleer Bill Russell	$500
1961-62 Fleer Jerry West	$700
1969-70 Topps Lew Alcindor	$550
1969-70 Topps Bill Bradley	$150
1969-70 Topps John Havilcek	$175
1969-70 Topps Jerry West	$100
1970-71 Topps Pete Maravich	$225
1971-72 Topps Rick Barry	$60
1972-73 Topps Julius Erving	$275
1973-74 Topps Kareem Abdul-Jabbar	$25
1974-75 Topps Bill Walton	$65
1974-75 Topps George Gervin	$60
1974-75 Topps Wilt Chamberlain	$30
1975-76 Topps Moses Malone	$50
1976-77 Topps Julius Erving	$55
1980-81 Topps Larry Bird/MagicJohnson	$450
1986-87 Fleer Michael Jordan	$1,000
1986-87 Fleer Patrick Ewing	$60
1986-87 Fleer Charles Barkley	$125
1986-87 Fleer Karl Malone	$60
1986-87 Fleer Hakeem Olajuwon	$140
1986-87 Fleer Isiah Thomas	$30
1986-87 Fleer Joe Dumars	$60
1987-88 Fleer Michael Jordan	$175
1987-88 Fleer Larry Bird	$30
1988-89 Fleer Michael Jordan	$50
1988-89 Fleer Scottie Pippen	$50
1988-89 Fleer Dennis Rodman	$45
1988-89 Fleer John Stockton	$30

Football Cards

1948 Bowman Sammy Baugh	$350
1950 Bowman Otto Graham	$450
1951 Bowman Tom Landry	$500
1952 Bowman-Large Frank Gifford	$475
1954 Bowman George Blanda	$175
1955 Topps All-American Knute Rockne	$325
1955 Topps All-American Jim Thorpe	$350
1955 Topps All-American Four Horsemen	$450
1955 Topps All-American Don Hutson	$200
1957 Topps Bart Starr	$400

1957 Topps Johnny Unitas $450
1957 Topps Paul Hornung $400
1958 Topps Jim Brown $400
1958 Topps Sonny Jurgensen $100
1959 Topps Alex Karras $40
1960 Fleer Jack Kemp $400
1960 Topps Johnny Unitas $80
1961 Fleer Jack Kemp $250
1961 Fleer Don Meredith $140
1961 Topps Jack Kemp $150
1962 Fleer George Blanda $55
1962 Topps Mike Ditka $200
1962 Topps Fran Tarkenton $200
1963 Fleer Len Dawson $250
1963 Fleer Lance Alworth $250
1963 Topps Bob Lilly $125
1965 Philadelphia Paul Warfield $75
1965 Topps Joe Namath $1,600
1966 Philadelphia Dick Butkus $185
1966 Philadelphia Gale Sayers $200
1966 Topps Joe Namath $350
1968 Topps Bob Griese $85

1969 Topps Brian Piccolo $75
1969 Topps Larry Csonka $80
1970 Topps Alan Page $40
1970 Topps O.J. Simpson $100
1971 Topps Terry Bradshaw $175
1972 Topps Roger Staubach $150
1973 Topps Franco Harris $50
1973 Topps Ken Stabler $60
1975 Topps Lynn Swann $45
1975 Topps Dan Fouts $50
1976 Topps Walter Payton $175
1977 Topps Steve Largent $60
1978 Topps Tony Dorsett $35
1979 Topps Earl Campbell $30
1981 Topps Joe Montana $175
1982 Topps Lawrence Taylor $30
1983 Topps Marcus Allen $25
1984 Topps John Elway $45
1984 Topps Dan Marino $125
1984 Topps John Elway $45
1984 Topps USFL Jim Kelly $100
1984 Topps USFL Steve Young $250
1984 Topps USFL Reggie White $100
1985 Topps Warren Moon $25
1986 Topps Jerry Rice $100
1989 Score Barry Sanders $60

Hockey Cards
1951-52 Parkhurst Maurice Richard $1,500
1951-52 Parkhurst Terry Sawchuk $1,000
1951-52 Parkhurst Gordie Howe $3,000
1955-56 Parkhurst Jacques Plante $700
1957-58 Parkhurst Henri Richard $350
1958-59 Topps Bobby Hull $3,000
1965-66 Topps Phil Esposito $400
1966-67 Topps Bobby Orr $1,700
1967-68 Topps Bobby Orr $800
1970-71 OPC Bobby Clarke $135
1971-72 OPC Marcel Dionne $125
1971-72 Topps Ken Dryden $100
1976-77 OPC Bryan Trottier $50
1978-79 OPC Mike Bossy $50
1979-80 OPC Wayne Gretzky $750
1979-80 Topps Wayne Gretzky $400
1980-81 OPC Mark Messier $175
1981-82 OPC Paul Coffey $85
1982-83 OPC Grant Fuhr $25
1985-86 OPC Mario Lemieux $375
1985-86 Topps Mario Lemieux $175
1986-87 OPC Patrick Roy $175
1986-87 Topps Patrick Roy $100
1988-89 OPC Brett Hull $55

1951 Bowman, Leo Durocher, #233.

TV Toys & Collectibles

When television began in the late 1940s, marketers figured out they could sell toys and other items based on TV characters. This was nothing new. The 1930s and 1940s radio characters had many premiums produced for the shows like *Little Orphan Annie* and *The Shadow*. Television, however, blew radio out of the water as the favored choice of entertainment. Television also produced many more toys and collectibles. Plus, television today is keeping many of these classic shows from gathering dust, with reruns on any number of stations.

Television toys and collectibles is one of the most fascinating and fastest growing areas in the marketplace. With about 4,000 different TV shows on the air since the age of television began, there are literally tens of thousands of items to collect. The price ranges for these items can be less than $10 (especially for items from newer shows) to hundreds of dollars for items from the 1950s, 1960s and 1970s.

Collectors often collect by show, by genre (Western, comedy, etc.) or by type of collectible, like board games or dolls.

Look for items in the best condition possible. On newer items—post-1970—look for collectibles in Near Mint condition or better. Items that are still in their original packaging are highly desirable. In fact, on post-1980 items, the market is very much geared toward items that are Mint in Box.

General Guidelines: Each era had its favorite shows and characters. These are often the most collectible today. Items to look for from the 1950s and earlier are those related to the cowboys—Gene Autry, Hopalong Cassidy, Roy Rogers and The Lone Ranger. Items from later Westerns, such as *Bonanza* and *Maverick*, are also popular.

The 1960s was the decade that might have seen the finest television shows ever made, as far as many are concerned. Among those with the most collectible toys are *Batman*, *Lost in Space*, *The Green Hornet*, *Man from U.N.C.L.E.*, *Hogan's Heroes*, *The Addams Family*, *The Munsters*, *The Beverly Hillbillies*, *Gilligan's Island*, *The Flintstones*, *I Spy* and *The Monkees*. Cool shows. Cool toys. These are classic shows that have a cult following, which contributes greatly to how in-demand the toys will be.

While the 1970s was a time of excessive bad taste and even worse television, there were actually some shows that spawned pretty neat toys, including *Charlie's Angels*, *The Six Million Dollar Man*, *The Bionic Woman*, *Battlestar Galactica*, *The Brady Bunch*, *The Partridge Family*, *CHiPs*, *M*A*S*H*, *Buck Rogers*, *Happy Days* and *Welcome Back Kotter*.

Items from 1980s and 1990s shows have proven less collectible, but *The X-Files*, *The Simpsons* and *Beverly Hills 90210* are a few current shows with toys and other memorabilia that may prove collectible in the future.

Monkeemobile, 1960s, Corgi, $225 Excellent.

Colorforms, Lazer Blazers 3-D Holographic Stickers,
    MIP, 1983 .... $7
Comic Book, #1-3, Marvel, 1984, NM, each $5
Doll, Mr. T, 12", Galoob, 1983 .... $75
Grenade Toss $40
Halloween bag, "Loot Bag," plastic, 6" x 10", Unique
    Industries, Mr. T $2
Kite, Mr. T, Hi-Flyer, MIP $15
Lunch box and thermos, steel, 1985 .... $35
Off-Road Attack Cycle $40
Party hats, four cones, nice graphics, 1983, MIP $7
Paperback book, #1 Defense Against Terror, 1983 .... $6
Puzzle, Mr. T, 18" x 24", MIP $9
Storybook coloring book, 8" x 8" $5
Storybook comic, large, 1983 .... $5

Addams Family
Bank, Thing, 1964 .... $60
Figure, Lurch, Remco, 1960s, NM $150
Figure, Morticia, Remco, 1960s, NM $350
Figure, Lurch, Uncle Fester, 1960s, NM $350
Kit, Haunted House, 1964, Aurora, MIB $775
Lunch box and Thermos, steel, 1974 .... $100
Paperback book, Homebodies, 1st edition, Pocket Books,
    1964, NM $20
Magazine, Monster World #9, 1966, NM $30

ALF
Board game, The ALF Board Game, Coleco Games,
    1987 .... $9
Booklet, *The Great ALFonso*, 1987 .... $4
Coloring book, *ALF Helps Out*, Alien Prod., unused,
    1988 .... $9
Comic book, Vol. 1, #8, Star Comic, 1988, EX $4
Comic book, Vol. 1, #21, Star Comic, 1988, NM $5
Doll, plush, 18", Alien Prod., 1986, EX $15
Doll, plush, clip-on, 4" $5
Doll, plush, with suction cups, 7", Applause, 1989 .... $8
Folder, heavy cardboard, 9-1/2" x 12-1/2", ALF in suit
    and tie, Alien Prod., 1987 .... $6
Halloween costume, 1986, MIB $15

VALUE LINE

A-Team
Board Game, Parker Bros., 1984, EX $13
Card game, The Adventures With B.A., Parker Bros., 1983,
    orig box $12

Hand puppets, plush, 12", Burger King premium, Alien Prod., 1988, each $6

Lunch box, plastic $20

Paperback book, *Day at the Fair*, 1987, EX $4

Paperback book, *Mission to Mars*, 1987, EX $4

PVC figures, 3", Wendy's premiums, 1990, each $3

Refrigerator magnet, 2-1/4" x 2", Burger King premium, 1988 .... $4

All in the Family

Game, Archie Bunker's Card Game, 1971, NM $15

Goblet, Archie Bunker For President, 6" h x 4" d, 1972, NM $15

Magazine, *People*, 3/27/78, NM $5

Paperback book, *Edith Bunker's Cookbook*, 1971, EX $5

Pinback button, Archie Bunker For President Pinback, 1970s, EX $12

Record, 1971, EX $11

Batman

Bat Chute with 4" bat figure, Ideal, 1966, MIP $125

Card game, 6" x 10", 1965, Ideal, MIB $55

Colorforms, 1966, EX $75

Costume, Burt Ward's yellow satin cape $3,500

Escape Gun, NM on card, 1966 .... $48

Figure, Mego, Catwoman $325

Fork and spoon, Imperial, 1966, EX, for pair $50

Mighty Mouse figure, 1970s, Dakin, $45 Excellent.

Hand puppet, 1965, Ideal, MIB $85

Lunch box and Thermos, steel, 1966 .... $225

Mug, milk glass, 1966 .... $30

Photos, b&w 8" x 10" glossies, 1966, each $7

Pin, 3", Batman & Robin Society Charter Member, MT .. $40

Pix-A-Go-Go, Embree Toys, 1966, EX $100

Place mat, vinyl, 1966m EX $60

Record, Robin figural 45 rpm, cardboard sleeve, 1966, EX $25

Record, TV theme and other songs, Panda, 1966 .... $25

Rubber stamp set, 1960s, Kellogg's, NM $200

Secret Print Putty, print book and magic paper, 1966, MT $95

Slippers, brown and tan, child's, 1966, EX $65

Transistor radio, works, with box, 1973, overall EX $65

View-Master pack, 1966 .... $30

Wallet, vinyl, 1966 .... $65

Battlestar Galactica

Activity book, 1978, EX $5

Board game, Parker Brothers, 1979, MT $15

Book, hardcover, Berkley, 1978 1st edition $8

Colonial Stellar Probe (missile firing), MIB $65

Colonial Viper, MIB $90

Comic book, Battlestar Galactica, Vol. 1, No. 4, Maximum Press, 1994 .... $4

Comic book, Battlestar Galactica, No. 5, Marvel, 1979 ..... $6

Die-cast vehicles, Larami, 1978, each $6

Glasses, premiums, 1979, each $15

Figure, Adama, MIP $40

Figure, Boary, Mattel, 1979, MIP $85

Figure, Imperious Leader, MIP $15

Figure, Ovion, MIP $40

Figure, Starbuck, MIP $40

Galactica Cylon Raider/Colonial Viper, MIB $90

Hand-held electric game, MT $70

Lunch box and Thermos, steel, 1978 .... $60

Paperback book, 1978, NM $5

Puzzle, MIB $10

Remote Controlled Cylon Raider, works, MT $90

Space Glider $10

Space Glow Putty $10

Trading card set, 132 cards, Topps, 1978 .... $28

Wallet $5

Beverly Hillbillies

Board game, Standard Toykraft, 1963, NM $50

Book, *The Saga of Wildcat Creek*, Whitman TV, 1963, NM $10

Card game, Milton Bradley, 1963, EX $15

Colorforms, no booklet, 1963, NM $75

Coloring book, kangaroo on cover, Whitman, 1964, EX .. $25

Fan card, b&w, Donna Douglas, facsimile signature, 1960s, NM $10

Lunch box, steel, EX $160

Magazine, *Saturday Evening Post*, 2/2/63, NM $15

Magazine, *TV Guide*, 7/11/70, VG $8

Paper doll booklet, Elly May, uncut, Whitman, 1963, NM $65

Paper doll booklet, cast, Whitman, 1964, EX $50

Record, *The Beverly Hillbillies*, Harmony, 1968, sealed .. $50
Trading card wrapper, O-Pee-Chee, 1963, NM $125
View-Master, Elly May Starts to School, 1963, NM $50

Beverly Hills 90210
Book covers, three in pack, 1991, MT $15
Booklets, 3" x 5" paperbacks, each $3
Bookmarks, Book Bites, photo-shaped, set of four, 1991 $15
Cereal box, Honey Nut Cheerios, 20 oz., 1991, NM $10
Cologne spray $12
Decoration kit, nine cardboard character shapes to
    punch out, MT $10
Doll, Brenda, Mattel, 1991, 12", MIB $75
Doll, Dylan, Mattel, 1991, 12", MIB $75
Dream plates, 6" x 12" plastic license plates, photo of
    Dylan, David or Brandon, MIP, each $15
Frisbee, Wham-O, 1991 MIP $15
Game, Entangle, Cardinal, MT $25
Gift-wrapping paper, Cleo, 1991, MT on roll $6
Gift Bag, cast photos, Cleo, 1991 .... $10
Lipstick and nail polish set $12
Paperback books, 1990s, each $5
Pencils, set of three, Fasco, 1991, MIP $10
Pillow, Dylan, heart-shaped, Nikry, 1991, NM $20
Poster, Dylan, O.S.P., 1991, MT $10
Poster set, Honey Nut Cheerios mail-away set of four,
    10" x 13", MT $25

Bionic Woman
Bank, plastic, 1976, EX $45
Beauty Salon, MIB $55
Board game, 1976, EX $28
Comic Book, Charlton, Vol. 1, #1, October 1977, light
    cover wear $10
Doll, Bionic Woman Fembot doll, MIB $200
Lunch box and Thermos, steel, 1977 .... $60
Outfit, Peach Dream Outfit, MIP $20

Blossom
Doll, Blossom, Tyco, 1993, MIB $25
Doll, Joey, 1993, MIB $25
Doll, Six, 1993, MIB $25
Paper doll booklet, 1994, MT $15
Puzzle, 1993, NM $5
View-Master, 1993, MIP $5

Bonanza
Book, Big Little Book, The Bubble Gum Kid, Whitman,
    1967, NM $15
Book, Whitman TV, Killer Lion, 1966, NM $15
Book, hardcover, Heroes of the Wild West, Whitman,
    1970, NM $10
Coloring book, Artcraft, EX $10
Comic book Gold Key #24, 1967, EX $10
Fan card, Lorne Green, sepia, facsimile auto, 1960s,
    NM $10
Figure, Ben with palomino, American Character, 1966,
    NM $150
Figure, Hoss with stallion, American Character, 1966,
    NM $200
Figure, Little Joe with Pinto, American Character, 1966,
    NM $200

Lunch box and Thermos, steel, 1968 .... $250
Paperback book, #1, *Winter Grass*, 1968, EX $10
Paperback book, #2, *Ponderosa Kill*, 1968, VG $7
Record, *Ponderosa Party Time*, 1968, EX $15

Buck Rogers
Comic book, Gold Key #3, September 1979, light cover
    wear $8
Comic book, Whitman #15, 1982 .... $6
Figure, Ardella, 1979, MIP $30
Figure, Killer Kane, 1979, MT $12
Figure, Tigerman, 1979, MIP $30
Figure, Wilma Dearing, MIP $65
Lunch box and Thermos, steel, 1979 .... $60
Model kit, Marauder $50
Model kit, Starfighter $60
Prop, original, rifle used in series $600
Trading card set, 88 cards, no stickers, Topps, 1979 .... $15

Captain Kangaroo
Presto Slate on board, 1960s, EX $28
Record, 45 rpm, 1957 .... $22
Record, 45 rpm, 1962 .... $18

Charlie's Angels
Doll, Cheryl Ladd, Mattel, 12", 1978, MIP $45
Doll, Farrah Fawcett-Majors, in swimsuit, Remco, 12",
    1977, MIB $50
Doll, Kate Jackson, Mattel, 12", 1978, MIP $45
Doll, Kelly, Hasbro, 9", MIP $45
Doll, Kris, Hasbro, 9", MIP $45
Doll, Sabrina, Hasbro, 9", MIP $45
Fashion Tote, 10" h, pink cylinder with "Charlie's
    Angels" printed on background, holds Hasbro dolls
    and accessories, 1978, NM $20
Lunch box and Thermos, steel, 1978 .... $50
Magazine, *TV Guide* with Smith, Ladd and Jackson,
    2/18/78, NM $25
Magazine, *TV Guide* with Smith, Ladd and Hack,
    12/29/79, EX $10
Model kit, Mobile Unit Van $70
Story book, *A Golden All-Star Book*, NM $20

CHiPs
Coloring book, Playmore Pub, 1983 MT $10
Die-cast Patrol Van, 1980, MIP $25
Figure, Jimmy Squeaks, 3-3/4", MIP $15
Figure, Jon, 3-3/4", MIP $15
Figure, Jon, 8", Mego, MIP $40
Figure, Ponch, 3-3/4", MIP $15
Figure, Ponch, 8", Mego, MIP $40
Figure, Sarge, 3-3/4", MIP $15
Figure, Wheels Willy, 3-3/4", MIP $15
Magazine, *TV Guide*, 1/30/82, EX $5
Model kit, Helicopter, MIB $25
Model kit, Jon's 4x4 Chevy, MIB $25
Motorcycle for 8" figures, MIB $45
Sunglasses $12
Wallet, MT on EX card $20

Donny & Marie
Activity book, Donny, 1973, VG $5
Coloring book, 1973, EX $20

Lunch box and Thermos, vinyl, 1977 .... $135
Marie's Travel Case, Osbro, 1977, NM $35
Paperback book, *Goin' Coconuts*, 1978, NM $10
Paper doll booklet, Donny & Marie, uncut, 1977, NM..... $15
Record, *Disco Train*, 1976 EX $5

Dr. Kildare
Bobbing head doll, 1960s $150
Book/Whitman TV, *Assigned to Trouble*, 1963, VG $8
Comic book, #5, 1964, NM $10
Paperback book, *Dr. Kildare*, 1960 VF $10

Dukes of Hazzard
Coloring book, 1981, MT $12
Finger Racers, Knickerbocker, 1981, MIP $15
I.D. set, Gordy, 1981, MIP $20
Lunch box and Thermos, Coy and Vance version, 1983,
   NM $50
Magazines, *TV Guide*, 7/12/80 or 5/1/82, NM, each $10
Model kit, General Lee, original issue, MIB $50
Plate, Melmac, 7", logo and color photo, 1981 .... $16
Puzzle, MIB $20
Record, 45 rpm, photo sleeve, MT, sealed $12
Record, *Now or Never*, John Schneider, 1981 NM $10
Talking Story Book with record, 1981, MT $10
Trading card set #3, 44 cards, Donruss, 1982, MT $25
View-Master, No. 2, 1982, on card $10

Emergency
Board game, Milton Bradley, 1973, EX $20
Fireman's helmet, plastic, 1970s, EX $60
Lunch box and Thermos, steel, 1973 .... $80
Record, *Great Adventures*, NM $28
Halloween costume, Collegeville, 1975 NM $45

Family Affair
Book, *Buffy Finds a Star*, Whitman, 1970, NM $10
Coloring book, Mrs. Beasley, uncolored, NM $20
Comic book, #10, 1972, NM $8
Lunch box and Thermos, steel, 1969 .... $90
Paperback book, *Buffy's Cookbook*, 1971, MT $15
Paper dolls, 1970, MIB $68
Paper dolls, Buffy & Mrs. Beasley, 1970, MIB $65
Paper dolls, Mrs. Beasley, 1970, uncut, EX $35
Sheet music, *River Song*, 1973, EX $5

Flintstones
Book, Giant Durabook, *Wilma & Betty and The
   Snallygaster Hunt* 1973, NM $10
Book, Little Golden Book, *Pebbles Flintstone*, 1963, NM . $8
Book, Little Golden Book, *The Flintstones*, 1961, NM.... $10
Book, Whitman Tell-A-Tale, *Pebbles Flintstone's ABCs*,
   1976, EX $5
Book, Whitman Tell-A-Tale, *The Rubbles and Bamm-
   Bamm*, 1965, VG $5
Comic book, Carlton, Vol. 1, #3, EX $8
Comic book, Gold Key, 1970, #56, G $5
Comic book, The Great Gazoo, #1, NM $5
Comic book, Marvel, 1978, #4, EX $7
Doll, Pebbles, 15", 1963, Ideal, EX $100
Figure, Fred, Bamm-Bamm, 1970, 7", NM $60
Figure, Barney, Dakin, 1970, 7-1/4", NM $50
Figure, Dino, Dakin, 1970, 7-3/4", NM $70

Figure, Fred, Dakin, 1970, 8-1/4", NM $50
Figure, Pebbles, Dakin, 1970, 8", NM $50
Flip book, *It's About Time*, 1977, NM $8
Happy Meal Toys, set of five, 1994, NM, for set $20
Horn, 1960s $65
Jell-O mold, 1988 .... $7
Lunch box and Thermos, steel, 1973 .... $175
Paddy Wagon motorized kit, 1961, Remco, MIB $290
Paper dolls, Pebbles and Bamm-Bamm, Whitman, 1971,
   MT $25
Push puppet, Dino, 1960s, NM $70
Push puppet, Hoppity, 1960s, NM $70
Tin wind-up, Barney, 3-1/2" l, Marx, 1960s, EX $175
Tin wind-up, Fred riding Dino, 18" l, Marx, 1962, NM . $600

Flying Nun
Board game, 1968, VG $65
Doll, 4", Hasbro, 1960s, MIP $75
Doll, 11", Hasbro, 1967, MIP $150
Figure, flies, MT on VG display box, Ray Plastic Co.,
   1970 .... $125
Lunch box and Thermos, steel, 1968 .... $225

Gomer Pyle USMC
Board game, NM $55
Comic books, #1-3, 1966, VG, each $8
Lunch box and Thermos, steel, 1966 .... $235
Paperback book, *Gomer Pyle U.S.M.C.*, 1965, VG $5
Trading cards, 1965, NM, each $1
Record, *Shazam! Gomer Pyle U.S.M.C.*, Columbia 1965,
   NM $25

Green Hornet
Book, Whitman TV, *Disappearing Doctor*, 1966, NM $35
Engraved stainless steel spoon and fork set, MT $50
Flicker disk, 8", 1966 .... $100
Lunch box and Thermos, steel, 1967 .... $550
Playing cards, deck $45

Happy Days
Colorforms, 1976, VG $5
Coloring Book, *Fonzie, A Cool Coloring Book*, 1976,
   NM $15
Lunch box and Thermos, steel, 1977 .... $60
Puzzle, The Fonz, HG Toys, 1976, NM $20
Paperback books, #1-6, NM, each $5
Record, 45 rpm, *Happy Days/Cruisin' with the Fonz*,
   1976, NM $5

Hardy Boys
Activity book, *Super Sleuth Word Finds*, 1977, EX $5
Booklet, *The Secret of Shaun: Parts I and II*, NM, set $20
Iron on, Shaun Cassidy, MT $10
Lunch box and Thermos, steel, 1977 .... $70
Pants, Shaun Cassidy's image printed onto fabric of right
   leg, Sears, 1977, EX $25
Record case for 45 rpms, 1978, VG $15
Record player, repaired, 1977, VG $20
Record, *The Hardy Boys*, 1978, VG $10
Sticker, 8" x 10", Shaun, 1977, MT $5

Howdy Doody
Belt buckle, figural head, metal, 1960s, VG $30
Game, Electric Doodler, 1950s, EX $135

Lunch box, steel, 1954 .... $450
Kung Fu
Book, paperback, #1, *The Way of the Tiger*, 1974, VG $5
Lunch box and Thermos, steel, 1974 .... $100
Target set, 1975, MIP $40
Trading card box, empty, Topps, 1973, NM $65
Trading card set, 60 cards, Topps, 1973, NM $100
Laugh-In
Brunch bag, vinyl, 1968, NM $60
Coloring book, unused, 1960s, VG $12
Lunch box and Thermos, steel, 1969, helmet on back $125
Lunch box and Thermos, steel, 1969, trike on back $175
Paperback book, #1, 1960s, EX $12
Paper doll booklet, Saalfield, 1969, MT $40
Record, 1960s, EX $20
View-Master set with envelope, no booklet, 1968, VG $20
Laverne & Shirley
Coloring book, Playmore, 1983, NM $8
Doll, Mego, Laverne, MIB $75
Doll, Mego, Lenny, MIB $125
Doll, Mego, Shirley, MIB $75
Doll, Mego, Squiggy, MIB $125
Fan card, cast, facsimile signatures, Paramount $10
Paperback book, #1, 1976, NM $10
Paperback book, #3, 1976, NM $15
Lost in Space
Board game, Milton Bradley, 1965, EX-NM $120
Coffee mug, Lost in Space logo, newer $12
Lunch box and Thermos, steel, 1967 .... $600
Original costume, Billy Mumy's orange velour top
    with brown velour detailing $2,000
Original costume, 2nd season, Billy Mumy's purple
    velour tunic, yellow dickie, lavender wool Swiss ski
    pants $7,500
Original costume, Billy Mumy's tiny gray futuristic
    tunic $7,500
Robot, wind-up, Masudaya, 1984, 4-1/2" h, MIB $25
Robot, Masudaya, 1984, 16" h, MIB $160
View-Master reel set, 1967 .... $155
M*A*S*H
Dog tags, stainless steel $15
Fan photo, cast, NM $10
Figure, B.J., 3-3/4", MIP $20
Figure, Col. Potter, 3-3/4", MIP $20
Figure, Father Mulcahy, 3-3/4", MIP $20
Figure, Hawkeye, 3-3/4", MIP $20
Figure, Hot Lips, 3-3/4", MIP $20
Figure, Winchester, 3-3/4", MIP $20
Model kit, helicopter $15
Model kit, The Swamp $15
Paperback books, various, 1970s, each $3
Trading card set, 66 cards, Donruss, 1982 .... $55
Vodka bottle, MIB $30
Man from U.N.C.L.E.
Car, Corgi, EX $80
Car, Husky, blue, VG $30
Figure, Napoleon Solo, 12", MIB $225
Lighter/gun, opens to reveal fake radio, 1965 .... $195

Archies figures, 1975, Marx, $15 each Mint no Package.

Lunch box and Thermos, steel, 1966 .... $225
Magazine, *TV Guide*, March 19, 1966, G+ $20
Model, Illya Kuryakin, Aurora, MIB $200
Paperback books, 1960s, EX, each .... $8-$12
Secret Print Putty, 1965, MT on VG card $95
Walkie talkie, 3-1/2" x 2-1/2", plastic, Gabriel Toys,
    1966, EX $125
Monkees
Lunch box and Thermos, vinyl, 1967 .... $500
Record, *Barrel Full of Monkees*, 1971, NM $75
Record, *Greatest Hits*, 1976, NM $10
Trading cards, 44 cards in first series set, 1966, NM $75
Mork & Mindy
Card game, 1978 .... $20
Lunch box and Thermos, steel, 1979 .... $35
Magazine, *Dynamite*, #56, without record, 1979, MT $5
Paperback book, 1979, NM $5
Puffy stickers, card of six, 1979, MT $3
Sleeping Bag, NM $20
T-shirt, Mork, MT in sealed back, 1978 .... $14
The Munsters
Book, *The Great Camera Caper*, 1965, NM $15
Figure, Lily, Remco, 1964, EX $225
Figures, plastic, 3", newer, any character, MT, each $7
Lunch box and Thermos, steel, 1965 .... $400
Trading card display box, empty, Leaf, 1964, EX $125
The Partridge Family
Board game, 1970s, complete, VG $75
Coloring Book, Artcraft, 1970, NM $35
Coloring Book, Saalfield, 1970, VG $25
Lunch box and Thermos, steel, 1971 .... $75
Magazine, *Tiger Beat*, 10/71, David on cover, NM $40
Magazine, *Tiger Beat*, 3/72, cast on cover, NM $40
Paperback books, 1971-1973, NM, each .... $5-$15
Posters, Topps, 1971, MT, each $20
Records, 45 rpm, NM, each .... $10-$20
Trading card pack, unopened, O-Pee-Chee, 1971 .... $25
Pee-Wee Herman
Colorforms, complete $32

Coloring book, Scholastic, 1979, NM $10
Doll, talking with pull string, MIB $125
Doll, talking with pull string, Mint loose $75
Figure, Pee Wee's pet Pterri, 13", MIP $125
Figure, Chairry, MIP $42
Figure, Cowboy Curtis, MIP $45
Figure, 6", King of Cartoons, MIP $32
Figure, 6", Pee Wee, MIP $32
Figure, 6", Pee Wee with scooter, MIP $65
Figure, Randy and Globey, MIP $42
Lunch box and Thermos, plastic, 1987 .... $25
Trading card box, empty, 1989 .... $5
Trading card set, 1989 .... $10
View-Master reels $10

Petticoat Junction
Comic book, #1, Dell, 1964, VG $10
Paper doll booklet, 1964, EX $45

Ren & Stimpy
Card Game, 1992, MIP $15
Cereal box, contains ad for R&S shorts, 1993, NM $10
Cereal premium, target toss, 1994, MT $20

S.W.A.T.
Cap gun, .45, 1975, MT on VG card $25
Model, police helicopter, 1977, NM $15
Paperback book, #1, Crossfire, 1975 .... $5
Puzzle, 1975, MT $15
Rifle, 1975, with card attached, NM $20

Scooby Doo
Book, *Scooby Doo and the Haunted Doghouse*, 1975,
    VG $10
Burger King premiums, 1996, set of four $10
Coloring Book, 1982, VG $10
Comic book, Charlton, #5 .... $5
Comic book, Gold Key, #21 .... $5
Little Golden Book, *Scooby Doo and the Pirate Treasure*,
    1974, NM $15
Lunch box and Thermos, steel, 1973 .... $80
Paperback book, *Scooby Doo and the Stolen Treasure*,
    1982, MT $10
Radio, Scooby Doo, 1970s, MT $50
View-Master, That's Snow Ghost, 1972, MT $12

Six Million Dollar Man
Bionic Action Club Kit, photo and certificate, 1973,
    NM $15
Bionic Transport and Repair Station $55
Board game, complete, 1975, EX $20
Coloring book, 1975, NM $15
Figure, Bionic Bigfoot, Kenner, MIP $120
Figure, Maskatron, Kenner, MIP $70
Figure, Steve Austin, Kenner, MIP $70
Lunch box and Thermos, steel, 1974 .... $65
Mission Control Center, MIB $100
OSI Headquarters, MIB $100
Paperback book, *Secret of Bigfoot Pass,* 1976, EX $5
Trading card pack, Holland, 1975, MT $10

Soupy Sales
Pin, Soupy Sales Society charter member, 3", 1960s,
    MT $22

Sheet music, *The Mouse*, 1965, EX $10
Wonder Book, 8-1/2" x 11", picture on front, 1965, VG .. $20
"V"
Figure, Mark Singer character, Spain, 1984, MIP $25
Paperback book, autographed by author George W.
    Proctor, 1985, NM $15
Walkie talkies, Nasta/Power-tronic, 1984, MIB $150
Sound pistol and holster, Arco, 1984, MIP $65
Trading cards box, unopened, 36 packs $40

Welcome Back Kotter
Classroom, Mego, MIB $170
Doll, John Travolta, Mego $75
Folders, set of five, 1976, MT $25
Lunch box and Thermos, steel, 1977 .... $50
Paperback book, #3, *The Super Sweathogs*, 1976, NM $5
Paper doll box, Toy Factory, 1976, MIP, each $25
Puzzle, Kotter, frame tray, 1977, MT $15
Puzzle, cast, frame tray, 1977, MT $15
View-Master, talking, GAF, 1976, NM $20

Miscellaneous Shows
Adam-12, Comic books, Whitman, 1974, NM, each $15
Avengers, paperback books, #1-8, Berkley, EX, each $8
Bewitched, board game, complete, 1965, EX $185
Dark Shadows, record, 1969, EX $25
Davy Crockett, child's vest, 1950s, EX $45
Dragnet, Jack Webb official badge, Knickerbocker, 1955,
    MIB $135
Hogan's Heroes, Signal sender/compass set, 1977,
    Harmony, MIP $35
H.R. Pufnstuf, comic book, #8, Whitman, 1972, NM $30
I Dream Of Jeannie, Halloween costume, Ben Cooper,
    1974, NM in EX box $35
Kojak, toy gun on keychain, MIP $20
Lassie, plush doll, 13" long, with original tags, rubber
    face, 1950s, EX $60
Leave It To Beaver, Little Golden Book, Whitman, 1959,
    EX $20
Magnum, P.I., trading card set, 1983, NM $20
Mod Squad, comic book, #3, 1969, VG $18
My Favorite Martian, Martian Magic Tricks, boxed set,
    1964, EX $200
Patty Duke, board game, 1964, EX $85
Punky Brewster, coloring book, Golden, 1986, NM $5
Space: 1999, paperback, #8, 1976, NM $5
Starsky & Hutch, book, *The Starsky & Hutch Story*, 1977,
    NM $20
T.J. Hooker, wallet, cuffs and badge, 1982, MIP $10
That Girl, paperback book, 1971, EX $8
Twin Peaks, paperback book, *The Secret Diary of Laura
    Palmer*, 1990, EX $8
Untouchables, paperback book, 1964, EX $5
Vega$, binoculars, 1978, MIP $20
The Waltons, hardcover book, #1, Whitman, 1975, NM .. $10
Zorro, dominoes with Zorro on horse, colorful 6" x 9"
    box, Halsam Products, 1950s, EX $65

VALENTINES

No one knows exactly when the first observance of St. Valentine's Day was held, but Geoffrey Chaucer noted it in 1375. England's Henry VIII, one of history's most-married monarchs, declared Valentine's Day a holiday in 1537.

Early cards celebrating St. Valentine's Day were handmade, often containing both handwritten verses and hand-drawn pictures. Many cards also were hand colored and contained cutwork.

Commercially-printed verses and artwork were available as early as 1820. Mass production of machine-made cards featuring chromolithography began after 1840.

By 1850, layers of lace, ribbons and sentiments were applied to the messages by a cottage-industry contingent of women who sold their wares to local merchants for display in their shops. In 1847, Esther Howland of Worcester, Mass., established a company to make hand-decorated valentines. They had a small "H" stamped in red in the top left corner. Howland's company eventually became the New England Valentine Company.

Lace paper was invented in 1834, and until 1860 many lacy cards were made.

Embossed paper was used in England after 1800. Embossed lithographs and woodcuts developed between 1825-1840, with early examples being hand colored.

Die-cut cards and novelty items were plentiful until the start of World War I. Elaborate fold-out or "layered" valentines, which can range in price today from $40 to $50 for prime examples, evolved into self-mail postal card versions by 1920. These postcard examples range in price from $2 to $20.

Most of the collectible valentines found today were made between 1900 and 1914, are freestanding and consist of layers of die cuts. These include pull-downs, pullouts, pop-ups and foldouts.

Pull-downs are made of cardboard die cut into fancy, lacy, colored shapes that create multi-dimensional images such as boats, ships, cars, planes or gardens. Early examples pulled down from the middle; later pieces, which are not quite as elaborate as their predecessors, come down from the front.

Honeycomb tissue was used a great deal on pullouts, which open out and are free-standing on a honeycomb base or easel back. Some of these open to form a circular design. The most valuable ones are those with a center column and a honeycomb base and canopy top. Tissue used on the early pieces was usually white, soft pink, blue or green; during the 1920s red or soft red tissue was used.

Two other popular styles are flats and hangers. Flats are easy to find and often have fancy die-cut borders, embossing and an artist-designed center of a pretty girl. Hangers are cards with silk ribbon at the top for hanging. A string of pretty die-cuts on a ribbon is called a charm string.

Bitter comic valentines were made as early as 1840, but most are from the post-1900 period. These cards make fun of appearance, occupation or personality and also embraced social issues of the day. Comic character valentines feature comic strip characters or the likes of Snow White, Mickey Mouse, Superman or Wonder Woman.

General Guidelines: Thousands of types of valentines have been created throughout the years; many have survived in scrapbooks. Collectors tend to focus on cards made before 1930, with special emphasis on the 19th century.

Mechanical cards, those with moving parts, are especially valued by collectors. Almost any pre-1950s mechanical valentine is worth collecting if in complete, clean working condition. But in most cases, condition is more important than age.

Themes and styles popular among collectors of valentines include Art Deco, comics, transportation, mechanical, lace and honeycomb (with paper fold-outs).

Prices can ranged from as low as $1 for a World War II era die-cut example to $100 or more for Aquatint, pull-down or puzzle examples from the 1830s.

Clubs
•National Valentine Collectors' Association
 P.O. Box 1404, Santa Ana, CA 92702.

Contributor to this section: Evalene Pulati

Schanaer, German pop-up valentine, 4-1/2" x 4-1/2", die-cut.

Animated

World War II sailor boy in boat, 5" x 8" $15
World War II soldier boy standup $15
1920s, children with bear, seesaw $18
1920s, girl playing piano, 6" $13
1923, small walking doll, 4" $14

Comic

McLoughlin

4" x 6", 1900 .... $7.50
8" x 10", sheet, sgd CJH, 1914 .... $9
10" x 15", sheet, occupational $18
Unknown maker, 8" x 10", sheet, 1925 .... $5

Die-cut, small

Artist sgd

Brundage $9
Clapsaddle $10
Heart shapes, girls $5

Die-cut valentine, folding, three dimensional, 3-7/8" x 6-7/8".

Flat

Art Nouveau

3" x 5", emb girls $5
4x 4", emb, fancy $8
Heart Shape, child, 1920s $4

Folder

Fancy borders, birds, 1914 .... $9
Lacy cutwork edges, verse $10
Tied with silk ribbon, 1920 .... $8

Hanger and String

Hanger

3" x 4", cutwork edge, litho, 1910 .... $10
5"x 5", Art Nouveau, heart, silk ribbon $10
8" x 8", fancy, artist signed, 1905 .... $15

String

4 pcs, 3" x 3", artist signed $35
5 pcs, 2" x 4", sweet children $45

Honeycomb Tissue

Beistle

Early 1920s, pale red $15
1926, honeycomb base and top, red $10

Temple Love

Honeycomb base only $18
Honeycomb base and top $25
Wide-eyed children playing house $25

Paper Lace

American

1890, McLoughlin, layered folder $20
3" x 5", c1900, orig envelope $25
6" x 9", two added lace layers $25
8" x 10", c1910, two layers $35
Boxed, fancy scraps, ribbons $45
Early, hand-done, scraps, ribbons $55
c1870, 5" x 7", simple lace folder $20
c1885, simple lace folder $13

Pull-Down

1910, horse-drawn wagon $165
c1910, auto, layered, very large $125
Pre-World War I, German auto, 5" x 8" $65

1920s

Auto, cute children $75
Dollhouse, elaborate $85
Floral, children, 4 layers $55
Garden, layered, fancy $75
Three layers
Artist die cut $45
Flowers $18

1930s

Children
Fancy background $27.50
2 layers $20
Windmill background $25
Hearts $65

Pullout

Flowers in vase, opens out, 1920s $20
Garden scene, children, 7" x 10" $55
Gondola, children, honeycomb base, 1930s $35

Lighthouse, opens out, 1920s $25
Sea plane, opens out, 1920s $25
Ship, 7" x 12", honeycomb base $75
Tunnel of Love
Honeycomb base $28
Honeycomb base and top $35
Silk Fringed
Prang
3" x 5", double-sided, 1880s $15
5" x 7", fancy padded front $25
Tuck
3" x 5", double-sided, c1900 .... $13
5" x 7", artist sgd, c1890 .... $20
Unmarked, small, 1900 .... $8
Standup with Easel Back
Airport scene, children traveling $18
Automobile, windows open, small $10
Cherub with heart $5
Children
Die-cut, fancy $13
Dollhouse, 1925 .... $15
Figural $5
Sledding, flat $8
Fancy, silk inserts, 10" x 14", 1900 .... $10
Flat, flapper, 8", c1920s $8

Flower basket
Cherub $15
Pasteboard, 1918 .... $8
Layered parchment, 5" x 8", c1910 .... $15
Schoolroom scene, children at desks $18
Sports figures, 7" h $8
World War I doughboy, 6" h $10
World War II soldier and sailor boys, 8" h $10
Victorian Novelty
Animated, doll, head reverses, large $85
Die-cut
Children, fancy, boxed $25
Musical instrument, large $55
Parchment
Children, umbrella $75
Layered, ribbons $55
Silk, cherubs $75
Wood, telephone, small, boxed $75

Mechanical stand-up valentine, c. 1910, 3-5/8" x 5-7/8".

Post war valentine, late 1940s.

VEHICLE TOYS

Vehicle toys — from airplanes to buses to cars and trucks — come in every shape, size, scale and medium. Collectors never run out of choices, and that's why toy vehicle collecting never slows down.

History: Arcade, A.C. Williams and Hubley were major makers of cast-iron vehicles in the late 1800s. These sturdy vehicles have been known to sell for $10,000 or more for prime examples. From the mid-1900s, large toy trucks were made of pressed steel and cast metal by companies like Buddy L, Structo, Tonka and Smith-Miller.

Marx and numerous Japanese companies produced tin vehicles, while Auburn specialized in rubber toys.

Smaller die-cast vehicles came on the scene in the 1920s with Tootsietoys leading the way. Other highly collectible die-cast vehicles are Corgi, Dinky, Mattel's Hot Wheels and Matchbox. Today these small scale die-cast vehicles enjoy a high level of interest among collectors for their size, detail and relative affordability.

General Guidelines: Rarity is a key factor with cast-iron and steel vehicles from the 1930s and earlier — therefore Near Mint or better examples can cost almost as much as an actual automobile. Vintage cast iron is almost never found in Mint condition, so imperfections may be more acceptable than those found on a small die-cast car.

Defects in die-cast vehicles may lessen their value 25 percent or more.

Boxes are hard to come by for earlier vehicles, but almost all collectors of modern vehicles desire original packages.

Numerous body style and color variations can greatly affect vehicle pricing. Vehicles in rarer colors will be worth more. Sure-fire winners among vehicle toys are those bearing advertising logos or character images, such as a Buddy L Coca-Cola truck, a Corgi Batmobile or James Bond car, Marx's Charlie Chaplin car or Tootsietoy's Buck Rogers destroyer.

Anything from the 1940s or earlier is worth picking up if the price is right. But beware of the many current reproductions in cast iron and other metals.

Trends: Values remain strong for vehicle toys of all kinds. Demand for die-cast examples including Hot Wheels, Johnny

Lightning and Matchbox has been on the rise as many children who grew up with these toys are reaching their late 20s and early 30s.

Attempting to meet this nostalgic collector demand, some replicas and reissues are reaching the retail and secondary marketplaces at reasonable prices. By contrast, while values for cast-iron toys haven't experienced drastic declines, they will bear close watching as their main collecting audience ages.

Clubs
•American International Matchbox
532 Chestnut St., Lynn, MA 01904

•Aviation Toys
P.O. Box 845, Greenwich, CT 06836

•Dinky Toy Club of America
P.O. Box 11, Highland, MD 20777

•Hot Wheels Collectors Club
6735 Hammock Rd., #105
Port Richey, FL 34668

•Toy Car Collectors Club
33290 W. 14 Mile Rd., #454
West Bloomfield, MI 48322

TIPS OF THE TRADE

• Budget and space are two important considerations for beginning collectors. Older cast-iron vehicles usually require more room due to their large size; by comparison, Matchbox toys can easily be displayed on a shelf.

• Decide how you wish to build your collection, possibly based on a particular era (the 1930s), manufacturer (Buddy L), type (trucks) or kind of vehicles (die-cast).

• Vehicle toys are classified by the materials used in manufacturing — cast iron, pressed steel, tin litho, die-cast metal, rubber and plastic.

• Toys in complete working condition in original boxes command top prices.

Demon, 1970, Mattel Hot Wheels, $15.

VALUE LINE

Prices listed are for items in Near Mint condition. Certain variations (such as color or accessories) may increase value. Cars in original boxes or packaging command a premium.

Arcade (cast-iron, 1920s-1930s)

Checker Cab	$1,200
DeSoto Sedan	$250
Limousine Yellow Cab	$1,300
Reo Coupe	$5,000
Sedan	$250

Allis-Chalmers Tractor	$150
Oliver Spreader	$1,200
International Dump Truck	$1,250
Mack Gasoline Truck	$2,200
White Delivery Truck	$3,300
White Moving Van	$13,500
Panama Dumpt Wagon	$600

Auburn (rubber, 1930s-1940s)

Telephone Truck	$75
Earth Mover	$30
Police Cycle	$100
Clipper Plane	$25
Battleship	$30
Race Car	$25
John Deere Tractor	$50
Army Jeep	$15

Buddy L (pressed steel, 1920s-1960s)

Hydraulic Aerial Truck	$1,100
Water Tower Truck	$6,000
Aerial Tower Tramway	$2,700
Cement Mixer on Wheels	$1,500
Cement Mixer on Treads	$4,500
Husky Tractor	$100
Giant Digger	$500
GMC Brinks Bank Set	$450
Trench Digger	$5,000
Highway Construction Set	$400
Borden's Milk Delivery Van	$275
Buddy L Milk Farms Truck	$500
Coca-Cola Delivery Truck	$150
Coal Truck	$2,000
GMC Coca-Cola Route Truck	$400
Giraffe Truck	$125

GOING MOBILE

The following are some of the leading collectible vehicle toy manufacturers:

AC Williams
Arcade
Auburn
Bandai
Buddy L
Corgi
Dinky
Ertl
Hubley
Marx
Mattel (Hot Wheels and Matchbox)
Nylint
Smith-Miller
Structo
Tonka
Tootsietoy
Winross
Wyandotte

Ice Truck	$1,300
Jewel Home Service Truck Van	$275
Kennel Truck	$125
Traveling Zoo	$150
U.S. Mail Truck	$575

Corgi (die-cast, 1950s-1960s)

Austin London Taxi	$35
Batmobile (several variations)	$200-$650
Batcopter	$100
Batboat	$100
Bedford Car Transporter	$150
Bedford Military Ambulance	$150
Beatles Yellow Submarine	$500
Bentley Continental	$110
Chevrolet Camaro SS	$75
Captain Marvel Porsche	$50
Charlie's Angels Van	$50
Circus Set	$1,000
Citroen Le Dandy Coupe	$175
Chitty Chitty Bang Bang	$450
Corvette Sting Ray	$125
Fiat 1800	$60
Giant Daktari Set	$650
James Bond Lotus Esprit	$100
James Bond Moon Buggy	$525
James Bond Aston Martin (several variations)	$75-$300
Lamborghini Miura	$75
Man from U.N.C.L.E. THRUSH-Buster	$500
Lunar Bug	$80
Penguinmobile	$65
Popeye's Paddle Wagon	$525
Spider-Bike	$100
Supermobile	$75

Mattel Hot Wheels (die-cast, 1960s-1970s)

Most 1990s regular issue cars	$1-$5
1990s Treasure Hunt series	$20-$65
Jack Rabbit special	$55
Odd Job	$600
Buzz Off	$90
Captain America	$100
Mongoose Funny Car	$160
Porsche 911, redline	$40
Snake Funny Car	$275
S'cool Bus	$750

Lincoln Touring Cars, 1924, A.C. Williams, $600 Excellent.

Volkswagen Beach Bomb (w/rear surfboards) $4,500
Volkswagen Beach Bomb (w/side surfboards) $275

Keystone (large scale steel, early 1900s)

U.S. Army Truck $1,300
Moving Van $2,000
Water Pump Tower Truck $1,600
Air Mail Plane $3,000
Ambulance $2,000
Wrecker $1,500
World's Greatest Circus Truck $10,000
Police Patrol $1,600

Marx (tin, 1930s-1960s)

Flying Zeppelin, wind-up $400
China Clipper plane, wind-up $250
Battleship, USS Washington $225
Donald Duck Disney Dipsy Car $895
Dick Tracy Police Car $400
Amos 'n Andy Fresh Air Taxi, wind-up $1,600
Charlie McCarthy Benzine Buggy $950
Nutty Mad Car $225
Tricky Taxi, wind-up $375
Yogi Bear Car $195
Sparkling Climbing Tractor, wind-up $300
Doughboy Tank $400
Mack Army Truck $300
Willy's Jeep $200
U.S. Mail Truck $400

Matchbox (die-cast, 1960s-1970s)

Most 1990s regular issues .... $1-$5
Aston Martin DB2 Saloon $40
Bedford Low Loader $100
Boss Mustang $6
Cement Mixer $45
Coca-Cola Lorry $150
Dumper Truck $25
Flying Bug $10
Ford Prefect $90
Greyhound Bus $30
Hovercraft $12

Lamborghini Miura $50
Lotus Racing Car $20
MG Midget $75
NASA Tracking Vehicle $5
Pontiac Trans Am $4
Rolls-Royce Phantom V $30
Volkswagen Microvan $40

Structo (pressed steel, early 1900s)

Sky King Airplane $1,500
Roadster $2,000
Moving Van $950
Excavator $950
Climbing Military Tank $1,100

Tonka (pressed steel, 1950s-1960s)

Steam Shovel $210
USAF Ambulance $250
Road Grader $125
Carnation Milk Van $400
Back Hoe $250
Star-Kist Tuna Box Van $700
Hydraulic Dump Truck $300
Gambles Pickup Truck $300

Minute Maid Box Van, 1955, Tonka, $400 Excellent.

GMC Bank of America Truck, 1949, Smith-Miller, $165 Excellent.

WALLACE NUTTING FURNITURE

Wallace Nutting (1861-1941) is probably best known to the general collecting public for the millions of hand-colored pictures he sold during the early 20th century. Nutting was also a widely-published author, writing nearly 20 books between 1918 and 1936.

Nutting's love of antiques led to his least profitable, but perhaps most important, business venture — reproducing antique furniture. Even as early as 1915 the finest examples of American antiques were frequently unobtainable, having already been gathered by wealthy individuals, private collections or public museums. Nutting realized that if he was having difficulty locating certain furniture, so were other collectors. So he decided to reproduce them himself.

Beginning in 1918, Nutting began reproducing Windsor chairs. Not a craftsman himself, Nutting had his most talented employees take the original chairs apart very carefully and measure each leg, stretcher, spindle and seat. They would analyze its special features and then reproduce each piece exactly.

His pieces were handmade and hand-finished five to seven times in a light maple or darker mahogany natural wood color. Some colored paint washes in black, red, yellow and green were also available but rarely used; few surviving examples are known today.

The earliest Nutting furniture was marked with a four- by six-inch paper label (1918-1922) that clearly identified the piece as a Nutting reproduction. The label was placed in an out-of-sight, yet still easy-to-find location (underside of a Windsor seat, inside of a drawer or back of a case piece).

Between 1922 and 1924, Wallace Nutting furniture was reproduced by another company which had purchased Nutting's business and the right to use his name. The paper label was eliminated during this period and the script-branded signature was introduced. Although furniture marked with the script branded signature is still highly collectible, it usually sells for less than the paper label and block-branded signature furniture, as its quality was generally not as high as Nutting's earliest (1918-22) and later (1925-1930s) period reproductions.

After repurchasing his business in 1924, Nutting restored his extremely high reproduction standards and began marking his furniture with a block-branded signature. The script-branded signature was in a cursive-style handwriting; the block-branded signature was in large capital block letters.

Wallace Nutting furniture is easily identifiable by the mark. The only exceptions to this are if the paper label was removed, or if it was impossible to affix a paper label, such as on a few 1918-1922 pieces (like a rush-seated chair). When a label could not be affixed the piece was identified with a paper tag attached with a thin wire. Once the tag was removed, there was no other formal Wallace Nutting identification on the piece.

Nutting's standard for high quality drove production costs prohibitively high and, with the onset of the Great Depression, relatively few people could afford a $600 chest or a $1,200 secretary desk. Although Nutting continued selling from inventory until his death in 1941, for all practical purposes, production of new designs stopped by the early 1930s.

Wallace Nutting.

General Guidelines: Chairs are the most common Wallace Nutting furniture, especially Windsor chairs.

"Case" pieces, such as highboys, lowboys, chests of drawers, secretary desks and blanket chests are among the rarest Nutting pieces. Also, the more difficult a piece was to produce, the higher the original cost. And the higher the original cost, the fewer pieces that Nutting produced; these are the rarest today.

Script-branded furniture may be worth anywhere from 25 to 35 percent less than an identical piece bearing a paper label or block-branded signature.

Nutting furniture can generally be dated according to its markings: paper label, 1918-22; script-branded signature, 1922-24; paper label and block-branded signature, 1925-26; block-branded signature only, 1927-1930s.

Condition is extremely important. Items in the best condition will bring the best prices.

Trends: Many people consider Wallace Nutting furniture undervalued today. Based upon the high quality, limited number of pieces, wide recognition of the Wallace Nutting name, and the fact that no more Wallace Nutting furniture will ever be produced, many people consider the Nutting furniture market poised and ready to take off, similar to the Shaker and Mission furniture markets of the 1980s.

Reproduction Alert: Although Wallace Nutting furniture has not been reproduced, some makers have created "fake" Wallace Nutting pieces with a block-branded signature. This has been a limited problem and should not be of any major concern to collectors.

Studying a Wallace Nutting General Catalog will provide a visual reference for the piece and provide sizing information.

Each piece of Wallace Nutting furniture was produced to exact specifications. A #326 Windsor Side Chair should look exactly like, and be of the exact same dimensions as, the #326 shown in the catalog. Any change in dimensions or features should suggest that the piece has either been altered or could be a fake.

Contributor to this section: Michael Ivankovich, P.O. Box 2458, Doylestown, PA 18901.

Publications

The Guide to Wallace Nutting Furniture, Michael Ivankovich.

Wallace Nutting General Catalog, Supreme Edition, Wallace Nutting. This is a reprint of Nutting's 1930 Furniture Sales Catalog and is the best visual reference book of Wallace Nutting reproduction furniture.

Wallace Nutting: A Great American Idea, Wallace Nutting. This is a reprint of the 1922 Wallace Nutting Script Furniture Catalog. This shows all Wallace Nutting furniture reproduced using the script-branded signature.

Use reference books to help accurately identify Wallace-Nutting furniture.

Wallace Nutting's Windsors: Correct Windsor Furniture, Wallace Nutting. Background information on Nutting's reproduction techniques. This is a reprint of Nutting's 1918 first Paper Label Furniture Catalog.

VALUE LINE

#17 Windsor Tripod Candlestand, Block Brand $525
#21 Maple Screw (Whirling) Candlestand, Block Brand $990
#22 Cross-Based Candlestand, Block Brand $575
#28 1-1/2" Treenware Open Salt Dish, Impressed Brand $155
#31 Curly Maple Candlestick (single), Unmarked $95
#31 Curly Maple Candlestick (single), Impressed Brand $175
#101 Windsor Round Stool, Block Brand $300
#102 Windsor Oval Stool, Paper Label $250
#164 Brewster Rushed Three-Legged Stool, Script $385
#166 15" Rushed Maple Stool, Block Brand $300
#168 22" Rushed Maple Stool, Block Brand $425
#301 Windsor Side Chair, Block Brand $525
#305 Windsor Bent-Rung Bowback Windsor Side Chair, Bamboo Turnings, Block Brand $800
#310 Windsor Slipper Side Chair, Paper Label $550
#326 Windsor Fan Back Side Chair, Script Brand & Paper Label $550
#377 Three-Slat Back Side Chair, Block Brand $385
#392 Four-Slat Ladderback Side Chair, Block Brand $475
#393 Pilgrim Side Chair, Block Brand $360
#401 Windsor Continuous Arm Chair, Block Brand .... $650-$1,200
#408 Windsor Bent Arm Chair, Block Brand
#411 Brewster Arm Chair, Script Brand $1,000
#412 Pennsylvania Windsor Comb Back Arm Chair, Block Brand $1,400
#414 Windsor Low Back Arm Chair, Block Brand & Paper Label $525
#415 Windsor Comb Back Arm Chair, Block Brand .... $750-$1,500
#419 Windsor Double Comb Back Arm Chair, Paper Label .... $750-$1,500
#421 Windsor Rocking Arm Chair, Script Brand $1,100

WESTERN AMERICANA

Once limited to the Western U.S., a love of the American cowboy has swept across America and even into Europe and Australia. Virtually everything associated with life on the frontier is desirable, from silver spurs and Stetson hats to six-shooters.

History: From the Great Plains to the Golden West and from the mid-19th century to the early 20th century, the American West was viewed as the land of opportunity by settlers. Key events caused cataclysmic changes — the 1848 Gold Rush, the opening of the Transcontinental railroad, the silver strikes in Nevada, the Indian massacres and the Oklahoma land rush. By 1890, the West of the cowboy and cattle was dead; Indians had been relocated onto reservations.

The romance did not die. Novels, movies and television, whether through the Ponderosa or Southfork, keep the romance of the West alive. Oil may have replaced cattle, but the legend remains.

General Guidelines: Value depends on condition, rarity and maker. Items of generic manufacture carry a cheaper price tag than items displaying the mark of a prominent maker. Those pieces decorated with silver or elaborate designs have more value than plain examples. Also, items associated with people (clothing, spurs, hats, holsters) are in stronger demand than horse-related items such as bridles and bits.

Watch for bogus name brands being stamped on "generic" chaps, gun belts, saddles, etc., to increase their value. Examine items marked "Meanea, Cheyenne, Wyoming" especially closely. There have also been reports of recently-made spurs from Korea being altered and artificially aged to look like vintage Western models. Exercise usual caution and judgment before investing.

Saddles

Made by the major manufacturers of the day — Meanea, Gallatin and Collins of Cheyenne, Wyo., or Frazier and Gallup of Pueblo, Colo. — saddles from 1870-1900 are typically known as "slick fork" models. Prices range from $500 and up. Saddles of generic manufacture, originally sold through general merchandise catalogs like Sears & Roebuck or Montgomery Ward are not as desirable.

Commanding top dollar are saddles made by Heiser, Main & Winchester and Edward Bohlin, a Swedish immigrant who became known as the "saddle maker to the stars."

Spurs

There are two main schools of Western spur designs. Generic iron spurs from the late 1800s generally sell in the $100 to $500 range.

"California-style" spurs were heavily influenced by Mexican artists in old California. Sometimes called "cowboy jewelry," they are the most elaborate of spurs, typically lighter in weight and design with fine, elegant engraved silver inlays. They typically sell for $1,000 to $5,000 a pair. California-style spurs by major makers demand higher prices; they include G.S. Garcia, Mike Morales, L.D. Stone, Rafael Gutierrez and Jose Figueroa, among others.

1940s silver parade saddle outfit by McCabe Silversmiths of Hollywood, complete with chaps, gun, rig, vest and spurs. The entire ensemble sold for $71,500 at the Mesa Wild West Auction.

A pair of 1902 G.S. Garcia presentation spurs sold for $46,200 at a High Noon auction in Mesa, Arizona, setting a new world record.

The other major school is the "Texas-style" spur. The Texas spurs are heavier in design and have bolder silver decorations. Famous makers include McChesney, J.O. Bass, Bischoff and Kelly Brothers. Expect to pay at least $150 for a pair and $400 to $1,500 for the more ornate, silver-overlay spurs. Especially nice items are spurs adorned with Western silver decorations — steer heads, arrows, snakes, stars and playing card suits.

Boots

Collectors consider the late 1940s and early 1950s to be the golden age of cowboy boot art. Colorful boot designs of the period featured bright butterflies, cactus, eagles or other Western symbols. Boots range in price from $50 to over $1,000.

Chaps

Chaps range in price from $300 to $2,000 and higher. The straight-leg "shotgun" variety chaps were the most popular with the working cowboy of the late 1800s. Rather plain in design, they typically have fringe running the length of the leg and large patch pockets. These are usually priced in the $600 to $1,500 range. Chaps with fancy studding and designs, and those from respected makers, bring the higher prices.

A more elaborate style of chaps, known as "batwings" because of their shape, popular with cowboys from the 1890s through the 1920s, were as were the distinctive "woolies," those hairy-looking chaps often worn by cowboys on television and in the movies. Ornately decorated batwing chaps can bring from $1,500 to $5,000, while fancy woolies in nice condition with a maker's mark can sell for $2,500 and higher.

These heavily-studded chaps—covered with more than 2,100 nickel studs—set a world record by fetching $5,600 in the Cody auction.

Holsters and Gun Belts

Traditionally gun belts and holsters held little value for gun collectors, but now the leather rigs are often more valuable than the guns they once carried. Very popular with cowboy collectors, they frequently command some of the highest prices of all Western collectibles. Values range from $100 to over $250 for a simple generic model originally sold by catalog, to thousands of dollars for fancier models.

Among the more desirable makers are Meanea, Heiser and Myres, worth between $500 and $2,000. Fancy models decorated with silver bring higher prices.

Cowboy Hats

Available in many different styles, authentic cowboy hats from the 1870s to the 1930s are generally found for between $60 and $500. Stetson cowbow hats always bring top prices. The classic Stetsons with a five-inch brim, high crown and "pencil-rolled" edge sell in the $500 to $1,000 range. Vintage sombreros are also popular. An elaborately embroidered Stetson sombrero once sold at a Scottsdale show for a record $4,400.

THE SWASTIKA IN WESTERN TERMS

Although its positive meaning was lost with the onslaught of Adolf Hitler, the swastika actually has a long-standing association with prosperity and good luck. Greeks used it on their coins, and the Pueblo and Navajo Indians of the Southwest have used the symbol for centuries.

From them white settlers quickly adopted the swastika as a bearer of good luck. Cowboys applied it to their bandannas, chaps and spurs, among other items. Much of this gear was destroyed when the swastika came to represent the Nazi party, and so cowboy swastika items — although they were not rare — have become relatively scarce.

Chaps, Bohlin, batwin style, brown, tooled billet (belt), engraved SS buckle, mounted with eight 1878 silver dollars $1,980

Chaps, Hamley, wide, over 1,000 metal studs, c1919 . $4,510

Gun belt and holster, Bohlin, two-tone floral carved, large engraved SS buckle $1,260

Holster and gun, fast dreq, Colt SA 38-40 revolver, used by stunt man Mark Swain $2,200

Holster and gun, Visalia, .38-caliber Smith & Wesson revolver, made for Alamedo County Sheriff's Posse, 1930s $3,850

Spurs, silver mounted, Bohlin, Hollywood, McChesney, #125-2, tooled leather Bohlin straps .. $3,400

Spurs, silver mounted, Cox, John, Canon City, prisoner #4307, 4" l shanks, fancy nickel-spotted leather straps by R.T. Frazier Saddlery Co., CO .. $13,200

Spurs, silver mounted, Garcia, G.S., #44, early mark, 14-point rowels $7,150

Spurs, silver mounted, Eddie Hulbert, Montana, Cheyenne-style heel band, engraved button design, 2-1/4" 18-point rowels $11,600

Spurs, silver mounted, Mike Morales, California-style, engraved shield, snowshoes and eagle motif $5,500

Spurs, silver mounted, Phillips & Gutierrez, eagle bit $5,610

Spurs, silver mounted, Qualey Bros., fully engraved, card-suit design, raised silver buttons, tooled leather straps $12,100

Spurs, silver mounted, L.D. Stone, marked "1900," silver-mounted drop shank, engraved button heel band, silver inlaid rowels, orange 2-1/4" domed-button beaded conchos, basketweave leather straps $6,050

Spurs, silver mounted, Jesus Tapia, c1916 .... $23,650

Spurs, silver mounted, Wauley Bros. $12,100

California style spurs such as these G.S. Garcia rattle snake pattern spurs typically sell for $2,000 to $8,000.

Two pairs of Gene Autry's boots brought $1,870 and $2,640 at a High Noon auction.

This silver saddle and accessories brought $71,500 at auction.

WORLD'S FAIR COLLECTIBLES

Fairs date back to the Middle Ages when people would travel many miles to view the street vendors who displayed their wares—tools, spices, armor, gold, expensive silks and countless crafts. The Great Exhibition of 1851 in London marked the beginning of the World's Fair and Exposition movement. The airplane, telephone and Ferris wheel — as well as the ice cream cone and hot dog — are among the many advancements that have been introduced at world's fairs.

History: The first world's fair, The Great Exhibition in London, was the brainchild of Prince Albert, husband of Queen Victoria. He wanted to gather all the civilized nations of the world under one roof, and did so in a gigantic building called the Crystal Palace. Designed by Joseph Paxton to resemble the underside of a water lily, the building consisted of a cast iron frame filled with glass panels. The event attracted 14,000 exhibitors from all over the world displaying fine arts, expensive furniture, delicate porcelain, cut glass, machinery, Colt guns and printing presses. After a successful 23-week run, the building was dismantled, moved to Sydenham and reopened in 1854.

The first world's fair in America was held in 1853 in New York City and was also called the Crystal Palace. It was built on farmland that is now the corner of Sixth Avenue and 42nd Street.

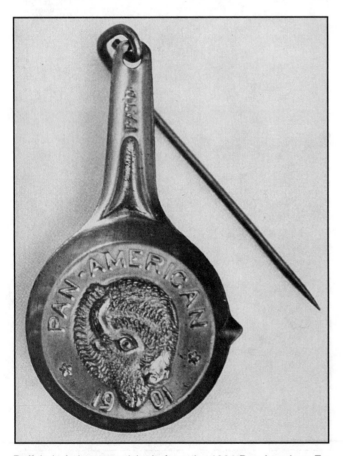

Buffalo in frying pan stick pin from the 1901 Pan-American Exposition; stamped, copper-plated, 1-1/2" in length.

Unlike its namesake, it was not very successful, even though P.T. Barnum was one of its large investors and Otis displayed his new Safety Elevator. The building burned down a few years later and immortalized ina print by Currier & Ives titled "The Burning of the Crystal Palace."

To date there have been over 100 recognized fairs and expositions, of which about 50 are considered to have been major events. Many renowned inventions have debuted and major events have occured at fairs, such as:

- 1876 (Centennial Exposition, Philadelphia) the telephone was first displayed
- 1889 (Int. Universal Exposition, Paris) Gustav Eiffel built his miraculous tower
- 1893 (World Columbian Exposition, Chicago) the first and still largest Ferris wheel appeared, as well as Cracker Jacks
- 1901 (Pan-American Exposition, Buffalo) President McKinley was assassinated
- 1904 (Louisiana Purchase Exposition, St. Louis) First gave us iced tea, ice cream cones and hot dogs on a bun
- 1925 (Exposition of Decorative Arts and Modern Industries, Paris) best remembered for its dramatic display of Art Deco
- 1933-34 (Century of Progress, Chicago) gave the world Sally Rand and her famous "Fan Dance"
- 1939-40 (World's Fair of Tomorrow, New York City) introduced television

General Guidelines: Among the most collectible items to look for are paper ephemera (tickets, fair guidebooks, posters, postcards), ruby red glass (and other glassware) and spoons.

Items from the more historically significant world's fairs have become highly collectible, but even souvenirs from these events can be purchased inexpensively. Items from the first few world's fairs scarcely turn up for sale, which has added to their value. Likewise, items from fairs held in the second half of the century are not as valuable as those of the earlier fairs and expositions.

Prices almost always are higher in the city or area where an exposition was held.

Condition also determines value. Markings on items should identify which fair the souvenir is from. Familiarize yourself with the main buildings and features of the early fairs and expositions. The Eiffel Tower, for example, adorns many items from the 1889 Paris Exposition, and the Trylon and Perisphere were associated with the 1939 New York World's Fair.

Items from local and state fairs have little value, except to collectors of local (city or state) memorabilia.

Contributor to this section: Mike Pender, World's Fair Collector's Society, P.O. Box 20806, Sarasota, FL 34276-3806.

VALUE LINE

1851, London Crystal Palace (the Great Exposition)
Book, *The Great Exposition*, by Tally $100
Cup, porcelain, white ground, blue picture of Crystal
   Palace $125
Pipe, white clay, picture of Crystal Palace on bowl $175

1853, New York Crystal Palace
Coin, so-called dollar, 1-7/8", obv Liberty seated, rev
   picture of Crystal palace $300
Print, "The Burning of the Crystal Palace," Currier &
   Ives $300

1876, Philadelphia (Centennial Exposition)
Book, history of the centennial, 6" x 9" 874 pages $75
Booklet, Centennial Book, 2-1/2" x 3", 16 pgs., issued
   by Orange Judd Co. $15
Inkwell, glass, Memorial Hall $100
Shoe, frosted glass, Gillinder $40
Stevengraph, 1-1/2" x 9-3/4", Lincoln $125
Stevengraph, 1-1/2" x 9-3/4", Washington $125
Textile, Memorial Hall, eagle on top, star border
   18-1/2" x 24-1/2" $75
Ticket, 2-1/4" x 4", "Admit One" $10
Trade card, Traveler's Insurance Co., color $22

1889, Paris (International Universal Exposition)
Clock, Eiffel Tower shape, 19", cast iron, alarm $400
Guide book $40
Textile, 22" x 22" bird's eye view of fair $65

1893, Chicago (World's Columbian Exposition)
Advertising trade card, Traveler's Insurance Co. (color).. $22
Barber bottle, 4-1/2"d, 10-1/2"h, bulbous, gold-imprinted
   Columbus medal $150
Bell, etched glass, frosted handle $65
Cane, pull-out map of World's Columbian Exposition... $350
Change tray $30
Doll furniture, chairs, sofas, soft lead, price for each
   piece $35
Fan, hand, large $50

Glass, 3-1/2"h, clear, frosted white inscription "World's
   Fair Agricultural Building" and building illustration .. $10
Guide book $35
Imprinted handkerchief, small $20
Large wooden cane $100
Matchsafe, Columbus head $125
Medal, brass, two piece, "Wisconsin—Columbian
   Exposition 1893" $20
Medallion, 1-1/2"d, brass, emb $16
Medallion, 1-3/4"d, Ferris wheel, aluminum $35
Paperweight, Liberty Bell, fused glass, "Made at World's
   Fair by Libbey Glass Co." $82
Periodical, The Youth's Companion $30
Pop-Up, 12-1/8" x 10-1/4", Electrical Building, Hall of
   Mines, Wisconsin State Building $150
Print, set of 12, 15-3/4" x 11-1/2", architecture, color,
   "Book of Builders," 1894 .... $100
Puzzle, egg shape, silvered brass, Christopher Columbus
   portrait on one end, inscribed 1492-1892 .... $50
Mines, Wisconsin State Building $150
Ruby red glass tumbler, tall $50
Sterling silver demitasse Spoon $20

Playing cards from the 1933 Chicago World's Fair (Century of Progress); view of Belgian Village.

Sugar spoon $25
Ticket, admission, Manhattan Day, NY, Oct. 21, 1893 .... $38
Token, Ferris wheel $25
Toothpick Holder, 2-1/2"d, 2-3/4"h, ruby glass,
    thumbprint $85
Woven silk bookmark $100

1898, Omaha (Trans-Mississippi Exposition)
Handkerchief, embroidered $6.50
Souvenir cup, ruby flashed $58
Pin, 2"d, Nebraska Day, Oct. 19, 1898 .... $60
View book, 5" x 6-3/4" $25

1901, Buffalo (Pan-American Exposition)
Frying pan, 4"l, aluminum.............................. $25
Letter opener, buffalo.................................... $30
Mug, 5" h, beer, stoneware $225
Poster, 25" x 48", Maid of the Mist................. $1,200
Souvenir book $25
Stickpin, frying pan shape, emb buffalo head $36
Vase, 6"h, Indian Congress............................. $175
Whiskey glass, etched, "Pan-American Exposition
    1901," orig. round box $60

1904, St. Louis (Louisiana Purchase Exposition)
Book, Universal Exposition, 9 1/2" x 12", 81 pgs. $30
Card, 3" x 5" litho, tin, full color aerial panorama illus.,
    company text and logo on reverse, issued by
    American Can Co. $45

Stoneware mug from the 1893 World's Columbian Exposition in Chicago.

Clock, 10" h, shaped like Festival Hall $1,800
Corset, original box $30
Handkerchief, 10" x 10", various prints embroidered on
    one corner $35
Matchsafe, Jefferson and Napoleon, SP $85
Matchsafe, plated, relief scenes.................... $55
Official guide book $25
Pitcher, 6"h, ruby glass $200
Plate, clear, lattice design $25
Playing cards, deck $100
Pocket knife, Cascade Gardens $125
Ruby red glass tumbler, tall $50
Shaker, ruby flashed, two in one, inside glass bladder
    holds pepper, salt on outside $99
Spooner, custard, enamel flowers $65
Tobacco canister, black aluminum $50
Toy, egg, 2" h, tin multicolored picture of Ferris wheel ... $75
Tray, 3-1/4" x 5", litho, tin, issued by American Can Co. $50
Tumbler, 5"h, milk glass................................. $30

1915, San Francisco (Panama-Pacific International Exposition)
Book, Art of the Exposition, 6" x 9" $25
Buttons, two coat, two sleeve, price for four-pc set $25
Medals, 1-3/4" d, opening day and closing day, ribbons,
    colorful, price for pair $125
Pin, 2-1/4" l, 1915 Pan-Pac Closing Day, brass hanger
    bar with attached silk ribbon $35
Watch Fob, leather, black, holds diecut brass poinsettia .. $75

1926, Philadelphia (Sesquicentennial Exposition)
Book, Sesqui-Centennial, 6-1/2" x 9-1/4", 500-plus pgs. $35
Compact, 2-1/2"d, Liberty Bell in center $50
Lamp, 8"h, 4"w, glass Liberty Bell shade $60
Pin, blue Liberty Bell, "Crane's Ice Cream Served
    Everywhere—Keep Cool During The Fair" adv $12.50
Pinback button, 1-1/4" d, multiple designs $25
Ring, metal, silvered, diecut Liberty Bell underneath
    seated eagle, patriotic motifs, inscribed "1776
    Sesquicentennial 1926" $35

1933, Chicago (Century of Progress)
Booklet, 5-1/4" x 8", Ford At The Fair, 24 pgs, issued
    by Ford Motor Co. $25
Card set, building and exhibit ext. views, self-mailer
    design packet forder with snap fastener, set of 20
    cards, unused $18
Change tray, 4-1/2" d, round, bronzed, 12 relief buildings
    and fountain, box $22
Cigarette case, 3-1/4" x 6-1/2", Art Deco, red and black
    coffee cup, Stewart's Private Blend, marked "Made in
    Bavaria" $75
Cookbook, The Wonder Book of Good Meals $20
Crumb set, engraved with World's Fair pavillions, white
    metal $25
Guide book, 1933 Century of Progress, Art Deco cover .. $24
Key, 8-1/2"l, metal, "Key to Chicago World's Fair 1933 . $20
Map, Milwaukee Road Railway, price for set of five $55
Medallion 2-5/8", bronze, Emil Zettler sculpture, MIB ... $75

DIRECTORY OF AUCTION HOUSES

The following is a representative, but not all inclusive, list of nationwide auction houses. For information on upcoming auctions, contact the auction house directly.

Noel Barrett Antiques & Auctions
P.O. Box 3006193 Carversville Rd.
Carversville, PA 18913
215-297-5109

Bill Bertoia Auctions
2413 Madison Ave.
Vineland, NJ 08360
609- 692-1881

Block's Box
P.O. Box 51
Trumbull, CT 06611
206-926-8448

Butterfield & Butterfield
7601 Sunset Blvd.
Los Angeles, CA 90046
213-850-7500

Christie's
502 Park Ave.
New York, NY 10022
212-546-1000

Continental Auctions
P.O. Box 193
Sheboygan, WI 53082
920-693-3371

William Doyle Galleries
175 E. 87th St.
New York, NY 10128-2205
212- 427-2730

Dumouchelle Art Galleries
409 East Jefferson Ave.
Detroit, MI 48226
313-963-6255 / 313-963-0248

Eldred's
P.O. Box 796
East Dennis, MA 02641-0796
508- 385-3116

Guernsey's
108 East 73rd St.
New York, NY 10021
212-794-2280

Hake's Americana & Collectibles
P.O. Box 1444
York, PA 17405-1444
717-848-1333

Randy Inman Auctions
40 College Ave.
P.O. Box 726
Waterville, ME 04901
207-872-6900

James D. Julia Auctioneers Inc.
Rte. 201, Skowhegan Rd.
P.O. Box 830
Fairfield, ME 04937
207-453-7125

Just Kids
310 New York Ave.
Huntington, NY 11743
516-423-8449

Leland's
36 E. 22nd St., 7th Floor
New York, NY 10010
212-545-0800

Manion's Auction House
PO Box 12214
Kansas City, KS 66112-0214
913-299-6692

Mapes Auctioneers & Appraisers
1600 Vestal Parkway West
Vestal, NY 13850
607-754-9193

McMasters Doll Auctions
P.O. Box 1755
Cambridge, OH 43725
614-432-4419

Mid-Hudson Auction Galleries
One Idlewild Ave.
Croton-On-Hudson, NY 12520

New England Auction Gallery
Box 2273-T
West Peabody, MA 01960
508-535-3140

Richard Opfer Auctioneering Inc.
1919 Greenspring Dr.
Lutherville Timonium, MD 21093-4113
410-252-5035

Phillips Fine Art & Auctioneers
406 East 79th St.
New York, NY 10022
212-570-4830

Lloyd W. Ralston
173 Post Rd.
Fairfield, CT 06430
203-255-1233

Skinner Inc.
357 Main St.
Bolton, MA 01740-1104
508-779-6241/ 617-350-5400

Smith House
P.O. Box 336
Eliot, ME 03903
207-439-4614

Sotheby's
1334 York Ave. at 72nd St.
New York, NY 10021
212- 606-7370 / 212- 606-7000

Theriault's
P.O. Box 151
Annapolis, MD 21404
800-638-0422

Toy Scouts
137 Casterton Ave.
Akron, OH 44303
330-836-0668

Withington Inc.
RD2 Box 440
Hillsboro, NH 03244
603-464-3232

YOUR GUIDES TO COLLECTIBLES

NEW

NEW

NEW EDITION

NEW EDITION